ays of Being "Religious"

Achieving an Integrated Self Through Creative Interaction	Social and Economic Justice as an Ultiamte Concern	The Ne... ...u Through Technocracy	Creating the Full Life Through Sensuous Experiences
• loneliness • alienation (loss of identity) • the experience of de-personalization • hypocrisy (facades) and insincerity	• the inhumanity of the status quo; i.e., the inhumanity of the social political/economic institutions • the existence of injustice and inequality • failure to recognize basic civil (human) rights	• chaos and confusion ("Whirl is King"): lack of temporal/spacial orientation vis a vis one's physical existence; environmental rootlessness or disorientation; ignorance of or failure to perceive one's spacio-temporal orientation • helplessness: inability to control one's environment • death (biological)	• abstraction: insensitivity to sensuous form • incapacity for feeling; sense of sterility, lifelessness • atrophy of feeling; an antisceptic existence • sterility of imagination (boredom)
• love (trust, understanding, concern) • relatedness • personal integrity (having no several selves) • the capacity to receive, respond to, and enjoy interpersonal relations • the unique personhood of self and others • relatedness regarded as the supreme reality	• justice • social relationships as constitutive of true humanity • institutions having the capacity for rapid social reform • universal capacity for moral integrity • innate human right to economic welfare	• physical comfort and security; preparation for all contingencies • immortality (biological) • efficiency and order • unlimited technology (man as maker, homo faber) • unlimited technical control • truth as explicit, precise, universal, and objective	• the power of senuous experience(s) • the priority of aesthetic reality • the creativity of man's imagination; thus, not being bound by what is considered the "norm"
• attention to one's immediate response to others • delight in human relationships • growth in terms of self-acceptance • truth experienced as empathic response	• a vision of a just society • commitment to implement the vision of a just society • a strong sense of moral responsibility; • responsivity to human needs	• attention to discovery of empirical regularities (the laws of nature) • quest for objectivity • pragmatic theory of truth (ideas as instruments, or tools, which do or do not "work well") • rejection of intuitive, sensuous or personal life styles • satisfaction derived from the production of a new environment • personal relationships subordinated to efficient team efforts	• intense attention to sensuous realities • immediacy of perception • pursuit of direct experience(s), of vivid experience(s) • form as vehicle for "the moment of truth"
• mental health movements • group therapy • criticism of institutions which restrict interpersonal relationships • social education toward sympathetic understanding of deviance	• decisions made through rational discussion • social action to implement moral decisions • formation of just (moral/social/political/economic institutions	• social commitment to this-worldly utopia • institutionalization of technology: technological specialist who directs mass support technodramas as propaganda	• indifference to social convention • anti-rationalism • selective centers for mutual encouragement ("gathering places") • avant-garde advocacy of new values

Ways of Being Religious

readings for
a new approach to religion

Frederick J. Streng,
Charles L. Lloyd, Jr.,
Jay T. Allen

*Southern Methodist University
Dallas, Texas*

PRENTICE-HALL, INC., ENGLEWOOD CLIFFS, NEW JERSEY

Library of Congress Cataloging in Publication Data

Streng, Frederick J   comp.
    Ways of being religious.

        Includes bibliographical references.
        1. Religion—Collections. I. Lloyd, Charles L.
1935- joint comp. II. Allen, Jay T., 1934-
joint comp. III. Title.
BL25.S65   208   72-7388
ISBN 0-13-946277-5

        1. Religion—Collections. I. Lloyd, Charles L.,
1935- joint comp.   II.   Allen, Jay T., 1934-
joint comp.   III.   Title.

© 1973 by Prentice-Hall, Inc.
Englewood Cliffs, New Jersey

Printed in the United States of America

10   9   8   7

PRENTICE-HALL INTERNATIONAL, INC., *London*
PRENTICE-HALL OF AUSTRALIA, PTY. LTD., *Sydney*
PRENTICE-HALL OF CANADA, LTD., *Toronto*
PRENTICE-HALL OF INDIA PRIVATE LIMITED, *New Delhi*
PRENTICE-HALL OF JAPAN, INC., *Tokyo*

To Truth-seekers,
Path-finders,
and Peace-makers

Table of Contents

Preface xi

Introduction:
What Is Religion? 1

Definitions Determine Our Course, 1 •
Guidelines for a Venture, 6 •
The Reality of the Religious Life, 12 •
Practical Considerations Governing This Study, 16

I
Rebirth through
Personal Encounter with the Holy 23

ADVOCACY 26

1. I Am Blessed But You Are Damned, 26 •
2. Biblical Examples of Divine Encounter, 29 •
3. Miki's Divine Experience, 31 •
4. A Buddhist's Vision in Tibet, 34 •
5. Experience of the Lord, St. Teresa, 39 •

6. Experience of the Divine Mot..er, Sri Ramakrishna, *43* •
7. An Account of Divine Revelation, *J. Smith, 47* •
8. The. Inner Ecstasy, *M. Bach, 50* •
9. Descent of the Spirit at a Pentacostal Meeting,
A. S. McPherson, 54 •
10. "Amazing Grace," *J. Newton, 59* •
11. Psalms 25 and 96, *60* •
12. Love for Allah, *'Abdullah al-Ansari, 62* •
13. In Praise of Krishna, *64* •

INTERPRETATION 67

14. Importance of Prayer for Knowing God, *N. Ferré, 68* •
15. On Personal Knowledge of God's Nature, *E. Brunner, 71* •
16. The Awesome and Fascinating Mystery, *R. Otto, 77* •

CRITIQUE 86

17. On Man's Self-Denial in the Face of the Holy as a
Psychological Illness, *P. Berger, 87* •
18. On the Justification of Claims Based on Religious
Experience, *C. B. Martin, 89* •

II
Creation of Community
through Myth and Ritual 97

ADVOCACY *100*

1. Initiation and Puberty Rites, *J. S. Mbiti, 100* •
2. Periodic Worship of the Zunis, *R. Benedict, 106* •
3. The Mythic Structure of Classical Judaism, *J. Neusner, 113* •
4. Myth, Ritual, and History in Christianity, *St. Paul, 119* •
5. Celebration and Renewal: The Catholic Mass, *123* •
6. Myth, Ritual, and National History Seen
in "Two American Sacred Ceremonies," *C. Cherry, 132* •

INTERPRETATION *141*

7. Reflections on Origins, *W. Otto, 141* •
8. The Sacred and the Profane, *J. E. Smith, 145* •
9. Symbols as Vehicles of the Sacred, *V. Warnach, 149* •
10. Rituals: Sacred and Profane—An Anthropological
Approach, *A. F. C. Wallace, 155* •

CRITIQUE *160*

11. Obsessive Acts and Religious Practices, *S. Freud, 160* •
12. The Biological Function of Myth, *J. Campbell, 168* •
13. The Ethics of Belief, *W. K. Clifford, 174* •

III
Living Harmoniously
through Conformity
to the Cosmic Law *181*

ADVOCACY *185*

1. On *Li* (Rites, Propriety, Rules of Decorum), *Hsün Tzu, 185* •
2. Precepts for Children, *E. Kaibara, 187* •
3. The Laws of Manu, *189* •
4. Psalm 19, *193* •
5. Qur'an, Suras 107 and 4, *195* •
6. Unwise and Untimely? *M. L. King, Jr., 197* •

INTERPRETATION *203*

7. Chinese Religion, *L. G. Thompson, 203* •
8. *Li:* Rites and Propriety, *N. E. Fehl, 210* •
9. What *Karma* Explains, *C. Humphreys, 219* •
10. Hindu *Dharma, S. Radhakrishnan, 224* •
11. Ethical Culture, *D. S. Muzzey, 234* •
12. The *Shari'ah* of Islam, *K. Cragg, 237* •

CRITIQUE *241*

13. On the Religious Sanction of Social Fictions, *P. Berger, 241* •
14. Morality as Social Convention, *R. Taylor, 254* •

IV
Spiritual Freedom
through Discipline (Mysticism) *261*

ADVOCACY *264*

1. On the Nature of Pure Consciousness, *Shankara, 264* •
2. The Way of Mindfulness, *Nyanaponika Thera, 269* •

3. Interviews with Yasutani Roshi, *280* •
4. Dialogue between Ch'an Master Yung-Chia and the Patriarch, *286* •
5. Master Hu Tzu and the Shaman, *Chuang Tzu, 288* •
6. Right Conduct on the Way to God, *Abu'l-Qasim al-Qushayri, 290* •
7. The Silence, *N. Kazantzakis, 296* •

INTERPRETATION 299

8. Introduction to Yoga, *S. K. Majumdar, 299* •
9. Can Superconsciousness Be Imparted? *Swami Akhilananda, 299* •
10. Training in Zen, *Abbot Z. Shibayama, 310* •
11. Different Paths, Different Goals, *N. Smart, 314* •

CRITIQUE 319

12. On Determining Truth, *H. Feigl, 319* •
13. On Whether Mystical Insight is an Adequate Solution to Suffering, *D. C. Vijayavardhana, 325* •

TRANSITION SECTION
The Shift to
Nontranscendent Ultimates *333*

1. The "Immortalist," *F. Nietzsche, 334* •
2. On Faith as Illusion, *W. T. Stace, 337* •
3. A Humanist Manifesto, *343* •
4. Evolution and Transhumanism, *J. Huxley, 346* •
5. Ethics without Religion, *K. Nielsen, 351* •
6. The Lost Dimension in Religion, *P. Tillich, 355* •

V
Attaining an Integrated Self
through Creative Interaction *359*

ADVOCACY *362*

1. Education in Approval, *A. S. Neill, 362* •
2. Education and Ecstasy, *G. B. Leonard, 366* •

3. Eupsychia—The Good Society, *A. Maslow, 374* •
4. On the Religious Character of "Integrity Groups,"
O. H. Mowrer, 378 •

INTERPRETATION *384*

5. On the Religious Function of the Mental Health
Movement, *J. Seeley, 384* •
6. Man's Search for Himself, *R. May, 390* •
7. Psychoanalyst—Physician of the Soul, *E. Fromm, 399* •

CRITIQUE *405*

8. On Man as God's Creation—Not Man's, *A. C. Outler, 405* •
9. Nice People or New Men, *C. S. Lewis, 412* •

VI
Achievement of Human Rights
through Political and Economic Action *417*

ADVOCACY *420*

1. Bread and Freedom, *A. Camus, 420* •
2. Agenda for a Generation, Students for a Democratic Society, *423* •
3. Human Being and Social Alienation, *J. Cone, 429* •
4. The Revolutionary as the Moral Ideal, *Liu Shao-Ch'i, 435* •
5. Toward Revolutionary Humanism, *D. Dellinger, 442* •
6. Female Liberation and Revolution, *R. Dunbar, 446* •

INTERPRETATION *452*

7. The Civil State, *J. J. Rousseau, 452* •
8. The Revolted, *C. Oglesby, 454* •
9. Revolutionary Immortality, *R. J. Lifton, 461* •
10. A Passion for Justice, *R. Clark, 467* •

CRITIQUE *472*

11. Religion and Morality, *J. E. Smith, 472* •
12. The Spiritual Source of Morality, *S. Radhakrishnan, 478* •

VII
The New Life
through Technocracy *481*

ADVOCACY *484*

1. How to Make the World Work, *R. B. Fuller, 484* •
2. The Immortalist, *A. Harrington, 488* •
3. Chart of the Future, *A. Clarke, 494* •
4. On Programming Society, *B. F. Skinner, 497* •

INTERPRETATION *508*

5. On the Meaning of the Technological Revolution, *V. C. Ferkiss, 508* •

CRITIQUE *519*

6. The Present Evolutionary Crisis, *Sri Aurobindo, 519* •
7. Modern Technology as an Expression of Rebellion, *E. Brunner, 531* •

VIII
Enjoyment of the Full Life
through Sensuous Experience *543*

ADVOCACY *545*

1. The Religion of Man, *R. Tagore, 545* •
2. Letting Go, *R. Kaiser, 552* •
3. Turning On, *R. Gustaitis, 557* •
4. High Priest, *T. Leary, 561* •

INTERPRETATION *570*

5. Do Drugs Have Religious Import? *H. Smith, 570* •
6. Nature, Man, and Woman, *A. Watts, 580* •
7. The Aesthetic in Religious Experience, *F. D. Martin, 589* •

CRITIQUE *598*

8. Guilt in the Social Sciences, *O. H. Mowrer, 598* •
9. Sin and Sensuality, *R. Niebuhr, 605* •

Index *613*

Preface

THERE ARE MANY RELIGIOUS BOOKS and books on religion. Most authors and readers are aware of the limitations of written materials for exposing religious meaning and power. Only if readers exercise a creative imagination and attempt to sharpen their sensitivities will they perceive "between the lines" power, insight, and truth in religious expressions. This is true regarding this book also. The data presented here express people's wrestling with questions about themselves and life that have no universally accepted answers; they expose some of the options for realizing the abundant life, ultimate freedom, and true holiness together with some basic criticisms that have been voiced regarding both religious goals and the means of realizing these goals. Nevertheless, the options will not become live for the reader unless he is to some degree able to identify with the intention found there. To the extent that these materials provide an opportunity for people to engage various religious options—to that extent the editors will have accomplished their goal.

The editors gratefully acknowledge the cooperation of two fine secretaries, who during the past three years have gone far beyond the usual secretarial tasks in helping to prepare these materials: Ms. Teresa Gundy and Mrs. Barbara Harper. Also we want to thank the chairman of the Religion Department, Southern Methodist University, Dr. Joseph Tyson, for his encouragement and support of an experimental course for which this approach to religion and some of these materials were initially used by undergraduates. In a similar vein we want to recognize those students who through their enthusiasm for, participation in, and critical reaction to the organization and content of this book discovered the richness and ambiguities of religious life.

Frederick J. Streng
Charles L. Lloyd, Jr.
Jay T. Allen

Introduction: What Is "Religion"?

Definitions Determine Our Course

An African proverb, from the Ganda tribe in central Uganda, states, "He who never visits thinks his mother is the only cook." As with most proverbs, its meaning is larger than the explicit subjects referred to—in this case food and visiting. It suggests that a person is much the poorer for not having had exposure to and acquaintance with the ways of other people.

This book is an attempt to encourage and to make it possible for students to visit (literally, "to go see") some of the religious expressions of mankind. All of us have had some acquaintance with religious people, just as we have tasted our mother's food. But do we really understand very well what it means to be religious? The "Father of the Scientific Study of Religion," Max Mueller, once said: "He who knows one religion understands none." That is perhaps too extreme a statement as it stands, and yet it says about the study of religion what the African proverb says about the knowledge of life in general—that we sacrifice much if we confine ourselves to the familiar.

If a visit is to be fruitful, the "traveler" must do more than just move from place to place. He must respond to what he sees. But what is it that shapes the way we respond to new experiences? Our perception of things

1

is often colored by our previous attitudes toward them. In this case, what do you, the reader, expect from an exposure to various expressions of religion? What sorts of things do you expect to see? How do you think you will respond to them? If you were asked to define, to illustrate, or to characterize religious behavior, how would you do so? The answers to these questions, of course, reflect your *pre*-conceptions. To become conscious of your preconceptions, ask yourself the following four questions.

Does your definition* reduce *religion to what you happen to be acquainted with by accident of birth and socialization? Perhaps that goes without saying. It may be true of anyone's "off-the-cuff" definition of religion. However, we ask this question to encourage you to consider whether your definition has sufficient *scope*. Is it broad enough to include the religious activities of human beings throughout the world? In surveying university students we have commonly gotten responses to the question, "What is religion?" as follows: "Being Christian, I would define it [religion] as personal relationship with Christ." "Religion [is]: God, Christ, and Holy Ghost and their meaning to each individual." Other students think of worship rather than belief. In this vein, one edition of Webster's dictionary, in the first of its definitions, describes religion as "the service and adoration of God or a god as expressed in forms of worship." If we were to accept any of the above definitions, many people in the world would be excluded— people who regard some of their most important activities as religious, but who do not focus upon a deity. That is to say, not all religions are theistic. It remains to be seen, of course, whether and to what extent this is true. But let us all be warned of taking our habits or our dictionary as the sole resource for defining religion. In some areas, the main lines of significant understanding are already well established. Therefore we have no serious quarrel with Webster's definition of food as "nutritive material taken into an organism for growth, work, or repair and for maintaining the vital processes." But in religion, interpretive concepts are more problematical. Therefore we are suspicious of the adequacy of the dictionary's definition of religion.

Another common way to define religion is to regard it as "morality plus stories," or "morality plus emotion." These are ways of asserting that religion has to do mainly with ethics, or that its myths merely support the particular ethical views of a people. There are, of course, persons for whom religion has been reduced to ethics, as when Thomas Paine stated (in *The Rights of Man*) : "My country is the world, and my religion is to do good." But we should be cautious in assuming that this testimony would do for all religious people.

A final example of a definition of religion that begins with personal experience is one that claims: "Religion is a feeling of security"; or, as one student put it: "Religion is an aid in coping with that part of life which man does not understand, or in some cases a philosophy of life enabling man to live more deeply." In locating the basis of religion in man's need for a sense of security, this approach suggests that the deepest study of religion is through psychology. It has been dramatically expressed by the psychiatrist and writer C. G. Jung when he wrote: "Religion is a relationship to the highest or strongest value...the value by which you are possessed unconsciously. That psychological fact which is the greatest power in your system is the god, since it is always the overwhelming psychic factor which is called god" (*Psychology and Religion,* p. 98). Although this understanding of religion expresses a very important point, many theologians and religious philosophers point out that an interpretation that reduces all of religious experience to psychological, biological, or social factors omits the central reality exposed in that experience—the Sacred or Ultimate Reality. Thus, a student of religion should keep open the question of whether a familiar interpretation of religious life that fits into a conventional, social science perspective of man is adequate for interpreting the data.

Does your definition reflect a **bias** *on your part—positive or negative— toward religion as a whole, or toward a particular religion?* There are many examples of biased definitions that could be cited. Some equate religion with superstition, thus reflecting a negative evaluation. One man defined religion as "the sum of the scruples which impede the free exercise of the human faculties." Another hostile view of religion is to see religion as a device of priests to keep the masses in subjection and themselves in comfort. Similarly, Karl Marx, while not actually attempting to define religion, called it "the opiate of the people," again reflecting a bias against (all) religion.

Still others, in defining religion, are stating their concept of *true* religion as opposed to what they regard as false or pagan faiths. Henry Fielding, in his novel *Tom Jones,* has the provincial parson Mr. Thwackum saying, "When I mention religion I mean the Christian religion; and not only the Christian religion, but the Protestant religion; and not only the Protestant religion, but the Church of England." Some Christians assume that their personal conviction comprises a definition of religion, so that religion is regarded as "the worship of God through His Son Jesus Christ," or "a personal relationship with Christ." A Muslim can point out that the essence of religion is to make peace with God through complete submission to God's will, a submission that he will insist is brought to fulfillment in Islam. (In Arabic the word "Islam" means "submission," "peace," "safety," and "salvation.")

Therefore the student interested in reflecting on religious experience that includes more than a single institutional or cultural expression should remember the distinction between descriptive (neutral) and evaluative definitions. A descriptive definition attempts to be as inclusive as possible about a class of items, such as religious forms. An evaluative definition, on the other hand, reflects one's own criteria for truth or falsity, for reality or illusion. In "visiting" religious people, we suggest that you delay making an evaluation until you have understood why their expressions and processes have profound meaning for them—however strange those expressions may seem to you. In the final analysis, each person must evaluate different religious alternatives; but one of our goals in bringing together the material in this volume is to provide you with a variety of options—a variety that is reduced if you limit religion to any single historical expression.

Obviously, the believer who advocates one religion to the exclusion of all others differs sharply from one who rejects all. Nevertheless, if either accepts his own convictions about what is best or worst in religion as a description of what religion in fact is everywhere and for everyone, he exhibits a common indifference to unfamiliar, and therefore potentially surprising, religious patterns. As a believer (or skeptic), you have a right to declare your own understanding of what is most important, most real, in religion. This declaration is, in fact, essential, for it guides you in your quest for whatever is most real in life. As a student, on the other hand, you have an obligation to carry your studies as far as necessary to include all relevant data. In this role, your obligation is not only to your own perception of value but also to a common world of understanding in which men of many religious persuasions can converse with each other. "But," you might ask, "what am I to do if I am both a student and a believer (or skeptic)?" This is an important question, and we shall attempt to deal with it later. For the moment, simply keep in mind the difference between the roles of student and of advocate.

Does your definition **limit** *religion to what it* **has been in the past, and nothing else, or does your definition make it possible to speak of emerging forms of religion?** In asking this question, we should observe two striking facts of the history of religion: there was a time when some present religions did not exist, and some of the religions which once emerged no longer exist (for example, the Egyptian and Babylonian religions). Human history, then, has witnessed the emergence and abandonment of several religions.

Even religious traditions that have maintained a sense of continuity over vast stretches of time (Hinduism, Buddhism, Judaism, Christianity, for example) have undergone important changes. Is it really as obvious as we tend to think that they are essentially the same now as they were at their origins? Do the terms naming these traditions even today point to a single entity, however complex? You are familiar with at least some instances of religious warfare *within* the Christian tradition. Roman Catholics have persecuted and killed Lutherans; Lutherans have persecuted and killed Calvinists; Calvinists, Anglicans; Anglicans, Quakers; and most have returned the act with interest. Are all of these groups expressions of "the one true church"? Are some more Christian than others? Is there only one form of Christianity? Are new movements violations of the tradition? Or is the one who speaks to his own time the one who is most faithful to the genius of his tradition? These questions can be asked of all religious traditions. All have experienced change and diversity. Furthermore, it seems likely that this will continue, and that new religious traditions will emerge. Therefore, the conventions of the past cannot be regarded as the limits of future religious forms.

In part because history has witnessed the emergence and internal changes of many religions, anthropologists and cultural historians commonly suggest that religion (and human culture in general) has attained only its adolescence. Likewise, philosophers and religious thinkers in both East and West point to the anxiety and tensions today that are expressed in political, social, economic, and intellectual upheaval. They raise a question of whether or not man's moral, psychic, and evaluative resources can catch up with his self-destructive potential seen in technologically advanced weapons and psychological-chemical techniques for social control. The most hopeful of these philosophers perceive the present turmoil as a lack of "maturity" in human consciousness, and express the hope that it is not too late (quite) to change the direction of man from self-destruction to self-fulfillment.

From this perspective most of mankind's experience is still in the future. The history of religious life to the present is only a beginning. But the basis of these projections is the recognition that man's survival requires him to recognize religious dynamics and processes for evaluations as major forces in human life. Should not a definition of religion aid us in looking at contemporary phenomena to see if any new ways of being religious are emerging? At least it should not inhibit persons with an interest in this matter, and we think an introduction to religion should encourage such reflection.

Does your definition have sufficient precision? Are there any limits to the scope of religion, or are the limits so vague that they fail to mark out an object of study? In an attempt to be as broadminded as possible, many definitions are like a student's statement that religion is "the means man has of coping with his world." Or they are similar to the claim that religion is "believing in a way of life which involves understanding and caring for others," or "religion is love." Such definitions tell us a good deal, but without some qualification they might refer to many other expressions of human life than specifically religious ones. In order to find a focus and a set of limitations at the outer circumference of that focus, we need to designate what are those essential elements of religion that will expose the *religious* meaning of the evidence we look at.

Guidelines for a Venture

When one has "visited" (seen) a wide range of religious life, from all parts of the world and throughout human history, it becomes apparent that religion is a way of life that involves many processes—all of which, in different ways, are directed to a common end. The goal is to reach a state of being that is conceived to be the highest possible state or condition. Religion is the general term for the various ways by which people seek to become changed into that highest state. We understand *religion as a means toward ultimate transformation*. By this we are not claiming that every activity you think of as religious will in fact transform you ultimately. It might, but that is not our point. We mean that *any* reasonably specific means that *any* person adopts with the serious hope and intention of moving toward ultimate transformation should be termed "religious." We think it possible to speak of all religious activity (Eastern and Western, past, present, and emerging) without reducing religion to what is merely familiar to us and without putting a value judgment on one or more religions. Later on, we will outline our selection of the "means" which constitute the primary subject matter of the following chapters. As you might imagine, it is this selection that gives each chapter its distinctive character and the whole book its range. But before we get to that issue, we need to take a more detailed look at the definition we have just proposed. Let us take each key term or phrase and reflect on its meaning:

1. Religion as a means toward *ULTIMATE* transformation
2. Religion as a means *TOWARD* ultimate *TRANSFORMATION*
3. Religion as a *MEANS* toward ultimate transformation

**Religion as a Means
toward ULTIMATE Transformation**

The term "ultimate" points to what a religious person holds to be "real," to what has such significance that people define their lives on its terms. Whatever is "ultimate" is that without which life would be meaningless and dead because of such common human experiences as physical death, unfulfilled hopes, and the discomfort derived from a sense of not belonging. In this context, the "ultimate" is a power or force in man's life that is recognized by the religious person to undergird, to condition, to encompass life. This appears in the form of words, actions, social relations, and states of consciousness; and its distinguishing mark is that it is so real that one recognizes its power to have been effective before as well as after one has become conscious of it. This is recognized as the reality that (who) estab-

lishes a whole and integrated person who then exists in a mutually beneficial relation with other people and with nature. In traditional religious
expressions, the ultimate character of what is experienced as fully real is
expressed by such terms as God, the Holy One, *Dharma, Nirvana, Sattva,
Tao, Kami* as well as the general concepts "sacred" or "divine" or "transcendent." In conventional English speech the term "ultimate" is synonymous
with "complete," "final," "comprehensive," "total," "absolute," "most,"
"maximum," "supreme."

Religion as a Means
TOWARD Ultimate TRANSFORMATION

The term "transformation" implies that human life necessarily presents
all of us a comprehensive task. This task may be variously conceived; one
may speak of it as the quest for salvation, enlightenment, perfection, fulfillment, or joy, but the distinctively religious claim is that it cannot be
escaped. In using the phrase "toward...transformation," then, we refer
not only to "conversion experiences" especially prominent in prophetic
(Western) religious traditions but also to significant changes that may
happen either suddenly or slowly, individually or communally, in people's
lives. Put more vividly, the claim is that one is threatened by illusion, but
that he can move toward truth; by death, but that he can move toward
life; by chaos, but that he can move toward meaning; by self-destruction,
but that he can move toward an abundant life. These are, no doubt, concerns of the nonreligious man as well. But the nonreligious man fails (or
refuses) to acknowledge the fundamental and comprehensive character of
these tasks. He thinks of his humanity simply as given; the religious man
insists that authentic humanity, although conditioned, must nevertheless be
attained, released, or granted. Put more strongly, in the eyes of the religious
man, one who fails to undertake this fundamental and comprehensive task
is not merely threatened, inconvenienced, or condemned—he is, as yet, only
potentially human. Some religious communities even say that he is subhuman.

How does one study the process of "ultimate transformation"? In one
sense, the activity designated by this term seems beyond empirical study,
for it takes place within or through activities that have a variety of other,
less comprehensive or incisive meanings. On the other hand, it encompasses
so much—the totality of the religious man's life—that we scarcely know
where to begin. It seems that our attempt to focus study on the intention
of the religious man has netted us little, for we now confront the same
problem that has always faced students of religion who go beyond con-
fessional or doctrinal boundaries. Let us call this problem the *paradox of
too little and too much.*

On the one hand, the activities or features of the religious object or aim are notoriously difficult to describe. Deities are not commonly available for public inspection. The insights of mystics seem always to confound language. And the harmonies of universal order and obligation that some men proclaim seem quite unconvincing to others. On the other hand, if we move from the religious object or aim to the behavior of believers, we are inundated by a veritable sea of claims and activities, many of them mutually incompatible. Students of religion have often felt as defeated by the seeming chaos of human religiousness as by the elusiveness of their intended object. The seeming paradox of too little and too much is fundamental to the study of religion. And a viable program for that study must find some way to order and interpret the data without sacrificing either the peculiar nature of the religious "object" or the immense variety of religious behavior.

To deal with these issues, we need a transcultural terminology by means of which we can perceive religion to be a distinctive impulse of the human being as such. Being religious is in some way prior to being American or Egyptian or Chinese. This does not mean that all religions are "really" alike. Far from it. It does mean, however, that the most important religious difference between a classical Confucian and a Southern Baptist does not lie only in the difference between Chinese and American culture. Rather, we should look for ways of describing this difference that cannot be stated and verified simply on the basis of history, language, or attitudes peculiar to each culture.

To anticipate our argument a bit, we can illustrate this point briefly as follows. The key difference between a Confucian and a Baptist does not lie in their derivation from different founders—important as this may be. It does not lie even in the difference between their beliefs—important as this certainly is. The most important *religious* difference between them is that the Confucian develops his understanding of life primarily by stressing the importance of obedience to a set of ethical norms, whereas the Baptist develops his primarily through the worship of a sacred figure perceived in a certain way. The difference between ethics and worship as activities central to one's life is not primarily a difference between Chinese and Western (or American) cultures. It is a distinction that applies *within* as well as between the two cultures. Therefore, in selecting this as the key distinction, we are not imposing the categories of one culture or one religion on another. We are using terms that express possibilities of human existence as such. In this way we can indicate significant differences between religious activities without violating the integrity of that common world of understanding which is the student's primary duty to preserve. The terms by which we order the material bring into focus those "means" through which we understand the religious life of man.

Religion as a MEANS
toward Ultimate Transformation

What is meant by "means"? In our study of religious data, we have found several sets of activities that are uncommonly effective in ordering the raw data of life into recognizable, intelligible, transcultural religious patterns. We call these sets "means." And we have based each of the following chapters on a particular "means." Thus, we seek to explore the ways of being religious, the means people have used and are using to achieve ultimate transformation. It is self-evident that no single university course could be exhaustive in its coverage of religious materials. We are therefore selective. Because our concern is with the dynamics of religious transformation rather than with a survey of interesting and strange religious activities and ideas, we have focused upon prominent or dominant cultural alternatives that could be relevant to contemporary man. We have also attempted to provide both geographical and historical diversity. Therefore, we have identified eight possible "ways of being religious": four representing the great religious traditions of the East and West and four representing a more contemporary and humanistic orientation. In each case we have tried to capture the "way" by a sentence-title:

A. Traditional (Western and Eastern) Ways:
   1. Rebirth Through Personal Encounter with the Holy
   2. Creation of Community Through Myth and Ritual
   3. Living Harmoniously Through Conformity with the Cosmic Law
   4. Spiritual Freedom Through Discipline (Mysticism)
B. Contemporary, Humanistic Ways:
   5. Attaining an Integrated Self Through Creative Interaction
   6. Achievement of Human Rights Through Political and Economic Action
   7. Conquest of Life's Inadequacies Through Technocracy
   8. Enjoyment of the Full Life Through Sensuous Experiences

We wish to make clear that we do not feel these eight ways exhaust the processes (ways, means) for being religious. At best, we would like to indicate that there are a number of religious processes, and that the differences are important for understanding both the different forms of religion and the nature of the ultimate claims made by various people. We think this constitutes a new and valuable approach to the study of religion.

The first means we call "rebirth through personal encounter with the Holy." One who seeks through prayer or meditation to receive some word, some vision, some experience of the Divine Presence is pursuing this path. Naturally, it matters a great deal both to him and to the observer whether or not he is praying to Krishna, to Allah, to the "Father of our Lord

Jesus Christ," or to Apollo. But if the one thing that matters to him more than anything else is that he should have some form of direct encounter with his deity, then he is engaged in the same *type* of religious activity as are those who worship different deities (or spirits) in this way. Do not mistake us. We are not saying that they are engaged in the same religion—only in the same *type* of religious activity. Within the same religion, one will usually find several major types of religious activity, to one degree or another.

The remaining means we will state somewhat more briefly. The second means we call "creation of community through myth and ritual." It differs from the first in its appearance primarily in being public and traditional rather than private and spontaneous. In this means, rites, symbols, and stories are held to have unique power to establish one's world. The third way we call "living harmoniously through conformity to cosmic law." This places a heavy emphasis on religious ethics. Note, however, that this way has no monopoly on ethics. Every type has an ethic. But only the third views obedience to law in everyday life as the primary expression of religious life. The fourth way we call "spiritual freedom through discipline." It features psychophysical techniques of meditation leading to liberation from illusion and anxiety. This way is sometimes referred to as mysticism. In each of these traditional types we present examples from as wide a geographical and chronological range as space allows.

The last four means perhaps require a word of special explanation. We refer to them as nontraditional means toward ultimate transformation. To some readers the term "nontraditional" may not seem strong enough. To them, these means may not seem religious at all. And they may be particularly upset by the insistence on the part of some advocates for these nontraditional means that they deny all transcendent claims. If this bothers you, let us say that we appreciate your concern at this point. We certainly do not mean to say that simply anything at all is religious. Nor are we fond of intellectual fads. But we do want to insist that virtually any act at all *can* be religious. And in a period as unstable, as searching, as changing as ours, we want to be open to any developing pattern of activity whose spokesmen promise to inform and nurture new, distinctive patterns of the religious life.

The key issue is this: Can there be a process of life transformation that can claim ultimacy without also claiming (or implying) contact with some transcendent agency, order, or state? Can one become "new" or perfect without moving outside or beyond the programs, techniques, beliefs, or states that have a meaning entirely within the daily round of affairs that are or reasonably might be familiar to all of us? It seems that at least some people think this is possible. They profess no belief in a divine being or beings. They anticipate no rewards or punishments beyond this life.

They claim no revelations and they offer no way "out" of the normal round of human affairs. And yet they appear to be confident that some program, policy, or technique which avoids all these sacred claims will fulfill not only their lives but also the lives of others. They may even be willing to die (or kill) for them. Shall we say without further investigation that these people are all frauds, quacks, or incompetents? You may, for instance, believe that they are. But do you *know* that they are? Apart from this, however, can these be called "religious" matters? That is indeed the question. If religion is to be understood as a means of ultimate transformation and if the term "ultimate transformation" is to have significant empirical meaning, then these programs for which so much has been hoped, risked, and achieved must be included. Therefore in full knowledge of the uncertain and intellectually risky character of this undertaking, we propose the four following nontraditional means toward ultimate transformation (numbered five through eight).

"The topic for today is: What is reality?"

By Henry Martin, from *Saturday Review*, May 29, 1971. Copyright 1971 by Saturday Review, Inc. Reprinted by permission of Saturday Review, Inc.

The first of these (and the fifth in our overall scheme) focuses on "attaining an integrated self through creative interaction." It features the possibilities that certain sorts of direct, personal encounter provide for healing sick lives and enriching or gracing our day-to-day existence. The sixth way emphasizes "achievement of human rights through political and economic action." It differs from the previous way primarily in its more systematic, more coercive, more public character. The seventh way promises "conquest of life's inadequacies through technocracy." Of all the four non-traditional means, it is perhaps the most opposed to the traditional meanings of religion because it eliminates all forms of submission or passivity. We call the last way "enjoyment of full life through sensuous experiences." In this means, attention is drawn toward the transforming power of art, body awareness, and the use of psychedelic drugs.

Let us caution you against certain hasty generalizations that might be drawn from this eight-fold typology. The first is that any single "way of being religious" should not be identified with any single religious tradition. A particular "way" finds expression in various religions, and a variety of ways is found in every religion. This, of course, would not preclude a judgment that a particular tradition has been generally dominated by one or two ways, or that during a certain period of its history some ways have dominated others. The second is that although we have tried to include a wide variety of material from different religious traditions, the particular selections chosen are not intended to provide a representation of the total breadth of options within any given religious tradition. The selections have been chosen to expose as clearly as possible the common characteristics of a particular way. This remark leads to the final caution, which is that just as religious traditions are often a combination of different ways, so many particular religious expressions are combinations of them. Thus you should not be frustrated in finding religious expressions in your everyday experience that cannot be pigeon-holed neatly into one or another type. The purpose of describing types is not to reduce the wide variety of data into abstract (perfect) ideas; rather it is to understand better the variety by allowing for significant differences not only in form but also in the processes or mechanisms of being religious.

The Reality of the Religious Life

Thus far we have defined the field of study and indicated the framework through which we will select and order the data. One might say that this definition and framework constitute the "soul" and the "skeleton" respectively of the religious life. We want you now to consider the dynamics, the active process, the spiritual metabolism that expresses the "soul" and animates the "skeleton." In this activity lies the reality of the religious life. Apart from this reality, the framework we have laid out would be dead and irrelevant. What cannot be lived need not be studied. Therefore we now hope to show how the guidelines of thought sketched out above can lead you to appreciate and to understand the reality of the religious life.

First we will state how this approach to studying religion requires one to treat the variety of experessions as significant in their own right. Then we will consider various risks and benefits that might befall a student who embarks on a study so conceived.

Understanding the Believer's World

How does the adoption of a particular religious "means" affect one's perception of and response to the basic problems of and resources for full, human life? We are aware of the variety of answers proposed to the question of life's meaning. What may be less obvious is that people differ as much regarding formulation of the problems to be faced as they do in their understanding of the resources available for their solution. Is the problem man's indifference to God's presence (as suggested in the first means)? His hostility to divine revelations (second means)? His breech of natural law (third means)? His illusions regarding meaning in an indifferent world (fourth means)? His unresponsiveness to people around him (fifth means)? His failure to use the resources of technology (seventh means)? In any case we can see how the adoption of a particular means shapes one's understanding of where the "real" issues are. Furthermore, notice the ways in which a particular means shapes one's behavior, both as an individual and as a member of society. Is one's religious activity continuous or occasional, private or public, organized or spontaneous, democratic or hierarchical, authoritarian or free? These are the alternatives that shape the appearance of the religious life. Taken together with the believer's own understanding of what the issues are, they describe religious structures of the believer's journey toward ultimate transformation.

If one is to take the believer's world seriously, he must accept the reality of that world in the terms provided by him. One must, at least provisionally, grant to that world the independence the believer claims for it. Consider it, perhaps, a loan of imaginative capital which you extend to him. If he fails to return the loan with interest, then you can cross him off your list as a bad risk. But to withold from the first the credit he claims as his due is to prejudge the issue. To put this differently, he cannot show you his accomplishments if you insist on receiving reports only from his competitors. At least consider the possibility that the religious world has within its own domain the resources for understanding religious belief and behavior that are most appropriate for them and most illuminating when applied to them. An approach that denied this from the first would necessarily fail to recognize and to appreciate either a potentially real independence of religious life or a significant autonomy to the several different religious means (ways, structures, types).

Taken on its own terms, the religious world arises as a response to a need peculiar to itself. This need or drive cannot be reduced to one that belongs to another realm of life. It is not a disguised form of some other activity. As a religious being, one seeks not sex, security, or social identity, but a means that provides ultimate transformation. His basic drive is simply an "appetite" for fulfilling and meaningful activity, or most generally, for a high quality of life. When this drive is directed toward ultimacy, completeness, or perfection, it appears as religious activity. In the grip of this appetite human beings raise questions about the ultimate character, origin, and authority of truth, duty, and meaning. Through imagination, symbolism, and certain states of consciousness they step beyond the simple factuality of their lives. They conceive what they might have been but were not; what they might be but are not. Thus, while man is admittedly both physically and socially conditioned, his capacity to reflect on his existence provides him with a leverage on fate that denies final determinism. From the possibility of reflection arises the reality of freedom. In this freedom from impersonal determination, man discovers and exercises his religious drive.

The interpreter's problem is to order the human expressions of this drive without distorting or overlooking their freedom, distinctiveness, and irreducible variety. It is obvious, from this point of view, that those who reduce religious life to social, psychological, or biochemical functions fail to understand its distinctive character. It may be less obvious, but still true, that those who conceive all religious thought and behavior as expressions of a single religious essence also fail to understand it. In the readings that follow, many social scientists commit the former error, and many advocates and their interpreters in Chapters I through IV commit the latter. Therefore, as you study the material that follows, we caution you to consider each religious expression with this question in mind: "What are the ways or means by which man's religious capacities are being expressed here?" This question will help you to understand both the distinctive character and the manifold expressions of religious life.

For instance, some religious expressions assume that the center of religious life lies in the performance of some ritual (for example, sacrament, sacrifice) or in the acknowledgment of some conception of deity (for example, creeds). Even religious traditions that promote different rituals or espouse different creeds have in common the convictions that the correct ritual or belief is primary to the religious life. Yet others whose intention is to realize the ultimate in a personal, inner way maintain that an individual will not realize the fullness of being until he breaks the bonds of all rituals and symbols by transcending them in an altered state of consciousness (as in Yoga or Zen). Both of these groups are religious. And yet the dispute between them is fundamental. One cannot set out to resolve the differences between them by imposing the basic attitudes of one on the other. If one focuses his attention either on the innate power of some symbols and rituals to structure the devotee's cosmos or on the power of transconventional states of awareness to free one from illusion, he destroys the basic structure of the alternate process of ultimate transformation.

Therefore we stress the *means* of ultimate transformation to expose the elements of a given "way" and to indicate how it is that there are basic differences as well as similarities among religious expressions. By locating the differences and similarities within the processes or mechanisms of acquiring religious values, you can wrestle directly with the issues involved in making ultimate decisions. From this encounter with the basic issues, you can become self-conscious that you are yourselves participating in processes of decision in your own "religious" or "antireligious" stances. This awareness can also grow as you become acquainted with options for making ultimate decisions which your culture or sub-culture group has not previously made available.

The Power of the Religious World: Risks and Benefits of Study

We have asked you to enter into the believer's world and to take it seriously. Before you do, you should realize that you may run some risks on this course. If you take this world seriously, you should be aware that the believer always approaches religious knowledge with care. In his view sacred truth is power; it is not to be profaned by irreverent or casual study. One who appreciates this point of view and yet continues his study will be aware of the risks he runs. "How absurd," you might say. "Are you going to warn us about walking under ladders and in front of black cats, too?" Nevertheless, our warning is serious. You cannot control this data without being changed by your response to it. Already, in response to our warning, you are "engaged" with a statement that may offend you. If you allow your irritation to fix the meaning of "religion," the response you intended as a shield may well function simply as a mist. For example, if you say, "Religion is just a bunch of rituals people go through because they are supposed to," you will never perceive the symbolic power believers have found in ritual; you will not be able to grasp the informing and transforming power imparted to common acts (for example eating and drinking) when they are incorporated into ritual. To put this most generally, to evade the warning is to miss the power, and to miss the power is to misapprehend the dynamics of the religious life. This limitation of your vision is damaging enough to you as a student. But it is even more damaging in that it may blind you to the reality of your own ritual acts, the repetitious patterns that structure your life at unconscious levels. Such deception can prevent you from realizing new and creative relationships with other people because it conceals from you the very possibility of their existence. Thus, one risk of our confrontation with the religious claim is that we may close off avenues leading toward a fuller humanity. Thoughtlessly accepting the familiar as the limit of the real, we often fail to grasp new possibilities of life.

The study of religion is dangerous, secondly, because you will be exposed to theories and practices that can destroy long-standing values which have provided comfort. Insight into human religious capacity might change your whole perspective on what is to be valued in the world. To probe into the possibilities of different levels of consciousness may call into question criteria of truth that previously provided an orientation and meaning. To listen to another person express deeply felt religious convictions that are based on quite different revelations or authorities than your own might lead you to convert to his position or perhaps to doubt that there is *any* profound meaning in life. The study of different ways of being religious may be painful, then, because one is thereby confronted with the strange, the different, with the not-self. This requires stretching mental and emotional capacities and sometimes tearing attitudinal and social fabrics.

This is the risk we take when we engage other persons seriously, especially in the domain of values and religious consciousness. For to engage another person at this level is to deal with those things he regards as most important—as ultimate. We can easily recognize that some words and phrases in religious discussion evoke strong feelings for some and uncanny discomfort for others: "God is love." "I take refuge in the Buddha." "God is the one god." "You are that [Atman]." For the adherent of any one of these phrases, the phrase is significant because it is part of him. If the student of religion denies the power of such a phrase in moulding the self-identity of the adherent, he will miss a major part of the reality expressed by a religious person. In a serious engagement with another person, we ask ourselves if we have been false to ourselves; we ask such questions as: How do I know what is right? What difference does it make? Do I really have a choice? What are the likely results of avoiding all dependence on authority, observation, and reasoning? The ideas, descriptions, and assertions you will be reading in this volume have been important for those who affirm them. Therefore you should be sensitive to the importance of the data you are about to engage. As you read the material try not only to enter into the thought patterns and emotional tone of the material, but from time to time ask yourself what you are feeling in response to the images you are constructing.

Besides the risks we have recounted, there are gains to be made in serious encounter with the dynamics of religion. The first is that you will extend your awareness to include options of religious life which you did not perceive before. Likewise, you may see dimensions of familiar religions that previously were hidden or vague. This new capacity will provide you with a more solid basis for making value judgments than before. In addition, you

"Who am I and where am I going?"

By Henry Martin, from *Saturday Review,* July 3, 1971.
Copyright 1971 by Saturday Review, Inc. Reprinted by
permission of Saturday Review, Inc.

may gain a therapeutic recognition that you are not alone in your own
spiritual quest and development. Other human beings have confronted life
with the question: Why? Others have felt dislocated in a meaningless
treadmill, or rejected due to a lack of love, or frustrated from a burdensome
ancestral hand. Others have lived in social groups that perceive strangers
as enemies, and make war out of fear for themselves. Others have wondered, "What's it all about?" Even those people who have disturbing
answers to these questions are responding to a human situation that has
some relation to our own. And when we recognize that at least some of the
people who at first appeared strange and different are at least as sensitive,
perceptive, moral, compassionate, and passionate as we are, we will realize
that the rejection of old familiar truths or the desire to investigate new

possibilities with imaginative hopes are not merely reflections of freakish, neurotic, or immoral tendencies; rather, we are exploring varieties of consciousness.

Practical Considerations
Governing This Study

Given the above theoretical approach to the field of religion, how does one go about studying it—exactly? Just what materials are we to put in this book, and how are you to study them? These are the questions we shall consider in this fourth and last section of this introduction. Regarding our part of this problem, there are two questions. First, what range of material should we include? The range of religious data is enormous. Should we attempt to sample the whole range? One who says "Yes" to this question, must abandon any attempt to cover social context or historical development. This is an important loss, for the religious life is nothing less than the attempt to meet the actual problems of life encountered under particular circumstances with a means of transforming power. One can understand this attempt only through the study of its full, historical context. Nevertheless, we have chosen to sample the whole range of religious life rather than to study any particular example or set of examples in historical depth. We do this for two reasons: (1) A systematic approach introduces the student more rapidly to an overview of the field; (2) This approach enables a student to examine the dynamics of religion. Such an examination is useful not only for the insight it yields on its own but also for its clarification of the religious options available in any life situation. Therefore we have attempted to include material from as wide a geographical, cultural, and chronological context as space allows.

The second part of our problem concerns the mechanics for the presentation of the believer's case. Should we speak for him, or should we allow him to speak for himself? And in either case should we listen to his critics too? These questions are once again made pressing by the enormity of the field. It would be in one sense most efficient for us to speak for the believer. We have, after all, proposed a systematic framework for the ordering and interpretation of religious data. We could, therefore, in company with other advocates of a systematic approach, write a textbook rather than edit a book of readings, relying on brief quotations and footnotes for illustration and evidence. Nevertheless, we have chosen to set up a dialogue in which believers and their critics speak from their own positions.

If religion is to be an independent field of study, a student must rely upon and check his knowledge against what is commonly referred to as "primary data," or "primary source material." Such data constitute direct expression of the subject under investigation, and are the original data upon which anyone's knowledge of the subject matter rests. In biography a person's letters and diary would be primary material; for example, Joseph Smith's account of the revelation imparted to him. Accounts of his life by second persons, whether sympathetic or not, are secondary material. Likewise, we are treating as primary material data that believers treat as basic to their religious life, such as selections from scriptures and revered texts. In this case the central question is not their historical reliability but their role in the dynamics of religious life. In those cases where accounts of key religious activities are not available from believers themselves, we have accepted firsthand accounts of sympathetic observers; for example, R. Benedict's account of Zuni ceremonies in Chapter II. The selections that meet the above criteria serve to expose the various "ways of being religious" and make up the bulk of the material.

We emphasize this sort of material in the hope that you will become sensitive to the differences of terms and thought patterns that the adherents themselves use. We believe that there is a unique benefit in listening to a spokesman in his or her own words, or in a sympathetic firsthand description that includes a believer's own words; for this material contains important nuances that do not come through a general interpretation. This material should also heighten the character of a dialogue between the spokesmen and you, because the basic material is directly before you without exclusive dependence on another interpreter.

Each chapter also contains secondary materials: sympathetic interpretation or general description of a religious orientation. This material is written by scholars who try to interpret primary material within a given context, which includes not only religious commitment but also cultural history and sociological or psychological study. It is included to expose the implications and presuppositions of the religious life described in the primary materials. Sometimes through different perspectives, each of these interpretations provides insight into, and exposes various dimensions of, the material. The authors of these materials may not be "believers," but have credentials of experience and scholarly acumen for providing us with perspectives about subject matter that may otherwise be more difficult to understand in a short amount of time.

A third type of readings that we feel is important for exposing the procedures and processes of evaluating ultimate choices is the critique or criticism of a "way of being religious." Each chapter's collection of data regarding a way of being religious includes at least two critiques of the assumptions and claims of the advocates for that particular way. These critiques include criticisms stemming from an alternate "religious" view or from empirical and rational criteria. They are chosen to raise the basic issues of religious conviction. For instance, a common religious issue that is explored in every case is: What are valid criteria for judging truth? But in the first chapter, this question is formulated to focus on the validity of claims regarding personal transcendent awareness of the Holy; in the second, it focuses on the validity of the claims that religious symbols are more than social conventions or neurotic obsessions; in the third, it focuses on the validity of the claim that there is an eternal order of life which prescribes "natural" physical and social limitations on any individual person. Also in the subsequent ways, the dynamics of each way influences the formulation of this issue.

The critiques provide a radically different perspective for interpreting the assertions and implications of each "way of being religious." They are often threatening in their rejection of the assumptions made by religious advocates; but we agree with M. H. Hartshorne when he suggests a need for a critical assessment of religious claims due to the fact that religion is often identified with uncritical and authoritarian beliefs. He describes the controversial nature of religious commitments:

> In every age religion has had its detractors and critics. We might expect this for at least two reasons. In the first place, religion, like every other human institution, is liable to human vanity, folly, and error. In the second place, we cannot exist as human beings without thinking— and to think is to question, to probe, to criticize. Inevitably religious men have resisted such criticism. We do not welcome doubt, especially where our religious beliefs are in question. Faith in our gods is the foundation of our lives—the source of meaning and value by which we fashion the stuff of our living, the ground we cannot surrender without the loss of our selves. Men are never so defensive as in behalf of their gods; self-criticism is not a virtue of religious men. Our criticism of religion seldom extends to our own gods; our stones crash with shattering force upon the altars of alien deities, but the images that grace our secret shrines are rarely in jeopardy. Indeed, the gods of our own households are so jealously guarded that ordinarily they are hidden even from our own view.[1]

However offensive criticisms may be, we think they should not be neglected in an introduction to religion. By their radically different point of view, they remind us of the important role interpretation plays in understanding religious people. They raise questions and problems of which we might be unaware under the spell of a believer or a sympathetic interpreter. As might be expected, a critique of one way sometimes includes the assumptions of another way, and the defense of a spokesman is often, in one sense, implicitly a critique of another way. Our concern in presenting these materials is, first, to make as strong a case as possible for a way of being religious by letting the advocates give witness to its power and provide some justification for its validity, and, then, to juxtapose these claims with views whose valuational definitions are radically different—thus involving you in a decision situation yourself.

Regarding the second part of the question raised at the beginning of this section, you might ask: How do I recognize a religious process? What are those elements that form the structure by which one identifies a process? Below are some practical suggestions for locating the elements of a structure.

1. Assume that the religious data that you are observing have meaning for the adherent. Let us assume that (a) there is a "logic" or pattern of meaning in the data rather than mere chaos or meaninglessness, and that (b) meaning is expressed in the configuration or patterning that different elements have, with some elements being more important than others. These more important elements are the determining (pivotal) features in relation to which secondary elements have their significance.

2. Ask a question of the data regarding the "intention" of the activities described or expressed (for example prayer, meditation, a religious vision). This suggests that the religious act or claim is not a dead, static entity, but rather the crystallized form (for example, book of prayer, yogic posture, or narration of a conversion experience) of a process, a dynamic experience that creates a new possibility of existence.

3. Keep in mind some basic religious questions for which the believer is seeking (and finding) an answer in the materials presented: (a) What is the nature of existence (or man)? (b) What is the nature of ultimate reality (truth, or ideal)? (c) How can I know and become that ultimate reality?

4. Look for answers to the above questions in the data by becoming sensitive to the phrase, terms, and arguments that expose the basic elements of the structure—which structure will relegate some concerns to a secondary place and thus provide meaning in terms of the central elements. For example, in both the ways "personal encounter of the Holy" and "freedom through spiritual discipline," there is an emphasis on individual, personal realization of the ultimate. However, in the former there is the experience of God as that which is totally different from man, to which man responds in awe, submission, and faith; man by nature is unable to aid Divine grace in his salvation. In the latter case, however, ultimate reality is thought already to be within man waiting to be uncovered, which man can do by avoiding his own corrupting, limiting action that blinds him to the truth; here the ideal is often termed freedom and enlightenment rather than joyful servitude and

obedience. The differences in the structures of these two processes, then, is seen to rest on the differences of the means or way of becoming properly related to God or realizing the ultimate reality within oneself.

5. Attempt to think with the thoughts and concepts of the advocates, and try to feel their emotional tone. Be sensitive to the danger of imposing the interpretation of your own religious awareness (or lack of it) on the data, since two phenomena may appear to be alike but actually be quite different. In other words, become self-conscious of the position from which you are observing or from which you are beginning to participate.

In sum, we hope that these materials will provide you access to spokesmen, sympathetic interpreters, and critics of various traditional and nontraditional ways of ultimate transformation; that the organization into different ways will expose the basic assumptions and elements of adopting a particular way; and that by "visiting with" both those who affirm and those who reject a particular way, you will have explored, rejected, or affirmed, and even developed your own basic procedures for deciding ultimate issues. By including some examples from traditional and nontraditional religious life we hope to expose contemporary possibilities of religious life. Through a focus on the different processes we can use today, we hope to probe into the assumptions, norms, and the potential for human consciousness and social expression that are at the foundation of religious meaning and joy.

NOTES

1. M. H. Hartshorne, *The Faith to Doubt: A Protestant Response to Criticisms of Religion,* (Englewood Cliffs, N.J.: Prentice-Hall, Inc., 1963), pp. 1, 2.

* Footnotes at the bottom of the page are the editors' footnotes, and are normally limited to clarifying particular names and terms. The footnotes marked in the text with numbers are provided by the authors of the selections, and are placed at the end of each selection.

I

Rebirth Through Personal Encounter with the Holy

"When man takes the initiative, his discourse on God becomes a discourse on himself; therefore, a meeting with God cannot be serious unless it is God who takes the initiative. If an Other is there, standing in front of man, it is up to this Other to reveal himself, to speak and make himself understood. God is an irruption, an unanticipated occurrence in man's life. All anticipations are in reality only anticipations of oneself."
(Jacques Durandeaux, Living Questions to Dead Gods, trans. Wm. Whitman [New York: Sheed & Ward, 1968], pp. 86–87.)

WE BEGIN OUR PORTRAYAL of religious types with that type which we call "rebirth through encounter with the Holy." We are speaking of a special kind of encounter. It is distinguished from others not only by its object—the Holy—but also by its role—to rescue, sustain, and direct the believer in all his living. From this point of view, the one thing a human being simply cannot do without is personal encounter with the mysterious but glorious "Other" on whom all things depend.

• One who adopts this point of view and makes it dominate all aspects of his life will exhibit a pattern of behavior and attitude which will be constant even across denominational, ethnic, or cultural lines. He will understand his basic problem to be separation from the Holy. If he is unhappy, ashamed, or unsuccessful, he will interpret his distress as a sign of his separation from the Holy One(s). Apart from hope of some special help, he would despair. But he will characteristically understand reality to be such that help is available. Its source is the all-sufficiency of the Divine. The Holy One(s) can do simply anything, and the activity of the Divine at least in part transcends our comprehension. At any time the divine power can break into the mundane round of impoverished existence and transform it. Therefore one need never lack hope. On the other hand, the efficient or practical ordering of one's life will not seem especially important.

This understanding of one's basic situation is both expressed and clarified by the religious means open to the believer. Knowing that his sole hope lies in a power beyond his comprehension and control, the believer adopts the role of humility, supplication, and openness in relation to God. He hopes for an incursion of the divine which he expects to be dramatic, unpredictable, uncanny, and perhaps even bizarre. Viewed collectively, a religious movement in which personal experience is primary will be individualistic, anti-institutional, exuberant, and aggressive (at least in matters it perceives as having religious significance). Various aspects of this pattern are illustrated and discussed in the following selections. We hope they will help you to see both the inner coherence of the pattern and the extent to which it is a feature of human life as such rather than of one or more cultures.

ADVOCACY

1. I Am Blessed
but You Are Damned

This autobiographical account of a 19th-century American slave's "call" from God exposes the importance of the experience itself in one's perception of the difference between the perverted existence that one usually accepts as normal and the blessed life. In what visual and emotional terms does the slave Morte experience God? What changes took place in Morte's self-image and activities as a result of the experience?

One day while in the field plowing I heard a voice. I jumped because I thought it was my master coming to scold and whip me for plowing up some more corn. I looked but saw no one. Again the voice called, "Morte! Morte!" With this I stopped, dropped the plow, and started running, but the voice kept on speaking to me saying, "Fear not, my little one, for behold! I come to bring you a message of truth."

Everything got dark, and I was unable to stand any longer. I began to feel sick, and there was a great roaring. I tried to cry and move but was unable to do either. I looked up and saw that I was in a new world. There were plants and animals, and all, even the water where I stooped down to drink, began to cry out, "I am blessed but you are damned! I am blessed but you are damned!" With this I began to pray, and a voice on the inside began to cry, "Mercy! Mercy! Mercy!"

As I prayed an angel came and touched me, and I looked new. I looked at my hands and they were new; I looked at my feet and they were new. I looked and saw my old body suspended over a burning pit by a small web like a spider web. I again prayed, and there came a soft voice saying, "My little one, I have loved you with an everlasting love. You are this day made alive and freed from hell. You are a chosen vessel unto the Lord. Be upright before me, and I will guide you unto all truth. My grace is sufficient for you. Go, and I am with you. Preach the gospel, and I will preach with you. You are henceforth the salt of the earth."

I then began to shout and clap my hands. All the time a voice on the inside was crying, "I am so glad! I am so glad!" About this time an angel appeared before me and said with a loud voice, "Praise God! Praise God!" I looked to the east, and there was a large throne lifted high up, and thereon sat one, even God. He looked neither to the right nor to the left. I was afraid and fell on my face. When I was still a long way off I heard a voice from God saying, "My little one, be not afraid, for lo! many wondrous works will I perform through thee. Go in peace, and lo! I am with you always." All this he said but opened not his mouth while speaking. Then all those about the throne shouted and said, "Amen."

I then came to myself again and shouted and rejoiced. After so long a time I recovered my real senses and realized that I had been plowing and that the horse had run off with the plow and dragged down much of the corn. I was afraid and began to pray, for I knew the master would whip me most unmercifully when he found that I had plowed up the corn.

About this time my master came down the field. I became very bold and answered him when he called me. He asked me very roughly how I came to plow up the corn, and where the horse and plow were, and why I had got along so slowly. I told him that I had been talking with God Almighty, and that it was God who had plowed up the corn. He looked at me very strangely, and suddenly I fell for shouting, and I shouted and began to preach. The words seemed to flow from my lips. When I had finished I had a deep feeling of satisfaction and no longer dreaded the whipping I knew I would get. My master looked at me and seemed to tremble. He told me to catch the horse, stumbling down the corn rows. Here again I became weak and began to be afraid for the whipping. After I had gone some distance down the rows, I became dazed and again fell to the ground. In a vision I saw a great mound and beside it or at the base of it, stood the angel Gabriel. And a voice said to me, "Behold your sins as a great mountain. But they shall be rolled away. Go in peace, fearing no man, for lo I have cut loose your stammering tongue and unstopped your deaf ears. A witness shalt thou be, and thou shalt speak to multitudes, and they shall hear. My word has gone forth, and it is power. Be strong, and lo! I am with you even until the world shall end. Amen."

I looked, and the angel Gabriel lifted his hand, and my sins, that had stood as a mountain, began to roll away. I saw them as they rolled over into the great pit. They fell to the bottom, and there was a great noise. I saw old Satan with a host of his angels hop from the pit, and there they began to stick out their tongues at me and make motions as if to lay hands on me and drag me back into the pit. I cried out, "Save me! Save me, Lord!" And like a flash there gathered around me a host of angels, even a great number, with their backs to me and their faces to the outer world. Then stepped one in the direction of the pit. Old Satan and his angels, growling with anger and trembling with fear, hopped back into the pit. Finally again there came a voice unto me saying, "Go in peace and fear not, for lo! I will throw around you a strong arm of protection. Neither shall your oppressors be able to confound you. I will make your enemies feed you and those who despise you take you in. Rejoice and be exceedingly glad, for I have saved you through grace by faith, not of yourself but as a gift of God. Be strong and fear not. Amen."

I rose from the ground shouting and praising God. Within me there was a crying, "Holy! Holy! Holy is the Lord!"

I must have been in this trance for more than an hour. I went on to the barn and found my master there waiting for me. Again I began to tell him of my experience. I do not recall what he did to me afterwards. I felt burdened down and that preaching was my only relief. When I had finished I felt a great love in my heart that made me feel like stooping and kissing the very ground. My master sat watching and listening to me, and then he began to cry. He turned from me and said to me, in a broken voice, "Morte, I believe you are a preacher. From now on you can preach to the people here on my place in the old shed by the creek. But tomorrow morning, Sunday, I want you to preach to my family and neighbors. So put on your best clothes and be in front of the big house early in the morning, about nine o'clock."

I was so happy that I did not know what to do. I thanked my master and then God, for I felt that he was with me. Throughout the night I went from cabin to cabin, rejoicing and spreading the news.

The next morning at the time appointed I stood up on two planks in front of the porch of the big house and, without a Bible or anything, I began to preach to my master and the people. My thoughts came so fast that I could hardly speak fast enough. My soul caught on fire, and soon I had them all in tears. I told them that God had a chosen people and that he had raised me up as an example of his matchless love. I told them that they must be born again and that their souls must be freed from the shackles of hell.

Ever since that day I have been preaching the gospel and am not a bit tired. I can tell anyone about God in the darkest hour of midnight, for it is written on my heart. Amen.

2. Biblical Examples of Divine Encounter

The personal awareness of Divine presence is one of the basic religious themes in the Jewish and Christian traditions. The examples given here focus on the inescapable Presence who thrusts Himself into the lives of individuals and a community. As you read these excerpts from the Bible, note the attitude of the people who personally experience the Holy. Do they feel dependent on something or someone radically different from themselves? Are they attracted to this Other force? Do they fear

From *The Complete Bible: An American Translation*, trans. J. M. Powis Smith and a group of scholars (Chicago: The University of Chicago Press, Copyright 1923, 1927, 1948; published 1939; sixteenth impression 1960), Isaiah 6: 1–8; *Good News for Modern Man* 3rd edition (New York: American Bible Society, 1966), Acts 11:1–18, 9:1–19.

it? What other emotions are expressed? How intense is their involvement?

In the year that King Uzziah died, I saw the Lord sitting upon a throne, high and uplifted, with the skirts of his robe filling the temple. Over him stood seraphim, each having six wings, with two of which he covered his feet, with two he covered his loins, and with two he hovered in flight. And they kept calling to one another, and saying, "Holy, holy, holy, is the Lord of hosts; The whole earth is full of his glory."

And the foundations of the thresholds shook at the sound of those who called, and the house filled with smoke.

Then said I, "Woe to me! for I am lost; For I am a man of unclean lips, And I dwell among a people of unclean lips; For my eyes have seen the King, the Lord of hosts."

Then flew one of the seraphim to me, with a red-hot stone in his hand, which he had taken with tongs from the altar; and he touched my mouth with it, and said, "See! this has touched your lips; So your guilt is removed, and your sin forgiven."

Then I heard the voice of the Lord saying, "Whom shall I send, And who will go for us?"

Whereupon I said, "Here am I! send me." (Isaiah 6:1–8)

The apostles and the brothers throughout all of Judea heard that the Gentiles also had received the word of God. When Peter went up to Jerusalem, those who were in favor of circumcising Gentiles criticized him: "You were a guest in the home of uncircumcised Gentiles, and you even ate with them!" So Peter gave them a full account of what had happened, from the very beginning:

"I was praying in the city of Joppa, and I had a vision. I saw something coming down that looked like a large sheet being lowered by its four corners from heaven, and it stopped next to me. I looked closely inside and saw four-footed animals, and beasts, and reptiles, and wild birds. Then I heard a voice saying to me, 'Get up, Peter; kill and eat!' But I said, 'Certainly not, Lord! No defiled or unclean food has ever entered my mouth.' The voice spoke again from heaven, 'Do not consider anything unclean that God has declared clean.' This happened three times, and finally the whole thing was drawn back up into heaven. At that very moment three men who had been sent to me from Caesarea arrived at the house where I was staying. The Spirit told me to go with them without hesitation. These six brothers also went with me to Caesarea and we all went into the house of Cornelius. He told us how he had seen an angel standing in his house who said to him, 'Send someone to Joppa to call for a man whose full name is Simon Peter. He will speak words to you by which you and all your family will be saved.' And when I began to speak, the Holy Spirit came down on them just as on us at the beginning. Then I remembered what the Lord had said: 'John baptized with water, but you will be baptized with the Holy Spirit.' It is clear that God gave those Gentiles the same gift that he gave us when we believed in the Lord Jesus Christ; who was I, then, to try to stop God!" When they heard this, they stopped their criticism and praised God, saying, "Then God has given to the Gentiles also the opportunity to repent and live!" (Acts 11:1–18)

In the meantime Saul kept up his violent threats of murder against the disciples of the Lord. He went to the High Priest and asked for letters of introduction to the Jewish meeting houses in Damascus, so that if he should find any followers of the Way of the Lord there, he would be able to arrest them, both men and women, and take them back to Jerusalem.

On his way to Damascus, as he came near the city, a light from the sky suddenly flashed all around him. He fell to the ground and heard a voice saying to him, "Saul, Saul. Why do you persecute me?" "Who are you, Lord?" he asked. "I am Jesus, whom you persecute," the voice said. But get up and go into the city, where you will be told what you must do." Now the men who were traveling with Saul had stopped, not saying a word; they heard the voice but could not see anyone. Saul got up from the ground and opened his eyes, but could not see a thing. So they took him by the hand led him into Damascus. For three days he was not able to see, and during that time he did not eat or drink anything.

There was a disciple in Damascus named Ananias. He had a vision, in which the Lord said to him, "Ananias!" "Here I am, Lord," he answered. The Lord said to him: "Get ready and go to Straight Street and look in the house of Judas for a man from Tarsus named Saul. He is praying, and in a vision he saw a man named Ananias come in and place his hands on him so that he might see again." Ananias answered: "Lord, many people have told me about this man, about all the terrible things he has done to your people in Jerusalem. And he has come to Damascus with authority from the chief priests to arrest all who call on your name." The Lord said to him: "Go, for I have chosen him to serve me, to make my name known to Gentiles and kings, and to the people of Israel. And I myself will show him all that he must suffer for my sake."

So Ananias went, entered the house and placed his hands on Saul. "Brother Saul," he said, "the Lord has sent me—Jesus himself, whom you saw on the road as you were coming here. He sent me so that you might see again and be filled with the Holy Spirit." At once something like fish scales fell from Saul's eyes and he was able to see again. He stood up and was baptized; and after he had eaten, his strength came back. (Acts 9:1–19)

3. Miki's Divine Experience

The experience of a divine encounter sometimes poses a problem for the person who undergoes it. In this description of "the True and Original God" who reveals his saving power through a Japanese housewife, Miki, we note not only the extraordinary experience of the encounter but the reluctance of Miki (Mee-kee) to become the "Shrine of God and mediatrix between God the Parent and men." Despite the hesitancy of Miki and members of her family to obey the Divine command, they submitted to the divine spirit when they realized their protest was to no avail. As a result of this special revelation Miki became the foundress of one of the "New Religions," called The Religion of Divine Wisdom (Tenrikyo). The events that took place over several months are summarized here by a Western scholar of Tenrikyo, Henry van Straelen. What can you infer from this selection of the relation between the divine and ordinary human reality?

It happened during the autmn of 1837 that Miki's eldest son Shūji, while he was working in the field, was suddenly overcome by a tremendous pain in one of his legs. Doctors were called in, but they were of no avail. A yamabushi 山伏, an itinerant priest, called Nakano Ichibei 中野市兵衛, was asked to practise a kind of mystical ritualism upon the patient, using a certain woman Soyo そよ as medium; the pain stopped immediately. However, some time later the pain started even fiercer than before; ritualisms were again applied with the same temporary success. These strange proceedings of renewed attacks and subsequent relief happened at least some 8 times. In so far as Miki was concerned, signs of strange phenomena began to cast their shadow. Repeatedly she felt as if her body were being shaken. One author remarks here that Miki began gradually to attune herself to the movements of the Universe.[1] He does not explain these mysterious words and it seems as if every reader is free to make his own interpretations. About a year later Miki and her husband Zembei and their son Shūji became victims of a painful experience. The itinerant priest was again called in, but since Mrs. Soyo was absent, Miki herself acted as medium. While the ritual proceeded, suddenly one of the heavenly deities forced himself upon the hospitality of Miki. The expression of her face became severe and her whole appearance took a dignified air. When asked what deity had descended upon her, she replied:" *Ten no Shōgun* 天の 将軍 the Heavenly General." At this the *yamabushi* reverently asked: "Who are you, Heavenly *Shōgun,* who descended upon this woman? Then a voice was heard: *"Ware wa moto no Kami, jitsu no Kami nari,* 我は 元の神 実の神なり, I am the True and Original God. I have a predestina-

From *The Religion of Divine Wisdom: Japan's Most Powerful Religious Movement,* Henry Van Straelem (Kyoto: Veritas Shoin, 1957), pp. 40–43.

tion to this Residence. Now I have descended from Heaven to safe [*sic*] all human beings. I want to take Miki as *Tsuki-Hi's yashiro* 月日の社 Shrine of God and mediatrix between God the Parent and men."[2]

All the bystanders were struck with awe. When Miki's husband came to his senses, he vehemently asked the deity to withdraw himself, pleading that his wife was a mother of four children who needed all her attention. However, the deity was stubborn and even menaced the whole family with extinction if his divine invitation should not be accepted.

In the usual Japanese way, a family council was held to which were invited also friends and religious authorities. After three days of thorough deliberation, they came to the final conclusion that nothing else could be done but to accept the divine invitation. Only after this conclusion was made the foundress recovered from her trance. At the same time all the members of the family felt themselves completly recovered from pain and sickness. This very day is considered as being the foundation day of Tenri-kyō. It was 26th of the 10th month of the 9th year of *Tempō* 天保 (1838), when Miki was 41 years old. In numerous publications Tenrikyō authors try to give all sorts of mystical interpretations why exactly this particular date and this particular year have been selected by the deity. But since I am afraid that Western readers will not be able to catch up with their (I should nearly say) mystical reasoning, I may be allowed to bypass these interpretations in silence.

This first revelation, which according to the Tenrikyō believers was given to Nakayama Miki, was only the beginning of a long chain of divine intimacies between the Gods and this elected woman. Only a short time after this first heavenly descension, a new and strange happening occurred at the house of Miki. One night, while she was sleeping in her room, a big noise was suddenly heard just above her. When she got up she had the feeling as if she had been placed under some heavy pressure. Later she explained that the 10 deities—who as the reader will see later,* play such prominent rôles in Tenrikyō's cosmogony—had forced themselves upon her in succession; first *Kunitokotachi-no-Mikoto* 国床立命 and then the other nine deities. We may safely accept that during the visits of these 10 deities the first seeds were sown in Miki's mind about the origin of this world and of mankind, which knowledge would ripen in later years to a fantastic jungle of trees and plants as we shall see later.

The very place where all these mysterious happenings had occurred forms today the center of Tenrikyō's worship, for in this place the *kanrodai*, an 8.2 feet column consisting of 13 different hexagonal layers, has been erected as a kind of eternal remembrance of the divine happenings. We read in the canonical writings: "This house is the residence where I created men and the universe. Here I came down for the revelation of mankind."[3] At this point of the biographies of Miki, the authors unanimously stress the fact that it must by now be clear that Tenrikyō is a revealed religion, just as well as Islam and Christianity.

---

* The material referred to has not been included.

From this time on, Miki by Divine Command began to practice charity so much that she got into trouble with her husband and with all her relatives. She began to give away all family treasures, funiture and even food that had been stored up in her house. Everyone tried to stop Miki's charitable prodigality, but without success. Many neighbours and villagers were convinced that she was possessed by a fox, a badger or some other evil spirit. Mr. Zembei was advised to take stern measures. One day he ordered her to put on a white dress and to place herself before the family shrine. Here before the spirit of his ancestors, he called her to attention and threatened her with persecution. However, the elected one remained obstinate, nay, became more than ever convinced of her divine mission, and her generosity became even greater. During this time it often happened that Mr. Zembei got up in the night and took the family sword in his hand in order to drive away the evil spirit of his wife, for he really thought that she had become insane or possessed by some evil spirit.

In the biography of the foundress written by the first patriarch of Tenrikyō, Nakayama Shinjirō 中山新治郎, we read how Miki one day addressed her husband as follows: "Upon divine command I wish our house to be pulled down. If you refuse you are opposing God's will." When Mr. Zembei refused this extraordinary request of his wife, the foundress became ill and was unable during 20 days to take any food or drink. A family council was held once again to discuss what steps should be taken for the recovery of the patient. As a consequence, the divine will was invoked and they received promptly the answer to tear down the house. People were called in to start the demolition upon which Miki recovered suddenly. On seeing this, the members of the family thought to have given sufficient proof of their good will and they stopped further demolition of the house. However, this seems to have been contrary to the divine command, because the foundress became ill once again. A new family council was held and we hear of another divine oracle, demanding solemnly once again to tear down not only a part but the whole house. At this pertinent request of the deity, the members of the family council became angry and they insulted the divine spirit with such words as: "You are only a god who brings troubles and who impoverishes people (*bimbōgami* 貧乏神). You can never be the true God, for only an evil spirit can cause man to suffer. We request you to go out of her."[4] The biographers tell us that at this refusal the sufferings of the foundress became so great that the members of the family could see no other solution but to submit to the divine request. And once again the foundress was restored to health.

NOTES

1. From *Oya-Sama* 教祖様, by Serizawa Kōjirō 芹沢光治郎 in *Tenri Jihō* 天理時報
2. *Tenrikyō Kyōten*, p. 3
3. *Ofudesaki* おふでさき, VI 55 & 56.
4. From *Hinagata Shikan* ひながた私観, by Matsuoka Kunio, 松岡国雄, p. 21.

4. A Buddhist's Vision in Tibet

The religious pilgrim's progress characteristically has both disappointments and moments of deep, rich, tranquil insight. In the following selection one of the latter is recorded by Lama Anagarika Govinda when he was a student on the quest for Truth. Born in Germany, his quest carried him to Ceylon, India, and finally to Tibet where eventually he became a member of the Buddhist Kargyüpa Order. He is the author of several books on Buddhism that are available in English. The scene of the following account is in a room of a monastery. This room had been dedicated to the celestial bodhisattva Maitreya, who is called "Friend" because he responds to prayers and is expected at the end of this era as the revealer of truth for all. Compare this account to Isaiah's vision in the temple (reading 2).

The sun had not yet set, so that it was too early to go to bed, and actually I did not feel sleepy. It was agreeable to stretch one's legs after a long day's ride, and so I remained at rest. As my eyes fell on the freshly plastered wall opposite me, I observed the irregular surface, and it seemed to me as if it had a strange life of its own.

At the same time I became conscious that this room, in spite of its emptiness, had something that appealed to me in an extraordinary way, though I was unable to discover any reason for it. The gloomy weather and the poor prospects for the following day were in no way conducive to an elated state of mind. But since I had entered this room my depression had vanished and had given place to a feeling of great inner peace and serenity.

Was it the general atmosphere of this ancient sanctuary, which from the cave of a pious hermit had grown in the course of centuries into a monastery in which uncounted generations of monks had lived a life of devotion and contemplation? Or was it owing to the special atmosphere of this room that the change had taken place in me? I did not know.

I only felt that there was something about the surface of this wall that held my attention, as if it were a fascinating landscape. But no, it was far from suggesting a landscape. These apparently accidental forms were related to each other in some mysterious way; they grew more and more plastic and coherent. Their outlines became clearly defined and raised from the flat background. It was like a process of crystallisation, or like an organic growth; and the transformation which took place on the surface of the wall was as natural and convincing as if I had watched an invisible sculptor in the creation of a life-size relief. The only difference was that the invisible sculptor worked from *within* his material and in all places at the same time.

From *The Way of the White Clouds* by Lama Govinda (London: Hutchinson Publishing Ltd., 1966), pp. 48–52.

Before I knew how it all happened, a majestic human figure took shape before my eyes. It was seated upon a throne, with both feet on the ground, the head crowned with a diadem, the hands raised in a gesture, as if explaining the points of an intricate problem: it was the figure of Buddha Maitreya, the Coming One, who already now is on his way to Buddhahood, and who, like the sun before it rises over the horizon, sends his rays of love into this world of darkness, through which he has been wandering in innumerable forms, through innumerable births and deaths.

I felt a wave of joy passing through me, as I had felt in the presence of my Guru,* who had initiated me into the mystic circle (*mandala*) of Maitreya and had caused his images to be erected all over Tibet.

I closed my eyes and opened them again: the figure in the wall had not changed. There it stood like a graven image, and yet full of life!

I looked around me to assure myself that I was not dreaming, but everything was as before: there was the projecting rock in the wall to the right, my cooking utensils on the ground, my luggage in the corner.

Again my glance fell upon the opposite wall. The figure was there—or was I mistaken? What I saw was no more the figure of a compassionately preaching Buddha but rather that of a terrifying demon. His body was thick-set and bulky, his feet wide apart, as if ready to jump: his raised, flamelike hair was adorned with human skulls, his right arm stretched out in a threatening gesture, wielding a diamond sceptre (*vajra*) in his hand, while the other hand held a ritual bell before his chest.

If all this had not appeared before me like a skillfully modelled relief, as if created by the hand of a great artist, my blood would have frozen with terror. But as it was I rather felt the strange beauty in the powerful expression of this terrifying form of Vajrapāni, the defender of truth against the powers of darkness and ignorance, the Master of Unfathomed Mysteries.

While I was still under the spell of this awe-inspiring figure, the diamond sceptre transformed itself into a flaming sword, and in place of the bell the long stem of a lotus-flower grew out of the left hand. It grew up to the height of the left shoulder, unfolded its leaves and petals, and upon them appeared the book of wisdom. The body of the figure had in the meantime become that of a well-formed youth, sitting cross-legged on a lotus-throne. His face took on a benign expression, lit up with the youthful vigour and charm of an Enlightened One. Instead of the flaming hair and the human skulls, his head was adorned with the Bodhisattva-crown of the Five Wisdoms. It was the figure of Mañjuśrī, the embodiment of active wisdom, who cuts through the knots of doubt with the flaming sword of knowledge.

After some time a new change took place, and a female figure formed itself before my eyes. She had the same youthful grace as Mañjuśrī, and even the lotus, which grew from her left hand, seemed to be the same. But instead of wielding the flaming sword her opened right hand was resting on the knee of her right leg, which was extended, as if she were about to descend from her lotus-throne in answer to some prayer of supplication.

---

* Spiritual teacher.

The wish-granting gesture, the loving expression of her face, which seemed to be inclined towards some invisible supplicant, were the liveliest embodiment of Buddha Sakyamuni's words:

From THE GODS OF NORTHERN BUDDHISM, by Alice Getty. Charles E. Tuttle Company, Tokyo, Japan, copyright 1962. Illustrations from the collection of Henry H. Getty. Used by permission.

"Like a mother, who protects her child, her only child, with her own life, thus one should cultivate a heart of unlimited love and compassion towards all living beings."

I felt deeply moved, and trying to concentrate my whole attention upon the lovely expression of her divine face, it seemed to me as if an almost imperceptible, sorrowful smile was hovering about her mouth, as though she wanted to say: "Indeed, my love is unlimited; but the number of suffering beings is unlimited too. How can I, who have only one head and two eyes, soothe the unspeakable sufferings of numberless beings?"

Were these not the words of Avalokiteśvara which reverberated in my mind? Indeed, I recognised in Tārā's face the features of the Great Compassionate One, out of whose tears Tārā is said to have sprung.

And, as if overpowered by grief, the head burst and grew into a thousand heads, and the arms split into a thousand arms, whose helping hands were stretched out in all directions of the universe like the rays of the sun. And now everything was dissolving into light, for in each of those innumerable hands there was a radiating eye, as loving and compassionate as that in the face of Avalokiteśvara; and as I closed my eyes, bewildered and blinded by so much radiance, it struck me that I had met this face before: and now I knew—it was that of the Coming One, the Buddha Maitreya!

When I looked up again everything had disappeared; but the wall was lit up by a warm light, and when I turned round I saw that the last rays of the evening sun had broken through the clouds. I jumped up with joy and looked out of the window. All the gloom and darkness had disappeared. The landscape was bathed in the soft colours of the parting day. Above the green pastures of the valley there rose the brown- and ochre-coloured slopes of rocky mountains, and behind them appeared sunlit snow-fields against the remnants of dark purple clouds, now and then lit up by lightning. A distant rumbling from beyond the mountains showed that Vajrapāni was still wielding his diamond sceptre in the struggle with the powers of darkness.

Deep below me in the valley I saw my horses grazing, small as toys, and not far from them rose the smoke of a camp-fire, where the men were preparing their evening meal. From the cave temple came the deep, vibrating sound of a big bass-drum. It came like a voice out of the bowels of the earth, like a call from the depths to the light above: the light that conquers all darkness and fear of the eternal abyss.

And out of the gladness of my heart words formed themselves spontaneously like a prayer and a pledge:

'Who art Thou, Mighty One,
Thou, who art knocking
at the portals of my heart?
Art Thou a ray of wisdom and of love,
emerging from the dazzling aura
of a silent Muni,*
illuminating those

---

* Monk.

whose minds are ready
to receive the noble message
of deliverance?

Art Thou the Coming One,
the Saviour of all beings,
who wanders through the world
in thousand unknown forms?

Art Thou the messenger
of one who reached the shore
and left the raft for us
to cross the raging stream?*
Whoever Thou may be,
Mighty Enlightened One:
wide open are the petals
of my heart,
prepared the lotus-throne
for Thy reception.

Do I not meet Thee
everywhere I go?—
I find Thee dwelling
in my brothers' eyes;
I hear Thee speaking
in the Guru's voice;
I feel Thee
in the mother's loving care.

Was it not Thou,
who turned the stone to life,
who made Thy Form
appear before my eyes,
whose presence sanctified
the rite of initiation,
who shone into my dreams
and filled my life with light?

Thou Sun of Thousand Helping Arms,
All-comprehending and compassionate,
O Thousand-Eyed One, Thou,
whose all-perceiving glance,
while penetrating all,
hurts none, nor judges, nor condemns,
but warms and helps to ripen,
like fertile summer rain.

---

* A common Buddhist metaphor is the raging stream of life which one can cross
safely by the raft of Buddhist teaching and practice.

Thou Light!
Whose rays transform and sanctify
compassionately
our weakness even;
Turning death's poison thus
into the wine of life—

Wherever in the sea
of hate and gloom
A ray of wisdom
and compassion shines:
There I know Thee,
O Mighty One!

Whose radiant light
leads us to harmony,
Whose peaceful power
overcomes all worldly strife.

O Loving One!
Take this my earthly life
and let me be reborn
in Thee!'

5. Experience of the Lord, St. Teresa

This selection is taken from the spiritual autobiography of St. Teresa of Jesus (1515–1582), one of the best-known and most influential Roman Catholic mystics. In this portion of the work she describes the highest state of prayer, as she has experienced it. Her career was striking not only for the complexity and intensity of her devotional life but also for her work as a religious reformer and as a founder of new chapters for her religious order. (She was a Carmelite nun.) Her career as a whole, therefore, included strong elements not only of personal experience of the Holy but also of themes we shall consider in

From *The Life of the Holy Mother Teresa of Jesus* in *The Complete Works* of Saint Teresa, Vol. 1, trans. and ed. by E. Allison Peers from the critical edition of P. Silverio de Santa Teresa, C. D. (New York: Sheed & Ward, Inc., 1946), pp. 119f, 121, 125f, 128f. Published in three volumes by Sheed & Ward, Inc., New York. Used by permission of the publisher.

the next chapter. Furthermore, this excerpt itself shows some elements of the religious type we shall consider in the fourth chapter. The term "mysticism" is often used to cover both of these types (and perhaps others, not considered in this book, as well). In both these religious types, personal experience is prominent. The key feature that places this account under the heading "personal experience of the Holy" is St. Teresa's conviction that the source of the power she experienced was external to her. What understanding of the Holy is stated in or implied by this selection? Why was St. Teresa sometimes afraid of the Lord's "favors" to her? What reasons might she give to rebut the claim that these experiences were the product merely of her own mind?

I should like, with the help of God, to be able to describe the difference between union and rapture, or elevation, or what they call flight of the spirit, or transport—it is all one. I mean that these different names all refer to the same thing, which is also called ecstasy. It is much more beneficial than union: the effects it produces are far more important and it has a great many more operations, for union gives the impression of being just the same at the beginning, in the middle and at the end, and it all happens interiorly. But the ends of these raptures are of a higher degree, and the effects they produce are both interior and exterior. May the Lord explain this, as He has explained everything else, for I should certainly know nothing of it if His Majesty had not shown me the ways and manners in which it can to some extent be described.

Let us now reflect that this last water* which we have described is so abundant that, were it not that the ground is incapable of receiving it, we might believe this cloud of great Majesty to be with us here on this earth. But as we are giving Him thanks for this great blessing, and doing our utmost to draw near to Him in a practical way, the Lord gathers up the soul, just (we might say) as the clouds gather up the vapours from the earth, and raises it up till it is right out of itself (I have heard that it is in this way that the clouds or the sun gather up the vapours)[1] and the cloud rises to Heaven and takes the soul with it, and begins to reveal to it things concerning the Kingdom that He has prepared for it. I do not know if the comparison is an exact one, but that is the way it actually happens.

In these raptures the soul seems no longer to animate the body, and thus the natural heat of the body is felt to be very sensibly diminished: it gradually becomes colder, though conscious of the greatest sweetness and

---

* She has been developing the image of the soul as a garden tended to God's glory. The levels of prayer are thus compared to various ways in which the garden might be watered. The last and best water, corresponding to the fourth stage of prayer, is the cloudburst sent by God's grace.

delight. No means of resistance is possible, whereas in union, where we are on our own ground, such a means exists: resistance may be painful and violent but it can almost always be effected. But with rapture, as a rule, there is no such possibility: often it comes like a strong, swift impulse, before your thought can forewarn you of it or you can do anything to help yourself; you see and feel this cloud, or this powerful eagle, rising and bearing you up with it on its wings.

You realize, I repeat, and indeed see, that you are being carried away, you know not whither. For, though rapture brings us delight, the weakness of our nature at first makes us afraid of it, and we need to be resolute and courageous in soul, much more so than for what has been described. For, happen what may, we must risk everything, and resign ourselves into the hands of God and go willingly wherever we are carried away, for we are in fact being carried away, whether we like it or no. In such straits do I find myself at such a time that very often I should be glad to resist, and I exert all my strength to do so, in particular at times when it happens in public and at many other times in private, when I am afraid that I may be suffering deception. Occasionally I have been able to make some resistance, but at the cost of great exhaustion, for I would feel as weary afterwards as though I had been fighting with a powerful giant. At other times, resistance has been impossible: my soul has been borne away, and indeed as a rule my head also, without my being able to prevent it: sometimes my whole body has been affected, to the point of being raised up from the ground. . . .

When I tried to resist these raptures, it seemed that I was being lifted up by a force beneath my feet so powerful that I know nothing to which I can compare it, for it came with a much greater vehemence than any other spiritual experience and I felt as if I were being ground to powder. It is a terrible struggle, and to continue it against the Lord's will avails very little, for no power can do anything against His. At other times His Majesty is graciously satisfied with our seeing that He desires to show us this favour, and that, if we do not receive it, it is not due to Himself. Then, if we resist it out of humility, the same effects follow as if we had given it our entire consent.

These effects are very striking. One of them is the manifestation of the Lord's mighty power: as we are unable to resist His Majesty's will, either in soul or in body, and are not our own masters, we realize that, however irksome this truth may be, there is One stronger than ourselves, and that these favours are bestowed by Him, and that we, of ourselves, can do absolutely nothing. This imprints in us great humility. Indeed, I confess that in me it produced great fear—at first a terrible fear. One sees one's body being lifted up from the ground; and although the spirit draws it after itself, and if no resistance is offered does so very gently, one does not lose consciousness at least, I myself have had sufficient to enable me to realize that I was being lifted up. The majesty of Him Who can do this is manifested in such a way that the hair stands on end, and there is produced a great fear of offending so great a God, but a fear overpowered by[2] the deepest love, newly enkindled, for One Who, as we see, has so deep a love for so loathsome a worm that He seems not to be satisfied by literally drawing the soul to Himself, but will also have the body, mortal though it is, and befouled as is its clay by all the offences it has committed. . . .

I can testify that after a rapture my body often seemed as light as if all weight had left it: sometimes this was so noticeable that I could hardly tell when my feet were touching the ground. For, while the rapture lasts, the body often remains as if dead and unable of itself to do anything: it continues all the time as it was when the rapture came upon it— in a sitting position, for example, or with the hands open or shut. The subject rarely loses consciousness: I have sometimes lost it altogether, but only seldom and for but a short time. As a rule the consciousness is disturbed; and, though incapable of action with respect to outward things, the subject can still hear and understand, but only dimly, as though from a long way off. I do not say that he can hear and understand when the rapture is at its highest point—by "highest point" I mean when the faculties are lost through being closely united with God. At that point, in my opinion, he will neither see, noi hear, nor perceive; but, as I said in describing the preceding prayer of union, this complete transformation of the soul in God lasts but a short time, and it is only while it lasts that none of the soul's faculties is able to perceive or know what is taking place. We cannot be meant to understand it while we are on earth—God, in fact, does not wish us to understand it because we have not the capacity for doing so. I have observed this myself. . . .

I believe myself that a soul which attains to this state neither speaks nor does anything of itself, but that this sovereign King takes care of all that it has to do. Oh, my God, how clear is the meaning of that verse about asking for the wings of a dove[3] and how right the author was—and how right we shall all be!—to ask for them! It is evident that he is referring to the flight taken by the spirit when it soars high above all created things, and above itself first of all; but it is a gentle and a joyful flight and also a silent one.

What power is that of a soul brought hither by the Lord, which can look upon everything without being ensnared by it! How ashamed it is of the time when it was attached to everything! How amazed it is at its blindness! How it pities those who are still blind, above all if they are persons of prayer to whom God is still granting favours! It would like to cry aloud to them and show them how mistaken they are, and sometimes it does in fact do so and brings down a thousand persecutions upon its head. Men think it lacking in humility and suppose that it is trying to teach those from whom it should learn, especially if the person in question is a woman. For this they condemn it, and rightly so, since they know nothing of the force by which it is impelled. Sometimes it cannot help itself nor endure failing to undeceive those whom it loves and desires to see set free from the prison of this life; for it is in a prison, nothing less—and it realizes that it is nothing less—that the soul has itself been living.

It is weary of the time when it paid heed to niceties concerning its own honour, and of the mistaken belief which it had that what the world calls honour is really so. It now knows that to be a sheer lie and a lie in which we are all living. It realizes that genuine honour is not deceptive, but true; that it values what has worth and despises what has none; for what passes away, and is not pleasing to God, is worth nothing and less than nothing.[4]

NOTES

1. The bracketed sentence is found in the margin of the autograph in St. Teresa's hand.
2. *Envuelto...*
3. Psalm liv. 7 (A.V. lv. 6).
4. Cf. *St. John of the Cross,* I, 25: "All the creatures are nothing; and their affections, we may say, are less than nothing.... The soul that sets its affections upon the being of creation is likewise nothing in the eyes of God, and less than nothing." (*Ascent of Mount Carmel,* 1. iv.)

6. Experience of the Divine Mother, Sri Ramakrishna

One of the most extraordinary saints in 19th-century India was the Hindu devotional-mystic Ramakrishna. He is regarded by his followers as an avatar *(divine incarnation). His immediate disciples founded the Ramakrishna Mission, which has various centers in the West under the name The Vedanta Society. This excerpt depicts some of his experiences as a young man when he was expected to serve as a priest in a temple at Dakshineshwar, near Calcutta. Contrary to the expectations of his superiors, his priestly duties were continually interrupted by his experiences of the Holy Power in the form of the goddess Kali, whom he addresses as "Mother." Note the intensity of the personal relationship Ramakrishna has with her. This relationship is made especially striking when you recall that he understood Kali to be "the appalling Power that makes and unmakes the universe." Why does Ramakrishna not comply with the expectations of conventional worship?*

From *Ramakrishna and His Disciples* by Christopher Isherwood (New York: Simon and Schuster, Inc.). Copyright 1959, 1961, 1962, 1963, 1964, 1965 by The Vedanta Society of Southern California. Reprinted by permission of Simon & Schuster, Inc. and The Vedanta Society of Southern California. pp. 64–68.

As the months of this year, 1856, went by, Ramakrishna's spiritual efforts became more and more intense. Addressing the image of (the goddess) Kali in the temple, he exclaimed piteously: "Mother, you showed yourself to Ramprasad and other devotees in the past. Why won't you show yourself to me? Why won't you grant my prayer? I've been praying to you so long!" And he wept bitterly.

"Oh, what days of suffering I went through!" Ramakrishna used to say, as he recalled this period in after-years. "You can't imagine the agony of my separation from Mother! But that was only natural. Suppose there's a bag of gold in a room and a thief in the next room, with only a thin partition in between. Can the thief sleep in peace? Won't he try to burst through that wall and get at the gold? That was the state I was in. I knew Mother was there, quite close to me. How could I want anything else? She is infinite happiness. Beside her, all the world's wealth is nothing."

Often, before the shrine, he became absorbed and stopped the performance of the ritual; sitting motionless for hours at a time. Because of this, some of the temple officials became impatient with him; others laughed at him for a half-crazy fool. But Mathur* was impressed. And he told the Rani: "We have got a wonderful devotee for the worship of our Goddess; very soon, he will awaken her."

Before long, Mathur was proved right. This is how Ramakrishna describes the experience: "There was an unbearable pain in my heart, because I couldn't get a vision of Mother. Just as a man wrings out a towel with all his strength to get the water out of it, so I felt as if my heart and mind were being wrung out. I began to think I should never see Mother. I was dying of despair. In my agony, I said to myself: 'What's the use of living this life?' Suddenly my eyes fell on the sword that hangs in the temple. I decided to end my life with it, then and there. Like a madman, I ran to it and seized it. And then—I had a marvellous vision of the Mother, and fell down unconscious. ... It was as if houses, doors, temples and everything else vanished altogether; as if there was nothing anywhere! And what I saw was an infinite shoreless sea of light; a sea that was consciousness. However far and in whatever direction I looked, I saw shining waves, one after another, coming towards me. They were raging and storming upon me with great speed. Very soon they were upon me; they made me sink down into unknown depths. I panted and struggled and lost consciousness."

It is not quite clear from Ramakrishna's narrative whether or not he actually saw the form of Mother Kali in the midst of this vision of shining consciousness. But it would seem that he did; because the first words that he uttered on coming to himself were "Mother, Mother!"

After this vision, Ramakrishna was so absorbed that he was often unable to perform the temple worship at all. Hriday had to do it for him. Hriday was so disturbed by the mental condition of his uncle that he

---

* Mathur Mohan was the son-in-law of Rani Rasmani, a wealthy, pious woman who built the temple building in which Ramakrishna worshipped.

called in a doctor to treat him. It would be interesting to know what form the treatment took. Needless to say, it was quite ineffectual.

On the days when Ramakrishna was able to perform the worship, a strange phenomenon would occur. "No sooner had I sat down to meditate," he later recalled, "than I heard clattering sounds in the joints of my body and limbs. They began in my legs. It was if someone inside me had keys and was locking me up, joint by joint, turning the keys. I had no power to move my body or change my posture, even slightly. I couldn't stop meditating, or go away elsewhere, or do anything else I wanted. I was forced, as it were, to sit in the same posture until my joints began clattering again and were unlocked, beginning at the neck, this time, and ending in my legs. When I sat and meditated, I had at first the vision of particles of light like swarms of fireflies. Sometimes I saw masses of light covering everything on all sides like a mist; at other times I saw how everything was pervaded by bright waves of light like molten silver. I didn't understand what I saw, nor did I know if it was good or bad to be having such visions. So I prayed anxiously to Mother: 'I don't understand what's happening to me. Please, teach me yourself how to know you. Mother, if *you* won't teach me, who will?' "

In such statements, we hear the artless accents of Ramakrishna, and they convey, more vividly than any words of his contemporaries, the personality he was more and more completly assuming; that of a child of the Divine Mother. Childlike, he now obeyed the will of the Mother in everything, no matter how trivial, and was utterly careless of what the world might think of his behaviour.

And now he had begun to see the Mother frequently. He saw her within the temple and outside it, without any longer having to make an effort of will in his meditation. He no longer saw an image in the temple but the form of Mother herself. Later, he described how "I put the palm of my hand near her nostrils and felt that the Mother was actually breathing. I watched very closely, but I could never see her shadow on the temple wall in the light of the lamp, at night. I used to hear from my room how Mother ran upstairs, as merry as a little girl, with her anklets jingling. I wanted to be sure that she'd really done this, so I went outside. And there she was, standing on the veranda of the second floor of the temple, with her hair flying. Sometimes she looked towards Calcutta and sometimes towards the Ganges."

Hriday has left us a description of his relations with Ramakrishna at this time, and of his uncle's astonishing behaviour. "You felt awestruck when you entered the Kali Temple in those days, even when Uncle wasn't there—and much more so when he was. Yet I couldn't resist the temptation of seeing how he acted at the time of the worship. As long as I was actually watching him, my heart was full of reverence and devotion; but when I came out of the temple, I began to have doubts and ask myself: 'Has Uncle really gone mad? Why else should he do such terrible things during the worship?' I was afraid of what the Rani and Mathur Babu would say when they came to hear of it. But Uncle never worried. . . . I didn't venture to speak to him much, any longer; my mouth was closed by a fear I can't describe. I felt that there was some kind of barrier between us. So I just looked after him in silence, as best I could. But I was afraid he'd make a scene, some day."

Hriday's fears were certainly justified. He continues: "I saw how Uncle's chest and eyes were always red, like those of a drunkard. He'd get up reeling from the worshipper's seat, climb on to the altar, and caress the Divine Mother, chucking her affectionately under the chin. He'd begin singing, laughing, joking and talking with her, or sometimes he'd catch hold of her hands and dance.... I saw how, when he was offering cooked food to the Divine Mother, he'd suddenly get up, take a morsel of rice and curry from the plate in his hand, touch the Mother's mouth with it and say: 'Eat it, Mother. Do eat it!' Then maybe he'd say: 'You want me to eat it—and then you'll eat some afterwards? All right, I'm eating it now.' Then he'd take some of it himself and put the rest to her lips again, saying: 'I've had some. Now you eat.'

"One day, at the time of the food-offering, Uncle saw a cat. It had come into the temple, mewing. He fed it with the food which was to be offered to the Divine Mother. 'Will you take it, Mother?' he said to the cat."

The appalling Power that makes and unmakes the universe may also be known in the aspect of an indulgent Mother whom one can laugh with and pester for favours like a child. And that Power is everywhere present—within the air around us, within an image in a temple, within a stray cat. These are the simple and overwhelming truths which Ramakrishna was demonstrating by his seemingly insane actions. No wonder the orthodox temple officials were outraged! They sent a message of complaint to Mathur, who was away from Dakshineswar at the time. Mathur replied that he would soon return to see and judge for himself; in the meanwhile, Ramakrishna was to be allowed to continue the worship. Shortly after this, Mathur did return, unannounced. He went into the Kali Temple while Ramakrishna was making the offering. What Mathur saw convinced him that he was in the presence not of insanity but of great holiness. He gave orders that Ramakrishna was not to be interfered with on any account. "Now the Goddess is being truly worshipped," he said to the Rani.

But the confidence which Mathur and his mother-in-law felt in Ramakrishna was to be put to an even more severe test. One day, the Rani paid a visit to Dakshineswar, bathed in the Ganges and went into the temple for the worship. Ramakrishna was already there. The Rani asked him to sing some of the songs in praise of the Mother which he sang so beautifully and with such ecstatic devotion. Ramakrishna sang for a while. Then suddenly he stopped, turned to the Rani and exclaimed indignantly: "Shame on you—to think such thoughts even here!" And so saying he struck the Rani with the palm of his hand.

Immediately there was a commotion. The women attendants of the Rani who were present began to scream for help. The gatekeeper and various officers of the temple came running up, ready to seize Ramakrishna and drag him out of the shrine. They only awaited the Rani's order. But the Rani herself remained calm; and Ramakrishna was now quietly smiling. "He is not to blame," the Rani told the officers. "Leave him alone."

For she already knew why Ramakrishna had struck her. Instead of listening to the song, she had actually at that moment been thinking about a lawsuit in which she was involved. She only marvelled that Ramakrishna could have known what was in her mind. Later, when her attendants exclaimed at his insolence, she replied gravely and humbly: "You don't understand—it was the Divine Mother herself who punished me and enlightened my heart." And she forbade them ever to refer to the incident again.

7. An Account of Divine Revelation, J. Smith

> *When religious authorities contradict each other, one who seeks to know the divine may sometimes seek for direct experience of it. It is just this situation which Joseph Smith (1805–1844), the founder of the Mormon church (or Church of Jesus Christ of the Latter-day Saints) describes in this excerpt. The outcome of such personal quests, as in this case, may be highly significant. What means does Smith use to find religious truth? How does this experience affect his standing in his community? What similarities to his situation does he find in Paul's account of his own vision?*

During this time of great excitement, my mind was called up to serious reflection and great uneasiness, but though my feelings were deep and often poignant, still I kept myself aloof from all these parties, though I attended their several meetings as often as occasion would permit. In process of time my mind became somewhat partial to the Methodist Sect, and I felt some desire to be united with them but so great were the confusion and strife among the different denominations, that it was impossible for a person young as I was, and so unacquainted with men and things, to come to any certain conclusion who was right and who was wrong.

My mind at times was greatly excited, the cry and tumult were so great and incessant. . . .

From *The Pearl of Great Price: A Selection from the Revelations, Translations, and Narrations of Joseph Smith,* Joseph Smith (Salt Lake City: The Church of Jesus Christ of Latter-day Saints, 1949), pp. 47–50.

In the midst of this war of words and tumult of opinions I often said to myself, What is to be done? Who of all these parties is right, or, are they all wrong together? If any one of them be right, which is it, and how shall I know it?

While I was laboring under the extreme difficulties caused by the contests of these parties of religionists, I was one day reading the Epistle of James, first chapter and fifth verse, which reads: "If any of you lack wisdom, let him ask of God, that giveth to all men liberally, and upbraideth not; and it shall be given him."

Never did any passage of scripture come with more power to the heart of man than this did at this time to mine. It seemed to enter with great force into every feeling of my heart. I reflected on it again and again, knowing that if any person needed wisdom from God, I did; for how to act I did not know, and unless I could get more wisdom than I then had, I would never know; for the teachers of religion of the different sects understood the same passage of scripture so differently as to destroy all confidence in settling the question by an appeal to the Bible.

At length I came to the conclusion that I must either remain in darkness and confusion, or else I must do as James directs, that is, ask of God. I at length came to the determination to ask of God, concluding that if He gave wisdom to them that lacked wisdom, and would give liberally, and not upbraid, I might venture.

So in accordance with this, my determination to ask of God, I retired to the woods to make the attempt. It was on the morning of a beautiful, clear day, early in the spring of eighteen hundred and twenty. It was the first time in my life that I had made such an attempt, for amidst all my anxieties I had never as yet made the attempt to pray vocally.

After I had retired to the place where I had previously designed to go, having looked around me, and finding myself alone, I kneeled down and began to offer up the desires of my heart to God. I had scarcely done so, when immediately I was seized upon by some power which entirely overcame me, and had such an astonishing influence over me as to bind my tongue so that I could not speak. Thick darkness gathered around me, and it seemed to me for a time as if I were doomed to sudden destruction.

But exerting all my power to call upon God to deliver me out of the power of this enemy which had seized upon me, and at the very moment when I was ready to sink to despair and abandon myself to destruction— not to an imaginary ruin, but to the power of some actual being from the unseen world, who had such marvelous power as I had never before felt in any being—just at this moment of great alarm, I saw a pillar of light exactly over my head, above the brightness of the sun, which descended gradually until if fell upon me.

It no sooner appeared than I found myself delivered from the enemy which held me bound. When the light rested upon me I saw two personages, whose brightness and glory defy all description, standing above me in the air. One of them spake unto me, calling me by name, and said, pointing to the other—"This is my Beloved Son, hear Him!"

My object in going to inquire of the Lord was to know which of all the sects was right, that I might know which to join. No sooner, therefore, did I get possession of myself, so as to be able to speak, than I asked the Personages who stood above me in the light, which of all the sects was right—and which I should join.

I was answered that I must join none of them, for they were all wrong and the Personage who addressed me said that all their creeds were an abomination in His sight, that those professors were all corrupt; that "they draw near to me with their lips, but their hearts are far from me, they teach for doctrines the commandments of men, having a form of godliness, but they deny the power thereof."

He again forbade me to join with any of them; and many other things did He say unto me, which I cannot write at this time. When I came to myself again, I found myself lying on my back, looking up into heaven. . . .

Some few days after I had this vision, I happened to be in company with one of the Methodist preachers, who was very active in the before mentioned religious excitement; and, conversing with him on the subject of religion, I took occasion to give him an account of the vision which I had had. I was greatly surprised at his behavior; he treated my communication not only lightly, but with great contempt, saying it was all of the devil, that there were no such things as visions or revelations in these days; that all such things had ceased with the apostles, and that there would never be any more of them.

I soon found, however, that my telling the story had excited a great deal of prejudice against me among professors of religion, and was the cause of great persecution, which, continued to increase, and though I was an obscure boy, only between fourteen and fifteen years of age, and my circumstances in life such as to make a boy of no consequence in the world, yet men of high standing would take notice sufficient to excite the public mind against me, and create a bitter persecution, and this was common among all the sects—all united to persecute me.

It caused me serious reflection then, and often has since, how very strange it was that an obscure boy of a little over fourteen years of age, and one, too, who was doomed to the necessity of obtaining a scanty maintenance by his daily labor, should be thought a character of sufficient importance to attract the attention of the great ones of the most popular sects of the day, and in a manner to create in them a spirit of the most bitter persecution and reviling. But strange or not, so it was, and it was often the cause of great sorrow to myself.

However, it was nevertheless a fact that I had beheld a vision. I have thought since, that I felt much like Paul, when he made his defense before King Agrippa, and related the account of the vision he had when he saw a light and heard a voice; still there were but few who believed him; some said he was dishonest, others said he was mad, and he was ridiculed and reviled. But all this did not destroy the reality of his vision. He had seen a vision, he knew he had, and all the persecution under heaven could not make it otherwise; and though they should persecute him unto death, yet he knew, and would know to his latest breath, that he had both seen a light and heard a voice speaking unto him, and all the world could not make him think or believe otherwise.

So it was with me. I had actually seen a light, and in the midst of that light I saw two Personages, and they did in reality speak to me, and though I was hated and persecuted for saying that I had seen a vision, yet it was true; and while they were persecuting me, reviling me, and speaking all manner of evil against me falsely for so saying, I was led to say in my heart: Why persecute me for telling the truth? I had actually seen a vision, and who am I that I can withstand God, or why does the world think to make me deny what I have actually seen? For I had seen a vision; I knew it, and I knew that God knew it, and I could not deny it, neither dared I do it, at least I knew that by so doing I would offend God and come under condemnation.

8. The Inner Ecstasy,
M. Bach

The selections we have included thus far have been drawn from other times and places. But the experience itself, the religious type featured in this chapter, is not at all foreign to the United States today. One of its most striking recently reported forms is that of "speaking in tongues." In this selection, Marcus Bach, a highly educated American, author of numerous books and director of the Foundation for Spiritual Understanding, describes his first personal experience of speaking in tongues or "glossolalia." According to Bach, how does one "get the Baptism"? What happens when one "gets the Baptism?" From this point of view, what does it mean to "know" Jesus?

"*The Baptism, Lord! The Baptism for my friend! Father, the Baptism for my good friend and brother!*"

The words were a prayer, a chant, an impassioned plea drumming on into a loss of time. Actually it may have been only five minutes, ten minutes, but however long, it was an eternity. I was kneeling on the hard floor of the printery, hunched over an office chair, head in my arms.

The droning voice was that of my friend Joseph, kneeling at another chair nearby. His words were a prayer-wheel turning, "*The Baptism, Lord!*

Reprinted by permission of The World Publishing Company from *The Inner Ecstasy* by Marcus Bach. Copyright © 1969 The World Publishing Company by Marcus Bach, pp. 11–13, 15–19.

The Baptism for my friend!" The supplication jogged the silent presses, stirring up the embalmed scent of printer's ink.

I was all too conscious, too aware of things. "You don't get the Baptism by remembering where you are," I told myself. "You don't get it in a printer's shop on a Saturday afternoon, or by smelling smells, or seeing in your mind's eye your Hungarian friend kneeling like a wound-up saint. You don't get it by wanting what you want, the Baptism, and not getting it because you say you want it. The robot in your brain is too awake. Your mind is too rational. You don't get it until you let go and let the Holy Ghost get through."

I wouldn't let go, nor would I let anyone get through. Who had the right to get through to me? Who was close enough to me, whom did I trust enough to be with me when I went out-of-my-mind? Was that what it was, an out-of-mind experience? Hypnosis? Self-hypnosis? Possession? Hysteria? No, not really. "You can't say that," I warned myself. "Forgive me, God, for thinking such things. I have seen the Baptism too often. I know what it does for people. I know how much I need it."

I *had* seen people "get the Spirit" or the "Baptism" all around me in my four months in this Pentecostal parish. I had seen them get it at Sunday morning services and at evening meetings and at midweek sessions when the faithful testified. When someone at these Holy Ghost assemblies shouted "Praise you, Jesus!" it sparked a fire that pounced upon the worshipers, a Pentecostal fire, burning without consuming, consuming without burning, as the Bible said.

"The Baptism, Lord! Father, the Baptism for my friend and brother!"

Many a worshiper at the Sunday services was overcome. Some of them actually passed out, but they claimed it was sheer joy. At first the quaking bodies and the spurted cries of "Bless you, Jesus!" and the babble of "unknown tongues" shocked the devil out of me, coming as I had from the staid and silent ranks of my traditional Reformed-Evangelical church, but after a while I saw the rapture.

Came a day when I *felt* the rapture but only by remote control. I felt the rapture that was not really *the* rapture and I knew it wasn't. Joseph told me it wasn't. I caught the warmth of the fire, but not the flames. You *had* to let go to really get the "tongues of fire." You had to go out-on-mind and into Spirit. And whom would I trust to see *me* in-the-Spirit? Whom would I want around to hear *my* babbling? Whom did I love enough to let him be a witness to *my* tears and to spy on God-only-knows what else I might reveal?...

"The Baptism, Lord! The Baptism for my friend! The Baptism for my good friend and brother!"

It was no use. I was reaching out for something which wasn't out but *in.* I cursed my ungullible mind for hanging on to reason, while my ego praised me for not going out-of-my-mind. My body grew tense. Tense and tenser to a breaking point.

A strange thing was happening. I was feeling light, relaxed, trancelike. I was aware that my lips were moving and that I was mumbling incoherently. Something was using my vocal cords, jabbering something through me. Short, sharp, stabbing gasps were getting the upper hand, taking me over, clearing a spiral path with a jargon I did not understand. *"Koina kara, lamani, mera!"*

"The Baptism for my good friend and brother!"

Joseph's voice. My voice. God's voice. It was all one. *"Koina, lamani karana!"* Not my words. Not my language. It was by no means I who was speaking into my nestled arms. This was what the Pentecostals called the unknown tongue or glossolalia.

I was conscious of what was happening, but as I contemplated this, the I that I thought I knew began moving out of range, moving into shadows, forced into retreat by an oncoming blob of light. My body was shaking. I was hot and cold. An ecstatically pleasant, thrilling surge of passion swept through me as if the Holy Ghost, whatever it was, had finally found an entry and was rushing in to take control.

The shaft of light was real and visible behind my tightly closed eyes. The more I tried to block it out, the more intense it became. The more I let go of my resistance to it, the faster it took form, setting up a blur of whirling scenes: violins, churches, pulpits, classrooms, crowds of people battling for and against my search for the Baptism.

In fantasy the word *BAPTISM* flashed before me on the rollers of a huge black printing press. The cylinders began to turn while the type had its own horizontal, back-and-forth movement in a wild, whirligig way, transferring itself instantly to spotlessly white sheets of paper raining from the sky. *BAPTISM, BAPTISM, BAPTISM.* I read the word over and over. Then the papers caught fire, burning up the churches and the people in my reeling brain, and exploding in a blinding flash.

Overpowered and overcome, I felt my arms lifted up in sheer delight. I raised my head and saw as in a mist Joseph with arms outstretched, fingers stiff, face radiant with approbation, exclaiming through his tears, "Praise the Lord! Praise the *Lord!"* I knew what I was doing but had no idea why I was doing it. All I know was that when I saw Joseph standing that way and when I answered his exclamation with a rush of gibberish welling up from deep inside me, I burst into hysterical laughter and weeping and sprawled to the floor in freedom and delight. *"Isbana el erra modana! Gurashi! Gurashi!"*

It was insanely wonderful. For the first time in my life a liberty beyond understanding and a joy that knew no bounds had hold of me. Just to lie on the floor and roll on the floor and shout prayers to God in a voice and words that only He could recognize, that only He could have put in my heart in the first place, to know that for once there was no separation between us, no quarrel, no quibbling about what is good or bad, true or false, white or black, pure or sinful, knowing only that whatever is, is right, that must have been what I was talking about in my "unknown tongue."

"Sona machina lanah, jura, lura, manakilira!"

The outpour of heavenish words, the volleys of Spirit-loaded phrases washed out every frustration and barrier that had ever kept me from saying,

"Lord, I believe!" I was saying it now in a "language of the Spirit" of which I understood not a single word. Mine was a feeling, a feeling that I was being *spoken through.*

"Spoken through, Joseph! Do you hear?" I shouted while my face was wet with tears.

"I hear!" Joseph cried. "I hear! Halleluiah!"

"This is the silliest thing in the world!" I heard myself say. *"Spoken through!* The silliest, loveliest, most wonderful thing in all the world! *Spoken through!"*

My words were drowned in a flood of ecstatic laughter. It *was* the silliest thing. I was again being spoken through. Words spewed out of me so thick and fast that in the midst of them I heard myself cry out, "I am Ishmael's spring!" The expression came from the same source from which I was getting all my "wisdom and power." From the Holy Spirit. Straight from the Holy Spirit, the Paraclete, Third Person of the Trinity. *Praise the Lord!*

How I had wanted to be a public speaker. How I had studied public speaking. How I had tried to learn and memorize a speech and now, my body trembling under the Baptismal power, I was explosive with the oratory of the prophets and I was voicing the language of the seers. *"Areada monoseena! Gurabsi! Llama ni sana! Mooranus, mooranus!"*

It was all mine. Everything I needed to know was mine. Anything I ever wanted to be was mine, even to being as great a violinist as my dear friend Joseph. All mine.

Joseph was clapping his hands and doing a little dance. Now he was singing:

> What shall save us from our sins?
> Nothing but the blood of Jesus!
> What shall make us pure within?
> Nothing but the blood of Jesus?

Out of the rapturous shock of the Baptism I took Joseph's hands. Whispering our "Praise the Lord!" we threw our arms around each other.

No one understands this, I told myself, only those who have experienced it. My church had no idea of the wonder of it. My church talked about conversion and changed lives and twice-born men and all the other phrases, but when you get the Baptism, when you stand with someone else who has it, when you "know as you are known," no one understands that unless he's had it.

"Right, Joseph?" I asked. "Isn't that the way it is? It can't be explained. You *can't* put it into words. You can't even *talk* about it. It doesn't make *sense* to people. God Almighty, it makes all things *new.* Old things are passed *away. Bless you, Jesus!"*

"Bless you, dear Jesus!" Joseph whispered.

"Bless you, dear Jesus!" I responded, overawed with wonder.

I walked away. "Bless you...dear Jesus." There was an anguish in me, a strange, deep, sudden anguish. I wanted to "cry myself out" as the

Pentecostals say, and I did. I wept without being ashamed. I had never spoken those words before, *"Bless you, dear Jesus."* At least never with a sense of feeling and believing. Never with the love that filled me now. I never really had communication with Jesus. I never knew Him. He had never come to life. He had always been a hazy kind of shadow-god. Even when I wanted to believe, I could not believe that He was as pure and sweet and divine as some people said He was. He was too good to be true. But now, *"Bless you, dear Jesus."*

First the anguish, then the ecstasy. It took me the remainder of the day and a prayer session with Joseph and most of the night to find the key to all this, but now for the first time my inner self confronted the world, making it clear to me that God and I were big enough to take on anything that the world had to offer. That, I was sure, was a secret that only Jesus knew.

9. Descent of the Spirit at a Pentecostal Meeting, *A.S. McPherson*

> *Vivid personal experience has long been a feature of Protestant evangelism in America. And this selection recounts an episode in the work of one of the best-known evangelists of recent times, Aimee Semple McPherson (1890–1944), founder of the Four Square Gospel. To the elements of prayer and glossolalia, which we have seen above, she adds preaching as well. And the combination of these in an intense and relatively long period of public witness and personal experience characterizes Pentecostal worship to this day. What leads her to describe one who has this experience as "slain under the power"? Why did she consider it so important for people who were already church members to hear her witness? What can you infer of her attitude toward society at large from this excerpt?*

Upon first arrival* this seemed a most discouraging field. No one but this precious colored sister was known to have received the baptism of the Holy Spirit according to Acts 2:4. Though we walked for blocks, not a hall could we find to rent, but I kept praying, and though everyone else doubted my call, I knew that God had sent me. Finally word came from the Swedish church that we would be welcome to open meetings there during the week.

From *This Is That* by Aimee Semple McPherson (Los Angeles: Echo Park Evangelistic Association, Inc., 1923), pp. 43–46, 91–97.
* At Corona, Long Island, near New York City, during World War I.

The second night the church was filled to the door, though church members had been warned by their ministers to keep away from the Pentecostal people and have nothing to do with those folks who talked in tongues. Just one week from the day meetings were opened the break came. A Sunday School teacher from one of the large churches, a man whose sound Christian standing had been known for years, was the first to receive the baptism. The wife of a leading citizen was the second, and when the altar call was given scores from the audience, which was made up entirely of church members, gathered about the altar.

Never having seen a Pentecostal meeting, they were very stiff and did not know how really to get hold and seek the Lord. Knowing that their ministers had warned them that this was all hypnotism, however, I was very careful not to lay hands upon, or speak to the seekers, but prayed by my own chair earnestly:

"Oh, Lord, send the power. Lord, honor your Word just now."

Then it was that Mrs. John Lake, who had risen from the altar and taken her seat in the audience again, suddenly fell under the power, with her head upon her husband's shoulder. In alarm the people said:

"She has fainted. Run and get some water." But I knew she hadn't fainted, and I kept on praying:

"Lord, send the power. Baptize her just now."

Quite a crowd had gathered round her, but before they could get back with the water, praise the Lord, her lungs began to heave with the power, her chin began to quiver, and she broke out speaking with other tongues to the amazement and delight of all.

On and on she spoke, in such a clear, beautiful language, her face shining with the glory of the Lord. One would say to another:

"What do you think of it?" and others would say:

"Oh, isn't it wonderful, marvelous! How I wish I had the same experience!"

The news of this well-known sister's baptism quickly spread through the town. The next night three were slain under the power and came through speaking in tongues, and thus the meetings increased in power, numbers and results each night.

After preaching in the church one week, Pastor W. K. Bouton invited us to his church to preach on a Thursday night. (After warning his people not to come near our meetings he had come himself.)

The Lord had convinced him of the truth that there was something deeper yet for himself and his church.

The night on which we spoke at his church I had to ask the Lord not to let me be afraid or overawed by the visiting ministers who sat behind me on the platform, and to give me liberty and power in preaching His Word and He never fails. He remembers our weakness, praise His name.

As I spoke, hearty "Amens" and "Hallelujahs" came from all over the church. I felt that I must preach the truth without compromise or fear at least once in this church as they might never ask me again. When finished I took my seat, not presuming to give an altar call in someone else's church.

The Minister rose and said:

"How many of you people believe what Sister McPherson has said to be the truth, feel that you have not received the baptism of the Holy Siprit in the Bible way, and would like to receive this experience? Lift your hands."

They tell me that every hand in the church went up. (My eyes were so full of tears of joy I really could not say).

The people rose from their seats and flocked up the aisles, gathered completely round the chancel rail, inside the chancel, right behind the pulpit, and prayed between the pews and all over the church for the baptism of the Holy Sprit. What a glorious sight it was! This church had been kept clean from concerts and suppers and worldly amusements. Through their consecrated pastor they had been brought up to the place where they were just ready to be swept into the fullness of the Spirit's power.

Three received the baptism that night. One lady fell by the organ, another at the other side of the church. Then two brothers who had not been on speaking terms with each other for over a year were seen talking to each other in the center of the church. One had asked the other, with tears in his eyes, to forgive him, and immediately fell back in his brother's arms under the power of the Holy Spirit. Alarmed, his brother lowered him to the floor.

I do not believe the scenes in that dear church could be described this side of heaven. Each time some one fell under the power the people would run to that side of the church. When some one would fall on the other side they would turn and go over there. It was all so new and strange.

The Pastor, however, did not run to look as the rest did, but kneeled by his pulpit with his hands over his face, looking through his fingers every once in a while to keep a watch on proceedings. (Laughing over it together later, when he had received his baptism, I told him it appeared as though he believed in the verse that told us to "watch and pray.") .He was yearning for the power of God, and yet naturally fearful lest his people should be led into confusion and error.

Seeing the questions and excitement of the people as the power of God prostrated their dear ones, the enemy whispered:

"Well, you will never have an invitation back to this church now. There never was anyone stretched out under the power on that green carpet before. They will never ask you back here again."

Oh, ye of little faith, wherefore did ye doubt?

At midnight, when the meeting was beginning to break a little, the Pastor touched me on the arm and said:

"Sister, we have talked this over with the officials and the church is yours for as long as you want it, and when you want it. When shall we have the next meeting?"

"Tomorrow night," I replied.

Tomorrow night found the church not only filled to the doors, but the vestry and Sunday School rooms as well,—this night seven received the baptism. The Minister invited me to preach the Bible evidence of the baptism

—speaking in other tongues as the Spirit gives utterance—and to take full liberty in every way.

During altar service he kneeled, looking through his fingers once in a while, at the strange proceedings taking place in his dignified congregation. Sinners broke down and wept their way to Jesus' feet—Protestants and Catholics alike. Such praying and calling upon the name of the Lord, the minister feared would result in the people's being arrested for disturbing the peace.

The third night nineteen received the baptism of the Holy Spirit. Down they went right and left, between the seats, in the aisles, in front of the chancel rail, up on the platform. Oh, Glory!

One night, while praying with a young lady who was receiving the baptism, I happened to catch the minister's eye as he was watching and beckoned him to come where he could really see and hear. He kneeled beside the young lady whom he knew well as a devoted Christian worker, and soon saw her face suffused with heavenly glory as she was filled with the Spirit and broke out speaking with other tongues and praising the Lord. As he watched and listened a wistful look came over the brother's face and without a word he went round to his pulpit again and kneeling down with closed eyes, lifted his hands and began to pray.

"Oh, Lord, fill me. Oh, Lord, fill me." Over and over he prayed this simple prayer in earnestness and humility before the Lord. The Spirit kept impressing me to go and pray for him. At first I hesitated, feeling my unworthiness, but at last I went and kneeled behind him and began to pray as simply as he:

"Lord, fill him."

"Lord, fill me," he would cry.

"Lord, fill him," was the prayer that filled my soul.

I do not know how long we kept on praying thus, but I do know that when I opened my eyes it seemed almost too good to be true. The minister was swaying from side to side, and soon fell backwards under the power and rolled off the little step and lay under the glorious power of the Lord, just inside the chancel rail.

Someone spoke to his wife, who had been sitting in the audience, and said:

"Oh, there goes William!"

This was too much and with one bound she was in the aisle and ran to the front sobbing imploringly:

"Oh, Will, Will, speak to me. Speak to me."

Kneeling beside her I was praying with all my might that the Lord should baptize this dear Pastor as it would mean so much to the entire church and in fact the whole town. Fearful lest she should disturb him, I said:

"Oh, my dear, you wouldn't disturb him while he is under the power, for the world, would you?"

"Oh, but he's dying. He's dying!" she wailed. "I know he's going to die!"

"Oh, no, he is not dying," I hastily explained. "This is the power of the Holy Spirit, dear. He is safe in the arms of Jesus and if you watch a few minutes you will see him receive the Holy Spirit, I am sure."

"Oh, but I know he is dying! He had a vision once before and he almost died then! Will! Will! speak to me!" she implored.

I doubt if I could have restrained her much longer, but just at that tense moment, when the congregation were gathered round in breathless circles, leaning over the chancel rail, some even standing on the pews to see over the others' shoulders, Pastor W. K. Bouton was filled with the blessed Holy Spirit and gave such a Christ-exalting message as one seldom hears in this old world. The glory of God filled the place. The presence of the Lord penetrated the very air.

People fell to the floor here and there through the audience. Strong men sobbed like babies, and when at last the Pastor rose to his feet he walked up and down the platform, and said:

"Oh, friends, I have to preach!" And preach he did, under the inspiration of the Holy Spirit, telling the people that "This Is That," commanding them to be filled with the Spirit, to get oil in their lamps and prepare for the coming of the Lord.

In the two weeks that followed practically the entire congregation from pulpit to the door, besides members who came in from other churches, were baptized with the Holy Spirit and were afire with the Spirit of Evangelism.

All the trustees except one were swept through to the baptism. This one held aloof for some time, saying:

"Oh, I don't believe that all this noise and shouting and falling under the power is necessary. I believe in the Holy Spirit, but not in this enthusiastic manner."

"Well, brother, even if you don't understand it all now, do not sit back here in the seats. Come up to the altar. You feel it will be all right to seek more of Jesus, don't you?"

"Oh, yes, I will seek more of the Lord," he replied. "That's all right," and he took his place with the others at the altar.

It was only a few minutes later while praying—with the seekers, and they were going down one by one under the mighty rushing wind of the heavenly gales that were sweeping from heaven, that we heard a great shout, and something struck the floor with a thump.

Making my way as quickly as possible to the place where this great roaring was coming from, I found its source of origin was none other than the trustee who had but shortly before declared that all of this noise and shouting was unnecessary. I doubt if there was anyone in the church who made as much noise as he. He shook from head to foot; his face was aglow with heaven's light; he fairly shouted and roared forth as the Spirit gave him utterance, his heart was filled with joy and glory.

One brother who had thought it unnecessary to have a religion of real heart warmth and glory shouted God's praises for hours after he had been filled, and coming to me as I was on the sidewalk, just leaving for home, said, as he shook with the power:

"S-S-Sister M-M-McPherson, w-w-will I ever b-be able to t-talk- in E-English again?" and away he went with other tongues again. Oh, hallelujah! Sometimes the greatest doubters get the biggest baptisms and the people who despise noise make the most noise of all when they receive this old-time power.

10. Amazing Grace,
John Newton

As you read (or sing) through this old "gospel" hymn, imagine its being sung at a revival meeting such as the one described above. What meaning would it have for those who have been "slain under the power"? How does it express their understanding of the religious life? This hymn is still in Methodist and Baptist hymnals. Do you think it is sometimes out of place in the contemporary worship of large denominations? Why?

SALVATION

Amazing Grace

AMAZING GRACE. C. M.

GRACE

188

JOHN NEWTON, 1725-1807

Early American Melody

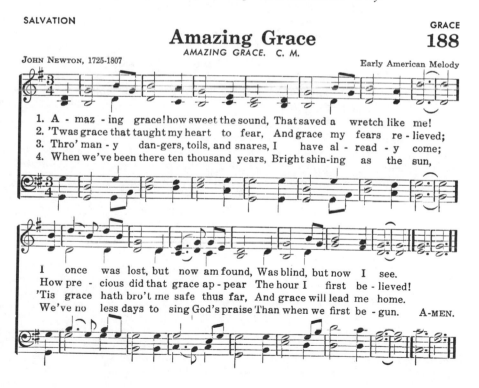

1. A - maz - ing grace! how sweet the sound, That saved a wretch like me!
2. 'Twas grace that taught my heart to fear, And grace my fears re - lieved;
3. Thro' man - y dan-gers, toils, and snares, I have al - read - y come;
4. When we've been there ten thousand years, Bright shin-ing as the sun,

I once was lost, but now am found, Was blind, but now I see.
How pre - cious did that grace ap - pear The hour I first be - lieved!
'Tis grace hath bro't me safe thus far, And grace will lead me home.
We've no less days to sing God's praise Than when we first be - gun. A-MEN.

11. Psalms 25 and 96

*The Psalms of the Hebrew and Christian scriptures have shaped
Western piety for centuries. Their authorship, date, and original
use(s) are disputed. Nevertheless, their continuing importance
to both public worship and private devotions in the West cannot
be doubted. From the variety of religious expressions displayed
in this complex work, we have selected two that portray basic
themes of personal experience: supplication and praise. In
Psalm 25 what is being sought? Can you infer from this psalm
why the psalmist hopes for the Lord's favor? In Psalm 96 why
is the psalmist praising God? Whom does he invite to join
in his praise?*

Psalm 25

Unto thee, O LORD my God, I life up my heart.
In thee I trust: do not put me to shame,
  let not my enemies exult over me.
  No man who hopes in thee is put to shame;
  but shame comes to all who break faith without cause.
    Make thy paths known to me, O LORD;
    teach me thy ways.
  Lead me in thy truth and teach me;
    thou art God my saviour.
  For thee I have waited all the day long,
    for the coming of thy goodness, LORD.
Remember, LORD, thy tender care and thy love unfailing,
    shown from ages past.
  Do not remember the sins and offences of my youth,
  but remember me in thy unfailing love.
  The LORD is good and upright;
therefore he teaches sinners the way they should go.
  He guides the humble man in doing right,
  he teaches the humble his ways.
  All the ways of the LORD are loving and sure
    to men who keep his covenant and his charge.
    For the honour of thy name, O LORD,
  forgive my wickedness, great as it is.
  If there is any man who fears the LORD,
  he shall be shown the path that he should choose;
  he shall enjoy lasting prosperity,
  and his children after him shall inherit the land.

From *The New English Bible.* © the Delegates of the Oxford University Press
and the Syndics of the Cambridge University Press, 1961, 1970. Reprinted by permission. Pp. 628–29 (Psalm 25), and pp. 695–96 (Psalm 96).

The LORD confides his purposes to those who fear him,
and his covenant is theirs to know.
My eyes are ever on the LORD,
who alone can free my feet from the net.

Turn to me and show me thy favour,
for I am lonely and oppressed.
    Relieve the sorrows of my heart
    and bring me out of my distress.
Look at my misery and my trouble
    and forgive me every sin.
Look at my enemies, see how many they are
    and how violent their hatred for me.
Defend me and deliver me,
do not put me to shame when I take refuge in thee.
Let integrity and uprightness protect me,
    for I have waited for thee, O LORD.
O God, redeem Israel from all his sorrows.

Psalm 96

Sing a new song to the LORD;
    sing to the LORD, all men on earth.

Sing to the LORD and bless his name,
    proclaim his triumph day by day.
    Declare his glory among the nations,
        his marvellous deeds among all peoples.
Great is the LORD and worthy of all praise;
    he is more to be feared than all gods.
    For the gods of the nations are idols every one;
    but the LORD made the heavens.
    Majesty and splendour attend him,
    might and beauty are in his sanctuary.

Ascribe to the LORD, you families of nations,
ascribe to the LORD the glory and might;
    ascribe to the LORD the glory due to his name,
bring a gift and come into his courts.
    Bow down to the LORD in the splendour of holiness,
    and dance in his honour, all men on earth.
Declare among the nations, 'The LORD is king.
    He has fixed the earth firm, immovable;
    he will judge the peoples justly.'
Let the heavens rejoice and the earth exult,
    let the sea roar and all the creatures in it,
    let the fields exult and all that is in them;

then let all the trees of the forest shout for joy
before the LORD when he comes to judge the earth.
He will judge the earth with righteousness
and the peoples in good faith.

12. Love for Allah,
'Abdullah al- Ansari

*This poem by the 11th-century Persian poet Abdullah al-Ansari
expresses in forms appropriate to Muslim faith a piety rooted
in personal experience of the Holy. Do you see themes in this
poem that also appear in the hymn and psalms above? According
to this poem, what matters most in human life? What matters least?*

Thou, Whose breath is sweetest perfume to the
    spent and anguished heart,
Thy remembrance to Thy lovers bringeth ease for every smart.
Multitudes like Moses, reeling, cry to earth's remotest place
"Give me sight, O Lord," they clamor, seeking to
    behold Thy face.
Multitudes no man hath numbered, lovers, and afflicted all,
Stumbling on the way of anguish, "Allah, Allah" loudly call.
And the fire of separation sears the heart and burns the breast,
And their eyes are wet with weeping for a love that gives
    not rest.
"Poverty's my pride!" Thy lovers raise to heaven
    their battle-cry,
Gladly meeting men's derision, letting all the world go by.
Such a fire of passion's potion Pir-i-Ansār* quaffing feels,
That distraught, like Layla's lover**
    through a ruined world he reels.
Oh God, accept my plea,
And to my faults indulgent be.
Oh, God, all my days have I spent in vanity,
And against my own body have I wrought iniquity.

Reprinted with permission of the publisher from *Islam,* edited by John Alden
Williams (New York: George Braziller, Inc., 1961). Copyright © 1961 by John
Alden Williams. Pp. 142–143.
    * Another name for the author.
    ** A reference to Layla and her lover Majnun, portrayed in the popular romance,
Layla and Majnun, written by the 12th-century AD Persian poet Hajji Khalifa.

Oh God, do Thou bless
    for this is not given to any man;
And do Thou caress,
    for this no other can.

Oh God, though succory is bitter,
    yet in the garden with the rose it blends;
And though 'Abdullah be a sinner
    yet is he among Thy friends.
Oh God, Thou saidst, "Do this," and didst not let me;
Thou badest, "Do this not," and didst permit me.

Small profit was my coming yesterday:
Today life's market's not more thronged or gay.
Tomorrow I shall go unknowing hence.
Far better were it to have stayed away.

Know that God Most High has built an outward
    Ka'ba* out of mud and stone,
And fashioned an inward Ka'ba of heart and soul alone.
The outward Ka'ba Abraham did build,
The inward Ka'ba was as the Lord Almighty willed.

Oh God, in gold and silver the rich take pride:
The poor resign themselves to *We do decide.*
    (Sūra 43:31)

Oh God, all other men are drunk with wine:
The wine-bearer is my fever.
Their drunkenness lasts but a night,
While mine abides forever.[1]

NOTES

1. A. J. Arberry, *Islamic Culture* (India, 1936), pp. 369 89.

---

   * The central Muslim sanctuary, at Mecca, believed by Muslims to have been built by the patriarch Abraham.

13. In Praise of Krishna

Lord Krishna is one of the most widely worshipped deities of Hinduism. He is symbolized not only as a noble warrior who establishes order through destruction of evil but also as the divine lover whose intimate caresses satisfy the deepest desires of man. This excerpt is from some devotional lyrics of the Vaishnavas (devotees of Vishnu; Vishnu appeared in several incarnations, one of which was Krishna). The lyrics were composed during the rise of the devotional movements in Bengal (14–17th centuries), but are still popular today among Bengali Vaishnavas in a form of worship called kirtan *(praise). The scene given here portrays the ecstasy felt by the beautiful young woman Radha when she is with her beloved, her longing for him when he is absent, and her preparation for his return. As in the Song of Songs of the Hebrew Bible, sensuous and religious imagery are intermingled; for example, Radha's passion and man's yearning for God. Perhaps as one author has suggested, man's yearning for a twin of flesh is a reflection of some primordial, long-forgotten lust, and pain of separation. How many images can you list from the last four readings which believers have used to express the character of their experience?*

[Radha's friend describes the meeting of the beloved and her Lord:]

Her cloud of hair eclipses the luster of her face,
    like Rahu* greedy for the moon;
the garland glitters in her unbound hair, a wave of
    the Ganges in the waters of the Yamuna.
How beautiful the deliberate, sensuous union of the
    two; the girl playing this time the active role,
riding her lover's outstretched body in delight;
her smiling lips shine with drops of sweat; the god
    of love offering pearls to the moon.
She of beautiful face hotly kisses the mouth of her
    beloved; the moon, with face bent down, drinks of the
    lotus.
The garland hanging on her heavy breasts seems like a
    stream of milk from golden jars.

From *In Praise of Krishna*, trans. Edward C. Dimock, Jr. and Denise Levertov. Copyright © 1967 by the Asia Society, Inc. Reprinted by permission of Doubleday & Company, Inc. and Jonathan Cape Ltd. Pp. 56–58, 65–66.

* In Indian legend an eclipse of the moon is understood to be the demon Rahu's attempt to devour the moon.

The tinkling bells which decorate her hips sound the
triumphal music of the god of love.

From IN PRAISE OF KRISHNA, by Edward C. Dimock
and Denise Leverton, editors. Copyright © 1967 by
The Asia Society, Inc. Reprinted by permission of
Doubleday and Company, Inc.

[Radha speaks:]
Beloved, what more shall I say to you?
In life and in death, in birth after birth
you are the lord of my life.
A noose of love binds
my heart to your feet.
My mind fixed on you alone, I have offered you everything;
in truth, I have become your slave.

In this family, in that house, who is really mine?
Whom can I call my own?
It was bitter cold, and I took refuge
at your lotus feet.
While my eyes blink, and I do not see you,
I feel the heart within me die. . . .

[She speaks:]

Let the earth of my body be mixed with the earth
my beloved walks on.
Let the fire of my body be the brightness
in the mirror that reflects his face.
Let the water of my body join the waters
of the lotus pool he bathes in.
Let the breath of my body be air
lapping his tired limbs.
Let me be sky, and moving through me
that cloud-dark Shyama*, my beloved. . . .

[Later, reflecting on the return of Lord Krishna, Radha says:]

When my beloved returns to my house
I shall make my body a temple of gladness,
I shall make my body the altar of joy
and let down my hair to sweep it.
My twisting necklace of pearls shall be the intricate
sprinkled design on the altar,
my full breasts the water jars,
my curved hips the plantain trees,
the tinkling bells at my waist the young shoots of the mango.
I shall use the arcane arts of fair women in all lands
to make my beauty outshine a thousand moons. . . .

The moon has shone upon me,
the face of my beloved.
O night of joy!

Joy permeates all things.
My life: joy,
my youth: fulfillment.

Today my house is again home,
today my body is my body.
The god of destiny smiled on me.
No more doubt.

---

* Another name for Krishna.

Let the nightingales sing, then,
let there be myriad
rising moons, let Kama's*
five arrows become five thousand
and the south wind

softly, softly blow:
for now my body has meaning
in the presence of my beloved.

From IN PRAISE OF KRISHNA, by Edward C. Dimock
and Denise Leverton, editors. Copyright © 1967 by
The Asia Society, Inc. Reprinted by permission of
Doubleday and Company, Inc.

INTERPRETATION

The materials thus far have presented accounts of religious experiences
without attempting to explain, interpret, or justify them. But these tasks
cannot be avoided indefinitely, however offensive they may be to believers.
Regardless of confidence in or devotion to the sacred power encountered
by a believer, sooner or later he must (1) distinguish correct from incorrect
responses to it, and (2) relate his experience to aspects of his own life
where its practical consequences may not be entirely clear, to separately
existing systems of thought in his own or (sometimes) other cultures, and
to a public that has not shared and is not sympathetic toward his experience.

Given the necessity for interpretation, the main question for this section arises: How can one hope to *understand* in finite and managcable
terms the mystery, the sovereignty, and the Otherness of the sacred reality

---

* The Indian god of love.

one has encountered? The interpreters included in this chapter attempt this in basically two ways. They reflect on:

1. the general character of the "Object" of the encounter, hoping to distinguish Him (Her?) from all others (reading 15 by Brunner);
2. the subject's own experience; i.e., its psychological character or its role in his religious life (readings 14 and 16 by Ferré and Otto).

14. Importance of Prayer for Knowing God, N. Ferré

In this excerpt, the late, widely influential Protestant theologian, Nels Ferré (1908–1971), makes perhaps the strongest claim for prayer in this chapter: "Unless we meet God in prayer, we never meet Him . . ." Only in this way, finally, can people be real. *He notes that religious leaders often rely on prayer as their principle resource, and he quotes with approval the suggestion that Jesus' death itself might be understood as a form of prayer. Why is it, according to Ferré, that prayer is the primary means of man's access to God? What images does he use to describe true prayer? How does he account for believers' sometimes frequent disinclination to pray? Why does he consider prayer more important than good works ("do-gooding")?*

Prayer is the main highway to making religion real. Unless we meet God in prayer we never meet Him, for prayer is meeting God. Unless we meet Him, He can never become real to us. A person can be fully real to us only as we get to know him personally. No amount of mere talking or thinking about him can take the place of knowing face to face. Not even the most intimate correspondence with a "pen pal" can substitute for knowing him in person. To learn to know God, then, we must learn to pray. If we have prayed and still do not know Him, we need to learn to pray aright.

Long ago Descartes uttered the famous words, 'I think, therefore I am." Even though he might doubt everything else, he felt sure of being the one thinking. Today, however, the existentialists tell us that Descartes was too intellectual. Life, they say, is more a matter of decisions. According to this approach Descartes should have written, "I decide, therefore I am!"

From *Making Religion Real* by Nels F. S. Ferré. Copyright © 1955 by Harper & Row, Publishers, Inc., pp. 51–56.

Nathaniel Micklem, the renowned Oxford scholar, has pointed out, nevertheless, that since prayer is man's main relation to God, he who prays knows the deepest truth; that is to say, "I pray, therefore I am." We are real in proportion to our right relation with God; and we are in right relation to Him in accordance with our praying.

The great men of God have been examples of prayer. They moved the world nearer to God mostly by the way they prayed. They came to be near God by the way they prayed and praying, they took the world part way with them. A young man who was writing his doctoral dissertation on the work of an illustrious preacher recounted that on passing through the preacher's city, he decided on the spur of the moment to call on him between trains. The visit was in vain, however, for the minister's secretary had orders to admit no one during his hour of prayer. His congregation may never have seen him on his knees, but they none the less felt his power. The saints of God have always been giants of prayer.

Peter Taylor Forsyth, one of the most eminent among recent Christian thinkers, suggested that the "priestliness of Christ was a priestliness of prayer" and that even "the atoning death of his deity" was "prayer and complete self-renunciation." On all the great occasions of his life Jesus is reported to have prayed. At the end of his ministry Gethsemane could become a victory of prayer because in the wilderness at the beginning of his mission he had prayed down his basic temptations. Jesus entered his ministry praying and he died praying. Gandhi died on his way to prayer. St. Francis developed a prayer life so real that when one of his followers eavesdropped on him, he heard the saint say nothing all night except "my God, my God." Life can offer no higher reward or usefulness than having religion become real through prayer.

People have a right to know why there is need for prayer. If God both knows our needs and wants to meet them, what real use can there be for prayer?

We should pray because God Himself has made prayer the way to His own presence. God does not force fellowship on us. He loves us enough to respect our freedom. Companionship is not consummated except by mutual free will. God longs to be loved because He is our Father; to help us He waits only for our willingness to receive. The heart of prayer is communion with God. Such communion requires that we accept God in the same way that He is ever ready to accept us.

We need to pray too because God respects our privacy. For our sake God hides Himself. Sometimes we think that God is merely hidden to our blind eyes. We believe that if we could see things as they really are we should find God everywhere. God, however, is not only hidden because of our imperfect sight; He also cannot be found precisely because He is not there. He hides Himself for the very purpose that we might become real. God does not want us to be puppets; He creates us to become living children. Our own children sometimes need to be free from parental participation. God never becomes guilty of "mom-ism," a selfish mother's refusing to let the child think or act by himself. Some people, to be sure, who pray "Father" really mean "Mamma"! But God never stoops to encouraging apron-string prayers!

We often think of God's presence as operating like atmospheric pressure, equally present everywhere. Is not God, we say, on the golf course as well as in the prayer meeting? But if He were, why should we pray for His holy presence? Why, if such were the case, should the Bible urge us, "Call upon me and I will be near"? Why should Jesus then have promised that where two or three should be gathered in his name he would himself be with them? No! God is personally present only to praying people. God is present only in the Spirit. When we are in the Spirit we are in a state of prayer.

To be in the Spirit is to be in communion with God regardless of how we have that communion, whether in words or silence, in worship or work. To be sure, God is always and everywhere present as the one who creates, sustains and controls the world. But as such He is not *personally* present. We can meet God personally only in communion with Him *and such communion is prayer.*

We also need to pray for the sake of finding light on our way. How we need light! I have heard a friend tell unforgettably a boyhood experience of cruising with his father off the rocky coast of Maine. Night had closed in as they approached the particularly treacherous reef that guarded the harbor's mouth. To their horror no light burned in the little lighthouse that should have given them their direction. Fuel was running low; they could hardly put out to sea again. Death waited in the darkness of the unseen, jagged rocks. Then a light! The smallest beam, perhaps a temporary lantern, but enough to give direction and to guide them safely into harbor.

But light seems hard to get. The difficulty, strangely enough, is because we are afraid of it. When we were children we were afraid of the dark. As we grow up we become afraid of the light, for the light shows us up. We want to fool ourselves. We want to believe that there are easier ways than his whose life was the light of men. The light shows that the way of love is the way of God. The way of God is the narrow path of truth. To follow it would cost all we have and all that we want to keep away from God and others.

Light seems hard to obtain because the kind of light we are seeking is light on how to get, to keep and to enjoy things for ourselves. Between us and the true light we puff up a smokescreen of anxiety as a protection of all that we hold dear. How can light pierce so dense a cloud of fear? Only an acceptance of God's love, that perfect love which casts out fear, can dissolve our inner anxieties and deliver us from outer pressures. True prayer gives us the fearlessness that brings rightness and brightness of heart. When we pray, we see things as they are, in their true light. The most objective person in the world is the one who has learned to pray, "Thy will be done."

Another reason for prayer is our need to receive power for good. Much of what we take for goodness is merely our foolish attempts to set things straight; meddling with God's order. Since we feel guilty within, we want to please God and, so to speak, to earn credit with Him. Therefore, we strive to outdo one another in good works. To be sure, God sees our intention; He knows how complicated our motives are. While most of do-gooding, however, never amounts to much, prayer, if it be genuine, makes the difference. How then does prayer give us power for good?

No one has ever seen power as such. We have seen the display of power in mighty waves that toss huge ocean liners like a chip—or in the little woman who runs the church. Power is not a thing. Power is the expression of some process or person. It is the ability to do something, to control something, or to direct something. While all power is ultimately from God, He shares some of it with us in order that we might become responsibly free. Besides, inasmuch as we need to do things together, having power also teaches us community concern.

We are free, of course, to go contrary to God's intention in using our power. We may become irresponsible and careless, or we may become concerned mostly about our own ease or pleasure. Irresponsible use of power, however, increases the world's problems and sufferings. Darting about doing good in our own way, apart from God's design for the common good, we introduce more trouble than we solve. When, on the contrary, in prayer we learn of God's way and therefore direct our small decisions in line with His large ones, we work according to God's real intention for the world and obtain power for lasting good. Prayer is opening our little lives to the power of God that we might gain and use more of it for the common good.

We should also pray to get love. To pray for love is to pray for God since God is love. At the outset we saw that we should pray in order to find God personally present. He is so present only in love. God is love and we are made for love. When we pray, therefore, if we pray for love, we find both God and ourselves. . . .

15. On Personal Knowledge of God's Nature, E. Brunner

> *Emil Brunner (1889–1966) was a Swiss Protestant theologian who argued against the contemporary assumption in many intellectual circles that truth, although always extending beyond any particular formulation, is a product of human effort.*

From *The Christian Doctrine of God* by Emil Brunner. Translated by Olive Wyon. Copyright, MCML, by W. L. Jenkins, The Westminster Press. Used by permission. Pp. 117–26.

According to Brunner, the knowledge of God is not knowledge about something; rather, it is communication with Someone who initiates all knowledge of Himself. He insists that the God revealed in the Christian scriptures stands always both beyond and above human reason. Note his insistence that God's mystery is not due to our ignorance, but to His essential nature—that it is "unfathomable." What is the meaning of this paradox, that "the better we know God, the more we know and feel that His Mystery is unfathomable"? Does this assertion help interpret the primary data you have studied? Why does Brunner argue that God's Name cannot be turned into a definition? Why does he assert that impersonal, abstract, "philosophical" conceptions of God are "idolatrous"?

The Nature of God and His Attributes

The phrase, "The Doctrine of God," must sound strange to any un-prejudiced person. How can *man* undertake to formulate a doctrine of God? If there is one point which is clear from the very outset it is this: that God is not an "object" which man can manipulate by means of his own reasoning; He is a Mystery dwelling in the depths of "inaccessible Light." *Favete linguis!* "God is in His Temple.... All within keep silence, Prostrate lie with deepest reverence...." "Calmly to adore the Unfathom-able" (Goethe)—this, surely, would be more fitting than the effort to construct a "doctrine of God." Do we not read in the Book of Judges: "Wherefore askest thou after My Name, seeing it is wonderful?"[1] And does not the Commandment of the Old Testament against "graven images" bear the same meaning, i.e., that we have no right to compare God with anything known to us: that He is incomparable, and therefore cannot be known? A man who thinks he can instruct others about God has forgotten what he is supposed to be doing.

But when we say this we have already begun to know God, and to teach men about Him. For *this* precisely is the knowledge of God, and the doctrine of God, namely, that He is incomparable, and that He cannot be defined. We are here confronted by a remarkable dialectic, which will accompany us throughout the whole of our study of dogmatics. The better we know God, the more we know and feel that His Mystery is unfathom-able. The doctrine which lays the most stress upon the Mystery of God will be nearest to the truth.

It is precisely this fact which distinguishes the God of the Biblical revelation from the gods and divinities of paganism. The gods of the heathen are not really mysterious, because they can be "known" within the sphere of that which is natural and given, whether in the processes of the world of nature or in the mind of man. Their mystery is the mystery of nature, of the Self, of the world, and therefore it is not the mystery of that which is genuinely supernatural. Through the Biblical revelation we dis-cover that what we can "learn" to know as "God" by our own unaided efforts is not the True God, precisely because we acquire this "knowledge" by our own efforts. Even the "Unfathomable" which the agnostic sets in the place of God is not a real mystery, but simply denotes the limitations of our knowledge, a fact of which we are fully aware, and one which it is not at all difficult to perceive. One who is only aware of this limitation is not yet aware how mysterious God is. The thought of that limitation to our knowledge, the idea of the Unfathomable which we can acquire by our own unaided efforts, has therefore no power at all to inspire us with genuine reverence, for there is here a confusion of ideas: the conception of that which has not yet been perceived, of the riddle of the universe, and the idea of that which in principle cannot be discovered by man's searching, these two fundamentally different ideas have unconsciously merged into one another. That which we can see to be "unfathomable" is an emptiness, not a fullness. It makes us "resigned," it does not bring us fulfilment. It does not bring us to our knees, and it moves neither heart nor will. It does not draw us to Itself; the only effect it has is that we do not further concern ourselves with something we cannot know. Agnosticism is not an attitude of reverence but of indifference.

Conversely, what the Biblical revelation teaches us is that the very *mystery* can only be understood as a genuine *mystery* by means of revelation. We do not fully realize how unknowable, how mysterious God is until we meet Him in His revelation. Here alone do we understand that all our own processes of knowing, just because they are our own, do not create the true knowledge of God, since through them—whether in a profound or in a superficial way—we remain in our own sphere. The nature divinity is not really mysterious, nor is the god of reason or of Spirit, which we conceive within the sphere of our reason, of our mind, of our Self; He alone is mysterious who comes to us from a region beyond all spheres known to us, who breaks through the barriers of our own experience of the world and the Self, and enters into our world as one who does not belong to it.

From the standpoint of our own knowledge Faust is perfectly right: "Who can name Him, and who can confess 'I know Him'? The name is an echo, resounding amid clouds of fragrant incense, concealing a heavenly glow." But this Nameless One is certainly not the truly Mysterious One; the Mysterious One is He who makes His Name known to us in His own revelation. . . .

We ask: Why is it that in the Bible this incomparable significance is attached to the idea of the "Name" of God? Strangely enough this question is rarely discussed by theologians, and still less often is it satisfactorily answered. We here anticipate our answer—which will be fully worked out in the following pages—by this summary statement: this high significance is ascribed to the idea of the "Name of God" within the Biblical revelation because it gathers up, in a simple way which everybody can understand, certain decisive elements in the reality of revelation: God stands "over against us"; we stand "over against" Him: God is not an "It" but a "Thou"; who addresses us; He makes Himself known through

His self-revelation; He manifests Himself to us in order that we may call upon Him and have communion with Him. The "Name" of God covers both the revealed Nature of God and His revealing action; the foundation of this revelation in Being and in Act is the Divine will to sovereignty and communion, the purpose of which is the glory of God and communion with God. Thus the Biblical conception of the "Name," and the "manifestation of the Name," contains the meaning of the whole Biblical doctrine of God. We must now proceed to define this in more detail, showing the foundation for our statements.

(1) God is known only where He Himself makes His Name known. Apart from this self-manifestation He is unknowable; from our point of view He is remote, inaccessible. The "Name" is that which is peculiar to Himself, it is that which distinguishes Him from all else, that which cannot be expressed by any general conception; which is not an object of human knowledge of any kind; we cannot discover it by the exercise of our own faculty of reason; it is a knowledge which—in the strict sense of the word—can only be *given*.

The Greek Fathers made a great mistake (and this error bore disastrous fruit) in turning the Name of Yahweh (and especially the Name as described by the Elohist writer in the narrative of the revelation of the Divine Name on Horeb[2]) into an ontological definition. The words "I AM THAT I AM" ought not to be translated in the language of speculative thought, as a definition: "I AM HE WHO IS." To do this not only misses the meaning of this statement, but it turns the Biblical idea of revelation into its opposite. The "Name" which cannot be defined is turned into a definition. The meaning of the Sacred Name is precisely this: I am the Mysterious One, and I will to remain so; I AM THAT I AM, I AM the Incomparable, therefore I cannot be defined nor named. This description is similar to that in the Book of Judges, which is intended to warn man off "holy ground": "Why askest thou thus after My Name?" God is the Unknown God, until He makes Himself known.[3]

This does not mean that pagans have no knowledge of God at all; such a foolish statement, and one which is utterly contrary to experience, does not occur anywhere in the Bible. But it does mean that those who do not possess the historical revelation, those to whom God has not made known His Name, do not know Him truly, do not know Him in such a way that they are in communion with Him. The pagan—or what comes to the same thing in the end—philosophical knowledge of God, does not create communion with God, because it is not knowledge of the God—since He makes Himself known—creates communion with Himself.

Even the man to whom God has not made His Name known is not without a certain knowledge of God; for a knowledge of the Creator forms part of the creaturely existence of man.[4] But this possibility of knowing God is not sufficient to remove the sinful blindness of man. It extends to the point of making man "without excuse," but it does not suffice to bring him to glorify God and to enter into communion with Him. In sinful man this natural knowledge of God becomes necessarily the delusion of idolatry, or—what amounts to the same thing in principle—the abstract, impersonal idea of God. Man who is left alone with Nature and with himself does not know the true God, because he does not know the God of revelation, the God whose Nature it is to be the Revealer, the one who communicates Himself. God in His Self-communication—that is *the Name of God*; hence where God does not make His Name known, He cannot be known aright.

(2) Secondly, the concept, the "Name" of God, suggests further that God is Person: He is not an "It"; He is our primary "Thou." That which we can think and know by our own efforts is always an object of thought and knowledge, some *thing* which has been thought, some *thing* which has been known. therefore it is never "Person." Even the human person is never truly "person" to us so long as we merely "think" it; the human being only becomes "person" to us when he speaks to us himself, when he manifests the mystery of his being as a "thou," in the very act of addressing us. . . .

(3) The communication of a name is the disclosure of one's self to the other, and thus the establishment—or at least the beginning—of a personal relation and communion. When one gives oneself to be known, one gives oneself away. There is an element of truth in that primitive magical idea—which can be discerned even in the Old Testament—that with the disclosure of the name one gives away something of oneself, and that, conversely, to know the name of a person gives one a power over him. In the divine revelation of the Name there lies a twofold truth: God gives Himself to those to whom He reveals Himself, and these, for their part, now have a certain right to Him—even though it is a right which has been given them —those to whom He makes His Name known have become "His own." They can and may now call upon Him. He gives them free access to His Majesty, which otherwise could not be approached. The disclosure of a name creates communion. Therefore the disclosure of the Name of God is consummated in the self-offering of the Revealer. "I have manifested Thy Name unto the men whom Thou gavest Me..." says Jesus on the night before His Crucifixion, and in anticipation of it. There, too, He also tells us the purpose of this manifestation of the "Name"; "Keep through Thine own Name those whom Thou has given Me, *that they may be one, as we are.*" When Yahweh manifests His Name He makes the Covenant with Israel; when Jesus in His own Person makes known fully and finally the personal mystery of God, He establishes communion between the Holy God and sinful man.

Even in that apparently primitive and anthropomorphic passage in the Book of Exodus where Yahweh promises to "proclaim the Name of the Lord" to Moses, this proclamation of the Name of God by God Himself is connected with the sovereign, freely electing, grace of God: "I will be gracious to whom I will be gracious, and will show mercy on whom I will show mercy." God's self-manifestation is the act by which God steps out of the sphere of His own glory and self-sufficiency, in which the One who exists *for Himself alone* becomes the One who exists *for us.*

Or rather, it is the act in which God shows us that He is the One who eixsts "for us." In that He gives His Name He graciously summons us to make use of His Name, by calling upon Him. He wills to be present to us, when we call upon Him: "Call upon Me in the day of trouble: I will deliver thee, and thou shalt glorify Me."[5] The disclosure of the Name establishes the connexion which man may and should use henceforth. And only through the fact that God becomes for us the One upon whom it is possible to call, does He become to us a real "Thou," the truly personal God.

(4) Thought that has been led on philosophical abstractions therefore finds the concept of the Name of God, and the revelation of the Name, to be an anthropomorphic degration, making God finite, which cannot be permitted. This is quite in order, it would indeed be very suprising if such a protest were not made. Only we must be clear how far this goes, how fundamental it is. Then we perceive that behind this reproach of "anthropomorphism" lies nothing less than the rejection of revelation, and this means the rejection of the truly personal God. The self-sufficient reason will not admit anything that comes from a sphere beyond its own possibilities. It wishes to remain isolated; it has no desire to receive; it will only acknowledge as truth that which, from the very outset, belongs to its own sphere.

People who think like this want to keep their minds closed to all that comes to them from outside the sphere of reason, the sphere, that is, which they can control by their own thought; they do not wish to see it opened from outside. They recognize only the truth which they already know, and that which can be verified by means which are at man's disposal. They have no intention of admitting that there could be such a thing as "given" truth. They will accept as truth only that which they can attain for themselves, but not that which approaches them from without. They will only receive—and this is the same thing in the end—monological and not dialogical truth, only truth which is preceded by the words: "I think," but not that which is prefaced by the words: "Here it is!" that is, truth which they can only receive in this way. Thus this habit of thought is rooted in the self-sufficiency of the isolated "I": *Cogito, ergo sum.*

But the revelation of the Name of God means the end of this self-sufficient isolation of the Self, the end of this truth which is shut up within the Self, the end of this unbroken continuity, of this truth which can be attained by the efforts of man alone. Revelation means that this self-centred circle has been broken down; the truth comes in its own way and in its own power, to you. You do not possess it, it is not in you, it is given to you. It is not that *you* are the starting-point, and *God* is the End, but that *God* is the starting-point, and *you* are the end of the movement. That which is disclosed does not start with *you,* the subject, as if that which you know were your own object of knowledge, but the disclosure starts from the other, from the non-Self, but which, precisely because it opens and is not opened, is not an object, not something which has been thought but it is a subject: the "Thou" who opens His heart unto you, and in so doing becomes the power which breaks down your self-centred isolation and makes an end of your self-sufficiency.

This is the decision, which is accomplished in faith in the revelation of the Name, and in the One who reveals His Name; what is at stake is the autonomy of the human personality. If this is retained, then no faith is possible; the zone of self-sufficiency is unbroken, the message of the God who manifests His Name is rejected as "anthropomorphism." But if, on the other hand, the revelation of the Name is believed, then the autonomy of the *cogito ergo sum* is rejected; the Self is no longer the final court of appeal, but the Divine Thou. Then self-sufficiency is no longer the standard of all truth, but the final highest truth is now truth which has been given, and this truth becomes real and living in God's approach to man, in the gracious movement of God towards man.

NOTES

1. Judges 13:18 (R.V.)
2. Exodus 3:14ff.
3. Grether, [*Name u. Wort Gottes im Alten Testament,* 1934], pp. 6ff. and Eichrodt, *Theologie Des Alten Testaments,* I, pp. 89ff.
4. Romans 1:19.
5. Psalms 50:15.

16. The Awesome
and Fascinating Mystery,
R. Otto

Rudolf Otto (1869–1937) was a Protestant theologian and professor of systematic theology (Germany) whose book, The Idea of the Holy *(1917, German; 1923, English translation) is now regarded as a "classic" statement on the nature of religious life. Otto hoped to avoid a merely sectarian statement of what religion is. He tried to draw from his study of many religious experiences a statement of the distinctive attitudes or responses which could account for the major features of all "religious"*

Adapted from *The Idea of the Holy* by Rudolf Otto, trans. J. W. Harvey and published by Oxford University Press, 1958, pp. 12–20, 23–29, 31–32.

behavior. He emphasized the awareness of the "numinous," a word coined from the Latin "numen" ("divine spirit"), and used by Otto to refer to the experience of the awesome mystery of God—external to man, awe-inspiring, terrible, holy, sacred—to which man responded with "creature-feeling." Note that Otto analyzes the adjective "awesome" (tremendum) first: the mystery of God is awesome because of its (1) awefulness, (2) overpoweringness (or majesty), and (3) energy or urgency. Secondly, God is mysterious because of his (4) wholly otherness, and (5) fascination. This five-fold schema is used by Otto to analyze systematically the experience of God. Note how he distinguishes religious emotions from each other and from nonreligious emotions; and how he defines aspects of the sacred reality by reference to these emotions. Why does Otto insist that certain emotional responses provide the basis for the only true knowledge of God? What are the qualities of God that require a certain way of knowing Him? What human responses are characteristic of those who stand in God's presence?

"Mysterium Tremendum"

THE ANALYSIS OF "TREMENDUM"

Let us consider the deepest and most fundamental element in all strong and sincerely felt religious emotion. Faith unto salvation, trust, love—all these are there. But over and above these is an element which may also on occasion, quite apart from them, profoundly affect us and occupy the mind with a wellnigh bewildering strength. Let us follow it up with every effort of sympathy and imaginative intuition wherever it is to be found, in the lives of those around us, in sudden, strong ebullitions of personal piety and the frames of mind such ebullitions evince, in the fixed and ordered solemnities of rites and liturgies, and again in the atmosphere that clings to old religious monuments and buildings, to temples and to churches. If we do so we shall find we are dealing with something for which there is only one appropriate expression, *"mysterium tremendum."* The feeling of it may at times come sweeping like a gentle tide, pervading the mind with a tranquil mood of deepest worship. It may pass over into a more set and lasting attitude of the soul, continuing, as it were, thrillingly vibrant and resonant, until at last it dies away and the soul resumes its 'profane', non-religious mood of everyday experience. It may burst in sudden eruption up from the depths of the soul with spasms and convulsions, or lead to the strangest excitements, to intoxicated frenzy, to transport, and to ecstasy. It has its wild and demonic forms and can sink to an almost grisly horror and shuddering. It has its crude, barbaric antecedents and early manifestations, and again it may be developed into something beautiful and pure and glorious. It may become the hushed, trembling, and speechless humility of the creature in the presence of—whom or what? In the presence of that which is *mystery* inexpressible and above all creatures.

It is again evident at once that here too our attempted formulation by means of a concept is once more a merely negative one. Conceptually *mysterium* denotes merely that which is hidden and esoteric, that which is beyond conception or understanding, extraordinary and unfamiliar. The term does not define the object more positively in its qualitative character. But though what is enunciated in the word is negative, what is meant is something absolutely and intensely positive. This pure positive we can experience in feelings, feelings which our discussion can help to make clear to us, in so far as it arouses them actually in our hearts.

The Element of Awefulness

Tremor is in itself merely the perfectly familiar and 'natural' emotion of fear. But here the term is taken, aptly enough but still only by analogy, to denote a quite specific kind of emotional response, wholly distinct from that of being afraid, though it so far resembles it that the analogy of fear may be used to throw light upon its nature. There are in some languages special expressions which denote, either exclusively or in the first instance, this "fear" that is more than fear proper. The Hebrew *hiqdish* (hallow) is an example. To "keep a thing holy in the heart" means to mark it off by a feeling of peculiar dread, not to be mistaken for any ordinary dread, that is, to appraise it by the category of the numinous. But the Old Testament throughout is rich in parallel expressions for this feeling. Specially noticeable is the "*emah* of Yahweh" ("fear of God"), which Yahweh can pour forth, dispatching almost like a daemon, and which seizes upon a man with paralysing effect.... Compare Exodus 23:27—"I will send my fear before thee, and will destroy all the people to whom thou shalt come..."; also Job 9:34; 13:21 ("let not his fear terrify me"; "let not thy dread make me afraid"). Here we have a terror fraught with an inward shuddering such as not even the most menacing and overpowering created thing can instil. It has something spectral in it....

Of modern languages English has the words "awe," "aweful," which in their deeper and most special sense approximate closely to our meaning. The phrase, "he stood aghast," is also suggestive in this connexion.... [The] antecedent stage [of "religious dread" or "awe"] is "daemonic dread" (cf. the horror of Pan) with its queer perversion, a sort of abortive offshoot, the "dread of ghosts." It first begins to stir in the feeling of "something uncanny," "eerie," or "weird." It is this feeling which, emerging in the mind of primeval man, forms the starting point for the entire religious development in history. "Daemons" and "gods" alike spring from this root, and all the products of "mythological apperception" of "fantasy" are nothing but different modes in which it has been objectified. And all ostensible explanations of the origin of religion in terms of animism or magic or folk-psychology are doomed from the outset to wander astray and miss the real goal of their inquiry, unless they recognize this fact of our nature—primary, unique, underivable from anything else—to be the basic factor and the basic impulse underlying the entire process of religious evolution.

Not only is the saying of Luther, that the natural man cannot fear God perfectly, correct from the standpoint of psychology, but we ought to go farther and add that the natural man is quite unable even to "shudder" (*grauen*) or feel horror in the real sense of the word. For "shuddering" is something more than "natural," ordinary fear. It implies that the mysterious is already beginning to loom before the mind, to touch the feelings. It implies the first application of a category of valuation which has no place in the everyday natural world of ordinary experience, and is only possible to a being in whom has been awakened a mental predisposition, unique in kind an ddifferent in a definite way from any "natural" faculty. And this newly-revealed capacity, even in the crude and violent manifestations which are all it at first evinces, bears witness to a completely new function of experience and standard of valuation, only belonging to the spirit of man.

Before going on to consider the elements which unfold as the "tremendum" develops, let us give a little further consideration to the first crude, primitive forms in which this "numinous dread" or awe shows itself. It is the mark which really characterizes the so-called "religion of primitive man," and there it appears as "daemonic dread." This crudely naive and primordial emotional disturbance, and the fantastic images to which it gives rise, are later overborne and ousted by more highly developed forms of the numinous emotion, with all its mysteriously impelling power. But even when this has long attained its higher and purer mode of expression it is possible for the primitive types of excitation that were formerly a part of it to break out in the soul in all their original naivete and so to be experienced afresh. That this is so is shown by the potent attraction again and again exercised by the element of horror and "shudder" in ghost stories, even among persons of high all-round education. It is remarkable that the physical reaction to which this unique "dread" of the uncanny gives rise is also unique, and is not found in the case of any "natural" fear or terror. We say: "my blood ran icy cold," and "my flesh crept." The "cold blood" feeling may be a symptom of ordinary, natural fear, but there is something non-natural or supernatural about the symptom of "creeping flesh." And any one who is capable of more precise introspection must recognize that the distinction between such a "dread" and natural fear is not simply one of degree and intensity. The awe or "dread" *may* indeed be so overwhelmingly great that it seems to penetrate to the very marrow, making the man's hair bristle and his limbs quake. But it may also steal upon him almost unobserved as the gentlest of agitations, a mere fleeting shadow passing across his mood. It has therefore nothing to do with intensity, and no natural fear passes over into it merely by being intensified. I may be beyond all measure afraid and terrified without there being even a trace of the feeling of uncanniness in my emotion. . . .

Though the numinous emotion in its completest development shows a world of difference from the mere "daemonic dread," yet not even at the highest level does it belie its pedigree or kindred. Even when the worship of "daemons," has long since reached the higher level of worship of "gods," these gods still retain as *numina* something of the "ghost" in the impress they make on the feelings of the worshipper, viz. the peculiar quality of the "uncanny" and "aweful," which survives with the quality of exaltedness and sublimity or is symbolized by means of it. And this element, softened though it is, does not disappear even on the highest level of all, where the worship of God is at its purest. Its disappearance would be indeed an essential loss. The shudder reappears in a form ennobled beyond measure where the soul, held speechless, trembles inwardly to the farthest fibre of its being. It invades the mind mightily in Christian worship with the words: "Holy, Holy, Holy"; it breaks forth from the hymn of Tersteegen:

> God Himself is present:
> Heart, be stilled before Him:
> Prostrate inwardly adore Him.

The "shudder" has here lost its crazy and bewildering note, but not the ineffable something that holds the mind. It has become a mystical awe, and sets free as its accompaniment, reflected in self-consciousness, that "creature-feeling" that has already been described as the feeling of personal nothingness and submergence before the awe-inspiring object directly experienced.

The referring of this feeling of numinous tremor to its object in the numen brings into relief a property of the latter which plays an important part in our Holy Scriptures, and which has been the occasion of many difficulties, both to commentators and to theologians, from its puzzling and baffling nature. This is the ...*orge,* the Wrath of Yahweh, which recurs in the New Testament as *orge theou* [wrath of God], and which is clearly analogous to the idea occurring in many religions of a mysterious *ira deorum* [God's anger]. To pass through the Indian Pantheon of gods is to find deities who seem to be made up altogether out of such an *orge;* and even the higher Indian gods of grace and pardon have frequently, beside their merciful, their "wrath" form. But as regards the "wrath of Yahweh," the strange features about it have for long been a matter for constant remark. In the first place, it is patent from many passages of the Old Testament that this "wrath" has no concern whatever with moral qualities There is something very baffling in the way in which it "is kindled" and manifested. It is, as has been well said, "like a hidden force of nature," like stored-up electricity, discharging itself upon anyone who comes too near. It is "incalculable" and "arbitrary." Anyone who is accustomed to think of deity only by its rational attributes must see in this "wrath" mere caprice and wilful passion. But such a view would have been emphatically rejected by the religious men of the Old Covenant, for to them the Wrath of God, so far from being a diminution of His Godhead, appears as a natural expression of it, an element of "holiness" itself, and a quite indispensable one. And in this they are entirely right. This *orge* is nothing but the *tremendum* itself, apprehended and expressed by the aid of a naive analogy from the domain of natural experience, in this case from the ordinary passional life of men. "Wrath" here is the "ideogram" of a unique emotional moment in religious experience, a moment whose singularly daunting and awe-inspiring character must be gravely disturbing to those persons who will recognize nothing in the divine nature but goodness, love, and a sort of confidential intimacy, in a word, only those aspects of God which turn toward the world of men. . . .

The Element of "Overpoweringness" (Majestas")

We have been attempting to unfold the implications of that aspect of the mysterium tremendum indicated by the adjective, and the result so far may be summarized in two words, constituting, as before, what may be called an "ideogram," rather than a concept proper, viz. "absolute unapproachability."

It will be felt at once that there is yet a further element which must be added, that, namely, of "might," "power," "absolute overpoweringness." We will take to represent this the term *majestas,* majesty—the more readily because anyone with a feeling for language must detect a last faint trace of the numinous still clinging to the word. The *tremendum* may then be rendered more adequately *tremenda majestas,* or "aweful majesty." This second element of majesty may continue to be vividly preserved, where the first, that of unapproachability, recedes and dies away, as may be seen, for example, in mysticism. It is especially in relation to this element of majesty or absolute overpoweringness that the creature-consciousness, of which we have already spoken, comes upon the scene, as a sort of shadow or subjective reflection of it. Thus, in contrast to "the overpowering" of which we are conscious as an object over against the self, there is the feeling of one's own submergence, of being but "dust and ashes" and nothingness. And this forms the numinous raw material for the feeling of religious humility. . . .

The Element of "Energy" or Urgency

There is, finally, a third element comprised in those of *tremendum* and *majestas,* awefulness and majesty, and this I venture to call the "urgency" or "energy" of the numinous object. It is particularly vividly perceptible in the *orge* or "wrath"; and it everywhere clothes itself in symbolical expressions—vitality, passion, emotional temper, will, force, movement, excitement, activity, impetus. These features are typical and recur again and again from the daemonic level up to the idea of the "living" God. We have here the factor that has everywhere more than any other prompted the fiercest opposition to the "philosophic" God of mere rational speculation who can be put into a definition. And for their part the philosophers have condemned these expressions of the energy of the numen, whenever they are brought on to the scene, as sheer anthropomorphism. . . .

For wherever men have been contending for the "living" God or for voluntarism, there, we may be sure, have been non-rationalists fighting rationalists and rationalism. It was so with Luther in his controversy with Erasmus; and Luther's *omnipotentia Dei* [omnipotence of God] in his [essay] *De Servo Arbitrio* is nothing but the union of "majesty"—in the sense of absolute supremacy—with this "energy," in the sense of a force that knows not stint nor stay, which is urgent, active, compelling, and alive. In mysticism, too, this element of "energy" is a very living and vigorous factor at any rate in the "voluntaristic" mysticism, the mysticism of love, where it is very forcibly seen in that "consuming fire" of love whose burning strength the mystic can hardly bear, but begs that the heat that has scorched him may be mitigated, lest he be himself destroyed by it. And in this urgency and pressure the mystic's "love" claims a perceptible kinship with the *orge* itself, the scorching and consuming wrath of God; it is the same "energy," only differently directed. "Love," says one of the mystics, "is nothing else than quenched wrath.". . .

THE ANALYSIS OF "MYSTERIUM"

"A God comprehended is no God." (Tersteegen)

We gave to the object to which the numinous consciousness is directed the name *mysterium tremendum,* and we then set ourselves first to determine the meaning of the adjective *tremendum*—which we found to be itself only justified by analogy—because it is more easily analysed than the substantive idea *mysterium.* We have now to turn to this, and try, as best we may, by hint and suggestion, to get to a clearer apprehension of what it implies.

The "Wholly Other"

It might be thought that the adjective itself gives an explanation of the substantive; but this is not so. It is not merely analytical; it is a synthetic attribute to it; i.e., *tremendum* adds something not necessarily inherent in *mysterium.* It is true that the reactions in consciousness that correspond to the one readily and spontaneously overflow into those that correspond to the other; in fact, anyone sensitive to the use of words would commonly feel that the idea of "mystery" (*mysterium*) is so closely bound up with its synthetic qualifying attribute "aweful" (*tremendum*) that one can hardly say the former without catching an echo of the latter, "mystery" almost of itself becoming "aweful mystery" to us. But the passage from the one idea to the other need not by any means be always so easy. The elements of meaning implied in "awefulness" and "mysteriousness" are in themselves definitely different. The latter may so far preponderate in the religious consciousness, may stand out so vividly, that in comparison with it the former almost sinks out of sight; a case which again could be clearly exemplified from some forms of mysticism. Occasionally, on the other hand, the reverse happens, and the *tremendum* may in turn occupy the mind without the *mysterium.*

This latter, then needs special consideration on its own account. We need an expression for the mental reaction peculiar to it; and here, too, only one word seems appropriate, though, as it is strictly applicable only to a "natural" state of mind, it has here meaning only by analogy: it is the word "stupor." *Stupor* is plainly a different thing from *tremor;* it signifies blank wonder, an astonishment that strikes us dumb, amazement absolute. Taken, indeed, in its purely natural sense, *mysterium* would first mean merely a secret or a mystery in the sense of that which is alien to us, uncomprehended and unexplained; and so far *mysterium* is itself merely an ideogram, an analogical notion taken from the natural sphere, illustrating, but incapable of exhaustively rendering, our real meaning. Taken in the religious sense, that which is "mysterious" is—to give it perhaps the most striking expression—the "wholly other"..., that which is quite beyond the sphere of the usual, the intelligible, and the familiar, which therefore falls quite outside the limits of the "canny," and is contrasted with it, filling the mind with blank wonder and astonishment....

Even on the lowest level of religious development the essential characteristic...lies...in a peculiar "moment" of consciousness, to wit, the *stupor* before something "wholly other," whether such an other be named "spirit" or "daemon" or "deva," or be left without any name. Nor .does it make any difference in this respect whether, to interpret and preserve their apprehension of this "other," men coin original imagery of their own or adapt imaginations drawn from the world of legend, the fabrications of fancy apart from and prior to any stirrings of daemonic dread.

In accordance with laws of which we shall have to speak again later, this feeling or consciousness of the "wholly other" will attach itself to, or sometimes be indirectly aroused by means of, objects which are already puzzling upon the "natural" plane, or are of a surprising or astounding character; such as extraordinary phenomena or astonishing occurrences or things in inanimate nature, in the animal world, or among men. But here once more we are dealing with a case of association between things specifically different—the "numinous" and the "natural" moments of consciousness—and not merely with the gradual enhancement of one of them— the "natural"—till it becomes the other. As in the case of "natural fear" and "daemonic dread" already considered, so here the transition from natural to daemonic amazement is not a mere matter of degree. But it is only with the latter that the complementary expression *mysterium* perfectly harmonizes, as will be felt perhaps more clearly in the case of the adjectival form "mysterious." No one says, strictly and in earnest, of a piece of clockwork that is beyond his grasp, or of a science that he cannot understand: "That is 'mysterious' to me."

It might be objected that the mysterious is something which is and remains absolutely and invariably beyond our understanding, whereas that which merely eludes our understanding for a time but is perfectly intelligible in principle should be called, not a "mystery," but merely a "problem." But this is by no means an adequate account of the matter. The truly "mysterious" object is beyond our apprehension and comprehension, not only because our knowledge has certain irremovable limits, but because in it we come upon something inherently "wholly other," whose kind and character are incommensurable with our own, and before which we therefore recoil in a wonder that strikes us chill and numb.

This may be made still clearer by a consideration of that degraded offshoot and travesty of the genuine "numinous" dread or awe, the fear of ghosts. Let us try to analyse this experience. We have already specified the peculiar feeling-element of "dread" aroused by the ghost as that of grisly horror. Now this grisly horror obviously contributes something to the attraction which ghost-stories exercise, in so far, namely, as the relaxation of tension ensuing upon our release from it relieves the mind in a pleasant and agreeable way. So far, however, it is not really the ghost itself that gives us pleasure, but the fact that we are rid of it. But obviously this is quite insufficient to explain the ensnaring attraction of the ghost-story. The ghost's real attraction rather consists in this, that of itself and in an uncommon degree it entices the imagination, awakening strong interest and curiosity; it is the weird thing itself that allures the fancy. But it does this, not because it is "something long and white" (as someone once defined a ghost), nor yet through any of the positive and conceptual attributes which fancies about ghosts have invented, but because it is a thing that "doesn't really exist at all," the "wholly other," something which has no place in our scheme of reality but belongs to an absolutely different one, and which at the same time arouses an irrepressible interest in the mind.

But that which is perceptibly true in the fear of ghosts, which is, after all, only a caricature of the genuine thing, is in a far stronger sense true of the "daemonic" experience itself, of which the fear of ghosts is a mere off-shoot. And while, following this main line of development, this element in the numinous consciousness, the feeling of the "wholly other," is heightened and clarified, its higher modes of manifestation come into being, which set the numinous object in contrast not only to everything wonted and familiar (i.e., in the end, to nature in general), thereby turning it into the "supernatural," but finally to the word itself, and thereby exalt it to the "supramundane," that which is above the whole world-order.

The Element of Fascination

The qualitative *content* of the numinous experience, to which "the mysterious" stands as *form* is in one of its aspects the element of daunting "awefulness" and "majesty," which has already been dealt with in detail; but it is clear that it has at the same time another aspect, in which it shows itself as something uniquely attractive and *fascinating*.

These two qualities, the daunting and the fascinating, now combine in a strange harmony of contrasts, and the resultant dual character of the numinous consciousness, to which the entire religious development bears witness, at any rate from the level of the "daemonic dread" onwards, is at once the strangest and most noteworthy phenomenon in the whole history of religion. The daemonic-divine object may appear to the mind an object of horror and dread, but at the same time it is no less something that allures with a potent charm, and the creature, who trembles before it, utterly cowed and cast down, has always at the same time the impulse to turn to it, nay to even make it somehow his own. The "mystery" is for him not merely something to be wondered at but something that entrances him; and besides that in it which bewilders and confounds, he feels a something that captivates and transports him with a strange ravishment, rising often enough to the pitch of dizzy intoxication; it is the Dionysiac-element in the numen.

The ideas and concepts which are the parallels or "schemata" on the rational side of this non-rational element of "fascination" are love, mercy, pity, comfort; these are all "natural" elements of the common psychical life, only they are here thought as absolute and in completeness. But important as these are for the experience of religious bliss or felicity, they do not by any means exhaust it. It is just the same as with the opposite experience of religious infelicity—the experience of the *orge* or "wrath" of God:—both alike contain fundamentally non-rational elements. Bliss or beatitude is more, far more, than the mere natural feeling of being comforted, of reliance, of the joy of love, however these may be heightened and enhanced. Just as "wrath," taken in a purely rational or a purely ethical sense, does not exhaust that profound element of *awefulness* which is locked in the mystery of deity, so neither does "graciousness" exhaust the profound element of *wonderfulness* and rapture which lies in the mysterious beatific experience of deity. The term "grace" may indeed be taken as its aptest designation, but then only in the sense in which it is really applied in the language of the mystics, and in which not only the "gracious intent" but "something more" is meant by the word. This "something more" has its antecedent phases very far back in the history of religions.

CRITIQUE

Implicit in our procedure so far has been a basic assumption. We have assumed that religion, whatever else it may be, is also an activity of man. This observation seems simple enough, but it has important consequences for our study. As an activity of man, religion is open to the observation and study of everyone, believer and nonbeliever alike. Naturally the believer insists that his activity can be properly understood only by reference to some agency, order, or state of affairs not open to the normal or common observations of man. This is especially true of the religious type we have been studying in this chapter. But some observers dispute this claim. They argue, in effect, that believers have misinterpreted their experience—that it has another, and perhaps quite different, meaning from that proposed. We deal with two such approaches here.

17. On Men's Self-denial in the Face of the Holy as a Psychological Illness, P. Berger

In our materials so far, believers have interpreted their submission to the Other as the appropriate response of a limited, mortal being to a power far beyond his/her understanding. In this excerpt, Berger, a widely read contemporary sociologist at the New School for Social Research, suggests that this submission has an altogether different meaning—that of psychological illness. He borrows a term from the field of psychology to describe this illness—masochism. To what extent are the testimonials in Chapter I vulnerable to this criticism? How would you determine whether an extraordinary experience having many of these characteristics was the expression of genuine religious experience or of psychological illness?

Every society entails a certain denial of the individual self and its needs, anxieties, and problems. One of the key functions of nomoi* is the facilitation of this denial in individual consciousness. There is also an intensification of this self-denying surrender to society and its order that is of particular interest in connection with religion. This is the attitude of masochism, that is, the attitude in which the individual reduces himself to an inert and thinglike object vis-á-vis his fellowmen, singly or in collectivities or in the nomoi established by them. In this attitude, pain itself, physical or mental, serves to ratify the denial of self to the point where it may actually be subjectively pleasurable. Masochism, typically in conjunction with its complementary attitude of sadism, is a recurrent and important element of human interaction in areas ranging from sexual relations to political discipleship. Its key characteristic is the intoxication of surrender to an other—complete, self-denying, even self-destroying. Any pain or suffering inflicted by the other (who, of course, is posited as the sadistic counterpart to the masochistic self—absolutely dominating, self-affirming, and self-sufficient) serves as proof that the surrender has indeed taken place and that its intoxication is real. "I am nothing—He is everything—and therein lies my ultimate bliss"—in this formula lies the essence of the masochistic attitude. It transforms the self into nothingness, the other into absolute reality. Its ecstasy consists precisely in this double metamorphosis, which is profoundly liberating in that it seems to cut all at once through the ambiguities and anguish of separate, individual subjectivity confronting

---

From *The Sacred Canopy* by Peter L. Berger. Copyright © 1967 by Peter L. Berger. Reprinted by permission of Doubleday & Company, Inc. and of Faber and Faber Ltd. from *The Social Reality of Religion*. Pp. 55–57.

* Social law.

the subjectivities of others. The fact that the masochistic attitude is inherently predestined to failure, because the self cannot be annihilated this side of death and because the other can only be absolutized in illusion, need not concern us here. The important point for our immediate considerations is that masochism, by its radical self-denial, provides the means by which the individual's suffering and even death can be radically transcended, to the point where the individual not only finds these experiences bearable but even welcomes them. Man cannot accept aloneness and he cannot accept meaninglessness, he finds a paradoxical meaning in self-annihilation. "I am nothing—and therefore nothing can hurt me," or even more sharply: "I have died—and therefore I shall not die," and then: "Come, sweet pain, come, sweet death"—these are the formulas of masochistic liberation.

"Just who does he think he is?"

The masochistic attitude originates in concrete relations with individual others. The lover, say, or the master is posited as total power, absolute meaning, that is, as a *realissimum* into which the tenuous realities of one's own subjectivity may be absorbed. The same attitude, however, can be extended to collectivities of others and, finally, to the nomoi represented by these. It can be sweet to suffer pain at the hands of one's lover—but it can also be sweet to be punished by the sovereign authority of the state. Finally, the self-denying submission to the power of the collective nomos can be liberating in the same way. Here, the concrete other of social experience is vastly magnified in the personifications of collective order. Thus it may not only be sweet to die for one's country—provided, of course, that one has the proper patriotic viewpoint. Needless to add, the same extension of the masochistic attitude may take on a religious character. Now the other of the masochistic confrontation is projected into the immensity of the cosmos, takes on cosmic dimensions of omnipotence and absoluteness, and can all the more plausibly be posited as ultimate reality. The "I am nothing—He is everything" now becomes enhanced by the empirical un-availability of the other to whom the masochistic surrender is made. After all, one of the inherent difficulties of masochism in human relations is that the other may not play the sadistic role to satisfaction. The sadistic fel-lowman may refuse or forget to be properly all-powerful, or may simply be incapable of pulling off the act. Even if he succeeds in being something of a credible master for a while, he remains vulnerable, limited, mortal—in fact, remains human. The sadistic god is not handicapped by these empirical imperfections. He remains invulnerable, infinite, immortal by definition. The surrender to him is *ipso facto* protected from the contingencies and uncertainties of merely social masochism—for ever.

18. On The Justification of Claims Based on Religious Experience, *C. B. Martin*

One may attack a religious claim not only on psychological but also on philosophical grounds. C. B. Martin, Professor of Philosophy at the University of Sydney, presents this second type of critique. He has in mind certain recent advocates of the position that religious knowledge rooted in experience is beyond philosophical attack. This position, although not strictly required by the religious type presented in this chapter, is highly compatible

Reprinted from C. B. Martin, *Religious Belief.* © 1959 by Cornell University. Used by permission of Cornell University Press. Pp. 66–67, 71–75, 83–86.

with it and often defended by those who find in personal experience of the Holy the primary feature of religion. (Recall the selection by Brunner, reading 15.) Therefore, Martin's arguments against it will be relevant to claims that believers of this type will be at least inclined to make. His main point is that claims that are beyond criticism are necessarily psychological rather than existential. (Note, Martin does not intend the term "existential" to imply the position(s) called "existentialism." He is talking instead about truth claims.) Why, according to Martin, is it insufficient to rely simply on one's own impressions to support truth claims? If one's own experience is, at least potentially, suspect, how does he know what to assert as true? Suppose a believer offered you a course of activity (for example, prayer) which he said would lead you to have roughly the same sort of intense but incomprehensible experiences he has had. Suppose further that you entered on this course of activity and had these experiences. Could you say, according to Martin, that the believer had established his religious claim as true—at least as far as you were concerned? Why or why not?

. . . The alleged theological way of knowing may be described as follows: I have direct experience (knowledge, acquaintance, apprehension) of God; therefore I have valid reason to believe that God exists. By this it may be meant that the statement "I have had direct experience of God, but God does not exist" is contradictory. If so, the assertion that "I have had direct experience of God" commits one to the assertion that God exists. From this it follows that "I have had direct experience of God" is more than a psychological statement, because it claims more than the fact that I have certain experiences—it claims that God exists. On this interpretation the argument is deductively valid. The assertion "I have direct experience of God" includes the assertion "God exists." Thus, the conclusion "Therefore, God exists" follows tautologically.

Unfortunately, this deduction is useless. If the deduction were to be useful, the addition of the existential claim "God exists" to the psychological claim of having religious experiences would have to be shown to be warrantable, and this cannot be done.

Consider the following propositions: (1) I feel as if an unseen person were interested in (willed) my welfare. (2) I feel an elation quite unlike any I have ever felt before. (3) I have feelings of guilt and shame at my sinfulness. (4) I feel as if I were committed to bending all my efforts to living in a certain way. These propositions state only that I have certain complex feelings and experiences. Nothing else follows deductively. The only thing that I can establish beyond possible correction on the basis of having certain feelings and experiences is that I have these feelings and sensations. No matter how unique people may think their experience to be, it cannot do the impossible. . . .

The believer has had certain unusual experiences, which, presumably, the unbeliever has not had. If "having direct experience of God" is made synonymous with "having certain religious experiences," and the believer has had these and the unbeliever has not, then we may say that the believer's knowledge is incommunicable to the unbeliever in that it has already been legislated that in order to know what the direct experience of God is one must have had certain religious experiences. "To anyone who has no such awareness of God, leading as it does to the typically religious attitudes of obeisance and worship, it will be quite impossible to indicate what is meant; one can only hope to evoke it."[1] Reading theological textbooks and watching the behavior of believers is not sufficient.

The theologian has made the analogy above hold at the cost of endangering the existential claim about God which he hoped to establish. If "knowing color" is made synonymous with "having color sensations" and "having direct experience of God" is made synonymous with "having certain religious experiences," then it is certainly true that a blind man cannot "know color" and that a nonreligious man cannot "have direct experience of God." By definition, also, it is true that the blind man and the nonreligious man cannot know the meaning of the phrases "knowing color" and "having direct experience of God," because it has been previously legislated that one cannot know their meaning without having the relevant experiences.

If this analogy is kept, the phrases "knowing color" and "having direct experience of God" seem to make no claim beyond the psychological claims about one's color sensations and religious feelings.

If this analogy is not kept, there is no sense in the comparison of the incommunicability between the man of normal vision and the blind man with the incommunicability between the believer and the unbeliever.

If "knowing color" is to be shaken loose from its purely psychological implications and made to have an existential reference concerning features of the world, then a whole society of tests and checkup procedures, which would be wholly irrelevant to the support of the psychological claim about one's own color sensations, become relevant. For example, what other people see, the existence of light waves, and the description of their characteristics, which needs the testimony of research workers and scientific instruments, all must be taken into account.

Because "having direct experience of God" does not admit the relevance of a society of tests and checking procedures, it tends to place itself in the company of the other ways of knowing which preserve their self-sufficiency, "uniqueness," and "incommunicability" by making a psychological and not an existential claim. For example, "I seem to see a piece of blue paper,"[2] requires no further test or checking procedure in order to be considered true. Indeed, if Jones says, "I seem to see a piece of blue paper," he not only needs no further corroboration but cannot be shown to have been mistaken. If Smith says to Jones, "It does not seem to me as if I were seeing a piece of blue paper," this cannot rightly raise any doubts in Jones's mind, though it may express Smith's doubts. That is, Smith may feel that Jones is lying. However, if Jones had said, "I see a piece of blue paper," and Smith, in the same place and at the same time, had replied, "I do not see a piece of blue paper," or, "It does not seem to me as if I were now seeing a piece of blue paper," then Smith's remarks can rightly raise doubts in Jones's mind. Further investigation will then be proper, and if no piece of paper can be felt and other investigators cannot see or feel the paper and photographs reveal nothing, then Jones's statement will be shown to have been false. Jones's only refuge will be to say, "Well, I certainly seem to see a piece of blue paper." This is a perfect refuge, because no one can prove him wrong, but its unassailability has been bought at the price of making no claim about the world beyond the claim about his own experience of the moment.

The closeness of the religious statement to the psychological statement can be brought out in another way, as follows. When one wishes to support the assertion that a certain physical object exists, the tests and checking procedures made by Jones himself are not the only things relevant to the truth of his assertion. Testimony of what others see, hear, and so on is also relevant. That is, if Jones wanted to know whether it was really a star that he saw, he could not only take photographs, look through a telescope, and the like but also ask others if they saw the star. If a large proportion of a large number of people denied seeing the star, Jones's claim about the star's existence would be weakened. Of course, he might still trust his telescope. However, let us now imagine that Jones does not make use of the tests and checking procedures (photographs and telescopes) but is left with the testimony of what he sees and the testimony of others concerning what they see. In this case, it is so much to the point if a large number of people deny seeing the star that Jones will be considered irrational or mad if he goes on asserting its existence. His only irrefutable position is to reduce his physical object claim to an announcement concerning his own sensations. Then the testimony of men and angels cannot disturb his certitude. These sensations of the moment he knows directly and immediately, and the indirect and nonimmediate testimony of men and angels is irrelevant. Absolute confidence and absolute indifference to the majority judgment is bought at the price of reducing the existential to the nonexistential.

The religious claim is similar to, though not identical with, the case above in certain important features. We have seen that there are no tests or checking procedures open to the believer to support his existential claim about God. Thus, he is left with the testimony of his own experience and the similar testimony of the experience of others. And, of course, he is not left wanting for such testimony, for religious communities seem to serve just this sort of function.

Let us imagine a case comparable to the one concerning the existence of a physical object. In this case Brown is a professor of divinity, and he believes that he has come to know of the existence of God through direct experience of God. In order to understand the intricate character of what Professor Brown is asserting we must imagine a highly unusual situation. The other members of the faculty and the members of Professor Brown's religious community suddenly begin sincerely to deny his, and what has been their own, assertion. Perhaps they still attend church services and pray as often as they used to do, and perhaps they claim to have the same sort of experiences as they had when they were believers, but they refuse to accept the conclusion that God exists. Whether they give a Freudian explanation or some other explanation or no explanation of their experiences, they are agreed in refusing to accept the existential claim (about God) made by Professor Brown. How does this affect Professor Brown and his claim? It may affect Professor Brown very deeply—indeed, he may die of broken-hearted disappointment at the loss of his fellow believers. However, the loss of fellow believers may not weaken his confidence in the truth of his assertion or in the testimony of his experience. In this matter his experience may be all that ultimately counts for him in establishing his confidence in the truth of his claim about the existence of God. It has been said that religious experience carries its own guarantee, and perhaps the account above describes what is meant by this.

It is quite obvious from these examples that the religious statement "I have direct experience of God" is of a different status from the physical object statement "I see a star" and shows a distressing similarity to the low-claim assertion "I seem to see a star.". . .

If I am sitting at my desk and someone asks me if there is an ash tray on my desk, *all* that I have to do is have a look and say "Yes" or "No." But whether or not I know there is an ash tray on my desk is not to be read off simply from what my eyes at that moment told me. For if my eyes can tell me the truth they can tell me a lie, and the difference here would not be decided by what they tell. For me really to have seen and known there was an ash tray, other people must have been able to have seen it if they had looked. If I have only the testimony of my eyes and discount all else, then that testimony is mute concerning the existence of what is external. My eyes can tell me (in an hallucination) of the presence of an ash tray when there is no ash tray.

When someone uses the sentence "I see an ash tray" in such a way that he counts as relevant to its truth *only* his visual experience at the time, he is talking *only* about that experience, though the sentence has the form of making a statement about an ash tray. It does not help if he calls it a "cognitive experience" or if he says that he "anyhow *does* know" or if he says that his experience is "self-authenticating" or is a "direct encounter." We cannot allow a speaker any final authority in the account of how he is using his sentences. If such special dispensation were allowable, conceptual confusion would be rare indeed.

Similarly, I have argued, when someone uses the sentence "I have or have had direct experience of God" in such a way that he counts as relevant to its truth *only* his experience at the time, he is talking *only* about that experience, though the sentence has the form of making a statement about the presence of God, and neither does it help if he calls it a "cognitive experience."

From the fact that someone uses the sentence "I see an ash tray" so that he is talking *only* about his visual experience, nothing at all follows about whether or not he is actually seeing an ash tray in front of him. His *statement* may be only about his visual experience itself, and his actual *situation* may be that of seeing the ash tray. Also, from the fact that some-one uses the sentence "I have or have had direct experience of God" in such a way that he is talking *only* about his experience at the time, nothing at all follows about whether or not he is actually experiencing the presence of a supernatural being. His *statement* may be only about his experience itself, and his actual *situation* may be that of experiencing the presence of a supernatural being.

The religious person will want, in what he says, to be able to distinguish between a "delusive" and a "veridical" experience of God. The experience should be due to the actual presence of God and not due only to a drug or to self-deception or to the action of Satan. Therefore he must use his sentence to refer to more than an experience that is, in principle, com-patible with these and other similar causes.

What makes a form of experience a way of knowing? It is often sug-gested that the mystic who "sees" God is like a man (in a society of blind men) who sees colors. It is claimed that each has a form of experience and a way of knowing that others lack. Let us now work out this analogy. A society of blind men is told by one of its members that he has come to have a form of experience and a way of knowing by means of which he has been able to discover the existence of things not discoverable by ordinary experience. He says that these things have a *kind* of size (not just like size as it is felt by the blind) and a *kind* of shape (not just like shape as it is felt by the blind); he further says that these things are somehow "every-where" and that they cannot expect to understand what these things are like and what he means by experiencing them unless they themselves have these experiences. He then tells them of a procedure by which they will be able to discover for themselves the existence of these things. He warns them that these things do not always reveal themselves when the procedure is carried out, but, if a person is sufficiently diligent and believes strongly enough in their existence, he will probably come to know by means of unique and incomparable experiences of the existence of these things.

Some people, with faith and diligence, submit themselves to the re-quired procedure, and some of these are rewarded by a kind of experience they have not known before. Color shapes float before them—things that they cannot touch or feel and that are beyond the reach of their senses, and things that may be present to one of their group and not experienced by the others, things that may as well be everywhere as anywhere, since they are locatable only in the sense of being "before" each observer to whom they appear. These people cannot correlate this new form of experience with the rest of experience, they cannot touch or smell these "things." Indeed, they "see" visions, not things. Or rather these people have no way of *knowing* the existence of the things that may or may not exist over and above the momentary experiences. May these experiences all the same be "cognitive"? Yes and no. Yes, there may be something, they know not what, responsible for their having these experiences. No, their experiences are not a way of *knowing* about this something. For the experience of a colored shape that needs no corroboration by the experience of others similarly placed, and that is not related to one's other senses, is not in itself a way of knowing what in the world is responsible for this experience even if there is something beyond the condition of the "observer" that is so responsible. So far, even the people concerned have no *way of knowing* what more is involved than the fact of their experiencing momentary "visions."

I have not denied that the religious mystic may have experiences that others do not. Neither have I denied that there might be some external agency responsible for these experiences. What I have denied is that the mystic's possession of these experiences is in itself a way of knowing the existence or nature of such an agency.

NOTES

1. H. H. Farmer, *Towards Belief in God* (London: S. C. M. Press, 1942), Part III, p. 40.
2. I shall call such statements "low-claim assertions."

Even if you experience something you will not "know" it.

(HOW DO YOU GET TO KNOW Anything then?)

II

Creation of Community
Through Myth
and Ritual

...[T]he liturgy is the summit toward which the activity of the
Church is directed; at the same time it is the fountain from
which all her power flows. For the goal of apostolic works is that
all who are made sons of God by faith and baptism should
come together to praise God in the midst of His Church, to
take part in her sacrifice, and to eat the Lord's supper.

The liturgy in its turn inspires the faithful to become "of
one heart in love" when they have tasted to their full of the
paschal mysteries; it prays that "they may grasp by deed what
they hold by creed." The renewal in the Eucharist of the covenant
between the Lord and man draws the faithful into the compelling
love of Christ and sets them afire. From the liturgy, therefore,
and especially from the Eucharist, as from a fountain, grace
is channeled into us; and the sanctification of men in Christ
and the glorification of God, to which all other activities of
the Church are directed as toward their goal, are most powerfully
achieved. (Taken from The Documents of Vatican II, ed. Walter
Abbott, S. J. Trans. Msgr. Joseph Gullugher [New York: Guild
Press, 1966], p. 143.)

ALL HUMAN EXPERIENCE, religious experience included, finds expression in some form. In Chapter I we considered a type of religion in which particular symbols and ritual had little importance. In this chapter we will look at others who feel differently about this. When religious concern shifts from the subjective experience of the moment to the proper form of its expression, we move from one "type" of religion to one of at least two other "types." The first of these we call "Creation of Community Through Myth and Ritual." The movement from experience to myth and ritual should not be understood as a movement from content to form or from inner to outer. Although not entirely inappropriate, these contrasts are, nevertheless, misleading, for each "type" has both a public and a private aspect. Each type perceives the whole range of human life from its own point of view and responds to it in ways that show consistent structural features even across the lines of tradition and culture.

To the believer of the myth and ritual type, the problem that threatens all human life is that of alienation from Reality (sin). In his view the "natural" order is essentially imperfect. It lacks the vitality and coherence essential to its continued existence. It runs down, dies, decays. To live in such an order is death. To trust in it is folly. To choose it is sin. It is a derivative world. Therefore, one can hope for life only if he can tap the essentially real, the creative source of being, from which the world of ordinary experience was and is derived. The attempt here is not so much to abolish the natural order (as, for instance, through abstinence or catastrophe) as to reconcile it with its source, to redeem it through that subordination to the Real which is its proper destiny.

This understanding of the situation is both expressed in and clarified by the means which believers of this type use to enact it. Because the Divine Act (perhaps at the beginning of time or at a special moment of fulfillment in history, or both) is understood to be both the source and the inner reality of all things, the believer seeks to conform himself to that act. He finds in his tradition stories that recount it, symbols that embody it, and rituals to enact it. (Note, we are considering the believer's view of this tradition—not its origin as defined by historical study.) Given these models of the real, he is—or seeks to be—faithful. He orders his life, worships, sacrifices, and celebrates, according to the pattern of the divine. In that faithfulness, together with his trust in the priority of the divine to the ordinary or everyday, he derives his hope.

A community devoted to myth and ritual patterns will give particular attention to those individuals who administer and preserve the sacred rites and tradition—the priests or seers. They will, in some measure, be set apart. They will have special training, privileges, and responsibilities. Furthermore, this society will be especially careful to preserve its traditions and its holy places or implements. Without specially endowed persons, it would be cut off from all truth, for the Divine Act(s) is/are thought to have been revealed "in the beginning." Without sacred symbols, the knowledge will (or at least may) be useless, for it is not intellectual comprehension, but the power of the symbols to connect the profane world with the sacred, that is important. As a consequence of these concerns and the understanding they express, the myth-and-ritual-believer always knows that he is part of a religious community. His faith may well be strong, but it is not primarily his experience that he trusts. His faith is molded by a specific form or manifestation of Divine love and power. He believes the traditions, he serves the cult, and he seeks divine aid as, and only as, the member of a religious community.

ADVOCACY

1. Initiation and Puberty Rites,
J. Mbiti

One of the most widespread set of rites is that of initiation. Whether sacred or secular, the initiation rite signifies a change in status or identity. From the standpoint of the initiating community (for this is always a communal act even when performed secretly), the initiated one has become a new person; he is only then fully present to some dimension of life basic to that community. Although initiations always involve some degree of training and testing, they vary widely in their forms. Of these, some of the most dramatic are those which involve the cutting of the sexual organs, and we have included several examples of this in the following selection. It is taken from an introduction to traditional African thought by John S. Mbiti, a black, African Christian who is Professor of Religious Studies at Makerere University, Kampala, Uganda. Note his stress on the simultaneously personal and corporate character of the initiation ceremonies. According to Mbiti, how does one become adult in tribal society? What meaning do you think the physical pain and its surrounding apprehension has for the initiates? Have you undergone any ceremonies of initiation? If so, were there any similarities between it and the ones described here? Do you see any functional similarities between conversion (Chapter I) and initiation?

...The rites of birth and childhood introduce the child to the corporate community, but this is only the introduction. The child is passive and has still a long way to go. He must grow out of childhood and enter into adulthood both physically, socially and religiously. This is also a change from passive to active membership in the community. Most African peoples have rites and ceremonies to mark this great change, but a few do not observe initiation and puberty rites. The initiation of the young is one of the key moments in the rhythm of individual life, which is also the rhythm of the corporate group of which the individual is a part. What happens to the single youth happens corporately to the parents, the relatives, the neighbours and the living-dead.

Initiation rites have many symbolic meanings, in addition to the physical drama and impact. We can mention some of the religious meanings before we come to concrete examples. The youth are ritually introduced to the art of communal living. This happens when they withdraw from other people to live alone in the forest or in specifically prepared huts away from the villages. They go through a period of withdrawal from society, absence from home, during which time they receive secret instruction before they are allowed to rejoin their relatives at home. This is a symbolic experience of the process of dying, living in the spirit world and being reborn (resurrected). The rebirth, that is the act of rejoining their families, emphasizes and dramatizes that the young people are now new, they have new personalities, they have lost their childhood, and in some societies they even receive completely new names.

Another great significance of the rites is to introduce the candidates to adult life: they are now allowed to share in the full privileges and duties of the community. They enter into the state of responsibility: they inherit new rights, and new obligations are expected of them by society. This incorporation into adult life also introduces them to the life of the living-dead as well as the life of those yet to be born. The initiation rites prepare young people in matters of sexual life, marriage, procreation and family responsibilities. They are henceforth allowed to shed their blood for their country, and to plant their biological seeds so that the next generation can begin to arrive.

Initiation rites have a great educational purpose. The occasion often marks the beginning of acquiring knowledge which is otherwise not accessible to those who have not been initiated. It is a period of awakening to many things, a period of dawn for the young. They learn to endure hardships, they learn to live with one another, they learn to obey, they learn the secrets and mysteries of the man-woman relationship; and in some areas, especially in West Africa, they join secret societies each of which has its own secrets, activities and language.

We shall now consider concrete examples of initiation rites. The details will obviously differ considerably, but the basic meaning and significance are generally similar. For most peoples the initiation rites take place during puberty, but there are places where they are performed either before or after puberty. For this reason it is incorrect to speak of them as "puberty rites."

AKAMBA INITIATION RITES

There are three parts to Akamba initiation rites, the first two being the most important. Formerly, everybody had to go through these first two, but only a small number of men went through the third which was performed when the men were over forty years old. Without being initiated, a person is not a full member of the Akamba people. Furthermore, no matter how old or big he is, so long as he is not initiated, he is despised and considered to be still a boy or girl.

Children go through the first stage of initiation rites when they are about four to seven years of age. The ceremony takes place in the months of August to October, when it is dry and relatively cool. Boys undergo circumcision, and girls undergo clitoridectomy. The date for the ceremony is announced in a given region, and when it arrives all the candidates are gathered together by their parents and relatives at the home where the ceremony is to take place. Specialist men circumcise the boys, and specialist women perform the operation on the girls; and a special knife is used in each case. The physical cutting takes place early in the morning. The foreskin of the boy's sexual organ is cut off; and a small portion of the girls' clitoris is similarly removed. Men gather round to watch the boys, and women to watch the girls. The operation is painful, but the children are encouraged to endure it without crying or shouting, and those who manage to go through it bravely are highly praised by the community. Afterwards there is public rejoicing, with dancing, singing, drinking beer and making libation and food offerings to the living-dead. In course of the following few weeks, while the wound is healing, relatives come to visit the initiated boys and girls, bringing them presents of chickens, money, ornaments and even sheep and cattle by those who can afford them.

That is the first stage of the initiation: what does it signify and mean? The cutting of the skin from the sexual organs symbolizes and dramatizes separation from childhood: it is parallel to the cutting of the umbilical cord when the child is born. The sexual organ attaches the child to the state of ignorance, the state of inactivity and the state of potential impotence (asexuality). But once that link is severed, the young person is freed from that state of ignorance and inactivity. He is born into another state, which is the stage of knowledge, of activity, of reproduction. So long as a person is not initiated, he cannot get married and he is not supposed to reproduce or bear children. The shedding of his blood into the ground binds him mystically to the living-dead* who are symbolically living in the ground, or are reached at least through the pouring of libation on to the ground. It is the blood of new birth. The physical pain which the children are encouraged to endure, is the beginning of training them for difficulties and sufferings of later life. Endurance of physical and emotional pain is a great virtue among Akamba people, as indeed it is among other Africans, since life in Africa is surrounded by much pain from one source or another. The presents given to the initiates by their relatives, are tokens of welcome into the full community. They also demonstrate and symbolize the fact that now the young people can begin to own and inherit property, they are entitled to new rights and can say, "This is my property," even if they own it jointly with the corporate group. Owning property leads eventually to the next important stage, which is the period of marriage.

The dancing and rejoicing strengthen community solidarity, and emphasize the corporateness of the whole group. It is only after this first initiation rite that young people are allowed to join in public dances. Making of offerings and libation to the living-dead emphasizes and renews the link

---

* "The *living-dead* is a person who is physically dead but alive in the memory of those who knew him as well as 'alive' in the world of spirits. So long as the living-dead is thus remembered, he is in a state of *personal immortality*." Mbiti, p. 32.

between human beings and the departed, between the visible and invisible worlds. It is to be noted here, however, that children whose parents die before they are initiated, are initiated at a much later age than usual. It is not quite clear why this must be so, perhaps it is in order to allow the children more time to grow since initiation thrusts upon them great responsibilities.

There is no set period between the first and the second initiations, but the latter can take place any time between a few weeks after the first initiation and the age of fifteen or so. The first is primarily physical, the second is mainly educational. The ceremony for the second (known as the "great" or "major" initiation) is sponsored by a household from where there are no initiates at the time, and this is a great privilege which the people concerned consider to be granted them by their living-dead. The ceremony lasts from four to ten days, during part of which the candidates are secluded from the public and live in huts built away from the villages. They are accompanied by supervisors and teachers, to whom is delegated the responsibility of introducing the candidates to all matters of manhood and womanhood. The Akamba describe this duty as "brooding over the initiates," the way that birds brood over their eggs before hatching On the first day the candidates learn educational songs and encounter symbolic obstacles On the second day they have to face a frightening monster known as "*mbusya*" (rhinoceros) In some parts of the country only the boys go through this experience, while in other parts both boys and girls do. This is a man-made structure of sticks and trees, from the inside of which some-one makes fearful bellows like those of a big monster. The initiates do not know exactly what it is, for that is one of the secrets of the ceremony. Afterwards they are not allowed to divulge the matter to those who have not been initiated. They face this "rhinoceros" bravely, shooting it with bows and arrows in order to destroy it the way they would destroy a similar enemy. That night, the man and woman who performed the operation at the first ceremony, have a ritual sexual intercourse; and the parents of the candidates have a ritual sexual intercourse on the third and seventh nights.

On the third day, the initiates rehearse adult life: boys go hunting with miniature bows and arrows, and girls cut small twigs (which symbolize firewood for the home). Later the same day the original operators at the first ceremony spit beer over the candidates to bless them, and the children return to their "home" in the bush. Here they must overcome objects that are placed before them. Each boy is given a special stick, which he must retain; and that evening a dance for the initiates takes place. With their special sticks the boys perform symbolic sexual acts upon the girls; and on the following day, they are examined on the meaning of riddles and puzzles carved on the sticks or drawn on sand. Afterwards the boys fetch sugar-canes, this being a form of permitted "stealing" acceptable and necessary for that particular purpose; and with the sugar-cane they make beer for their incumbents.

On the fifth day the initiates and their incumbents go to a sacred tree, usually the fig or sycamore tree on the banks of a river. The supervisors take a little amount of sap from the tree and give it to each candidate. The initiates pretend to eat it; and thereafter they may now eat all the foods which otherwise they had been forbidden to eat during the previous day. At this tree the operators make a small cut on the sexual organs of the initiates, and beer is poured on the organs.

The sixth day is spent peacefully. On the seventh day, the boys make a mock cattle raid, while the girls cry out that the enemies have come. The ceremony may end at that point, and the young people now return to their individual homes. The parents have a ritual sexual intercourse that night.[1]

This long description is intended to illustrate, at some detail, the significance of the initiation rite. Certain meanings clearly emerge from this ceremony. Corporate living is instilled into the thinking of the young people by making them live together in the special huts in the woods. This experience is like a miniature community. The incumbents play the role of the elders; and it is extremely important that the young respect and obey the older people whether they are their immediate parents or not. Seclusion serves to make the candidates concentrate on what they are experiencing and doing, and becomes like a re-enaction of death. It is a new rhythm for the young people as well as for their wider community. When seclusion is over they emerge as qualified and legally recognized men and women who may establish families, become mothers and fathers and defend their country—hence the mock raid attack and the symbolic sexual act that are part of the ceremony. The frightening ordeal of the "rhinoceros" is a psychological device partly to emphasize the seriousness of the occasion, and partly to drive out fear from the candidates so that in time of danger they do not flee away but take courage to defend themselves and their families. The riddles carved on the special sticks or drawn on sand are symbols of knowledge, to which the candidates now have full access. The initiates are now entitled to know every secret of tribal life and knowledge, apart from what is known to exclusive groups. The rite at the sacred tree is a reminder of the religious life, and a symbolic visit to the living-dead and the spirits who are thought to live there. The occasion is a renewal of the link with the Zamani period, the link with the spiritual realities and a reminder that the living-dead are "present" with them. Permission to eat the foods which the initiates were previously forbidden to eat is a symbolic and dramatic way of opening up for them the full participation in all the affairs of the nation. The slight cut on the sex organs at the sacred tree indicates the sacredness of sex, in the sight of God, the spirits, the living-dead and the human community. The return home is like an experience of resurrection: death is over, their seclusion is ended, and now they rejoin their community as new men and women, fully accepted and respected as such. Their parents have a ritual sexual intercourse as the final seal of the ceremony, the symbolic gesture that their own children are fertile, that their children are now initiated and authorized to carry on the burning flame of life, and that a new generation is now socially and educationally born.

Akamba men have still a third initiation rite, when they are over forty years of age. Only a few of them actually undergo this ceremony, and it is so secret that little is known about it by those who have not participated in it. It is like a ritual mystical experience, and there are grades through which the candidates go after they have finished with the actual rite. Among other things the rite involves very severe tests of endurance and going through great torment. During that stage the men perform acts which are not regarded as their own, since candidates are in a state of having "lost" themselves. The ceremony is performed in secret, away from the villages, and the initiated men are under such strong oath of secrecy that even those who later become Christians are unwilling to divulge what actually happens.

MAASAI INITIATION RITES

Among the Maasai, circumcision rites take place every four to five years, for young people aged between twelve and sixteen. All those who are circumcised together form a lifelong age-group, and take on a new special name. As preparation for the ceremony, all the candidates first assemble together, covered with white clay and carrying no weapons. Then they spend about two months moving about the countryside. On the day before the ceremony the boys wash themselves in cold water. When their foreskin is cut off, the blood is collected in an ox hide and put on each boy's head. For four days the boys are kept in seclusion, after which they emerge dressed like women and having their faces painted with white clay and heads adorned with ostrich feathers. A few weeks later, when their sex organs have healed, the heads are shaved and the boys now grow new hair and can become warriors. Girls have their ceremony in which a portion of their sex organ is cut or pierced. They adorn their heads with grass or leaves of a special tree (doom palm). When their wounds have healed, the girls can get married; and in some parts of the country they also have their heads shaved.[2]

In this example we see the same type of meaning as among the Akamba. The underlying emphasis is separation from childhood and incorporation into adulthood. Cutting or piercing the sex organ, and the shaving of the head, symbolize the break from one status and entry into another. The smearing of the face with white clay is the symbol of a new birth, a new person, a new social status. When the ceremony is over, the men begin their career as warriors: they may now defend their country or raid other peoples. The women are ready to get married and often do so immediately. So the rhythm of a new generation is dramatized and played. The young people who have been initiated together become mystically and ritually bound to each other for the rest of their life: they are in effect one body, one group, one community, one people. They help one another in all kinds of ways. The wife of one man is equally the wife of other men in the same age-group; and if one member visits another he is entitled to sleep with the latter's wife, whether or not the husband is at home. This is a deep level of asserting the group solidarity, and one at which the individual really feels that "I am because we are; and since we are, therefore I am." This solidarity creates or provides a sense of security, a feeling of oneness and the opportunities of participating in corporate existence.

NOTES

1. D. N. Kimilu, *Mukamba Waw'o* (Nairobi 1962), p. 30f.; Middleton, I, p. 88f.
2. A. van Gennep, *The Rites of Passage* (E.T. 1960), p. 85 f.

2. Periodic Worship of the Zunis,
R. Benedict

> *Ceremonies and ritual actions give religious significance not only to key moments in the life of individuals but also to recurring moments in the life of society. In this description of religion in one American culture—the Zunis of New Mexico—we can observe especially well the role of sacred things (prayers, dances, gods, priests, and so forth) in the ordering of the community's life. Zuni communal life is organized around various cults—priesthoods, tribal masked god societies, and medicine societies. This excerpt, drawn from the work of a famous American anthropologist, includes her discussion only of the first two of the three interlocking cults. Note the emphasis on correct form in ritual, the role of priests in their sacred function and in society at large, the goods sought through ritual, and the importance of the sacred realm for society generally. In what way(s) is worship for the Zunis like or unlike the examples of religious activity in Chapter I?*

The Zuñi are a ceremonious people, a people who value sobriety and inoffensiveness above all other virtues. Their interest is centred upon their rich and complex ceremonial life. Their cults of the masked gods, of healing, of the sun, of the sacred fetishes, of war, of the dead, are formal and established bodies of ritual with priestly officials and calendric observances. No field of activity competes with ritual for foremost place in their attention. Probably most grown men among the western Pueblos give to it the greater part of their waking life. It requires the memorizing of an amount of word-perfect ritual that our less trained minds find staggering, and the performance of neatly dovetailed ceremonies that are charted by the calendar and complexly interlock all the different cults and the governing body in endless formal procedure.

The ceremonial life not only demands their time; it preoccupies their

From Ruth Benedict, *Patterns of Culture* (New York: Houghton Mifflin Co., 1934), pp. 59–69.

attention. Not only those who are responsible for the ritual and those who take part in it, but all the people of the pueblo, women and families who 'have nothing,' that is, that have no ritual possessions, centre their daily conversation about it. While it is in progress, they stand all day as spectators. If a priest is ill, or if no rain comes during his retreat, village gossip runs over and over his ceremonial missteps and the implications of his failure. Did the priest of the masked gods give offence to some supernatural being? Did he break his retreat by going home to his wife before the days were up? These are the subjects of talk in the village for a fortnight. If an impersonator wears a new feather on his mask, it eclipses all talk of sheep or gardens or marriage or divorce.

This preoccupation with detail is logical enough. Zuñi religious practices are believed to be supernaturally powerful in their own right. At every step of the way, if the procedure is correct, the costume of the masked god traditional to the last detail, the offerings unimpeachable, the words of the hours-long prayers letter-perfect, the effect will follow according to man's desires. One has only, in the phrase they have always on their tongues, to "know how." According to all the tenets of their religion, it is a major matter if one of the eagle feathers of a mask has been taken from the shoulder of the bird instead of from the breast. Every detail has magical efficacy.

Zuñi places great reliance upon imitative magic. In the priests retreats for rain they roll round stones across the floor to produce thunder, water is sprinkled to cause the rain, a bowl of water is placed upon the altar that the springs may be full, suds are beaten up from a native plant that clouds may pile in the heavens, tobacco smoke is blown out that the gods "may not withhold their misty breath." In the masked-god dances mortals clothe themselves with the "flesh" of the supernaturals, that is, their paint and their masks, and by this means gods are constrained to grant their blessings. Even the observances that are less obviously in the realm of magic partake in Zuñi thought of the same mechanistic efficacy. One of the obligations that rest upon every priest or official during the time when he is actively participating in religious observances is that of feeling no anger. But anger is not tabu in order to facilitate communication with a righteous god who can only be approached by those with a clean heart. Its absence is a sign of concentration upon supernatural affairs, a state of mind that constrains the supernaturals and makes it impossible for them to withhold their share of the bargain. It has magical efficacy.

Their prayers also are formulas, the effectiveness of which comes from their faithful rendition. The amount of traditional prayer forms of this sort in Zuñi can hardly be exaggerated. Typically they describe in ritualistic language the whole course of the reciter's ceremonial obligations leading up to the present culmination of the ceremony. They itemize the appointment of the impersonator, the gathering of willow shoots for prayer-sticks, the binding of the bird feathers to them with cotton string, the painting of the sticks, the offering to the gods of the finished plume wands, the visits to sacred springs, the periods of retreat. No less than the original religious act, the recital must be meticulously correct.

> Seeking yonder along the river courses
> The ones who are our fathers,
> Male willow,
> Female willow,
> Four times cutting the straight young shoots,
> To my house
> I brought my road.
> This day
> With my warm human hands
> I took hold of them.
> I gave my prayer-sticks human form.
> With the striped cloud tail
> Of the one who is my grandfather,
> The male turkey,
> With eagle's thin cloud tail,
> With the striped cloud wings
> And massed cloud tails
> Of all the birds of summer,
> With these four times I gave my prayer-sticks human form.
> With the flesh of the one who is my mother,
> Cotton woman,
> Even a poorly made cotton thread,
> Four times encircling them and tying it about their bodies.
> I gave my prayer-sticks human form.
> With the flesh of the one who is our mother,
> Black paint woman,
> Four times covering them with flesh,
> I gave my prayer-sticks human form.

Prayer in Zuñi is never an outpouring of the human heart. There are some ordinary prayers that can be slightly varied, but this means little more than that they can be made longer or shorter. And the prayers are never remarkable for their intensity. They are always mild and ceremonious in form, asking for orderly life, pleasant days, shelter from violence. Even war priests conclude their prayer:

> I have sent forth my prayers.
> Our children,
> Even those who have erected their shelters
> At the edge of the wilderness,
> May their roads come in safely,
> May the forests
> And the brush
> Stretch out their water-filled arms
> To shield their hearts;
> May their roads come in safely;

May their roads all be fulfilled,
May it not somehow become difficult for them
When they have gone but a little way.
May all the little boys,
All the little girls,
And those whose roads are ahead,
May they have powerful hearts,
Strong spirits;
On roads reaching to Dawn Lake
May you grow old;
May your roads be fulfilled;
May you be blessed with life.
Where the life-giving road of your sun father comes out,
May your roads reach;
May your roads be fulfilled.

If they are asked the purpose of any religious observance, they have a ready answer. It is for rain. This is of course a more or less conventional answer. But it reflects a deep-seated Zuñi attitude. Fertility is above all else the blessing within the bestowal of the gods, and in the desert country of the Zuñi plateau, rain is the prime requisite for the growth of crops. The retreats of the priests, the dances of the masked gods, even many of the activities of the medicine societies are judged by whether or not there has been rain. To "bless with water" is the synonym of all blessing. Thus, in the prayers, the fixed epithet the gods apply in blessing to the rooms in Zuñi to which they come, is "water-filled," their ladders are "water-ladders," and the scalp taken in warfare is "the water-filled covering." The dead, too, come back in the rain clouds, bringing the universal blessing. People say to the children when the summer afternoon rain clouds come up the sky, "Your grandfathers are coming," and the reference is not to individual dead relatives, but applies impersonally to all forbears. The masked gods also are the rain and when they dance they constrain their own being—rain—to descend upon the people. The priests, again, in their retreat before their altars sit motionless and withdrawn for eight days, summoning the rain.

From wherever you abide permanently
You will make your roads come forth.
Your little wind blown clouds,
Your thin wisp of clouds
Replete with living waters,
You will send forth to stay with us.
Your fine rain caressing the earth,
Here at Itiwana,[1]
The abiding place of our fathers,
Our mothers,
The ones who first had being,
With your great pile of waters
You will come together.

Rain, however, is only one of the aspects of fertility for which prayers are constantly made in Zuñi. Increase in the gardens and increase in the tribe are thought of together. They desire to be blessed with happy women:

> Even those who are with child,
> Carrying one child on the back,
> Holding another on a cradle board,
> Leading one by the hand,
> With yet another going before.

Their means of promoting human fertility are strangely symbolic and impersonal, as we shall see, but fertility is one of the recognized objects of religious observances.

This ceremonial life that preoccupies Zuñi attention is organized like a series of interlocking wheels. The priesthoods have their sacred objects, their retreats, their dances, their prayers, and their year-long programme is annually initiated by the great winter solstice ceremony that makes use of all the different groups and sacred things and focuses all their functions. The tribal masked-god society has similar possessions and calendric observances, and these culminate in the great winter tribal masked-god ceremony, the Shalako. In like fashion the medicine societies, with their special relation to curing, function throughout the year, and have their annual culminating ceremony for tribal health. These three major cults of Zuñi ceremonial life are not mutually exclusive. A man may be, and often is, for the greater part of his life, a member of all three. They each give him sacred possessions "to live by" and demand of him exacting ceremonial knowledge.

The priesthoods stand on the highest level of sanctity. There are four major and eight minor priesthoods. They "hold their children[2] fast." They are holy men. Their sacred medicine bundles, in which their power resides, are, as Dr. Bunzel says, of "indescribable sanctity." They are kept in great covered jars, in bare, inner rooms of the priests' houses, and they consist of pairs of stoppered reeds, one filled with water, in which there are miniature frogs, and the other with corn. The two are wrapped together with yards and yards of unspun native cotton. No one ever enters the holy room of the priests' medicine bundle except the priests when they go in for their rituals, and an elder woman of the household or the youngest girl child, who go in before every meal to feed the bundle. Anyone entering, for either purpose, removes his moccasins.

The priests, as such, do not hold public ceremonies, though in great numbers of the rites their presence is necessary or they initiate essential first steps in the undertaking. Their retreats before their sacred bundle are secret and sacrosanct. In June, when rain is needed for the corn, at that time about a foot above the ground, the series of retreats begins. In order, each new priesthood going "in" as the preceding one comes out, they "make their days." The heads of the sun cult and of the war cult are included also in this series of the priests' retreats. They must sit motionless, with their thoughts fixed upon ceremonial things. Eight days for the major priesthoods, four for the lesser. All Zuñi awaits the granting of rain during these days, and priests blessed with rain are greeted and thanked by everyone upon the street after their retreat is ended. They have blessed their people with more than rain. They have upheld them in all their ways of life. Their position as guardians of their people has been vindicated. The prayers they have prayed during their retreat have been answered:

> All my ladder-descending children,
> All of them I hold in my hands,
> May no one fall from my grasp
> After going but a little way.
> Even every little beetle,
> Even every dirty little beetle
> Let me hold them all fast in my hands,
> Let none of them fall from my grasp.
> May my children's roads all be fulfilled;
> May they grow old;
> May their roads reach all the way to Dawn Lake;
> May their roads be fulfilled;
> In order that your thoughts may bend to this
> Your days are made.

The heads of the major priesthoods, with the chief priest of the sun cult and the two chief priests of the war cult, constitute the ruling body, the council, of Zuñi. Zuñi is a theocracy to the last implication. Since priests are holy men and must never during the prosecution of their duties feel anger, nothing is brought before them about which there will not be unanimous agreement. They initiate the great ceremonial events of the Zuñi calendar, they make ritual appointments, and they give judgment in cases of witchcraft. To our sense of what a governing body should be, they are without jurisdiction and without authority.

If the priesthoods stand on the level of greatest sanctity, the cult of the masked gods is most popular. It has first claim in Zuñi affection, and it flourishes today like the green bay tree.

There are two kinds of masked gods: the masked gods proper, the kachinas; and the kachina priests. These kachina priests are the chiefs of the supernatural world and are themselves impersonated with masks by Zuñi dancers. Their sanctity in Zuñi eyes makes it necessary that their cult should be quite separate from that of the dancing gods proper. The dancing gods are happy and comradely supernaturals who live at the bottom of a lake far off in the empty desert south of Zuñi. There they are always dancing. But they like best to return to Zuñi to dance. To impersonate them, therefore, is to give them the pleasure they most desire. A man, when he puts on the mask of the gods, becomes for the time being the supernatural himself. He has no longer human speech, but only the cry which is peculiar to that god. He is tabu, and must assume all the obligations of anyone who is for the time being sacred. He not only dances, but he observes an esoteric retreat before the dance, and plants prayersticks and observes continence.

There are more than a hundred different masked gods of the Zuñi pantheon, and many of these are dance groups that come in sets, thirty or forty of a kind. Others come in sets of six, coloured for the six directions— for Zuñi counts up and down as cardinal points. Each of these gods has individual details of costuming, an individual mask, an individual place in the hierarchy of the gods, myths that recount his doings, and ceremonies during which he is expected.

The dances of the masked gods are administered and carried out by a tribal society of all adult males. Women too may be initiated "to save their lives," but it is not customary. They are not excluded because of any tabu, but membership for a woman is not customary, and there are today only three women members. As far back as tradition reaches there seem not to have been many more at any one time. The men's tribal society is organized in six groups, each with its kiva or ceremonial chamber. Each kiva has its officials, its dances that belong to it, and its own roll of members.

Membership in one or the other of these kivas follows from the choice of a boy's ceremonial father at birth, but there is no initiation till the child is between five and nine years old. It is his first attainment of ceremonial status. This initiation, as Dr. Bunzel points out, does not teach him esoteric mysteries; it establishes a bond with supernatural forces. It makes him strong, and, as they say, valuable. The "scare kachinas," the punitive masked gods, come for the initiation, and they whip the children with their yucca whips. It is a rite of exorcism, "to take off the bad happenings," and to make future events propitious. In Zuñi whipping is never used as a corrective of children. The fact that white parents use it in punishment is a matter for unending amazement. In the initiation children are supposed to be very frightened, and they are not shamed if they cry cloud. It makes the rite the more valuable.

NOTES

1. "The Middle," the ceremonial name of Zuni, the center of the world.
2. That is, the people of Zuni.

3. The Mythic Structure of Classical Judaism, J. Neusner

In this excerpt, Jacob Neusner (Professor of Religious Studies, Brown University) speaks of the liturgical (ritual) materials as the "most widely present and meaningful" phenomenon of Judaism. Through an examination of two such rituals—the marriage ceremony and the festival of Passover—he shows how they illustrate "the mythic structure of classical Judaism." How is God experienced and understood in the Judaic myth? Note that what is "Real" for a Jew is not obvious or on the face of things, but is revealed by the Judaic myth. The Jew "views secular reality under the mythic aspects of eternal, ever-recurrent events."

In a history of nearly forty centuries, the Jews have produced rich and complex religious phenomena. Indeed, Judaic religious and historical data, like those of other religions, may seem at the outset to defy adequate description. The varieties of historical setting, ritual, intellectual and religious expression, literary and theological literature—these can scarcely be satisfactorily apprehended in the modest framework of a lifetime of study. In working toward a definition of any religion, one must confront the same formidable complexities.

Our operative criteria of selection ought to be, What phenomena are most widely present and meaningful? What, further, is important as a representation of the reality both viewed and shaped by "Judaism"? The answers surely cannot be found only in philosophical, legal, mystical, or theological literature produced by and for a religious elite. We cannot suppose sophisticated conceptions of extraordinary men were fully grasped by common folk. Theological writings, while important, testify to the conceptions of reality held by only a tiny minority. The legal ideals and values of Judaism were first shaped by the rabbis, a class of religious virtuosi, then imposed upon the life of ordinary people. Excluding learned theological and legal writings, the religious materials best conforming to our criteria are liturgical. The myths conveyed by prayer and associated rituals were universal, everywhere present and meaningful in the history of Judaism. Of greatest importance, they provide the clearest picture of how Jews in archaic times envisioned the meaning of life and of themselves.

Before proceeding, we had best clarify the meaning of "mythic structure." By myth, historians of religion do *not* mean, "something which is not true." They mean, in Streng's words, "that the essential structure of reality manifests itself in particular moments that are remembered and repeated from generation to generation."[1] These moments are preserved in myths. This meaning is wholly congruent to the Judaic data we shall now consider. If, in general, myth has the power to transform life because "it reveals the truth of life," as Streng says,[2] then what is the nature of Judaic myth?

If a myth is present, it must be everywhere present, somehow hidden in every ceremony and rite, every liturgy, every sacred gesture and taboo. We must be able to locate it in commonplace, not merely extraordinary, events of piety. Liturgy provides the clearest and, at the same time, the most reliable evidence of the structure of Judaic myth. . . .

. . . For the Jew the most intimate occasion is the marriage ceremony. Here a new family begins. Individual lover and beloved celebrate the uniqueness, the privacy of their love. One should, therefore, expect the nuptial prayer to speak of him and her, natural man and natural woman. Yet the blessings that are said over the cup of wine of sanctification are as follows:

> Praised are You, O Lord our God, King of the universe, Creator of the fruit of the vine.
>
> Praised are You, O Lord our God, King of the universe, who created all things for Your glory.
>
> Praised are You, O Lord our God, King of the universe, Creator of man.
>
> Praised are You, O Lord our God, King of the universe, who created man and woman in his image, fashioning woman from man as his mate, that together they might perpetuate life. Praised are You, O Lord, Creator of man.
>
> May Zion rejoice as her children are restored to her in joy. Praised are You, O Lord, who causes Zion to rejoice at her children's return.
>
> Grant perfect joy to these loving companions, as You did to the first man and woman in the Garden of Eden. Praised are You, O Lord, who grants the joy of bride and groom.
>
> Praised are You, O Lord, our God, King of the universe, who created joy and gladness, bride and groom, mirth, song, delight and rejoicing, love and harmony, peace and companionship. O Lord our God, may there ever be heard in the cities of Judah and in the streets of Jerusalem voices of joy and gladness, voices of bride and groom, the jubilant voices of those joined in marriage under the bridal canopy, the voices of young people feasting and singing. Praised are You, O Lord, who causes the groom to rejoice with his bride.[3]

These seven blessings say nothing of private people and of their anonymously falling in love. Nor do they speak of the community of Israel, as one might expect on a public occasion. In them are no hidden sermons, "to be loyal to the community and faithful in raising up new generations in it." Lover and beloved rather are transformed from natural to mythical figures. The blessings speak of archetypical Israel, represented here and now by the bride and groom.

Israel's history begins with creation, first, the creation of the vine, creature present in the place of the natural world. Creation is for God's glory. All things speak to nature, to the physical as much as the spiritual, for all things were made by God, and the Hebrew ends, "who formed the *Adam*." All things glorify God; above all creation is man. The theme of ancient paradise is introduced by the simple choice of the word "Adam," so heavy with meaning. The myth of man's creation is rehearsed: man and woman are in God's image, together complete and whole, creators of life, "like God." Woman was fashioned from man, together with him to perpetuate life. And again, "blessed is the creator of man." We have moved, therefore, from the natural world to the archetypical realm of paradise. Before us we see not merely a man and a woman, but Adam and Eve.

But this Adam and this Eve also are Israel, children of Zion the mother, as expressed in the fifth blessing. Zion lies in ruins, her children scattered:

> If I forget you, O Jerusalem, may my right hand forget its skill...if I do not place Jerusalem above my greatest joy.

Adam and Eve cannot celebrate together without thought to the condition of the mother, Jerusalem. The children will one day come home. The mood is hopeful, yet sad as it was meant to be, for archaic Israel mourns as it rejoices, and rejoices as it mourns. Quickly, then, back to the happy occasion, for we do not let mourning lead to melancholy: "Grant perfect joy to the loving companions," for they are creators of a new line in mankind, the new Adam, the new Eve, and their home— may it be the garden of Eden. And if joy is there, then "praised are you for the joy of bride and groom."

The concluding blessing returns to the theme of Jerusalem. This time it evokes the tragic hour of Jerusalem's first destruction. When everyone had given up hope, supposing with the end of Jerusalem had come the end of time, only Jeremiah counseled renewed hope. With the enemy at the gate, he sang of coming gladness:

> Thus says the Lord:
> In this place of which you say, "It is a waste, without man or beast," in the cities of Judah and the streets of Jerusalem that are desolate, without man or inhabitant or beast,
> There shall be heard again the voice of mirth and the voice of gladness, the voice of the bridegroom and the voice of the bride, the voice of those who sing as they bring thank-offerings to the house of the Lord...
> For I shall restore the fortunes of the land as first, says the Lord.
>   —*Jeremiah 33:10–11*

The closing blessing is not merely a literary artifice or a learned allusion to the ancient prophet. It is rather the exultant, jubilant climax of this acted-out myth: Just as here and now there stand before us Adam and Eve, so here and now in this wedding, the olden sorrow having been rehearsed, we listen to the voice of gladness that is coming. The joy of this new creation prefigures the joy of the Messiah's coming, hope for which is very present in this hour. And when he comes, the joy then will echo the joy of bride and groom before us. Zion the bride, Israel the groom, united now as they will be reunited by the compassionate God—these stand under the marriage canopy.

In classical Judaism, who is Jewish man? He is an ordinary, natural man who lives within a mythic structure, who thereby holds a view of history centered upon Israel from the creation of the world to its final redemption. Political defeats of this world are by myth transformed into eternal sorrow. The natural events of human life, here the marriage of ordinary folk, are by myth heightened into a reenactment of Israel's life as a people. In marriage, individuals stand in the place of mythic figures, yet remain, after all, a boy and a girl. What gives their love its true meaning is the myth of creation, destruction, and redemption, here and now embodied in that love. But in the end, the couple goes to bed: the sacred and secular are in most profane, physical love united.[4]

The wedding of symbol and reality, the fusion and confusion of the two—these mark the classical Judaic experience, shaped by myths of creation, Adam and Eve, the Garden of Eden, the equally mythic memory of the this-worldly destruction of an old, unexceptional temple. Ordinary events, such as a political and military defeat or success, are changed into theological categories such as divine punishment and heavenly compassion. If religion is a "means of ultimate transformation," rendering the commonplace into the paradigmatic, changing the here and now into a moment of eternity and of eternal return, then the marriage liturgy serves to exemplify what is *religious* in Judaic existence.

. . . At the festival of Passover, in the spring, Jewish families gather around their tables for a holy meal. There they retell the story of the Exodus from Egypt in times long past. With unleavened bread and sanctified wine, they celebrate the liberation of slaves from Pharaoh's bondage. How do they see themselves?

> *We* were the slaves of Pharaoh in Egypt; and the Lord our God brought us forth from there with a mighty hand and an outstretched arm. And if the Holy One, blessed be He, had not brought our fathers forth from Egypt, then surely we, and our children, and our children's children, would be enslaved to Pharaoh in Egypt. And so, even if all of us were full of wisdom and understanding, well along in years and deeply versed in the tradition, we should still be bidden to repeat once more the story of the exodus from Egypt; and he who delights to dwell on the liberation is a man to be praised.[5]

Through the natural eye, one sees ordinary folk, not much different from their neighbors in dress, language, or aspirations. The words they speak do not describe reality and are not meant to. When Jewish people say of themselves, "We were the slaves of Pharaoh in Egypt," they know they never felt the lash; but through the eye of faith that is just what they have done.

It is *their* liberation, not merely that of long-dead forebears, they now celebrate.

To be a Jew means to be a slave who has been liberated by God. To be Israel means to give eternal thanks for God's deliverance. And that deliverance is not at a single moment in historical time. It comes in every generation, is always celebrated. Here again, events of natural, ordinary life are transformed through myth into paradigmatic, eternal, and ever-recurrent sacred moments. Jews think of themselves as having gone forth from Egypt, and Scripture so instructs them. God did not redeem the dead generation of the Exodus alone, but the living too—especially the living. Thus the family states:

> Again and again, in double and redoubled measure, are we beholden to God the All-Present: that He freed us from the Egyptians and wrought His judgment on them; that He sentenced all their idols and slaughtered all their first-born; that He gave their treasure to us and split the Red Sea for us; that He led us through it dry-shod and drowned the tyrants in it; that He helped us through the desert and fed us with the manna; that He gave the Sabbath to us and brought us to Mount Sinai; that He gave the Torah to us and brought us to our homeland— there to build the Temple for us, for atonement of our sins.[6]
>
> This is the promise which has stood by our forefathers and stands by us. For neither once, nor twice, nor three times was our destruction planned; in every generation they rise against us, and in every generation God delivers us from their hands into freedom, out of anguish into joy, out of mourning into festivity, out of darkness into light, out of bondage into redemption.[7]
>
> For ever after, in every generation, *every man must think of himself as having gone forth from Egypt* [italics mine]. For we read in the Torah: "In that day thou shalt teach thy son, saying: All this is because of what God did for me when I went forth from Egypt." It was not only our forefathers that the Holy One, blessed be He, redeemed; us, too, the living, He redeemed together with them, as we learn from the verse in the Torah: "And He brought us out from thence, so that He might bring us home, and give us the land which he pledged to our forefathers."[8]

Israel was born in historical time. Historians, biblical scholars, archaeologists have much to say about that event. But to the classical Jew, their findings, while interesting, have little bearing on the meaning of reality. The redemptive promise that stood by the forefathers and *stands by us* is not a mundane historical event, but a mythic interpretation of historical, natural events. Oppression, homelessness, extermination, like salvation, homecoming, renaissance—these are this-worldly and profane, supplying headlines for newspapers. The myth that a man must think of himself as having gone forth from Egypt (or, as we shall see, from Auschwitz) and as being redeemed by God renders ordinary experience into a moment of celebration. If "we, too, the living, have been redeemed," then the observer no longer witnesses only historical men in historical time, but an eternal return to sacred time.

The "going forth" of Passover is one sort of exodus. Another comes morning and night when Jews complete their service of worship. Every synagogue service concludes with a prayer prior to going forth, called *Alenu,* from its first word in Hebrew. Like the Exodus, the moment of the congregation's departure becomes a celebration of Israel's God, a self-conscious, articulated rehearsal of Israel's peoplehood. But now it is the end, rather than the beginning, of time that is important. When Jews go forth, they look forward:

> Let us praise Him, Lord over all the world;
> Let us acclaim Him, Author of all creation.
> He made our lot unlike that of other peoples;
> He assigned to us a unique destiny.
> We bend the knee, worship, and acknowledge
> The King of kings, the Holy One, praised is He.
> He unrolled the heavens and established the earth;
> His throne of glory is in the heavens above;
> His majestic Presence is in the loftiest heights.
> He and no other is God and faithful King,
> Even as we are told in His Torah:
> Remember, now and always, that the Lord is God;
> Remember, no other is Lord of heaven and earth.
> We, therefore, hope in You, O Lord our God,
> That we shall soon see the triumph of Your might,
> That idolatry shall be removed from the earth,
> And false gods shall be utterly destroyed.
> Then will the world be a true kingdom of God,
> When all mankind will invoke Your name,
> And all the earth's wicked will return to You.
> Then all the inhabitants of the world will surely know
> That to You every knee must bend,
> Every tongue must pledge loyalty.
> Before You, O Lord, let them bow in worship,
> Let them give honor to Your glory.
> May they all accept the rule of Your kingdom.
> May you reign over them soon through all time.
> Sovereignty is Yours in glory, now and forever.
> So it is written in Your Torah:
> The Lord shall reign for ever and ever.[9]

In secular terms, Jews know that in some ways they form a separate, distinct group. In mythical reality, they thank God they enjoy a unique destiny. They do not conclude with thanks for their particular "being," but sing a hymn of hope that he who made their lot unlike that of all others will soon rule as sovereign over all. The secular difference, the unique destiny, is for the time being only. When the destiny is fulfilled, there will be no further difference. The natural eye beholds a social group, with some particular cultural characteristics defining that group. The myth of peoplehood transforms *difference* into *destiny*.

The existence of the natural group means little, except as testimony to the sovereignty of the God who shaped the group and rules its life. The unique, the particular, the private—these now are no longer profane matters of culture, but become testimonies of divine sovereignty, pertinent to all men, all groups. The particularism of the group is for the moment alone; the will of God is for eternity. When that will be done, then all men will recognize that the unique destiny of Israel was intended for everyone. The ordinary facts of sociology no longer predominate. The myth of Israel has changed the secular and commonplace into a paradigm of true being.

NOTES

1. Frederick J. Streng, *Understanding Religious Man* (Belmont, Calif.: Dickenson Publishing Co., 1968), p. 56.
2. Streng, p. 57.
3. *A Rabbi's Manual*, ed. by Jules Harlow (New York: The Rabbinical Assembly, 1965), p. 45. The "seven blessings" said at a wedding are printed in traditional Jewish prayer books.
4. I must stress that in classical times the marriage ceremony included provision for bride and groom to consummate their marriage with sexual intercourse while left in private for an appropriate period. Nowadays, the privacy is brief and symbolic, to be sure.
5. Trans. Maurice Samuel, *Haggadah of Passover* (New York: Hebrew Publishing Co., 1942), p. 9.
6. Samuel, p. 26.
7. Samuel, p. 13.
8. Samuel, p. 27.
9. *Weekday Prayer Book*, pp. 97–98.

4. Myth, Ritual, and History in Christianity, St. Paul

Around 54 to 58 A.D., the apostle Paul wrote letters to the Christian congregations in Rome and in Corinth. In the letter to Rome, here placed first, he proclaimed the death and resurrection of Jesus Christ to be a divine act through which all men could be saved from death (which would be inevitable due to sin), reconciled to God, and brought into new life. Two

From *Today's English Version of the New Testament*, Third Edition, Romans 5:1–6:11, pp. 376–79; I. Cor. 11:23–32, pp. 419–20. Copyright © The American Bible Society, 1966. Used by permission of the publisher.

central images of Christian faith—Adam and Christ—here become paradigmatic images for Christians, in the same sense that the exodus and Sinai are paradigmatic for the Jews. (A "paradigm" is a pattern, example, or model. Or, as Paul says, Adam was a "figure" of the one who was to come.) Adam's sin and Jesus' crucifixion are understood not only as particular events of the past but also as controlling images through which the believer grasps and responds to the meaning of his present existence. Note that through the sacrament of baptism the Christian dies to sin and becomes "alive to God in union with Christ Jesus," thus manifesting both the form and the continuing power of these events. In the excerpt from the letter to the Corinthians, the sacramental power of Jesus' words and acts is asserted in still another way. The communion meal is portrayed as a means by which one may share in the sacred reality of the Savior's life. This means of communion is understood to be so effective and the reality of that life so far above mundane existence that to approach the sacrament without faith or reverence was to risk even death. Does Paul say that the power of the sacrament is dependent on the believer's faith? Do you believe that acts can transform life only if done with prior understanding and conviction?

Romans 5:1–6:11

5 Now that we have been put right with God through faith, we have peace with God through our Lord Jesus Christ. He has brought us, by faith, into this experience of God's grace, in which we now live. We rejoice, then, in the hope we have of sharing God's glory! And we also rejoice in our troubles, because we know that trouble produces endurance, endurance brings God's approval, and his approval creates hope. This hope does not disappoint us, because God has poured out his love into our hearts by means of the Holy Spirit, who is God's gift to us.

For when we were still helpless, Christ died for the wicked, at the time that God chose. It is a difficult thing for someone to die for a righteous person. It may be that someone might dare to die for a good person. But God has shown us how much he loves us; it was while we were still sinners that Christ died for us! By his death we are now put right with God; how much more, then, will we be saved by him from God's wrath. We were God's enemies, but he made us his friends through the death of his Son. Now that we are God's friends, how much more will we be saved by Christ's life! But that is not all; we rejoice in God through our Lord Jesus Christ, who has now made us God's friends.

ADAM AND CHRIST

Sin came into the world through one man, and his sin brought death with it. As a result, death spread to the whole human race, because all men sinned. There was sin in the world before the Law was given; but where there is no law, no account is kept of sins. But from the time of Adam to the time of Moses death ruled over all men, even over those who did not sin as Adam did by disobeying God's command.

Adam was a figure of the one who was to come. But the two are not the same, because God's free gift is not like Adam's sin. It is true that many men died because of the sin of that one man. But God's grace is much greater, and so is his free gift to so many men through the grace of the one man, Jesus Christ. And there is a difference between God's gift and the sin of one man. After the one sin came the judgment of "Guilty"; but after so many sins comes the undeserved gift of "Not guilty!" It is true that through the sin of one man death began to rule, because of that one man. But how much greater is the result of what was done by the one man, Jesus Christ! All who receive God's abundant grace and the free gift of his righteousness will rule in life through Christ.

One righteous act sets all men free and gives them life

From *Good News for Modern Man* (New York: American Bible Society, 1966). Reprinted by permission of the American Bible Society.

So then, as the one sin condemned all men, in the same way the one righteous act sets all men free and gives them life. And just as many men were made sinners as the result of the disobedience of one man, in the same way many will be put right with God as the result of the obedience of the one man.

Law was introduced in order to increase wrongdoing; but where sin increased, God's grace increased much more. So then, just as sin ruled by means of death, so also God's grace rules by means of righteousness, leading us to eternal life through Jesus Christ our Lord.

DEAD TO SIN BUT ALIVE IN CHRIST

6 What shall we say, then? That we should continue to live in sin so that God's grace will increase? Certainly not! We have died to sin—how then can we go on living in it? For surely you know this: when we were

Set free from the power of sin

From *Good News for Modern Man* (New York: American Bible Society, 1966). Reprinted by permission of the American Bible Society.

baptized into union with Christ Jesus, we were baptized into union with his death. By our baptism, then, we were buried with him and shared his death, in order that, just as Christ was raised from death by the glorious power of the Father, so also we might live a new life.

For if we became one with him in dying as he did, in the same way we shall be one with him by being raised to life as he was. And we know this: our old being has been put to death with Christ on his cross, in order that the power of the sinful self might be destroyed, so that we should no longer be the slaves of sin. For when a person dies he is set free from the power of sin. If we have died with Christ, we believe that we will also live with him. For we know that Christ has been raised from death and will never die again—death has no more power over him. The death he died was death to sin, once and for all; and the life he now lives is life to God. In the same way you are to think of yourselves as dead to sin but alive to God in union with Christ Jesus.

1 Corinthians 11:23–32

For from the Lord I received the teaching that I passed on to you: that the Lord Jesus, on the night he was betrayed, took the bread, gave thanks to God, broke it, and said, "This is my body, which is for you. Do this in memory of me." In the same way, he took the cup after the supper and said, "This cup is God's new covenant, sealed with my blood. Whenever you drink it, do it in memory of me." For until the Lord comes, you proclaim his death whenever you eat this bread and drink from this cup.

It follows, then, that if anyone eats the Lord's bread of drinks from his cup in a way that dishonors him, he is guilty of sin against the Lord's body and blood. So then, everyone should examine himself first, and then eat the bread and drink from the cup. For if he does not recognize the meaning of the Lord's body when he eats the bread and drinks from the cup, he brings judgment on himself as he eats and drinks. That is why many of you are sick and weak, and several have died. If we would examine ourselves first, we would not come under God's judgment. But we are judged and punished by the Lord, so that we shall not be condemned together with the world.

5. Celebration and Renewal: The Catholic Mass

The celebration of Christ's death and resurrection has always been the distinguishing act of Christian liturgy. For Roman Catholicism, this celebration finds its central expression in the Mass. Here Jesus' death is understood as a sacrifice, and its redeeming power becomes available to, and effective in, the believer. The believer's own faith and prayers are involved in this enactment, but without the priestly reenactment of the sacrifice, the communicant's worship is thought to be defective. The independent reality of God's act in time (Christ) has its counterpart in the independent reality of the Church's corporate worship (the Mass.)

Within the Mass, the most sacred passages are called the "Canon." This word derives from the Greek word for measuring rod, and indicates the enduring, unchanging character of these passages. They remained, in fact, virtually unchanged from the 7th century A.D. *to the Second Vatican Council, several years ago. During most of this time, with the exception of certain special occasions, the Canon of the Mass was recited silently by the priest. As you will observe, this feature has been substantially changed. In reading this item (which includes the Canon), note the sequence of prayers and the particular acts of the priest. In what way do they symbolize key stages in the drama of salvation? What does the believer understand to be happening in this celebration?*

"Holy Communion" from *Sunday Missal Prayerbook and Hymnal* (New York: Catholic Book Publishing Co., Inc.), pp. 39–48. Used by permission of the International Committee on English in the Liturgy (ICEL), Washington, D. C.

Eucharistic Prayer No. 4*

℣.** The Lord be with you.   (STAND)

℟.   **And also with you.**

℣.   Lift up your hearts.

℟.   **We lift them up to the Lord.**

℣.   Let us give thanks to the Lord our God.

℟.   **It is right to give him thanks and praise.**

PREFACE

Father in heaven, it is right that we should give you thanks and glory:
you alone are God, living and true.
Through all eternity you live in unapproachable light.
Source of life and goodness, you have created all things, to fill your creatures
    with every blessing
and lead all men to the joyful vision of your light.
Countless hosts of angels stand before you to do your will;
they look upon your splendor
and praise you, night and day.
United with them, and in the name of every creature under heaven,
we too praise your glory as we sing (say):

SANCTUS   [*First Acclamation of the People*]

Holy, holy, holy Lord, God of power and might,
heaven and earth are full of your glory.
    Hosanna in the highest.
Blessed is he who comes in the name of the Lord.
    Hosanna in the highest.   (KNEEL)
                                              [*Praise to the Father*]

Father, we acknowledge your greatness:
all your actions show your wisdom and love.
You formed man in your own likeness
and set him over the whole world
to serve you, his creator,
and to rule over all creatures.
Even when he disobeyed you and lost your friendship
you did not abandon him to the power of death,
but helped all men to seek and find you.
Again and again you offered a covenant to man,
and through the prophets taught him to hope for salvation.

---

* The Communion rite may be introduced by one of four different eucharistic
prayers.

** The priest says the words marked by ℣; the congregation responds with words
marked by ℟.

Father, you so loved the world
that in the fullness of time you sent your only Son to be our Savior.
He was conceived through the power of the Holy Spirit, and born of the
   Virgin Mary,
a man like us in all things but sin.
To the poor he proclaimed the good news of salvation,
to prisoners, freedom,
and to those in sorrow, joy.
In fulfillment of your will
he gave himself up to death;
but by rising from the dead,
he destroyed death and restored life.
And that we might live no longer for ourselves but for him,
he sent the Holy Spirit from you, Father,
as his first gift to those who believe,
to complete his work on earth
and bring us the fullness of grace.

[Invocation of the Holy Spirit]

Father, may this Holy Spirit sanctify these offerings.
Let them become the body and blood of Jesus Christ our Lord
as we celebrate the great mystery
which he left us as an everlasting covenant.

[The Lord's Supper]

He always loved those who were his own in the world.
When the time came for him to be glorified by you, his heavenly Father,
he showed the depth of his love.
While they were at supper,
he took bread, said the blessing, broke the bread
and gave it to his disciples, saying:
Take this, all of you, and eat it:
this is my body which will be given up for you.

In the same way, he took the cup, filled with wine.
He gave you thanks, and giving the cup to his disciples, said:
Take this, all of you, and drink from it:
this is the cup of my blood,
the blood of the new and everlasting covenant.
It will be shed for you and for all men
so that sins may be forgiven.
Do this in memory of me.

[*Memorial Acclamation*]

Priest: Let us proclaim the mystery of faith.

PEOPLE:*

(A)   **Christ has died,**
      Christ is risen,
      Christ will come again.

(B)   **Dying you destroyed our death,**
      rising you restored our life.
      Lord Jesus, come in glory.

(C)   **When we eat this bread and drink this cup,**
      we proclaim your death, Lord Jesus,
      until you come in glory.

(D)   **Lord, by your cross and resurrection**
      you have set us free.
      You are the Savior of the world

[*The Memorial Prayer*]

Father, we now celebrate this memorial of our redemption.
We recall Christ's death, his descent among the dead,
his resurrection, and his ascension to your right hand;
and, looking forward to his coming in glory, we offer you his body and
     blood,
the acceptable sacrifice which brings salvation to the whole world.
Lord, look upon this sacrifice which you have given to your Church;
and by your Holy Spirit, gather all who share this bread and wine
into the one body of Christ, a living sacrifice of praise.

[*Intercessions: For the Church*]

Lord, remember those for whom we offer this sacrifice,
especially *N.,* our Pope,
N., our bishop, and bishops and clergy everywhere.
Remember those who take part in this offering,

---

* One of the following responses is used.

those here present and all your people,
and all who seek you with a sincere heart.

[For the Dead]

Remember those who have died in the peace of Christ
and all the dead whose faith is known to you alone.

[In Communion with the Saints]

Father, in your mercy grant also to us, your children,
to enter into our heavenly inheritance
in the company of the Virgin Mary, the mother of God,
and your apostles and saints.
Then, in your kingdom, freed from the corruption of sin and death,
we shall sing your glory with every creature through Christ our Lord,
through whom you give us everything that is good.

Through him,
with him,
in him,
in the unity of the Holy Spirit,
all glory and honor is yours,
almighty Father,
for ever and ever.

[Concluding Doxology]

All reply: **Amen.**

COMMUNION RITE

To prepare for the paschal meal, to welcome the Lord, we pray for forgiveness and exchange a sign of peace. Before eating Christ's body and drinking his blood, we must be one with him and with all our brothers and sisters in the Church.

Lord's Prayer   (STAND)

Priest: Let us pray with confidence to the Father in the words our Savior
            gave us:

Priest and **PEOPLE:**
   Our Father, who art in heaven,
   hallowed be thy name;
   thy kingdom come;
   thy will be done on earth as it is in heaven.
   Give us this day our daily bread;
   and forgive us our trespasses
   as we forgive those who trespass against us;
   and lead us not into temptation,
   but deliver us from evil.

Priest: Deliver us, Lord, from every evil,
            and grant us peace in our day.
            In your mercy keep us free from sin
            and protect us from all anxiety
            as we wait in joyful hope
            for the coming of our Savior, Jesus Christ.

PEOPLE: For the kingdom, the power, and the glory are yours, now and
   for ever.

Sign of Peace

The Church is a community of Christians joined by the Spirit in love. It needs to express, deepen, and restore its peaceful unity before eating the one Body of the Lord and drinking from the one cup of salvation. We do this by a sign of peace.

   The priest says the prayer for peace:
Lord Jesus Christ, you said to your apostles:
I leave you peace, my peace I give you.
Look not on our sins, but on the faith of your Church,
and grant us the peace and unity of your kingdom
where you live for ever and ever.

PEOPLE: Amen.
Priest: The peace of the Lord be with you always.

PEOPLE: And also with you.
Deacon (or priest) :
> Let us offer each other the sign of peace.

The people exchange a sign of peace and love, according to local custom.

Breaking of the Bread

Christians are gathered for the "breaking of the bread," another name for the Mass. In communion, though many we are made one body in the one bread, which is Christ.

> *The priest breaks the host over the paten and places a small piece in the chalice, saying quietly:*

May this mingling of the body and blood of our Lord Jesus Christ bring eternal life to us who receive it.

PEOPLE: *Meanwhile the people sing or say:*

> **Lamb of God, you take away the sins of the world:**
> > **have mercy on us.**
> **Lamb of God, you take away the sins of the world:**
> > **have mercy on us.**
> **Lamb of God, you take away the sins of the world:**
> > **grant us peace.**

> *The hymn may be repeated until the breaking of the bread is finished, but the last phrase is always:* "Grant us peace."

Prayers Before Communion

We pray in silence and then voice words of humility and hope as our final preparation before meeting Christ in the Eucharist.

> *Before communion, the priest says quietly one of the following prayers:*

Lord Jesus Christ, Son of the living God,
by the will of the Father and the work of the Holy Spirit
your death brought life to the world.
By your holy body and blood
free me from all my sins and from every evil.
Keep me faithful to your teaching,
and never let me be parted from you.

OR: Lord Jesus Christ,
> with faith in your love and mercy
> I eat your body and drink your blood.
> Let it not bring me condemnation,
> but health in mind and body.

> *Holding the bread elevated slightly over the paten and facing the people, the priest says:*

Priest: This is the Lamb of God
who takes away the sins of the world.
Happy are those who are called to his supper.

Priest and **PEOPLE:** (once only):
Lord, I am not worthy to receive you,
but only say the word and I shall be healed.

Reception of Communion

Before receiving communion, the priest says quietly: May the body of Christ bring me to everlasting life. May the blood of Christ bring me to everlasting life. *He then gives communion to the people.*
Priest: The body of Christ.

Communicant: **Amen.**

Communion Song

The Communion Psalm or other appropriate Song or Hymn is Sung while Communion is given to the faithful. If there is no singing, the Communion Verse is said.

Silence After Communion   (SIT)

After communion there may be a period of silence, or a song of praise may be sung.

Prayer After Communion   (STAND)

The priest prays in our name that we may live the life of faith since we have been strengthened by Christ himself. Our Amen makes his prayer our own.
Priest: Let us pray.

Priest and people may pray silently for a while. Then the priest says the prayer after communion. . . .

At the end. **PEOPLE: Amen.**

CONCLUDING RITE

We have heard God's Word and eaten the body of Christ. Now it is time for us to leave, to do good works, to praise and bless the Lord in our daily lives.

Blessing **(STAND)**

After any brief announcements (sit), the blessing and dismissal follow:

Priest: The Lord be with you.

PEOPLE: And also with you.

Priest: May almighty God bless you, the Father, and the Son, ✠ * and the Holy Spirit.

PEOPLE: Amen.

Dismissal

Deacon (or priest):
(A) Go in the peace of Christ.
(B) The Mass is ended, go in peace.
(C) Go in peace to love and serve the Lord.

PEOPLE: Thanks be to God.

* Congregation makes the sign of the cross.

6. Myth, Ritual, and National History Seen in Two American Sacred Ceremonies, C. Cherry

The religious character of a ritual will not always be fully apparent even to those who respond to it with conviction. Nor is the locus of myth necessarily in the distant past, even when symbols prominent in it are drawn from an ancient tradition. The occasion on which the ritual is enacted and the experiences through which the meaning of the symbols is rendered specific may give a ceremony a meaning well beyond that which is precedented by tradition or anticipated by its participants. These are points that Conrad Cherry, a historian at Pennsylvania State University, would have us keep in mind when we look at our own history. According to Cherry, a new religion has appeared among us, a religion of the American nation. But we have failed to recognize it, partly because of its long entanglement with Protestant Christianity and partly because it has so formed our identity that we think of it as "natural." What leads him to say that the Memorial Day service and the funeral for Senator Robert Kennedy represent rites of a national religion even though these were largely composed of traditional rites and symbols? What is the primary belief, the central image of the national religion? Through what institutions does it find expression? Does he give any examples of religious opposition to the national religion?

The Memorial Day celebration is an American sacred ceremony, a religious ritual, a modern cult of the dead. Although it shares the theme of redemptive sacrifice with Christianity and other religions, and although its devotees would insist that the God invoked is the God of Judaism and Christianity, the Memorial Day rite is a national service that unites Protestants, Catholics and Jews beyond their differences. Lloyd Warner has described the essential function of the rite:

> Each man's church provides him and those of his faith with a set of beliefs and a way of acting to face these problems [of our own, our friends' and all men's deaths]; but his church and those of other men do not equip him with a common set of social beliefs and rituals which permit him to unite with all his fellows to confront this common and most feared of all his enemies. The Memorial Day rite and other sub-

From Conrad Cherry, "Two American Sacred Ceremonies, Their Implications for the Study of Religion in America," *American Quarterly,* Vol. 21, 1969 741–45, 748–53. Published with permission of the author and the Trustees of the University of Pennsylvania.

sidiary rituals connected with it form a cult which partially satisfies this need for common action on a common problem. It dramatically expresses the sentiments of unity of all the living among themselves, of all the living to all the dead, and of all the living and dead as a group to the gods.[1]

Joined with the unifying and existential problem-solving function of the cult is the conviction repeatedly expressed by the speakers that the United States has been given the providential burden of acting as guardian and preserver of freedom. American soldiers have presented themselves as sacrifices on the altar of history so that America's God-given task of rescuing oppressed peoples might not fail, so that she may continue to be a beacon of freedom to all the world, so that the sacred principles contained in the Declaration of Independence and the Constitution might remain untarnished.

There are, of course, large segments of American society that feel little or no affinity with the Memorial Day ceremony. Many citizens in the larger cities, in fact, have never witnessed the celebration of Memorial Day as a sacred event. These portions of our society are doubtless inclined to dismiss the celebration as the vestige of a village tribalism. And even those who are personally acquainted with the ceremony as a sacred event may be offended by the Legionnaire super-patriotism, frequently involved in the rite, which calls down the blessing of God on all-things-American simply because they are American and which defends "American freedoms" while at the same time undermining the freedom to dissent from and criticize particular national commitments. Memorial Day is not America's only sacred ceremony, however, and is not the only way Americans as citizens come to terms with death. In her funerals for great men, especially her political leaders, America has created another religious ceremony that meets anxiety over death in a corporate way and that transcends sectarian religious differences. The recent funeral for Senator Robert F. Kennedy was one such ceremony.

After Senator Kennedy's death on June 6, 1968, hundreds of thousands of Americans waited outside St. Patrick's Cathedral in New York City to pay their last respects, and millions of citizens who could not take their places in those long lines were able to assume a kind of presence there through their television sets. By way of television they witnessed the funeral, followed the funeral train at its points of passage to Washington and grieved with the family at the burial. Once again in the 1960s Americans participated in a ceremony honoring a leader who had been stopped by an act of destructive violence. In the funeral Robert Kennedy was vested with a meaning that derived from his "American dream" or his vision of American destiny. His funeral was another sacred ceremony in which the dilemma of death was met corporately, religious differences were transcended and death was construed in terms of America's destiny under God. The day of the funeral, unlike Memorial Day, was altogether a holy day, completely devoid of mixture with a holiday spirit. And because of the suddenness and circumstances of Kennedy's death, the intensity of emotion elicited by the funeral was undoubtedly much greater than that called forth by a Memorial Day ceremony. Nevertheless, many of the same themes, symbols and invocations were present.

Senator Kennedy's funeral was obviously a religious affair; it was "religious" in the sense in which most Americans think of that term since it had the trappings of one of the traditional Western religious communities. It was, after all, a Roman Catholic funeral mass. It was at the same time a civic-religious ceremony that appealed to Americans regardless of their denominational persuasions. The occasion was one in which the Catholic doctrines of hope, resurrection and heavenly reward for a life well lived were drawn upon as resources of comfort by a mourning Kennedy family and other Christians. It was also an occasion when the Kennedys and numerous other Americans found a degree of comfort in the conviction that Robert Kennedy had met his death in the midst of an endeavor to secure freedom for all Americans and thereby fulfill that portion of America's destiny.

The funeral liturgy affirmed life in the face of death. "For those who have been faithful all the way, life is not ended but merely changed. And when this earthly abode dissolves, an eternal dwelling place awaits them in Heaven." Senator Edward Kennedy, quoting from and commenting on a speech by his brother, offered a different kind of affirmation:

> "Our future may lie beyond our vision, but it is not completely beyond our control. It is the shaping impulse of America that neither faith nor nature nor the irresistible tides of history but the work of our own hands matched to reason and principle will determine our destiny."
>
> There is pride in that, even arrogance, but there is also experience and truth, and in any event it is the only way we can live. That is the way he lived. That is what he leaves us.
>
> My brother need not be idealized or enlarged in death beyond what he was in life. He should be remembered simply as a good and decent man who saw wrong and tried to right it, saw suffering and tried to heal it, saw war and tried to stop it.[2]

Those words invited their hearers to a hope and a sense of social responsibility in a way that the promise of an "eternal dwelling place" alone could not.

In his eulogy Archbishop Terence J. Cooke sensed the national religious meaning of the occasion and of Robert Kennedy's life and death. The message was certainly sensitive to the deep personal loss that the Kennedy family had sustained and appropriately commented on Robert Kennedy as devoted husband, father and son. The liturgy's reference to eternal life after death was cited at the beginning and at the end of the eulogy, providing the frame for the substance of the address. The greater part of Archbishop Cooke's eulogy, however, placed Robert Kennedy in the context of an American dream and was a challenge to Americans to prevent the waste of Kennedy's life by fulfilling that dream.

Although Robert Kennedy could have chosen a much less arduous manner of life, the Archbishop said, it was because he was driven by the ideal of building "a better world for his fellow man" that he accepted the demanding challenge of public service. "We admire the ability to identify so that Negro people spoke of him as one of ours. We admire his vision in confronting the problems of poverty and civil rights." It was a dream that he had for America that evoked this admiration and enlisted his followers: "the dream of an America purged of prejudice, assuring freedom for all her citizens, a land of truly equal opportunity." The proper response to this man's tragic death, therefore, is to occupy ourselves with his dream of America's destiny. "Our sense of shame and discouragement tears alone will not wash away. Somehow by the grace of God, and with the strength that still lies deep within the soul of America, we must find the courage to take up again the laborious work to which Senator Kennedy devoted all his energies, the building of a great and honorable nation. Especially in this hour we must keep faith with America and her destiny and we must not forsake our trust in one another." Participation in America's historic destiny is the socially responsible way to meet Senator Kennedy's death. "We have always believed in our national destiny marked by unity in lofty ideals. We believe that our country came into existence to secure the blessings of freedom, equality and peace for ourselves and those who will come after us."[3]

In this funeral Americans joined in a sacred ceremony, the scope of which crossed denominational religious boundaries. Many citizens had participated in another such ceremony only a few weeks earlier at the funeral for Dr. Martin Luther King Jr., and in still another a few short years earlier at the funeral for President John F. Kennedy. American history is, in fact, replete with leaders who have been canonized in the national consciousness as examplars of American ideals and as particular bearers of America's destiny under God. When those leaders have met violent deaths they have become, in the national memory as well as in the ceremonies and speeches that surround their deaths, martyrs for the American cause, even in some cases redeemers.[4]

Dissimilarities between the two sacred ceremonies examined here are not to be denied. In addition to those differences in emotional climate, already noted, there are differences in content. The human "freedom" for which the supreme sacrifice has been made and which constitutes the essence of American destiny does not, for example, have the same meaning in the two ceremonies. In the Memorial Day celebration it means the freedom of all peoples of the world to share in American democratic principles and the freedom and duty of Americans to enforce or safeguard those principles around the world. In the Kennedy funeral "freedom" stands for the civil right of all American citizens to enjoy full and equal participation in their society. Despite such important differences, the two ceremonies have in common a symbolic, thematic and ritualistic structure. Both are cults of the dead in which the living are united with one another, the living are united with the dead and all are united with God and what are believed to be his purposes in history. Both ceremonies stress the belief that God has in store—has always had in store—for this nation a special destiny for which the supreme sacrifice has been made and to the fulfillment of which all Americans must dedicate themselves. And both rites are able to unite Americans beyond their religious divisions. . . .

Bellah and Mead believe the national religion to be a phenomenon that in itself is worthy of study.* Their suggestions, together with inferences from the sacred ceremonies sketched above, indicate the questions that must be answered by the student of American religion before the full picture of the civic faith will emerge.

1. *What are the beliefs that make up the national religion?*

When dealing with any religion it is a highly dubious practice to detail beliefs in isolation from their historical and cultural settings, and this is especially the case for a civil religion which has no formal creed. Nevertheless, certain beliefs continually turn up in American sacred ceremonies.

One belief around which many other convictions cluster is the sense of America's special destiny under God. This is a central theme in Memorial Day ceremonies, funerals for American leaders and the inaugural addresses of U.S. presidents. The belief that America is a "New Israel," a people newly chosen by God to carry out his historical purposes and serve as an example to the nations, has been a conviction of the American people from the colonial settlements to the present. It is so pervasive a theme in the national life that it has passed into the "realm of motivational myths."[5] That is, it provides a religious outlook on history and its purpose, and by finding a place in the feelings and choices as well as in the ideas of American citizens, it can move the people to action. Variations on the theme of American destiny under God have been numerous. The sacred ceremonies described above represent two versions: America is the nation destined to act as missionary and defender of democratic principles around the world (in the Memorial Day ceremony) : or America is the nation elected to serve the world as an example of freedom by extending full citizenship to all within her boundaries (in the funeral).[6] Historians have long been aware of the diverse ways in which Americans have interpreted their divine mission as they have met a series of formidable challenges: the settlement of a frontier, the formation of a new nation, the extension of empire, the winning of wars, the preservation of peace.[7] Yet an examination of the theme of American destiny in the cultic and mythic context of the national religion and in terms of the relation of the theme to the larger belief structure of the national faith is a task that still demands the effort of historian, anthropologist, literary critic and philosopher of religion.

Clues to other beliefs in the national religion are found in official national documents. The God-references in the Declaration of Independence, for example, frequently appear in the rhetoric of American sacred ceremonies—the "Laws of Nature and of Nature's God" that entitle any people to independence, the claim that all men "are endowed by their Creator

---

* The references are to Robert N. Bellah, a contemporary American sociologist, and Sidney E. Mead, an historian, both of whom have an interest in the religious aspects of American history.

with certain inalienable Rights," the appeal to "the Supreme Judge of the world for the rectitude of our intentions," the urging of a "firm reliance on the protection of divine Providence."[8] The redemptive value for the nation of human sacrifice is another conviction that arises in public sacred ceremonies and that is preserved in sacred documents like the Gettysburg Address. Analysis of beliefs such as these requires the same responsible care as the examination of the beliefs of any other religion.

2. *What are the source of the beliefs and symbols of the national religion?*

Any portrait of the American civil religion must use the colors of both biblical history and the history of America. The deepest source of most of the symbols, beliefs and rituals of the religion lies in the Old and New Testaments. But the more immediate source is the history of the nation, or certain events of that history which have been judged revelatory. In the Memorial Day ceremony and in Kennedy's funeral, the images of God's deliverance of and demands upon his chosen people and the rebirth that can issue from sacrificial death are definitely biblical images. But they are given immediacy by being translated into events of national history. God's demands upon his chosen people become demands upon America at this particular juncture of her history; redemptive sacrifice becomes the sacrifice of American war dead and martyrs. Biblical events serve as the archetypes, but the immediate events of revelation (those paradigmatic events by which the participants in the national religion interpret the meaning of their national life and the purposes of God in history) are events in the American experience.

Where there are events of revelation, there are usually sacred scriptures, redeemers and saints. Who would deny that in the national memory Lincoln has become a Christ figure and Washington both Moses and Joshua, both the deliverer of the American people out of bondage and the leader of the chosen people into the promised land of independence? Or who would deny that the Gettysburg Address serves as a sacred scripture, preserving the sacrificial meaning of the Civil War? On the other hand, where have these persons and scriptures been treated fully as religious in their own right, as parts of a religious tradition?

3. *What is the institutional framework of the national religion?*

A study of the institutions of the national religion must take seriously the argument of John Smylie that the nation itself gradually assumed the traditional role of the church for most Americans. As these shores were inundated by a host of diverse religious organizations and as our laws made clear that no one religious denomination could operate as the established national religion, the word "church" made sense to Americans only in the plural. The one, universal church had no institutional visibility and no state support. Lacking special endorsement by the state, the American churches gave up the functions normally associated with the universal church. But, Smylie insists, where the churches moved out the nation moved in. "Gradually in America the nation emerged as the primary agent of God's meaningful activity in history. Hence Americans bestowed on it a catholicity of destiny similar to that which theology attributes to the universal church." Early colonial groups believed that their own church covenants were vehicles of God's action in history, but eventually the Declaration of Independence, the Constitution and the Bill of Rights became the covenants that bound together the people of the nation and secured to them God's blessing, protection and call to historic mission.[9]

The public schools must also be counted as major institutions of the national religion and as objects of study for those who would understand the role that this religion plays in American society. The public schools have provided the place of instruction (often, admittedly, the place of unexamined propaganda) in the traditions of the national faith. Certainly until recent efforts at redirection, the schools were unabashedly Protestant in their prayers, morning devotions and general religious orientation. But they were also the depositories and purveyors of the events and documents of the national religion. Is it really accurate to view the Supreme Court rulings forbidding devotional Bible reading and prayer as attempts to "secularize" the schools? Are not those rulings an effort to disentangle the practices and beliefs of the diverse American religions (including, according to the Court, the "religion of secularism") from those of the civil religion, rather than an attempt to put an end to the national faith in the schools? In the texts and classrooms students are still instructed in the basic documents of the civil religion (including their references to God and providence), the religion's heroes and martyrs are still celebrated on their birthdays and on Memorial Day, the American ceremonial calendar is still observed.[10]

American churches and synagogues have also provided an institutional haven for the national religion. The Americanization of churches and synagogues has been so well documented that it only needs mentioning here. To a great extent the churches of this land have come to abide by the suggestion of the Founding Fathers that the different religious groups should exist not only for the sake of their own beliefs and practices but should also assume responsibility for maintenance of the public order, the dissemination of the "essentials of every religion" (e.g., the existence of God, the reward of virtue), and the promotion of the public welfare. The consequent presence of the American flag in the churches, the celebration of national events by religious groups and the frequent mixing of biblical and American-sacred history in sermons are some of the obvious signs that the national religion has found a home in the American churches. The obvious signs are often misleading, however, for the history of the relationship between the national religion and the denominations has been complex.

4. *What is the relation between the national religion and other religions in America?*
Beginnings of an answer to this difficult question can be indicated by noting that there have been at least three modes of relationship.

One type of relation is apparent in our two sacred ceremonies. There, sectarian religious beliefs do not intrude; in fact, religious differences are transcended to the plane of a national faith made up of symbols and beliefs that Americans hold in common. The symbolism does have its deepest source in the biblical tradition of the denominations, but that is the tradition of the nonsectarian national religion as well. At any rate, the symbolism is so woven into the fabric of national history that it loses any potentially sectarian color. In this relationship, therefore, the national religions is rather clearly differentiated from the denominations. An American may be a Methodist, a Conservative Jew or a Roman Catholic and at the same time participate in the civil religion—and without insisting that the civil religion be expressed in specifically Methodist, Jewish or Catholic terms.[11]

Although this type of relationship has had its defenders from Jefferson and Franklin to Lincoln to Dewey, only recently has it become a vital option in American life. Only after Protestantism lost its powerful grip on the public life of the nation did the national religion begin to dislodge itself from Protestant articulation and custody. During the 19th century and well into the 20th, leading spokesmen for the national faith couched its beliefs in terms that were unmistakably Protestant. Another type of relationship between the civil religion and other religions, therefore, has a long historical precedent, though that precedent is in the process of being broken. It is marked by a rather thorough blending of a generalized Protestantism with the national religion. The Protestantism is "generalized" in that it is nondenominational. Its representatives tend to define America as a "Christian civilization," but their Christianity is seldom big enough to include Roman Catholicism.[12] It took such factors as the impact of non-Protestant immigrants, an enlightened Supreme Court determined to de-Protestantize the public schools, and a pluralization of values in many regions of American life through modern means of communication to break through this confusion of Protestantism and the religion of America. "Not until the modern period, when Catholics and Jews and others have come into full and unabashed participation in the public life of the nation, as symbolized by the 1960 election, has the old Protestant culture-religion been frontally challenged."[13]

Finally, the national religion and other religions in America have existed in a relationship of tension. The most obvious instances of the tension appear in those sects, like the Jehovah's Witnesses, that spurn patriotic symbols, reject American sacred ceremonies and refuse to allow the nation to function for them as a "church." One would also have to add the clergy and scholars within the Christian and Jewish mainstream who have insisted that any civil religion is a distortion of their prophetic faith, as well as those persons deeply involved in an ecumenical movement that hopes to cross both national and cultural barriers. There is no evidence, however, that the tension has ever grown to the point where the national religion has been seriously weakened in its appeal to the masses of American society.

NOTES

1. W. Lloyd Warner, *American Life, Dream and Reality* (Chicago, 1953), p. 24.
2. From a transcript of the eulogy as printed in the New York Times, June 9, 1968.
3. All quotations from a transcript of the eulogy. *Ibid.*
4. The most obvious example of the latter is Lincoln. Since Lincoln's assassination occurred on Good Friday, hundreds of speakers on the following Sunday were quick to note that assassination day was also crucifixion day. Said one: "Jesus Christ dies for the world; Abraham Lincoln dies for his country." Cf. the apotheosizing of Jefferson who dies on Independence Day, discussed in Merrill D. Peterson, *The Jefferson Image in the American Mind* (New York, 1960), pp. 3ff.
5. The phrase is Sidney Mead's in his discussion of the theme, *The Lively Experiment* (New York, 1963). Cf. Russel B. Nye, *This Almost Chosen People* (East Lansing, 1966), pp. 164–65.
6. Cf. Clinton Rossiter, "The American Mission," *American Scholar,* XX (1950–51), 19–28.
7. There is a wealth of literature on this subject, but see esp. Nye, *op. cit.*; Edward M. Burns, *The American Idea of Mission* (New Brunswick, 1957); Perry Miller, *Errand into the Wilderness* (Cambridge, 1956)); Albert K. Weinberg, *Manifest Destiny* (Gloucester, Mass., 1958); Merle Curti, *The Roots of American Loyalty* (New York, 1946); Reinhold Niebuhr & Alan Heimert, *A Nation So Conceived* (New York, 1963); Ernest Lee Tuveson, *Redeemer Nation* (Chicago, 1968).
8. See Bellah, "Civil Religion in America," *Daedalus,* XCVI (Winter 1967), pp. 1–6, for a comparison of these beliefs with the inaugural address of John F. Kennedy.
9. John Edwin Smylie, "National Ethos and the Church," *Theology Today,* Oct. 1963, 313–18.
10. For a similar, more detailed discussion of religion in the public schools see Robert Michaelsen, "The Public Schools and 'America's Two Religions,'" *A Journal of Church and State,* Autumn 1966, pp. 380–400.
11. Cf. Robert Bellah's discussion of John F. Kennedy's inaugural address, pp. 1–3.
12. For a typical expression of this view in the 19th century see the popular and oft-delivered address by that influential Congregational minister, Lyman Beecher, *A Plea for the West* (Cincinnati, 1835).
13. Franklin H. Littell, "The Churches and the Body Politic," *Daedalus,* XCVI (Winter 1967), 33.

INTERPRETATION

7. Reflections on Origins, *W. Otto*

In this portion of his work on the Greek god Dionysius, the German scholar of Greek culture and religion, Walter F. Otto (d. 1958) asks us to consider cultus *as a singular and marvelous creation of man which expresses a primitive but total sense of the sacred. For Otto, "cultus" refers not only to ritual but also to everyday social expressions that are derived from the act of worship. Otto scorns interpreters who fail to see its originality and power. The glories of mythic imagination and religious art that are often viewed today as profound expressions of faith, he views as secondary by-products of an original sense of communion in which man's own body, his gesture or dance, was the vehicle of the sacred Presence. How does he use the image of a cathedral in the first paragraph of this selection? What attitudes or convictions does he seem to value least for the study of* cultus? *What does he propose as the true test of greatness?*

The somewhat childish explanation of cultus which states that it is an imitation of myth certainly does the significance of *cultus* no justice. And yet modern theory has misunderstood and disparaged this explanation more than have all previous speculations and reveries. Completely dominated and blinded by the self-confidence of the rational and technical civilization of its time, modern theory has never recognized the astonishing dimensions of *cultus,* grasping merely that part of its living essence which a mind receptive only to what is useful would grasp of the living essence of a cathedral. Were the phenomenon of artistic creation completely lost to us at some time, we would first have to approach it with wonder before we would dare to penetrate to its meaning. So, the phenomenon of *cultus,* which has, as a matter of fact, been lost to us except for a few ancient remnants, should awaken in us, above all, a deep sense of awe.

Cultus as a totality belongs to the monumental *creations* of the human spirit. To get a proper perspective of it, we must rank it with architecture, art, poetry, and music—all of which once served religion. It is one of the great languages with which mankind speaks to the Almighty, speaking to Him for no other reason than that it must. The Almighty or "God" did not earn these names of Almighty or God only by striking fear into man and forcing him to win His Good will by favors. The proof of His greatness is the power it engenders. Man owes the highest of which he is

From Walter F. Otto, *Dionysius: Myth and Cult,* trans. Robert B. Palmer (Bloomington: Indiana University Press, 1965), pp. 18–23.

capable to the feeling of His presence. And this highest is his power to speak, a power which bears witness to the marvelous encounter through which it is conceived and brought into being. Every manifestation also unlocks the soul of man, and this immediately results in creative activity. Man must give utterance to the feeling of awe which has seized him. There was a time when he did this by building temples, a form of expression which the gigantic undertaking of cathedral construction has continued even into the centuries which lie before us. One can call them the habitations of godhead, and yet this term expresses only an insignificant part of their great meaning. They are the mirror, the expression of the Divine, born of a spirit which must express itself in plastic form when the splendor of greatness has touched it.

The most sacred of these great languages is the language of *cultus*. Its age lies far behind us, and it is really not surprising that it is precisely its language which has become more alien to us than all the others. It testifies that the Almighty was so near that man had to offer his own being as the form in which this proximity could be expressed—an expression that the other languages were called upon to create, from a greater distance, through the media of stone, color, tones, and words. For this reason they have become more powerful as the proximity of deity disappeared, while *cultus* slowly lost its vitality. But it continued as the companion of other languages for thousands of years, and many of its forms still had the power, even in later ages, to evoke a deity whose presence they had summoned up in time past.

None of this contradicts the fact that the deity is offered something in *cultus* which will delight it, something which should have value for it. None of it contradicts the fact that this is accompanied by man's natural wish to be blessed by the good will of deity. Wherever men are united by awe and love, the first impulse of reverence and giving is the need to express great emotion. Yet if we suspect self-interest, we consider the giver's sentiments to be base or his piety unwarranted. But must the vulgar intrigues and sentiments of mankind give us the model for man's intercourse with the gods? If so, let us stop using words as awe-inspiring as "faith" and "worship." Let us not speak of "Greater Events," and us not prostitute the name of religion by using it to describe a superstitious delusion and its mercenary exploitation. The man who permits himself to speak of greatness should know that its surest sign is that great emotions must respond to it.

The forms of *cultus* are determined by the proximity of deity. Hence many of them have the characteristics of immediate communion with it. Sacrifice makes its appearance as a gift which deity is to receive, a repast in which it is to participate. Prayer is a salutation, a eulogy, or a request. But the position which the worshipper assumes, his physical acts, are unquestionably older than his words and more primal expressions of his feeling that the god is present. Its force we can no longer conceive of by considering the emotion of which man in our experience is capable.

That which he later built out of stones to honor God (and his cathedrals still tell us of this today), that very thing *he, himself,* once was, with his arms stretched out to heaven, standing upright like a column or kneeling. And if, in the course of centuries, the only element which remained generally understood in the infinite meaning of that act was the act of supplication, just a tiny remnant of that meaning, then that is merely an example of the same poverty of understanding from which other forms of *cultus* also suffered in later ages.

The rite of the blood sacrifice is a creation whose greatness we can still experience, even though its significance was, for the most part, already lost in the time when it was still being practiced. Recent theories—regardless of whether they resort to the analogy of the *"do ut des"** thesis or more complex ways of thought—only prove that the entire conception of this rite could not have sprung from motives which stem from our rational being. If we were in a position to feel once more what it means for a god to be in our immediate presence, only an experience of this imminence could open our eyes. Even to hope for such an experience is presumptuous. But this should not make us incapable of recognizing, in the powerful drama of the animal which sheds its life-blood, the expression of a state of mind, the sublimity of which can be found paralleled only in the great works of art. Nothing makes less sense than to confuse the element of expediency, which is never completely lacking in any genuine act of creation, with the spirit which has produced the created whole. To do this is to take the process of fossilization for the process of life. The more the creative spirit is eclipsed, the more prominent interest and utility always become.**

If we were to adhere to the utility thesis, we would have absolutely no way of of dealing with those acts of *cultus* for which the analogies of our own existence would no longer permit us to divine a purpose. I think of dances, processions, dramatic scenes of highly divergent types. Let us not be confused any longer by the barren ideology with which the members of retrograde cultures presume to explain their customs which still survive but are no longer understood. The serious observer cannot doubt that the dances and evolutions of *cultus* were set into motion and given form by a contact with the Divine. They were so filled with its presence, so transported, that they often no longer expressed the human condition but the reality and activity of the god, himself. Thus later it was said that man was imitating the god and his history. That is still by far the most logical explanation. The idea we like so much today—that man wanted to be transformed into a god—coincides, at best, with a late interpretation. If God were really there, what better thing could man have done than become, in himself, the living monument of His presence?

---

* Literally, "Give so as to get [something in return]." It implies a bargaining relationship.

** In this connection recall the accounts of worship in which acts or symbols of sacrifice are important (readings 4, 5, and 6 especially).

But God had, as yet, no history which could be related and imitated. His myth lived in cult activity, and the actions of *cultus* expressed in plastic form what He was and what He did. Before the faithful visualized the image of their God, and gave verbal expression to His life and works, He was so close to them that their spirit, touched by His breath, was aroused to holy activity. With their own bodies they created His image. His living reality was mirrored in the solemnity of their actions long before this mute or inarticulate myth was made eloquent and poetic.

The great era of this myth, strictly speaking, dawned only after *cultus* began to lose its original freshness and creative vitality and become fixed. At that time great sculptors drew anew from the same divine abundance out of which practices of *cultus* had arisen. In its emotion-filled richness they found a diversity of Being and Becoming which *cultus* had not made apparent. But the same reality which was expressed in cult institutions was present in the singers, too, who unquestionably created song out of just that element of the existence, effect, and fortunes of this reality which the sponsors of the cult—that is to say, the community—had had to experience in the consummation of the cult.

Living reality is always inexhaustible. Other people may have received in the presence of godhead holy laws and most secret wisdom, but the Greek genius was given the key to a great theatre, whose scenes revealed the wonders of the world of the gods with a clarity which is unparalleled. The sacred Being, which, in the cult of every god, led irresistibly to ritual, became clear, and was revealed in an abundance of forms. The limitless meaning of godhead stepped into the light of living forms—comparable to that which occurred later in a new form in the fine arts.

That is the way of the Greeks. Are we to call it less religious than others because here faith in God does not reveal laws, penance, and the denial of the world, but the sacredness of Him who is and the great circles of Being in which gods, as eternal form, are active? This prejudice, of course, lies at the heart of all research up to now, and for this reason everything which myth created had to be interpreted as a product of the poetic imagination, without the realization that our task is understanding the religion of the *Greek* spirit.

For this religion, myth, as such, is no less of a witness than *cultus*. Actually, it yields more information because the forms of *cultus* are less well known to us and are, unfortunately, all too often obscure. The language of myth, on the other hand, is not only more mobile but also more distinct. To be sure, it reached its point of perfection in those ages in which the singers were no longer the spokesmen for the spirit of the community but had received the revelation of deity as individuals. In the course of the years, moreover, man has used his poetic imagination to subject myth to arbitrary and personal interpretations, meddlesome speculations, and the naive desire he has always had to rationalize everything. Viewed as a whole, however, it still remains the noblest phenomenon of Greek religion.

8. The Sacred and the Profane, J. E. Smith

In this selection, John E. Smith, chairman of the department of philosophy at Yale University since 1961, draws our attention to a distinctive feature of religious rituals. He notes that they tend to cluster at points of transition in human life. Why should this be so? In the course of answering this question he suggests that we adopt a certain understanding of the relation between the sacred and the profane. What does Smith mean by the term "celebration"? Why, according to him, are critical transitions in human life especially appropriate for the recognition and celebration of the sacred? How does the effort to maintain contact with the sacred through myth and ritual differ from the efforts of such evangelists as Aimee Semple McPherson (Chapter I, reading 9)? What does Smith mean by "profane existence"? Does he consider it an evil thing? What term best describes, for Smith, the relation between the sacred and the profane?

The key to understanding the holy in experience is to be found in the contrast between the ordinary activities of human life—waking, nourishing ourselves, working, replenishing our energy through taking rest and recreation—and those special times or junctures in life that are set apart from the ordinary course of events and "celebrated" as having some peculiar meaning and seriousness about them. These special times, sometimes called the "crises" or turning points in life, are regarded in all cultures as extraordinary times that are somehow set apart from the rest of life. The time of being born, the time of attaining puberty or entering into adult life, the time of initiation into the social community or of confirmation (baptism, etc.) into the religious community, the time of choosing a vocation, the time of marriage, the time of giving birth, the time of death; these are the special times at which the holy becomes manifest.* Identifying these events in human life as turning points endowed with peculiar significance because they involve the holy is a far easier task than expressing precisely what it is about them that causes us to set them apart and to celebrate them. The idea of *celebration* furnishes an initial key, as does also the fact that times for celebration are marked off as "holidays," in religious language, "holy days."

Celebration here does not mean primarily making merry or escaping from the daily round through enjoyment, although festive eating and

---

From *Experience and God* by John E. Smith. Copyright © 1968 by Oxford University Press, Inc. Reprinted by permission. Pp. 57–62.

* In this connection, recall some of the readings in this chapter: initiation (1), marriage (3), baptism (4), and death (5).

drinking are generally associated with the celebration of the extraordinary events in a person's life. Celebration means being awed, fascinated, and even overpowered by the special events as a result of acknowledging that they are times when a sense of the mystery of all being and of one's own being is forced upon us. There is the sense that at these times we are in the presence of the supremely powerful, what has control over our destiny, what is the supremely important reality that is alone worthy of worship. The utter fascination of such occasions gives rise to celebration, a form of ritual intended to preserve or perpetuate the record of the event and its power. The effort at preservation within the act of celebration has two aspects: first, there is the actual *marking off* of the event as something more than an event beside others and its removal from the cycle of anonymous events of the daily round; second, there is the aim of *retaining* the event in memory, of keeping it from passing away by associating with it other experiences that intensify its quality. Except for marriage and childbirth, the distinguishing feature of each of the crucial junctures of life is that they cannot be repeated; there is a "once-for-all" character about them that stands in marked contrast to the ordinary events of life taking place again and again.

The existence of crucial events in the cycle of human life has been acknowledged in all cultures, and they have always been set apart and celebrated because of their peculiar significance. What remains to be made clear is precisely why these events should be of special importance for understanding the holy in human experience. The answer is twofold: in the first place, these events have been called, aptly enough, "crises" in human life because they are times when the purpose of life as such comes into question and when we have the sense that life is being judged, not in its details, but as a whole; in the second, the crisis times fill us with a sense of the finitude and frailty of man, of our creatureliness, of our dependence upon resources beyond our own, and of our need to find a supremely worshipful reality to whom we can devote ourselves without reserve. In both cases it is the source and quality of our being that is forced into the foreground of our consciousness; the crisis times are filled with power because for the time being they set at nought all preliminary concerns and direct our thoughts away from the banality of ordinary life to dwell, with awe and proper seriousness, upon the mystery of life itself. It is of the utmost importance to notice that in the records of many primitive religions the times of crisis are regarded as "dangerous" times, because it is at such times that the natural order comes in contact with or is touched by the unseen world and its power. Apart from the crudity and superstition often associated with such beliefs, there remains an important truth in these interpretations. It is as if the times of crisis were so many openings into the depth of life, into its ground, its purpose, its finite character. Ordinary life, "profane" existence, just because it is subjected to habit and routine, remains on the surface and covers the depth. A life that exists only on the surface gradually loses the capacity to acknowledge or to respond in awe to life in its depth and must be shocked into a realization of the holy on the special occasions when the holy ground of life is celebrated. A completely profane existence is one in which the ordinary events of life, no matter how bizarre, exciting, cruel, tragic they may be in themselves, exclude all sense of awe and mystery, so that even the crisis times themselves become ordinary times occasions for merriment or "relaxation," and the depth aspect of life no longer has any meaning. Whether it is possible to achieve a complete profanization of life remains a question, but for many people the times of crisis have lost their power and no longer elicit an acknowledgment of the holy ground of all life.

Profane existence means an existence which is open, manifest, transparent, obvious, taken for granted, ordinary, and thus lacking all mystery and power. Ordinary occasions are precisely those that do not involve matters of "life and death" so that they fail to quicken in us an attitude of contemplation over the mystery of life itself and its purpose. It is not that profane life is valueless or that it should be degraded or despised; on the contrary profane existence forms by far the largest part of our life, but in contrast with the crucial times, the daily round of events is ordinary enough and gives no occasion for wonder or special concern. In the ordinary events there is no question of a judgment on life as a whole. We do not celebrate the ordinary events because they do not arrest us; we do not see in them any reason for preserving them or for setting them apart. The profane stands over against the holy, not because it is sordid or "unclean," but because it is ordinary and harbors no mystery, nor calls forth the sense that beyond and beneath our life is a holy ground.

The basic relation between the holy and the profane may be summed up by saying that the holy provides the final purpose giving point and poignancy to all the details of profane existence, while the profane is the body of life and the medium through which the holy is made fully actual. Profane existence serves as a critical testing ground for the holy, in the sense that unless the holy takes historical form and becomes related to life in the world it may be dissipated in aesthetic enjoyment or contemplation that leaves life unaffected. The holy, on the other hand, is the standard for judging the profane since the holy provides us with a vision of what life should be, and thus reveals the extent to which mundane existence falls short of its ideal. The mutual involvement of the holy and profane is best understood by considering each as it might be if it existed all alone.

Profane life without the holy would be untouched by devotion to any but finite and limited objects—self, family, profession, nation—and such life would be without conviction about a final purpose for existence and devoid of a sense of dependence upon a transcendent source of existence. There would be no sense of the mystery of being; life would simply be given as one form of existence among others and, while life could well embrace the enjoyment of goods and values within the cycle of both nature and culture, it would not be viewed as the expression of a more than human purpose or power. Such visions of an ideal form of life as there would be would have to be constructed, in understanding and imagination, from the facts of natural existence. There would be no other source of information, so to speak, to illuminate human life and furnish insight into what man was "meant to be."

The holy without the profane, on the other hand, would become a sphere of pure "spirit" in which the transcendent holiness would be celebrated without concern for its embodiment in historical existence. Were the whole of life swallowed up in sacred existence, we would have a model of what the holy all by itself would mean. Religion would be the entire reality and profane life would have no being at all. Religion would remain in merely implicit form, there being no profane existence to give it actuality. If the profane without the holy means that life is bereft of spirit or depth, the holy without the profane would mean the cessation of life altogether.*

There is a limit to the insight that can be gained by supposing what is contrary to fact. Actual life embraces both the holy and the profane and the question concerns neither one nor the other taken in isolation, but the proper connections between them. The two have independent natures *vis à vis* each other in the sense that neither can be dissolved into the other, and yet they must be brought into some mutual relationship. The holy is not to be set entirely apart in a special sphere where it loses its critical power and where its judgment upon profane life is lost or nullified. On the other hand, the holy has to be set apart; it must not become too familiar or fall to the level of what is ordinary. That is, the attempt to interpret the holy as merely the "soul" or "spirit" of the profane in a way that does not allow for a due sense of awe in the presence of the holy is bound to fail. The holy stands over against the profane at the same time that it manifests itself in and illuminates the purpose of the profane. The crucial events of life in which the holy is present require special celebration through the ritual and symbolism of positive religion; if this does not happen, the holy gradually declines in significance and in power. The limit of this process is the profanation of life or, in terms more frequently used, the totally secularized society. It is impossible to maintain the holy merely as an idea or a general pervading spirit; actual celebration is required so that, insofar as the holy coincides with religion, religion must take on a positive and visible form in a cult and church. The church exists as the means of giving shape to the celebration of the holy. There is literally a life of religion, but it cannot exist merely alongside of profane life; the truth lies in interpenetration rather than co-existence.

---

* Keep this point in mind when we deal with Zen in Chapter IV, where a similar observation will lead to a different conclusion.

9. Symbols as Vehicles of the Sacred, V. Warnach

> *In this reading, Warnach, a contemporary Roman Catholic theologian, is concerned to explain the sense in which sacred power (Christ) is active in the Eucharist (Mass). The key feature of his argument is his distinction between sign and symbol. The importance of the latter is that it is a sensible reality through which a "higher transcendent reality" is thought to be present and active. Note that the cultic sacrifice has three stages. What transformations take place in its course? How does Warnach explain the failure of the bread and wine to undergo any change visible to a chemist? Is the whole affair primarily psychological (that is, subjective)?*

SYMBOL AND REALITY

The modern usage of the word "symbol" and its derivative is very confusing. It is frequently used to mean a pure sign (whether a semantic sign, or a logical or scientific expression, figure or term), for something which is not immediately present. The function of a sign, however, is to bring to mind the reality for which it stands. This reality is something essentially different from the sign itself. Signs are abstract and in the logic of intention, for instance, they stand at the greatest possible distance from reality. The word "symbol" is also used of the images by which we refer to supersensual realities. If we then go on to use "symbol" of "emblems" such as flags, coats of arms, insignia, and so on, this is because these, too, represent an institution office or group which has some sort of power or influence. In depth-psychology "symbol" is used of suppressed elements of conscious life or of the sublimated forms by which drives manifest themselves in dreams, neurotic traits and awkward behavior. "Symbol" here involves a greater degree of reality than the earlier examples and borders of its full significance as seen in religious and artistic traditions. Here, especially in the older cultures, it does not mean an abstract instrument of our understanding but principally a means by which a higher, frequently divine, reality is made present or accessible—a means therefore by which living contact with the "other" world can be achieved. Symbol properly so called, therefore, is not something man has chanced upon, nor the result of human invention as are most signs, but owes its symbolic character either to the created or natural order (natural symbol) or to God's

From "Symbol and Reality in the Eucharist," by Victor Warnach, in *The Breaking of Bread,* edited by Pierre Benoit, Roland E. Murphy, and Bastiaan van Iersel, Volume 40 of *Concilium: Theology in the Age of Renewal* (New York: Paulist Press, 1969), pp. 85–88, 95–100.

presence in saving history.[1] The two worlds of God and man, heaven and earth, spirit and matter meet preeminently in the religious symbol. Even the etymology of *symbolon,* from *symballein* (to cast together), suggests this.

The "real symbol," the full correct meaning of "symbol," is therefore a form that can be experienced by the senses and through which a higher transcendent reality announces itself as present and active.[2] It is distinguishable from a sign in that it is of its nature a self-expression in which something of the reality of what is expressed, or expresses itself, is present or "appears." For this reason it is distinguishable from the mere expression through which some inner experience spontaneously becomes visible but whose nature can only be gathered from its effects. To be sure, as an exact phenomenological analysis shows, both the significative and the expressive function are included within the complex phenomenon of the symbol. Nevertheless its fundamental character derives from its roots in space and time; it must be the visible and sensible "appearance" (*epiphaneia*)—as an ontological presence—of a (higher) being. The use of "appearance" here neither weakens nor questions the reality of the symbolic presence—a conclusion too frequently found in platonic thinkers. Rather it emphasizes the inadequacy of the material levels of being by indicating that spiritual (pneumatic) being cannot be directly present in space and time since its nature is essentially beyond the bounds of space and time. A symbol, accordingly, is the making visible and present of a reality, of its nature divisible, in a form that though inadequate, discloses what it signifies.

Our conception of what a symbol is, therefore, determines whether we see a contradiction between symbol and reality, or can conceive of the possibility of a synthesis encompassing and complementing both aspects. This latter possibility is easier to visualize if we avoid a static limitation of our concepts of "real" and "symbol"; for in worship especially the symbols are often symbolic actions, or even symbolic or mystery dramas in which the "primal deeds" or saving events can begin to realize themselves in the present.

In any case the Bible has a realistic conception of symbol; it recognizes the fact of the pure real symbol, and this not just as a meaningless survival from a heathen cult, but as a God-given means for communicating with him. The uniqueness of the means can be appreciated from the fact that the term *symbolon* is used only twice in the Greek Bible and on both occasions in a derogatory sense (Hos. 4, 12; Wis. 2, 9). Yet the Bible contains clear references to the symbolical and to the fact of the symbolical function. . . .

THE TRANSFORMATION AT THE CONSECRATION

The real symbol, whose roots in sacred history we have indicated, leads us to a greater understanding of the mystery of the eucharist. Not only the eucharistic gifts but also the sacred actions are symbols in the strict sense, for the reality symbolized is actually present in both.[3]

If we start with the eucharistic event we can see there, as in all cultic sacrifices, a process that has three phases: gifts are brought or offered, they are set apart for God and they are consecrated for his acceptance. Corresponding to these three cult acts there are the three existential "moments": the self-offering (renunciation), the transformation (movement from the profane to the sacred realm), and the union with God (communion).[4] The bread and wine in the eucharist are offered, therefore, as signs of our own self-offering. As such they already have a symbolic value in their own right, if only in a very preliminary sense. The sacrifice of the Mass does not really consist of our gifts or self-offering; rather both are symbols through which the sacrifice of Christ accomplishes itself. What we have to offer, however valuable and noble, can never effect salvation and sanctification. We are expected to offer gifts and, above all, ourselves,[5] but these are useless if they do not become part of Christ's sacrifice. Though it is God who invites us to offer gifts, it is he alone who, through the Spirit of Christ, sanctifies and consecrates them. Our offerings are themselves God's gift to us and so must always become thanksgiving (*eucharistia*) for these offerings and for all the works of creation and salvation.

This thanksgiving "in the name of Jesus" is the efficacious word which transforms and consecrates the offerings—it "eucharistizes" them as Justin said.[6] They then become *symbola,* visible manifestations of the sanctified body and blood of the crucified Christ. The unique saving sacrifice becomes a saving and sanctifying presence among us.

The Mass is not just a sacrificial action, it is also a sacrificial *meal.* That is why we offer food. But this food now has a very different meaning. It functions not just to nourish and strengthen man's body so that he can prolong his earthly life, but principally to feed the "inner man," not just his "soul" but the whole of his human nature so as to prepare him for the "other" true eternal life with God.

There is therefore at least a threefold change in the fundamental significance of the bread and wine: (1) prior to the consecration they function as signs of our self-offering; after it they realize the presence in a symbol of Christ's sacrifice on the cross; (2) bread and wine become more than purely natural nourishment; they are "spiritual food" (1 Cor. 10, 3); (3) as part of a meal they constitute a table-fellowship among those present, but in communion the eucharistic gifts unite us first to Christ, then through him with one another in the one spiritual body of the Church....

If we try to situate the eucharist within saving history we perceive that it is the meeting place of the descent (*katabasis*) of the self-emptying (*kenosis*) and the ascent (*anabasis*) to glorification (*doxa*). To be more precise: the paschal mystery is realized in the eucharist to the extent that it also contains that unique *kairos,* that irrevocable all-embracing turning point in Christ's course through his sacrificial death to a new life. The path which stretches from his incarnation to the criminal's death on a cross is expressed in the sacrament by him, emptying himself under the forms of bread and wine, so that the eucharist can be valued as a new incarnation of Christ. Its meaning stems from the "perpetuation"[7] of his unique sacrifice and from the fellowship (*koinonia*) of the sacred meal.

The natural creative power of selfless love changes the earthly materials of bread and wine in their innermost being, making them like a window through which shines the self-offering and glorification of the dying and risen Lord—visible to those with faith. Just as Jesus' visible body was his historical and personal manifestation (*species*) in his temporal existence, so the eucharistic gifts are the manifestation (*species*) of Christ in his transition to the world of God. We, too, must share in this unique transition if we wish to be saved.

Although we can parallel the "form" of bread and wine and the human form of the "fleshly body" (Col. 1, 22), there are nevertheless essential differences between the historical and the sacramental manifestations of Christ: (1) the body which the *Logos* took from the Virgin is only a "symbol" for the present Lord in a derivative sense, whereas the bread and wine, because of their institution and consecration, are proper cult symbols and consequently make him present; (2) the presence of Christ in the sacrament is not historical or spatio-temporal but real and "substantial" (or better, personal) which as sacramental or pneumatic is beyond space and time, as the encyclical *Mysterium Fidei* emphasized.[8] This spiritual or pneumatic form of existence is not less real but rather more fully real. In contrast to an impoverished and empty idea of reality to be found in positivism, Christian realism has always seen in spiritual being its highest and richest form, positively surpassing space and time by overflowing their boundaries. Matter is not thereby denied value or turned into spirit. It is illumined and made radiant through the spirit, brought to its true fulfillment in the unity and completeness (*pleroma*) of Christ's spiritual body. So our sacrificial gifts undergo a radical (ontological) transformation which leaves their form (species) unaltered as the manifesting medium, while radically altering their being, giving them totally new relationships and connections.

What we mean can be clarified and to some extent justified by a short consideration of the fundamental ontological structure of things. Modern science and scientifically orientated philosophy considers bread and wine to be a mixture of organic and inorganic materials which cannot properly speaking be called "substances" (that is, entities relatively independent in their own being but not their origin). The true substance of bread and wine is rather the cosmos "not yet as" a system of purely physical foces and fields but as the nature (*physis*) transformed by man.

Bread and wine represent together, in a picture, a world fashioned by human resources. They are especially suitable therefore to symbolize (in a broad sense) human self-offering. They are the principal materials by which men are nourished and they imply man's limitation to this world. Naturally they are typical of human offerings since Melchizedek's time, if not long before that.

In the present saving order our human offerings become meaningless unless they are part of the one saving sacrifice of Christ. He has therefore taken our useless gifts and made them his own, his own sacrifice of body and blood, thus linking them with his very being which is by nature one of sacrificial love. In this way they are changed ontologically and become the "species" of a different "substance."[9] The ground and the meaning of their being, that is, their "substance" is no longer the cosmos; it is Christ himself, the Lord of the cosmos, who makes these "forms" (*species*) into a self-manifestation.[10] Bread and wine, therefore, become his body and blood; through them he really and sacramentally "appears," offering himself here and now. The cult-symbol finds in this rite its highest realization. In this sense one can really speak of "transubstantiation," meaning that instead of the substance of the cosmos Christ himself bears bread and wine as his "species," so that they express him and he becomes their "substance."

NOTES

1. In this we differ from S. Wisse who in his learned study *Das religiöse Symbol* (Essen, 1963) describes symbol as "the sensible form by which one expresses one's experience of the transcendent holiness of God" (p. 48). We would agree that in a real symbol both the expressive and the sign function are at work, but we would insist that it is not subjective experience but an objective determination and institution that gives a symbol its character, thus uniting the symbol with that which is symbolized on an ontological level. Wisse has logically to refuse to accept this (pp. 159–73) and consequently considers the sacraments to be "exceptions" (p. 172; cf. pp. 47; 207f.).

2. On this we agree with K. Rahner (*The Theology of the Symbol*, in *Theological Investigatives IV* (1966) pp. 227–52) although Rahner's conception of symbol is wider than ours as it includes all reality: "Being is of itself necessarily symbolic since it must 'express' itself in order fully to find its own nature" (p. 224).

3. The word "actio" whose cultic significance O. Casel first drew attention to ("Actio in liturgischer Verwendung," in *Jahrb. f. Liturgiewiss.,* 1 [1921], pp. 34–9) is met with also in the *Instructio* mentioned in note 10 (n. 3c) and quite generally in theological literature including the Letter of the German bishops (n. 440) mentioned in note 13. [Author's note not included.]

4. On this point see our work on religious phenomenology: *Vom Wesen des kultischen Opfers,* in *Opfer Christi und Opfer der Kirche,* ed. B. Neunheuser (Düsseldorf, 1960), pp. 29–74, esp. pp. 61–5.

5. Even M. Luther had allowed this in a qualified sense, see V. Warnach, "Das Meßopfer als ökumenisches Anliegen," in *Lit. u. Möncht.* 17 (1955), pp. 66–9; H. B. Meyer, *Luther und die Messe* (Paderborn, 1965), pp. 137–72. The "crisis" among theologians trying to understand the Offertory makes them tend to reduce its significance, or even to eliminate it altogether (see the Dutch Catechism referred to in note 13, pp. 335, 340). Although it is no autonomous unit, but only preparatory to the eucharistic celebration, bread and wine are offered so that they may be changed into the body and blood of Christ (N. M. Denis-Boulet, *Analyse des rites et des prières de la Messe,* in *L'égilse en prière,* ed. A. G. Martimort (Paris, 1965[3]), pp. 377f.; nevertheless, the offering belongs to the unified structure of the Mass (J. A. Jung-

mann, *op, cit.,* p. 367f.; Th. Schnitzler. *Der römische Meßkanon* (Freiburg
i. Br., 1968), pp. 29–31. cf. pp. 88f.). On the meaning of the Offertory:
W. J. Grisbrooks, "Oblation at the Eucharist," in *Studia liturg.* 3 (1964),
pp. 227–39; 4 (1965) pp. 37–55; A. M. Argenti, "El ofertorio en la celebra-
cion de la eucaristia," in *Phase* 6 (1966), pp. 391–402; G. Oury, "La signifi-
cation de l'offertoire," in *Ami du clergé* 76 (1966), pp. 362–6. Even evan-
gelical theologians speak of the sacrificial offering of the Church, for instance,
M. Thurian, *L'Eucharistie* (Neuchâtel-Paris 1963), and the recent work by
H. Asmussen, *Christliche Lehre anstatt eines Katechismus* (Berlin-Hamburg,
1968), p. 108f; further references in W. Averbeck, *op cit.,* note 13, esp. p. 785.
[Author's note omitted.]

6. Justin, *Apol.* 1, 65. 67; cf. Irenaeus, *Adv. haer.* V, 2, 3; on this see O. Casel,
   Das christliche Opfermysterium (Graz. 1968), pp. 114f, 293–7, 315ff, 389–
   92, 395ff; and also J. Pascher, *Eucharistia* (Münster-Freiburg i. Br., 1953²),
   p. 122f.

7. See the same encyclical, p. 754, where it follows the *Constitution on the
   Liturgy* (n. 47). This word is not to be understood in a static sense, but
   in a dynamic one within the context of saving history.

8. So we have on p. 762: *per consecrationis verba (Dominus) sacramentaliter
   incipit praesens adesse...sub speciebus panis et vini.* This seems to be contradicted when it says later on: *sub quibus (speciebus) totus et integer
   Christus adest in sua physica "realitate" etiam corporaliter praesens, licet
   non eo modo quo corpora sunt in loco* (p. 766). But this only emphasizes
   the "bodily" reality of the presence of the Lord in a context where the non-
   spatial manner of the Lord's bodily presence is being emphasized. Even
   Thomas taught this: the body of Christ in the eucharist is *nullo modo...
   localiter* present *sed per modum substantiae* (S. T. III, 76, 5) or more
   precisely: *non per modum corporis, id est, prout est in sua specie visibili*
   but *prout est spiritualiter, id est, invisibili modo, et virtute spiritus (op. cit.,
   75, 1 ad 4.)* We can take as our basic assumption that the same (personal)
   body of Christ is: the "fleshly body" (Col. 1, 22, cf. 2, 11) of his earthly
   existence; the glorified (*doxa,* Phil. 3, 21) or "spiritual body" (1 Cor. 15,
   44) in heaven; the "one body in Christ" (Rom. 12, 5) of the Church;
   and the body under the appearances of bread and wine; all these are different analogous manifestations of the same reality. Consequently, one can
   say of the eucharistic mode of presence that it is neither physical and
   sensual, nor a material object, nor purely symbolic and abstract, nor just
   spiritual, but a real or sacramental symbol in that it manifests a spiritual
   (pneumatic) or personal reality to the believer through visible forms as a
   living and a life-giving presence. It cannot be separated from the cultic
   sacrifice and meal which the Church celebrates, and so from the spiritual
   and personal presence of the Lord working in her, himself present through his
   Spirit and his Word in the gifts, offering himself in the sacrifice and meal
   and enabling us to share in these. One can only quote from the immense
   literature on this: E. Schillebeeckx, *Die eucharistische Gegenwart* (full
   details in [author's original] note 10 [*Zur Diskussion über die Realpräsenz*
   (Dusseldorf, 1967)] and the review by J. Ratzinger in *ThQ* 147 (1967), pp.
   493–96. For what follows see L. Scheffczyk, "Die materielle Welt im Lichte
   der Eucharistie," in *Aktuelle Fragen zur Eucharistie,* ed. M. Schmaus (Munich,
   1960), pp. 156–79, and B. Welte's supplement on pp. 190–95, but noting that
   both authors proceed from ontological presuppositions different from ours.

9. The philosophical term, "substance," (or "substantial") is often used in the

sense of "nature" (*essentia, ousia*), or even in contrast to these latter to mean "subject" (*subiectum, hypokeimenon*), a usage which stems from Aristotelian usage. Consequently, the eucharistic event was described in the 12th century, and especially by Petrus Cantor, as a change of subject, that is, as a change in the (bodily) material (as distinct from the *forma materialis*) (S. H. Jorissen, *Die Entfaltung der Transsubstantiationslehre bis zum Beginn der Hochscholastik* [Munster, 1965], pp. 87–114), while one often translated transubstantiation into the German *"Wesensverwandlung"* (change of nature) as does also L. Scheffczyk (*op. cit.,* p. 168–70). It is our opinion, however, that what is affected here is not the subject (bearer) or the nature (contents) as such, but rather being which unites bearer and contents. It is in this sense that we speak of substance as the true or independent existent. It is here that we agree with the modern tendency to regard the substance of the eucharist as a person, or at least as personal; see for instance E. Schillebeeckx, *op cit.,* pp. 47f., 53f.; J. Ratzinger, "Das Problem der Transsubstantiation und die Frage nach dem Sinn der Eucharistie," in *ThQ* 147 (1967), p. 152.

10. The eucharistic change can be compared with the "transfiguration" of Christ on Tabor where the glorified Christ also appeared in *altera specie* (Lk. 9, 29; cf. 3, 22). J. M. R. Tillard (*op. cit.,* ["L'Eucharistie et le Saint Esprit," *Nouv. Rev. Theol.* 100 (1968), p. 135] note 7) has very clearly shown that the Spirit was at work in this change even though he does tend to enhance the role of the Spirit as the third person of the Trinity in contrast to that of the Spirit of Christ, to the neglect of the important role of the latter in saving history.

10. Rituals: Sacred and Profane—
An Anthropological Approach,
A. F. C. Wallace

With this excerpt from an article by Anthony F. C. Wallace (b. 1923), chairman of the department of anthropology at the University of Pennsylvania, we shift perspective. The three interpretive selections above, however different from each other they may be, all view myth and ritual positively. Wallace, on the other hand, attempts to view the subject dispassionately. Without considering questions of truth or falsity (at this point), he asks, in effect, "How does ritual function in society? What does it communicate and how is it learned?" To answer these questions, he discusses the "law of dissociation" and describes the ways in

From *Religion: An Anthropological View,* by Anthony F. C. Wallace. Copyright © 1966 by Random House, Inc. Reprinted by permission of Random House, Inc. Pp. 65–70.

which ritual illustrates it. In what sense, according to Wallace, are the goals of science and of religion the same? What is the law of dissociation and from what mechanisms does he distinguish it? How do Smith (reading 8) and Warnach (reading 9) account for that shift in attention from one realm of thought to another which Wallace refers to as "dissociation"? What might be a believer's response to Wallace's observation that ritual patterns are culturally dependent?

In human rituals the content of the communication is twofold: first, it is a statement of an intention; and second, it is a statement of the nature of the world in which the intention is to be realized. The conscious intentions of human rituals, as we have seen, can be broadly categorized as transformations of state in the technological, therapeutic (and anti-therapeutic), ideological (for social control), salvational, and revitalizational senses. But it must be recognized that several intentions can be expressed in the same act of communication, often on different levels of awareness. It has been the principal contribution of the psychoanalytical approach to ritual to emphasize that multiple intentions, sometimes congruent and sometimes contradictory, can be expressed by the same ritual act, and in the same ritual sequence. Furthermore, the "language" of ritual is, in a sense, extremely abstract, in that the rather arbitrary signals of which it is composed refer to extensive and complex ideas of value, structure, and transformation, whose verbal statement requires considerable time. The symbolism of ritual, therefore, is extremely elaborate and oft-times obscure, since it refers to intentions and beliefs that are complex and, in part, unconscious.

Thus the simple ritual act of crossing oneself, in Catholic custom, by touching the fingers to the forehead and chest in four, must be understood as a statement of intent to secure divine power as a protection against danger, spiritual or physical. The "sign of the cross," the extremities of which are indicated by the points touched, invokes the whole story of Christ and its complex meanings; the accompanying litany—"In the name of the Father, Son, and Holy Ghost, Amen"—asserts a particular theological conception and constitutes both a prayer and a primitive magical conception of power inherent in naming; the points of the body chosen are believed to be seats of particular spiritual function in man; and the nature of the danger to be warded off is obviously liable to be a complex combination of conscious threats. Thus, this simple act may be a statement of extremely complex intentions and is certainly an assertion of a world view which is embodied in an extraordinarily elaborate set of beliefs based both on ancient Christian mythology and even more ancient conceptions of magic. In some rituals, the connection between the signal and that to which it refers is more easily recognizable; one thinks particularly of rituals involving sexual and aggressive symbolism interpretable by the kind of logic implied in Freudian dream interpretation. Thus, for instance, the analyst interprets the Australian subincision ceremony, in which the penis is slit lengthwise to the urethra, as a statement of intent by men to secure female sexual parts and to achieve certain generative powers associated with feminity; and this interpretation has some support from native informants. But it is also a test and a sign of manhood, of admission to a social status that involves the acceptance of both rights and obligations; and these rights and obligations are defined, in part, in an extensive mythology. In general, then, we must recognize that "the" meaning of any ritual act is apt to be multiple rather than singular and that explanations of ritual which claim a simple singularity are almost invariably oversimplifications.

But even though the meaning of a rite is both highly particular and highly complex, it has always one other message, which is implicit rather than explicit. This is the message of organization. The stereotypy of ritual is orderliness raised to an extraordinary degree; rituals are predictable; the contingent probabilities of chains of events are near unity; the myth upon which the ritual is based describes a world in which chaos is being, or is to be, replaced by order. Furthermore, the content of ritual reduces the complex heterogeneity of reality to which the ritual refers, explains the mystic unity which lies behind phenomenological diversity in its realm of relevance. Thus ritual, and its supporting belief system, constitutes a world of symbols that is simple and orderly. This is hardly unexpected, as we have seen, for one of the principal functions of religion is to reduce anxiety and enlarge confidence, and to do this, the human (or non-human) organism participant must view his life and circumstances as a system so efficiently well-organized as to permit quick decision and confident action. An organism overwhelmed by information overload is incapable of discriminating response; ritual, by reducing the information content of experience below the often bewildering level of complexity and disorder with which reality confronts him, permits adaptive response. In this sense, the goal of science and the goal of religion and myth are the same: to create the image of a simple and orderly world.

The accomplishment of the ritual reorganization of experience thus is a kind of learning. It is a reprogramming, as it were, of a machine, sometimes done once for a given individual and not again, as in many rites of passage, and sometimes done repeatedly, as in those calendrically scheduled communal ceremonies which readjust values and perceptions and refocus attention. But the psychological mechanisms upon which ritual learning depends are not confined to the practice-and-reinforcement schedule which has been so carefully investigated by experimental psychologists. The ritual learning process, whether its effects be measured in years, as in the case of puberty rituals, or in hours or minutes, as in the case of certain technological rituals, seems to involve a special five-stage process, which invokes not so much the law of effect (as in conditioning and instrumental learning) or the law of repetition (as in imprinting) as what might be called the law of dissociation: the principle that cognitive and affective content can be restructured more rapidly and more extensively the more the perceptual cues from the environment associated with previous learning are excluded from conscious awareness and the more those immediately relevant to the elements to be reorganized are presented. How permanent such a new cognitive synthesis will prove to be depends, presumably, in part on the maintenance of the dissociation (by such devices as actual isolation from prior contacts and as the continued presentation of the selected matrix of cues, including suggestion) and in part on the reinforcement in the conventional learning sense. The stages of the ritual process of cognitive-and-affective restructuring are as follows:

1. *Prelearning.* At least some of the several elements to be reorganized in the new cognitive synthesis must be already present as a result of previous learning. Some knowledge of the standardized rights and obligations of the new role, for instance, is usually held by novitiates before a rite of passage; persons about to become possessed by a deity are aware of that being's interests and characteristics; persons hopeful of salvation know something of what the new identity would be like; the incipient prophet is already well stocked with a miscellany of criticism of the status quo and of recommendations for reform. But the cognitive content of relevant prelearning is internally contradictory and not sorted out from other cognitive material.

2. *Separation.* The ritualist separates himself, and/or is separated by others, from conscious awareness of irrelevant environmental information. This can be accomplished in several ways:

a) By deprivation of sensory contact with previously significant features of the environment through such devices as physical isolation, darkness, distracting noise;

b) By the use of drugs, such as mescaline, which interfere with the ability to assign meaning to previously familiar sensory data;

c) By the imposition of extreme physical stress—through pain, fatigue, sleeplessness, hunger and thirst, or even actual trauma or illness—which restricts attention;

d) By the presentation of monotonous and repetitive stimuli, such as drumming, flashing lights, dancing, which (as in hypnosis) induce a trance.

While the degree of separation of attention achieved by these methods can vary greatly—from the probably minor effect of simple withdrawal to a quiet, "sacred" place to the profoundly dissociative effect of drugs, complete sensory deprivation, extreme stress, or prolonged drumming—all these procedures seem to have the effect of facilitating cognitive restructuring.

3. *Suggestion.* Once the state of separation or dissociation (sometimes called trance) has been achieved, the cognitive material relevant to resynthesis can be readily recombined under the influence of direct suggestion from others or from one's self (the general instructions for resynthesis having been prelearned, as, for instance, in the case of the Plains Indian vision quest). Apparently, in the absence of any specific suggestion, a spontaneous sorting out of dissociated elements is possible, if one

can judge from the reported experience of prophets like Handsome Lake and the reports of experimental subjects in drug and sensory-deprivation experiments. Such a resynthesis may take the form of transient changes in mood, as in most technological rituals, or of an alternate, but only temporarily manifest, personality (as in those cases of temporary multiple personality which are interpreted by a theory of possession, as in Haitian voodoo); but it may also take the form of a hopefully permanent restructuring of beliefs and values, as in the radical mazeway resynthesis of the religious prophet or the identity transformations of rites of passage and of salvation.

4. *Execution.* After the achievement of resynthesis, the ritual subject will be expected, sooner or later, to act in accordance with the new cognitive structure. If "sooner," it may mean immediately, as in ritual possession and during the dissociated state; but if the new role is to be a permanent one played out in a secular context, its execution may be delayed until after the dissociated state is over, and the expectation may be for a permanent, lifelong change.

5. *Maintenance.* In cases of ritual possession, the resynthesis is implemented during the dissociated state, and is terminated with the end of those procedures which maintain the dissociation. The individual apparently retains a lower threshold for dissociation and personality alternation, however. In some instances, the maintenance of the new structure depends on posthypnotic suggestion; but this, by itself, usually does not remain effective for more than several weeks or months at most. Therefore, for "permanent" change, it is necessary either to renew, periodically, the ritual itself or to provide the subject with tangible cues from the ritual experience which will serve to maintain the new structure, or both. This provision of repetition of the ritual, even if in attenuated form, is recognized by evangelists, like John Wesley, who insist on their converts joining cells, congregations, or study groups who hold periodic meetings; and the provision of tangible reminders is, of course, effected by such devices as amulets, talismans, and medicine bundles, by special ornaments and uniforms, and by public symbols (like the cross). By such means as these, the survival of a resynthesis achieved under dissociation can be extended for a long period of time, perhaps indefinitely, even with minimal reinforcement (by a schedule of rewards or punishments).

The anthropologist should, in his consideration of this process, recognize that, although it invokes a specialized, and in Western eyes exotic, psychological mechanism for the achievement of cognitive change which seems to be independent of prior learning, and therefore of culture, it is in fact closely dependent upon culture. The prelearning, of course, will in large measure be by the learning of traditional culture and of various personal attitudes toward it, and the techniques and content alike of the suggestions are similarly closely related to culture. Thus, despite the connotations of individualistic spontaneity, of pathology, or of radical innovation which these mechanisms of resynthesis have for team-minded Western readers, they should not be viewed as either extraordinary or as non-cultural. The ritual process, as described above, is a universal human phenomenon and indeed is not restricted to man; what man has done has been to institutionalize this process, to develop it into particular forms which are, in fact, different in detail in each society. One—but only one—way of institutionalizing the ritual process is to interpret and apply it with the context of a belief in supernatural beings.

CRITIQUE

11. Obsessive Acts and Religious Practices, *S. Freud*

As we have seen in the critiques of Chapter I, religious life can be closely observed without being accepted as sacred or even as worthy. In this excerpt, Sigmund Freud (1856–1939), "the father of psychoanalysis" asserts that religious ceremonies (ritual, sacraments) are best understood as a form of a collective obsessional neurosis. The justification that believers give for participating in religious ceremonies, he argues, is a rationalization that does not reveal the true motives for these acts. He compares the resemblances between religious ceremonial acts common in the West and his clinical data of neurotics addicted to obsessive acts, and then suggests that both kinds of repetitive acts are motivated by repression of instincts. They are seen as protective measures to avoid anticipated punishment, expressing unconscious convictions of guilt. In what ways do the neurotic's obsessive acts and the believer's ceremonial acts resemble each other? Does Freud mention any differences in form or motivation? Do you think he has justification for calling neurosis "a private religious system," and religion "a universal obsessional neurosis"?

From "Obsessive Actions and Religious Practices" in *The Standard Edition of the Complete Psychological Works of Sigmund Freud,* Vol. IX, rev. and ed. James Strachey and *The Collected Papers of Sigmund Freud,* Vol. II, ed. Ernest Jones, M. D. (London: The Hogarth Press and The Institute of Psycho-Analysis and New York: Basic Books, Inc., Publishers, 1959), pp. 117–27. By permission of Sigmund Freud Copyrights Ltd., The Institute of Psycho-Analysis, The Hogarth Press Ltd., and Basic Books, Inc., Publishers.

Which readings in this section seem vulnerable to this interpretation, and to what degree are they vulnerable? Is Freud writing about what might *be true of* some *religion, or about what* is *true of* all *religion?*

I am certainly not the first person to have been struck by the resemblance between what are called obsessive actions in sufferers from nervous affections and the observances by means of which believers give expression to their piety. The term "ceremonial," which has been applied to some of these obsessive actions, is evidence of this. The resemblance, however, seems to me to be more than a superficial one, so that an insight into the origin of neurotic ceremonial may embolden us to draw inferences by analogy about the psychological processes of religious life.

People who carry out obsessive actions or ceremonials belong to the same class as those who suffer from obsessive thinking, obsessive ideas, obsessive impulses and the like. Taken together, these form a particular clinical entity, to which the name of "obsessional neurosis" ["*Zwangsneurose*"] is customarily applied.[1] But one should not attempt to deduce the character of the illness from its name; for, strictly speaking, other kinds of morbid mental phenomena have an equal claim to possessing what are spoken of as "obsessional" characteristics. In place of a definition we must for the time being be content with obtaining a detailed knowledge of these states, since we have not yet been able to arrive at a criterion of obsessional neuroses; it probably lies very deep, although we seem to sense its presence everywhere in the manifstations of the illness.

Neurotic ceremonials consist in making small adjustments to particular everyday actions, small additions or restrictions or arrangements, which have always to be carried out in the same, or in a methodically varied, manner. These activities give the impression of being mere formalities, and they seem quite meaningless to us. Nor do they appear otherwise to the patient himself; yet he is incapable of giving them up, for any deviation from the ceremonial is visited by intolerable anxiety, which obliges him at once to make his omission good. Just as trivial as the ceremonial actions themselves are the occasions and activities which are embellished, encumbered and in any case prolonged by the ceremonial—for instance, dressing and undressing, going to bed or satisfying bodily needs. The performance of a ceremonial can be described by replacing it, as it were, by a series of unwritten laws. For instance, to take the case of the bed ceremonial: the chair must stand in a particular place beside the bed; the clothes must lie upon it folded in a particular order; the blanket must be tucked in at the bottom and the sheet smoothed out; the pillows must be arranged in such and such a manner, and the subject's own body must lie in a precisely defined position. Only after all this may he go to sleep. Thus in slight cases the ceremonial seems to be no more than an exaggeration of an orderly procedure that is customary and justifiable; but the special conscientiousness with which it is carried out and the anxiety which follows upon its neglect stamp the ceremonial as a "sacred act." Any interruption of it is for the most part badly tolerated, and the presence of other people during its performance is almost always ruled out.

Any activities whatever may become obsessive actions in the wider sense of the term if they are elaborated by small additions or given a rhythmic character by means of pauses and repetitions. We shall not expect to find a sharp distinction between "ceremonials" and "obsessive actions." As a rule obsessive actions have grown out of ceremonials. Besides these two, prohibitions and hindrances (abulias) make up the content of the disorder; these, in fact, only continue the work of the obsessive actions, inasmuch as some things are completely forbidden to the patient and others only allowed subject to his following a prescribed ceremonial.

It is remarkable that both compulsions and prohibitions (having to do something and having *not* to do something) apply in the first instance only to the subject's solitary activities and for a long time leave his social behaviour unaffected. Sufferers from this illness are consequently able to treat their affliction as a private matter and keep it concealed for many years. And, indeed, many more people suffer from these forms of obsessional neurosis than doctors hear of. For many sufferers, too, concealment is made easier from the fact that they are quite well able to fulfil their social duties during a part of the day, once they have devoted a number of hours to their secret doings, hidden from view like Mélusine.[2]

It is easy to see where the resemblances lie between neurotic ceremonials and the sacred acts of religious ritual: in the qualms of conscience brought on by their neglect, in their complete isolation from all other actions (shown in the prohibition against interruption) and in the conscientiousness with which they are carried out in every detail. But the differences are equally obvious, and a few of them are so glaring that they make the comparison a sacrilege: the greater individual variability of [neurotic] ceremonial actions in contrast to the stereotyped character of rituals (prayer, turning to the East, etc.), their private nature as opposed to the public and communal character of religious observances, above all, however, the fact that, while the minutiae of religious ceremonial are full of significance and have a symbolic meaning, those of neurotics seem foolish and senseless. In this respect an obsessional neurosis presents a travesty, half comic and half tragic, of a private religion. But it is precisely this sharpest difference between neurotic and religious ceremonial which disappears when, with the help of the psycho-analytic technique of investigation, one penetrates to the true meaning of obsessive actions.[3] In the course of such an investigation the appearance which obsessive actions afford of being foolish and senseless is completely effaced, and the reason for their having that appearance is explained. It is found that the obsessive actions are perfectly significant in every detail, that they serve important interests of the personality and that they give expression to experiences that are still operative and to thoughts that are cathected with affect. They do this in two ways, either by direct or by symbolic representation; and they are consequently to be interpreted either historically or symbolically.

I must give a few examples to illustrate my point. Those who are familiar with the findings of psycho-analytic investigation into the psycho-neuroses will not be surprised to learn that what is being represented in obsessive actions or in ceremonials is derived from the most intimate, and for the most part from the sexual, experiences of the patient.

(*a*) A girl whom I was able to observe was under a compulsion to rinse round her wash-basin several times after washing. The significance of this ceremonial action lay in the proverbial saying: "Don't throw away dirty water till you have clean." Her action was intended to give a warning to her sister, of whom she was very fond, and to restrain her from getting divorced from her unsatisfactory husband until she had established a relationship with a better man.

(*b*) A woman who was living apart from her husband was subject to a compulsion, whenever she ate anything, to leave what was the best of it behind: for example, she would only take the outside of a piece of roast meat. This renunciation was explained by the date of its origin. It appeared on the day after she had refused marital relations with her husband—that is to say, after she had given up what was the best.

(*c*) The same patient could only sit on one particular chair and could only get up from it with difficulty. In regard to certain details of her married life, the chair symbolized her husband, to whom she remained faithful. She found an explanation of her compulsion in this sentence: "It is so hard to part from anything (a husband, a chair) upon which one has once settled."

(*d*) Over a period of time she used to repeat an especially noticeable and senseless obsessive action. She would run out of her room into another room in the middle of which there was a table. She would straighten the table-cloth on it in a particular manner and ring for the housemaid. The latter had to come up to the table, and the patient would then dismiss her on some indifferent errand. In the attempts to explain this compulsion, it occurred to her that at one place on the table-cloth there was a stain, and that she always arranged the cloth in such a way that the housemaid was bound to see the stain. The whole scene proved to be a reproduction of an experience in her married life which had later on given her thoughts a problem to solve. On the wedding-night her husband had met with a not unusual mishap. He found himself impotent, and "many times in the course of the night he came hurrying from his room into hers" to try once more whether he could succeed. In the morning he said he would feel ashamed in front of the hotel housemaid who made the beds, and he took a bottle of red ink and poured its contents over the sheet; but he did it so clumsily that the red stain came in a place that was very unsuitable for his purpose. With her obsessive action, therefore, she was representing the wedding-night. 'Bed and board'[4] between them make up marriage.

(*e*) Another compulsion which she started—of writing down the number of every bank-note before parting with it—had also to be interpreted historically. At a time when she was still intending to leave her husband if she could find another more trustworthy man, she allowed herself to receive advances from a man whom she met at a watering-place, but she was in doubt as to whether his intentions were serious. One day, being short of small change, she asked him to change a five-kronen[5] piece for her. He did so, pocketed the large coin and declared with a gallant air that he would never part with it, since it had passed through her hands. At their later meetings she was frequently tempted to challenge him to show her the five-kronen piece, as though she wanted to convince herself that she could believe in his intentions. But she refrained, for the good reason that it is impossible to distinguish between coins of the same value. Thus her doubt remained unresolved; and it left her with the compulsion to write down the number of each bank-note, by which it *can* be distinguished from all others of the same value.[6]

These few examples, selected from the great number I have met with, are merely intended to illustrate my assertion that in obsessive actions everything has its meaning and can be interpreted. The same is true of ceremonials in the strict sense, only that the evidence for this would require a more circumstantial presentation. I am quite aware of how far our explanations of obsessive actions are apparently taking us from the sphere of religious thought.

It is one of the conditions of the illness that the person who is obeying a compulsion carries it out without understanding its meaning—or at any rate its chief meaning. It is only thanks to the efforts of psycho-analytic treatment that he becomes conscious of the meaning of his obsessive action and, with it, of the motives that are impelling him to it. We express this important fact by saying that the obsessive action serves to express *unconscious* motives and ideas. In this, we seem to find a further departure from religious practices; but we must remember that as a rule the ordinary pious individual, too, performs a ceremonial without concerning himself with its significance, although priests and scientific investigators may be familiar with the—mostly symbolic—meaning of the ritual. In all believers, however, the motives which impel them to religious practices are unknown to them or are represented in consciousness by others which are advanced in their place.

Analysis of obsessive actions has already given us some sort of an insight into their causes and into the chain of motives which bring them into effect. We may say that the sufferer from compulsions and prohibitions behaves as if he were dominated by a sense of guilt, of which, however, he knows nothing, so that we must call it an unconscious sense of guilt, in spite of the apparent contradiction in terms.[7] This sense of guilt has its source in certain early mental events, but it is constantly being revived by renewed temptations which arise whenever there is a contemporary provocation. Moreover, it occasions a lurking sense of expectant anxiety, an expectation of misfortune, which is linked, through the idea of punishment, with the internal perception of the temptation. When the ceremonial is first being constructed, the patient is still conscious that he must do this or that lest some ill should befall, and as a rule the nature of the ill that is to be expected is still known to his consciousness. But what is already hidden from him is the connection—which is always demonstrable—between the occasion on which this expectant anxiety arises and the danger which it conjures up. Thus a ceremonial starts as an *action for defence* or *insurance, a protective measure.*

The sense of guilt of obsessional neurotics finds its counterpart in the protestations of pious people that they know that at heart they are miserable sinners; and the pious observances (such as prayers, invocations, etc.,) with which such people preface every daily act, and in especial every unusual undertaking, seem to have the value of defensive or protective measures.

A deeper insight into the mechanism of obsessional neurosis is gained if we take into account the primary fact which lies at the bottom of it. This is always *the repression of an instinctual impulse*[8] (a component of the sexual instinct) which was present in the subject's constitution and which was allowed to find expression for a while during his childhood but later succumbed to suppression. In the course of the repression of this instinct a special *conscientiousness* is created which is directed against the instinct's aims; but this psychical reaction-formation feels insecure and constantly threatened by the instinct which is lurking in the unconscious. The influence of the repressed instinct is felt as a temptation, and during the process of repression itself anxiety is generated, which gains control over the future in the form of *expectant* anxiety. The process of repression which leads to obsessional neurosis must be considered as one which is only partly successful and which increasingly threatens to fail. It may thus be compared to an unending conflict; fresh psychical efforts are continually required to counterbalance the forward pressure of the instinct.[9] Thus the ceremonial and obsessive actions arise partly as a defence against the temptation and partly as a protection against the ill which is expected. Against the temptation the protective measures seem soon to become inadequate; then the prohibitions come into play, with the purpose of keeping at a distance situations that give rise to temptation. Prohibitions take the place of obsessive actions, it will be seen, just as a phobia is designed to avert a hysterical attack. Again, a ceremonial represents the sum of the conditions subject to which something that is not yet absolutely forbidden is permitted, just as the Church's marriage ceremony signifies for the believer a sanctioning of sexual enjoyment which would otherwise be sinful. A further characteristic of obsessional neurosis, as of all similar affections, is that its manifestations (its symptoms, including the obsessive actions) fulfil the condition of being a compromise between the warring forces of the mind. They thus always reproduce something of the pleasure which they are designed to prevent; they serve the repressed instinct no less than the agencies which are repressing it. As the illness progresses, indeed, actions which were originally mostly concerned with maintaining the defence come to approximate more and more to the proscribed actions through which the instinct was able to find expression in childhood.

Some features of this state of affairs may be seen in the sphere of religious life as well. The formation of a religion, too, seems to be based on the suppression, the renunciation, of certain instinctual impulses. These impulses, however, are not, as in the neuroses, exclusively components of the sexual instinct; they are self-seeking, socially harmful instincts, though, even so, they are usually not without a sexual component. A sense of guilt following upon continual temptation and an expectant anxiety in the form of fear of divine punishment have, after all, been familiar to us in the field of religion longer than in that of neurosis. Perhaps because of the admixture of sexual components, perhaps because of some general characteristics of the instincts, the suppression of instinct proves to be an inadequate and interminable process in religious life also. Indeed, complete backslidings into sin are more common among pious people than among neurotics and these give rise to a new form of religious activity, namely acts of penance, which have their counterpart in obsessional neurosis.

We have noted as a curious and derogatory characteristic of obsessional neurosis that its ceremonials are concerned with the small actions of daily life and are expressed in foolish regulations and restrictions in connection with them. We cannot understand this remarkable feature of the clinical picture until we have realized that the mechanism of psychical *displacement,* which was first discovered by me in the construction of dreams,[10] dominates the mental processes of obsessional neurosis. It is already clear from the few examples of obsessive actions given above that their symbolism and the detail of their execution are brought about by a displacement from the actual, important thing on to a small one which takes its place—for instance, from a husband on to a chair.[11] It is this tendency to displacement which progressively changes the clinical picture and eventually succeeds in turning what is apparently the most trivial matter into something of the utmost importance and urgency. It cannot be denied that in the religious field as well there is a similar tendency to a displacement of psychical values, and in the same direction, so that the petty ceremonials of religious practice gradually become the essential thing and push aside the underlying thoughts. That is why religions are subject to reforms which work retroactively and aim at a re-establishment of the original balance of values.

The character of compromise which obsessive actions possess in their capacity as neurotic symptoms is the character least easily detected in corresponding religious observances. Yet here, too, one is reminded of this feature of neuroses when one remembers how commonly all the acts which religion forbits—the expressions of the instincts it has suppressed—are committed precisely in the name of, and ostensibly for the sake of, religion.

In view of these similarities and analogies one might venture to regard obsessional neurosis as a pathological counterpart of the formation of a religion, and to describe that neurosis as an individual religiosity and religion as a universal obsessional neurosis. The most essential similarity would reside in the underlying renunciation of the activation of instincts that are constitutionally present; and the chief difference would lie in the nature of those instincts, which in the neurosis are exclusively sexual in their origin, while in religion they spring from egoistic sources.

A progressive renunciation of constitutional instincts, whose activation might afford the ego primary pleasure, appears to be one of the foundations of the development of human civilization.[12] Some part of this instinctual repression is effected by its religions, in that they require the individual to sacrifice his instinctual pleasure to the Deity: "Vengeance is mine, saith the Lord." In the development of the ancient religions one seems to discern that many things which mankind had renounced as 'iniquities' had been surrendered to the Deity and were still permitted in his name, so that the handing over to him of bad and socially harmful instincts was the means by which man freed himself from their domination. For this reason, it is surely no accident that all the attributes of man, along with the misdeeds that follow from them, were to an unlimited amount ascribed to the ancient gods. Nor is it a contradiction of this that nevertheless man was not permitted to justify his own iniquities by appealing to divine example.

NOTES

1. See Löwenfeld (1904). [According to that author (Die psychischen Zwang-serscheinungen, Wiesbaden, p. 8) the term *"Zwangsvorstellung"* ("obses-sional idea" or simply "obsession") was introduced by Krafft-Ebing in 1867. The concept (and the term) "obsessional neurosis" originated (on the same authority, ibid., 296 and 487) from Freud himself. His first published use of it was in his first paper on anxiety neurosis (1895b).]*

2. [A beautiful woman in mediaeval legend, who led a secret existence as a water-nymph.]

3. See the collection of my shorter papers on the theory of the neuroses published in 1906 [*Standard Ed.* 3.]

4. [In German *"Tisch und Bett"* ("table and bed"). Cf. a paper on fairy tales in dreams (1913d), *Standard Ed.*, **12**, 282, footnote 3.]

5. [Equivalent at that time to four shillings or a dollar.]

6. [Freud discussed this case again at considerable length in Lecture XVII of his *Introductory Lectures* (1916–17).]

7. [The German word used here for "sense of guilt" is *"Schuldbewusstsein,"* literally "consciousness of guilt"—This seems to be the earliest explicit appearance of the "unconscious sense of guilt" which was to play such an important part in Freud's later writings—e.g. at the beginning of the last chapter of *The Ego and the Id* (1923b). The way had been prepared for the notion, however, very much earlier, in Section II of the first paper on "The Neuro-Psychoses of Defence" (1894a).]

8. [*"Triebregung."* This appears to be Freud's first published use of what was to be one of his most used terms.]

9. [This passage foreshadows the concept of "anticathexis," which is developed at length in Section IV of the paper on "The Unconscious" (1915e), *Standard Ed.*, **14**, 180 ff.]

---

* The bracketed material is in the Strachey edition.

10. See *The Interpretation of Dreams* (1900a), Chapter VI, Section B [*Standard Ed.*, **4,** 305 ff.].
11. [Freud had already described this mechanism in his book on jokes (1905c), near the end of Section 11 of Chapter II. He often recurred to the point— for instance, in the "Rat Man" analysis (1909d), *Standard Ed.*, **10,** 241, and in the metapsychological paper on repression (1915d), ibid., **14,** 157.]
12. [This idea was expanded by Freud in the paper on sexual ethics written about a year later (1908d), p .186 ff. below.]

12. The Biological Function
of Myth,
J. Campbell

> *Joseph Campbell is an American scholar whose field of interest is symbolism, myth, and world literature. In this excerpt from his work, he directs our attention to the uniformity of mythical themes around the world. He seeks not only to describe but also to explain this uniformity. Although his treatment of myth is sympathetic, in effect it constitutes a serious challenge to this type of religion as ultimate. He makes use of some striking metaphors in order to portray what he believes is the function of mythology: Mythology has a "biological function"; society, with its myths, is a kind of "second womb"; myths function like marsupial pouches; and "myth is everywhere the womb of man's specifically human birth." What does he mean by such assertions? Does man have to pay a price ("misbirth") for living in the "second womb" of mythology? What does Campbell think of the doctrine of rebirth in Christianity?*

How mythology functions, why it is generated and required by the human species, why it is everywhere essentially the same, and why the rational destruction of it conduces to puerility, become known the moment one abandons the historical method of tracing secondary origins and adopts the biological view (characteristic of the medical art of psychoanalysis), which considers the primary organism itself, this universal carrier and fashioner of history, the human body. As Róheim states in his brilliant monograph *The Origin and Function of Culture:*

> The outstanding difference between man and his animal brethren consists in the infantile morphological characters of human beings, in the prolongation of infancy. This prolonged infancy explains the traumatic

From *Psychoanalysis and Culture* by George B. Wilbur and Warner Muensterberger, eds. Copyright 1965 by International Universities Press, Inc.

character of sexual experiences which do not produce the like effect in our simian brethren or cousins, and the existence of the Œdipus Complex itself which is partly a conflict between archaic and recent love objects. Finally, the defence mechanisms themselves owe their existence to the fact that our Soma (Ego) is even more retarded than the Germa (Id) and hence the immature Ego evolves defence mechanisms as a protection against libidinal quantities which it is not prepared to deal with.[1]

"Man," as Adolf Portmann of Basel vividly phrases it, "is the incomplete creature whose style of life is the historical process determined by a tradition."[2] He is congenitally dependent on society and society, commensurably, is both oriented to and derived from the distinctive psychosomatic structure of man. This structure, furthermore, is rooted not in any local landscape, with its economic-political potentials, but in the germa of a widely distributed biological species. Whether on the ice of Baffin Land or in the jungles of Brazil, building temples in Siam or cafés in Paris, "civilization," as Dr. Róheim shows, "originates in delayed infancy and its function is security. It is a huge network of more or less successful attempts to protect mankind against the danger of object-loss, the colossal efforts made by a baby who is afraid of being left alone in the dark."[3] In such a context, the symbolical potentialities of the various environments are at least as important as the economic; symbolism, the protection of the psyche, no less necessary than the nourishment of the soma. Society, as a fostering organ, is thus a kind of exterior "second womb," wherein the postnatal stages of man's long gestation—much longer than that of any other placental—are supported and defended.

One thinks of the marsupial pouch, likewise auxiliary to a foetal development that overreaches the intrauterine possibilities of the species. The young of the kangaroo, for example, born after a gestation period of but three weeks, measure an inch in length and are entirely naked and blind; their hind limbs are undeveloped, but the forelimbs are robust with claws. William King Gregory, of the American Museum of Natural History, describes the climbing of these little creatures, by means of their sturdy forelimbs, up the mother's belly, immediately upon birth, and into her pouch, where they reach for the teats, one of which each eventually seizes. The tip of the teat then expands within the mouth, so that the young cannot be released. "Thus the marsupials," Gregory summarizes, "specialized in the early and brief internal development of the embryo, which depends for food chiefly upon its own yolk-sack and which completes its development after birth while attached to the teat. The higher or placental mammals gave the young a longer and better uterine development and a more flexible system of nursing, with greater maternal responsibility."[4]

The marsupials (kangaroo, bandicoot, wombat, oppossum, etc.) represent an intermediate stage between monotremes (the duck-billed platypus, spiny anteater of Australia, etc.), whose progeny, like those of reptiles, are born from eggs, and placentals (mice, antelopes leopards, gorillas, etc.), whose young appear only after a comparatively long gestation period within the mother (made possible by the placenta) and at birth are almost ready for life. Man, biologically, is a placental. The period of gestation, however, has become again inadequate—indeed, even less adequate than that of the marsupials; for instead of the mere few months spent by the young kangaroo in the auxiliary womb of its mother's' pouch, the infant *Homo sapiens* requires years before it can forage for its food, and as many as twenty before it looks and behaves like an adult.

George Bernard Shaw played on this anomaly in his biological fantasy *Back to Methuselah,* where he viewed man, in Nietzsche's manner, as a bridge to the superman. Looking forward to the year 31,920 A.D., he showed us the birth from a huge egg of a pretty girl, who, in the twentieth century, would have been thought to be about seventeen.[5] She had been growing within the egg for two years; the first nine months, like the nine of the present gestation period of the human embryo, recapitulated the biological evolution of man; the remaining fifteen then matured the organism, briefly but securely, to the condition of the young adult. Four years more, spent among youthful playmates in the sort of childhood that we remain in today until seventy, would terminate when her mind changed and the young woman, tiring suddenly of play, became wise and fit for the wielding of such power as today, in the hands of children, is threatening to wreck the world.

Human adulthood is not achieved until the twenties: Shaw put it in the seventies: not a few look ahead to Purgatory. Meanwhile, society is what takes the place of the Shavian egg.

Róheim has indicated the problem of man-growing-up, no matter where—defense against libindinal quantities with which the immature ego is not prepared to deal;[6] and he has analyzed the curious "symbiotic mode of mastering reality,"[7] which is the very fashioner, the master builder, of all human societies. "It is the nature of our species," he writes, "to master reality on a libidinal basis and we create a society, an environment in which this and only this is possible."[8] "The psyche as we know it, is formed by the introjection of primary objects (super-ego) and the first contact with environment (ego). Society itself is knitted together by projection of these primary introjected objects or concepts followed by a series of subsequent introjections and projections."[9] This tight-knitting of defensive fantasy and external reality is what builds the second womb, the marsupial pouch that we call society. Hence, though man's environment greatly varies in the corners of the planet, there is a marvelous monotony about his ritual forms. Local styles of the century, nation, race, or social class obviously differ; yet what James Joyce calls the "grave and constant in human sufferings,"[10] remains truly constant and grave. It arrests the mind, everywhere, in the rituals of birth, adolescence, marriage, death, installation and initiation, uniting it with the mysteries of eternal recurrence and of man's psychosomatic maturation. The individual grows up not only as a member of a certain social group, but as a human being.

THE IMAGE OF A SECOND BIRTH

Rites, then, together with the mythologies that support them, constitute the second womb, the matrix of the postnatal gestation of the placental

Homo sapiens. This fact, moreover, has been known to the pedagogues of the race, certainly since the period of the Upanishads, and probably since that of the Aurignacian caves. In the Mundaka Upanishad we read, for example: "There are two knowledges to be known—as indeed the knowers of Brahman are wont to say: a higher and also a lower. Of these, the lower is the Rig Veda, the Yajur Veda, the Sama Veda, the Atharva Veda, Pronunciation, Ritual, Grammar, Definition, Metrics, and Astrology. The higher is that whereby the Imperishable is apprehended."[11] "Those abiding in the midst of ignorance, self-wise, thinking themselves learned, hard smitten, go around deluded, like blind men led by one who is himself blind. Thinking sacrifice and merit the chiefest thing, naught better do they know. . . . But they who practise austerity and faith in the forest, the peaceful knowers who live on alms, depart passionless through the door of the sun, to where is that immortal Person, even the imperishable Spirit."[12]

In India the objective is to be *born* from the womb of myth, not to remain in it, and the one who has attained to this "second birth" is truly the "twice born," freed from the pedagogical devices of society, the lures and threats of myth, the local *mores,* the usual hopes of benefits and rewards. He is truly "free" (*mukti*), "released while living" (*jivan mukti*) ; he is that reposeful "superman" who is man perfected—though in our kindergarten of libidinous misapprehensions he moves like a being from another sphere.

The same idea of the "second birth" is certainly basic to Christianity also, where it is symbolized in baptism. "Except a man be born of water and of the spirit, he cannot enter into the kingdom of God. That which is born of the flesh is flesh; and that which is born of the Spirit is spirit."[13] One could ask for no more vivid rendition of the doctrine of the two wombs: the womb of the mammal and the womb of perfected man.

Within the Christian Church, however, there has been a historically successful tendency to anathematize the obvious implications of this idea, and the result has been a general obscuration of the fact that regeneration means going beyond, not remaining within, the confines of mythology. Whereas in the Orient—India, Tibet, China, Japan, Indo-China, and Indonesia—everyone is expected, at least in his final incarnation, to leave the womb of myth, to pass through the sun-door and stand beyond the gods, in the West—or at least throughout the greater part of the Judaeo-Christian–Mohammedan development—God remains the Father, and none can step beyond Him. This accounts, perhaps, for the great distinction between the manly piety of the Orient and the infantile of the recent Occident. In the lands of the truly "twice born" man is finally superior to the gods, whereas in the West even the saint is required to remain within the body of the Church, and the "second birth" is read rather as being born *into* the Church than born out of it. The historical result was a shattering of this particular marsupial pouch in the fifteenth century.

There is no need to multiply examples of the rebirth motif in the philosophies and religious rites of the civilized world. The Neoplatonic and Taoist philosophies, the Greek Mysteries, the myths and rites of Phoenicia, Mesopotamia, and Egypt, as well as those of the Celts and Germans,

Aztecs and Mayas, abound in applications of the idea. Nor is it less prominent in the myths and rites of the primitive peoples of the world. "Death and rebirth," declares Róheim, "are the typical contents of all initiation rites."[14]

Among the Keraki of New Guinea bull-roarers play a prominent role in the ceremonies of initiation. The boys are made to sit with their eyes covered by the older men and then the bull-roarers begin to sound. The boys think they are hearing the voice of the presiding crocodile-deity of the ritual; the sound comes nearer, at though the monster were approaching to swallow them, and when it is directly over their heads, the old men's hands are removed and the boys see the bull-roarers.[15] Thus they become aware, abruptly, of the source of the sound that throughout their childhood had been thought to be the voice of a living monster.

Such sudden awakenings are characteristic of the tradition of initiation everywhere. What for the child were disciplinary terrors become the symbolic implements of the adult who knows. Nevertheless, the result is not that the symbols are understood as frauds; on the contrary, the bull-roarers of the Keraki receive food offerings.[16] They are divinities: the guardians of the Way of life. "At the creation of the world," said a medicine man of the Pawnee of Kansas and Nebraska, "it was arranged that there should be lesser powers. Tirawaatius, the mighty power, could not come near to man, could not be seen or felt by him, therefore lesser powers were permitted. They were to mediate between man and Tirawa."[17] The myths and paraphernalia of the rites of passage represent such powers, and so are informed with the force of the source, support, and end of existence.

The fact that some of the burials of the Mousterian cave men include implements and joints of meat suggests that the idea of regeneration beyond the veil of life must have been entertained some fifty thousand years B.C. Later paleolithic burials with the corpse in the crouch-position of the foetus in the womb give point to the same theme by stressing the idea of a second birth. And, finally, the picture of a dancing, masked medicine man in the Aurignacian cave of the Trois Fréres, Arlège, France, suggests that there must have been, fifteen thousand years ago, initiates aware of the force and meaning of the symbols. It would perhaps be going too far to suggest that in any primitive society pedagogues, or mystagogues, can have existed whose reading of the rebirth idea drove as far as that of the Hindus; nevertheless, it cannot be denied that in primitive mythologies and rites we find the image of the sun-door, the clashing rocks, death and resurrection, the Incarnation, the sacred marriage and father atonement, employed not haphazardly but in the same relationships as in the myths of the higher cultures.[18]

> The actual unity of folklore represents on the popular level [declared Ananda K. Coomaraswamy] precisely what the orthodoxy of an élite represents in a relatively learned environment. The relation between the popular and the learned metaphysics is, moreover, analogous to and partly identical with that of the lesser to the greater mysteries. To a very large extent both employ one and the same symbols, which are

taken more literally in the one case and in the other understood parabolically: for example, the "giants" and "heroes" of popular legend are the titans and gods of the more learned mythology, the seven-league boots of the hero correspond to the strides of an Agni or a Buddha, and "Tom Thumb" is no other than the Son whom Eckhart describes as "small, but so puissant." *So long as the material of folklore is transmitted, so long is the ground available on which the superstructure of full initiatory understanding can be built.*[19]

Whether, in any given culture, the individual is enabled to be really born again or required to remain spiritually foetal until released from purgatory, myth is everywhere the womb of man's specifically human birth: the long-tried, the tested matrix within which the unfinished being is brought to maturity; simultaneously protecting the growing ego against libidinal quantities which it is not prepared to deal with and furnishing it with the necessary foods and saps for its normal, harmonious unfoldment. Mythology fosters a balanced intuitive and instinctive, as well as rational, ontogenesis, and throughout the domain of the species the morphology of this peculiar spiritual organ of *Homo sapiens* is no less constant than that of the well-known, readily recognizable human physique itself.

THE ANXIETY OF THE MISSION

Misbirth is possible from the mythological womb as well as from the physiological: there can be adhesions, malformations, arrestations, etc. We call them neuroses and psychoses. Hence we find today, after some five hundred years of the systematic dismemberment and rejection of the mythological organ of our species, all the sad young men, for whom life is a problem. Mythology leads the libido into ego-syntonic channels, whereas neurosis (to cite, once again, Géza Róheim) "separates the individual from his fellows and connects him with his own infantile images."[20] Psychoanalysis and certain movements in contemporary art and letters represent an effort to restore the biologically necessary spiritual organ. Blake, for example, Goethe and Emerson, saw the need for it. Their effort was to restore the poet to his traditional function of seer and mystagogue of the regenerative vision. James Joyce has supplied the whole blueprint. The morphology of the organ will remain the same as ever, but the materials of which it is composed and the functions served will have to be those of the new world: the materials of the machine age and the functions of the world society that is today in its throes of birth—as myth.

NOTES

1. Géza Róheim, *The Origin and Function of Culture*, p. 17.
2. Adolf Portmann, "Das Ursprungsproblem," *Eranos-Jahrbuch 1947* (Zurich: Rhein Verlag, 1948), p. 27.
3. Róheim, *The Origin and Function of Culture*, p. 100.
4. William King Gregory, "Marsupialia," *Encyclopaedia Britannica*, 14th edition, XIV: 975–76.

5. George Bernard Shaw, *Back to Methuselah* (New York: Brentano's, 1921), pp. 235 ff.
6. Róheim, *The Origin and Function of Culture*, p. 17.
7. *Ibid.*, p. 81.
8. *Ibid.*
9. *Ibid.*, p. 82.
10. James Joyce, *A Portrait of the Artist as a Young Man* (New York: The Viking Press, 1964 ed.), p. 204.
11. *Mundaka Upanisad* 1.1. 4–6. Translation by Robert Ernest Hume, *The Thirteen Principal Upanishads* (London: Oxford University Press, 1921), pp. 366–67.
12. *Ibid.*, 1.2. 8–11, in Hume. *op. cit.*, pp. 368–69.
13. John 3:5–6
14. Géza Róheim, *The Eternal Ones of the Dream* (New York: International Universities Press, 1945), p. 116.
15. Richard Thurnwald, "Primitive Initiations- und Wiedergeburtsriten," *Eranos-Jahrbuch 1939* (Zurich: Rhein-Verlag, 1940), pp. 364–66. This entire volume, by the way, should be consulted by anyone doubting the universality of the rebirth idea.
16. *Ibid.*, p. 369.
17. Alice C. Fletcher, *The Hako: A Pawnee Ceremony,* Twenty-second Annual Report, Bureau of Americancan Ethnology (Washington, D.C., 1904), Part 2, p. 27.
18. *Cf.* Jeff King, Maud Oakes, and Joseph Campbell, *Where the Two Came to Their Father: A Navaho War Ceremonial,* The Bollingen Series I (New York: Pantheon Books, 1943).
19. Ananda K. Coomaraswamy, "Primitive Mentality," *Figures of Speech or Figures of Thought* (London: Luzac, 1946), p. 220. The italics are Dr. Coomaraswamy's.
20. Róheim, *The Origin and Function of Culture*, p. 93.

13. The Ethics of Belief,
W. K. Clifford

As we noted in Chapter I, a religious type can be attacked not only on the ground of its social or psychological functioning but also on the ground of its philosophical adequacy. It is this sort of attack presented here by the Victorian intellectual, critic, and mathematician W. K. Clifford (1845–1879). An honest man, he asserts, will assent only to those claims that he can support by evidence and critical reason. Authority, ancient tradition, purity

From William K. Clifford, "The Ethics of Belief," in *Lectures and Essays,* Leslie Stiphen and Frederick Pollock eds. (New York: MacMillan and Co., 1886), pp. 342–49, 352–53.

of character, and degree of personal power are all subordinate to the above criteria. Note that this position is incompatible with a myth and ritual type as here conceived, for it insists that all claims must be supported by evidence which Smith (in selection 8) would describe as "profane." On whom is the duty for critical thought placed? Why does Clifford believe the duty of reason to be so important? How do you think Clifford would deal with assertions regarding the efficacy of Christian sacraments such as those found in readings 4, 5, and 9 above?

[N]o one man's belief is in any case a private matter which concerns himself alone. Our lives are guided by that general conception of the course of things which has been created by society for social purposes. Our words, our phrases, our forms and processes and modes of thought, are common property, fashioned and perfected from age to age; an heirloom which every succeeding generation inherits as a precious deposit and a sacred trust to be handed on to the next one, not unchanged but enlarged and purified, with some clear marks of its proper handiwork. Into this, for good or ill, is woven every belief of every man who has speech of his fellows. An awful privilege, and an awful responsibility, that we should help to create the world in which posterity will live. . . .

It is not only the leader of men, statesman, philosopher, or poet, that owes this bounden duty to mankind. Every rustic who delivers in the village alehouse his slow, infrequent sentences, may help to kill or keep alive the fatal superstitions which clog his race. Every hard-worked wife of an artisan may transmit to her children beliefs which shall knit society together, or rend it in pieces. No simplicity of mind, no obscurity of station, can escape the universal duty of questioning all that we believe.

It is true that this duty is a hard one, and the doubt which comes out of it is often a very bitter thing. It leaves us bare and powerless where we thought that we were safe and strong. To know all about anything is to know how to deal with it under all circumstances. We feel much happier and more secure when we think we know precisely what to do, no matter what happens, than when we have lost our way and do not know where to turn.* And if we have supposed ourselves to know all about anything, and to be capable of doing what is fit in regard to it, we naturally do not like to find that we are really ignorant and powerless, that we have to begin again at the beginning, and try to learn what the thing is and how it is to be dealt with—if indeed anything can be learnt about it. It is the sense of power attached to a sense of knowledge that makes men desirous of believing and afraid of doubting.

This sense of power is the highest and best of pleasures when the belief on which it is founded is a true belief, and has been fairly earned by investigation. For then we may justly feel that it is common property,

---

* This is also Wallace's point (reading 9), but Clifford sees it as the main problem to be overcome, whereas Wallace viewed it as one possible social stratagem.

and holds good for others as well as for ourselves. Then we may be glad, not that *I* have learned secrets by which I am safer and stronger, but that *we men* have got mastery over more of the world; and we shall be strong, not for ourselves, but in the name of Man and in his strength. But if the belief has been accepted on insufficient evidence, the pleasure is a stolen one. Not only does it deceive ourselves by giving us a sense of power which we do not really possess, but it is sinful,, because it is stolen in defiance of our duty to mankind. That duty is to guard ourselves from such beliefs as from a pestilence, which may shortly master our own body and then spread to the rest of the town. What would be thought of one who, for the sake of a sweet fruit, should deliberately run the risk of bringing a plague upon his family and his neighbours?

And, as in other such cases, it is not the risk only which has to be considered; for a bad action is always bad at the time when it is done, no matter what happens afterwards. Every time we let ourselves believe for unworthy reasons, we weaken our powers of self-control, of doubting, of judicially and fairly weighing evidence. We all suffer severely enough from the maintenance and support of false beliefs and the fatally wrong actions which they lead to, and the evil born when one such belief is entertained is great and wide. But a greater and wider evil arises when the credulous character is maintained and supported, when a habit of believing for unworthy reasons is fostered and made permanent. If I steal money from any person, there may be no harm done by the mere transfer of possession; he may not feel the loss, or it may prevent him from using the money badly. But I cannot help doing this great wrong towards Man, that I make myself dishonest. What hurts society is not that it should lose its property, but that it should become a den of thieves; for then it must cease to be society. This is why we ought not to do evil that good may come; for at any rate this great evil has come, that we have done evil and are made wicked thereby. In like manner, if I let myself believe anything on insufficient evidence, there may be no great harm done by the mere belief; it may be true after all, or I may never have occasion to exhibit it in outward acts. But I cannot help doing this great wrong towards Man, that I make myself credulous. The danger to society is not merely that it should believe wrong things, though that is great enough; but that it should become credulous, and lose the habit of testing things and inquiring into them; for then it must sink back into savagery.

The harm which is done by credulity in a man is not confined to the fostering of a credulous character in others, and consequent support of false beliefs. Habitual want of care about what I believe leads to habitual want of care in others about the truth of what is told to me. Men speak the truth to one another when each reveres the truth in his own mind and in the other's mind; but how shall my friend revere the truth in my mind when I myself am careless about it, when I believe things because I want to believe them, and because they are comforting and pleasant? Will he not learn to cry, "Peace," to me, when there is no peace? By such a course I shall surround myself with a thick atmosphere of falsehood and fraud, and in that I must live. It may matter little to me, in my cloud-castle of sweet illusions and darling lies; but it matters much to Man that I have made my neighbours ready to deceive. The credulous man is father to the liar and the cheat; he lives in the bosom of this his family, and it is no marvel if he should become even as they are. So closely are our duties knit together, that whoso shall keep the whole law, and yet offend in one point, he is guilty of all.

To sum up: it is wrong always, everywhere, and for any one, to believe anything upon insufficient evidence.

If a man, holding a belief which he was taught in childhood or persuaded of afterwards, keeps down and pushes away any doubts which arise about it in his mind, purposely avoids the reading of books and the company of men that call in question or discuss it, and regards as impious those questions which cannot easily be asked without disturbing it—the life of that man is one long sin against mankind.

If this judgment seems harsh when applied to those simple souls who have never known better, who have been brought up from the cradle with a horror of doubt, and taught that their eternal welfare depends on *what* they believe, then it leads to the very serious question, *Who hath made Israel to sin?*

It may be permitted me to fortify this judgment with the sentence of Milton[1]—

"A man may be a heretic in the truth; and if he believe things only because his pastor says so, or the assembly so determine, without knowing other reason, though his belief be true, yet the very truth he holds becomes his heresy."

And with this famous aphorism of Coleridge[2]—

"He who begins by loving Christianity better than Truth, will proceed by loving his own sect or Church better than Christianity, and end in loving himself better than all."

Inquiry into the evidence of a doctrine is not to be made once for all, and then taken as finally settled. It is never lawful to stifle a doubt; for either it can be honestly answered by means of the inquiry already made, or else it proves that the inquiry was not complete.

"But," says one, "I am a busy man; I have no time for the long course of study which would be necessary to make me in any degree a competent judge of certain questions, or even able to understand the nature of the arguments." Then he should have no time to believe.

THE WEIGHT OF AUTHORITY

Are we then to become universal sceptics, doubting everything, afraid always to put one foot before the other until we have personally tested the firmness of the road? Are we to deprive ourselves of the help and guidance of that vast body of knowledge which is daily growing upon the world, because neither we nor any other one person can possibly test a hundredth part of it by immediate experiment or observation, and because it would not be completely proved if we did? Shall we steal and tell lies because we have had no personal experience wide enough to justify the belief that it is wrong to do so?

There is no practical danger that such consequences will ever follow from scrupulous care and self-control in the matter of belief. Those men who have most nearly done their duty in this respect have found that certain great principles, and these most fitted for the guidance of life, have stood out more and more clearly in proportion to the care and honesty with which they were tested, and have acquired in this way a practical certainty. The beliefs about right and wrong which guide our actions in dealing with men in society, and the beliefs about physical nature which guide our actions in dealing with animate and inanimate bodies, these never suffer from investigation; they can take care of themselves, without being propped up by "acts of faith," the clamour of paid advocates, or the suppression of contrary evidence. Moreover there are many cases in which it is our duty to act upon probabilities, although the evidence is not such as to justify present belief; because it is precisely by such action, and by observation of its fruits, that evidence is got which may justify future belief. So that we have no reason to fear lest a habit of conscientious inquiry should paralyse the actions of our daily life.

But because it is not enough to say, "It is wrong to believe on unworthy evidence," without saying also what evidence is worthy, we shall now go on to inquire under what circumstances it is lawful to believe on the testimony of others; and then, further, we shall inquire more generally when and why we may believe that which goes beyond our own experience, or even beyond the experience of mankind.

In what cases, then, let us ask in the first place, is the testimony of a man unworthy of belief? He may say that which is untrue either knowingly or unknowingly. In the first case he is lying, and his moral character is to blame; in the second case he is ignorant or mistaken, and it is only his knowledge or his judgment which is in fault. In order that we may have the right to accept his testimony as ground for believing what he says, we must have reasonable grounds for trusting his *veracity,* that he is really trying to speak the truth so far as he knows it; his *knowledge,* that he has had opportunities of knowing the truth about this matter; and his *judgment,* that he has made proper use of those opportunities in coming to the conclusion which he affirms.

However plain and obvious these reasons may be, so that no man of ordinary intelligence, reflecting upon the matter, could fail to arrive at them, it is nevertheless true that a great many persons do habitually disregard them in weighing testimony. Of the two questions, equally important to the trustworthiness of a witness, "Is he dishonest?" and "May he be mistaken?" the majority of mankind are perfectly satisfied if *one* can, with some show of probability, be answered in the negative. The excellent moral character of a man is alleged as ground for accepting his statements about things which he cannot possibly have known. A Mohammedan, for example, will tell us that the character of his Prophet was so noble and majestic that it commands the reverence even of those who do not believe in his mission. So admirable was his moral teaching, so wisely put together the great social machine which he created, that his precepts have not only been accepted by a great portion of mankind, but have actually been obeyed. His institutions have on the one hand rescued the negro from savagery, and on the other hand have taught civilisation to the advancing West; and although the races which held the highest forms of his faith, and most fully embodied his mind and thought, have all been conquered and swept away by barbaric tribes, yet the history of their marvellous attainments remains as an imperishable glory to Islam. Are we to doubt the word of a man so great and so good? Can we suppose that this magnificent genius, this splendid moral hero, has lied to us about the most solemn and sacred matters? The testimony of Mohammed is clear, that there is but one God, and that he, Mohammed, is his Prophet; that if we believe in him we shall enjoy everlasting felicity, but that if we do not we shall be damned. This testimony rests on the most awful of foundations, the revelation of heaven itself; for was he not visited by the angel Gabriel, as he fasted and prayed in his desert cave, and allowed to enter into the blessed fields of Paradise? Surely God is God and Mohammed is the Prophet of God.

What should we answer to this Mussulman? First, no doubt, we should be tempted to take exception against his view of the character of the Prophet and the uniformly beneficial influence of Islam: before we could go with him altogether in these matters it might seem that we should have to forget many terrible things of which we have heard or read. But if we chose to grant him all these assumptions, for the sake of argument, and because it is difficult both for the faithful and for infidels to discuss them fairly and without passion, still we should have something to say which takes away the ground of his belief, and therefore shows that it is wrong to entertain it. Namely this: the character of Mohammed is excellent evidence that he was honest and spoke the truth so far as he knew it; but it is no evidence at all that he knew what the truth was....

To consider only one other such witness: the followers of the Buddha have at least as much right to appeal to individual and social experience in support of the authority of the Eastern saviour. The special mark of his religion, it is said, that in which it has never been surpassed, is the comfort and consolation which it gives to the sick and sorrowful, the tender sympathy with which it soothes and assuages all the natural griefs of men. And surely no triumph of social morality can be greater or nobler than that which has kept nearly half the human race from persecuting in the name of religion. If we are to trust the accounts of his early followers, he believed himself to have come upon earth with a divine and cosmic mission to set rolling the wheel of the law. Being a prince, he divested himself of his kingdom, and of his free will became acquainted with misery, that he might learn how to meet and subdue it. Could such a man speak falsely about solemn things? And as for his knowledge, was he not a man miraculous with powers more than man's? He was born of woman without the help of man; he rose into the air and was transfigured before his kinsmen; at last he went up bodily into heaven from the top of Adam's Peak. Is not his word to be believed in when he testifies of heavenly things?

If there were only he, and no other, with such claims! But there is Mohammed with his testimony; we cannot choose but listen to them both. The Prophet tells us that there is one God, and that we shall live for ever in joy or misery, according as we believe in the Prophet or not. The Buddha says that there is no God, and that we shall be annihilated by and by if we are good enough. Both cannot be infallibly inspired; one or other must have been the victim of a delusion, and thought he knew that which he really did not know. Who shall dare to say which? and how can we justify ourselves in believing that the other was not also deluded?

We are led, then, to these judgments following. The goodness and greatness of a man do not justify us in accepting a belief upon the warrant of his authority, unless there are reasonable grounds for supposing that he know the truth of what he was saying. And there can be no grounds for supposing that a man knows that which we, without ceasing to be men, could not be supposed to verify.

NOTES

1. *Areopagita.*
2. *Aids to Reflection.*

III

Living Harmoniously Through Conformity with the Cosmic Law

The correct manner of dealing with every life problem that arises, . . . , is indicated by the laws (dharma) of the caste (varna) to which one belongs, and of the particular stage-of-life (āśrama) that is proper to one's age. One is not free to choose; one belongs to a species—a family, guild and craft, a group, a denomination. And since this circumstance not only determines to the last detail the regulations for one's public and private conduct, but also represents (according to this all-inclusive and pervasive, unyielding pattern of integration) the real ideal of one's present natural character, one's concern as a judging and acting entity must be only to meet every life problem in a manner befitting the role one plays. Whereupon the two aspects of the temporal event—the subjective and the objective—will be joined exactly, and the individual eliminated as a third, intrusive factor. He will then bring into manifestation not the temporal accident of his own personality, but the vast, impersonal, cosmic law, and so will be, not a faulty, but a perfect glass: anonymous and self-effacing. For by the rigorous practice of prescribed virtues one actually can efface oneself, dissolving eventually the last quirk of impulse and personal resistance—thus gaining release from the little boundary of the personality and absorption in the boundlessness of universal being. Dharma is therefore fraught with power. It is the burning point of the whole present, past, and future, as well as the way through which to pass into the transcendental consciousness and bliss of the purest spiritual Self-existence. (From Heinrich Zimmer, Philosophies of India, *J. Campbell, ed., [New York: Meridian Books, 1957], pp. 152–53.)*

THE WAY OF BEING RELIGIOUS focused on in this chapter emphasizes social morality. It is epitomized in the statement: "Actions speak louder than words." As in the former two types of religious life, we find a transcendent reality from which all material things, thoughts, and actions have come; however, we will see—especially in the case of Chinese morality—this transcendent reality does not have to be regarded as a person. Rather it is a neuter Cosmic Law or Natural Order. Although the Chinese material refers to ancestral spirits in advocating the use of rites, the ancestors are not ultimate. Likewise, the material from the Hindu *Law of Manu* personifies somewhat the source of everything, but it is clear that this source is in every form of existence and is not another being. When human beings are ignorant of the Cosmic Law or the Principle of Life, or when they intentionally oppose the natural flow of the Natural Rhythm that brought the universe itself into existence, they hurt themselves and even destroy themselves. Thus, just as a person will drop to his death when he steps from a twentieth story window instead of taking the slow way down the elevator or the stairway, so when a person breaks the *natural* relationships between parents and children, men and women, teachers and students, people and animals, and (in some cases) lower and higher social-economic power groups in a community, human life will be in disharmony. Such disregard for the natural order will lead to an imbalanced social organism in which a relatively small group has all the benefits, or to such social evils as stealing, killing, adultery, and fear of other people.

Like the second way of being religious, there is a deep concern for developing a social community, and the principles for developing the sense that an individual realizes his highest potential through social responsibility are known and preserved by a special professional group. However, unlike the second way, which emphasized the unique power of sacramental actions and of conformity to the Divine models expressed in a myth, in the third way there is the assumption that the Cosmic Law is *by nature* already within the person and physical phenomena so that the means for attaining the highest spiritual joy is cultivating one's true nature as part of the social-physical organism (that is, the world). Every human act should expose a person's place in the eternal order of things. This is done by imitating the actions of the ancient seers who perceived the eternal principle in a former "golden age." Through persistent cultivation, one's true self matures and expresses itself spontaneously. Especially the leaders of society, by cultivating the eternal virtues, stimulate harmony and prosperity of a society.

Under the heading of advocacy we are including both ancient and contemporary expressions of daily living that express an eternal order. Our basic models come from the Confucian tradition in China and Japan (readings 1, 2, 7, and 8) and from the concern with *dharma* (law, truth, principle) in the orthodox Hindu tradition of India (readings 3 and 10). Another article (reading 9) is applicable to the religious traditions of India and the Far East. Nevertheless it is important to note the concern for ethical social obligation in Western religions (readings 4, 5, 6, and 12). In these latter cases we should recognize the merging of "this way of being religious" with that found in the last chapter in that the social responsibility is based on God's creation and self-revelation of His will. One Western representative who rejects a theistic basis for religion is also included (reading 11). The critiques focus on two central issues: (1) Is there really a universal eternal moral order? and (2) Are not the particular cultural claims for the transcendent nature of their traditional forms merely self-deceptions intended to legitimize inequalities in the status quo?

ADVOCACY

1. On *Li*
(Rites, Propriety, Rules of Decorum),
Hsün Tzu

> *One of the most famous Confucian thinkers is Hsün Tzu, who
> flourished between 298–238 B.C. His writings are collected in a
> book of thirty-two chapters called simply* Hsün Tzu. *Among
> the Confucians he is noted for his rational justification of social
> responsibility and his realistic view of human life and its goals. He
> emphasized education in proper social relationships through
> example of government officials, through art, social courtesies,
> and deference, and through ritual activity among the masses.
> The cultivation of righteousness as defined by the rules of
> conduct that were set by the Confucian literati was the means
> for living in harmony with the eternal order. (See reading 8
> for an explanation of the importance of* li *in the Chinese cultural
> tradition.) Note that the Chinese word* li *is translated in two
> different ways in the following except: as "rules of decorum,"
> in which individual and social conduct is emphasized, and as
> "rites," in which the focus is on social and private ritual.
> According to Hsün Tzu, does a concern with* li *eliminate deep
> personal experience? In what way do rites draw attention to
> "the most important things in life"? Do you agree that following
> prescribed rules of conduct allow many more people in society
> to satisfy their desires than when socially approved rules of
> conduct are broken?*

Whence do the rules of decorum arise? From the fact that men are born
with desires, and when these desires are not satisfied, men are bound to
pursue their satisfaction. When the pursuit is carried on unrestrained and
unlimited, there is bound to be contention. With contention comes chaos;
with chaos dissolution. The ancient kings disliked this chaos and set the
necessary limits by codifying rules of decorum and righteousness, so that
men's desires might be satisfied and their pursuit be gratified. In this way
it was made certain that desires were not frustrated by things, nor things
used up by desires. That these two should support each other and should
thrive together—this is whence the rules of decorum arise....

Rites (*li*) rest on three bases: Heaven and earth, which are the source
of all life; the ancestors, who are the source of the human race; sovereigns

---

From *Hsün Tzu: Basic Writings,* trans. Burton Watson, in *Sources of Chinese
Tradition,* ed. Wm. T. de Bary *et al.* (New York: Columbia University Press,
1960), pp. 122–24. Used by permission of the publisher.

and teachers, who are the source of government. If there were no Heaven and earth, where would life come from? If there were no ancestors, where would the offspring come from? If there were no sovereigns and teachers, where would government come from? Should any of the three be missing, either there would be no men or men would be without peace. Hence rites are to serve Heaven on high and earth below, and to honor the ancestors and elevate the sovereigns and teachers. Herein lies the three-fold basis of rites. . . .

In general, rites begin with primitive practices, attain cultured forms, and finally achieve beauty and felicity. When rites are at their best, men's emotions and sense of beauty are both fully expressed. When they are at the next level, either the emotion or the sense of beauty oversteps the other. When they are at still the next level, emotion reverts to the state of primitivity.

It is through rites that Heaven and earth are harmonious and sun and moon are bright, that the four seasons are ordered and the stars are on their courses, that rivers flow and that things prosper, that love and hatred are tempered and joy and anger are in keeping. They cause the lowly to be obedient and those on high to be illustrious. He who holds to the rites is never confused in the midst of multifarious change; he who deviates therefrom is lost. Rites—are they not the culmination of culture? . . .

Rites require us to treat both life and death with attentiveness. Life is the beginning of man, death is his end. When a man is well off both at the end and the beginning, the way of man is fulfilled. Hence the gentleman respects the beginning and is carefully attentive to the end. To pay equal attention to the end as well as to the beginning is the way of the gentleman and the beauty of rites and righteousness. . . .

Rites serve to shorten that which is too long and lengthen that which is too short, reduce that which is too much and augment that which is too little, express the beauty of love and reverence and cultivate the elegance of righteous conduct. Therefore, beautiful adornment and coarse sackcloth, music and weeping, rejoicing, and sorrow, though pairs of opposites, are in the rites equally utilized and alternately brought into play. Beautiful adornment, music, and rejoicing are appropriate on occasions of felicity; coarse sackcloth, weeping, and sorrow are appropriate on occasions of ill-fortune. Rites make room for beautiful adornment but not to the point of being fascinating, for coarse sackcloth but not to the point of deprivation or self-injury, for music and rejoicing but not to the point of being lewd and indolent, for weeping and sorrow but not to the point of being depressing and injurious. Such is the middle path of rites. . . .

Funeral rites are those by which the living adorn the dead. The dead are accorded a send-off as though they were living. In this way the dead are served like the living, the absent like the present. Equal attention is thus paid to the end as well as to the beginning of life. . . .

Now the rites used on the occasion of birth are to embellish joy, those used on the occasion of death are to embellish sorrow, those used at sacrifice are to embellish reverence, those used on military occasions are to embellish dignity. In this respect the rites of all kings are alike, antiquity and the present age agree, and no one knows whence they came. . . .

Sacrifice is to express a person's feeling of remembrance and longing, for grief and affliction cannot be kept out of one's consciousness all the time. When men are enjoying the pleasure of good company, a loyal minister or a filial son may feel grief and affliction. Once such feelings arise, he is greatly excited and moved. If such feelings are not given proper expression, then his emotions and memories are disappointed and not satisfied, and the appropriate rite is lacking. Thereupon the ancient kings instituted rites, and henceforth the principle of expressing honor to the honored and love to the beloved is fully realized. Hence I say: Sacrifice is to express a person's feeling of remembrance and longing. As to the fullness of the sense of loyalty and affection, the richness of ritual and beauty—these none but the sage can understand. Sacrifice is something that the sage clearly understands, the scholar-gentlemen contentedly perform, the officials consider as a duty, and the common people regard as established custom. Among gentlemen it is considered the way of man; among the common people it is considered as having to do with the spirits.

2. Precepts for Children, E. Kaibara

> *Confucian morality has been a dominant social force not only in China but also in Japan. An example of a Japanese thinker advocating Confucianism is found in Ekken Kaibara (1630–1714), who sought to state Confucian ethics in a simple manner that could be understood by everyone. In the previous selection, Hsün Tzu maintained that proper social (moral) action depends on nature (heaven and earth), ancestors, and nobility (sovereigns and teachers). In the following excerpt Kaibara emphasizes the interrelation of man and nature, pointing out that the Confucian virtue of benevolence (Chinese jen, Japanese jin, "human-heartedness," "humane-ness") includes benevolence toward nature. Also, as many Confucians before him, Kaibara emphasizes the virtue of filial service (hsiao). Why is man indebted to nature? What is the basic aim of human life? Note the practical expressions of "following the way of heaven" in everyday events. Can you sense why he claims that it would be improper to cut trees and grass out of season?*

From Ekken Kaibara, "Precepts for Children," in *Sources of Japanese Tradition*, ed. R. Tsunoda et al. (New York: Columbia University Press, 1958), pp. 376–77. Used by permission of the publisher.

All men may be said to owe their birth to their parents, but a further inquiry into their origins reveals that men come into being because of nature's law of life. Thus all men in the world are children born of heaven and earth, and heaven and earth are the great parents of us all. The *Book of History** says, "Heaven and earth are the father and mother of all things" (T'ai-shih 1). Our own parents are truly our parents; but heaven and earth are the parents of everyone in the world. Moreover, though we are brought up after birth through the care of our own parents and are sustained on the gracious bounty of the ruler, still if we go to the root of the matter, we find that we sustain ourselves using the things produced by nature for food, dress, housing, and implements. Thus, not only do all men at the outset come into being because of nature's law of life, but from birth till the end of life they are kept in existence by the support of heaven and earth. Man surpasses all other created things in his indebtedness to the limitless bounty of nature. It will be seen therefore that man's duty is not only to do his best to serve his parents, which is a matter of course, but also to serve nature throughout his life in order to repay his immense debt. That is one thing all men should keep in mind constantly.

As men mindful of their obligation constantly to serve nature in repayment of this great debt, they should not forget that, just as they manifest filial piety in the service of their own parents, so they should manifest to the full their benevolence toward nature. Benevolence means having a sense of sympathy within, and bringing blessings to man and things. For those who have been brought up on the blessings of nature, it is the way to serve nature. It is the basic aim of human life, which should be observed as long as one lives. There should be no letting up on it, no forgetting of it. Benevolence in the service of nature and filial piety are one in principle: it is a principle which must be known and observed by anyone insofar as he is a man. There is none greater than this, none more important. All men living in their parents' home should expend themselves in filial service to their father and mother; and serving their lord should manifest single-minded loyalty to him. Just so, living as we do in the wrap of nature, we must serve nature and manifest to the full our benevolence. For a man to be unaware of this important duty, to let the days and years pass idly by and let one's life go for naught, is to make oneself unworthy of being a man. Indeed, how can anyone who would be a man ignore this fact? It is in this that the way of man lies. Any way apart from this cannot be the true way.

To persist in the service of heaven means that everyone who is a man should be mindful of the fact that morning and evening he is in the presence of heaven, and not far removed from it; that he should fear and reverence the way of heaven and not be unmindful of it. He should not, even in ignorance, oppose the way of heaven or commit any outrage against

---

* One of the Confucion classics, which was revered as "scripture"—though without the sense of having been Divine revelation.

it. Rather, following the way of heaven, he should be humble and not arrogant toward others, control his desires and not be indulgent of his passions, cherish a profound love for all mankind born of nature's great love, and not abuse or mistreat them. Nor should he waste, just to gratify his personal desires, the five grains and other bounties which nature has provided for the sake of the people. Secondly, no living creatures such as birds, beasts, insects, and fish should be killed wantonly. Not even grass and trees should be cut down out of season. All of these are objects of nature's love, having been brought forth by her and nurtured by her. To cherish them and keep them is therefore the way to serve nature in accordance with the great heart of nature. Among human obligations there is first the duty to love our relatives, then to show sympathy for all other human beings, and then not to mistreat birds and beasts or any other living things. That is the proper order for the practice of benevolence in accordance with the great heart of nature. Loving other people to the neglect of parents,* or loving birds and beasts to the neglect of human beings, is not benevolence.

3. Laws of Manu

The most famous code of Hindu law and jurisprudence is the Laws of Manu. According to orthodox Hindu pandits, it was composed several millennia ago, though contemporary historians place its composition between 600 B.C. and 300 A.D. Manu is the name both of one or more semi-divine beings of mythology and of a compiler of legal doctrines. The first verses in the following selection indicate the high reverence in which Manu's words are held. According to the subsequent sections of the quoted material, the social law is derived from the very nature of things. Society is seen to be composed of four classes: Brāhmaṇa *(Brahmins, or priest-seers),* Kshatriya *(rulers, protectors),* Vaiśya *(farmers and merchants), and* Sūdra *(servants, common laborers). Those persons born into the first three classess have the right and obligation to do certain sacred rituals whereby they are "born again." Thus they had two births, a physical one and a religious one, and were called "twice-born." Note that*

---

* Filial piety (*hsiao*) required that even after marriage a son's primary responsibility was to his parents, not his wife or children.

From *The Laws of Manu with Extracts from Seven Commentaries,* trans. G. Bühler, in *Sacred Books of the East,* ed. G. Max Müller, Vol. XXV (Oxford: Clarendon Press, 1886), pp. 1, 2, 24–31.

this code of laws is given to avoid a disruption of the natural order, and to inform human beings about good conduct, which is the root of all spiritual discipline (austerity). According to this text, what are the blessings that result from fulfilling one's duty? How important is it to be learned in the sacred verses—that is, the Veda (Śruti)? How can a person learn what are the rules for marriage, eating, duties to kings, and other basic social activities?

CHAPTER I

1. The great sages approached Manu, who was seated with a collected mind, and, having duly worshipped him, spoke as follows:

2. "Deign, divine one, to declare to us precisely and in due order the sacred laws of each of the (four chief) castes (*varṇa*)* and of the intermediate ones.

3. "For thou, O Lord, alone knowest the purport, (i. e.) the rites, and the knowledge of the soul, (taught) in this whole ordinance of the Self-existent (*Svayambhū*), which is unknowable and unfathomable."

4. He, whose power is measureless, being thus asked by the high-minded great sages, duly honoured them, and answered, "Listen!"...

87. In order to protect this universe He, the most resplendent one, assigned separate (duties and) occupations to those who sprang from his mouth, arms, thighs, and feet.

88. To Brāhmaṇas he assigned teaching and studying (the Veda), sacrificing for their own benefit and for others, giving and accepting (of alms).

89. The Kshatriya he commanded to protect the people, to bestow gifts, to offer sacrifices, to study (the Veda), and to abstain from attaching himself to sensual pleasures;

90. The Vaiśya to tend cattle, to bestow gifts, to offer sacrifices, to study (the Veda), to trade, to lend money, and to cultivate land.

91. One occupation only the lord prescribed to the Śūdra, to serve meekly even these (other) three castes.

92. Man is stated to be purer above the navel (than below); hence the Self-existent (Svayambhū) has declared the purest (part) of him (to be) his mouth.

93. As the Brāhmaṇa sprang from (Brahman's) mouth, as he was the first-born, and as he possesses the Veda, he is by right the lord of this whole creation.

94. For the Self-existent (*Svayambhū*), having performed austerities, produced him first from his own mouth, in order that the offerings might be conveyed to the gods and manes** and that this universe might be preserved.

---

* The printing of Sanskrit terms has been changed from the original printing to comply with the present most commonly used transliteration style.

** The spirits of ancestors.

95. What created being can surpass him, through whose mouth the gods continually consume the sacrificial viands and the manes the offerings to the dead?

96. Of created beings the most excellent are said to be those which are animated; of the animated, those which subsist by intelligence; of the intelligent, mankind; and of men, the Brāhmaṇas;

97. Of Brāhmaṇas, those learned (in the Veda); of the learned, those who recognise (the necessity and the manner of performing the prescribed duties); of those who possess this knowledge, those who perform them; of the performers, those who know the Brahman.

98. The very birth of a Brāhmaṇa is an eternal incarnation of the sacred law; for he is born to (fulfil) the sacred law, and becomes one with Brahman.

99. A Brāhmaṇa, coming into existence, is born as the highest on earth, the lord of all created beings, for the protection of the treasury of the law.

100. Whatever exists in the world is the property of the Brāhmaṇa; on account of the excellence of his origin the Brāhmaṇa is, indeed, entitled to it all.

101. The Brāhmaṇa eats but his own food, wears but his own apparel, bestows but his own in alms; other mortals subsist through the benevolence of the Brāhmaṇa.

102. In order to clearly settle his duties and those of the other (castes) according to their order, wise Manu sprung from the Self-existent, composed these Institutes (of the sacred law).

103. A learned Brāhmaṇa must carefully study them, and he must duly instruct his pupils in them, but nobody else (shall do it).

104. A Brāhmaṇa who studies these Institutes (and) faithfully fulfils the duties (prescribed therein), is never tainted by sins, arising from thoughts, words, or deeds.

105. He sanctifies any company (which he may enter), seven ancestors and seven descendants, and he alone deserves (to possess) this whole earth.

106. (To study) this (work) is the best means of securing welfare, it increases understanding, it procures fame and long life, it (leads to) supreme bliss.

107. In this (work) the sacred law has been fully stated as well as the good and bad qualities of (human) actions and the immemorial rule of conduct, (to be followed) by all the four castes (varṇa).

108. The rule of conduct is transcendent law, whether it be taught in the revealed texts or in the sacred tradition; hence a twice-born man who possesses regard for himself, should be always careful to (follow) it.

109. A Brāhmaṇa who departs from the rule of conduct, does not reap the fruit of the Veda, but he who duly follows it, will obtain the full reward.

110. The sages who saw that the sacred law is thus grounded on the rule of conduct, have taken good conduct to be the most excellent root of all austerity.

111. The creation of the universe, the rule of the sacraments, the

ordinances of studentship, and the respectful behaviour (towards Gurus), the most excellent rule of bathing (on return from the teacher's house),

112. (The law of) marriage and the description of the (various) marriage-rites, the regulations for the great sacrifices and the eternal rule of the funeral sacrifices,

113. The description of the modes of (gaining) subsistence and the duties of a Snātaka,* (the rules regarding) lawful and forbidden food, the purification of men and of things,

114. The laws concerning women, (the law) of hermits, (the manner of gaining) final emancipation and (of) renouncing the world, the whole duty of a king and the manner of deciding lawsuits,

115. The rules for the examination of witnesses, the laws concerning husband and wife, the law of (inheritance and) division, (the law concerning) gambling and the removal of (men nocuous like) thorns,

116. (The law concerning) the behaviour of Vaiśyas and Śūdras, the origin of the mixed castes, the law for all castes in times of distress and the law of penances,

117. The threefold course of transmigrations, the result of (good or bad) actions, (the manner of attaining) supreme bliss and the examination of the good and bad qualities of actions,

118. The primeval laws of countries, of castes (jāti), of families, and the rules concerning heretics and companies (of traders and the like)—(all that) Manu has declared in these Institutes.

119. As Manu, in reply to my questions, formerly promulgated these Institutes, even so learn ye also the (whole work) from me.

CHAPTER II

1. Learn that sacred law which is followed by men learned (in the Veda) and assented to in their hearts by the virtuous, who are ever exempt from hatred and inordinate affection.

2. To act solely from a desire for rewards is not laudable, yet an exemption from that desire is not (to be found) in this (world): for on (that) desire is grounded the study of the Veda and the performance of the actions, prescribed by the Veda.

3. The desire (for rewards), indeed, has its root in the conception that an act can yield them, and in consequence of (that) conception sacrifices are performed; vows and the laws prescribing restraints are all stated to be kept through the idea that they will bear fruit.

4. Not a single act here (below) appears ever to be done by a man free from desire; for whatever (man) does, it is (the result of) the impulse of desire.

5. He who persists in discharging these (prescribed duties) in the right manner, reaches the deathless state and even in this (life) obtains (the fulfilment of) all the desires that he may have conceived.

---

* A snātaka is a young man who has finished his religious training; the completion is marked by a ritual bath called *snāna*.

6. The whole Veda is the (first) source of the sacred law, next the tradition and the virtuous conduct of those who know the (Veda further), also the customs of holy men, and (finally) self-satisfaction.

7. Whatever law has been ordained for any (person) by Manu, that has been fully declared in the Veda: for that (sage was) omniscient.

8. But a learned man after fully scrutinising all this with the eye of knowledge, should, in accordance with the authority of the revealed texts, be intent on (the performance of) his duties.

9. For that man who obeys the law prescribed in the revealed texts and in the sacred tradition, gains fame in this (world) and after death unsurpassable bliss.

10. But by Śruti (revelation) is meant the Veda, and by Smriti (tradition) the Institutes of the sacred law: those two must not be called into question in any matter, since from those two the sacred law shone forth.

11. Every twice-born man, who, relying on the Institutes of dialectics, treats with contempt those two sources (of the law), must be cast out by the virtuous, as an atheist and a scorner of the Veda.

12. The Veda, the sacred tradition, the customs of virtuous men, and one's own pleasure, they declare to be visibly the fourfold means of defining the sacred law.

13. The knowledge of the sacred law is prescribed for those who are not given to the acquisition of wealth and to the gratification of their desires; to those who seek the knowledge of the sacred law the supreme authority is the revelation (Śruti).

4. Psalm 19

Jewish thought and life has expressed a deep sense that the world in which man lives manifests both the glory and law of the Lord. One of the resounding themes in Jewish religious reflection is the relationship between God's righteousness, which was the foundation of His covenant with the people of Israel, and his power, by which all things were made. In this joyous song credited to David, King of Israel during its "golden age," both the physical and social worlds are seen to be under the sovereignty of God. Does the "law of the Lord" seem to David more of a restriction, or more of a capacity of life-fulfillment? In what ways is the law of the Lord like the Confucian li *and the Hindu* Laws of Manu? *In what ways are they different?*

From *The New English Bible* © the Delegate of the Oxford University Press and the Syndics of the Cambridge University Press, 1961, 1970. Reprinted by permission. Pp. 623–24.

Psalm 19

The heavens tell out the glory of God,
the vault of heaven reveals his handiwork.
One day speaks to another,
night with night shares its knowledge,
and this without speech or language
or sound of any voice.
Their music goes out through all the earth,
their words reach to the end of the world.

In them a tent is fixed for the sun,
who comes out like a bridegroom from his wedding canopy,
rejoicing like a strong man to run his race.
His rising is at one end of the heavens,
his circuit touches their farthest ends;
and nothing is hidden from his heat.

The law of the LORD is perfect and revives the soul.
The LORD's instruction never fails,
and makes the simple wise.
The precepts of the LORD are right and rejoice the heart.
The commandment of the LORD shines clear
and gives light to the eyes.
The fear of the LORD is pure and abides for ever.
The LORD's decrees are true and righteous every one,
more to be desired than gold, pure gold in plenty,
sweeter than syrup or honey from the comb.
It is these that give thy servant warning,
and he who keeps them wins a great reward.

Who is aware of his unwitting sins?
Cleanse me of any secret fault.
Hold back thy servant also from sins of self-will,
lest they get the better of me.
Then I shall be blameless
and innocent of any great transgression.

May all that I say and think be acceptable to thee,
O LORD, my rock and my redeemer!

5. Qur'an, Suras 107 and 4

*For the Muslim the Qur'an (sometimes transliterated Koran)
is the Word of God, given at various times, but culminating in
the revelation to His prophet Mohammed. As such it is the
source for the belief and daily ethic of the Islamic world. A basic
understandnig of God in the Qur'an is that He is the creator of
a unitary and purposeful order in the universe which ideally
expresses the harmony of His will. Within this order man is to
live his everyday life (in every thought and action) in compliance
with the Divine Will. Many of the suras (chapters) in the
Qur'an include moral principles and exhortations, with the clear
warning that if a person fails to heed God's will, he or she will
face an awesome punishment at the final Day of Judgment
("the Doom"). According to the short Sura 107 reprinted below,
what sorts of ethical attitudes and actions result in God's final
punishment? Does this passage suggest that all prayer is
unimportant? What indications do you find in Sura 4 that
certain social relations are part of a Divine order? What is the
result of human transgressions and sins? What are some of the
positive ethical admonitions given? From the standpoint of the
final verses, is perfect justice possible? If so, what is the source
of it?*

Sura 107
CHARITY

In the Name of God, the Merciful, the Compassionate

Hast thou seen him who cries lies to the Doom?
That is he who repulses the orphan
and urges not the feeding of the needy.

So woe to those that pray
and are heedless of their prayers,
to those who make display
and refuse charity.

Sura 4
WOMEN

O believers, consume not your goods
between you in vanity, except there be

From THE KORAN INTERPRETED, by Rabindranath Tagore, trans. A. J.
Arberry (New York: The Macmillan Company and London: Allen & Unwin Ltd.,
© 1955), pp. 105, 106, and 351.

trading, by your agreeing together.
And kill not one another. Surely God is
    compassionate to you.
But whosoever does that in transgression
and wrongfully, him We shall certainly
roast at a Fire; and that for God is
    an easy matter.
If you avoid the heinous sins that
are forbidden you, We will acquit you
of your evil deeds, and admit you by
        the gate of honour.

Do not covet that whereby God in bounty
has preferred one of you above another.
To the men a share from what they have earned,
and to the women a share from what they
have earned. And ask God of His bounty;
        God knows everything.

To everyone We have appointed heirs
of that which parents and kinsmen leave,
and those with whom you have sworn compact.
So give to them their share; God is witness
        over everything.

Men are the managers of the affairs of women
for that God has preferred in bounty
one of them over another, and for that
they have expended of their property.
Righteous women are therefore obedient,
guarding the secret for God's guarding.
And those you fear may be rebellious
admonish; banish them to their couches,
and beat them. If they then obey you,
look not for any way against them; God is
        All-high, All-great.
And if you fear a breach between the two,
bring forth an arbiter from his people
and from her people an arbiter, if they
desire to set things right; God will
compose their differences; surely God is
        All-knowing, All-aware.

        Serve God,
    and associate naught with Him.

Be kind to parents, and the near kinsman,
and to orphans, and to the needy,

and to the neighbour who is of kin,
and to the neighbour who is a stranger,
and to the companion at your side,
and to the traveller, and to that your
right hands own. Surely God loves not
    the proud and boastful
such as are niggardly, and bid other men
to be niggardly, and themselves conceal
the bounty that God has given them.
We have prepared for the unbelievers
    a humbling chastisement,
and such as expend of their substance
to show off to men, and believe not
in God and the Last Day. Whosoever
has Satan for a comrade, an evil
    Comrade is he.
Why, what would it harm them, if they
believed in God and the Last Day, and
expended of that God has provided them?
    God knows them.
Surely God shall not wrong so much as the
weight of an ant; and if it be a good deed
He will double it, and give from Himself
    a mighty wage.

6. Unwise and Untimely?
M. L. King, Jr.

*One of the characteristics of the third type of religiousness is the
living of every moment as a part of a social organism. The flow
of social existence is ordered by social norms held to be "natural,"
and often held so deeply that they are accepted without question.
At times in the history of a culture certain social structures are
established, which then for a while are taken for granted or are
defended as "natural." Such was slavery in early American
history, and the development of "untouchability" in late medieval
India. However, in both of these cases there were powerful voices
raised questioning the rightness of the status quo, and appeals
were made to a "higher law" that was established in the nature*

From Martin Luther King, Jr., "Unwise and Untimely?" A Letter from Eight
Alabama Clergymen to Martin Luther King, Jr. and his reply to them on order
and common sense, the law and justice, nonviolence and love (Nyack, New York:
Fellowship of Reconciliation, n.d.), pp. 3–4, 7–8, 11–13.

*of life and that took precedence over "man's corruption" of social
relationships. Thus, such social-political leaders as Martin Luther
King, Jr. in the United States and Mahatma Gandhi in India
questioned social practices they found around them even to the
point of intentionally breaking the law. In this selection we see
King appealing to God's divine law and to the findings of
social scientists in denouncing practices which, according to
Alabama statutes and customs, were legal and just.*

*Before his assassination in 1968, Martin Luther King, Jr. was
the leader of nonviolent protests against social and economic
injustices experienced by black people in America. Several times
he broke segregation laws in the South in order to test the
constitutionality of these laws, or engaged in marches even when
denied permits to do so by the authorities, and found himself in
jail on many of these occasions. This excerpt comes from a letter
he wrote while in jail and which was intended as a reply to an
open letter published by eight Alabama clergymen who regarded
his nonviolent demonstration to be "unwise and untimely" because
they provoked violent reactions by those opposed to King's call
for justice. How does King justify coming into Birmingham from
Atlanta and Montgomery, where he had previously been located?
How does he justify his acts of lawbreaking, thereby calling into
question the moral sense of his critics? How does he distinguish
a just from an unjust law? Note the similarities between his
conception of social justice and that of the previous selection.
Does he seem to you to be opening the door to anarchy by his
conviction that human laws may properly be violated by those
who serve a higher law? How does he answer the charge of
"extremism"? What benefits to the social order does King claim
for his actions?*

I am in Birmingham because injustice is here. Just as the eighth century prophets left their little villages and carried their "thus saith the
Lord" far beyond the boundaries of their home towns; and just as the
Apostle Paul left his little village of Tarsus and carried the gospel of Jesus
Christ to practically every hamlet and city of the Graeco-Roman world, I
too am compelled to carry the gospel of freedom beyond my particular home
town. Like Paul, I must constantly respond to the Macedonian call for aid.

Moreover, I am cognizant of the interrelatedness of all communities
and states. I cannot sit idly by in Atlanta and not be concerned about
what happens in Birmingham. Injustice anywhere is a threat to justice
everywhere. We are caught in an inescapable network of mutuality, tied
in a single garment of destiny. Whatever affects one directly affects all
indirectly. Never again can we afford to live with the narrow, provincial
"outside agitator" idea. Anyone who lives inside the United States can never
be considered an outsider anywhere in this country.

You deplore the demonstrations that are presently taking place in Birmingham. But I am sorry that your statement did not express a similar concern for the conditions that brought the demonstrations into being. I am sure that each of you would want to go beyond the superficial social analyst who looks merely at effects, and does not grapple with underlying causes. I would not hesitate to say that it is unfortunate that so-called demonstrations are taking place in Birmingham at this time, but I would say in more emphatic terms that it is even more unfortunate that the white power structure of this city left the Negro community with no other alternative. . . .

BREAKING THE LAW

You express a great deal of anxicty over our willingness to break laws. This is certainly a legitimate concern. Since we so diligently urge people to obey the Supreme Court's decision of 1954 outlawing segregation in the public schools, it is rather strange and paradoxical to find us consciously breaking laws. One may well ask, "how can you advocate breaking some

"Frankly, doctor, don't you think it's time to get off this civil rights kick and get back to the fundamental teachings of Christianity?

Reproduced by special permission of *Playboy* Magazine; Copyright © 1968 by Playboy.

laws and obeying others?" The answer is found in the fact that there are two types of laws: There are *just* and there are *unjust* laws. I would agree with Saint Augustine that "An unjust law is no law at all."

Now what is the difference between the two? How does one determine when a law is just or unjust? A just law is a man-made code that squares with the moral law or the law of God. An unjust law is a code that is out of harmony with the moral law. To put it in the terms of Saint Thomas Aquinas, an unjust law is a human law that is not rooted in eternal and natural law. Any law that uplifts human personality is just. Any law that degrades human personality is unjust. All segregation statutes are unjust because segregation distorts the soul and damages the personality. It gives the segregator a false sense of superiority, and the segregated a false sense of inferiority. To use the words of Martin Buber, the great Jewish philosopher, segregation substitutes an "I-it" relationship for the "I-thou" relationship, and ends up relegating persons to the status of things. So segregation is not only politically, economically and sociologically unsound, but it is morally wrong and sinful. Paul Tillich has said that sin is separation. Isn't segregation an existential expression of man's tragic separation, an expression of his awful estrangement, his terrible sinfulness? So I can urge men to disobey segregation ordinances because they are morally wrong.

Let us turn to a more concrete example of just and unjust laws. An unjust law is a code that a majority inflicts on a minority that is not binding on itself. This is difference made legal. On the other hand a just law is a code that a majority compels a minority to follow that it is willing to follow itself. This is sameness made legal.

Let me give another explanation. An unjust law is a code inflicted upon a minority which that minority had no part in enacting or creating because they did not have the unhampered right to vote. Who can say that the legislature of Alabama which set up the segregation laws was democratically elected? Throughout the state of Alabama all types of conniving methods are used to prevent Negroes from becoming registered voters and there are some counties without a single Negro registered to vote despite the fact that the Negro constitutes a majority of the population. Can any law set up in such a state be considered democratically structured?

These are just a few examples of unjust and just laws. There are some instances when a law is just on its face and unjust in its application. For instance, I was arrested Friday on a charge of parading without a permit. Now there is nothing wrong with an ordinance which requires a permit for a parade, but when the ordinance is used to preserve segregation and to deny citizens the First Amendment privilege of peaceful assembly and peaceful protest, then it becomes unjust.

You spoke of our activity in Birmingham as extreme. At first I was rather disappointed that fellow clergymen would see my nonviolent efforts as those of the extremist. I started thinking about the fact that I stand in the middle of two opposing forces in the Negro community. One is a force of complacency made up of Negroes who, as a result of long years of oppression, have been so completed drained of self-respect and a sense of "somebodiness" that they have adjusted to segregation, and, of a few Negroes in the middle class who, because of a degree of academic and economic security, and because at points they profit by segregation, have unconsciously become insensitive to the problems of the masses. The other force is one of bitterness, and hatred and comes perilously close to advocating violence. It is expressed in the various black nationalist groups that are springing up over the nation, the largest and best known being Elijah Muhammad's Muslim movement.* This movement is nourished by the contemporary frustration over the continued existence of racial discrimination. It is made up of people who have lost faith in America, who have absolutely repudiated Christianity, and who have concluded that the white man is an incurable "devil." I have tried to stand between these two forces saying that we need not follow the "do-nothingism" of the complacent or the hatred and despair of the black nationalist. There is the more excellent way of love and nonviolent protest. I'm grateful to God that, through the Negro church, the dimension of nonviolence entered our struggle. If this philosophy had not emerged, I am convinced that by now many streets of the South would be flowing with floods of blood. And I am further convinced that if our white brothers dismiss as "rabble rousers" and "outside agitators" those of us who are working through the channels of nonviolent direct action and refuse to support our nonviolent efforts, millions of Negroes, out of frustration and despair, will seek solace and security in black nationalist ideologies, a development that will lead inevitably to a frightening racial nightmare.

Oppressed people cannot remain oppressed forever. The urge for freedom will eventually come. This is what happened to the American Negro. Something within has reminded him of his birthright of freedom; something without has reminded him that he can gain it. Consciously and unconsciously, he has been swept in by what the Germans call the *Zeitgeist*,** and with his black brothers of Africa, and his brown and yellow brothers of Asia, South America and the Caribbean, he is moving with a sense of cosmic urgency toward the promised land of racial justice. Recognizing this vital urge that has engulfed the Negro community, one should readily understand public demonstration. The Negro has many pent up resentments and latent frustrations. He has to get them out. So let him march sometime; let him have his prayer pilgrimages to the city hall; understand why he must have sit-ins and freedom rides. If his repressed emotions do not come out in these nonviolent ways, they will come out in ominous expressions of violence. This is not a threat; it is a fact of history. So I have not said to my people "get rid of your discontent." But I have tried to say that this normal and healthy discontent can be channelized through the creative outlet of nonviolent direct action. Now this approach is being dismissed as extremist. I must admit that I was initially disappointed in being so categorized.

---

* That is, the Black Muslims in America.
** Spirit of the time.

EXTREMISTS FOR LOVE

But as I continued to think about the matter I gradually gained a bit of satisfaction from being considered an extremist. Was not Jesus an extremist in love—"Love your enemies, bless them that curse you, pray for them that despitefully use you." Was not Amos an extremist for justice —"Let justice roll down like waters and righteousness like a mighty stream." Was not Paul an extremist for the gospel of Jesus Christ—"I bear in my body the marks of the Lord Jesus." Was not Martin Luther an extremist— "Here I stand; I can do none other so help me God." Was not John Bunyan an extremist—"I will stay in jail to the end of my days before I make a butchery of my conscience." Was not Abraham Lincoln an extremist—"This nation cannot survive half slave and half free." Was not Thomas Jefferson an extremist—"We hold these truths to be self-evident, that all men are created equal." So the question is not whether we will be extremist but what kind of extremist will we be. Will we be extremists for hate or will we be extremists for love? Will we be extremists for the preservation of injustice—or will we be extremists for the cause of justice? In that dramatic scene on Calvary's hill, three men were crucified. We must not forget that all three were crucified for the same crime—the crime of extremism. Two were extremists for immorality, and thusly fell below their environment. The other, Jesus Christ, was an extremist for love, truth, and goodness, and thereby rose above his environment. So, after all, maybe the South, the nation and the world are in dire need of creative extremists.

I had hoped that the white moderate would see this. Maybe I was too optimistic. Maybe I expected too much. I guess I should have realized that few members of a race that has oppressed another race can understand or appreciate the deep groans and passionate yearnings of those that have been oppressed and still fewer have the vision to see that injustice must be rooted out by strong, persistent and determined action. I am thankful, however, that some of our white brothers have grasped the meaning of this social revolution and committed themselves to it. They are still all too small in quantity, but they are big in quality. Some like Ralph McGill, Lillian Smith, Harry Golden and James Dabbs have written about our struggle in eloquent, prophetic and understanding terms. Others have marched with us down nameless streets of the South. They have languished in filthy roach-infested jails, suffering the abuse and brutality of angry policemen who see them as "dirty nigger lovers." They, unlike so many of their moderate brothers and sisters, have recognized the urgency of the moment and sensed the need for powerful "action" antidotes to combat the disease of segregation.

INTERPRETATION

7. Chinese Religion, L. G. Thompson

In order to understand the power of daily social life for expressing Ultimate Reality in China and India we need to examine some basic concepts in these cultures. Note especially the lack of a monotheistic deity in these interpretations of cosmic order. In the first selection of this section, Thompson (Professor of Asian Studies, University of Southern California) quickly surveys a number of key concepts in Chinese religion. Especially important for our study is the ancient Chinese understanding that man is part of an eternal bipolar flow of energy (yin–yang) in the ever-changing universe. The religious ideal illustrated here is that every human being should live according to universal structures seen in the regularity of the natural cycles of life—the seasons, day–night, and birth–growth–death—which have their corresponding natural structures in social life. To live in the natural rhythm of life is to live in the Tao, the cosmic law. This sense of participation in a universal harmony (a Gestalt *cosmology) is an attitude that links both the peasant and the intellectual in Chinese society. Everyday life is seen as an organic whole, a worthy and orderly process, within which man should be perfectly at home. How does "familial morality" illustrate the effort to participate in a natural harmony? Note that moral perfection is not just an abstract, impossible ideal; rather it is a mark of the truly religious man. How does Thompson distinguish Chinese religion from Christianity? What examples of virtue (jen) come to mind from your own experience?*

The Naturalistic Universe. The universe of the ancient Chinese was naturalistic, in the sense that it was characterized by the regularity which Western philosophy has called "law"—but it lacked the Western assumption of an outside "lawgiver."[1] Three features of this regularity were conspicuous to the ancients: first, the cyclical processes, such as night following day followed by night, or the rotation of the seasons; second, the process of growth and decline, exemplified by the waxing and waning of the moon; third, the bipolarity of nature. The latter meant not simply that everything had its opposite, but that opposites were necessary and complementary to each other. These opposites tended to merge into each other, and even to

become each the opposite of its former self. The ground or fundamental stuff of the universe was seen to be homogeneous, and all particular phenomena were individualized through these processes. The third process was no doubt the latest to be grasped as a principle, being by far the most sophisticated.

In fact, once the third principle was recognized it could be seen to account for the other two, which were merely operational aspects of this all-inclusive one. As a principle, it was one of the most fruitful and useful ever devised by the mind of man for making sense out of the infinite multitude of diverse facts in the universe. Today, described as positive and negative electrical charges, it is the basis of "matter" according to science (we are not suggesting that the ancient Chinese knew about electricity); in traditional China, expressed through the concepts of *yang* and *yin,* bipolarity constituted the specific characteristic of Chinese metaphysics. Once this principle had suggested itself, perhaps as early as 1000–500 B.C., the Chinese were able to develop a perfectly coherent theory of the cosmos. Nature was seen to operate through the interplay of light and darkness, heat and cold, male and female, and so forth. The *yang* (as represented by the first of each pair) and *yin* (the second of each pair) were not in absolute and permanent opposition to each other. They might best be described as definable phases in a ceaseless flow of change:

> When the sun goes the moon comes; when the moon goes the sun comes. The sun and moon give way to each other and their brightness is produced. When the cold goes the heat comes; when the heat goes the cold comes. The cold and heat give way to each other and the round of the year is completed. That which goes wanes, and that which comes

waxes. The waning and waxing affect each other and benefits are produced.[2]

It is significant that this bipolar world view did not, in its ancient, classical formulation, have anything to do with a struggle between basic principles of good and evil. *Yang* and *yin* were equally essential forces in the ceaseless dynamic of an impersonal universe.

In the material world produced through this process there was an infinite variety of phenomena, and the Chinese by late Chou times (fifth–third centuries B.C.) had, like other ancient peoples, overcome this confusion by classifying all things into what seemed to be irreducible elements. As a consequence of the principle of constant transformation embodied in the *yang-yin* theory, the Chinese concept of the primary elements was essentially different from that of the ancient Greeks. Instead of atoms —tiny particles of a certain kind of substance—the Chinese fixed on the fundamental *qualities* observed in things. These qualities were not static, but were ceaselessly interacting, transforming, and replacing each other. The Chinese word *hsing*, which has customarily been translated as "element," is actually a verb meaning to walk, to go, to act. There were five *hsing*, given in the "Hung Fan" chapter of *Shu Ching*[3] as water, fire, wood, metal, and earth (their order and mutual reactions differ in other texts). Thinking of *hsing* as verbal will help us to keep in mind their active nature (water overcoming fire, fire burning wood, and so forth); while thinking of *hsing* as adjectival will help us to understand their elemental nature (that is, all things may be categorized as either "watery," i.e., liquid; "fiery," i.e., gaseous; and so forth). So as to emphasize both of these aspects of the Chinese term, we shall throughout this book refer to the *hsing* as the five operational qualities. . . .

To modern man in the West it must require a great effort of the imagination to empathize with the traditional Chinese feeling. We are so accustomed to seeing the physical world as something "out there," as an environment (mostly hostile to us), or as a purely material object for our exploitation, that we can scarcely comprehend the Chinese sense of the wholeness of the universe, in which man is a part, only a part, and really a part. This intimate feeling of being at home in nature is shown in many ways in the traditional Chinese culture: in the philosophical writings, particularly the wonderful flights of Chuang Tzu (365–290 B.C.), as a perennial theme of poetry through the ages, and visually in those landscape paintings which place man in perspective as a tiny observer of the vast universe—an observer who is seeking to absorb himself in this universe.

In an integrated universe, it will occur to men to seek out the signs writ large in nature whereby they may confirm that human actions are in accord or discordant with the *tao* of this universe. In the *Shu Ching* we may read how these signs were interpreted by the Chou people:

> . . .the various verifications. . .are called rain, sunshine, heat, cold, wind and their seasonableness; when the five come in a complete way, and each in its order, all the plants are rich and luxuriant. If one (of them)

is complete to the extreme, it is baleful; if one is lacking to the extreme, it is baleful. (Some) are called the lucky verifications. Gravity—seasonable rain responds to it; orderliness—seasonable sunshine responds to it; wisdom—seasonable heat responds to it...(Some) are called unlucky verifications. Wildness—constant rain responds to it; incorrectness— constant sunshine responds to it; indolence—constant heat responds to it....
...What the king scrutinizes is the year (sc. as to its natural phenomena), the dignitaries and noblemen the months, the many lower officials the days (sc. for verification of their government). When in years, months and days the seasonableness has no...failings, the...many cereals ripen, the administration is enlightened, talented men of the people are distinguished, the house is peaceful and at ease.... What the common people scrutinize is the stars. There are stars which favour wind, there are stars which favour rain.... According as the moons follow the. (various) stars, there is wind and rain (sc. the people can judge the indications in the sky and so participate in the "verifications").[4]

The same text in another section gives a clear illustration of the specific application of the theory:

In the autumn, when there was great ripeness, when they had not yet reaped, Heaven made great thunder and rain with wind, all the grain laid itself down, great trees were uprooted. The people of the land greatly feared...[The cause was discovered to be a calumniation of the king's uncle, Regent Chou Kung. Thereupon the king said, weeping:] Formerly the prince [i.e., Chou Kung] toiled for the Royal house, but I, young man, have not...had the means of knowing it. Now Heaven has set in motion its terror in order to signalize Chou Kung's virtue. I, the little child, will in person go and meet him...When the king came out to the suburbs (sc. on his way to meet Chou Kung), Heaven rained and turned the wind and the grain all rose up. The two princes ordered the people of the state, in regard to all great trees which had been overthrown, to raise them all and earth them up. The year was then greatly...fruitful.[5]

Such a belief in the interactions of man (particularly represented in the person of the Son of Heaven, as the king was titled) and the rest of nature continued to be a basic aspect of the Chinese world view up to modern times. The reading of omens and portents was a pronounced feature of the Chinese religion.

It is surely this "gestalt cosmology" which gives to the world view of the native Chinese tradition its specific character. Lacking the premise of a God "out there" who created and controls the universe and requires man's worship, the typical Western form of religion did not develop. Lacking the theory that human souls are particularizations of the universal Atman, the typical Indian form of religion likewise did not develop. The Chinese religion, based on the premises we have outlined, developed on its highest level a mysticism perhaps not essentially different from the mysticisms of other religions, but nevertheless felt to be identification with tao, or Nature itself, and not with God, beyond or outside of Nature. The Chinese religion, while giving to Heaven power to punish man's misbehavior, defined this misbehavior as actions inimical to the harmonious workings of the universe. The Chinese religion conspicuously lacked the central concept of the ever-brooding presence of Almighty God, continuously attending to the sins and virtues of every individual, swift to save or damn, requiring submission, belief, faith, and adoration. . . .

Man to Man. When the naturalistic world view of the Chinese was focused upon man as man, it found its subject of central interest. The nature of human nature was always at the heart of Chinese philosophical discussion, with the result that ethics and social philosophy were more prominent than speculative thought. What it was to be a man, and what it was to be in various relationships with other men: these were the preoccupations of Chinese intellectuals through the ages. A few keen minds might wrestle with the abstruse problems of Buddhist philosophy, and many poetical minds turned to the pleasures of Taoist philosophy; but the main current was the humanistic rationalism of the Confucian School, which became the officially sanctioned doctrine in the mid-second century B.C.

. . . The religion of the family was the universal religious institution of China, and the ethical views of the Confucian tradition were essentially a rationalization and extension of the familial virtues. The principles of this familial morality were derived from natural relationships rather than abstract theory. By the early Chou dynasty the *Shu Ching* is referring to "the five classes," meaning fathers and mothers, eldest and younger brothers, and sons, and to the obligations of each "class." In *Meng Tzu,* there is a somewhat different but similarly homely classification attributed by the philosopher Mencius (390–305 B.C.) to the times of the semilegendary sage-emperor Shun:

> Between father and son there is affection; between prince and minister there is integrity; between husband and wife there is (?) a proper distance; between senior and junior there is proper precedence; between friend and friend there is faithfulness.[6]

And in the Confucian codes, *Li Chi* . . . , compiled in early Han (second century B.C.), yet a third form of the same domestic ethic is expressed:

> The father is merciful, the son filial; the elder brother is good, the younger brother submissive; the husband is upright, the wife complaisant; the adult is kind, the child obedient.[7]

This age-old familial morality, preached by Confucius and his principal followers and eventually enshrined in the Confucian Canon, came to permeate all of Chinese society. To the vast majority of the Chinese, who followed conventional careers, these precepts were the moral norm; to the minority who were different, it was this tradition from which they differed. Even Buddhist and Taoist monks and nuns, living apart from society, were still guided in their conduct largely by this Confucian family-style morality.

Above the level of the code of familial relationships was the body of ethical teachings meant for the "superior men," the small minority who received a literary education and who were thereby destined to govern the nation and to guide its cultural development. This higher tradition was directly inspired by the life and words of Confucius (551–479 B.C.). The Master exemplified the ideals by which all educated men should guide their conduct. He was a man to whom truth, honor, and the furtherance of just government meant everything. He stood for the good ways of the ancient sages. He sought all his life for a prince who would use him by putting his principles into practice; but when a ruler found expediency more profitable than principle Confucius left his service. Before Confucius, in China as in old Europe, a "gentleman" was a man of nobel blood; after Confucius, a gentleman was a man who possessed the *character* a gentleman should possess, regardless of his blood. This emphasis upon character, upon moral excellence, was the great contribution of Confucius to Chinese society.

The gentleman was to cultivate his own character, and, equally important, he was, like his Master, to put this highly cultivated character at the service of the State whenever this was feasible. The educated—those who mastered the Confucian Canon—served as officials, governing the untutored masses, a government that was in theory one of moral example rather than coercion. Confucius had said, "The Gentleman is like the wind; his inferiors are like grass. When the wind blows the grass must bend."[8] The full implication of this remarkable conception of government as moral example is seen in a passage near the beginning of the canonical *Ta Hsüeh (The Great Learning)*:

> The men of old who wished to make their bright virtue shine throughout the world first put in order their own states. In order to put in order their own states they first regulated their own families; in order to regulate their own families they first disciplined their own selves. In order to discipline their own selves they first rectified their own minds (or, hearts); in order to rectify their minds they first resolved sincerely upon their goals; in order to resolve sincerely upon their goals they first broadened their understanding of things to the utmost. The broadening of understanding to the utmost was accomplished by studying the nature of things.
>
> When they studied the nature of things then their understanding became complete; when their understanding was complete then they resolved sincerely upon their goals; when they were sincerely resolved upon their goals then their minds (or, hearts) were rectified. When their minds were rectified then they were able to discipline themselves; when they could discipline themselves then they could regulate their families; when they could regulate their families then they could put in order their own states; when their own states were in order then they could bring peace to the world.
>
> From the Son of Heaven (i.e., the emperor) down to the common people there is a single [principle]: discipline of the self is fundamental.

Thus, aside from their family religion, the educated elite in China had as their primary religious obligation the perfection of themselves to serve as moral paragons. The Confucian self-discipline was therefore quite different from the asceticism and yogic concentration of the Buddhist practice, or the breath-control, dietary, alchemical, and other techniques of religious Taoism.

Moral perfection was summed up in the term *jen* (pronounced like *run*), whose graph eloquently expresses its basic requirement: it is formed from the elements "man" and "two." From this composition of the word, translators have derived such renderings as "man-to-manness" and "human-heartedness," attempting to improve on older definitions such as "benevolence" or "goodness." There is actually no doubt that in common usage *jen* came to be no more than goodness or even just charity, but to Confucius it stood for such an exalted ideal that he had never known a person to whom the word could truly apply.

Aside from *jen,* the virtues stressed in the Confucian teachings are down to earth and easy to understand, or at least we can approximate them with the names of virtues familiar to Western morality: righteousness, loyalty, trustworthiness, modesty, frugality, incorruptibility, courtesy, learning and the like. If they seem like moral platitudes it is because they were practical ideals in the education of gentlemen destined to run the empire. The important thing to understand is that it was this *concentration upon character-building* which engaged the minds of the men who governed China and created her high culture. It was this which engaged them rather than other forms of the religious quest.

Finally we should note that in this naturalistic view of man there is no original sin, no inherent depravity from which man can only be lifted by a savior. There was, to be sure, a running debate throughout the history of Chinese philosophy as to whether human nature is good, bad, or morally neutral. But even those philosophers who proposed the second of these alternatives did not conceive of "badness" as a sort of taint, ineradicable except by divine grace. The majority view in the Confucian tradition was that given its authoritative expression by Mencius, who argued that human nature was inherently good. His greatest opponent was Hsün Tzu (340–245 B.C.), but Hsün Tzu merely insisted that men were inherently *inclined* towards evil and selfishness, and he believed that they would become good through education. The Confucian tradition subsequently blended these two views: the goodness of human nature was generally accepted in theory, while education was given the place of supreme importance in practice. In any case, there was no question of sinfulness and salvation in the Western sense.

NOTES

1. Joseph Needham has thoroughly developed this theme. See his *Science and Civilization in China* (Cambridge, England: Cambridge University Press, 1956), Vol. II, Chap. 18, "Human Law and the Laws of Nature in China and the West."
2. *Yi Ching,* "Hsi Tz'u," II.
3. "Hung Fan" is generally regarded as a late Chou addition.

4. *Shu Ching*, "Hung Fan," in *The Book of Documents*, B. Karlgren, trans., *Bulletin of the Museum of Far Eastern Antiquities* (Stockholm, No. 22, 1950), pp. 34–35.
5. *Ibid.*, "Kin t'eng," p. 36.
6. *Meng Tzu (Mencius)* IIIA. 4.8.
7. *Li Chi*, "Li Yün."
8. *Analects* XII, 19.

8. *Li:* Rites and Propriety, N. E. Fehl

> *How is an individual's virtuous action related to the natural rhythm of change in life? Can society be established without an appeal to a supreme creator of life? Is there a moral law without a lawgiver? In this excerpt from a study of Chinese cultural history, we find that* li *is a primary "cultural style" of life in China that provides an alternative to the usual institutional forms of religion found in the West. The author, professor of world history at The Chinese University of Hong Kong, focuses here on the social morality of Hsün Ch'ing (also called Hsün Tzu, whose views on* li *were expressed in reading 1 of this Chapter). Hsün Ch'ing, unlike some other Confucian spokesmen, held that man's nature was not good; in fact, men have a tendency toward evil. Also, he was a rationalist in his account of the origin of society, and tried to expurge legends of divine authority and ritual from morality. In this study of Hsün Ch'ing's view of* li, *then, we find no appeals to Divine encounter or revelation as the basis of the highest expression of life. How did the ancient sages learn the principles of life? How did Hsün Ch'ing interpret the differences in the physical and social realms? What does he mean when he urges men to "adopt Heaven's Fate"?*

From "Chou to China,"* the development of an empire from a confederation of clans with diverse pedigrees and economies, is the history of *li* 禮 (rites and propriety). *Li* is, in its broadest sense, the cultural heritage

---

From *Li: Rites and Propriety in Literature and Life* by Noah E. Fehl (Hong Kong: The Chinese University of Hong Kong, 1971), pp. 3, 165–71, 178–80. Used by permission of the author.

* The time from the beginning of the Chou Dynasty to the Chin Dynasty represents about a millennium of cultural life upon which grew the classical Chinese notions, which took form during the Han Dynasty (206 B.C.–220 A.D.).

of Chinese civilisation, the evolution of a cultural style. The history of *li* is the cultural history of pre-Han China. No English words such as "manners" or "propriety," "rites" or "ceremonial" translate the *li* of the *Li Chi*, the Han classic, generally rendered *The Book of Rites*. In part *li* takes the place of, rather than constitutes, what in the western or the middle eastern world is meant by religion or even morality. *Li* is an alternative to the specifically religious and the moral—an alternative so pervasive, persistent and successful in Chinese civilisation that Chinese as well as western Sinologists can find no better word than "moral" to define the perspective of Chinese philosophy and historiography.[1] . . .

The alternative to savagery (the survival of the vilest) is the way of the sage kings. They were the first to make distinctions, to discover man's evil nature, and to hate the disorder which was the inevitable result of a brutish struggle for satisfaction and survival. It was not that they were better or different from other men by nature. "The sage has his original nature in common with ordinary people; he is not different in this respect."[2] The nature of all men, of Yao and Shun, of Chieh and Chih is the same. The nature of the superior man and the inferior man is the same.[3] "The man on the street can become a Yü*—how about that! . . . What gave Yü the qualities of Yü was that he carried out benevolence, justice, obedience to the laws, and uprightness. . .everyman on the street has the nascent ability of knowing the principles of benevolence. . . . Everyone has the capacity of becoming a sage but not everyone exercises it."[4] While the sons of dukes and great officers may fall short of the mark of the superior man, the posterity of the common people may fulfill the demands of *li* and justice.[5] Therefore the paradox is the more striking. Vile man did form a society: he has, over the course of the centuries, created a civilisation. The achievement was not by virtue of some divine hero.[6] Yao, Shun and Yü were however the few who did take the decisive action that initiated a civilised society. Hsün Ch'ing** appears to have followed Mo-ti in suggesting that the initial step was that of assuming the power of rule.

> (They) knew that man's nature was evil, that it was partial, bent on evil, corrupt, rebellious, disorderly, without good government, hence they established the authority of the prince to govern man; they set forth clearly the rules of *li* and justice to reform him, they established laws and government to rule him, they made punishments severe to warn him, and so they caused the whole country to come to a state of good government and prosperity.[7]

Two points in this passage are of special interest: 1. man must be under authority: to seize rule, to establish the overlordship of a prince was the historical and necessary pre-condition of society;[8] 2. those who did, by seizing rule, form a society were men dedicated to the reform of human nature by the institution and enforcement, with severity if need be, of *li* and justice. Any man could have done this. But it is the "historical fact"

---

* Lengendary emperor of noble qualities.
** Hsün Ch'ing is another name for Hsün Tzu.

that it was the sage kings who did it. Hsün Ch'ing is saying: we have a society, notwithstanding this time of troubles, not because men are good— not because we have of ourselves achieved it—nor because of the good will of men at large in the past. We have *li* not because man is good but because he is evil. "For the carpenter's square and rule are produced because there is crooked wood; . . . Princes were established and *li* and justice became evident because man's nature is evil."[9] It was because of the towering achievement of the few, of the one man as it were, in each age who by wisdom and prodigious effort accumulated and united in himself power and justice. In so far as we are in any sense good it is because we are under the authority of the sage kings.[10]

There originated with the Sophists a similar reconstruction in Greek social theory. Sextus Empiricus preserves a fragment of Critias[11] wherein Sisyphus, the hero of this satyr drama, relates how the social life among men began when order was brought out of the chaos of conflicting individual ambitions by the discovery of statecraft and the institution of laws. Some wise men fashioned a code of behaviour which they attributed to the gods and imposed upon a lawless band with the sanction of the tale of an omniscient witness to all wrong doing. Thus they seized rule and established order. Hesiod had earlier identified the rise of human society from "a chaos like unto the bands of beasts" with the time that men were persuaded to sacrifice their own wanton wills to the rule of a just sovereign. Later Euhemerus developed Critias' theory with an emphasis upon the unique role of the sage king: "When the life of mankind was without order, those who so far excelled the rest in strength and intelligence, that all men lived subservient to their commands, being intent to gain for themselves a kind of superhuman and divine authority, were in consequence accounted gods by the populace."[12]

In both streams there is an underlying scepticism. Critias and Euhemerus were attempting a sociological theory, later developed by the early French positivists and Durkheim, of the origin of religion. Critias proposed that the myths and hence the gods also were created by sages in order to accomplish a noble purpose: a sanction greater and more effectual than law to restrain anti-social behaviour and establish the foundation of an orderly society. Thus the sage "introduced" the sweetest of all teachings; but the truth he kept concealed with fraudulent discourse. . . . And thus he quenched out lawlessness with laws.[13] Hsün Ch'ing would have preferred to expunge all legend prior to Yao from literature and its ritual influence from life. Yet if the old religious traditions cannot be extinguished then he would agree with Ssu-ma Ch'ien that ancient cultic deities should be historicised as human hero-sovereigns.[14]

As Hsün Ch'ing reconstructs the formation of a civilised society, the next step taken by the sage, after assuming rule, was to establish the rules of *li* and justice—to formulate the fundamental principles consonant with the 'nature' common to all and the distinctions which properly distinguish one class from another. In each case the inferior must be under the authority of the superior. How did they accomplish this great work? Though they had the same desires as others they were "different and superior to ordinary people in acquired learning."[15] It is implied that they were of higher intelligence.[16] We have in the *Ta Hsüeh* (Great Learning) the clue that their superior "wisdom" was acquired and not an endowment of intellect different in kind from that of other men.[17] First the ancients (sages) "investigated things and extended their knowledge." In this way they were guided toward sincerity, i.e., to seek what is reliable or can be depended upon.[18] By this certainty concerning the nature of things they were able to rectify or reform their own minds. In this sense, then, they were more "intelligent" than their fellows. Their great secret was enlightened self interest. By understanding themselves they knew others. They saw human nature (*hsing* 性) as the product of Nature (*t'ien* 天). The essence of man's nature they knew to be the emotions (*ch'ing* 情) which in reaction to the total environment (social as well as physical) gave rise to desires. Inevitably these led men into conflict. Hsün Ch'ing's prime illustration is the sexual drive: "if this be the case, then men will have the misfortune of losing their mates and the calamity of having to struggle to gain any sex relation. Hence for this reason intelligent men have introduced social distinctions."[19] Similarly, the *Ta Hsüeh* relates that when the ancient sages had rectified their own minds and cultivated (disciplined) their own persons, then they inaugurated the regulation of life within families, and from thence proceeded to the ordering of a state comprising family units. All this is remarkably consonant with the story of the first great cultural revolution which our anthropologists now tell us lay behind the origin of society.[20]

Presumably drawing upon this acquired self understanding, the sages discovered that men had different aptitudes, capacities and skills. Though all men had the same desires they could be distinguished by different abilities. The fundamental distinction in the *Hsün Tzu* is the differences which men exhibit in their capacities to develop ability. All could be equal, but some are wise and some stupid.[21] Hence each has his own kind or level of ability. Each is qualified for a particular kind of occupation.[22] Each has, as it were, his own way (*tao*), and it is this which he should follow. The *tao* of the common man is to exercise his strength in the fields so that he may become an expert farmer; of the merchant, to develop his knowledge of goods and their value; and of the mechanic, to cultivate his skill with tools that he may become an expert artisan.[23] Were it not for these distinctions there could be no society. Differentiation of competence and function is the *tao* of living in society. Society is possible only if there is a hierarchical structure of authority and functions. There is order, harmony and prosperity when the kindly rule of the superior and the respectful obedience of the subordinate are established.[24]

Hsün Ch'ing, following Confucius, Mo-ti and Mencius, reconstructed the rise of civilisation from the perspective of a failing feudalism and a pervasive failure of faith in its ideals. The thrust of his argument is somewhat different than that of earlier Confucians: not what should or could be the way of the restoration of the Chou so much as what are the pillars of any dynasty. For him one foundation of feudal society must in the nature of things be common to any social order. No society can exist without distinctions. First of all there is the distinction between man and animal. Second there are the orders of human society: the ruler and the ruled, the superior and the subordinate, father and son, elder and younger, and husband and wife. Finally there are the divisions of time: the uses of the day, the appropriate activities of the month, the season and the year. Though the last of these did not elicit his special concern, he did not overlook it, but with the former categories he dealt at length, and especially in connection with his development of the Confucian doctrine of the rectification of names (terms). As in the early Confucian school, "rectification" in the *Hsün Tzu* is achieved by reviving distinctions.[25] These distinctions are fundamental to society. They are the pre-condition of any economy and of any pattern of human relationship. "An able man cannot be skilled in more than one line, nor should he hold two offices. If people live alone and do not serve one another there will be poverty. If they live together without social distinctions there will be strife." If there is not the proper separation of the sexes and the regulation of sexual relations there will be a return to savagery.[26]

In Plato's *Republic,* imperfect societies are degenerate societies. Similarly Hsün Ch'ing interprets radical social change from the close of the Western Chou, accelerating in his own time, as a course of increasing disorder that could lead back to chaos. In the perfect society which he sees, in contrast to Plato, as having been realised in the past, particularly in the Hsia dynasty under Yü and in the Chou under the regency of Chou Kung, the king must be the sage or conversely the sage must be king.[27] Only if the son of the sage king is himself a sage should he succeed to the throne. "If not, and there is a sage among the high nobles (such as one of the three chief ministers), the rule should be continued by that sage. In short, on the death of a sage king, the rule must be carried on by whoever is sufficiently qualified."[28] The issue, as in the *Republic,* is to maintain the continuity of sage rule rather than the continuity of a dynasty.[29] Hsün Ch'ing's ideal state is feudal not "republican" and hence it is best for nobility and the people when the king's son is a sage. "If a Yao succeeds a Yao, what change is there?" Nevertheless a change of dynasty, an alternation in the government, is difficult. When this is not possible, when the emperor dies, the person who is able to carry the responsibility of the empire will naturally succeed him. In this, the distinctions of the rules of *li* and standards of justice are made complete, and what need is there of abdication.[30] . . .

There is an established order to which all men must be subservient if society is to survive. It is the special duty of the aristocrat, whether he be the warrior of Homer or the Confucian of superior learning to uphold by his monitions and exhibit in his life those principles and their ceremonial expression that hold society together.[31] An orderly society is the *summum bonum* of man. It is the greatest of human achievements and hence it is enough, whatever his lot, for man to be man.

I would conclude that a noble pessimism and sense of the *noblesse oblige* of the intellectual who spurned sentiment characterised the mind of Hsün Ch'ing in much the same way that we find this cast of mind expressed in the *apologia* for an orderly society in the Greek sceptical school of the Roman period. Both would say that if a man is not master of his fate, he is in a certain sense capable of controlling his response to whatever confronts him to the end that he may serve society. In a sense man's nature is his *ming*.* It is man's *ming* to have desires that cannot be fully satisfied if he is to be a member of a society, and man is not truly man apart from society. Further it is the *ming* of society to have distinctions. Hence *li* and justice are the *ming* which man has fashioned for himself within the limitations of his own nature and his total environment (heaven and earth and his fellowman). Thus Hsün Ch'ing can say that it was Heaven and Earth that gave birth to *li*.[32] Elsewhere he is more explicit: "Heaven and Earth are the source of life, *li* and justice the source of an ordered society; the source of *li* and justice is the superior man; and to follow them, to practice and study them and to love them greatly is the source of being a superior man."[33] In these passages Hsün Ch'ing seems to regard *li* as a categorical imperative grounded in something like a metaphysical first principle. It has cosmologically and historically three sources:

> Heaven and Earth gave it birth—this is a source; our ancestors (sage kings) made it fit the situation—this is a source; the princes and teachers formed (codified) it—this is a source. Without Heaven and Earth how could it be born? Without our ancestors, how could it be produced? Without rulers and teachers, how could it be given form? If one of these were lacking, men would be without peace. Hence the code of *li* on the one hand serves Heaven (the impersonal source of life and of humanity) and on the other, Earth; it honours our ancestors and magnifies the rulers and teachers—this is how *li* (itself) serves the three sources of the code of *li*.
>
> Hence the sovereigns have Heaven for their first ancestor; the feudal nobles dare not move or replace the family tablets; the officers and prefects have a fixed ancestral hall. They are distinguished by their honourable origin; and honourable origin is the source of virtue.'[34]

The passage is a concise summary, something like a creed, comprising many elements of Hsün Ch'ing's philosophy of life. Like all creeds, what is said waits upon interpretation; and it represents, with interpretation, what its author could in candour repeat in conformity with Confucius' own beliefs. With Confucius he holds Chou feudalism to be the one truly viable structure of human society and its government. Deviating from Confucius, he holds this conviction on the basis of an unknowable and impersonal heaven which stands for him as simply the designation of the immutable nature of things as they are, the inscrutable cause of effects observable in the sphere of human affairs that have their setting on earth which is in some way related to heaven.

> The fixed stars make their round; the sun and moon alternately shine; the four seasons come in succession.... We things acquire their germinating principle and are brought into existence.... We do not see

---

* Fate, eternal decree, necessity.

the cause of these occurrences but we do see their effects. The results of these changes are known, but we do not know the invisible soruce—this is what is meant by the work of Heaven. Only the sage does not seek to know Heaven.[35]

Hsün Ch'ing simply could not conceive of either a metaphysics or of a natural science.

> If one seeks to know the laws of the material world by using that wherewith he knows the nature of man, there is nothing to hinder him. ...In studying these laws, although he lived a myriad years, it would not be enough to embrace the changes of all things—he would be the same as a stupid man.[36]

For him the 'what', 'how' and 'why' of nature in our sense were meaningless questions. His only interest, which he felt should be that of all men, was in the question: what use can man make of the given? Neither could he conceive of any relevant or credible theology. "Instead of obeying Heaven and praising it, why not adopt Heaven's Fate (*T'ien Ming* 天命) and make use of it." By this response to the given, man can in some measure "control Heaven's seasons and Earth's material resources, and ultilise them." Not to attempt to penetrate the mystery of what lies behind things as they are, Ssün Ch'ing says, demythologising the old language of religion, "is what is meant by refraining from contesting in one's activities with Heaven."[37] Concluding the analysis of man's nature and the function of the mind cultivated by *li* and learning for mastery over the emotions and what limited control over external circumstance of natural phenomena and society is possible, the *Hsün Tzu* adds the simple observation: "What one meets in a specific situation is called Fate (*ming*)."[38]

NOTES

1. Kuei Fu, *Shuo Wên Chieh Tzǔ I Chêng* (Hupei, 1870), Vol. I, p. 11.
2. XXIII, 4, (D. p. 306). [Roman numerals refer to chapters in *Hsün Tzu*; data in parenthesis refer to H. H. Dubs' translation *The Works of Hsün Tzu* (Probsthain's Oriental Series Vol. XVI, London, 1928), reprinted by Ch'eng-wên Publishing Co., Taipei, 1966.]
3. XXIII, 6. (D. p. 310).
4. *Ibid.*, 7, 8. (D. pp. 312 f.). Similarly the *Li Chi:* "There is no such thing in the world as acquiring honourable position by birth" (XXVI, 18). Thung Chung-shu did not exempt even the emperor from being degraded if he failed to observe *li* and justice (*Ch'un Ch'iu Fan Lu* 春秋繁露 XIV, 70). See B. Watson, *op. cit.,* p. 23.
5. IX.
6. Yao, Shun and Yü shared with all men a propensity toward evil and all other men share with them the ability to distinguish between good and evil, defined in terms of the commonweal.
7. XXIII, 5. (D. p. 308).
8. The aspirant's question: "How do I sieze rule?" is so often the formal prelude to the doctrine of the several schools. *The Book of Lord Shang,* we are

told, is the record of Shang Yang's answer as he edged closer to the prince so that at last their knees were on the same mat. The plot of the historical romance the *Ta K'uang* chapter of the *Kuan Tzŭ* is the guidance given Duke Huan of Ch'i along the path to hegemony. Holding power or exercising rule, Kuan Chung advises, is a matter of setting up and enforcing a system of rewards and punishments for the several classes. First came the covenant, establishing the regime of rule (651), signed at K'uei-ch'u, then the instrument of rule, distinctions of classes and their appropriate rewards and punishments. (*Kuan Tzŭ*, "*Ta K'uang*," chapter 12, b–15a., trans. by Rickett, [*Kuan Tzŭ: A Repository of Early Chinese Thought* (Hong Kong, 1965)], pp. 66 ff.).

9. XXIII, 6. (D. p. 309).
10. See B. Watson's discussion of the far reaching role of the hero in Chinese history which he traces to Ssu-ma Ch'ien's preoccupation with the influence of the individual in history (*op. cit.*, p. 8). 'He was', Watson concludes, "a hero-worshipper who devoted much of his life to writing of the heroes of the past" (*Ibid.*, p. 35).
11. *Adversus Mathematicos* IX, 54. See my *Christian Judgment of Paganism in the First Three Centuries* (University of Chicago microfilm, 1950), pp. 92 ff.
12. *Ibid.*, IX, 17.
13. *Ibid.*, IX, 54. Euhemerus used Critias' theory in support of his thesis that the gods were all once men, possibly the strongest, most talented or even the most noble of their age, whose great contributions subsequently became legendary. Then cults were established and they were worshipped as deities. Hsün Ch'ing makes no claim for the divinity of the sage kings. Quite otherwise he insists that they were men in all ways sharing the same desires and the same basic capacity of all others whether of antiquity or the present. He was demythologising the traditions of Yao, Shun and Yü (who were originally local deities), as were also Critias and Euhemerus in respect of the early Greek cultic "heroes."
14. The Sung scholar, Li T'u, believed this to be too great a concession. Of the Grand Historian, he said: "he takes this factual approach and makes facts out of all the empty tales of the world" (trans. by Burton Watson, *op cit.*, p. 17).
15. XXIII, 4. (D. p. 306).
16. Fung Yu-lan, among the sparse comments of his compendial *History of Chinese Philosophy,* calls attention to Hsün Ch'ing's conclusion to his theory of the origins of society and the state (X, 2. D. p. 153): "Hence for these (reasons) intelligent men have introduced social distinctions." He remarks that the term "intelligent" should be specially noted, for it was by knowledge and intellectual insight, not because of a superior moral nature that the sages established *li* and justice (*op. cit.*, Vol. I, p. 296).
17. I, 4. Here Waley's comment on "The Book of Changes" is pertinent: "If I consult the tortoise and get a favourable response, that is my *tê*. It is my potential good luck, that is my *tê*. But it remains like an uncashed cheque unless I take the right steps to convert it into a *fu* 福, a material blessing." *Museum of Far Eastern Antiquities Stockholm:* Bulletin No. 5. (Stockholm, 1933), p. 136.
18. In the article quoted in fn. 28., Waley explains that our understanding of "sincerity" cannot have been the original meaning of 孚. In the oracle bones it seems generally to stand for "prisoner." He traces its semantic history from the "creature which carries its young (i.e., eggs) in its claws,

the "reliable character of the ant's weather prophecies," and the guarantee posited a hostage or a captive of war to the notion of what can be relied upon, the certain, and finally, the true. (*Ibid.*, p. 125).

19. X, 2. (D. p. 153).
20. See *Scientific American* (Sept., 1960)—a special issue on the origins and earliest development of the human species. See especially the article by Marshall D. Sahlins, "The Origin of Society"; Jacquetta Hawkes, *Prehistory: UNESCO History of Mankind's Cultural and Scientific Development* (New York, 1965), Vol. I, Pt. 1, pp. 177 ff.
21. X, 1. (D. p. 151).
22. X, 1. (D .p. 153).
23. IV, 23. (D. pp. 65 f.).
24. X, 1. (D. p. 152).
25. See Ying-shih Yü's review of T. Fukasu's article on the Confucian doctrine of rectification through distinction, *Revue Bibliographique de Sinologie*, Vol. 6 (Paris, 1967), p. 285.
26. X, 2. (D. pp. 152 f.). See quotation above, p. 218, of *Hsün Tzu* XXIII, (D. pp. 314 f.) on Shün's description of the decline of a society
27. *Republic*, VIII, 543. Similarly for Plato, when rule passes from the philosopher-king to the high command of a timarchy, the return to chaos has begun.
28. Fung Yu-lan comments: "This ideal is identical with that of Mencius, only Mencius, adds to it the concept of a Decree of Heaven, whereas *Hsün Tzu* remains purely rational" (Vol. I, pp. 30 f.).
29. In the ideal republic the philosopher-king would not belong to a dynastic house. He would not know his father, and hence the transmission of rule would in theory not involve the overthrow of a royal house but only the choice of the most capable successor, presumably from among the 'philosopher-ministers'.
31. For the story of Li-yang see *Huai Nan Tzu*, II, 13 (trans. by B. Watson). In this way, Cicero's sceptic in the *De Natura Deorum* and Sextus Empiricus exhort their followers and detractors, lies the realisation of whatever happiness is possible to anyone whether he has been blessed or cursed by fate or chance beyond others.
32. XIX, 3. (D. p. 219) notes that this passage appears in the *Ritual of the Senior Tai* as well as in the *Shu Ching*.
33. XX, 11. (D. pp. 134 f.).
34. XIX, 3. (D. p. 219 f.).
35. XVII, 13. (D. p. 175).
36. XXI, 14. (D. p. 276).
37. XVII, 13. (D. p. 174).
38. This line from chapter XXII ("On the Rectification of Terms") was probably not written by Hsün Ch'ing himself, but it is a concise summing up of what his disciples understood to be their master's disciplined disinterest in a problem which he held man had no ability to resolve. I am indebted to Professor Tang Chun-i for commentary on this quotation which I have used in the translation. 節 he points out meant originally sections of bamboo rather than divisions of time, space, or significant encounters which could be crucial in men's lives. 遇 he suggests can here have the force of "meeting" or "encounter."

What *Karma* Explains,
C. *Humphreys*

> *How is one to explain the apparent injustice of life? The*
> *recurring blight of war? The disorders of the mind? The*
> *seemingly needless loss of good hopes? In this excerpt a widely*
> *read Western advocate of Buddhism tries to convince the reader*
> *that a person can truly understand himself only if he recognizes*
> *that he lives under the "law of karma." Karma means "action"*
> *(deeds, works), and the "law of karma" states that every human*
> *experience is both the result of a former action and the*
> *conditioning force for the future—not only in this life but also*
> *in a future life. Many peoples, including those in the Indian*
> *religious traditions, have believed that when people die, a*
> *spiritual (moral) element continues to form the basis for another*
> *existence; rebirth follows rebirth on different (that is, higher*
> *or lower) planes (animal, human, demon, celestial powers). This*
> *entails a belief in reincarnation or transmigration of souls. The*
> *law of karma, like a law of physics, acts impersonally, so that a*
> *person must take responsibility for his present circumstances while*
> *conditioning his future toward a better life. How does the law*
> *of karma account for differences in opportunity among men,*
> *according to Humphreys? How does it relate to heredity, free*
> *will, "original sin," conscience, and the larger movements of*
> *history? What advantages does Humphreys claim in understanding*
> *the law of karma, for example, in modern psychology? To what*
> *degree do you think this claim has validity?*

Once the Law is reasonably understood it solves a large proportion of the problems which cloud our present mind, and certainly in the East, where Karma is as obvious as the law of gravity, these problems do not arise.

In the first place it explains the inequities and inequalities of daily life. Only Karma

> can explain the mysterious problem of Good and Evil, and reconcile
> man to the terrible *apparent* injustice of life. For when one unacquainted
> with the noble doctrine looks around him, and observes the inequalities
> of birth and fortune, of intellect and capacities; when one sees honour
> paid to fools and profligates, and their nearest neighbour, with all his
> intellect and noble virtues, perishing of want and for lack of sympathy;
> when one sees all this and has to turn away, helpless to relieve the un-

---

From *Karma and Rebirth* by Christmas Humphreys (London: John Murray Ltd., 1943), pp. 54–63.

deserved suffering, that blessed knowledge of Karma alone prevents him from cursing life and men, as well as their supposed Creator.[1]

On the other hand, nothing is more untrue than the cry that all men are born equal. They are not. Each is born with the burden, pleasant or unpleasant, of his own Karma, and no two men are equal, for no two are the same.

> All mankind is one family, but its members are of different ages. Therefore there is no equality of opportunity and no equality of responsibility. Although all are marching towards a common goal they cannot bear equal burdens, and would not be expected to if the Law of Karma were understood.[2]

In the same way Karma explains the problem of Original Sin. There is no problem, for there is no original sin. First causes are necessarily unknowable, and as the Buddha insisted again and again, discussion of such matters is unprofitable, as leading in no way to the heart's enlightenment. But the teaching of the Wisdom is clear. Evil is man-made, and is of his choosing, and he who suffers suffers from his deliberate use of his own free will. Cripples, dwarfs and those born deaf or blind are the products of their own past actions, and one's pity should be used, not in bewailing the injustice of their condition, but in assisting the new-born brain to appreciate its own responsibility and to produce new causes whose result will be the undoing of the evil whose results are manifest. Infant prodigies, on the other hand, are clearly the result of specialization in some particular line, and even special aptitudes and preferences are the outcome of the Law.

Conscience is a Karmic memory. The Essence of Mind is deathless, and its ray, the consciousness (*vinnana*) which moves from life to life, is a store-house of immensely complex memory. Even though the brain, which is new in each life, has forgotten the lessons of past experience, the inner mind remembers, and when temptation murmurs again of the pleasures of a certin low desire, the voice of memory replies, 'But what of the cost in suffering, the price that you paid?'

HEREDITY VERSUS ENVIRONMENT

Karma explains. " 'Karma' expresses, not that which a man inherits from his ancestors, but that which he inherits from himself in some previous state of existence."[3] In the same way, environment is a product of one's own past actions, for each new birth accords with the Karma therein to be discharged. All that is inherited from parents is the body, the outermost garment of the many-robed, essential man. The mind, or returning unit of consciousness, so far from being the product of its body's parents, chose those parents, and the body which they would provide for the working out of a portion of past Karma. Heredity is therefore the servant of Karma and not its substitute. By the law of affinity, the magnetic law of attraction

THE UNIVERSE IS LAWFUL TO THE CORE. (S. Radhakrishnan, The Hindu View of Life)

and repulsion, each new body attracts an appropriate "soul" or character, as each returning consciousness attracts or is attracted to a vehicle suitable for self-expression in the life to come. The staggering complexity of such elaborate choosing, allowing for period, race, sex, family and the compound circumstances of "environment," is a reason for the mind's humility before the Law, but no bar to its acceptance. If an automatic telephone exchange can be made to "choose" which of a dozen lines is the least "loaded" at the moment, how much more can the Namelessness in manifestation operate its own high purposes!

KARMIC CYCLES

Modern astronomy has reached considerable knowledge of the stellar cycles, and even modern astrology, the half-understood remains of a once esoteric and spiritual science, has much to say on planetary cycles and their effect on man. Indian philosophy has a complete record of 'Yugas', great and small, covering enormous periods of time, and of cycles, wheels within wheels, as regular as the ebb and flow of the tide. These cycles affect all planes of manifestation, the psychic and mental as well as the physical, but the law which governs these cycles cannot be understood save in the context of the wider, Karmic Law. The obvious example of the working of the Law on a mass unit of humanity is the rise and fall of races or sub-races, which may or may not be coincident with nations. Whole civilizations are known to have risen, flourished, reached a great height of culture and then decayed or, as in the case of the Khmers of Indo-China, suddenly disappeared. Modern Greece, though still, as the world now knows, a magnificent fighting nation, is not to be compared in culture with its classic forebear; Spain and Portugal are not what they were; Mexico has sunk to comparative insignificance. On the other hand, many a nation now at its prime has risen suddenly, and in the round of time will as surely fall. Ethnologists are always puzzled at the causes of a tribe's collapse and disappearance, and only an understanding of the Law of Karma-Rebirth will solve the mystery. It is not that a given tribe or race by hereditary evolution of its inherent abilities grows rapidly from mediocrity to genius, but that an ever higher standard of "souls" find in the rising race opportunity for their own development. In due course, when the cycle has reached its greatest height, these great ones, far on the road of genius in their several ways, begin to leave, and with the assistance of external causes, themselves Karmic, such as disease, sterility, conquest or moral decay, the race dies out.

THE CAUSE OF WAR

One of the obvious cycles is that of peace and war. War is an effect, the mass-effect of mass thinking, and once the cause is produced the effect is inevitable. The cause of war, as of all evil, is the 'Three Fires' burning in the human mind, desire, hatred and illusion. Hatred is born of illusion, that life is separate, the ignorance of man's essential unity, and desire, or its negative aspect, fear, is the product of and in turn engenders hate.

> Were no man to hurt his brother, Karma–Nemesis would have neither cause to work for, nor weapons to act through. It is the constant presence in our midst of every element of strife and opposition, and the division of races, nations, tribes, societies and individuals into Cains and Abels, wolves and lambs, that is the chief cause of the "ways of Providence."[4]

Hate is a force, a tremendous force, and mass hate slowly accumulates as a thunder-cloud in the sky. When the opposing thought-forms on the psychic plane have reached a point of over-loading it needs but the lightning flash to cause a discharge. But the analogy is insufficient. When the thunder-cloud has fallen the tension is over; the discharge itself does not, in the ordinary sense, produce another cloud. But in war there is hate, deliberate cruelty, revenge and lust. All these are causes, and each must bear its inevitable effect. Thus wars are the cause of wars, and a "war to end war" is one of the wilder illusions of the human mind.

Even in peace we are causing war.

> In our daily life we are competitive, aggressive, nationalistic, vengeful and self-seeking, which inevitably culminates in war. Intellectual and emotionally we are influenced and limited by the past, which produces the present reaction of hate, antagonism and conflict.... Until our own lives are no longer aggressive and greedy, and psychologically we cease from seeking security, and so breaking up the world into different classes, races, nationalities and religions, there cannot be peace.[5]

The cause of war, therefore, is the individual mind which, in its ignorance of man's essential unity, wants everything for itself and therefore hates and fears its fellow men. But this war is an everlasting war within, and until each human being has slain the foe within he will not find peace without. "The man who wars against himself and wins the battle can do it only when he knows that in that war he is doing the one thing which is worth doing."[6]

FORETELLING THE FUTURE

If the future is the past and present not yet come, then it should be as possible to predict the future as it is to predict the future weather, providing, and it is a very large proviso, that all the causal factors are known. But just as a meteorologist can only predict from his known facts, and there are usually factors of which he has no information, so the fortune-teller, whether he be an astrologer dealing in world astrology or some other type considering the affairs of an individual, can only calculate from known factors to the resultant effect which is not yet manifest. If a single factor is missing the whole calculation is worthless. Much "fortune-telling," however, is the work of persons whose psychic faculties, though quite untrained, are more awake than is usual in the Western world. They "feel," by means of cards or other devices for concentrating their faculties, the cloud of unexpected Karma in the aura, or psychic envelope, and try to read it. Being untrained they are seldom accurate, and though palmistry, physiognomy and the like might conceivably, at a later stage in man's evolution, develop into sciences, they are, at our present stage, a poor substitute for knowledge, even assuming that such knowledge is to be desired. But is it? Or does this morbid craving to lift the veil of the future lead but to a weakening of the will? Certainly it is a miserable substitute for the planned and purposeful development of all one's faculties by the conscious user of the Law. The first type wonders what the future will bring; the other decides it.

FURTHER ADVANTAGES

The advantages of working by the Law of Karma have no end. As already explained, the Law provides a graded sanction or reason for right living. At the worst, it is seen that it pays to be good; higher than this, it proves that men are in essence one, and that any deed which hurts one's neighbour or the commonweal is an injury to oneself; finally, it reveals a world or a plane of consciousness where right becomes the inmost law of being, and a man does right, not because it pays or because it avoids self-injury, but because, beyond all argument, he must.

Karma destroys the cause of envy and jealousy and the consequent ill-will, for your neighbour is more fortunate than you because he has earned a better fortune. It removes impatience, for when there is all but infinite time ahead, why worry the fretful hour? It largely removes the fear of death, for where there is inner conviction of rebirth and, by the law of affinity, reunion sooner or later with those one loves, why worry that the hour must come for leaving the present robes and resting, ere returning, robed anew, for fresh experience?

KARMA AND MODERN PSYCHOLOGY

Psychology, the Cinderella of Western science, is yet in its infancy, but any doctrine must sooner or later come to terms with it. Here is a fascinating field for research and experiment. Industrial psychologists, for example, are troubled with the problem of the 'accident prone' workmen who are always suffering or somehow being mixed up in unnecessary "accidents." An American scientist writes that "it has been completely proved, beyond all shadow of doubt, that the elimination of certain men from industrial plants met with a decrease if not a cessation of accidents in that plant." From the personal point of view these men may have "unconsciously-deliberately" caused the accidents; from the mass point of view they may be Karmic agents, that is, as W. Q. Judge defined it, "one who concentrates more rapidly than usual the lines of influence that bring about events, sometimes in a strange and subtle way."

Karma would seem to be the missing link in modern psychology. Surely "complexes" are only deposits in the unconscious from action and reaction in past lives, and "character deficiencies," gaps in the moral development of the patient, defy the physician's skill because none can implant in another's mind a virtue which, though there potentially, has not been developed in the lives gone by. In other words, the psychologist, however skilful his analysis, can only restore the position at birth, removing the knots and inhibitions of wrong thinking and leaving the patient free to resume the path of development with less impediment and wasted energy. The application of psychology to crime, and in particular juvenile delinquency, would be far easier if the psychologist appreciated that he must look further back than the criminal's childhood for the true cause of the crime, and the whole field of insanity should be revised in the light of the Karmic Law. These, however, are the exceptions, for the West has need of applying the Law to the many, not only to the few. The outlook on life of the "man in the street" could be utterly changed by a knowledge of Karma, and he who accepts it as a reasonable hypothesis will find by his own experience that the Law is true, and that he who uses it is master of life and death, and the sole custodian of his destiny.

NOTES

1. *The Secret Doctrine*, H. P. Blavatsky.
2. *The Scales of Karma*, Owen Rutter.
3. *Buddhism in Translations*, Henry Clarke Warren.
4. *The Secret Doctrine*, H. P. Blavatsky.
5. *Krishnamurti. Notes of a Talk in America.*
6. *Practical Occultism*, H. P. Blavatsky.

10. Hindu *Dharma*, S. Radhakrishnan

Does the notion of Karmic law necessarily lead to fatalism (total determinism) and to despair for a person sensitive to his own evil? Here Dr. Radhakrishnan (b. 1888), a noted Indian philosopher and former president of India (1962–67), advocates living according to the natural order of life (dharma), which balances personal expression (as set in the context of inherited capacities) with social responsibilities. This excerpt follows a discussion of the importance of the social order (law) according to Hindu orthodoxy, which divides society into four classes ("castes," varna, see reading 3)—plus the "outcastes," in a later development—and then marks off four stages of development

From *The Hindu View of Life* by S. Radhakrishnan (London: George Allen & Union Ltd., 1927), pp. 71–83. Used by permission of the publisher.

(aśrama) *in the lives of males belonging to the three highest classes: student, householder, "forest-dweller" for self-reflection and contemplation of ultimate truth, and wandering ascetic. (A woman finds her self-identity in relation to her father at birth, to her husband at marriage, and to her son if her husband dies before she does.) The religious implication of this social obligation is that one's highest duty is to express in daily life that action which is right for him according to sex, birth into a certain class, and stage of maturity. All this adds up, claims Radhakrishnan, to "a spiritual view of society as an organic whole." This, of course, places an emphasis on heredity and careful childhood training to maintain a sense of one's role in the family, society, and cosmic harmony. In this excerpt the author advocates social class distinctions within an organic view of society. Note that though Radhakrishnan states that "Caste on its social side is a product of human organization and not a mystery of divine appointment," the weight of his discussion about the importance of the distinctions between classes rests on their natural or inherent quality. Thus, he argues: "We may wish to change or modify our particular mode of being, but we have not the power to effect it." Do you agree that our "individualistic conception of society" tends to educate people toward egotistic materialism and expediency, and that an "organic view of society" would instruct people that service to fellowmen is a more religious purpose for social, political, and economic action? Do you agree that the development of social distinctions is a civilizing force? Would you agree that there is, as a matter of fact, a four-fold "caste organization" of (1) the cultural and spiritual guides, (2) military and political leaders, (3) economic classes, and (4) unskilled workers in every society? Do you think that Radhakrishnan's solution to the "class conflict" by cultivating the sense that all classes are part of an organic whole and thus mutually dependent on each other is a realistic solution?*

Indiscriminate racial amalgamation was not encouraged by the Hindu thinkers. The Hindu scriptures recognized the rules about food and marriage which the different communities were practising. What we regard as the lower castes have their own taboos and customs, laws and beliefs which they have created for themselves in the course of ages. Every member of the group enters into the possession of the inheritance bequeathed. It is the law of use and wont that distinguishes one group from its neighbours. Caste is really custom. Crude and false as the customs and beliefs of others may seem to us, we cannot deny that they help the community adopting them to live at peace itself and in harmony with others. It is a point of social honour for every member to marry within his own caste, and a 'low' caste woman would refuse to marry one outside her caste, even if he were from a "higher" one.

Though the Hindu theory of caste does not favour the indiscriminate crossing of men and women, interbreeding has been practised, largely unconsciously, and the essential differences of tribes were modified. Purely anthropological groups are found only among primitive and savage peoples, and not in the societies which play a part in the march of humanity. There has been a general infusion of foreign blood into the Hindu race, and within the race itself there has been a steady flow of blood from the Brahmin to the Caṇḍāla.* The inter-mixture of blood has been carefully regulated by means of *anuloma* and *pratiloma* marriages, though the tendency to indiscriminate crossing was not encouraged. While Manu recommends marriages of members of the same caste (*savarṇa*) he tolerates marriages of men with women of the "lower castes" (*anuloma*). Though he does not justify *pratiloma* marriages, i.e., marriages of women of the "higher" castes with men of the "lower," he describes the various progeny of such marriages. While they were not regarded as proper there is no doubt that they prevailed. Castes of a mixed type have been formed in order to regularize the position of groups originally proceeding from marriages forbidden or discountenanced by custom or law but condoned after a time. Some of the groups which are today regarded as "untouchable" are said to have arisen by indiscriminate crossing.

While we are dealing with this question, it may be observed that the Hindu system did not condemn all crossing as mischievous. When the stocks are of nearly the same level, crossing is highly beneficial. The deplorable example of the Eurasians is frequently quoted, but then the two stocks happen to be widely different. Besides, the circumstances which accompany their birth and training will damage the best of men. The white man who seduces an Indian nearly always abandons her when she becomes a mother, and the child coming into the world as the product of irregular mating, badly nourished and much despised, grows up generally in conditions which are not very desirable. Not only inheritance but environment also counts.

Yet the principle of *savarṇa* marriages is not unsound. It is a difficult question to decide whether the influence of heredity is so great as to justify *savarṇa* marriages only. The question of nature *versus* nurture is still hotly debated. Democrats are quite certain that it is not blue blood or inherited traits that make for the superiority of the upper classes. The Hindu view, however, has the support of ancient Greek thought and modern science. The Greeks believed in heredity and actually developed a theory of race betterment by the weeding out of inferior strains and the multiplication of the superior ones. As early as the sixth century B.C. the Greek poet Theognis of Megara wrote, "We look for rams and asses and stallions of good stock, and one believes that good will come from good; yet a good man minds not to wed the evil daughter of an evil sire.... Marvel not that stock of our folk is tarnished, for the good is mingling with the base." We are all familiar with Plato's views of biological selection as the best method of race improvement. Aristotle also believed that the state should encourage

---

* That is, from the highest social level to the lowest.

the increase of superior types. There has been during the eighteenth century an increasing insistence on the natural equality of men. Adopting the views of Locke and Rousseau, the thinkers of French and American declarations on human right, Buckle held that men were moulded by their environments as so much soft clay. Modern science, however, holds that this view exaggerates the influence of the environment. Progress does not depend on a mere change of surroundings. Darwin's teaching that evolution proceeds by heredity was taken up by Galton and other biologists like Weismann and De Vries, and the science of eugenics rests today on somewhat safe and sound foundations. The marvellous potency of the germ-plasm is shown by carefully isolating and protecting it against external influences when it steadily follows its predetermined course. Even when interfered with, it tends to overcome the opposition and resume its normal course. Every cell of our body contains tiny chromosomes, which practically determine our being, height and weight, form and colour, nervous organization and vital energy, temperament and intelligence. Half the number of chromosomes in every cell of our body comes from the father and half from the mother, and they transmit to us most faithfully the qualities of our parents. Any stupidity or insanity of our parents, grandparents or great-grandparents will be transmitted to our children and our children's children. The Hindu thinkers, perhaps through a lucky intuition or an empirical generalization, assumed the fact of heredity and encouraged marriages among those who are of approximately the same type and quality. If a member of a first-class family marries another of poor antecedents the good inheritance of the one is debased by the bad inheritance of the other, with the result that the child starts life with a heavy handicap. If the parents are about the same class the child would be practically the equal of the parents.[1] Blood tells. We cannot make genius out of mediocrity or good ability out of inborn stupidity by all the aids of the environment.

It does not, however, mean that nature is all and nurture is nothing. The kind of nurture depends on the group and its type. So long as we had the caste system, both nature and nurture co-operated. There is such a thing as social heredity. Each successive generation acquires by conscious effort the social acquisitions of the groups.

If we want to prevent the suicide of the social order, some restrictions have to be observed with regard to marital relations. Marriages should be, not necessarily in one's own caste but among members of approximately the same level of culture and social development. For castes also degenerate. As sons are expected to follow the calling of their fathers, superior individuals are not allowed to grow higher than the groups, and the inferior ones are not allowed to sink lower into their proper scale. Caste, as it is, has not made room for high-born incompetents and low-born talents. While every attempt should be made to energize the weak and the lowly by education and moral suasion, indiscriminate marriage relations do not seem to be always desirable.

Without creating great racial disturbances the Hindu spirit brought about a gradual racial harmony. The synthesis of caste started as a social organization of different ethnic types. There is no doubt that there are many animists who have not been assimilated by Hinduism. When Hindu India lost its independence its work of assimilation and reform stopped, though the present day Hindu leaders are slowly realizing their responsibilities towards them.

Caste was the answer of Hinduism to the forces pressing on it from outside. It was the instrument by which Hinduism civilized the different tribes it took in. Any group of people appearing exclusive in any sense is a caste. Whenever a group represents a type a caste arises. If a heresy is born in the bosom of the mother faith and if it spreads and produces a new type, a new caste arises. The Hindu Society has differentiated as many types as can be reasonably differentiated, and is prepared to accept new ones as they arise. It stands for the ordered complexity, the harmonized multiplicity, the many in one which is the clue to the structure of the universe.

Today many brilliant writers are warning us of a world-conflict of races. The rise of racial selfconsciousness is a peculiar phenomenon of our times. The coloured peoples are clamouring rightly for a share in the control of the world. Those who are politically subject are demanding political freedom. The conflict between emigration and immigration countries is highly acute. When the weak, the ignorant and the slothful races were wiped out or subordinated, it was argued in defence of this method that the savage races and the primitive peoples could not expect to remain undisturbed in their habitat, for the world cannot afford to let fields lie fallow and ore remain undug, and if the chance occupants of resourceful areas are too feeble and sluggish to develop them, their displacement by people who can redeem the waste places is necessary and right. The mere fact that in the chance wanderings of the race, a particular tribe happened to pitch its tent on a diamond field or an oil-well whose existence it had not guessed and whose use it had not understood, does not give that tribe an exclusive claim to its possession. No country belongs to itself. The needs of the world are the paramount consideration. But this argument is not applied to the present conditions. While the pressure of population draws masses of men from their countries to seek employment elsewhere, and while there are immense underpopulated areas requiring intelligent labour for the development of their resources, the adjustments are not allowed to take place. America, Australia, South Africa, etc, are forbidden lands to the coloured people. Latin America is very sparsely populated, and might easily contain ten times its present number and increase its production to an almost unlimited extent. There are territories which thirst for population and others which are overflowing with it, and yet pride of race and love of power are overriding all considerations of abstract justice and economic necessity. It is not my purpose here to deal with the practical difficulties in the way of an easy solution of the racial problem. They are great, but they can be solved only by the consciousness of the earth as one great family and an endeavour to express this reality in all our relationships. We must work for a world in which all races can blend and mingle, each retaining its special characteristics and developing whatever is best in it.

Very early in the history of Hinduism, the caste distinctions came to mean the various stratifications into which the Hindu society settled. The confusion between the tribal and the occupational is the cause of the perpetuation of the old exclusiveness of the tribal customs in the still stringent rules which govern the constitution of each caste. Caste on its social side is a product of human organization and not a mystery of divine appointment. It is an attempt to regulate society with a view to actual differences and ideal unity. The first reference to it is in the Purusa Sūkta, where the different sections of society are regarded as the limbs of the great self. Human society is an organic whole, the parts of which are naturally dependent in such a way that each part in fulfilling its distinctive function conditions the fulfilment of function by the rest, and is in turn conditioned by the fulfilment of its function by the rest. In this sense the whole is present in each part, while each part is indispensable to the whole. Every society consists of groups working for the fulfilment of the wants of the society. As the different groups work for a common end they are bound by a sense of unity and social brotherhood. The cultural and the spiritual, the military and the political, the economic classes and the unskilled workers constitute the four-fold caste organization. The different functions of the human life were clearly separated and their specific and complementary character was recognized. Each caste has its social purpose and function, its own code and tradition. It is a close corporation equipped with a certain traditional and independent organization, observing certain usages regarding food and marriage. Each group is free to pursue its own aims free from interference by others. The functions of the different castes were regarded as equally important to the well-being of the whole. The serenity of the teacher, the heroism of the warrior, the honesty of the business man, and the patience and energy of the worker all contribute to the social growth. Each has its own perfection.

The rules of caste bring about an adjustment of the different groups in society. The Brahmins were allowed freedom and leisure to develop the spiritual ideals and broadcast them. They were freed from the cares of existence, as gifts to them by others were encouraged and even enjoined. They are said to be above class interests and prejudices, and to possess a wide and impartial vision. They are not in bondage to the State, though they are consulted by the State. The State, as one of the groups in society, was essentially military in its organization. Its specific function was to preserve peace and order, and see to it that the different groups worked in harmony and no confusion of functions arose. The Government was an executive organization expected to carry out the best interests of the people. The Brahmins, as the advisors of the Government, point out the true interests of society.

The political and the economic life of the community is expected to derive its inspiration from the spiritual. This principle saved the State from becoming a mere military despotism. The sovereign power is not identified with the interests of the governing classes but with those of the people at large. While dharma represents the totality of the institutions by which the commonweal is secured and the life of the people is carried on,

Government is the political organization which secures for all the conditions under which the best life can be developed. The State did not include the other institutions, trade guilds, family life, etc, which were allowed freedom to manage their own affairs. It did not interfere with art, science and religion, while it secured the external conditions of peace and liberty necessary for them all. Today, the functions of the State are practically unlimited, and embrace almost the whole of social life.

In spite of its attachment to the principle of non-violence, Hindu society made room for a group dedicated to the use of force, the Kṣatriyas. As long as human nature is what it is, as long as society has not reached its highest level, we require the use of force. So long as society has individuals who are hostile to all order and peace, it has to develop controls to check the anti-social elements. These anti-social forces gather together for revolt when the structure of society is shaken by war or internal dissensions. It is a great tribute to the relative soundness of the social structure in Great Britain, in all its strata, that its industrial upheavals, such as the general strike of 1926, which continued for nine days, are marked by little criminality and rowdyism.

The economic group of the Vaiśyas were required to suppress greed and realize the moral responsibilities of wealth. Property is looked upon as an instrument of service. In the great days of Hinduism, the possessor of property regarded it as a social trust and undertook the education, the medical relief, the water supply and the amusements of the community. Unfortunately at the present day in almost all parts of the world the strain of money-making has been so great that many people are breaking down under it. Love of wealth is disrupting social life and is tending to the suppression of the spiritual. Wealth has become a means of self-indulgence, and universal greed is the cause of much of the meanness and cruelty which we find in the world. Hinduism has no sympathy with the view that "to mix religion and business is to spoil two good things." We ought not to banish spiritual values from life.

The unskilled workers and the peasants form the proletariat, the Śūdras. These castes are the actual living members of the social body each centred in itself and working alongside one another in co-operation. When a new group is taken into the fold of Hinduism, it is affiliated with one of the four castes. Many of the races from outside were accepted as Kṣatriyas. Mr Jackson writes: "Those Indians indeed have a poor opinion of their country's greatness who do not realize how it has tamed and civilized the nomads of Central Asia, so that wild Turcoman tribes have been transformed into some of the most famous of the Rajput royal races."[2]

The system of caste insists that the law of social life should not be cold and cruel competition, but harmony and co-operation. Society is not a field of rivalry among individuals. The castes are not allowed to compete with one another. A man born in a particular group is trained to its manner, and will find it extremely hard to adjust himself to a new way. Each man is said to have his own specific nature (*svabhāva*) fitting him for his own specific function (*svadharma*), and changes of dharma or function are not encouraged. A sudden change of function when the nature is against its proper fulfilment may simply destroy the individuality of the being. We may wish to change or modify our particular mode of being, but we have not the power to effect it. Nature cannot be hurried by our desires. The four castes represent men of thought, men of action, men of feeling, and others in whom none of these is highly developed. Of course, these are the dominant and not the exclusive characters, and there are all sorts of permutations and combinations of them which constitute adulterations (*sankara*) and mixture (*miśra-jāti*). The author of the *Bhagavadgītā* believes that the divisions of caste are in accordance with each man's character and aptitude.[3] Karma is adapted to *guṇa*, and our qualities in nature can be altered only gradually. Since we cannot determine in each individual case what the aptitudes of the individuals are, heredity and training are used to fix the calling. Though the functions were regarded as hereditary, exceptions were freely allowed. We can learn even from lowly persons. All people possess all qualities though in different degrees. The Brahmin has in him the possibilities of a warrior. The *ṛṣis* of old were agriculturists and sometimes warriors too.

The caste idea of vocation as service, with its traditions and spiritual aims, never encouraged the notion of work as a degrading servitude to be done grudgingly and purely from the economic motive. The perfecting of its specific function is the spiritual aim which each vocational group set to itself. The worker has the fulfilment of his being through and in his work. According to the *Bhagavadgītā,* one obtains perfection if one does one's duty in the proper spirit of non-attachment. The cant of the preacher who appeals to us for the deep-sea fishermen on the ground that they daily risk their lives, that other people may have fish for their breakfasts, ignores the effect of the work on the worker. They go to sea not for us and our breakfasts but for the satisfaction of their being. Our convenience is an accident of their labours. Happily the world is so arranged that each man's good turns out to be the good of others. The loss of artistic vitality has affected much of our industrial population. A building craftsman of the old days had fewer political rights, less pay and less comfort too, but he was more happy as he enjoyed his work. Our workers who enjoy votes will call him a slave simply because he did not go to the ballot-box. But his work was the expression of his life. The worker, whether a mason or a bricklayer, blacksmith or carpenter, was a member of a great co-operative group initiated into the secrets of his craft at an impressionable age. He was dominated by the impulse to create beauty. Specialization has robbed the worker of pride in craft. Work has now become business, and the worker wants to escape from it and seeks his pleasure outside in cinemas and television. While the social aspirations of the working classes for a fuller life are quite legitimate, there is unfortunately an increasing tendency to interpret welfare in terms of wealth. The claims of materialism are more insistent in the present vision of social betterment. The improvement of human nature is the true goal of all endeavour, though this certainly requires an indispensable minimum of comfort to which the worker is entitled.

We are now face to face with class conflicts. There has grown up an intense class consciousness with elements of suspicion and hatred, envy and jealousy. We are no more content to bring up our children in our own manner of life, but are insisting that all doors must be opened to those equipped with knowledge. The difficulties are due to the fact that some occupations are economically more paying, and all wish to knock at the paying doors. Democracy is so interpreted as to justify not only the very legitimate aspiration to bring about a more equitable distribution of wealth, but also the increasing tendency for a levelling down of all talent. This is not possible. There will always be men of ability who lead and direct, and others who will obey and follow. Brains and character will come to the top, and within the framework of democracy we shall have an aristocracy of direction. It is not true that all men are born equal in every way, and everyone is equally fit to govern the country or till the ground. The functional diversities of workers cannot be suppressed. Every line of development is specific and exclusive. If we wish to pursue one we shall have to turn our attention away from others. While we should remove the oppressive restrictions, dispel the ignorance of the masses, increase their self-respect, and open to them opportunities of higher life, we should not be under the illusion that we can abolish the distinctions of the genius and the fool, the able organizer and the submissive worker. Modern democracies tend to make us all mere "human beings," but such beings exist nowhere.

India has to face in the near future the perils of industrialism. In factory labour where men are mechanized, where they have little to do with the finished product, and cannot take any pleasure in its production, work is mere labour, and it does not satisfy the soul. If such mechanical work cannot be done by machines, if men have to do it, the less of it they have to do the better for them. The more the work tends to become mechanical and monotonous, the more necessary it is that the worker should have larger leisure and a better equipment for the intelligent use of it. The standard of employment must be raised not merely in wages, but in welfare. Mechanical work should be economically more paying than even that of the artist or the statesman. For in the latter case work is its own reward. In ancient India the highest kind of work, that of preserving the treasures of spiritual knowledge, was the least paid. The Brahmin had no political power or material wealth. I think there is some justice in this arrangement, which shows greater sympathy for those whose work is soul-deadening. We have also to remember that the economic factor is not the most important in a man's life. A man's rank is not to be determined by his economic position. Gambling peers are not higher than honest artisans. The exaltation of the economic will lead to a steady degradation of character. Again, we should not forget that the individuals who constitute the nation cannot all pursue the one occupation of political leadership or military power, but will be distributed into many employments, and these will tend to create distinctive habits and sympathies. Though there may be transfers from one group to another, they are not likely to be numerous.

We are not so certain today as we were a century ago that the individualistic conception of society is the last word in social theory. The moral advantages of the spiritual view of society as an organic whole are receiving greater attention. A living community is not a loose federation of competing groups of traders and teachers, bankers and lawyers, farmers and weavers, each competing against all the rest for higher wages and better conditions. If the members of the different groups are to realize their potentialities, they must share a certain community of feeling, a sense of belonging together for good or evil. There is much to be said from this point of view for the system of caste which adheres to the organic view of society and substitutes for the criterion of economic success and expediency a rule of life which is superior to the individual's interests and desires. Service of one's fellows is a religious obligation. To repudiate it is impiety.

Democracy is not the standardizing of everyone so as to obliterate all peculiarity. We cannot put our souls in uniform. That would be dictatorship. Democracy requires the equal right of all to the development of such capacity for good as nature has endowed them with. If we believe that every type means something final, incarnating a unique possibility, to destroy a type will be to create a void in the scheme of the world. Democracy should promote all values created by the mind. Each kind of service is equally important for the whole. Society is a living organism, one in origin and purpose though manifold in its operations. There can be no real freedom in any section or class in a society so long as others are in bondage. It is a truly democratic ideal that is uttered in the words, "May all cross safely the difficult places of life, may all see the face of happiness, may all reach that right knowledge, may all rejoice everywhere." While the system of caste is not a democracy in the pursuit of wealth or happiness, it is a democracy so far as the spiritual values are concerned, for it recognizes that every soul has in it something transcendent and incapable of gradations, and it places all beings on a common level regardless of distinctions of rank and status, and insists that every individual must be afforded the opportunity to manifest the unique in him. Economically we are a co-operative concern or brotherhood where we give according to our capacity and take according to our needs. Politically we enjoy equal rights in the sight of law, and these two enable us to attain true spiritual freedom. A just organization of society will be based on spiritual liberty, political equality and economic fraternity.

NOTES

1. An interesting record of one Martin Kallakak appeared in *Popular Science Siftings:* "Martin Kallakak was a young soldier in the Revolutionary War. His ancestry was excellent. But in the general laxity and abnormal social conditions of war-time he forgot his noble blood. He met a physically attractive but feeble-minded girl. The result of the meeting was a feeble-

minded boy. This boy grew up and married a woman who was apparently of the same low stock as himself. They produced numerous progeny. These children in turn married others of their kind, and now for six generations this strain has been multiplying. Since that night of dissipation long ago the population has been augmented by 480 souls who trace their ancestry back to Martin Kallakak and the nameless girl. Of these 143 have been feeble-minded, 33 have been immoral, 36 illegitimate, 3 epileptics, 3 criminals and 8 brothel-keepers. The original Martin, however, after sowing this appalling crop of wild oats, finally married a young Quaker woman of splendid talents and noble ancestry. From this union there have been 496 direct descendants. Many of them have been governors, soldiers, one founder of a great university, doctors, lawyers, judges, educators, land-holders, and useful citizens and admirable parents prominent in every phase of social life. The last one in evidence is now a man of wealth and influence."

2. *Indian Antiquary,* January 1911.
3. iii. 21: xvii. 13, 41, 45–6.

11. Ethical Culture,
D. S. Muzzey

Less well-known than Roman Catholicism, Protestantism, or Judaism in the West is a small humanist movement known as Ethical Culture. Like the authors in the previous readings, our representative figure from this movement, David Muzzey, affirms the existence of a moral law in the universe without tying this affirmation to any kind of theism. In fact, he explicitly rejects the creeds and myths of various Western religious traditions and asserts that it is the moral element which is the prior, and the only valid religious element, in these traditions. What weaknesses does he find in the Christian and Jewish traditions? Does he think that man is inherently capable of responding to the moral law? Compare the capacity for moral perfection with that found in the Confucian ideal. Do you agree that the most profound moral acts are independent of creeds or sacramental acts?

"The most powerful thing in the world," wrote Victor Hugo, "is an idea whose time has come." Quietly, persistently, inexorably that idea ripens into actuality like the fruit which matures in the vernal sun. The time for the emergence of a forward-looking, democratic, universal religion of ethics is at hand. The world is waiting for the sunrise of a common

From *Ethics as a Religion* by David S. Muzzey (New York: Simon & Schuster, Inc., 1951. Reprinted New York: Frederick Unger, 1967), pp. 85, 155–59.

faith which shall inspire its new-found and travail-born resolve to gather the nations into a common fold of humanity. How near or how distant the daybreak of that faith may be we do not know. But the signs of its dawning are multiplying every year that passes. The footprints of history are pointing toward that goal. The future is with ethical religion. . . .

The first postulate of ethical religion is the existence of a moral law in the universe, as permeating and indefeasible as the physical laws of nature. Belief in this moral law far antedates the rise of Christianity. Thousands of years ago the Egyptian sages recognized the binding force of this law, as we see from the pyramid texts and ethical precepts recorded in the late Professor Breasted's fascinating book, *The Dawn of Conscience.* For the Hebrews in their crude tribal state Jehovah was a local god of battles like the gods of neighboring tribes; but for the great prophets of Israel he became the incarnation of universal moral law. More than four centuries before the birth of Jesus the Greek tragedian Sophocles makes his heroine Antigone stand fearlessly up to King Creon and invoke, in justification of her defiance, a higher law than the king's edict: "Nor deemed I that thy decrees were of such force that a mortal could override the unwritten and unfailing statutes of heaven. For their life is not of yesterday or today, but from all time, and no man knows when they were first put forth." What were these "statutes of heaven" which Egyptian, Israelite and Greek long centuries ago, as well as Wordsworth and Emerson and Gandhi in recent times, have seen as binding on the conscience of man, but the majestic moral law which pervades the universe? It is the matrix of all just laws of mortal making. It is, in the language of Plato, the "idea" of law itself, "laid up in heaven"; transcendent, indefinable, inexorable, but so *real* to believing men that they have gone to the stake, faced wild beasts in the arena, and drunk the hemlock rather than disobey its commands.

But do not the synagogues and churches also exalt the moral law? Do they not also postulate a binding sense of obligation on the part of men to live up to its commands to the limit of their possibilities? Certainly they do. Yet there is a real difference between the postulate of moral law as held by synagogue and church and that held by the ethical religion. And the difference lies in the fact that for Judaism and Christianity the source of the moral law lies in certain historical events which seem to the Ethical Culturist to qualify, or to tend to qualify, its universality. For example, in Judaism it is the "Law of Moses"—the Torah and its supplements and commentaries—that gives a tone of particularism to moral law. The concept of a "chosen people," in spite of the injunction laid upon them to consider their "election" to Jehovah's favor as a mission to extend his commands to nations of the world, affects the moral law with an element of prescribed historic ritual which limits rather than commends its universality. Turn back, if you please, to the words of Joseph Klausner quoted near the beginning of Chapter Three* and see the traces of racialism and

---

* This refers to a chapter in Muzzey's book not included here.

legalism which still linger in the Jewish conception of the reign of moral law. Though the nations are not literally to be gathered to the holy hill of Zion, yet "the historic national culture" of the Jewish people is to continue, "the politico-spiritual Messianic ideal of Israel" is to be realized "in all its fulness," and the "ceremonial laws of Judaism...shall not be altogether abolished, since they serve to protect the existence of the nation." This is hardly the language of a universal moral law which transcends the accidents of race or ritual.

Nor does the Christian conception of the moral law wholly satisfy our ethical demands. This is because the Christianity (or perhaps one should say the "churchianity") developed by the church fathers and councils conditioned acceptable moral conduct upon theological belief. Emerson was ostracized by the Harvard Divinity School because in his address of 1838 to the students he declared that nothing was at last sacred to them but the integrity of their own minds. Virtue was virtue, from whatever source it came. But in the eyes of the church the virtues of the man who did not confess to having been "born again" by the grace of God were only manifestations of mundane pride.

This interposition of a theological sanction detracted from the majesty of moral law. For it made its universal and timeless authority, so magnificently stated in the plea of Antigone which we have quoted, subordinate to the authority of a dogma imposed by an institution which had grown to power in the midst of historical vicissitudes that greatly modified its primitive character. But ethics is independent of theological creeds. The universal moral law admits no impediment to its validity, no modification of its authority. It contains its own sanction.

A second postulate of ethical religion is the existence of a spiritual element in man's nature which makes him capable of seeking the fulfillment of the moral law in his daily conduct. It is on the ground of that capability that we attribute worth to him. And it is to that capability that the appeal of every worthy religion has been made. Certainly this was true of the religion taught by the Hebrew prophets and by Jesus. The latter throughout his ministry never ceased to exhort and *expect* men to turn from evil to righteousness. All his wonderful parables (the prodigal son, the good Samaritan, the friend at midnight, the workers in the vineyard, and the rest) were told to stimulate in his hearers the resolve to lead a better life. In the Sermon on the Mount there is not a single proposition of theological tenor; the "blessed" are those who manifest the *ethical* qualities of humility, purity of soul, love of peace, and hunger and thirst after righteousness.

How did it come about that the wholesome confidence in man's mental and moral capacities which characterized the great thinkers of antiquity, like Socrates, Plato, Aristotle, Epictetus and Seneca, yielded to the despairing doctrine of human impotence to cope with the challenge of destiny or take a single step toward spiritual growth? Gilbert Murray, in his *Five Stages of Greek Religion,* coined the phrase "the failure of nerve" to designate the period of intellectual and moral letdown that followed the age of Aristotle and Alexander the Great. The zest for constructive thinking was lost. Men lived on the leavings of great ages past. A soul-sickness spread like an epidemic, and the cult of savior-gods flourished in all parts of the Roman Empire. It was in this soil of intellectual and moral abdication that the seed of Christianity was sown. And the theologians of the early church, inevitably influenced by the "climate of opinion" of the age in which they lived, erected the doctrine of man's utter incompetence to enter on the path of righteousness except through the grace of the one Savior-God into the basic dogma of the church. If protests against the denial of the efficacy of man's own will and reason to guide him in the search for righteousness were raised here and there, they were silenced by the authority of the church. Thus, when an Irish monk named Pelagius asserted that man could take the initiative in procuring his salvation through good works, he was condemned as a heretic by St. Augustine in a blistering treatise against Pelagianism. Nor were the Protestant reformers like Luther and Calvin any less firm in their denunciation of the doctrine of man's competence, in his "natural" state of sin, to move toward virtue. The moral of the parable of the prodigal son escaped them.

OPTION

(12.) The *Shari'ah* of Islam, K. Cragg

*The word Shari'ah originally meant "the path leading to water,"
and thus it carries the connotation that it is the way to the source
of life. This source, which draws all creatures back to itself, is
none other than God, who shows and ordains the way to a full
life. Therefore, when people walk the path ordained by God
they automatically submit their wills to His. Ideally, the Muslim
(literally, the "submitter to God") patterns his everyday life
according to the will of Allah (God) as found in the divine
revelation (Qur'ān). The Qur'ān is the ultimate source of the
Shari'ah, or right path of social life. What areas of life, according
to Cragg, should be governed by Shari'ah? What threefold division
of this Shari'ah is given by the author? Note the five "pillars" or
"articles" of Islam mentioned, and especially the moral obligation
of almsgiving. Do you see any similarity in the importance and
religious role of Shari'ah and the Hindu dharma or Chinese li?*

From *The House of Islam* by Kenneth Cragg, pp. 45–48. © 1969 by Dickenson Publishing Company, Inc., Belmont, California. Reprinted by permission of the publisher.

There is, indeed, no more complete ethical theism than Islam. Its genius, we often find it said, is law rather than theology. The point is well made. But it would be truer to say that its strength lies in theology as law. It understands the world and man as set under God, constituted by creation, guided by revelation and summoned to submission. Awareness of God is, therefore, primarily awareness of obligation and accountability. Just as the law from Sinai set Jewry under the claims of the Divine Lordship within what they understood as sacred history, so the Divine law in Islam makes all life and activity the realm of God's authority and man's obedience. The knowledge Islam enjoys in the revelation has to do directly with the demands of God and only indirectly with His nature. Law, we may say, is religion and religion is law.

The general term embracing both is *Shari'ah,* or "way," or right path of action, both ritual and ethical. This is the Torah of Islam, received through the Prophet and elaborated in the first three centuries of Islam through the gathering experience of Muslims in its custody. Law is often denoted by a term earlier than *Shari'ah,* namely *Fiqh,* or "understanding." The *fuqahā',* or "legists," were the men of discernment who drew out, for actual jurisprudence, or life-direction and due order, the implications of the Divine will. The word *Fiqh* combines the twin ideas of directive and response, of God in command and man in surrender.

Total and inclusive as it is, this *islām,* or law-abidingness, of man within the structure of Divine direction is not properly seen as passive or servile. It belongs with the dignity of man as entrusted with the dominion (*khilāfah*) of the world, and as undertaking the *amānah,* or trust, of suzerainty under God. (See Surahs 2:30 and 33:72). The earth is the Lord's and not man's. But the 'empire' over it is given into man's hands and presupposes capacities of intelligence and freedom, as well as of loyalty. In that responsibility to God with and for the world, lies the issue of man's being.

The intelligent nature of man's *Fiqh,* or conformity to the Divine will, does not mean that the *Shari'ah* is derived from rationality. On the contrary, it is given by God and has no other ground. Even where its contents take their definition from sources other than the Qur'ān and tradition, they possess, nevertheless, the same revelatory and mandatory quality. The *Shari'ah* is what God commands and what men obey. The very legalism it may engender is, arguably, a lesser evil than the reduction of its imperative force. Submission is tested, exemplified, made concrete, even in exacting rituals and matters that reason may find pointless. One can more wholly register Divine demand by discerning no other point, of utility or arguability, in what it enjoins. The spirit that complains against the letter may soon have no more context in which either to complain or to attain. That debate, of course, continues—and not only in Islam.

In this way Muslims see in the *Shari'ah* an all-embracing sacred law, the source of which is God's will and the motive obedience to Him. Its content is understood, classically, as governing and determining all areas of life—personal, communal, social, civil, political and cultic. The strictly ritual and devotional provisions are the sacramental *foci* of what is throughout religious, in the sense that it is God-aware, God-responsive and God-ordained. One does not rightly speak of religion *and* morality, of morality *and* law: they are identical—though the problems implicit in seeing them so are serious and lively. There is a sense in which one can only equate law and life, religion and existence by neglecting either the ideals of the one or the realities of the other. But the hope of their identity is magnificent, provided we are alert to its perpetual frustration. There lies the whole inner tension of Islamic law and ethics.

The Godward relation of men, in this exceptionless quality, was, from the earliest centuries, understood as threefold. Things to be believed are given in *Imān*, or faith. It is the obligation of man to receive and confess them. Things to be done in rite and ordinance are given in *Dīn*, or religion. It is the duty of man to perform and do them. Things commanded as good and vetoed as evil are also given, in what Arabic calls: *Al-Amr bi-l-Ma'rūf* and *Al-Nahī 'ān al-Munkar*. It is the obligation of man to fulfill the one and abjure the other. In the whole *Sharī'ah* are the gathered prescriptions and regulations legislating for the whole complex range of human affairs and relationships.[1] By all these the innate calling, freedom, and stature of man, in body and soul, in family and society, in order and well-being, are to find their realization. Within the whole there are wide stretches of moral option or neutrality, where the *Sharī'ah* does not tediously enjoin, but yet hallows and conditions the choices and works of Muslim mankind.

The articles of faith, or *Īmān*, are God and His unity, the books, the prophets and messengers of God, angels as bearers of God's commands and revelation, the last day and judgment, and the Divine decree of good and evil, that is, the Divine criteria or determination, of reality and of destiny. There have been endless debates on these themes, not least the last, and a diversity of emphases and interpretation. But broadly they constitute the dogmatic structure of Islam, set the doctrinal texture of Muslim thought and give the house of Islam its characteristic temper of soul. It was the intention of our first three chapters to indicate their main significance and their historical genesis in seventh century Arabia.

The faith acceptance of the right Muslim, however, is summed up and articulated in the briefer *Shahādah,* or confession, prefaced by the singular: "*I* bear witness. . ."

To say: "There is no god but God and Muhammad is the *Rasūl** of God" is the first of the five articles, or "pillars," of *Dīn* and joins both faith and practice. Its personal, vocal avowal is the criterion of being Muslim, though from time to time inconsistency of conduct led purists to insist that it had to be corroborated by fidelity of life. Neglect of the rest of the *Sharī'ah* disqualified *Shahādah* also. At the crux of this issue was the range of *Niyyah,* or "intention," by which a valid confession had to be

---

* Prophet, messenger, apostle.

made. Three other pillars of religion, namely *Salāt* *Saum,* and *Ḥajj,* prayer, fast and pilgrimage, respectively, will be discussed in the next chapter. They belong under Law but may be studied as Liturgy.

The remaining pillar is *Zakāt,* or almsgiving—an institution which undergirds a whole philosophy of social responsibility in Islam. From a very early point, allegiance involved obligation to fellow Muslims who were poor or victimized. The help of the Medinan converts to the Meccan emigrés became an abiding theme of tradition and example. The needs of the original and growing community were for solidarity, mutuality, inter-dependence, and resources for propagation, as well as the sealing of ac-cessions. All these, as the phrase went, were "in the way of God." *Zakāt* was thus the cement of Islam, always joined with prayer in the double Quranic phrase: "Perform the *Salāt* and bring the *Zakāt,*" and willful withholding of it a sign of rebellion. The *jizyah,* or tax on non-Muslim minorities surviving under Islam was always carefully distinguished from *Zakāt,* thus further enforcing its communal character. Both the paying and the disbursing signalized participation in the household of the faith.

"Lend to God a good loan" says Surah 73:20. *Zakāt* is understood as a means to repentance and atonement, as a way of practical reconciliation, and as a parable of brotherliness. It also symbolizes those voluntary acts of generosity that season common life. As a tradition says: "A camel lent out for milk is alms, good works are alms, your smile to your neighbor is alms." These deeds, sometimes called *Sadaqāt,* to distinguish them from legal alms (though the term is not consistently held to that sense), should not, however, excuse the doer from *Zakāt* proper. The obligatory cannot rightly be displaced by the voluntary. Nor, in the eyes of literalists, can *Zakāt* be equated with state taxation for social welfare purposes, since then the element of obligatoriness is not of the *Sharī'ah,* but of the fiscal author-ity of the state. For most modern thinkers, nevertheless, the ideology ar-guable from this pillar of religion, namely an active social conscience, is regarded as achieved, under the different conditions of the modern world, by the sanctions of state action. The organization of the mosque and of the religious leadership cannot feasibly cope with the task of collecting and disbursing even a modest poor relief in the teeming, complex world of this century. It is surely not an un-Islamic doctrine that what is enjoined by religion can be organized and implemented by the political power.

At all events the intelligent enunciation of *Zakāt* today makes the case for socialist economy. The root meaning of the term is "to purify." Surah 9:103 says: "Take of their wealth an offering [*sadaqah*] to purify them and cleanse [*tuzakkihim*] them thereby." The doctrine is that property is validated as a private right and enjoyment, provided a portion of it is devoted to the common need, in token of the corporate awareness that should characterize all personal possession. This paid portion "purifies," that is, legitimizes, what is retained. Without this active conscience, re-tention and ownership would be impure and disqualified. The community has not only a stake in, but also a claim on, the individual's *amwāl* or substance. It is easy to see a direct line of argument from this central thesis of the faith to the Marxist doctrine of the labor theory of value, of the community as the source and context of all worth, and of a communal ownership of what is vital to common life. The last theme, however, must be subject to the implicit approval of ownership, once socially conscious, which is involved in the whole ordinance of *Zakāt*. The abolition of private ownership would terminate the feasibility of the pillar of *Dīn;* and that, argue the orthodox theorists, could never be the intention of God.

NOTES

1. The canonical sources of the Sharī'ah are involved in the tensions belonging with the Sunnī/Shī'ah controversies. . . .

CRITIQUE

13. On the Religious Sanction of Social Fictions, *P. Berger*

> *In this group of readings, taken from various cultures, there has been an emphasis on everyday social life as the essential expression of religious life. The human effort to live in a particular understanding of human rights and duties is sanctioned by appeals to divine law, universal ethical sensitivity, and cosmic order. But when Peter Berger, an American sociologist, looks at this process, he is struck not by the reality of the alleged cosmic law but rather by the persistent tendency of social groups to believe that their particular, local, and customary forms reflect, and are justified by, the universal order of nature. This tendency finds its chief expression in religion. Berger argues that it is the preponderant tendency of religion to bless as true and right any value or practice whatever that is basic to the life of some social unit. Note that Berger's critique is applicable to the public exercise of authority whether justified by an appeal to cosmic law, revelation, or mythic tradition. How is this function related to mechanisms of social control? How does it contribute to "bad faith"? What is wrong with living in an "okay world"?*

From *The Precarious Vision* by Peter L. Berger. Copyright © 1961 by Peter L. Berger. Reprinted by permission of Doubleday & Company, Inc. Pp. 102, 103, 105–6, 109–17, 119–22.

Would you agree with Berger that in America "religion functions overwhelmingly as an integrator" rather than as a transforming power of our society? Is it possible for societies that appeal to cosmic law to reform their practices while still appealing to an ultimate source of power?

...Religion is a social phenomenon, hence it must be studied as such. And the most important social consequence of religion is that its beliefs and practices unite into what Durkheim* called a "moral community" those who adhere to them. Durkheim went further than that and, in sharp distinction from other contemporary theories seeking to explain religion scientifically, maintained that society itself was both source and ultimate object of all religious devotion. Not only is religion an essentially social phenomenon, but what the religious devotee is ultimately worshiping is society itself, or rather its most awesome values. There are very few social scientists today who would defend this extreme position, and most would feel that at this point Durkheim's philosophical presuppositions tended to run ahead of his scholarly judgment.[1] However, the importance of Durkheim's study of religion lies not in this extreme position on the ultimate substance of religion but rather in the attention it drew to its actual functioning in society. Not only Durkheim himself but his disciples in the French school of sociology were greatly interested in what they called the "collective representations" of society. They stressed the fact that society could not be understood except with a grasp of the web of meanings, ideas, and values (that is, the "collective representations") which holds its members together. These "collective representations," taken together, constitute the "collective conscience" of a society—the basic moral consensus without which it would not exist.[2] In this collective conscience religion plays a crucial role. The deepest levels of the collective conscience are those which are sanctified through the religion which the society adheres to. By thus putting under its sanctions the most important elements of consensus, religion makes possible a moral community, and thus makes it possible for society to exist at all. Religion is not an accidental element of society, relating itself here and there to other social elements. Religion is essential to society, so much so that one could say that without religion in some form society could not exist....

This primary social function of religion also relates it in a very important way to the apparatus of social control. Sociologists speak of social control, a term coined by the American sociologist E. A. Ross,[3] to refer to the various techniques society develops in order to bring into line its recalcitrant members. Such techniques can be external devices, ranging from killing to social ostracism or gossip. However, as both role theory and the

---

* Emile Durkheim (1858–1917) was a French sociologist who held that religion was produced by social obligations claiming to have sacred sanctions. See his book *The Elementary Forms of the Religious Life,* trans. J. W. Swain (Glencoe: Free Press, 1947).

psychoanalytic approach have conclusively shown, the most important controls are internalized. In the process of socialization the value structure of society becomes the inner value structure of the individual conscience. Essentially the same process is meant when Mead refers to the "generalized other" as when Freud speaks of the "superego"—society no longer just confronts the child as an external reality but has become part and parcel of his inner self. No ongoing society can dispense with such a process of moral internalization. The external techniques of social control can be economically applied only if most people, having successfully internalized controls, stay in line quite naturally. To put this a little differently, a few hundred policemen are sufficient to preserve law and order in a city with many thousands of people. Why? Because most of these people will behave in a legal and orderly fashion in any case, even if they never see a policeman or think of one. But instead of the external cop they have a little, invisible cop sitting squarely in the middle of their heads. This is the metaphysical gentleman whom Freud called the "censor." This internal police force is not only more economical but far more efficient than the flesh-and-blood troopers. Without it any society is doomed, even if it uses the most brutal methods of physical repression.

The purpose of social control is to keep society going despite the occasional foibles and iniquities of its membership. One could say that social control has three lines of defense. The first line of defense is consensus, the common taken-for-grantedness of moral prescriptions and proscriptions, which, if it functions well, makes social control in its proper sense unnecessary. There will be no stepping out of line and thus no need for the techniques of bringing anyone back into line. The second line of defense is the internalized social-control machinery—if one prefers, the conscience. There may here be a strong desire to step out of the collective march, but the little cop keeps banging the naughty wish back into the speechless underworld whence it came. And even if the desire sometimes wins out, there is the potent poison of repentance and guilt, often a far more powerful control than the most grisly punishments inflicted from without. Finally, there is the third line of defense when the external means of coercion have to be brought into action. This is reserved for that minority whose immorality has proved stronger than both consensus and conscience. Now religion enters vitally into each of these lines of defense. At the first line, religion coordinates the moral consensus of society, systematizes it in a certain picture of human destiny, takes up the moral imperatives one by one, and calls them blessed. At the second line, religion provides the most uncomfortable pangs that conscience can inflict, involving one fatally in guilt not only against one's neighbor (who, after all, may be presumed to be a sinner too) but also against supernatural forces, which not only possess far more sinister means of retaliation than one's neighbor but may also be so offensively righteous that one cannot even argue with their threatened thunderbolts. At the third line, religion provides the ratification of the acts of coercion performed on behalf of society. Now it is quite possible that someone reads this interpretation, thinks of all the moral notions that are dearest to his heart, and then nods happily at the thought that religion protects them so effectively. In order to avoid such reassurance it ought to be emphasized most strongly that religion offers these services to society regardless of the moral contents involved. In other words, depending upon which society we are talking about, religion will thus defend cannibalism or vegetarianism, infanticide or love of children, slavery or universal brotherhood. The functionality of religion appears to be a formal characteristic of social reality and can exist as such irrespective of the character of the moral values which it integrates. . . .

It is not difficult to see how religion is related to the process of legitimation. Even in so-called secular states, or states that operate under a legal separation of state and church, the most powerful legitimations of power are the religious ones. This, of course, is most evident in acute crises of the political order, as in times of war or insurrection. As the drums roll before battle there is always a moment of silence in which the impending carnage is commended to the supernatural powers. The blessing of weapons is one of the most time-hallowed tasks of religious functionaries. But also in the routine exercise of power the availability of religious sanctions is important. Power very easily involves men in ultimate sacrifice and ultimate guilt. Therefore power requires the ideas by which men interpret their ultimate experiences, the ideas which motivate men to face death and which rationalize their guilt. It is not difficult to understand the profound proximity between throne and altar—even in states that have a republican form of government. Religion is one of the most important ingredients in theories of legitimacy.

Weber's concept of theodicy approaches the subject from a slightly different angle. As in other terms which Weber took from the vocabulary of religion, he uses the concept of theodicy in a way modified from its religious usage (where it means the problem of reconciling the idea of an omnipotent divinity with the existence of suffering or evil). Weber distinguishes between a theodicy of happiness and a theodicy of suffering. The former is the religious preoccupation of the fortunate, the latter that of their less privileged fellow men. Both theodicies are rationalizations of the social fact that some men live happily while others continue all their lives in wretchedness.

Perhaps the religion of the classical Graeco-Roman world provides one of the best examples of a theodicy of happiness. Those who lived in happiness were those favored by the gods. Not only was the shunning of the miserable an instinctive act of revulsion, but it was also a religious act. The miserable, those not favored by the gods, were religiously impure as well as socially despicable. Their wretchedness had about it a contagious quality and the happy had better stay away from it or they might themselves become infected with it. However, any religion which identifies divine blessing with earthly success provides this kind of theodicy. Thus the Brahmin in traditional Hindu society knows that his favored position is not just an accident of birth but is well earned as a result of good deeds in countless past reincarnations. Thus the Puritan of, say, the society of colonial New England could be self-righteously certain that his privileges were the bounty of an inscrutable providence, which sees fit to elect some men and damn others. And his latter-day secularized successor, established in a favorable position in American society, retains the same tendency to ascribe good fortune to virtue and its opposite to vice. This theodicy of happiness is, of course, closely related to the process of legitimation. Men want power, wealth, happiness, but they also want a theory which explains to them and to others that they are entitled to all these advantages. Religion frequently satisfies this need.

The theodicy of suffering performs an analogous function for those on the other side of the fence. While it is terrible to suffer it is even more terrible to suffer meaninglessly. Religion provides meaning for suffering. In this interpretation of the religion of the underdog Weber was strongly influenced by Marx on the one hand and by Nietzsche and Scheler on the other. With Marx he sees that religion, in providing a theodicy of suffering and thus relieving tensions within the social order, tends to preserve the *status quo*. This, for example, is why American slaveowners encouraged the conversion of imported Negroes to Christianity, why one of the first buildings put up in Southern mill villages was the church, and why the present authorities in South Africa encourage the activities of certain evangelists among the native population. With Nietzsche and Scheler, Weber perceived how in certain cases religion provides a focus for the pent-up resentments and hatreds of subjected groups, providing a rationalization for one's own impotence. Thus Christianity became for the slaveowner a means of social repression, but for the slave it was a means of psychological repression of his own instincts of rebellion. While society spits upon the slave, religion assists in the process by suggesting that he is despicable (thus legitimating the oppression) and at the same time providing an outlet for the slave's aggressions through a promise of supernatural bliss (thus fortifying the oppression against insurrectionary dangers). Where Weber differed from Marx and Nietzsche is in his refusal to regard these as universal functions of religion. There are important cases in which religion operates in society in a different way. One might think, for example, of the role of the Quakers in the underground railroads preceding the Civil War or the long nights of *voudun* drumming preceding the Haitian revolution. We are not concerned here with developing an exhaustive sociological theory of religion. It is important for us to bring out those functions of religion tending toward the maintenance of the social system, happily agreeing that there are exceptions and other possibilities.

However, even with these reservations the writer is convinced that the preponderant tendency of religion is to be socially functional rather than disfunctional. That is, religion will tend to provide integrating symbols rather than symbols of revolution. Religion will tend to legitimate power rather than to put it in question. Religion will tend to find rationalizations for social inequalities (both among the beneficiaries and the injured in these arrangements) rather than to seek their removal. This preponderant tendency has been well summarized by J. M. Yinger as follows:

"Insofar as it is accepted religion, by rite and symbol, gives emotional support to the fundamental values of a society; it softens the hardness of the struggle for scarce values by emphasizing values that can be achieved by all (e.g., salvation); and it lessens the tensions of those who have failed to achieve a desired level of a society's values by approved means by emphasizing supra-mundane values."[4]

Insofar as religion functions in this way, it is crucially related to the various fictions by which societies maintain themselves and thus crucially related to the problems of bad faith discussed in the last chapter. It might be added here that, whatever reservations one might make about the social role of religion in other societies, there can be no doubt that in America religion functions overwhelmingly as an integrator in the sense outlined above. We shall have occasion to take illustrations from the American scene further on, but for the moment we might just quote the apt characterization of American "civic religion" made by Will Herberg:

"Civic religion is a religion which validates culture and society, without in any sense bringing them under judgment. It lends an ultimate sanction to culture and society by assuring them that they constitute an un-equivocal expression of 'spiritual ideals' and 'religious values.' Religion becomes, in effect, the cult of culture and society, in which the 'right' social order and the received cultural values are divinized by being iden-tified with the divine purpose. Any issue of *Christian Economics,* any pronouncement of such organizations as Spiritual Mobilization, will pro-vide sufficient evidence of how Christian faith can be used to sustain the religion of '*laissez-faire* capitalism.' Similar material from Catholic and Jewish sources comes easily to hand, from 'liberal' quarters as well as from 'conservative.' On this level at least, the new religiosity pervading America seems to be very largely the religious validation of the social patterns and cultural values associated with the American Way of Life."[5]

We can fully agree with Herberg that this description fits contemporary American religiosity in the main and also that this constitutes a betrayal of Biblical faith. We would only add that there is nothing very unusual or surprising about this state of affairs. American religion stands here in a venerable tradition dating all the way back to the sacred rattles with which Neanderthal man encouraged himself to face the dinosaurs. In any case, we would contend that the analysis of religion as the great social integrator is of very special importance in contemporary America, and not only to spoilsport sociologists.

It will now be our task to show in somewhat greater detail how this social functionality relates to the problem of bad faith that was discussed in the last chapter. It is this which interests us here. It would be quite possible to approach the problem of the social fictions from other angles. For example, there is a philosophical problem inherent in the very term of fiction. What are fictions in the first place? How are fictions to be dis-tinguished from other forms of symbolizations? Are all fictions the same as illusions? We are not competent to discuss these questions philosophically. But we are not at the moment interested in the ontological status of social fictions. Our interest in these fictions is a strictly anthropocentric one.

More specifically, we do not ask what these fictions ultimately mean, but only in what way they contribute to bad faith and human inauthenticity. It is here that the place of religion becomes clear.

We can look again at this point at the case of capital punishment, that one event in which the bad faith and the murderousness of the social fictions come together with unusual clarity. The relationship between religion and capital punishment has been perceived very clearly by the atheist critics of religion since the eighteenth century. This relationship has been stated so succinctly by Albert Camus in our own time that we shall take the occasion of quoting at some length from his essay on the death penalty:

> "The verdict of capital punishment destroys the only indisputable human community there is, the community in the face of death, and such a judgment can only be legitimated by a truth or a principle that takes its place above all men, beyond the human condition. Capital punishment, in fact, throughout history has always been a religious punishment. When imposed in the name of the king, representative of God on earth, or by priests, or in the name of a society considered as a sacred body, it is not the human community that is destroyed but the functioning of the guilty man as a member of the divine community which alone can give him his life. Such a man is certainly deprived of his earthly life, yet his opportunity for reparation is preserved. The real judgment is not pronounced in this world, but in the next. Religious values, especially the belief in an eternal life, are thus the only ones on which the death penalty can be based, since according to their own logic they prevent that penalty from being final and irreparable: it is justified only insofar as it is not supreme."[6]

Perhaps, to evade the criticism that, after all, Camus was a hostile witness, we ought to also quote from a recent article by a respected Protestant churchman in this country in which precisely the same point is made, only with the opposite intention:

> "We who are supposed to be Christian, make too much of physical life. Jesus said, 'And do not fear those who kill the body but cannot kill the soul; rather fear him who can destroy both soul and body in hell' (Matt. 10:28). Laxness in law tends to send both soul and body to hell. It is more than a pious remark when a judge says to the condemned criminal: 'And may God have mercy on your soul.' The sentence of death on a killer is more redemptive than the tendency to excuse his crime as no worse than grand larceny."[7]

It is not surprising, in view of this, that churchmen have been among the most valiant defenders of capital punishment throughout so-called Christian history—except for the period of the early church, when any form of killing was regarded as unthinkable for Christians, and except for the scattered witness of such groups as the Quakers. It is not even necessary to go back to the atrocities of the Inquisition to be edified by this affinity between priests and hangmen. In the long discussion in the British Parliament about the modification and abolition of capital punishment, the bishops of the Church of England stood steadfastly for the retention of the gallows.[8] In 1810 the bishops voted the death penalty for a theft of five shillings.[9] And as recently as 1948 the Bishop of Truro suggested that capital punishment should be extended rather than abolished.[10] In the great debate over abolition of the death penalty in the House of Lords in 1956, both Anglican archbishops spoke for abolition, but only after carefully dissociating themselves from the argument that capital punishment was a wrong in itself and in the hope that a modification of it will, in the words of the Archbishop of Canterbury, "refound the death penalty on its only secure and legitimate foundation as an act expressing the general will of the community for the defence of society and for the solemn vindication of the laws of God."[11]

Leaving aside for the moment the difficulties which this traditional religious bloodthirstiness presents to adherents of a movement founded by an executed criminal, one may ask why this position exists and why it is so widespread among religious people. It is here that the relationship between religion and bad faith can be seen very sharply. We have discussed before how men put on magic cloaks for certain acts in society for which they claim moral immunity for their persons. But simply human conjury is not enough when it comes to some of the most terrifying acts. Now the alibi is not just that one does not do this personally but *qua* a particular kind of officeholder. Now the office itself must be transfigured by supernatural spookery. The act then takes on the quality of a divine intervention. Killing is such an act. In the same essay from which we quoted above, Camus mentions the inscription on the executioner's sword in Freiburg, in Switzerland: "Lord Jesus, Thou art the Judge." The meaning of the inscription is simple. It proclaims that the hangman is not doing the killing, neither is the judge, nor the jury, nor the good people of the canton watching the execution. The killer is Jesus Christ, who is absolutely just and therefore absolutely beyond questioning. As the executioner's sword comes down on the victim's neck, we can see in the one stroke an act of religious faith and one of bad faith inseparably linked.

It is in this fog of sanctified delusion that hangmen will shake the hand of their victim seconds before the execution, that priests will urge repentance on the victim to the last moment of the atrocity, that officials presiding over all this will afterward shake their heads and say, "I hated to do it!"—and that there will even be people who sympathize with them! But once more we find that the delusion (though for different reasons) is often shared by the intended victim too. If we may paraphrase Weber here, there is a theodicy of hanging and a theodicy of being hanged. A group of anthropologists who made a study of a community in the Deep South some twenty years ago have given us a bloodcurdling account of the way in which religion entered into the hanging of two Negroes.[12] The two men were sentenced to death for the murder of fellow Negroes. This is a crime for which Southern traditional jurisprudence rarely inflicted the death penalty, but preceding this trial there had been a number of Negro crimes and the general feeling in the community was that it was about time "to teach the niggers a lesson." As soon as the death sentence was pronounced everybody involved in the case was genuinely anxious that the two men "get religion." A number of preachers were employed to achieve the desired result. But only one of the two men obliged and died "reconciled." The other remained defiant to the end, making everybody feel quite uneasy and resentful against him for not playing the role expected of him. This is how the authors of the study interpret this anxiety on the part of the white authorities:

> "To the whites the execution ceremony is much more than the punishment of a Negro by a group of whites. It is a ritual sanctioned by God, that is, by the most important power of the total society, whereby the complete surbordination of the individual to the society is upheld. The proper role of the victim is one of complete subordination to the caste society and to God. He must confess his crime and seek for forgiveness, not of individuals who have been harmed, but of the total society. He must accept the rightness of this supreme white power which takes his life. If he fails in this role, if he does not pray and ask forgiveness, if he does not 'get religion,' he is denying the supreme authority and is rebelling against the society. He is a 'bitter' Negro."[13]

In the case of a Negro recently executed in a Southern state for "first-degree burglary" the prisoner, apparently half-crazed by fear, reported that in the night before his execution he had a vision of Jesus and that now he was ready to go. This account was received with great satisfaction by the chaplain attending him and duly reported by the newspapers throughout the state. It made everyone feel much better.

Religion here functions as the ultimate alibi of the murderer. It is the foundation stone of his bad faith. It was religion functioning in this way which caused the original outcry of the antireligious revolt of the eighteenth century: "Destroy the infamy!" But Voltaire, who wrote these words, could still say in another place, "If God did not exist, we should have to invent Him." It was only in the nineteenth century that this antireligious revolt reached its logical consequence in Mikhail Bakunin's paraphrase of Voltaire's words, "If God *did* exist, we would have to abolish Him!" It is not an accident that this same Bakunin was tormented by the existence of capital punishment and wrote a lengthy commentary upon its religious apologists. The divinity that Bakunin wanted to abolish is that age-old supreme being presiding over countless enactments of what is rightly called the supreme penalty. There is a section in a liturgical handbook for ministers of the Lutheran Church of Sweden printed in the nineteenth century which contains instructions for proper prayers and exhortations at hangings. This handbook includes a rubric which points out that although it may happen occasionally that an innocent man is hanged, the minister should point out to all concerned that no man is innocent before God and that all men deserve death for their sinfulness, so that, presumably, the injustice of this particular execution is of a relative nature. It may also be assumed that such pious observations made everyone feel much better— perhaps even the prisoner about to be hanged to the accompaniment of this liturgy!...

Religion, however, not only contributes to bad faith by providing moral alibis. In many situations it also assists the systematized delusions by which entire social groups succeed in hiding from themselves the true nature of

"I think war is nature's way!"

their situation. This, again, is a facet of religion that is peculiarly significant in contemporary American society. A brilliant analysis of this process
has recently been made by Arthur Vidich and Joseph Bensman in their
study of a small community in upstate New York.[14] The study presents us,
on the one hand, with a picture of rural America rapidly disintegrating
under the impact of contemporary economic, technological, and political
forces, and on the other hand, with a picture of the people of this fading
rural society tenaciously clinging to their old images of themselves. There
are various institutions in the community which reinforce these images
(which the authors call the "public ideology"). Among them the churches
are of crucial importance. They continue to proclaim the old virtues of
rustic life and, implicitly or explicitly, affirm that these virtues are still
operative in the present. Within the religious assemblages one can, then,
act (and presumably feel) as if the dynamics of the modern age had
left untouched the small town with its simple, neighborly, democratic

ways. In other words, the churches play a key role in the elaborate social-psychological process by which unpleasant realities are suppressed.

What Vidich and Bensman found in the small rural community can also be found in the new suburbs.[15] Here too we find at work a powerful "public ideology," with a strong family resemblance to that of the rural community, differing from it in that its function is not to preserve an old image but to create a new one in the teeth of reality. The reality of the suburbs is that of what sociologists call a *Gesellschaft*-type society—that is, a society in which people have transitory, superficial relations with each other, in which people cannot cast down deeper roots, in which most kinds of belonging (other than those within the immediate family) are very precarious. The ideology of the suburb refers itself to what sociologists call a *Gemeinschaft*-type society—that is, a society in which people belong to each other profoundly and with the totality of their persons, in which life is rooted in community, in which human relations are not fragmented or transient. It is interesting to observe how the ideology of the suburb resembles that of the small town. The image which both hold up is that of an earlier, more bucolic, and presumably better America. The small town pretends that this image is true and was always true of itself. The suburb pretends to create this fiction *ex nihilo*. Now, in the suburb too the churches function as a powerful reinforcement of this ideology. Very often the ideology is quite synthetic, the sophisticated product of the sales propaganda of the real-estate and development promoters. With the idyllic names of their projects (constant reiterations and recombinations of such rusticity-pregnant words like "forest," "woods," "brook," "meadow," and so forth) goes the picture of the friendly rural church, a monument of New Englandish cleanness and healthy propriety, where neighbors meet and where harmless gossip mixes with wholesome fun and where children can grow up to be upstanding citizens. Sometimes, as we know, the developers actually build the church (or churches). Religion is an important part of the fantasy being promoted. The reality of suburbia, of course, can be preceived only when we follow its inhabitants as they take off on their daily commuter trains. Then we see suburbia not against the background of agricultural beatitude but as the frantic escape from the murderous competition, the noise, nerves, ulcers, and cutthroat relationships of the big city. Religion in suburbia does not provide its clientele with the means to confront the reality in which they spend their crucial waking hours. Rather it provides an easy ratification of the various escape routes that converge in the suburban way of life. Religion is one of the allegedly recreational leisure-time activities, but it also gives positive sanction to all the others. The minister of the suburban church plays an important role here. He lives like all the others, shares their aspirations and tastes and most of their opinions, but in addition he is a certified man of virtue. He thus becomes the exemplary suburbanite, the one in whom the suburban way of life is vicariously and solemnly justified. This is a "real good" feeling when one meets him at a cocktail party.

This leads over into yet another way in which religion contributes to bad faith. In the preceding paragraphs we looked at the way in which religion reinforces certain specific delusions that men have about their social reality. But religion also reinforces in a general way, quite apart from ideological distortions, the notion that the world ones lives in is essentially and ultimately all right. For lack of a better term, we could say that religion ratifies the "okay world." Again, this is of great importance in America, though certainly not an exclusively American or even modern phenomenon. In this function, again, religion contributes to bad faith—or perhaps it would be more accurate here to use Heidegger's concept of inauthenticity. For in reality man does not live in an "okay world" at all. He rushes toward his own death on a course marked by indecipherable signs and surrounded on all sides by a darkness full of pain. He can become authentically human only if, in some way, he faces and comes to terms with this destiny. The "okay world" prevents precisely that. It thus contributes essentially to inauthenticity. To revert to a picture used before, it is a Potemkin village erected to provide the illusion of safety, sanity, and order.

It seems to the writer that this function of religion can already be observed in primitive cultures, for example in what anthropologists call "rites of passage." As the great crises of life succeed each other in the biography of the individual—birth, puberty, marriage, sickness, death—the community, through its religious ceremonialism, proclaims the assurance that all these events are taking place within a cosmos that is understood and somehow controlled by the social ritual. Malinowski has analyzed funerary ceremonialism in very similar terms—the proclamation of the continued presence and cohesiveness of the community against the potent threat of death.[16] W. Lloyd Warner, in his intensive study of Memorial Day ritual in America,* has given us a very similar interpretation applicable to our own society.[17] But it is not only the facing of death which provokes this reassuring response. Any experience of potential ecstasy (*ekstasis*) constitutes a threat to the "okay world" in which the routine business of society is enacted. Consequently, when crises threaten the everyday taken-for-granted routine of the individual and there looms the ecstatic possibility of confronting directly his own existence, society provides the rituals by which he is gently led back into the "okay world." Undoubtedly this process has very deep psychological roots, perhaps all the way back to the first time a mother bent over her terrified infant and whispered, "It's all right, it's all right, there's nothing to be afraid of!" For a moment then, the shadows are denied and the nightmares chased away. When we call this process inauthenticity we certainly are not suggesting that one ought to live in nightmares. But we live, in fact, in a world whose horizons on all sides are hidden in darkness, and our own lives are rushing toward this dark horizon. We must, therefore, face up to the night if we want to face up to our existence. And in speaking depreciatingly of the "okay world" we also do not wish to suggest that there is something wrong about men's quest for order, for an intelligible cosmos or for a meaning to their fate. Order is

---

* Compare Chapter II, item 5.

something that men seek, passionately desire, try to construct precariously in their own lives. Order is *not* something given, self-evident, secure. The "okay world" gives the latter impression, which is not only illusionary but which effectively stops the search for order before it has even started—in the illusion of already sitting safely in an oasis men abandon the search for paths through the wilderness.

NOTES

1. For a critique of Durkheim's position *cf.* Malinowski, *Magic Science and Religion,* pp. 37 ff.
2. Durkheim's French phrase could be translated as either "collective conscience" or "collective consciousness," but the latter translation is bound to be misleading. Durkheim did not hold a theory of a "group soul." The collectivity which interested him is a moral not a metaphysical fact.
3. E. A. Ross, *Social Control* (New York, The Macmillan Co., 1901).
4. Yinger, [*Religion, Society and the Individual* (New York: Macmillan Co., 1957)] p. 65.
5. Will Herberg, *Protestant–Catholic–Jew* (Garden City, N.Y., Doubleday & Company, Inc., 1955), pp. 279 f.
6. Albert Camus, "Reflections on the Guillotine," *Evergreen Review,* No. 12.
7. Jacob J. Vellenga, "Is Capital Punishment Wrong?", *Christianity Today,* October 12, 1959, p. 9.
8. Arthur Koestler, *Reflections on Hanging* (New York, The Macmillan Co., 1957), p. 169.
9. *Ibid.,* p. 166.
10. *Ibid.,* p. 41.
11. *Parliamentary Debates (Hansard),* Vol. 198, No. 115, July 10, 1956 (London, Her Majesty's Stationery Office). It may be added that in the United States, with the exception of the so-called "peace churches," the attitude of Protestant churches toward the issue has been largely one of indifference, although some national denominations have recently passed resolutions in favor of abolition.
12. A. Davis, B. G. Gardner and M. R. Gardner, *Deep South* (Chicago, University of Chicago Press, 1941), pp. 527 ff.
13. *Ibid.,* p. 533.
14. Arthur Vidich and Joseph Bensman, *Small Town in Mass Society* (Princeton, Princeton University Press, 1958).
15. *Cf.* J. R. Seeley, R. A. Sim and E. W. Loosley, *Crestwood Heights* (New York, Basic Books, Inc., 1956); William H. Whyte, Jr., *The Organization Man* (New York, Simon and Schuster, Inc., 1956); David Riesman, "The Suburban Sadness," in William M. Dobriner (ed.), *The Suburban Community* (New York, G. P. Putnam's Sons, 1958).
16. Malinowski, *Magic, Science and Religion,* pp. 29 ff.
17. W. Lloyd Warner, *The Living and the Dead* (New Haven, Yale University Press, 1959).

NOT RESPONSIBLE FOR ON TEST

14. Morality as
Social Convention,
R. Taylor

*Are the distinctions between good and evil discovered in the
same way as the difference between men and women or between
wood and metal? With this question Richard Taylor, Professor
of Philosophy at the University of Rochester, raises a basic question
for those advocates of morality who claim that their rules of
conduct are derived from natural (universal, eternal) distinctions.
In this excerpt he criticizes moral decisions that appeal to moral
principles—that is to implicit distinctions of good or bad in the
very nature of things. To the contrary, argues Taylor, man
designates some action as "good" or "bad" according to its
capacity for satisfying one or several desires and aims—and
because different men have different aims they differ on what
they label "good" and "bad." Why, according to Taylor, is
justification of a decision by appealing to some general principle
of universal rightness futile? Are you convinced that moral rules
and principles are no different than conventions of conduct,
such as traffic rules—except that they are hallowed by age? In
the* Laws of Manu *and the* Hsün Tzu *there was great concern
that if the morality and decorum based on the natural (eternal)
order were not upheld, then social disorder would threaten
man's existence. Does Taylor think that people should do what
they please without regard for social conventions?*

Probably the fundamental question of ethics concerns the status of its
basic ideas. Are the distinctions between good and evil, right and wrong,
and just and unjust discovered by men in the same way they discover the
difference between hot and cold and male and female? Or are they, unlike these, simply distinctions that are invented or created by men, like the
distinctions between married and unmarried, free man and slave, ruler
and ruled? Men, we know, create their own laws and customs and, no
doubt, their religions—in short, their conventions. Are these modeled on
any real distinction between right and wrong or between good and evil, or
are these merely derived from the conventions?

The Greeks, as we have seen, never answered this question with one
voice, but they certainly understood with enviable clarity what the question was and why it was important. Modern moralists, it seems fair to
say, have with few exceptions done less well, most of them merely assuming
an answer to it without really addressing themselves to the question. G. E.

Reprinted with permission of The Macmillan Company from *Good and Evil:
A New Direction* by Richard Taylor. Copyright © 1970 by Richard Taylor. Pp.
145–50, 163, 164, 172–75.

Moore, who for decades set the intellectual tone of philosophical ethics in several nations, declared the question "What is good?" to be the most fundamental and important question of moral philosophy; and after many pages of subtle distinctions he delivered his answer to this great question. The good, he gravely declared, is simply, *the good,* and that is the end of it.[1] It is probably fair to say that even the least moralist of antiquity had a better grasp of the problem than is displayed in that tautology.

If good and evil are natural qualities of things, then, as Plato rightly perceived, they must be highly elusvie ones, yielding themselves to human understanding only after the most difficult and painstaking philosophical inquiry. Plato embraced this conclusion, and in his *Republic* he permitted students of philosophy to consider goodness and justice only after many years of philosophical training. Until then, he thought, they were insufficiently equipped with the knowledge and understanding to perceive them.

The thing to see, however, is that both answers to the question are wrong. The distinction between good and evil is not a natural one that merely awaits the discovery of men, nor is it purely conventional, in the sense that it is arbitrarily created by this or that culture. Good and evil, as such, form no part of the framework of nature, as do darkness and light, for we have seen that they would find no place whatsoever in a world devoid of any living thing. At the same time, however, they do result, in a perfectly natural way, from certain facts of human nature that are evident to anyone, and along with them emerges every other moral distinction, such as right and wrong and just and unjust. And although these distinctions— right and wrong and just and unjust—do to some extent depend on human contrivance—because they arise only with the appearance of rules, which are man-made—they are not created by men capriciously or arbitrarily. They are always tailored, badly or well, to men's perception of good and evil. And that distinction is not, even by the broadest meaning of the term, a human fabrication. Man is not the measure of *all* things, because he is not the measure of himself. That men are the kind of beings they are is a fact of nature, and it is from that fact, given to men, that good and evil arise.

© 1968 United Features Syndicate, Inc.

For it is a fact that men are, as I have expressed it, conative beings. It is a fact that, by nature, men have nerves, and are therefore capable of feeling; that they have desires, wants, and needs; and, in short, that they pursue ends of all sorts, both trivial and great. Virtually every moment of any man's activity is aimed at something or other—at getting food, comfort, enjoyment, at building and removing, at getting something done. This is, indeed, the very nature of human activity.

When obstacles and threats to a man's activity are encountered, he deems them bad, and when things that assist in his goal-seeking are discovered, he deems them good. The objects of his desires are also deemed good, as the objects of his aversions are deemed bad. There is, moreover, one general purpose that every man normally has, and that is the preservation of himself and the enhancement of his well-being in numberless ways. There is, perhaps, no metaphysical reason *why* any beings should be of this nature, but it is a fact that men are. Their activity is directed toward this persisting goal and, together with it, toward numberless subordinate goals that are exceedingly diverse from one man to another. And it is just in the light of this fact that men draw the distinction between good and evil in the first place. A man regards those things as good that satisfy his conative nature, and bad, those that frustrate it. This is all that the distinction originally means, the very basis for even making the distinction to begin with. The distinction between good and evil could never have occurred to a race of beings incapable of pursuing any ends, who had no desires or aversions, and who had not, for example even an aversion to the feeling of pain. To such beings, everything would appear simply as given, not as something to shun or pursue; and this, it should be noted again, would remain true, no matter to what degree they might be endowed with reason and intelligence. Reason, by itself, can discern no good or evil in anything, but the will detects it at once.

At this point it may be enlightening to contrast again the two crude pictures of human nature with which we began. Figure 2 roughly portrays human nature as the moral rationalist and defender of a true morality conceives it:

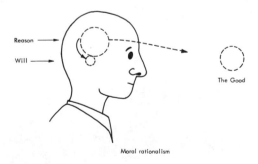

Moral rationalism

In this figure, man's reason has a two-fold function. In the first place, it understands nature, which simply means that it is by his reason that a man understands what is true, to whatever extent he does understand this. And incorporated in this understanding is his perception, however fallible, of the difference between good and evil. Thus, perceiving which things are good and which things are not, he directs his will to the pursuit of those that appear good and away from the things that seem bad. And this expresses the second function of reason: to *govern* the appetites and desires or—which is the same thing—the will, keeping it aimed at the good, insofar as this is possible, and away from the bad, to which it naturally tends. As we have seen, Socrates considered this conception of human nature so true and admirable that he deemed a man *unjust* to the extent that he lapsed from it. He supposed that the natural objects of appetite or desire are more often than not *bad*. The same idea is found in traditional Christianity and also was monumentally reinforced by Kant. Kant declared that nothing can be really morally worthwhile if it is at the same time satisfying to the will. The idea has, ever since, turned most moral philosophies quite upside down and seriously infected the attitudes even of men who are good.

Figure 3 crudely portrays human nature as I have described it, and I have called it the conception of moral voluntarism:

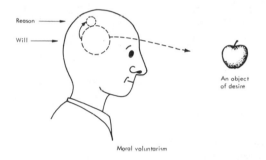

Moral voluntarism

According to this picture, too, it is by his reason that a man understands what is true, to whatever extent he does understand this. But embodied in such understanding are no *a priori* truths of morality. In fact, the understanding alone finds no distinction in nature between things that are good and things that are bad, because no such distinction exists independently of the will. Reason, accordingly, can in no way govern the will, directing it toward the attainment of what it perceives as good and away from what seems evil, for it lacks any such perception to begin with. As Figure 3 further shows, however, a man wills certain things; that is, he has desires and aims. There is no indication of why this is so; the picture only suggests that it is. And what one then perceives as assisting the will—that is, as satisfying his desires and aims—he pronounces good, and things that promise the opposite, he pronounces bad. But far from the reason *directing* the will toward whatever object it has—for example, toward self-preservation and the enhancement of one's well-being—the will by its very nature is directed to these things. No reason whatever can be given why it should be. It just is. And to the extent that anything can even metaphorically be described as being governed here, it is clearly the reason that is governed by the will. For it is the will that determines what any man shall declare to be good, and what he shall pronounce evil. The end or goal of a man's activity is set by the will, for to say that anything *is* a man's goal or the object of his desire is simply to say that it is willed. In this a man's reason has no voice whatsoever, and surely no power of veto. It is instead reduced to the humble office of devising the means to its attainment. If one is at all tempted to doubt this, let him ask himself at what point in his life he first rationally derived the conclusion that the preservation and enhancement of his life was a thing to be desired—thus making his first discovery of this hitherto unsuspected good—by what line of reasoning he was led to that conclusion, and approximately how soon thereafter he enlisted his will to the pursuit of that goal. And then, having seen the nonsense of this, let him ask the same question concerning the rest of his interests, desires, and goals—his recurring interest in eating, for instance, or in sex, or his persistent desires for possessions, status, or power, in case he has any obsessions with these. It was surely with such considerations as these in mind that Hume made his famous and sometimes reviled comment that reason is, and ought to be, a slave to the passions and can pretend to no other office.[2] ...

If what I am saying is correct, it follows that the usual, typical, and normal approach to questions or morality is basically wrong. When a man appears, perhaps to himself as well as to others, to have given a moral justification for a certain course of conduct by showing that it accords with some general principle of rightness, he has in fact done nothing of the sort. The principle to which he appeals is itself in need of justification, and (here is the rub) nothing under the sun can possibly justify that principle unless the course of action in question is itself seen to be right independently of that principle. When one appeals to a moral principle in justification of his decision, he only succeeds in changing the subject; he in no way justifies anything. He changes the subject to the principle itself, which now comes under scrutiny, and if, as is typical, this principle is "justified" by still another principle, then he only manages to change the subject still another time. This, I believe, is the basic reason why discussions of morality are so invariably inconclusive and no one's mind is really changed about anything. They involve a perpetual jump from one subject to another, getting further and further away from the issue originally raised, without hope of settling anything. We can also find here the basis for a very common illusion about moral problems: namely, that the answers to moral problems are very difficult to reach. Indeed they are, if they are sought in this way, for *that* kind of answer does not even exist. Still, people simply assume that the only allowable moral justification of an action must be in terms of some moral principle, and plenty of philosophers reinforce this assumption. Moral discussion therefore weaves tortuously from principle to principle, going about in circles, getting increasingly remote from the issue at hand, in a vain search for "the answer." Insofar as the answer exists at all, however, it lies right under one's nose, in the very action itself, and cannot possibly exist anywhere else. It is as if a man were to set forth from his cottage in search of his son, getting farther and farther away and still with nothing but misleading clues, until he finally gave up and came home to find the youngster in bed. ...

Moral principles are nothing but conventions, but they have the real and enormous value to life that conventions in general possess. They help men to get where they want to go. Without them social life would be impossible, and hence any kind of life that is distinctively human. Their justification is, therefore, a practical one and has nothing to do with moral considerations in the abstract. The moment such a principle ceases to have that value, the moment its application produces more evil than good, then it ceases to have any significance at all and ought to be scorned. Nothing is achieved, other than those dexterous feats of intellectual dishonesty called casuistry, by paying homage to the principle while redefining all the terms necessary to abate its effects. It is far simpler and more honest to declare: Here the principle ceases to work; let us cast it from view; we owe it nothing, and it is not going to coerce us.

The purely practical basis and the justification of rules of conduct are very obvious in the case of those that have not been so hallowed by age as to acquire in our minds the status of moral principles. Rules governing the movement of vehicular traffic are good examples. There is, for example, no ultimate moral principle from which it can be derived that cars should proceed on the right lane rather than the left of the highway. Countries that follow the opposite practice are not censured in our eyes. All that matters is that there be *a* rule, and the reason it matters is very obvious. General adherence to the rule enables people, quite literally, to get where they want to go. The rule minimizes hindrances, obstacles, and danger. It is for this reason, and this reason only, that it ought to be followed; its practical justification is its moral justification, and the whole of it. When, accordingly, circumstances arise such that adherence to the rule would cause more harm than good, its whole basis is swept away and it ought then to be disregarded. This is recognized by all in the case of an ambulance, under certain conditions, on an urgent mission. The driver of such a vehicle would be a fool who deemed it an unexceptionable principle to drive always in the manner prescribed by the rule, even though it was obvious that, in some situations, this would produce great harm. He would be no less a fool if he cast about for some higher principle to justify every departure from it. The only "principle" involved is a practical concern for human welfare. It is the only justification for the rule to begin with, and no other justification is required for departing from it, provided such a justification for the departure actually exists.

The case is no different with what men have come to think of as moral rules and principles, except that these are much older, have acquired the venerability bestowed by time, and have for the most part become embodied in religion. The rules against murder, adultery, bigamy, and so on have an obvious practical basis. Like traffic rules, they enable men to get where they want to go, with the minimum of hindrance and danger, although in not so literal a sense. "Enabling men to get where they want to go" means, here, enabling them to fulfill their various aims and purposes in such a way as to hinder as little as possible the pursuits of others. All such rules prohibit certain ends, or the means to them, in order that other more widespread and important pursuits may flourish. The general utility of the rule against murder, for instance, is too obvious to belabor. The utility of the prohibition of adultery and bigamy is hardly less obvious. Such rules tend, although not infallibly, to protect home life, in which most men have a deep interest, as well as the interests of children. As with all rules, however, they do not always work. Adherence to them can sometimes produce more harm than good, and in such circumstances the basis for adherence evaporates. It is probably the reluctance to face this fact that has led men to suppose that such rules have some origin other than practical utility. It is, once one has become accustomed to it, easier to follow the rule than to depart from it. It gives one a sense of security and innocence and relieves him of the necessity to think or to make difficult decisions. Men accordingly invent other sources for the rules, saying, for example, that they are delivered by God, or that they are derived from some eternal Moral Law.

Does a wise man, then, deal lightly with rules and conventions, following or departing from them as he pleases? Surely not. A general adherence to rules that is not slavish, unthinking, and mechanical, even in situations in which there seems to be no practical point to it, is perhaps a virtue, although certainly a minor one. It is by such general adherence to rules, just because they are rules, that social life is made regular and predictable, and this is itself a considerable source of security. If the members of any group know what the rules are and in general comply with them, then human relationships are enlivened and relieved of friction and uncertainties. This does not imply, however, that rules, even though one chooses to view them as principles of morality, are to be respected for their own sake and adhered to mechanically; for it always remains possible that the violation of a rule on a given occasion—the violation, if one likes, of a "fixed" moral principle—will still produce more good than harm. Putting the matter graphically, a man should really think twice before committing a murder, just as one should think twice before going through a red light. A man of very dull understanding might take this to mean that murder is considered to be no more significant than a traffic violation, but one of more sense will not fail to see its true meaning. The rules involved here have, certainly, not the same importance, but the justification of both is identical, and in neither case does that justification always hold.

NOTES

1. G. E. Moore, *Principia Ethica* (Cambridge University Press, 1956), pp. 3–14; 59–79.
2. David Hume, *A Treatise of Human Nature*. L. A. Selby-Bigge, ed. (Oxford, 1888), p. 415.

IV

Spiritual Freedom
Through Discipline
(Mysticism)

Meditational practices constitute the very core of the Buddhist approach to life. An intensely practical religion, Buddhism is by contrast inclined to treat doctrinal definitions and historical facts with some degree of unconcern. As prayer in Christianity, so meditation is here the very heartbeat of the religion.

Enlightenment, or the state of Nirvana, is, of course, the ultimate aim of Buddhist meditations. On the way to Nirvana they serve to promote spiritual development, to diminish the impact of suffering, to calm the mind and to reveal the true facts of existence. Increased gentleness and sympathy are among their by-products, together with an opening up to life's message, and a feeling that death has lost its sting.... (Edward Conze, Buddhist Meditation [*London: George Allen & Unwin Ltd., 1956*], *p. 11.)*

"MYSTICISM" IS A TERM that is used to describe a wide range of religious experience. It has been used to portray ecstasy, occult phenomena, extra-sensory perception, and personal communion with the divine (seen in the material in Chapter I), as well as the process and achievement of the ultimate illumination through mental-psychic discipline typified in Yoga and Zen. Without claiming that everyone should restrict his use of the term "mysticism" to meditative techniques and processes of illumination in the ascetic practices of Hinduism and Buddhism, we do want to indicate that there are important differences between various kinds of religious experiences called "mysticism," some of which can be seen by a comparison of the material in Chapters I and IV. First, of course, we must note the strong similarity between the materials in these chapters. Both focus on personal awareness of the Truth, and often mark the point of transformation by a moment of extraordinary insight or vision. In general, one could say that the opinions represented in these readings emphasize the crucial nature of inner experience, while Chapters II and III emphasize the outward and social forms of religious life as particularly important. (This, of course, does not mean that the materials in Chapters I and IV show no external expression in literature, symbols, images, ethics, communities, and tradition or that the materials in Chapters II and III show no concern for inner personal change, or self-disciplines to learn the truth about life.)

There are several important differences, however, between the structures of material in Chapters I and IV. In the readings in Chapter I, man is viewed as weak and sometimes corrupt in the face of the "wholly other" who is the source of creation and salvation; but in this chapter, especially in the readings on Eastern traditions, man uncovers the Eternal Truth within him. In Chapter I, referring to the awareness of the Holy Presence, man is considered to be "chosen" by the Divine; whereas in this chapter, illustrating the attainment of spiritual freedom through discipline, man corrects his vision by avoiding or overcoming the illusion he has created for himself. In the first chapter, the consequence of the awareness of the Holy is a desire to change the world as a prophet or revival preacher might do; in this chapter, concerning the attainment of spiritual freedom, the consequence is a preference to change the self in relation to the world. Last, in Chapter I, extraordinary visions are very important; in this chapter, in the spiritual disciplines of the East (Hindu, Buddhist, Taoist), extraordinary visions are not the most important events. Although they may be important at an early stage of spiritual progress, they are also considered to be egoistic mental projections. The highest superconscious knowledge is possible only when a person is not attached to any form. Then this lack of attachment to "things" (including mental forms of the Divine) transforms one's existence.

We begin with a classical Hindu statement and continue with three Buddhist selections—one by a Singhalese Theravada monk and two items from Zen. A short Taoist story distinguishing occult power from the highest wisdom follows, and then a selection from a (Muslim) Sufi manual. The first section ends with a lyric expression by the novelist Nikos Kazantzakis (author of *Zorba The Greek*). The interpretation section includes two readings on Hindu yoga (from a Vedanta perspective), a lecture by a Zen master, and an analysis of mystical paths in relation to their goals by a Western scholar. A typology of religious life as used in this book runs the risk of suggesting that the differences between religious traditions are unimportant; but this is not the case. Thus keep in mind that the cultural contexts out of which these various expressions arise are different. Some of the differences will appear in comparing the Hindu material with such subsequent selections as the Zen master's lecture and the Sufi explanation of how a person should progress on the "path of God." The critical selections include one analysis by a Western philosopher of science who questions whether or not one can call mystical intuition true "knowledge"; and a selection by a Singhalese Buddhist political commentator who questions the value of the monastic meditative life in light of contemporary social, economic, and political needs.

1. On the Nature of Pure Consciousness, *Shankara*

The personal realization of Ultimate Reality is hampered and even prevented by the self-imposed limitations that people place on themselves. One does not obtain true knowledge of the nature and source of all existence through intellectual distinctions or by investigating "things" that are external to oneself. According to Vedanta, true self-knowledge is that "I am the Supreme Brahman"—a kind of awareness in which Brahman is not the object of my knowledge, but the unmoving, unchanging source of both the knower and the object known. These are some of the claims made by the author of the next selection, who is the most famous of all Hindu Advaita (non-dual) Vedantic philosophers: Shankara (c. 788–838 A.D.). These verses are from the metric section of a small summary of Vedanta philosophy, and focus on the nature and realization of pure consciousness. How is the psychophysical activity of the ego in everyday experience related to the Ultimate Brahman? Why do so few people recognize that they are Brahman? What are the benefits from realizing one's true nature?

CHAPTER X
RIGHT CONCEPTION
OF THE NATURE OF CONSCIOUSNESS

1. I am the supreme *Brahman* which is pure consciousness, always clearly manifest, unborn, one only, imperishable, unattached and all-pervading like the ether and non-dual. I am, therefore, ever-free. Aum.[1]

From *Upadeshasāhāsri of Sri Sankarāchāya*, trans. Swāmi Jagadānanda, pp. 111–21. Used by permission of the publisher. Sri Ramakrishna Math, Mylapore, Madras-4, India.

2. Pure and changeless consciousness I am by nature devoid of objects (to illumine). Unborn and established in the Self I am all-pervading *Brahman* in the front, oblique, upward, downward and all other directions.

3. I am unborn, deathless, devoid of old age, immortal, self-effulgent, all-pervading and non-dual. Perfectly pure, having neither cause nor effect and contented with the one Bliss.[2] I am free. Yes.[3]

4. No perception whatever in waking, dream or deep sleep belongs to Me but it is due to delusion. For these states have no independent existence nor an existence depending[4] on the Self. I am, therefore, the Fourth[5] which is the Seer of all the three states and without a second.

5. As I am changeless the series producing pain viz., the body, the intellect and the senses are not Myself nor Mine. Moreover they are unreal[6] like dream-objects, there being a reason for inference that they are so.

6. But it is true that I have no change nor any cause of a change as I am without a second. As I do not possess a body I have neither sin nor virtue, neither bondage nor liberation, neither a caste nor an order of life.*

7. Beginningless[7] and devoid of attributes I have neither actions nor their results. Therefore I am the supreme One without a second. Though in a body I do not get attached on account of My subtleness[8] like the ether which, though all-pervading, does not get tainted.

8. Though I am the Lord[9] always the same in all beings, beyond the perishable and the imperishable,[10] and therefore the Supreme, the Self of all, and without a second I am considered to be of a contrary nature on account of Ignorance.

9. Not distanced[11] by anything from Itself and untouched by Ignorance, by false conceptions (of possessing a body etc.) and by actions the Self is very pure. Without a second and established in My real nature like the immovable ether I am (thought[12] to be) connected with the powers of seeing and other perceptions.

10. There is the saying of the *Sruti*[13] that one who has the sure conviction about oneself that one is *Brahman* is never born again. There being no[14] delusion, there is no birth. For, when the cause is not there there cannot be any effect.

11. False conceptions of people such as, 'mine,' 'this,' 'thus,' 'this is so,' 'I am so,' 'another is not so,' etc., are all due to delusion. They are never in *Brahman* which is auspicious, the same in all and without a second.

12. All grief and delusion are removed from those great souls when there arises the very pure[15] knowledge of the non-dual Self. It is the conclusion of those who know the meaning of the *Vedas* that there cannot be any action or birth in the absence of grief and delusion.[16]

13. It is the conclusion here (in the *Vedântas*) that one who, though perceiving[17] the world of duality in the waking state, does not,[18] as a man in deep sleep does not,[19] perceive it owing to duality being negated and who is (really) actionless even when (apparently) acting, is a man of Self-knowledge; but no one else is so.

14. This Right knowledge described by me is the highest because it is

---

* Contrast this statement with those in readings 3 and 10 of Chapter III.

ascertained in the *Vedântas*.* One becomes liberated and unattached (to actions) like the ether if one is perfectly convinced of this Truth.

CHAPTER XI

NATURE OF THE WITNESS

1. All beings are by nature pure Consciousness Itself. It is due to Ignorance that they appear to be different from It. Their (apparent) difference from It is removed by the teaching 'Thou art Existence.'[20]

2. The scriptures negate *Vedic* actions with their accessories[21] by saying 'Knowledge alone is the cause of immortality,[22] and that there is nothing else to cooperate with it (in producing liberation).'**

3, 4. How can there be any special[23] property in Me who am changeless by nature and witness the modifications of the minds of all without any exception? (How can again there be any change in Me) who witness the mind and its functions in the waking state as in dream? But as there is the absence[24] of both the mind and its functions in deep sleep I am Pure Consciousness, all-pervading and changeless.

5. Just as dreams appear to be true as long as one does not wake up, so, the identification of oneself with the body etc. and the authenticity of sense-perception and the like in the waking state continue as long as there is no Self-knowledge.

6. I am *Brahman* of the nature of pure Consciousness, without qualities, free from Ignorance, and free from the three states of waking, dream and deep sleep. Living in all beings like the ether I am the witness free from all their defects.

7. Ever free and different from names, forms and actions I am the supreme *Brahman,* the Self, consisting of pure Consciousness and always without a second.

8. Those who think themselves to be one with *Brahman* and at the same time to be doers and experiencers should be regarded as fallen from both Knowledge and duties. They are, no doubt, unbelievers (in the *Vedas*).

9. It must be accepted on the strength of the scriptures that the Self is *Brahman,* and that liberation accrues from Right Knowledge only, like the connection with the Self[25] of the results of sin and virtue, which, though unseen is admitted (on the same authority).

10. What are called (in the *Śruti*[26]) clothes coloured with turmeric etc. are nothing but mental impressions perceived by people in dream. (The Self, their[27] illuminator, must, therefore, be different from them and from the subtle body in which they lie.) So the Self, pure Consciousness, (the perceiver of doership etc.,) must be different from them[28] (in the waking state also).

11. Just as a sword taken out of its sheath is seen as it is, so, the Knower,

---

* The *Upanishads* are also called *Vedantas*.

** This verse rejects the essential sacred symbols and actions of the Hindu priestly tradition and is thus a rejection of the way of being religious described in Chapter II.

the Self, is seen[29] in dream in Its real and self-effulgent nature free from cause and effect.[30]

12. The real nature[31] of the individual (Self) who was pushed and awakened[32] has been described by the saying, "Not this,[33] not this" which negates all superimposition.

13. Just as objects of enjoyment like a great Kingship[34] etc. are super-imposed on Me in dream (and are unreal),[35] so, the two forms,[36] (the visible and the invisible) with the mental impressions,[37] are also superimposed on Me (and are similarly unreal).[38]

14. All actions are performed by the Self[39] which has identified Itself with the gross and the subtle bodies and which has the nature of accumu-lating[40] impressions. As I am of the nature[41] indicated by the *Sruti*, "Not this, not this," actions are nowhere[42] to be done by Me.

15. As actions have Ignorance for their cause there is no hope from them of immortality. As liberation is caused by right Knowledge (alone) it does not depend on anything else.[43]

16. But Immortality[44] is free[45] from fear and destruction. The individual Self (signified by the words) "dear[46] to one" is *Brahman*[47] (devoid of all attributes) according to the *Sruti*, "Not this, not this." Whatever[48] is thought to be different from It[49] should, therefore, be renounced together with all actions.

NOTES

1. The Sanskrit word *"Aum"* used in the text indicates that one realizes *Brahman* by meditating on it. See *Kathopanishad* 1.2.16, 17.
2. I.e., the Bliss of the Self.
3. The word in the Text indicates assent. The disciple accepts Brahman as the Self.
4. For they cannot have an existence dependent on the Self which is contrary to them in nature i.e., the Self is conscious while they are not so.
5. Fourth, because the Self is beyond the three states of waking, dream and deep sleep which are superimposed on It.
6. The argument is this. the series is not real as they are objects of knowledge like dream-objects which are known to be unreal.
7. *Bhagaved Gita,* 13.31.
8. I.e., having no form. See *Bhagavad Gita,* 13.32.
9. I.e., the cause. And therefore untouched by the defects of beings in whom I reside.
10. The unmanifested Power of *Brahman* which transforms itself into the mani-fested universe. See *Bhagavad Gita,* 15.16–18.
11. See footnote 1, p. 60. [Not included]
12. Through Ignorance.
13. *Kathopanishad,* 1.3.8.
14. For one has known the Self.
15. I.e., free from all doubts.
16. Ignorance implied by them.
17. Apparently.
18. I.e., does not perceive it to be real.

19. Duality gets merged in Ignorance in the case of deep sleep but in the case of Self-knowledge it gets negated in all the states.
20. *Brahman.*
21. The sacred tuft of hair on the head, the sacred thread, etc.
22. *Brihadaranyaka Upanishad,* 4.5.15.
23. E.g., agency, egoism, etc.
24. Therefore witnessing the mind and its functions is not in the nature of the Self.
25. The individual Self.
26. *Brihadaranyaka Upanishad,* 2.3.6.
27. The Knower, Knowing and the Known in dream.
28. I.e., from the subtle body and the impressions in it.
29. Not as an object.
30. I.e., the mind which assumes the forms of causes and effects in dream.
31. *Brahman* Itself.
32. *Brihadaranyaka Upanishad,* 2.1.15.
33. *Brihadaranyaka Upanishad,* 2.3.6.
34. *Brihadaranyaka Upanishad,* 2.1.18.
35. *Brihadaranyaka Upanishad,* 4.3.10.
36. *Brihadaranyaka Upanishad,* 2.3.1.
37. *Brihadaranyaka Upanishad,* 2.3.6.
38. For they are objects of Knowledge.
39. The individualized Self.
40. Owing to continual performance of actions. As a matter of fact the subtle body is the seat of mental impressions.
41. I.e., Pure Consciousness.
42. Neither in waking nor in dream; and also neither by nature nor by *Vedic* injunctions.
43. Actions etc.
44. *Brahman.*
45. If it were not so it would be capable of being produced by actions.
46. *Brihadaranyaka Upanishad,* 1.4.8 and 2.4.5.
47. Therefore *Brahman,* not different from the Self, is not capable of being realized by actions.
48. I.e., the ideas of "me" and "mine" with respect to it.
49. *Brahman.*

2. The Way of Mindfulness,
Nyanaponika Thera

Why is there war? Why do people suffer? Why is there so much discontent? To answer these questions, said the Buddha over 2,500 years ago, you must seek the causes, the "seeds" of suffering. Since then his followers have focused on solving the problems of life by controlling the cause of suffering that is found in a person's attitude, in his mind. Our contemporary. problems also—even those as public and pervasive as war—begin in the mind. Therefore the way of liberation is that of "mindfulness." This excerpt is by a Buddhist revered master from Ceylon. It is based on a handbook for Buddhist mental training, giving instruction derived from discourses revered as having been spoken by the Buddha himself. The Satipatthana (a Pali term which means "establishing mindfulness") method of meditation here described focuses on sharpening "mindfulness"—a process useful for all people but requiring a singlemindedness in practice that only a few are willing to achieve. Note the preliminary physical factors and mental attitude which aid in the attainment of mindfulness; and observe that practicing "mindfulness" includes becoming aware of shifts in attention and of choices in intention as well as sensory awareness of the present. This description of the meditation procedure, though consistent with Buddhist practice, was written with Westerners in mind. Do you think it represents a significant religious option for you? Would your answer change if the question were phrased: Does this practice appear to be a useful technique for personal self-development? In what sense and in what way (if any) can you say that Nyanaponika Thera intends to know Ultimate Reality? How would you describe the goal of the meditation activity described here?

A MESSAGE OF HELP

In the present era after two world wars, history seems to repeat its lessons to humanity with a voice more audible than ever, because the turbulence and suffering that, alas, are generally equivalent with political history, affect increasingly larger sections of mankind, directly or indirectly. Yet it does not appear that these lessons have been learned any better than before. To a thoughtful mind, more gripping and heart-rending than all

From Nyanaponika Thera, *The Heart of Buddhist Meditation: A Handbook of Mental Training Based on the Buddha's Way of Mindfulness* (London: Rider & Co., 1969; first published in 1962), pp. 19–21, 87–99. By permission of Hutchinson Publishing Group Ltd.

the numerous single facts of suffering produced by recent history, is the uncanny and tragic monotony of behaviour that prompts mankind to prepare again for a new bout of that raving madness called war. The same old mechanism is at work again: the interaction of greed and fear. Lust for power or desire to dominate are barely restrained by fear—the fear of man's own vastly improved instruments of destruction. Fear, however, is not a very reliable brake on man's impulses, and it constantly poisons the atmosphere by creating a feeling of frustration which again will fan the fires of hate. But men still bungle only with the symptoms of their malady, remaining blind to the source of the illness which is no other than the three strong Roots of Everything Evil (*akusala-mūla*) pointed out by the Buddha: greed, hatred and delusion.

To this sick and truly demented world of ours, there comes an ancient teaching of eternal wisdom and unfailing guidance, the Buddha-Dhamma, the Doctrine of the Enlightened One, with its message and power of healing. It comes with the earnest and compassionate, but quiet and unobtrusive question whether, this time, the peoples of the world will be prepared to grasp the helping hand that the Enlightened One has extended to suffering humanity through his timeless Teaching. Or will the world wait again till it has succeeded in conjuring up a new and still more gruesome ordeal that may well result in mankind's final decline, material and spiritual?

The nations of the world seem unthinkingly to assume that their reserves of strength are inexhaustible. Against such an unwarranted belief stands the universal Law of Impermanence, the fact of incessant Change, that has been emphasized so strongly by the Buddha. This Law of Impermanence includes the fact shown by history and by daily experience, that the external opportunities for material and spiritual regeneration, and the vital strength and inner readiness required for it, are never without limits, either for individuals or for nations. How many empires, mighty like those of our days, have not crumbled, and how many a man has not, in spite of his repentance and "best intentions," been confronted with an implacable "Too late!" We never know whether it is not this very moment or just this present situation that is opening to us the door of opportunity for the last time. We never know whether the strength that we still feel pulsating in our veins, however feebly, will not be the last capable of carrying us through our distressful plight. Hence it is this very moment that is most precious. "Let it not escape from you!" warns the Buddha.

The Message of the Buddha comes to the world as an effective way of help in present-day afflictions and problems, and as the radical cure for ever-present Ill. Some doubt may arise in the minds of Western men how they could be helped in their present problems by a doctrine of the far and foreign East. And others, even in the East, may ask how words spoken 2,500 years ago can have relevance to our "modern world," except in a very general sense. Those who raise the objection of distance in space (meaning by it, properly, the difference of race), should ask themselves whether Benares is truly more foreign to a citizen of London than Nazareth from where a teaching has issued that to that very citizen has become a familiar and important part of his life and thought. They should further be willing to admit that mathematical laws, found out long ago in distant Greece, are of no less validity to-day, in Britain or elsewhere. But particularly these objectors should consider the numerous basic facts of life that are common to all humanity. It is about them that the Buddha pre-eminently speaks. Those who raise the objection of the distance in time, will certainly recall many golden words of long-dead sages and poets which strike such a deep and kindred chord in our own hearts that we very vividly feel a living and intimate contact with those great ones who have left this world long ago. Such experience contrasts with the "very much present" silly chatter of society, newspapers or radio, which, when compared with those ancient voices of wisdom and beauty, will appear to emanate from the mental level of stone-age man tricked out in modern trappings. True wisdom is always young, and always near to the grasp of an open mind which has painfully reached its heights and has earned its chance to listen to it. . . .

In the following pages, information will be given about a course of strict meditative practice according to the Satipaṭṭhāna method. The course was held at the "Thathana Yeiktha,"[1] at Rangoon (Burma), under the guidance of the Venerable Mahāsi Sayadaw[2] (U Sobhana Mahāthera).

A course of practice at this meditation centre lasts usually one to two months. After that period the meditators are expected to continue the practice at their own abodes, in adaptation to their individual conditions of life. During the course of strict practice the meditators do not engage themselves in reading and writing, or any other work than that of meditation and the routine activities of the day. Talk is limited to the minimum. The lay meditators, at that institution, observe, for the duration of their stay there, the Eight Precepts (aṭṭhaṅga-sīla) which include, e.g., abstinence from taking solid food (and certain liquids, as milk, etc.) after twelve o'clock, noon.

A brief written statement on practical meditation, even if limited to the very first steps as is done here, cannot replace personal guidance by an experienced teacher who alone can give due consideration to the requirements and the rate of progress of the individual disciple. The following notes are therefore meant only for those who have no access to an experienced meditation master. The fact that their number will be very great, in the West as well as in the East, has induced the writer to offer these notes, with all their inherent shortcomings, as a practical supplement to the main body of the book.

It is a fundamental principle of the Satipaṭṭhāna method that the disciple should take his very first steps on the firm ground of his own experience. He should learn to see things as they are, and he should see them for himself. He should not be influenced by others giving him suggestions or hints about what he *may* see or is expected to see. Therefore, in the aforementioned course of practice, no theoretical explanations are given, but only the bare instructions about what to do and not to do, at the start of the practice. When, after some initial practice, mindfulness becomes keener, and the meditator becomes aware of features in his object of mindfulness which were hitherto unnoticed, the meditation master may, in individual cases, decide not merely to say (as usual), "Go on!" but indicate briefly the direction to which the disciple's attention may be turned with benefit. It is one of the disadvantages of a written statement that even these indications cannot be given, as they necessarily depend on the progress of the individual meditator at the start of his practice. Yet, if the instructions given here are closely followed, the meditator's own experience will become his teacher and will lead him safely onwards, though it has to be admitted that progress is easier under the direction of an experienced meditation master.

Soberness, self-reliance and an observant, watchful attitude are the characteristics of this meditative practice. A true Satipaṭṭhāna Master will be very reticent in his relationship with those whom he instructs; he will avoid seeking to "impress" them by his personality and making "followers" of them. He will not have recourse to any devices that are likely to induce auto-suggestion, hypnotic trance or a mere emotional exultation. Those who employ such means, for themselves or for others, should be known to be on a path averse to the Way of Mindfulness.

In taking up this practice, one should not expect "mystical experiences" or cheap emotional satisfaction. After one has made one's earnest initial aspiration, one should no longer indulge in thoughts of future achievements or hanker after quick results. One should rather attend diligently, soberly and exclusively to those very simple exercises which will be described here. At the outset, one should even regard them just as purposes in themselves, i.e., as a technique for strengthening mindfulness and concentration. Any additional significance of these exercises will naturally unfold itself to the meditator, in the course of his practice. The faint outlines of that significance which appear at the horizon of the meditator's mind, will gradually grow more distinct and finally become like commanding presences to him who moves towards them steadily.

The method outlined here falls into the category of Bare Insight (*sukkha vipassanā*), that is the exclusive and direct practice of penetrative insight, without the previous attainment of the meditative absorptions (*jhāna*).[3] The method aims, in its first stage, at a discernment of bodily and mental processes (*nāma-rūpa-pariccheda*) in one's own personality by one's own experience. An increasingly keen awareness of the nature of these processes, and a strengthened concentration (up to the degree of Accessor Neighbourhood Concentration; (*upacāra-samādhi*) will result in a deepening insight into the Three Characteristics fo existence—Impermanence, Suffering and Egolessness—gradually leading to the attainment of the Stages of Sanctity (*magga-phala*), that is to final Liberation. The approach to that final goal leads through the Seven Stages of Purification (*satta visuddhi*) which are treated in Buddhaghosa's *Path to Purification*.

PRELIMINARIES : PHYSICAL

Posture. The Western mode of sitting, on a chair with legs hanging, is rather unfavorable for one who wishes to sit in meditation for increasingly longer periods of time, without discomfort and without frequently shifting the body. When seated on a chair the beginner in self-control may easily yield to any slight wish to shift legs or body even before benumbedness of limbs calls for it; or he may keep legs or body too rigid and tense for physical and mental ease. In postures with legs bent, however, the rump rests on a broad and firm basis, the body forming a triangle. When legs are crossed or linked, it is not so easy to shift on the seat and there is little necessity for it. With practice one can maintain such a posture for long periods.

The best-known Yoga posture, with fully crossed legs, the *padmāsana* or lotus posture, is rather difficult for most Westerners. Though it is advantageous for meditations aiming at full mental absorption (*jhāna*) it is of less importance for the Satipaṭṭhāna practice. We shall, therefore, not describe it here, but turn to the description of two easier postures.

In the *vīrāsana* ("hero's posture") the bent left leg is placed on the ground and the right leg upon it, with the right knee resting on the left foot, and the right foot on the left knee. There is no crossing, only a bending of legs in this posture.

In the *sukhāsana* ("the comfortable posture") both bent legs are placed on the ground evenly. The heel of the left foot rests between the legs; the toes are between the knee bend of the right leg which provides, as it were, the outer frame of the left leg. Since there is no pressure on the limbs whatsoever, this posture is the most comfortable one, and is, therefore, recommended in the Burmese meditation centre aforementioned.

For comfort in either of these postures it is essential that the knees rest firmly and without strain on their support (the floor, the seat, or on the other leg). The advantages of a posture with legs bent are so considerable for an earnest meditator that it will be worth his effort to train himself in any such posture. But if these postures come not easily to him, it is advisable to allow for posture training a separate period of time which may be used to one's best ability, for reflection, contemplation or Bare Attention. For the sake of such posture training, however, one should not delay or disturb one's determined attempt to achieve and sustain a higher degree of mental concentration, and for that purpose one may use, for the time being, a mode of sitting that is comfortable, dealing as best as one can with the disadvantages mentioned before. One may, then, sit on a straight-backed chair of a height that allows the legs to be placed on the floor without strain.

When sitting with legs bent, one may place a pillow, a folded cloth or blanket under the lower back, bringing it level with the legs. The body should kept erect but not rigidly stiff or tense. The head should be slightly bent forward and the gaze should gently (not rigidly) rest where it naturally falls at that position of the head. One may place at that spot any small and simple object for focussing one's glance on it; preferably a geometrical shape like a cube or cone, without a shining or light-reflecting surface, and without anything else that may divert thoughts. Such a device is, of course, not a necessity.

Female meditators in the East do not sit in either of the postures with legs bent as described above, nor with legs crossed. They kneel on ample-sized, well-stuffed cushions, sitting on their heels, the hands resting on the knees.

As to the mode of sitting, the meditator will have to use his own discretion, and apply to his individual case the "clear comprehension of suitability."

Clothing should be loose, for instance at the waist. Before one starts with the meditation one should make sure that muscles are relaxed, for instance, neck, shoulders, face, hands, etc.

Eating. In the countries of Theravāda Buddhism, those who take up a strict course of full-time practice in a meditation centre, usually observe, among other rules, the sixth precept of the monk, that is they abstain from solid food and nourishing liquids after mid-day. For those, however, who work all day, this will hardly be practicable though it will be feasible for periods of meditation during a weekend or holidays. In any case, however, for one who wishes to take up in earnest regular meditative practice, it will be very desirable that he should be moderate in eating. It was not without reason that the Buddha recommended repeatedly "moderation in eating" to those devoted to meditation. Experience will confirm the benefits of it to those who are determined to make actual progress in meditation and are not satisfied with casual attempts.

PRELIMINARIES: THE MENTAL ATTITUDE

The aim of the meditative practice to be described here, is the highest which the teaching of the Buddha offers. Therefore, the practice should be taken up in a mental attitude befitting such a high purpose. The Buddhist meditator may begin with the recitation of the Threefold Refuge, keeping in mind the true significance of that act.[4] This will instil confidence in him, which is so important for meditative progress: confidence in the peerless Teacher and Guide, the *Buddha*; confidence in the liberating efficacy of his Teaching (*Dhamma*), and in particular the Way of Mindfulness; confidence aroused by the fact that there have been those who have realized the Teaching in its fullness: the Community of Saints (*ariya-sangha*), the Accomplished Ones (*arahats*). Such conviction will fill him with joyous confidence in his own capacity and will give wings to his endeavour. In such a spirit, the follower of these Three Ideals should start his meditation practice with the quiet but determined aspiration to attain the highest, not in a distant future but in this very life.

> *"I shall be going now the Path trodden by the Buddhas and the Great Holy Disciples. But an indolent person cannot follow that Path. May my energy prevail! May I succeed!"*

But also the non-Buddhist will do well to consider that, in following even partly the Way of Mindfulness, he enters ground that is hallowed to the Buddhist, and therefore deserving of respect. Such courteous awareness will help him in his own endeavours on the Way.

It will bring firmness to his steps on the Way if he makes a solemn aspiration like the following ones or any other that he may formulate for himself:

> For mind's mastery and growth effort must be made
> If once you see the need. Why not make it now?
> The road is clearly marked.
> May what I win bring weal to me and to all beings!

> Mind brings all happiness and woe. To conquer woe
> I enter now the Path of Mindfulness.
> May what I win bring weal to me and to all beings!

THE PROGRAMME OF PRACTICE

1. **Training in general mindfulness.** During a course of strict training the time of practice is the whole day, from morning to night. This does not mean that the meditator should all that time attend exclusively to a single, that is the primary subject, of meditation with which we shall deal below. Though he should certainly devote to it as much of the day and night as he possibly can, there will of course be pauses between the single spells of the main practice; and for beginners these pauses will be fairly frequent and of longer duration. But also during these intervals, be they long or short, the guiding rope of mindfulness must not be dropped or allowed to slacken. Mindfulness of all activities and perceptions should be maintained throughout the day to the greatest possible extent: beginning with the first thought and perception when awakening, and ending with the last thought and perception when falling asleep. This general mindfulness starts with, and retains as its centre piece, the Awareness of the four Postures (iriyāpatha-manasikāra), i.e., going, standing, sitting and lying down. That means, one has to be fully aware of the posture presently assumed, of any change of it (including the preceding intention to change it), of any sensation connected with the posture, e.g., pressure, i.e., touch consciousness (kāya-viññāṇa), and of any noticeable feelings of pain or ease ("Contemplation on Feeling"). For instance, when lying down for the night and waking up in the morning, one should be aware of one's reclining posture and of touch ("lying down, touching").

The meditator may not be able at once to attend mindfully to all or even a greater part of the activities and impressions of the day. He therefore may start with the postures alone and gradually extend the scope of mindfulness to all routine activities, as dressing, washing, eating, etc. This extension will come naturally when, after the first few days of full-time practice, the mind becomes calmer, observation keener and mindfulness more alert.

One example may illustrate how mindfulness may be applied correctly to a series of activities: a wish arises to clean the mouth in the morning, and one is aware of that wish (thought-conscious: "he knows mind and mental objects"); one sees the glass and water jug, at some distance (visual consciousness); one goes towards that place (posture-conscious); stops there (posture-conscious); stretches the hand towards the jug ("acting with clear comprehension when bending and stretching"); one grasps the jug (touch-conscious), etc.

While performing these activities, one should also notice the arising of any pleasant or unpleasant feelings ("Contemplation of Feeling"), of stray thoughts interrupting the flow of mindfulness (Mind Contemplation: "unconcentrated mind"), of lust (e.g., when eating; Mind Contemplation: "mind with lust"; Mind-object-Contemplation: Hindrance of Sense Desire, or Fetter arising through tongue and flavours), etc. In brief, one should be aware of all occurrences, bodily and mental, as they present themselves. In that way, one will attend to all four objects, or Contemplations, of Satipaṭṭhāna, during the day of practice.

Such a detailed application of Mindfulness involves a considerable slowing-down of one's movements which can be maintained only in periods of strict practice, and not, or only rarely, during every-day life. The experience, and the effects, of that slowing-down practice will, however, prove wholesome and useful in many ways.

In attending to those routine activities of the day, mindfulness need not be directed to all minute phases of them (as it should be with the principal subjects). By doing so, the slowing-down would be too great. It will be sufficient if mindfulness goes watchfully along with these activities, noticing only those details which present themselves without effort.

The initial purpose of this general application of Mindfulness is the strengthening of awareness and concentration to an extent enabling the meditator to follow the unceasing flow of variegated mental and bodily impressions and activities, for an increasingly long period and without a break of attention or without an *unnoticed* break. It will count as "uninterrupted mindfulness," if the meditator is not carried away by his stray thoughts, but if breaks of attention are noticed at once when they occur, or soon after. For the beginner, the standards of "general mindfulness" will be satisfied by that procedure.

2. The main practice with selected subjects. After one has attended mindfully to the various routine activities of the morning, one sits down on the meditation seat, being aware of one's preceding intention to sit down, the single phases of the act, and then of "touching" and "sitting." Now one turns one's attention to the regular *rising and falling movement of the abdomen,* resulting from the process of breathing. The attention is directed to the slight sensation of pressure caused by that movement, and not so visually observing it. This forms the *primary object (mūl' ārammaṇa)* of mindfulness, in the course of practice described here. It has been introduced into the practice by the Venerable U Sobhana Mahāthera (Mahāsi Sayadaw) as it was found to be very effective.

It should be well understood that one must not think *about* the movement of the abdomen, but keep to the bare noticing of that physical process, being aware of its regular rise and fall, in all its phases. One should try to retain that awareness without break, or without *unnoticed* break, for as long a period as possible without strain. The insight at which the method aims, will present itself to the mind spontaneously, as the natural result, or the maturing fruit, of growing mindfulness. The Meditation Master said: "The knowledge will arise by itself" (*ñāṇam sayam eva uppajjissati*). It will come in the degree in which, through sharpened awareness, features of the observed processes appear which were hitherto unnoticed. Insight arrived at in this way will carry the conviction conveyed by one's own indubitable experience.

Though it is the breathing which causes the abdominal movement, the attention directed to the latter must not be regarded as a variety of the "Mindfulness of Breathing" (*ānāpānasati*). In the practice described here the object of mindfulness is not the breath but just the rise and fall of the abdomen as felt by the slight pressure.

In the case of beginners, the abdominal movement is not always clearly noticeable at once and sometimes may remain distinct only for short recurring periods. This is nothing unusual and will improve in the course of diligent practice. As a help in making the movement of the abdomen perceptible more often and for a longer stretch, one may lie down; by doing so it will become more distinct. One may also place one's hand on the abdomen for tracing the movement first in that way; it will then be easier to keep track of it even when the hand is removed. If one feels it helpful, one may well continue the exercise in a reclining position, provided one can keep off sleepiness and lassitude. But, in between, one may try it repeatedly in the sitting posture.

Whenever the awareness of the abdominal movement ceases or remains unclear, one should not strain to 'catch' it, but should turn one's attention to *"touching"* and *"sitting."* This should be done in the following way. From the many points of contact, or better, perceptions of touch, that are present in the apparently uniform act of sitting—e.g., at the knees, thighs, shoulders, etc—six or seven may be chosen. The attention should turn to them successively, travelling, as it were, on that prescribed route, ending with the awareness of the sitting posture, and starting again with the same series: touching—touching—touching—sitting; touching—touching—touching—sitting. One should dwell on the single perception just for the length of these two-syllable words (spoken internally, and later to be abandoned when one has got into the time rhythm). It should be noted that the object of mindfulness is here the respective sensation, and not the places of contact in themselves, nor the words "touching-sitting." One may change, from time to time, the selection of "touches."

This awareness of "touching-sitting" is, as it were, a "stand-by" of the awareness of the abdominal movement, and is one of the secondary objects of the main practice. It has, however, a definite value of its own for achieving results in the domain of Insight.

When, while attending to "touching-sitting," one notices that the abdominal movement has become clearly perceptible again, one should return to it, and continue with that primary object as long as possible.

If one feels tired, or, by sitting long, the legs are paining or benumbed, one should be aware of these feelings and sensations. One should keep to that awareness as long as these feelings and sensations are strong enough to force attention upon them and to disturb the meditation. Just by the act of noticing them quietly and continuously, i.e., with Bare Attention, these feelings and sensations may sometimes disappear, enabling one to continue with the primary object. In the awareness of the disturbing sensations one stops short at the bare statement of their presence without "nursing" these feelings and thus strengthening them by what one adds to the bare facts, i.e., by one's mental attitude of self-reference, excessive sensitivity, self-pity, resentment, etc.

If, however, these unpleasant sensations, or tiredness, persist and disturb the practice, one may change the posture (noticing the intention and the act of changing), and resort to *mindfully walking up and down*. In doing so, one has to be aware of the single phases of each step. The sixfold division of these phases as given, e.g., in the Commentary to the Discourse, will be too elaborate for the beginner. It is sufficient to notice three (A) or two (B) phases. For fitting into a two-syllable rhythm it is suggested to formulate them as follows: A. 1. lifting, 2. pushing, 3. placing; B. 1. lifting, 2. placing, of the foot. Whenever one wishes to walk somewhat quicker, one may use the twofold division; otherwise the threefold one is preferable as affording a closer sequence of mindfulness, without a gap.

This practice of mindful walking is, particularly for certain types of meditators, highly recommendable both as a method of concentration and as a source of Insight. It may therefore be practised in its own right, and not only as a "change of posture" for relieving fatigue. In the Discourses of the Buddha we meet a frequently recurring passage, saying: "By day, and in the first and third watches of the night, he purifies his mind from obstructing thoughts, while *walking up and down* or *sitting*."

If walking up and down is taken up as a practice in its own right, it is desirable to have for that purpose a fairly long stretch of ground, either in the house (a corridor or two adjoining rooms) or outdoors, since turning around too often may cause disturbance in the continuous flow of mindfulness. One should walk for a fairly long time, even until one feels tired.

During the entire day of practice, stray thoughts, or an unmindful "skipping" of steps (in walking), phases or sequences of the abdominal movements, or of parts of any other activities, should be clearly noticed. One should pay attention to the fact whether these breaks in attention have been noticed at once after occurring, or whether, and how long, one was carried away by stray thoughts, etc., before resuming the original object of mindfulness. One should aim at noticing these breaks at once, and then returning immediately to one's original object. This may be taken as a measure of one's growing alertness. The frequency of these breaks will naturally decrease when, in the course of the practice, mental quietude and concentration improve. Growing competence in this practice of immediate awareness of breaks of attention will be a valuable help in the strenghtening of one's self-control, and in checking mental defilements (*kilesa*) as soon as they arise. Its importance for one's progress on the Path and one's mental development in general is evident.

One should not allow oneself to be irritated, annoyed or discouraged by the occurrence of distracting or undesirable thoughts, but should simply *take these disturbing thoughts themselves as (temporary) objects of one's mindfulness,* making them thus a part of the practice (through the Contemplation of the State of Mind). Should feelings of irritation about one's distracted state of mind arise and persist, one may deal with them in the very same way; that is, take them as an opportunity for the Contemplation of Mind-objects: the Hindrance of aversion, or of restlessness and worry. In this context the Meditation Master said: Since a multiplicity of thought-objects is unavoidable in ordinary life, and such defilements as lust, aversion, etc., are sure to arise in all unliberated minds, it is of vital importance to face these variegated thoughts and defilements squarely, and to learn how to deal with them. This is, in its own way, just as important as acquiring an increased measure of concentration. One should, therefore, not regard it as "lost time" when one is dealing with these interruptions of the methodical practice.

The same method should be applied to interruptions from outside. If there is, for instance, a disturbing noise, one may take brief notice of it as "sound"; if it was immediately followed by annoyance about the disturbance, one should register it, too, as "mind with anger." After that, one should return to the interrupted meditation. But if one does not succeed at once in doing so, the same procedure should be repeated. If the noise is loud and persistent and keeps one from attending to the subject of meditation, one may, until the noise ceases, continue to take it as an object of mindfulness, namely as one of the six sense-bases, within the frame of the Contemplation of Mind-objects: "He knows the ear and sound, and knows the fetter (annoyance) arising dependent on both..." In the fluctuations of sound one can observe 'rise and fall'; in its intermittent occurrence, its origination and disappearance, and its conditioned nature will become clear.

In that way, *disturbances of the meditative practice can be transformed into useful objects of the practice*; and what appeared inimical, can be turned into a friend and teacher.

Nevertheless, when the mind has been quieted or the outer disturbances have disappeared, one should return to the primary subject of meditation, since it is the sustained cultivation of it that will make for quicker progress.

Three to four hours of continuous mindfulness, i.e., without unnoticed breaks, are regarded as the minimum for a beginner undergoing a course of strict practice. This, of course, does not mean that three or four hours are sufficient for the whole day of practice. If one has "lost the thread" of mindfulness, be it after, or before, that minimal period, one should take it up again and again, and continue with the practice of sustained concentration, as long as possible.

Quiet sustained effort, without too much regard to bodily discomfort, is recommended, particularly during a course of strict practice. Often, when disregarding the first appearance of fatigue, one will discover behind it new resources of energy, a "second-wind." On the other hand, one should not go to extremes, and should allow oneself rest when effort ceases to be useful. These intervals of rest will also form parts of the practice (with less intense focussing) if one keeps mindful. The more natural and relaxed the flow of one's mindfulness is, or becomes, in following the continual arising and disappearing of its selected or variegated objects, the less fatigue will be caused by it.

When alertness grows one may also give particular attention to one's thoughts or moods of satisfaction or dissatisfaction, even if very subtle. They are the seeds of stronger forms of attraction and aversion, and of feelings of pride or inferiority, elation or depression. It is therefore important to get acquainted with them, to notice them and to stop them early. One should also avoid futile thoughts of the past or the future, as Satipaṭṭhāna is concerned with the present only.

The primary and secondary objects dealt with here (i.e., abdominal movement, touching-sitting, walking) are retained throughout the whole practice, i.e., during a strict course and afterwards, without anything being added in the way of new devices, etc. If there is persistent application to them, these simple exercises are capable of leading gradually to the highest results.

NOTES

1. Pronounce 'Yeeta'.
2. 'Sayadaw', a Burmese word, is a respectful way of addressing senior or learned Buddhist monks, and means 'great teacher'.
3. See page 85. [Not included here.]
4. See *The Threefold Refuge,* by Nānamoli Thera (a free tract of the Buddhist Publication Society, Kandy).

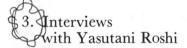

3. Interviews with Yasutani Roshi

Buddhism spread from India to South Asia and north to China and Japan. Despite various cultural developments resulting in different forms of Buddhism throughout the world, there are several common elements. One of these is the importance placed on meditation, which includes the development of a heightened sense of mental, emotional, and attitudinal factors that contribute to a person's consciousness of everyday experience. In Theravada Buddhism and Japanese Zen we find both a concern to apprehend those elements in one's personality that prevent him from living freely and joyously, and a training program through which one can develop skills in self-discovery.

The spiritual training in a Zen monastery includes a private interview between a master (roshi) and his disciple. These are usually regular, though brief, periods in which the roshi examines the disciple's progress, answers questions, and makes suggestions for more effective meditation. Prior to the interview the student has had lectures and general instruction in Buddhist thought and practice, and has meditated for some time on a koan—a word, phrase, or question that points to the ultimate truth. (See reading 10 for a Zen master's explanation of the importance of sitting in meditation.)

The following excerpt is from a series of interviews between a thirty-three-year-old Western woman and a contemporary eighty-year-old Soto Zen master, Yasutani Roshi. This woman's koan is "Who am I?" It has only recently been changed from the koan "mu" (emptiness, nothing), on which she had meditated for two years. Several sessions are given here; each new session is marked by . . . in the text. Do you think that the roshi's response to the woman's misgivings about her meditation was appropriate? What relationship does the roshi see between meditation and cultivating kindness? How is meditation different from philosophical reflection in resolving the problems of existence? What sense is there in saying that man is inherently "perfect" when most people experience themselves as "imperfect"?

ROSHI: Do you have any questions?

STUDENT: Yes. When I question myself "Who am I?" I say to myself, "I am bones, I am blood, I am skin." Where do I go from there?

ROSHI: Then ask yourself, "What is it that has this blood? What is it that has these bones? What is it that has this skin?"

STUDENT: It seems to me that I have to do two things: to become one with eating, for instance, as to ask myself, "Who is eating?" Is that right?

ROSHI: No, only question yourself as to who is eating. Your mind must become one mass of profound questioning. This is the quickest way to the realization of your True nature. Asking "Who am I?" is really no different from asking "What is mu?"

STUDENT: To be honest, I have no burning desire for kensho.* I wonder why. This bothers me.

---

* Enlightenment, literally: "seeing into one's own nature."

ROSHI: People who have been compelled to face painful life situations, such as the death of a beloved one, for example, are frequently precipitated into asking the most searching questions about life and death. This questioning gives rise to an acute thirst for Self-understanding so that they can alleviate their own as well as mankind's sufferings. With true enlightenment, disquiet and anxiety are replaced by inner joy and serenity. Listening to the Buddha's teachings in my lectures, you will develop within you a longing for Self-realization, which will grow deeper and deeper.

•   •   •

STUDENT: Last night during zazen* I was often troubled by the thought that my desire for enlightenment is weak. Why, I kept asking myself, do I not strive more intensely like so many around me? At one o'clock this morning I was ready to quit, though only four hours earlier I had determined to sit up in zazen all night. In the kitchen, where I went for a drink, I saw the old cook-nun washing clothes. Watching her, I felt ashamed of my own feeble efforts.

The other day you told me that those who have the strongest desire for enlightenment are people who have suffered in life. You said that they keenly wish kensho so as to relieve their own suffering as well as the suffering of others. The fact is that in my teens I experienced considerable suffering. Perhaps that is why I felt so compassionate toward others and why my friends and acquaintances often came to me for advice and help.

Some years later when I heard about Zen I began to practice it, after a fashion, in the United States. Then a few years ago I came to Japan, having given up my work in America, and began the traditional practice of Zen. The sympathy and compassion I had always felt toward people before I undertook zazen have dried up in me. I have experienced so much pain in Zen that I no longer think of saving anybody but myself. I hate having to suffer! So my life in Zen, far from making me sensitive to the sufferings of others and kindling in me a desire to save them, has destroyed whatever altruistic feelings I possessed, leaving me cold and selfish.

ROSHI: As I observe your face and manner, I see neither insensitivity nor selfishness—on the contrary, I see much that is Kannon-like. I am sure that most people who come in contact with you sense your natural warmth and feel well-disposed toward you. What you have described to me, rather than making you out to be cold-hearted and selfish, reveals a deepening of your natural sympathies, but all this lies outside your consciousness. One who thinks of himself as kind-hearted and sympathetic is truly neither.[1] That you no longer are consciously aware of these emotions only shows how deeply entrenched they have become.

There are many people who spend all their time giving aid to the needy and joining movements for the betterment of society. To be sure, this ought not to be discounted. But their root anxiety, growing out of their false

---

* Sitting meditation.

view of themselves and the universe, goes unrelieved, gnawing at their hearts and robbing them of a rich, joyous life. Those who sponsor and engage in such social betterment activities look upon themselves, consciously or unconsciously, as morally superior and so never bother to purge their minds of greed, anger, and delusive thinking. But the time comes when, having grown exhausted from all their restless activity, they can no longer conceal from themselves their basic anxieties about life and death. Then they seriously begin to question why life hasn't more meaning and zest. Now for the first time they wonder whether instead of trying to save others they ought not to save themselves first.

I assure you that you have not made a mistake in deciding to tread this path, and one day it will become clear to you. It is not selfishness to forget about saving others and to concentrate only on developing your own spiritual strength, though it may seem to be. The solemn truth is that you can't begin to save anybody until you yourself have become whole through the experience of Self-realization. When you have seen into the nature of your True-self and the universe, your words will carry conviction and people will listen to you.

STUDENT: But I become tired and discouraged so easily—the Way is terribly long and hard.

ROSHI: The Buddha's Way calls for energetic devotion and perseverance. When you stop to consider, however, that philosophers have been struggling for two or three thousand years to resolve the problem of human existence, without success, but that through asking "Who am I?" you can succeed where they have failed, have you cause to be discouraged? What activity or work in life is more urgent or compelling than this? By comparison everything else fades into insignificance.

STUDENT: I feel that way too; that's why I came to Japan to train in Zen.

ROSHI: You are different from most here. They come for a sesshin* because they hear Zen is remarkable and they want to grab it as quickly as they can and go about their business; therefore they strain themselves. They attack zazen with the fury of a sudden storm where the rain comes down in torrents and is swiftly carried away. But you, having made tremendous sacrifices for the sake of entering upon the Way of the Buddha, need not torture yourself. Your practice ought to be like rain gently dropping from the sky and seeping deep into the earth. With this state of mind you can sit patiently for four or five years, or even more, until you realize Truth in its fullness.

STUDENT: Is it because philosophers ask Why? and How? that they have been unable to resolve the problem of human existence?

---

* An intensive training session for about one week (though sometimes they last only a few days, or sometimes longer than a week) when one seeks his true Self-nature. Beginning with certain ceremonies, the days are divided into regular intervals (beginning at 3 A.M.) of long periods of meditation (zazen), formal lectures, and private interviews between master and student (as here presented).

ROSHI: Their investigations take them away from themselves into the realm of diversity—this is how philosophers and scientists work—whereas the question "Who am I?" precipitates you into an awareness of your fundamental solidarity with the universe.

STUDENT: I am ready to do whatever you say.

ROSHI: I feel that your training up to now has not been entirely suited to your temperament. However, you must not think that the time you have spent in Zen has been wasted; it has been valuable in more ways than you are aware. I also feel that, for the time being at least, you ought not to be struck with the kyosaku.*

STUDENT: I can't tell you how nervous it has made me. In the last place I was doing zazen I spent ninety-five percent of the time fighting my reaction to it.

ROSHI: Had it been possible for you to communicate with your last teacher the way you and I are now able to, thanks to this interpretation, a different practice might well have been assigned you. In any case, hereafter question yourself, "Who am I?" with sharp yet unruffled penetration.

●　　　●　　　●

ROSHI: Have you anything to say?

STUDENT: Yes. A few days after the last sesshin I suddenly realized in a new way that seeking excitement and pleasure and trying to avoid pain, which has been the story of my life, was senseless, since it was always followed by an aching hollowness. Now, even though this insight had come to me with great force, along with an exhilaration which persisted throughout the day, within a week the old feeling of the flatness and meaninglessness of life, together with a craving for excitement, returned. Is this natural or unnatural—?

ROSHI: To wish for a fuller, happier life than your present one is natural and commendable. What is not commendable is to despise your present state while yearning for a more exalted one. In giving yourself over wholly to whatever you are doing at the moment you can achieve a deeper and richer state of mind— Am I answering your question?

STUDENT: I haven't come to the crux of it yet. When I feel this way I want to get away from myself, to run off to a movie or to stuff myself with loads of rich food. My question is, should I indulge these desires or fight to repress them and continue with my zazen?

ROSHI: This is a most vital question. It is unwise either to repress your feelings severely or to indulge them wildly. There are people who, when they feel as you do, either get riotously drunk or eat themselves sick. Of course you are not that kind of person. The point is, it is all right to go to a movie occasionally if you go to one you enjoy and not to just any movie. Likewise, when you have an irresistible urge to treat yourself to a feast, eat food that you not only enjoy but that is nourishing as well, and don't overeat so that you are sick the next day. If you exercise moderation and judgment, you won't feel remorseful afterwards, reproaching your-

---

* A long flat paddle or stick.

self for having foolishly wasted valuable time which you could have utilized more profitably in zazen. You will be taken out of your doldrums and given a lift, and will be able to resume your practice with greater zest. But if you have feelings of self-disgust, they will give rise to a host of thoughts which will interfere with your practice. As your zazen deepens, however, all this will cease to be a problem to you.

•   •   •

STUDENT: If I understood you correctly, at one time you told me to keep my mind in my palm, another time to focus it in the region below the navel, and again, when I become sleepy, to place it between my eyes. I am confused. I don't even know what my mind is, so how can I put it in any of these places?

ROSHI: When I told you to put your mind in the palm of your hand, what I meant was to focus your *attention* at that point. You must not constantly change the focal point of your concentration. Both Dogen and Hakuin recommend focusing the mind in the palm of the hand. If you want to increase the intensity of your zazen, you can do so by directing your attention to your hara.* A good way to overcome sleepiness is to concentrate your attention between your eyes.

STUDENT: But what is Mind, anyway? I mean, I know what it is theoretically, because I have read many of the sutras and other books on Buddhism. But can I really find out what Mind is by asking "Who am I?"

ROSHI: A theoretical understanding of Mind is not enough to resolve the question "Who am I?" and through it the problem of birth-and-death. Such understanding is merely a portrait of reality, not reality itself. If you persistently question yourself "Who am I?" with devotion and zeal—that is to say, moved by a genuine desire for Self-knowledge—you are bound to realize the nature of Mind.

Now, Mind is more than your body and more than what is ordinarily called mind. The inner realization of Mind is the realization that you and the universe are not two. This awareness must come to you with such overwhelming certainty that you involuntarily slap your thigh and exclaim: "Oh, of course!"

STUDENT: But I don't know who it is that is asking "Who am I?" and not knowing this, or who it is that is being asked, how can I find out who I am?

ROSHI: The one asking the question is You and You must answer. The truth is, they are not two. The answer can only come out of persistent questioning with an intense yearning to know. Up to the present you have been wandering aimlessly, uncertain of your destination, but now that you have been given a map and have your bearings, don't stop to admire the sights—march on!

---

* "Center"—anatomically it refers to a spot in the lower abdomen, but it also refers to a psychological center that remains quiet while the personality responds to environmental conditions.

•   •   •

STUDENT: You have said that we are all inherently perfect—without a flaw. I can believe that in our mother's womb we are, but after birth we are anything but perfect. The sutras say that we are all beset by greed, anger, and folly. I believe that, because it is certainly true of myself.

ROSHI: A blind man, even while blind, is fundamentally whole and perfect. The same is true of a deaf-mute. If a deaf-mute suddenly regained his hearing, his perfection would no longer be that of a deaf-mute. Were this saucer on the table to be broken, each segment would be wholeness itself. What is visible to the eye is merely the form, which is ever-changing, not the substance. Actually the word "perfect" is superfluous. Things are neither perfect nor imperfect, they are what they are. Everything has absolute worth, hence nothing can be compared with anything else. A tall man is tall, a short man is short, that is all you can say. There is a koan where in reply to the question "What is the Buddha?" the master answers: "The tall bamboo is tall, the short bamboo is short." Kensho is nothing more than directly perceiving all this in a flash.

NOTES

1. Compare with Lao-tzu's "The truly virtuous is not conscious of his virtue. The man of inferior virtue, however, is ever consciously concerned with his virtue and therefore he is without true virtue. True virtue is spontaneous and lays no claim to virtue." (From the *Tao Teh Ching*, quoted by Lama Govinda in his *Foundations of Tibetan Mysticism*, p. 235.)

4. Dialogue Between Ch'an Master Yung-chia and the Patriarch

In the last interview we witnessed the struggle within a disciple to break the habitual structures of thought and self-perception. What would a dialogue between two enlightened persons look like? The following short dialogue is an example of "irrelevant questions and answers." It is one of more than a thousand such stories and dialogues in a famous Chinese Ch'an (Zen) text called The Transmission of the Lamp, *compiled by Tao-yüan in 1004 A.D. When reading this dialogue, keep in mind that*

From *Original Teachings of Ch'an Buddhism,* trans. by Chang-Yuan. Copyright © 1969 by Chang Chung-Yuan. Reprinted by permission of Pantheon Books, A Division of Random House, Inc. Pp. 27–28.

*normal discursive talk, which includes distinguishing between
"things," is regarded by meditation masters as having nothing
to do with realizing the true nature of existence. Talk is often
illusory, and has an uncanny power to trap a person when he
seeks to know himself (and all life) at the most profound level.
A common Buddhist expression of the highest spiritual wisdom
is "attainment of no-birth" or "attainment of no-movement,"
and the realization of "no-meaning." However these phrases
themselves and their supposed referrents can become an object
of selfish desire in which the spiritually blind will entangle
themselves. If this dialogue does not blow your mind after a
couple of readings, focus on Master Yung-chiu's replies after the
following questions of the Patriarch: "Why don't you attain
no-birth and free yourself from this speed?" "Are you not leaving
too soon?" and "Who is he who is aware of no-movement?"*

When he arrived there,* he shook his staff and held a vase in his hand;
he walked around the Patriarch three times and then stood still. The
Patriarch said to him:

"A Buddhist monk is he who follows the three thousand regulations and
performs the eighty thousand detailed duties.[1] Where do you come from,
sir? Why should you have such great self-pride?"

"Life and death are a serious matter," replied Yung-chia, "and death
follows life with terrible speed."

"Why don't you attain no-birth and free yourself from this speed?"
inquired the Patriarch.

"Attainment is no-birth, and basic freedom is never speedy," replied
Yung-chia.

"That's so! That's so!" exclaimed the Patriarch.

At this everyone in the assembly was astonished, and it was not until
then that Yung-chia observed the rule of bowing to the Patriarch.

A little while later he came to the Patriarch to bid him goodbye.

"Are you not leaving too soon?" asked the Patriarch.

"Basically, motion does not move. How can you say that I am leaving
too soon?" challenged Yung-chia.

"Who is he who is aware of no-movement?" asked the Patriarch.

"You, Master, are making this discrimination," replied Yung-chia.

"You have grasped very well the meaning of no-birth."

"How can no-birth have meaning?"

"If it has no meaning, who can differentiate it?"

"Even though one may differentiate it, it is still meaningless."

The Patriarch exclaimed, "Good! Good! Please stay here for at least
one night."

Therefore, the people of that time called Yung-chia's visit "Enlightenment from One Night's Lodging."

---

* When the monk Yung-chia arrived at the monastery of the Patriarch . . .

The following day Master Hsüan-ts'ê remained in Ts'ao-ch'i, but Yung-chia went down the hill back to Wên-chou.

NOTES

1. The three thousand regulations govern the proper way of walking, standing, sitting, and lying down. The eighty thousand detailed duties are rules concerning the four awe-inspiring deportments and many other aspects of the monk's behavior.

5. Master Hu Tzu
and the Shaman,
Chuang Tzu

> When a person searches for the true nature of existence, or the
> Original Source, he is confronted with various claims and
> demonstrations of insights by different sorts of people. There
> are some criteria of true insight that are common to various
> traditions. One of these criteria is that the truly enlightened is
> unconcerned with promotion or praise. (This disinterest in
> external display, of course, does not negate the serene
> self-confidence of a spiritual master when he affirms that he has
> realized the Source.) In the following excerpt from the sayings
> of the famous (Chinese) Taoist exponent Chuang Tzu, we
> observe how Lieh Tzu, a Taoist who—according to tradition—had
> learned to ride the wind, learns that even occult powers are weak
> when compared with manifesting emptiness. Does this story
> (plus the the final expository paragraph) show you how to bypass
> the outward forms for "the substance" of reality?

In Cheng there was a shaman of the gods named Chi Hsien. He could tell whether men would live or die, survive or perish, be fortunate or unfortunate, live a long time or die young, and he would predict the year, month, week,[1] and day as though he were a god himself. When the people of Cheng saw him, they dropped everything and ran out of his way. Lieh Tzu went to see him and was completely intoxicated. Returning, he said to Hu Tzu,[2] "I used to think, Master, that your Way was perfect. But now I see there is something even higher!"

From *Chuang Tzu: Basic Writings,* trans. Burton Watson (New York: Columbia University Press, 1964), pp. 92–95. Used by permission of the publisher.

Hu Tzu said, "I have already showed you all the outward forms, but I haven't yet showed you the substance—and do you really think you have mastered this Way of mine? There may be a flock of hens but, if there is no rooster, how can they lay fertile eggs? You take what you know of the Way and wave it in the face of the world, expecting to be believed! This is the reason men can see right through you. Try bringing your shaman along next time and I will show him who I am."

The next day Lieh Tzu brought the shaman to see Hu Tzu. When they had left the room, the shaman said, "I'm so sorry—your master is dying! There's no life left in him—he won't last the week. I saw something very strange—something like wet ashes!"

Lieh Tzu went back into the room, weeping and drenching the collar of his robe with tears, and reported this to Hu Tzu.

Hu Tzu said, "Just now I appeared to him with the Pattern of Earth— still and silent, nothing moving, nothing standing up. He probably saw in me the Workings of Virtue Closed Off.[3] Try bringing him around again."

The next day the two came to see Hu Tzu again, and when they had left the room, the shaman said to Lieh Tzu, "It certainly was lucky that your master met me! He's going to get better—he has all the signs of life! I could see the stirring of what had been closed off!"

Lieh Tzu went in and reported this to Hu Tzu.

Hu Tzu said, "Just now I appeared to him as Heaven and Earth—no name or substance to it, but still the workings, coming up from the heels. He probably saw in me the Workings of the Good One.[4] Try bringing him again."

The next day the two came to see Hu Tzu again, and when they had left the room, the shaman said to Lieh Tzu, "Your master is never the *same!* I have no way to physiognomize him! If he will try to steady himself then I will come and examine him again."

Lieh Tzu went in and reported this to Hu Tzu.

Hu Tzu said, "Just now I appeared to him as the Great Vastness Where Nothing Wins Out. He probably saw in me the Workings of the Balanced Breaths. Where the swirling waves[5] gather there is an abyss; where the still waters gather there is an abyss; where the running waters gather there is an abyss. The abyss has nine names and I have shown him three.[6] Try bringing him again."

The next day the two came to see Hu Tzu again, but before the shaman had even come to a halt before Hu Tzu, his wits left him and he fled.

"Run after him!" said Hu Tzu, but though Lieh Tzu ran after him, he could not catch up. Returning, he reported to Hu Tzu, "He's vanished! He's disappeared! I couldn't catch up with him."

Hu Tzu said, "Just now I appeared to him as Not Yet Emerged from My Source. I came at him empty, wriggling and turning, not knowing anything about 'who' or 'what,' now dipping and bending, now flowing in waves—that's why he ran away."

After this, Lieh Tzu concluded that he had never really begun to learn anything.[7] He went home and for three years did not go out. He replaced his wife at the stove, fed the pigs as though he were feeding people, and showed no preferences in the things he did. He got rid of the carving and polishing and returned to plainness, letting his body stand alone like a clod. In the midst of entanglement he remained sealed, and in this oneness he ended his life.

Do not be an embodier of fame; do not be a storehouse of schemes; do not be an undertaker of projects; do not be a proprietor of wisdom. Embody to the fullest what has no end and wander where there is no trail. Hold on to all that you have received from Heaven but do not think you have gotten anything. Be empty, that is all. The Perfect Man uses his mind like a mirror—going after nothing, welcoming nothing, responding but not storing. Therefore he can win out over things and not hurt himself.

NOTES

1. The ancient ten-day week.
2. The Taoist philosopher Lieh Tzu has already appeared on p. 26 above: ["Lieh Tzu could ride the wind and go soaring around with cool and breezy skill, but after fifteen days he came back to earth."] Hu Tzu is his teacher.
3. Virtue here has the sense of vital force. Cf. *Book of Changes, Hsi tz'u* 2: "The Great Virtue of Heaven and Earth is called life."
4. The language of this whole passage is, needless to say, deliberately mysterious. The term "Good One" may have some relation to the passage in the *Changes, Hsi tz'u* 1: "The succession of the yin and yang is called the Way. What carries it on is goodness."
5. Following the emendation and interpretation of Ma Hsü-lun.
6. According to commentators, the three forms of the abyss in the order given here correspond to the third, first, and second of Hu Tzu's manifestations.
7. That is, he had reached the highest stage of understanding.

6. Right Conduct on the Way to God,
Abū 'l-Qāsim al-Qushayrī
(English translation by *W. Paul McLean*)

> *The author of this brief treatment of the Sufi path was a prominent Muslim spiritual teacher who lived in the 11th century A.D. He might be called a "moderate" Sufi who saw ascetical-mystical Islam (taṣawwuf or Sufism) as the complement and crown of orthodox Islamic dogmatic theology and legal theory. Sufis lived in poverty and devoted themselves to prayer and meditation. They saw themselves as the "friends of God," and sought to manifest His will perfectly in every daily activity. The substance of the sections given here of the* Right Conduct on the

Way to God* *is broadly representative of Sufi thought and practice.*

Al-Qushayri observed elsewhere that the central element of the Sufi spiritual discipline is dhikr,** *here translated as "remembrance." In the religious context of Islam,* dhikr *means basically to remember God and to say His name. As illustrated in the following excerpt, "remembrance" was a practice that developed into a complete and comprehensive spiritual discipline in which the Sufi "emptied" himself, turning away totally from all things other than the Transcendent One. Three stages of remembrance are recognized. The initial stage of remembrance is commonly referred to as "remembrance of the tongue," in which concentration on God is coupled with repetition of one of his names. The practice of this* dhikr *then gives way to the next stage, the "remembrance of the heart." The process of "remembrance" moves continually from external expression to the inner life, so in the second stage the aspirant has lost normal awareness of his body or external stimuli. The ultimate act (third stage) of remembrance is "remembrance of the Secret," in which the place of the act of remembrance is the inmost center of man's being. The self-disclosure of God to man in his inmost self is the goal of the Sufi way. In the "remembrance of the Secret" the Sufi becomes, by the grace of God, one who lives and moves for, by, and in God.*

In common with other spiritual disciplines presented in this chapter, the Sufis use a number of techniques for overcoming ego-centered ignorance that keeps man from full awareness of truth and joy. These include tirelessly repeating a sacred sound (in this case God's name), reciting verses from Scripture (in this case the Qur'an), and leading a strict moral life. Likewise, the Muslim student shows complete trust in his spiritual master (shaykh); *he commonly meditates in solitude; and he participates in prescribed physical exercises and postures that help to regulate breathing rhythms and focus his attention.*

While mentioning the features that a Sufi aspirant shares with other saints on the mystic path, we should also call attention to the fact that there are some important differences between this strongly theistic, mystical tradition and those religious disciplines in which a notion of God plays a small role—for example, Zen or Yoga. Because of its position in Islam, Sufi experience has some characteristics of the material presented in the chapter "Rebirth through Personal Encounter with the Holy." For example, there is a clear recognition of the grace of God in

---

* Sections 1–4 and 6 translated from the critical edition of *Tartīb as-sulūk*, published by Fritz Meier in *Oriens* 16 (1963), pp. 15–22.

** The *"dh"* in *dhikr* represents a single Arabic consonent and should properly be pronounced like the *th* in the English word "this." However, this consonent is now almost universally pronounced by Arabs like the English "z."

spiritual insight and of the absolute quality of the Divine Will. In orthodox Islamic theology there is, therefore, a refusal to assert a total identification between the Divine Reality and the creature who seeks to lose his will in God's. Thus we find the caution expressed in Section VI.

What are the qualifications and functions of the shaykh *in directing the "remembrance" of the Sufi aspirant? What are some of the main difficulties encountered by the aspirant? How would you describe the peculiar "knowledge" achieved through the states of "passing away" and "remaining"? How would you relate such knowledge to that based on reliable report, sense observation, and discursive reasoning?*

SECTION I

The learned doctor Abu al-Qasim 'Abd al-Karim Ibn Hawazin al-Qushayri said:

It is necessary for anyone who would follow the Sufi path to be free of the entanglements of the lower world, to possess nothing, and to know what God requires of him in the recognition of His Unity and in obedience to His revealed law. Moreover, he must always be ritually pure in his person and his garments.

If he fulfills these preliminary conditions, let him become the spiritual pupil of one of the people who has trod the Way of God and who is devoted entirely to it, and let the novice occupy himself exclusively with God, in order that his master's teaching may be of benefit to him. For following one who has followed the Way of God is the surest and quickest way of progress. If he becomes the student of someone whose knowledge of the Way he does not completely trust, the aspirant may still amaze everyone and eventually arrive at his goal; but not with the same speed, because the endeavor of his master will not sustain him. He can thus be likened to the foal of a bad stallion, while the man with the fully worthy master can be likened to the foal of a noble stallion.

The master will impose as conditions upon the novice that he prefer poverty above wealth, humility above high rank, and God above all else. The master will further require of the novice that he eat, even if the Sufis have eaten and that he not say what he does not mean, even if the Sufis say it. Further, the novice must not show predilection for the easy life, even if those whom he sees around him in the convent seem to prefer it.*

Then, after the novice has accepted these conditions, his master will say to him: "I accept you as my pupil that I may lead you on the Way of God, to the degree that you are capable of Knowing it. I will not begrudge you what I know of it."

Thereafter, the master will proceed with the training of the novice and will order him to listen only to the master, and to see all of his spiritual states and all success as from God. And the master will say to his student:

---

* Note that the statements in this paragraph clearly establish the authority of the master and exemplify the special rigor of the Sufi "way."

"Say, 'Allāh, Allāh, Allāh.' "* He will order him to persist in this act of remembrance (*dhikr*) and to turn neither his eyes nor his thoughts to anything else. If something should distract the novice from his spiritual exercise, the novice must disregard it, even if it be the death of his parents. Of the acts of piety** he will perform only what is absolutely required, plus the two prostrations of the forenoon, and after every lesser ablution two acts of ritual prostration. He will give up various extraordinary religious activities and extended reading of the Qur'ān.

The novice will persevere in this formal act of remembering God until God so strengthens his will that while in remembrance of Him, he is withdrawn from all other things. Then he will be withdrawn from himself in the act of remembrance, and then will be withdrawn even from the act of remembrance itself. For a long time, sometimes he will not be self-conscious of the act of remembrance and at other times he will be self-conscious of the act.

He will continue to ascend through these alternations to another stage wherein he has a higher experience, in which the individual transcends*** the act of remembrance and these states. When he again arrives at the state of "remaining" (*baqā'*)† after being thus "withdrawn," his speech, hearing, and eyesight will have been taken from him, leaving only the faculty of the heart (*qalb*). The individual in such a state can no longer speak with his tongue. He now produces an utterance in the heart that is neither a knowledge nor an inner vision. But just as his tongue was speaking before, his heart will now utter the remembrance of God. This will continue until, whenever God wills, a higher experience occurs involving overwhelming fear of God; and in the grip of this experience, the aspirant will think that he has drawn near to God, and he will "pass away" (*fanā'*) in this state. He will alternate between the states of "passing away" and "remaining," and each time he is returned to the state of remaining the expressions of his heart in its remembrance of God will increase until eventually he experiences forms of remembrance of God coming from his heart in various tongues and in expressions that he has neither heard nor thought of before. He finds all of that in his heart until he imagines that all existent being is remembering God in various expressions from time to time, and the aspirant reaches such a state that, because of the overwhelming effects of his act of remembrance upon him, he cannot distinguish his individual act of remembrance of all existent beings, for he hears all of these forms of remembrance.

---

* "God, God, God." This is the first stage of remembrance, "the remembrance of the tongue."

** Such as certain fasts, daily ritual prayers, charitable assistance to the poor, teaching, and pilgrimage.

*** A more literal translation of this term (*fanā'*) is "passes away (from)."

† "State of remaining" refers to various levels of realization, each level achieved by withdrawal from the previous level. These levels always include both divinely bestowed attributes and a degree of discriminating awareness of the phenomenal world.

Thereafter, another level is reached of such character that were it to be tasted by anyone who had not trod this spiritual path he would surely die from the dread of God. This experience is such that the Sufi "passes away" (*fanā'*) and nothing of him remains. Then he will be restored to the state of remaining but the various states of his heart, those pertaining to the world of sense and others, will be removed from him and the very Secret of the Transcendent World will appear to him. Nothing now remains of man. There is only God. He (God) will appear like the sea by whose power the rivers come into being. And nothing other than God has any sovereignty. After this, no self-movement will belong to the man, while before this he moved himself in response to what happened to him. Now, if the sea which has appeared to him moves, the man moves, and if it rests, the man rests. And he (man) will only hear and see and witness what is manifest to him (from God). After this state has been reached, whatever is fleshly is utterly without dominion, as is the act of remembrance itself and all of the various inner states. Dominion belongs exclusively to the Creator, *viz.*, God Most High. In the course of these mystical states, before his achievement of this station which is the goal, the aspirant was seeing all existent being by a light given to him so that nothing in existence was hidden from him and he was seeing all of the beings of heaven and earth in a clear vision, but in his heart. He was not seeing anything during this time with his physical sight. Nor was this the "vision" of ordinary knowledge. Nay, if a particle of dust or an ant moved, he saw it.

SECTION II

When the aspirant is completely involved in the remembrance of the tongue, the act of remembrance becomes the remembrance of the heart. And when the heart remembers there occurs to him states which he perceives as coming from himself, nay, he hears from his heart names and forms of remembering God that he has never heard before nor read in a book—names and forms in various expressions and contrasting languages such as neither angel nor man has heard. Then if he perseveres in his intention and does not turn toward or pay attention to these psychic occurrences themselves, he will progress steadily until his effort ends in the remembrance of the inmost Secret (*sirr*).* If, on the other hand, he turns his attention to the experiences of these states that are happening to him, and considers their various types and these various forms of remembrance, and contemplates them and occupies himself with them, he has committed a grave breach of proper conduct; and he will be punished immediately. His first punishment will be the suspension of progress. He will be punished secondly, if he persists in this course, in that he will be returned to a [merely] external knowledge of these states, and he will gain such knowledge that he supposes that the knowledge of the First and the Last things has been disclosed to him. Then if he devotes himself to their

---

* In Sufi psychology, the "Secret" is the most subtle "core" of man's soul, the locus of the immediate vision of divine things.

knowledge, this devotion too is a violation of right conduct and he will deserve punishment. In this case, the punishment is that he is returned to the state of understanding. The basic difference between the state of understanding and that of knowledge is that the latter is an existent state occurring in the mind, while the former is contemplation of that knowledge. It is as if the understanding is self-consciousness of his knowledge of these matters. And if he contemplates the understanding, he has again violated the course of right conduct, and his punishment will be that he is returned to the state of heedlessness.

SECTION III

When the aspirant has undertaken the practices of remembering God with his tongue and his intention to remember God has become so strong that he persists in it assiduously, longing for and desiring it so completely that there remains no part of him not devoted to the remembrance of the tongue—when such a state has been achieved and the aspirant remembers God with his tongue while thinking of Him in his heart, there occur various states in which the aspirant imagines that he is growing and becoming great. He supposes indeed that he has become greater than any other thing. Thereupon, God causes his servant to be overtaken suddenly by an overwhelming experience of fear and He restrains him from his self-inflation and uproots and removes the feeling. Then He (God) restores him to his prior state, and when He restores him the aspirant returns to a condition stronger than the first, and grows great until it seems as though he is more exalted than before. He continues to alternate between these states (of inflation and contraction) in increasing strength, progressing with every breath and in every hour until an overwhelming experience of subjection to God takes place after perhaps years of practicing the remembrance of the tongue. And when God restores him after this passing away, the remembrance of the tongue is removed from him, and the servant finds only a weak remainder of his hearing and sight. Thereupon the act of remembrance is transferred to the heart and the aspirant hears the remembrance from his heart until he longs to be in a deserted place, for it seems to him that the people are listening to his inner remembrance of God with their ears. He does not know that no one other than he can hear his remembrance.

SECTION IV

The beginning of the act of remembrance in the members of the body is that the aspirant discovers a movement in his members so that there is no part of his flesh or bones in which there is not movement and quivering. Then these movements and quiverings become stronger until they take the form of voices and speech, so that the aspirant hears voices from all of his members and parts with the exception of his tongue because the tongue makes no utterance during these states. The aspirant will persist in his desire to think on God alone because he is certain that if he considers or seeks knowledge of these forms of remembrance he will remain in them. So he does not consider them until he has ascended beyond them. This experience takes place after the primary place of the act of remembrance is in the heart. In the state of remembrance with the tongue, the members have these movements and quiverings but not with this severity....

SECTION VI

The seekers of the ultimate goal have a serious problem.* It lies in the fact that there appears on occasion in the deepest recesses of their inwardness a speech that they do not doubt comes from God. Out of His kindness He speaks secretly and intimately with His friends. Then the innermost being of the man responds, and the man hears the response of his own inwardness and the statement from God. On another occasion such a communication may be accompanied by overwhelming dread of God and the inwardness of the man is silent in this case. Then too he may encounter a divine speech which is itself statement and response, the man having no part in it whatever. The man knows by mystical intuition, as though he saw himself in sleep, that he is not God, while he does not doubt that this is truly the speech of God. But if this subtle intuition of distinction should be temporarily obscured in the man, the sense of identification is momentarily removed in the state of the mystical unification. It is for this reason that one of the Sufis may say, "I am the Truth,"** while Abu Yazid*** said, "Praise be to me." In these cases, the men were not making claims for themselves. Rather, God was speaking directly through them in a state of which the finite individualities of the men has been utterly effaced.

7. The Silence, N. Kazantzakis

The spiritual goal of ultimate freedom has usually been rejected by the dominant institutional forms of Western religion during the past two thousand years. The form of inner spiritual development that has been most tolerated (and then carefully

---

From Nikos Kazantzakis, *The Saviors of God: Spiritual Exercises*, trans. K. Friar (New York: Simon and Schuster, 1960), pp. 127–31. Copyright © 1960 by Simon and Schuster, Inc. Reprinted by permission of the publisher.

* This problem is that ecstatic utterances are often misinterpreted, and considered blasphemous by conventional Muslims.

** This is a famous statement by the Sufi al-Hallaj, who was executed in the 10th century A.D. for such statements.

*** This is a famous Sufi of the 9th century A.D., who was noted for his controversial ecstatic utterances.

controlled) has been a personal awareness of the Divine that begins with God's self-revelation (see St. Teresa, reading 5 in Chapter I) in terms of the scripture and theology affirmed by a community of believers. Nevertheless, there have been thinkers and poets who sought to plumb the depth of their lives beyond their culture's conventions and who have left their thoughts in various Western literatures. A twentieth-century example of such a person is Nikos Kazantzakis, the famous Greek novelist. In 1923 he composed the first edition of The Saviors of God *while he was in Germany amid great political turmoil and personal spiritual agony, and then revised it a few years later, adding a section entiled "The Silence," reprinted here.*

These verses, together with other expressions of Kazantzakis' personal views, have been interpreted by some as nihilistic, but the editors of this volume feel such an interpretation is unjustified. "The Silence" is placed after a consideration of duties, an expression of the evolutionary movement from the ego to the cosmos, an ecstatic vision of God, and an entreaty for activity in the world. The whole effort, according to Kazantzakis, is a lyrical attempt at a post-Communist statement of faith. It is an appeal to strip one's self of an imaginary world that by its very delineation of what "is" negates life. It is a negation of negation—leading to the paradoxical result of freedom through despair of limited, "small-time" hopes and expectations.

The statements in this selection are not meant as philosophical or theological statements on which one can build a moral or religious system; rather they are strands of experience which a reader might catch hold of—which drop away as one is abandoned for another. Why is silence the ultimate stage of spiritual exercise?

THE SOUL OF MAN *is a flame, a bird of fire that leaps from bough to bough, from head to head, and that shouts: "I cannot stand still, I cannot be consumed, no one can quench me!"*

2. All at once the Universe becomes a tree of fire. Amidst the smoke and the flames, reposing on the peak of conflagration, immaculate, cool, and serene, I hold that final fruit of fire, the Light.

3. From this lofty summit I look on the crimson line which ascends—a tremulous, bloodstained phosphorescence that drags itself like a lovesick insect through the raincool coils of my brain.

4. The ego, race, mankind, earth, theory and action, God—all these are phantasms made of loam and brain, good only for those simple hearts that live in fear, good only for those flatulent souls that imagine they are pregnant.

5. Where do we come from? Where are we going? What is the meaning of this life? That is what every heart is shouting, what every head is asking as it beats on chaos.

6. And a fire within me leaps up to answer: "Fire will surely come one day to purify the earth. Fire will surely come one day to obliterate the earth. This is the Second Coming.

7. *"The soul is a flaming tongue that licks and struggles to set the black bulk of the world on fire. One day the entire Universe will become a single conflagration.*

8. *"Fire is the first and final mask of my God. We dance and weep between two enormous pyres."*

9. *Our thoughts and our bodies flash and glitter with reflected light. Between the two pyres I stand serenely, my brain unshaken amid the vertigo, and I say:*

10. *"Time is most short and space most narrow between these two pyres, the rhythm of this life is most sluggish, and I have no time, nor a place to dance in. I cannot wait."*

11. *Then all at once the rhythm of the earth becomes a vertigo, time disappears, the moment whirls, becomes eternity, and every point in space —insect or star or idea—turns into dance.*

12. *It was a jail, and the jail was smashed, the dreadful powers within it were freed, and that point of space no longer exists!*

13. *This ultimate stage of our spiritual exercise is called Silence. Not because its contents are the ultimate inexpressible despair or the ultimate inexpressible joy and hope. Nor because it is the ultimate knowledge which does not condescend to speak, or the ultimate ignorance which cannot.*

14. *Silence means: Every person, after completing his service in all labors, reaches finally the highest summit of endeavor, beyond every labor, where he no longer struggles or shouts, where he ripens fully in silence, indestructibly, eternally, with the entire Universe.*

15. *There he merges with the Abyss and nestles within it like the seed of man in the womb of woman.*

16. *The Abyss is now his wife, he plows her, he opens and devours her vitals, he transmutes her blood, he laughs and weeps, he ascends and descends with her, and he never leaves her.*

17. *How can you reach the womb of the Abyss to make it fruitful? This cannot be expressed, cannot be narrowed into words, cannot be subjected to laws; every man is completely free and has his own special liberation.*

18. *No form of instruction exists, no Savior exists to open up the road. No road exists to be opened.*

19. *Every person, ascending above and beyond his own head, escapes from his small brain, so crammed with perplexities.*

20. *Within profound Silence, erect, fearless, in pain and in play, ascending ceaselessly from peak to peak, knowing that the height has no ending, sing this proud and magical incantation as you hang over the Abyss:*

1 I BELIEVE IN ONE GOD, DEFENDER OF THE BORDERS, OF DOUBLE DESCENT,[1] MILITANT, SUFFERING, OF MIGHTY BUT NOT OF OMNIPOTENT POWERS, A WARRIOR AT THE FARTHEST FRONTIERS, COMMANDER-IN-CHIEF OF ALL THE LUMINOUS POWERS, THE VISIBLE AND THE INVISIBLE.

2 I BELIEVE IN THE INNUMERABLE, THE EPHEMERAL MASKS WHICH GOD HAS ASSUMED THROUGHOUT THE CENTURIES, AND BEHIND HIS CEASE-LESS FLUX I DISCERN AN INDESTRUCTIBLE UNITY.

3 I BELIEVE IN HIS SLEEPLESS AND VIOLENT STRUGGLE WHICH TAMES AND FRUCTIFIES THE EARTH AS THE LIFE-GIVING FOUNTAIN OF PLANTS, ANIMALS, AND MEN.

4 I BELIEVE IN MAN'S HEART, THAT EARTHEN THRESHING-FLOOR WHERE NIGHT AND DAY THE DEFENDER OF THE BORDERS FIGHTS WITH DEATH.

5 O LORD, YOU SHOUT: "HELP ME! HELP ME!" YOU SHOUT, O LORD, AND I HEAR.

6 WITHIN ME ALL FOREFATHERS AND ALL DESCENDANTS, ALL RACES AND ALL EARTH HEAR YOUR CRY WITH JOY AND TERROR.

7 BLESSED BE ALL THOSE WHO HEAR AND RUSH TO FREE YOU, LORD, AND WHO SAY: "ONLY YOU AND I EXIST."

8 BLESSED BE ALL THOSE WHO FREE YOU AND BECOME UNITED WITH YOU, LORD, AND WHO SAY: "YOU AND I ARE ONE."

9 AND THRICE BLESSED BE THOSE WHO BEAR ON THEIR SHOULDERS AND DO NOT BUCKLE UNDER THIS GREAT, SUBLIME, AND TERRIFYING SECRET:

THAT EVEN THIS ONE
DOES NOT EXIST!

NOTES

1. *Defender of the Borders, of Double Descent:* This refers in particular to Vasílius Diyenís Akrítas, a tenth-century Byzantine hero. *Diyenís* means "of double birth," for Akrítas' father was a Moslem and his mother a Christian Greek. *Akrítas* means "border guard" of the Empire.

INTERPRETATION

8. Introduction to Yoga, S. K. Majumdar

This excerpt expresses that form of spiritual discipline very often associated with India: yoga. The author, S. K. Majumdar, was born and raised in India. His training includes ten years of pilgrimage, study, and meditation in the Himalayas, and

Taken from *Introduction to Yoga* by Sachindra K. Majumdar (New Hyde Park, New York: University Books, 1964), pp. 56–60, 74–77.

*philosophical studies at Columbia University, New York.
Presently he is serving as the director of the Yoga Institute in
New York City, where he conducts classes in both hatha yoga
(physical exercise) and meditation. Yoga (literally "union")
is a term that has different specific meanings in different contexts;
here it refers to a physical and psychological discipline based on
one of several philosophical perspectives in orthodox Hinduism.
As a discipline, yoga is the realization of power as well as the
knowledge of reality, which is achieved in superconscious awareness
called samadhi. Keep in mind that according to Hindu
psychology, there can be different kinds of consciousness, some
regarded as being of a higher order than others. For example,
empirical perception or imaginary and rational construction
(vikalpa) are useful for an everyday level of awareness; but these
should not take precedence over spiritual insight (prajna) and
samadhi. Prajna is not just a better formulation of ideas, but
a release from the generally accepted "hypnotic" illusion (avidya)
most people accept as truth about themselves. How is samadhi
different from everyday experience? How is it that "concentration"
aids in freeing a person from ignorance? Why is yoga called an
"awakening"? What are some truths about one's Self that yoga
suggests we should come to know? Do you think Majumdar would
agree with Nyanaponika Thera (reading 2) that the most practical
solution to contemporary problems is to investigate the process
of man's apprehension of life? What do you think J. Campbell
(Chapter II, reading 11) would think of this position?*

Yoga is both knowledge and power. The search for knowledge is closely
related to the search for power. "Knowledge is power" is an ancient Sanskrit saying. Francis Bacon also made the same remark.

The power which a yogi seeks is the power that destroys basic or
philosophical ignorance. This power is the knowledge or realization of our
true nature. Such knowledge liberates us from those delusions which are
the cause of our weakness and suffering. However, through certain yogic
practices special powers of perception as well as power over natural forces
and things come to us. These powers are not without limit, nor are they
ever-lasting. Yoga regards the pursuit of such powers as unspiritual, as
creating further bondage and leading, ultimately, to suffering. . . .

Samadhi or superconscious experience is the key concept of yoga. Yoga
as philosophy is an interpretation of existence based on this experience; it
is life viewed in the perspective of *prajna,* or truth-filled wisdom, and the
estimation and organization of values in that perspective. It is also a
method for the progressive realization of man's supreme goal of truth. It is
therefore essential to have an understanding of samadhi, its relationship to
life and to the evolution of man.

All religions are ultimately based on experience of the beyond. A religion, as a creed, is not truth; it is only a way. People need creeds and
beliefs to organize their lives and give them sensible direction; society

needs institutions to preserve ideals and to guide men. But beliefs and institutions are not the resting places of the mind. It has been said: It is good to be born in a church but terrible to die in it. Beliefs are provisional, they acquire fresh meaning with experience. Besides, men do not know the meanings of their beliefs. God, heaven, and salvation mean different things to different individuals at different levels of development. No one has clear ideas about them.

> Real religion begins with experience. The test of a true religious experience is seen in the transformation of character and in the achievement of a clearer comprehension of the realities of existence.

When we come to the realm of religious experience we encounter many varieties which depend on the training and background of the individual involved. There is an infinite range. But as we move higher and higher into more universal areas, the differences in expression lessen and finally disappear. In the experience of pure Awareness, the distinction between knower and known is lost. One who achieves the experience exclaims, "I am the Truth," "I am Brahman," "Thy Self is Brahman." This is the experience of the pure Selfhood and is the highest form of samadhi, or superconsciousness. In yoga this is technically called *nirvikalpa* samadhi, or *asamprajnata* samadhi.

Superconsciousness has also been called cosmic or universal consciousness. In this state the limitations of consciousness, spirit or pure Self fall away. One discovers one's true identity as transcendent spirit and clearly perceives the basic unity of existence. Samadhi is the height of awareness and the essence of yoga; it is the perfect apprehension of Truth and the supreme achievement of man, his highest value. Yoga is also called samadhi. The Gita says:

> Gaining which man does not consider any other gain superior,
> And established in which he is not shaken by the greatest pain,
> Know that state above suffering to be yoga...

Some theologians have made a great fanfare about the superior value of dogmatic faith and the dualistic religious attitude based upon it. They regard mystic experience as subjective, personal and without social significance, maintaining that the relation of "I and Thou" is a more objective relationship which invests individual life and world history with meaning and worth. We have seen earlier that yoga assigns a superior value and deeper significance to the everyday concepts of personality and social activity. It accepts the distinction between subject and object on the practical plane. But, philosophically and scientifically speaking, the distinctions are superficial and not radical, i.e., they are not ultimately true or valid. People work intellectually with such distinctions; they are dogmas and creeds. As creeds they have their value and also their limitations. But if they are not seen in their proper light, they bar man's growth and lead to fanaticism, with all the evils which come in its train. Subject and object are two phases of the same spirit. What we generally call subject is actually an object, the psycho-physical complex, our apparent self and identity. The pure subject as awareness is opposed to nature, as light is to darkness. In nirvikalpa samadhi we have the experience of the pure unconditioned Selfhood or subject. Nature or object is an emanation of the pure subject.

The lower form of samadhi or superconscious experience is called *savikalpa* samadhi or *samprajnata* samadhi, i.e., cognitive samadhi. On this plane the mind knows objects with a degree of concentration which is called *ekagra* and which is extraordinary. Such concentration reveals the subtle or finer truths of nature, the underlying principles of things.

The superior samadhi, i.e., the nirvikalpa samadhi is also called the *nirodha* samadhi or the perfect arrest of all forms of mental functioning. Patanjali defines yoga in this manner. . . .

MIND AND THE FORMS OF AWARENESS

The function of the mind can be classified according to different principles. For example, we say that the mind can function not only on the conscious and preconscious planes, but also on the superconscious level. On this last level, the ordinary functions of the mind are completely arrested by the power of voluntary concentration. The feeling of "I" or the ego disappears on this plane and a person becomes established in his true being. He is no longer identified with the fluctuating states of the body or mind but discovers that his true nature is distinct from them. This superconscious state is the direct opposite of the egoless preconscious condition.

According to one system, the superconscious state has been described as a fourth state of awareness (*turiya*), distinguishing it from the states of deep sleep, dream and wakefulness. Still another view (as in Patanjali), differentiates pure awareness from five other forms of common mental function: right cognition (*pramana*), error (*viparyaya*), intellectual construction (*vikalpa*), memory (*smriti*), and sleep (*nidra*).

The last form of classification makes certain things clear. Superconscious knowledge, called prajna, is different not only from error, illusion, hypnotic trance, etc., but also from *right* knowledge, i.e., valid perceptions, inferences or communications. Thus it is different from "science" and "scientific" knowledge. Yogic knowledge, wisdom or perception is superior to the conceptual knowledge of science. Philosophical truth, in the sense of superconscious perception, is higher than scientific truth which is practically valid but not metaphysically true.

Vikalpa is a special type of mental function which deserves some comment since it has been generally misunderstood and mistranslated. *Vikalpa* designates empty concepts or intellectual constructs, i.e., those which have no objective counterpart but are nevertheless useful and to be found in all linguistic formulations. Such constructions are necessary for communication and practical, but they are no more than imaginings. Time and space, substance and quality are such notions. They are useful but unreal. There can be no language or statement without vikalpa. Linguistic truth is a relative truth. The "brute and stubborn facts" are burdened with a lot of wooly fiction.

Superconscious experience is the most immediate form of knowledge. This is the real intuitive knowledge of yoga. Such intuition is superior to reason, as reason is superior to the senses.

The perfect stillness of mind which is samadhi, is comparable to the smooth surface of a clear lake in which an object is mirrored perfectly without being broken up and distorted by waves. In an analogous manner, we perceive the clear reflection of the Self in the calm lake of the mind. Then we know our real Self (atman) in its pristine purity, for at all other times we are identified with the processes of the body and the mind.

The state of samadhi or perfect inwardness is achieved through the practice of concentration (abhyasa) and discrimination (vairagya), or detachment. . . .

I have spoken of truth and illusion in the preceding pages. It is therefore proper that I further clarify the meanings of these words and point out what they stand for in yoga philosophy.

Truth can be both perceptual (aparoksha) and conceptual (paroksha). Truth is both a fact and the quality of a statement. When yoga speaks of truth it means the ultimate or underlying fact of existence, the reality, or spirit. The experience which is ultimate and which is never contradicted by any other experience is the highest truth. This is the truth attainable by samadhi. Perception of truth shows up the illusory character of other experiences prior to it; therefore it is called prajna, the supreme knowledge, or wisdom. Knowledge here is not a theory or an abstract conception but a perception.

But there are levels of truth. First, there is truth on the rational and sense level. We lead our daily lives on this level. We know that what is presented to us by the senses is an appearance. There is something behind such appearances. Our reason gives us many theories in regard to the underlying facts and operations of nature. But they are never final. We have come to realize through rational investigation that in the very act of sensory observation we change and distort what we observe. We do not see or know the fundamental truth of things. The mystery remains and deepens and the usual notions, with which we carry on our practical life, are seen to be illusions. This awareness removes many prejudices and false beliefs, but is not important enough to give us true freedom.

There is another kind of illusion which surrounds our life until we wake up. It is the poor understanding of our selves, our nature and destiny. We live and act on the belief that we are individuals, but we do not know what this individuality is. We do not know what we really want. Today we may want one thing, tomorrow it is not enough for us, though we thought that if only we had it we would be happy all our life. Tastes and ideals change. Nothing is good for all time. The child's optimism gives away with the years to a sense of despair and disillusionment.

Recently (early in 1963) Bertrand Russell was interviewed for TV on the occasion of his ninetieth birthday. Asked to discuss the happiest period in his life, Russell replied that he had never been happier than he was at the moment. When the interviewer asked the reason, the philosopher replied that he now knew exactly what he wanted in life. If Bertrand Russell, with all his logic and clarity of mind, came to know at the age of ninety that the real meaning of his life lay in a humanistic concern transcending the limits and needs of his own individualistic existence, how much perception can be expected of others?

People do not realize the roots of their motivations and desires. They say they make conscious choices and decisions in life without realizing how much they are governed by unconscious universal forces. Under the influence of rage and passion, they often do things which they regret the rest of their lives. Seeking happiness by wrong means, they destroy the very conditions of happiness. A man who cannot respect himself, cannot be happy; he who rules others by fear cannot, himself be free from fear and anxiety. People who value power find that power, once achieved, does not satisfy the needs of the heart. Men cannot gain true love, affection, honor and respect by means of power.

Men are not fully awake. They like to live in dreams. They like to be told lies, to be told that they are loved and respected though in their hearts they know it is not so. This is what most people call life. They are so dependent, so helplessly alone, yet what an ego they have! One moment they shout and bluster, the next they weep and go down on their knees. A little praise and adulation transports them to the heavens; a little criticism and rebuke drives them to tears.

People do not live their lives, they are lived by it. They want to enjoy, they are enjoyed; they go out to catch, they get caught; they try to deceive, they are, themselves deceived; they want to be clever and prove themselves stupid.

Sensible persons realize late in life how they should have lived, but the time has already passed by.

Blindness about life and its goal is *avidya* or ignorance. *Avidya* is philosophical or metaphysical ignorance; basically, it is a false view of our Self, our true nature. Radical ignorance is shown in clinging to the notion of separate egohood and individuality, in regarding the impermanent as permanent, in identifying the process with reality. Because of this ignorance, man seeks peace, happiness and self-fulfillment through pursuit of worldly goods, pleasures, success and power.

Avidya is also called *Maya*. Avidya is a false view and not total ignorance. We live in a twilight zone, not in total darkness. Maya is no denial of plurality and change. But the world needs to be seen in the context of the Cosmos, the individual in the context of the universal, the person in the context of the impersonal, the many in the context of the one. Our practical world is not without light from the beyond. We do not have complete confidence in the world. The dangers, denials and doubts which surround the little island of life like a sea, challenge us to seek across the unknown. Ideals of love, truth and freedom lure us on to the shores of the beyond.

A real life is one which strives to be honest, to be in touch with the truths of our Self and the world. It is a life of growth, transformation of outlook, improvement of understanding. A sensible and creative life moves ever closer to the basic realities of existence and the universal concerns of history. When man finally stands on his unfailing inner strength, the rock of Self, then all doubts vanish, all bonds are broken, and he attains that imperturbable serenity of mind, that confidence of character, which is the true fruit of wisdom.

9. Can Superconscious Knowledge Be Imparted?
Swami Akhilananda

In contemporary Western philosophy and psychology there is often an implicit assumption that despite the variations in human experience the accounts of superconscious awareness can be best understood in terms of common factors having biological and social origins. In contrast, traditional Hindu psychology regards everyday experience as only a part of the potential of human awareness, indeed as a less than full use of man's capacity to know. Superconscious awareness cannot, from this latter perspective, be regarded as a psychological escape from "the real world," for both common everyday experience and neurosis are processes of consciousness quite different from superconscious awareness. Some of the basic distinctions have been discussed in the selection by Majumdar (reading 8), and should be kept in mind when reading this excerpt by a well-known contemporary Hindu teacher, Swami Akhilananda. A member of the Ramakrishna Order of India, Swami Akhilananda has lectured throughout the United States and is head of the Vedanta centers of Boston and Providence, R.I. What is the importance of the distinction between the "quantitative value" of mediate knowledge (or conceptually formulated information) and the "qualitative value" of spiritual realization? In what ways is the relationship between the guru (spiritual teacher) and the disciple important or not important for superconscious knowledge? Does the swami suggest that a person should experiment with spiritual practices for a few days to see if one likes them or not? What evidence is given for the transmission of "higher" knowledge from a guru to a disciple?

From *Hindu Psychology: Its Meaning for the West* by Swami Akhilananda, Copyright, 1946, by Harper & Row, Publishers, Inc. and 1948, by Routledge & Kegan Paul Ltd. of London. By permission of the publishers. Pp. 190–96.

There is a legitimate question in the minds of the vast majority of scientific thinkers as to whether or not superconscious knowledge can be imparted to others. If it is to be scientifically investigated it must be communicable. Many devout religious persons are of the opinion that this knowledge comes through the grace of God...consequently, it cannot be the object of scientific investigation, nor can it be communicated as one person gives an object to another. The history of religion proves to us that superconscious knowledge as well as the lower extrasensory perceptions, psychic and occult powers can be transmitted and received. Of course, there are certain necessary conditions to be fulfilled by the person who communicates them and the person who receives them. In the first place, every person who stumbles into certain extraordinary experiences, whether they are occult powers or higher superconscious realizations, cannot transmit these powers to others as effectively as it is desirable. When a person stumbles into spiritual experiences, he can have certain definite realization of the Ultimate Reality. Yet because he has not developed the technique and is not well established in it he cannot transmit that knowledge directly and immediately to others. He can, perhaps, describe some of his experiences and gives some idea of his personal realizations. On the other hand, when a man is thoroughly established in the superconscious, whether through certain practices or through divine grace, he can transmit this power and this knowledge to others—not as mediate knowledge but as direct perception.

It is true, however, that the exact nature of emotional reaction in certain spiritual realizations cannot be communicated and cannot be made enjoyable through oral expressions, just as the emotion of love cannot be qualitatively given to anyone. In order to understand the real effect of love, one must fall in love. A mother cannot communicate her inner emotion to anyone else. In order to understand a mother's love one has to be a mother. Similarly, spiritual realizations, whether they come almost instantly through divine intervention alone or through spiritual practice and divine intervention combined, cannot be communicated in their qualitative value, nor can they be fully described by human language as to their quantitative value, since they are unique experiences so far as the persons are concerned—just as the experience of love is unique.

It is also true that there are some systematic methods by following which one can reach these experiences. The so-called extrasensory perceptions, occult powers, and such other extraordinary display of mental or psychic powers can, of course, be expressed as prescribed by Patanjali in *Raja Yoga*. The higher superconscious realizations can also be reached by systematic methods, as Patanjali and other great religious leaders of other countries and religions prescribed, and which we studied in the last chapter.

The person who transmits or gives this knowledge is the *Guru* (teacher), and the person who receives it is the *shisya* (disciple). The *Guru* is not an ordinary teacher of the type we hear about in the church schools and other schools of the West. The conception of *Guru* is deep and significant in spiritual life. According to most of the Hindu authorities, one can hardly expect to reach the higher state of divine realization without the help of his *Guru*. Swami Brahmananda* says:

> It is not so easy without a *Guru*. The *Guru* is one who shows the path of God through a *mantram* (holy name). He gives the secret of spiritual practices. He watches over his disciple and protects him from going astray. A *Guru* must be a knower of Brahman.[1]

As a *Guru* is so essential to the spiritual development of his disciples, the required qualifications of the religious teacher should be understood.

As mentioned previously, a teacher of higher psychology or spiritual realization must be thoroughly established in those experiences to teach others. His mind must be fully illumined—first, through ethical practices and next, through practices of concentration, meditation, and such other disciplinary processes. When a man is established in higher realizations, his mind becomes completely colorless or free from all preconceived notions and impressions, and he can empty the contents of his mind at will. When he tries to impart suitable methods for spiritual practices and training to his disciple, he makes his mind completely free from all preconceived thoughts and ideas; and, consequently, he can immediately understand the very nature of his disciple. He can also understand the distinct qualities of that particular mind. A *Guru* must also inspire confidence and devotion within the student; the relation between these two persons must be extremely harmonious and loving. A teacher goes through the difficulties of imparting knowledge to the disciple only because of his intense love for him. To use the modern psychological term, there must be a "transference" of the highest type between the teacher and the disciple. This relationship is created not only because of the love between them but also because of the convictions of both. The teacher must have faith in his student, believing that the student is capable of learning what he is to teach. The teacher, through his deep understanding, also knows the future possibilities of the student, and his conviction and faith brings out the student's latent possibilities.[2]

The *shisya* (disciple), too, must have the necessary qualities for higher realization and development. In the first place, he must have confidence in the teacher and devotion and love for him. Then he must have the spirit of obedience and be ready to follow implicitly the advice and instructions of the teacher. This does not, however, preclude the questioning spirit. A student is always encouraged to ask questions. "Know That (Truth) by questioning" the Hindu scriptures tell us. The spirit of humility is the most important condition for spiritual development, however, although questions and inquiries are much encouraged in a real spiritual relationship between teacher and student. The student must also have perseverance and tenacity in order to continue the practices and discipline according to instructions. There are some persons who, out of curiosity, like to make a little experiment for a few days, and then they give up the practices. This

---

* Swami Brahmananda was the author's guru.

fickleness of attitude has been extremely discouraged by all religious psychologists. Patanjali regards this as one of the greatest obstacles to spiritual unfoldment. Swami Vivekananda strongly emphasized *shraddha* (dynamic faith and consequent action). Without this tenacious faith and consequent perseverance in practices, a student can hardly expect to have any of the higher realizations.

It is true that often students get discouraged because they cannot reach the goal as soon as they had expected. One can easily understand that the practice for higher realizations requires tremendous patience, as we have to struggle with the illusive and restless mind. Unfortunately, our minds are much agitated and colored by innumerable past experiences. Apart from that, the subconscious impressions (*samskaras*), the accumulated residuals of past thoughts and actions, are so strong that they agitate the mind all the time. Modern psychoanalysts and others find it amazing to what extent the subconscious states disturb the conscious mind. Indian psychologists thoroughly understand this factor. Consequently, they warn the students not to be disturbed or discouraged when they find that it is difficult to hold the mind on the object of concentration. Swami Brahmananda gives methods by which a disciple can be helped through such difficult periods:

These are the different stages through which the aspirant progresses. A man should begin from where he stands. If, for instance, an ordinary man is told to meditate on union with the Absolute Brahman,* he cannot grasp the truth of it; nor can he follow the instructions. He may make the attempt, but soon he will tire and give it up. However, if the same man is asked to worship God with flowers, perfume, and other accessories he will find that his mind gradually becomes concentrated on God and he will soon experience a joy in his worship. Through ritualistic worship, devotion to the performance of *japam*** grows. The finer the mind becomes, the greater is its capacity for higher forms of worship. *Japam* inclines the mind toward meditation. Thus the aspirant moves toward his Ideal by a process of natural growth.[3] This shows that a disciple needs careful attention in the early stages of spiritual development. The Guru removes difficulties of various types from the path of the disciples. However, there are "dark hours of the soul," as described by the Christian mystics; but the *Guru,* with his own spiritual insight, understands the inner struggles of his disciples and directs them accordingly. He fully realizes the pitfalls on the path of spiritual effort and warns against such discouragement. Patanjali, Swami Vivekananda, and others say that steady practice is absolutely necessary to overcome obstacles;[4] but when the teacher is qualified and the student is fit, then the result is positive. "Wonderful is its teacher, and (equally) clever the pupil. Wonderful indeed is he who comprehends it taught by an able preceptor."[5]

A great spiritual personality who is perfectly established in higher realizations can transmit this knowledge to a disciple even if the disciple has

---

* In Hinduism a term for the Ultimate Reality.
** A spiritual exercise of repeating prayers or the name of God. Sometimes a rosary is used to keep count of the repetitions.

not undergone vigorous spiritual practices. Sri Ramakrishna,* who was born in 1836 in India, could transmit spiritual power and various experiences immediately and directly to his disciples. His biography contains descriptions of such occurrences.[6] Swami Vivekananda was about eighteen years old when he first went to see Sri Ramakrishna. The great Master touched the chest of the young aspirant, who at once entered into the highest state of superconscious realization immediately and directly. He lost his physical consciousness in the realization of the Ultimate Reality. One day when Swami Brahmananda was rubbing oil on the body of Sri Ramakrishna, he too entered into superconscious realization spontaneously and immediately. He not only lost the consciousness of the external and objective world but he experienced the Ultimate Reality. On another occasion, this great Master wrote a name of God on the tongue of another disciple, who then had the realization of the personal aspect of God, his chosen Deity. We know from the history of that period that this great man had a peculiar power of awakening the latent possibilities of his disciples, and that innumerable men and women had their highest realizations from him either by a touch, a word, a wish, or even a glance. One of the greatest disciples of the Master, Swami Shivananda, told us that all of the disciples had the highest realization (*samadhi*) during the lifetime of the Master. Their lives prove to us without the least shade of doubt that they were well established in God either through realization of the personal (bodily) aspect or through the Impersonal (formless) aspect of God. These two types of realization are mentioned by St. Paul: "I knew a man in Christ... (whether in the body, I cannot tell; or whether out of the body, I cannot tell: God knoweth)."[7]

The supremely developed person not only can transmit this power immediately and directly to a disciple who has not performed spiritual practices, but even the disciples of these great teachers can awaken latent spiritual power and give the higher realizations when they are in that particular mood. We know definitely that Swami Vivekananda, Swami Brahmananda, and others transmitted this power on certain occasions to their disciples and devotees. It is explained by the religious psychologists of India that still lesser personalities can also help their disciples in awakening spiritual consciousness, provided they themselves are established in higher realizations and the students practice according to their advice and directions.

NOTES

1. *The Eternal Companion* (Hollywood: Vedanta Society of Southern California, 1944), p. 184.
2. *The Complete Works of Swami Vivekananda* (Mayavati, Almora, Himalayas: Advaita Ashrama, 1931), pp. 19–27.
3. *The Eternal Companion*, p. 103.

---

* This is the same Ramakrishna whose ecstatic experience is described in Chapter I, reading 6.

4. *Yoga Aphorisms of Patanjali* I:13.
5. *Katha Upanishad* II:7.
6. Romain Rolland, *The Life of Ramakrishna* (Mayavati, Almora, Himalayas: Advaita Ashrama, 1931).
7. II Corinthians 12:2.

10. Training in Zen, *Abbot Z. Shibayama*

> *Zen means "meditation." This excerpt is by the abbot of the beautiful Nanzenji Monastery in Kyoto, Japan. It exemplifies the use of stories, anecdotes, and descriptions of life in the training of beginners in Zen. Like the earlier expressions of meditation, this essay expresses the human capacity for realizing Truth through individual awareness; however, it also describes the spiritual desperation that both prompts and is actually induced by this discipline. Note the typical pattern of spiritual development by Zen masters. What are the three conditions required of a monk in training? What is a koan? What is the purpose of sanzen? Compare the anticipated goal, satori or kensho, to samadhi (reading 8). Why does the Zen master push the monk to his psychological, intellectual, and spiritual extremity? Does this Zen master encourage most people to take up the Zen discipline? Why (not)? How does "opening the wisdom eye" differ from a profound emotional state of oneness with everything? Do you see any difference between the awareness here described as* satori *and the personal awareness of the Holy expressed in Chapter I?*

Zen, especially Rinzai Zen, emphasizes the primary importance of religious experience which will satisfy the human spiritual yearning, and it maintains that the essence of religion lies in religious experience. In the days of the early Zen Masters, there were no fixed training methods, but they naturally went through their own inner spiritual darkness, followed by the moment of religious awakening. They were all real religious geniuses who could attain *satori* by themselves. . . .

Zen history tells us that Masters in the early days all came to the attainment of their *satori* by themselves by going through a natural and unique training process of their own. If we, however, try to summarize the processes of these Masters' spiritual development, we can find more or less similar patterns. Tokusan's case is a typical example. Namely, they first start with

From Zendei Shibayama, *A Flower Does Not Talk: Zen Essays,* trans. Sumiko Kudo (Tokyo: Charles E. Tuttle Co., 1970), pp. 34, 39–48.

an extremely intense religious quest; then comes hard, strong-willed search and discipline, which will be followed by spiritual crises, or a sense of the abyss; and finally, they experience the moment of awakening. These are the inner processes they generally go through.

Zen training originally followed individual and natural courses of development. Our ordinary life, however, is so complex that it is not possible for everyone of us to go through such an inner natural process of religious searching as the old great Masters did. Zen Masters wished to help students in future generations in their search for the Truth. Out of their compassion they reflected on their own training days and tried to find some helpful means for their fellow beings. Thus, as time went on, a pattern of Zen training as we have it today came to be established.

Zen monasteries in Japan are all institutions where Zen training thus established is actually being carried on. In any monastery, the following three conditions are particularly required of a training monk as indispensable requisites in Zen training:

> *1. To have a firm faith and commitment in undertaking one's training.* (大信根)
> *2. To have a strong will to carry on under hard discipline.* (大精進)
> *3. To have the Great Doubt—Spiritual Quest—which will be the prajna (true wisdom) basis in searching for the Truth.* (大疑団)

If any of the three is lacking, it is impossible for the monk to accomplish his Zen training; when these three requisites are present, day and night, he will be encouraged to carry on his discipline.

Under such spiritual conditions, monks go on with their training, practicing *zazen* (Zen meditation) and taking *sanzen* (personal Zen interview). In Zen, we have Soto Zen and Rinzai Zen, and their ways and methods of training are somewhat different. As I am a Rinzai Zen Master, here I am discussing Zen training in Rinzai.

Regularly in the morning and evening for several hours every day monks practice *zazen,* but they also engage in all sorts of work in daytime since a monastery is self-supporting.

Once in every month they have a special training period, of a week's duration, which is called *sesshin* in Japanese. During this *sesshin* period they exclusively do *zazen.* In addition to these regular monthly *sesshin,* at the beginning of December they have a special, most intensive training period to commemorate Sakyamuni Buddha's attainment of *satori.* At this greatest *sesshin,* a week is regarded as a day, that is, they just keep on doing *zazen* through a week's time without going to bed, although they are allowed to sleep in the sitting posture for a few hours at night.

Such hard *zazen* practice does not mean just to assume a quiet, full-lotus sitting posture. In addition to stopping physical movements, one is required to cast away all thoughts and consciousness of himself. He has to be actually in the state of no-thought, no-mind, and no-form, where there is neither the self that is sitting, nor the earth which is supporting him.

Old Zen Masters described such a state of no-thought and said, "Sheer darkness all over," or, "To be confined to an ice cave ten thousand miles thick." In other words, one is to be the True Self, or the true genuine absolute subjectivity that can no longer be objectified.

It may be easy to talk about somebody else's hard training and to describe his psychological development in training. It is most difficult, however, for anybody to actually go through such training. One has to be prepared to risk his life, and even then *satori* may not be accessible. Zen has been, therefore, described from olden days as the way for only a handful of geniuses.

Hakuin, the author of *The Song of Zazen,* was a Zen Master who had once had hard training days himself. He says it is like a mountain climber who has lost his footing while scaling a steep cliff. His life now hangs on a single vine to which he clings with all his might. Hakuin demands that he let go of the vine. In other words, he tells him to die once.

When Zen talks of no-mind or no-self, it does not refer to an idea nor engage in conceptual speculation. No-mind has to be experienced by each individual as an actual fact. It cannot be just easily accomplished. If one hesitates in his search because it is so difficult, then the time will never come for him to open his spiritual eye to a new world. At a monastery, therefore, a kind of artificial training method is used to encourage training monks: *koan* and *sanzen* are used.

Without going into a detailed explanation of the *koan,* they may be briefly described as sayings left by Zen Masters to show their own Zen experience. These sayings and phrases sound so irrational that our ordinary dualistic reasoning utterly fails to interpret them. For instance, they say:

> *"If you clap both your hands there is a sound; what is the sound of one hand clapping?"*
> *"See your Self before you were born!"* or
> *"Before Abraham I am"* can be a Zen *koan.*

This very irrationality of *koan,* which refuses all the intellectual approaches, plays a most important role in Zen training, for it makes us realize the limitations of our discriminating intellect and finally drives us to despair of it.

After a novice has exerted himself to learn how to sit in the full-lotus posture for a certain period of time, the Zen Master at a monastery will give him a *koan* and the novice will do *zazen* with the *koan,* which will drive him to despair of his knowledge and intellect until he will come to have the real Great Doubt, or Spiritual Quest. Zen training seeks to cast away all discriminating consciousness. This process of casting away one's discriminating consciousness is not at all easy, in practice. Therefore, at the monastery they take *sanzen* to help Zen studies.

Sanzen is a personal Zen interview with a Zen Master. The training monks go one by one into the Master's room, each approaching him in a traditional manner which must be strictly observed, and sits face to face with the Master, and presents the results of his discipline. It is a most serious occasion for the novice who is required to reveal all his Zen ability and spiritual insight to the Master. The outcome of his Zen training which he presents is not a conceptual conclusion, nor a result of reasoning or speculation: it must be the spirituality, or Zen attaining, he has reached by *zazen* and *koan*. It is natural, therefore, that a monk cannot be ready all the time to take *sanzen* in a satisfactory manner.

Even so, this *sanzen* takes place several times a day at the monastery during the *sesshin*, the intensive training period, and two or three times a day even on ordinary days. It can be easily imagined how difficult it is for the training monk. If a novice is not ready to take *sanzen* at all, several senior monks in the Zen Hall will forcefully drag him out and chase him to the room of the Master. The Master will spurn him and drive him out. Every day a novice has to go through such hard discipline. By encouragement given, and by his strong spiritual quest, his inner search is intensified. He puts his heart and soul into his training. He comes to the extremity where no logic and no verbalisms are of any avail. His eyes are open, yet he is not conscious of seeing. He has ears, but is not conscious of hearing. He is actually in the state of no-mind, no-thought, where there is neither the self nor the world.

Rinzai said, "Years ago when I was not awakened to the Truth, it was sheer darkness all over." He was in the abyss of unconsciousness before attaining *satori*.

When one is in such a condition, it is not unusual for all sorts of abnormal, morbid psychological phenomena and illusions to appear. From olden days, however, Masters have strongly warned us not to be attached to them, but to throw them away.

How long the dark night of unconsciousness will continue cannot be foreseen. It depends on each individual. All of a sudden, however, and quite unexpectedly, the moment of awakening comes to the monk. When this blessed moment is given, the abyss of unconsciousness is broken through.

Years ago, Zen Master Reiun, after thirty years of hard discipline, had this blessed moment of awakening when he saw a peach blossom in bloom. The unconscious self of Reiun revived as the True Self. Reiun was born anew in the world. He was the peach, and the universe was full of its fragrance; or rather, he was the universe itself now.

Master Kyogen, after a long search, came to the moment of awakening when he heard the sound of a stone hitting a bamboo. Here he was resounding throughout the universe as the rap of the stone.

A Japanese Zen Master in the Tokugawa period named Shido Bunan had a *waka* poem:

> *Die while alive, and be completely dead,*
> *Then do whatever you will, all is good.*

The aim of Zen training is to die while alive, that is, to actually become the self of no-mind, and no-form, and then to revive as the True Self of no-mind and no-form. In Zen training, therefore, what is most important is for one to revive from the abyss of unconsciousness. Zen training is *not* the emotional process of just being in the state of oneness, nor is it just to have the "feeling" of no-mind. *Prajna* wisdom (true wisdom) has to shine out after breaking through the extremity of the Great Doubt, and then still further training is needed so that one can freely live the Zen life and work in the world as a new man. At any rate, such deep spiritual experience has a great significance which we should not ignore in developing the spiritual culture of mankind today and in the future.

Hard training is carried on at Zen monasteries today with the purpose of reproducing in a novice the similar inner processes the old Zen Masters experienced. We have to be careful and serious in strictly and correctly adopting the training methods used.

In studying Zen, therefore, those who want to appreciate it as a cultural value, or as religious philosophy, can very well do so from such perspectives. Those, however, who want to experience it in themselves should be prepared to go through the hardship, and should never be tempted to follow an easy shortcut. Recently there have been people who talk about instant enlightenment, or those who take drugs in an attempt to experience *satori*. Whatever claims they may make, I declare that such approaches are not authentic, true Zen at all.

I should like to add a few last words here. True as it may be that Zen is really a supreme way to the Truth, it is obvious that not everyone can be expected to have the training required for attainment of the exquisite moment of *satori*. We have to admit that basic Zen is a very difficult way and only a handful of religiously endowed people under favourable conditions can attain *satori*.

11. Different Paths, Different Goals, N. Smart

What is mysticism? Are mystics all saying the same thing, even though they express their goals and procedures for spiritual enlightenment differently? In this excerpt Ninian Smart (Professor of Religious Studies, University of Lancaster, England) attempts to define mysticism by noting both the language that mystics use and the setting in which they use it. The excerpt includes three of his conclusions: (1) that spiritual discipline is of the

From Ninian Smart, *Reasons and Faiths* (New York: Humanities Press Inc., 1958 and London: Routledge & Kegan Paul Ltd.), pp. 55–56, 59–66. By permission of the publishers.

essence of mystical practice; (2) that the form of discipline chosen (language, procedure, prescriptions) determines the definition or conception of the state to be attained; and (3) that the mystic can intend this final state only indirectly. Why does Professor Smart insist that "union with Allah" and "gaining nirvana" cannot be said to be the same thing? Do you think that gaining skill in spiritual consciousness through a particular "path" or set of procedures will effect the outcome? Why is it impossible to strive for the bliss of nirvana directly? Would the Zen master Shibayama (reading 10) agree with Smart's assertion that "expectations of achievement militate against success"? Can you think of other everyday goals that can be pursued (successfully) only indirectly?

WHAT IS MYSTICISM?

Determining what mysticism is involves little more than a piece of prudent legislation about the word—a task unfortunately necessitated by the looseness and disrepute into which such words as "mystical" have fallen.[1] For we hear tell of "Hitler's mystical belief in the superiority of the *Herrenvolk*," etc., and of the "mystic influence of the stars," etc. Let us say that a mystical experience is one which is reported by a class of persons generally referred to as "mystics"—such men as Eckhart, St. John of the Cross, Plotinus, the Buddha, Śaṅkara and so on. Such men are characterized by spirituality and asceticism and pursue a certain method. Thus we do not wish to call Hitler or astrologers mystics in this sense nor their doctrines mystical. We should note too that it is quite possible for someone to have feelings of joy and exaltation in a religious context without having any experience properly describable as mystical; and certainly mysticism is far from religious enthusiasm. For a most important characteristic, one which we may regard for the purposes of linguistic legislation as the defining characteristic, of the mystic is that he undertakes a certain sort of mystical discipline. The following are a few main points typically made by such men: that they have achieved unspeakable bliss; that this experience is timeless and other-worldly; that it is gained after a long course of self-mastery and meditation (referred to as "the Path," "the Way," etc.); that upon attaining it they acquire a new vision of the world, etc.[2] . . .

NIRVĀṆA IS THE ACHIEVEMENT
OF A CERTAIN STATE

Literally, "nirvāna" means "waning away" (as of a flame) or "cooling off,"[3] and therefore suggests a connection with *taṇhā*, "burning" or "craving," which according to the Buddha's teaching is the cause of *dukkha*, "suffering" or "misery,"[4] and is conducive to rebirth. Thus the Four Noble Truths declare (i) that all existence is sorrowful; (ii) that the cause of sorrow is craving; (iii) that there is a means of destroying this craving; (iv) and that the way to the destruction of craving is the Noble Eightfold

Path. And with the destruction of craving, there will be no more rebirth, and one is thus freed from the ceaseless round of existence (*saṃsāra*). Thus there are four aspects of nirvāṇa which have to be noticed:

(*a*) Achieving the state of nirvāṇa involves destroying the fetters, depravities or intoxicating influences (*āsavas*) which implicate one in worldly existence; and thus involves the cultivation of good conduct, summed up in sections (iii) to (v) of the Eightfold Path as right speech, right activity and right livelihood.

(*b*) The destruction of the *āsavas* also involves spiritual training, summed up in sections (vi) and (vii) of the Path as right endeavour and right mindfulness (i.e., the struggle for self-mastery and continual watchfulness and self-awareness).

(*c*) These lead to mystical meditation (*samādhi*), summed up in section (viii) of the Path as right meditation.

(*d*) On death one attains to complete nirvāṇa, and there is no more rebirth.

We may thus refer to four achievements within the Eightfold Path: (*a*) the achievement of moral mastery; (*b*) the achievement of spiritual mastery; (*c*) the attainment of mystical bliss; (*d*) the arrival at death of one who has achieved the above and not fallen away (like the unfortunate Godhika who attained temporary release six times but fell away).[5] It should be noted that spiritual mastery is held to bring knowledge or insight—insight into the truth of the Four Truths. Thus (*b*) and (*c*) are often referred to respectively as the emancipation of knowledge, and the emancipation of heart and mind.[6] . . .

NIRVĀṆA, LIKE OTHER MYSTICAL STATES, IS A GOAL

Like other mystical states as reported, e.g., by Western mystics and Ṣūfīs, nirvāṇa is a goal, as is shown by the universal references to the conduct leading to them as "the Path," "the Way," etc. And this path involves a method (in Buddhism, right meditation). John Cassian, for example, one of the earliest Christian writers on mysticism is insistent that mysticism involves method.[7] Again the whole concept of *yoga* (i.e., yoking) is one of controlled attainment.

Nevertheless, the goals achieved in different mystical endeavours are not in a sense the same goal. Someone who had correctly performed the injunctions laid down by the Buddha would be likely to exclaim: "Now I have gained nirvāṇa," not "Now I have seen God" or "Now I am one with Brahman." This is not accountable in the following simple ways: The Buddhist has never heard of Allah or Brahman—or: The Buddhist and the others are trying to say the same thing in different ways—or even: The Buddhist thinks he has achieved one thing when he has *really* attained another.

It is not simply a matter of not having heard of Allah, for even if he had and he were a Buddhist he would still express himself by reference to nirvāna. Nor is it a case of different ways of saying the same thing, for, on the contrary, the difference of language is one of the vitally important differences. It is indeed this which perhaps more than anything else distinguishes the achievement of the Buddhist monk from that of the Sūfī. For in many other ways there are similarities of behaviour: and the subtle divergencies are crystallized by the use of differing concepts. For, first, each is embedded in different doctrinal schemes. And second, they are partly precipitated out of the rules for attaining the goals represented by the concepts. In fact, in the case of nirvāna, the concept is in a very great degree bound up with the Eightfold Path (*Allah* and *union with Allah* are less tightly bound to a path, since another strand enters here too). Thus, it can hardly be said of one who has obeyed *these* rules that he has attained to the goal precipitated out of *those* rules, that the *nibbuta* has gained the peace of God. Nor that he thinks he achieved one thing but has in fact achieved another. (Though there may be a missionary point in saying these things; but even so the real issue must be seen in the relative merits of doctrinal schemes.)

THE ATTAINMENT OF THE GOAL
AND ITS SETTING

From the foregoing it will be seen that it is absurd to entertain the possibility of stumbling, all unawares, on the mystic's bliss. For the latter is defined in large part by the procedure for getting there. Thus Plotinus' remark:

> It is pointless to say "Look to God" without giving instruction on how to look,[8]

is a stronger one than that of St. Thomas à Kempis when he said:

> What will it avail thee to argue profoundly about the Trinity if thou be void of humility and therefore displeasing to the Trinity?[9]

In the first case, talk about the divine will be empty without "unpacking" in terms of the Path; in the second, it will have content but no fruit. In the one case it will be pointless, in the other worse than pointless.

Thus propositions about the attainment of nirvāna need, for their verification, attention to their setting. Just as, in understanding "He scored a goal" we must look to the setting of a game conducted according to certain rules; and in understanding "He found the solution" we must look to a situation of search, so too with "He attained nirvāna" we must attend to the setting. Even if a boy were kicking a football about by himself and then deftly shot it between the posts, we could only understand this as a goal on the supposition that he was pretending to play a game; even if someone while watching an opera were to cry "I know the answer," we could only understand this oddly-situated solution by reference to another situation, some search that this Archimedes had been conducting. So too it would hardly make sense to speak of someone's realizing nirvāna unless certain conditions had previously been fulfilled, unless, so to speak, the stage had been set. Thus these conditions are not merely (or perhaps even) to be thought of as causal conditions, for unless they obtain it is *inappropriate* to say that nirvāṇa has been achieved. One must advance along the Eightfold Path. To verify the proposition "He has attained nirvāṇa" one must consult the rules. . . .

We may state the matter succinctly thus: The nature of the goal is revealed in the rules enjoined for its attainment, which are affected not merely by differing conceptions of the mystical journey, but also by differing features in the doctrinal schemes. Further, the attainer of the goal must intend to, in the sense that he deliberately submits to the enjoined rules, with the hope or intention of attaining the goal. The pre-arrival conditions which have to be fulfilled before the claim to have achieved nirvāṇa can be entertained are: the attainment of moral and spiritual mastery, as under stages (i) to (vii) of the Eightfold Path. Hence the claim is not a simple one to have had some particular experience or experiences: for the setting involved in the claim stretches well before the time of blissful rapture and the achievement is the achievement of a particular sort of goal. . . .

A QUALIFICATION: NIRVĀNA
A SPECIAL KIND OF GOAL

It is at this point convenient to mention a further complication to what has been depicted so far. The bliss is hoped for but not strictly intended. For in saying that bliss is the mystic's goal, we may well be confronted with the objection that spiritual teachers commonly impress upon their pupils that they are not to expect to gain such bliss. In Zen Buddhism this is particularly clearly (though paradoxically) insisted on: our target must be hit without aiming;[10] and we may compare the general Buddhist doctrine that we must fight free not merely from sensual desires, but also from *vibhavataṇhā*, the thirst for release from existence. How then can we call such bliss (and its consequent state of tranquillity) a goal? Maybe it is thus: we cannot be sure of attaining the goal, and so we should not expect to; but we can hope for it, and put ourselves upon the Path. For expectations of achievement militate against success. But this is not the whole story. For there is something even logically wrong about speaking of intending something which we are not sure is within our power (that is, reasonably certain it is such that we might be able to achieve). We cannot intend to realize nirvāṇa, but we can hope that setting ourselves on the Path may bear fruit. In this respect the hope of nirvāṇa is somewhat like the hope of happiness: we would gladly be happy, but it is not a practical aim which we can set ourselves.

NOTES

1. Not only in our day has this group of words fallen in disrepute: in the Age of Enlightenment also. "The word 'mystic' was synonymous with 'crazy dreamer.' Kant called mysticism 'Afterphilosophie,' which means as much

as 'pseudo-philosophy' or 'sham philosophy'." (J. M. Clark, *The Great German Mystics*, p. 26.)

2. There may be some objection to describing the mystical goal as one of *bliss*. For instance, it is sometimes said to be beyond bliss, since bliss implies enjoyment and if the mystic seeks enjoyment he will not find it. Also "bliss," like similar words, has a tendency towards debasement in usage. Though other expressions might serve, such as "peace" (see Prof. Shoson Miyamoto, *The Philosophical Basis of Peace in Buddhism*, Atti del VIII Congresso Internazionale di Storia delle Religioni, pp. 198–200), "ecstasy" (E. Underhill, *Mysticism*, ch. viii), etc., "bliss" has the advantage of being the common translation of the Sanskrit *ānanda,* frequently used of the mystical state (see, e.g., *Taittirīya Upan.*, II.8.1) and also used to describe an aspect of the nature of Brahman; and it is a reasonable word for the Pāli *sukha,* used in connection with nirvāna. Further, it is necessary here to give a somewhat schematic account of mystical bliss, in order that we may have a model of the mystical strand.

3. The Pāli term is *nibbāna,* but I use "nirvāna" as being more familiar to English readers. The latter, the Sanskrit expression, being one of a group meaning "release," need not have a specifically Buddhist sense—for the Brāhmanist, nirvāna would be union with Brahman.

4. *taṇhā*=Skrt. *trsnā; dukkha*=Skrt. *duhkha.*

5. *Samyutta Nik.*, i.109.

6. *ceto,* see E. J. Thomas, *The History of Buddhist Thought*, p. 121.

7. *Confessions*, xiv.

8. *Enneads*, II.9.15.

9. *Imitatio Christi*, I.1.3.

10. See, passim, E. Herrigel's strikingly beautiful book, *Zen in the Art of Archery*. Also in characterizing the goal as (short-term) bliss rather than, say, serenity we slightly simplify matters, since the supreme state is sometimes said to be "beyond bliss" (see later, pp. 98, 99 [Not included]).

CRITIQUE

12. On Determining Truth, *H. Feigl*

This excerpt is the first of the critiques of Chapter IV. The author, Herbert Feigl, is a contemporary American philosopher of science. His purpose is to suggest that whatever else mysticism is (for example, it may be a powerful emotional experience; it

From Herbert Feigl, "Philosophy of Science," in *Philosophy*, by Roderick M. Chisholm, et al., © 1964 by the Trustees of Princeton University. Reprinted by permission of Prentice-Hall, Inc., Englewood Cliffs, New Jersey. Pp. 478–80, 483–84, 524, 526–28, 534–536.

may produce radical reorientations in one's life style and attitudes), it is not a method for arriving at knowledge, if one means by "knowledge" what scientists or empiricists mean—namely, some thing that can be empirically validated. Thus, as in the case of the personal awareness of the Holy (Chapter I), so in the attainment of spiritual freedom, the question of verifying the claims made by mystics has been raised. The author is committed to the idea that the procedures of scientific investigation are normative for any inquiry that seeks knowledge of reality, and rejects claims to knowledge based on any experience that departs from those procedures. He distinguishes, for example, between an "emotive appeal" and an informative claim. He asserts the necessity of objective ("intersubjective") facts. Do you think that "genuine knowledge-claims" should be limited to claims that can be verified by intersubjective tests? (Do you recognize different kinds of knowledge, for example, of "understanding" in historical and psychological studies, as contrasted with "explanations" in the physical sciences?) In the final section, Feigl also excludes value judgments from the realm of knowledge (for they are matters of "commitment" instead), and denies that one can hope to know anything by attaining some sort of identity with it. Do you think Feigl has sufficiently supported his conclusion that "the mystical claims of transcendence are untenable"? And is the "wish to know what reality is 'absolutely' and 'intrinsically' " a misguided one? Why or why not? What would the advocates of this chapter think of Feigl's argument?

The line of demarcation between science and religion requires special consideration because of the truth-claims that are explicitly made especially in those religions that are connected with a theology. The same sort of question arises in regard to the boundary between science and metaphysics. Unfortunately the word "metaphysics" is used in at least six different senses.[1] What I have in mind here is the sort of knowledge-claims that are transcendent in that they are in principle irrefutable (and as some would add, unconfirmable) by any kind of empirical evidence. This is presumably what many philosophically unsophisticated people have in mind when they say that theological and metaphysical assertions can be neither proved nor disproved, and hence that they are a matter of faith. At this point we encounter a good deal of disagreement among the philosophers of science. The logical positivists and the logical empiricists have for a long time maintained that assertions that are absolutely beyond the possibility of test are devoid of factual meaning and that whatever significance they have consists in their evocative expressions and appeals, i.e., in their pictorial, emotional, and motivational potencies, but that they could not have any cognitive (factual, empirical) reference. This implies that questions concerning the truth of such assertions cannot even arise. Other, less radical thinkers merely say that immunity to test removes metaphysical and theological truth-claims from the domain of the empirical sciences, but not from the domain of the cognitively meaningful. In short, the issue is between adopting a criterion of (factual) meaningfulness versus a criterion of demarcation. The pragmatist-operationist tendencies in this country favor the former. If there is no difference that *makes* a difference in observable consequences between the affirmation and the denial of a given statement, then this statement is not a genuine proposition at all, but a sentence, i.e., a sequence of words that may express or arouse mental images and emotions, influence attitudes, or stimulate action. In such cases we are precluded from asking how reliable the statement is in the light of evidence —and this for the simple reason that we have (often unwittingly) made the statement immune to any kind of test, and thus "proof against disproof." As the positivists have emphasized, it is not only pointless but strictly meaningless to ask questions that we have so conceived as to make them in principle unanswerable. Problems of this sort are guaranteed 100 per cent insoluble! All this is relevant not only for the critique of traditional theology and the speculative metaphysical systems propounded by the philosophers throughout the ages. It is also most pertinent for the type of metaphysical admixtures that we find again and again in the history of scientific ideas. Doctrines concerning absolute space and time, absolute substance, the ether theories, certain conceptions of causal necessity, of vital forces and entelechies, of the human soul or mind, of group minds, etc. have sometimes been so conceived as to make them in principle immune to even the most indirect or incomplete tests. It is this sort of intellectual self-stultification to which the radical empiricists object, and which they attempt to remove by closer attention to the functions of language and the types of significance. There is no question that in ordinary discourse the cognitive and the emotive (pictorial, emotional, and motivative) types of significance are usually combined or fused. The positivistic critique admits the fusion, but warns against the confusion of one type of significance with the other. What the positivists object to is the mistaking of emotive appeals for factual meanings. Sentences in religious discourse, for example, may serve the purposes of exhortation, fortification, edification, or consolation, but they do not communicate *information*. Similarly, many a metaphysician mistakes the wish for experience with the quest for reliable knowledge. Intuitive and mystical "insights" may consist in powerful emotional experiences, they may even produce radical reorientations in one's attitude toward the values and ideals of human life, but they are by themselves not a basis for the validation of knowledge-claims. To the radical empiricist (positivist, operationist), religion may indeed be a way of life, an attitude of devotion to certain moral ideals, but neither religion nor theology can be considered as a branch of knowledge parallel (or superior) to scientific knowledge. The factual sciences as we understand them nowadays make genuine knowledge-claims precisely because they are so conceived as to make them susceptible to severely scrupulous tests....

The examples from psychological and historical knowledge illustrate something that is important for all scientific knowledge: that verifications or refutations are almost always *indirect,* as well as incomplete. They also show that the sort of tests we apply must utilize evidence that can be ascertained *intersubjectively.* This is at least part of what is meant by the much vaunted "objectivity of science." It amounts to the demand that knowledge-claims, if they are to be *scientific,* must be in principle open to tests by any observer, sufficiently equipped with the requisite instruments and with the intelligence to perform the tests and to interpret their results. The significance of this requirement becomes clearer if we ask what it excludes. It obviously excludes the sort of dogmatism that answers the question "How do you know?" by simply asserting "I just know." This answer is clearly taboo among responsible scientists, as it should be taboo also among rational thinkers in any intellectual domain. The implications for intuition or mystical insight are obvious. The *occurrence* of intuitive or mystical experiences is not to be denied. It can itself be intersubjectively certified. But no matter how much agreement there may be in the intuitive experience of a great number of individuals, this by itself does not validate the knowledge-claims concerning anything over and above those experiences. If the defender of intuitive knowledge then goes on to say that the immediate intuitive experience or mystical insight provides *evidence* for the inference of something beyond, e.g., the existence of an absolute, a God, or the like, then the scientific attitude demands that we scrutinize this claim. The mentioned experiences may well be evidence for something beyond themselves, but this may turn out to be something perfectly natural, such as the infantile situation of man, or unconscious remnants thereof.

The requirement of intersubjective testability also rules out as scientifically meaningless (if we adopt the meaning criterion), or as beyond the scope of science (if we are satisfied with a criterion of demarcation) any speculations about disembodied minds. If part of our mental life were to continue beyond our bodily death, it might well be possible to verify this *subjectively.* But if we assume that there can be no physical manifestation of such a surviving mind, then intersubjective tests are in principle impossible. . . .

Some behaviorists were inclined to deny the existence of mental phenomena altogether—and were thus close to a materialistic outlook. But the majority of behaviorists were only methodologically oriented, and refused to commit themselves on what they regarded as the metaphysical question of the status of mental entities and their relation to behavior or neural processes. The behavior of animals and human beings, under various conditions of previous positive or negative reinforcement, strength of drives, stimulus patterns, etc., could be examined in a completely objective manner. Psychology in this sense became part of general biology. Some psychologists and a good many philosophers raised a storm of objections. It was said that psychology, having lost its soul (with the abandonment of theological and metaphysical speculations), later had lost its consciousness and finally its mind. . . .

Finally, I shall discuss briefly the assertion that the natural sciences are value-free or value-neutral, whereas the social sciences are invariably evaluative. This notion is prima facie plausible for two reasons: First, many historians, sociologists, and economists do make evaluations—moral or nonmoral, as the case may be. Second, investigation into the relations of the conditions to the consequences of social action serve as a basis for planning, guidance, or control. Perhaps more than any one else, John Dewey opposed the dualism of fact and value, already very clearly seen by Hume and emphasized, developed, and subjected to more penetrating analyses by the logical empiricists. This issue is discussed elsewhere in this volume in William Frankena's essay on "Ethical Theory"; that is indeed where it properly belongs, but it is also relevant here. The issue of science and evaluation has been discussed briefly by Carnap and Reichenbach, as well as by other philosophers of science of logical empiricist convictions. As they (and I with them) see it, it is one thing to *study evaluations* and valuative attitudes in the manner in which psychologists, anthropologists, sociologists, and historians pursue this task, but it is another thing to *make evaluations*. The logical empiricists staunchly maintain that, while the first task is a legitimate and important part of the social sciences, the second is part of the life process itself, and not a scientific activity at all. For even if we had complete knowledge concerning what conditions produce what consequences (or what means ensure with what probabilities and what utilities certain ends), it is an extrascientific question what consequences we *ought* to desire, or what ends we *should* aim at. It is admitted that knowledge regarding the probabilities and utilities in question is indispensable for rational action. But the evaluation of the utilities and of the purposes of action must at some point become a matter of commitment rather than of knowledge. Many of our fundamental commitments are so much taken for granted as a matter of course that we are interested only in the—admittedly vital and indispensable—information regarding means-ends relations. Thus we emphatically prefer the perpetuation of human life on our planet to its extermination, or we prefer health to sickness, fairness to injustice, and so on. But these are commitments, matters of attitude, which in and by themselves are not susceptible to scientific justification. Of course, as commitments and attitudes they can be studied by social scientists. Their historical development and possibly their causal explanation may be disclosed by scientific study. But to questions of ethics—e.g., why we ought to perpetuate human life rather than destroy it—there are no answers that science can validate. Any attempt in this direction is bound to beg the question at issue.

There have been occasional voices saying that the whole scientific enterprise rests on evaluations. It has even been maintained that the scientific method involves ethical decisions. I believe that those views that would, as it were, turn the tables are generated by certain confusions. It should be clear that both a saint and a scoundrel can utilize the best scientific information for their very different purposes. And while of course commitment to the aims of science in a sense underlies all scientific activities, it is in itself not part of the knowledge-claims of science. It is equally clear that even though value judgments play a role in the selection of problems and of techniques with which to attack them, such value judgments do not as such become part of the corpus of science. They are essentially like the considerations of utility and probability that enter into rational planning for practical action. In this sense they pertain to the pursuit of the scientific enterprise but not to its cognitive content. . . .

Proponents of mystical intuition, be it religious or metaphysical, often claim that their insights attain an "Absolute Reality" that is in principle beyond the possibility of scientific investigation. This is usually accompanied by the admission that the language of the mystic is unavoidably meta-phorical or allegorical, and that there is something completely ineffable about "ultimate reality." But equally characteristic of this outlook is the assertion that mystical insight consists in an identification or coalescence of the knowing subject with its object of knowledge. From the point of view of the vast majority of philosophers of science, these contentions reveal that the very word "knowledge" as used by the mystic for his trans-empirical insights means something utterly different from what this word means in common life and in science. Strict identification of the knowing subject with the to-be-known object is a logically incoherent notion. The best sense one can make of it is that immediate experience provides "ac-quaintance" with the qualities of consciousness. But as soon as we represent even only the relations of these qualities among each other in propositional form, we make knowledge-claims in the ordinary sense. And if the mystic maintains that he uses his extraordinary experiences as data that "indicate" a transempirical reality, then we are back again in the arena of scientific criticism. The question then is whether the intuitive experiences of the mystic are not susceptible to perfectly naturalistic (e.g., psychological) ex-planations that, if valid, would render any supernatural explanations super-fluous. Although no one can afford to be dogmatic in these matters, it seems plausible that the powers of scientific explanation, combined with those of logical analysis, are sufficient to show that the mystical claims of transcendence are untenable. But it may well be granted that mystical experience, just like religious experience more generally, can be extremely influential in the formation of one's attitude toward life and human affairs in moral and social respects.

The thinking of most modern American philosophers of science in regard to all the alleged "limitations of science" is that of a cautious optimism. Tremendous difficulties have been overcome and are continually being overcome by the ingenuity of the experimenters and the theorists. Many a problem that appeared as an unsolvable "riddle of the uni-verse" only some eighty years ago has been successfully approached by the advance of scientific knowledge. The origin of the universe is responsibly discussed by modern astrophysics and cosmology. The question of the origin of life, in the light of recent biochemical research, is no longer so deep a mystery as it used to be. The relations of mind and body have been considerably illuminated by the progress of psychophysiology, and by epistemological reflections. The nature of force and matter is increasingly disclosed by the results of modern physics. The wish to know what reality is "absolutely" and "intrinsically" is misguided in that it strives for mystical "identification" rather than for relational knowledge—the only kind of knowledge that is responsible and intelligible. If there are any absolutely unsolvable problems, they seem to be of our own making. They arise out of confusions that can be dispelled by logical analysis.

NOTES

1. One may distinguish the following types of "method": (1) intuitive, (2) deductive, (3) inductive-synthetic, (4) dialectical, (5) categorial-analytic, (6) transcendent.

(13.) On Whether Mystical Insight Is an Adequate Solution to Suffering, *D. C. Vijayavardhana*

One common criticism of mysticism is that it encourages its followers to withdraw from the world into an irrelevant asceticism and selfish contemplation; that it shows selfish concern with one's own spiritual freedom instead of fulfilling the higher ethic of helping other people. In this excerpt, a Ceylonese Buddhist layman criticizes the present Buddhist community (sangha) in his country for placing so much emphasis on the ideal of the monk (bhikkhu) and on ascetic virtues, and states his conviction that such an emphasis is a degenerate departure from the Buddha's original teaching. The "revolt in the temple" of which he speaks is against this departure, and he calls instead for a "reborn Buddhism," which would be a "Social Religion" in which good deeds predominate. Forget yourself, yes, but in the service of others: that is the transformation he encourages people to make, the only form of egolessness he cares to justify. Why does he feel that the emphasis on monastic virtues is wrong? To what norms does he appeal? Could this critique be used as a testimonial in one of the earlier chapters? Compare this Buddhist solution to present-day ills with Nyanaponika Thera's claim (in reading

From *The Revolt in the Temple* by D. C. Vijayavardhana (Colombo, Ceylon: Sinha Publications, 1953), pp. 582–88. Reprinted by permission of Mrs. Rukmini Beligammana.

2) that only by controlling the arising of suffering in the person can human life be significantly transformed. Last, note that, aside from expressing a common criticism of mysticism, this excerpt illustrates the point that exactly what was meant by the Buddha's teaching is still open to question.

The popularity of the teaching of the Buddha was mostly due to its offering an immediate escape from the sorrows of life. In the age of the Buddha men of keen intellect and deep feeling were asking: What does all this weary round of existence mean? And the Buddha addressed his appeal to the men who were longing for a way of escape, a resort to Nirvana here and now itself, the peace of mind of self-forgetful activity. The world with all its sufferings seems adapted to the growth of goodness. The Buddha does not preach the mere worthlessness of life or resignation to an inevitable doom. His is not a doctrine of despair. He asks us to revolt against evil and attain a life of finer quality, an Arahata state.

Originally a bhikkhu went forth as a preacher and taught the Doctrine to the people. The Buddha had exhorted His disciples to wander and preach the Truth for the welfare and liberation of the multitude, as He loved His fellow creatures and had compassion on them. Such was the ideal of the bhikkhu, as it was understood during the three centuries after the Buddha's death. But it seems that the Sangha began to neglect certain important aspects of it in the second century B.C., and degenerated from the lofty ideal set before them by the Master. They became too self-centred and contemplative, and did not evince the old zeal for missionary activity among the people. They cared only to "save their own skins." They were indifferent to the duty of teaching and helping all human beings. They became cold and aloof, a saintly and serene, but an inactive and indolent monastic order. They ceased to exist or existed in an undefinable, inconceivable sphere somewhere or nowhere, and were lost to the world of men as friends and helpers.

The lack of warmth and the passionlessness of the Theravāda ideal are not inspiring. Disgust of life does not represent all that is substantial in the life of man. In the "Khaggavisana Sutta,"* family life and social intercourse are strictly prohibited, and we cannot reach our goal by means of a life of love and activity. "To him who leads a social life, affections arise and the pain which follows affection," says the *Sutta Nipata*. Again, a wise man "should avoid married life as if it were a burning pit of live coals." The *Visuddhi Magga*** tells us that "meditation in the cremation ground brings many exquisitive virtues." These ideas cannot be reconciled

---

* A section of the Pali Buddhist canonical text *Sutta Nipata* (*A Collection of Discourses*), which advises a *bhikkhu* to avoid the pleasures and entanglements of common social life.

** *Path of Purification,* a famous Theravada summary commentary, written in the 4th century A.D. by the monk Buddhaghosha.

with the Buddha's original teachings, of which even the first discourse declared that asceticism was "gloomy, unworthy and profitless."

This tendency towards spiritual selfishness amongst the Sangha is exhibited in the later Pali literature. The *Dhammapada** exalts self-control, meditation and absense of hatred, but it also exhibits an attitude of contempt for the common people and remoteness from their interests. Most poets of the *Theragatha*** only stirke the note of personal salvation; they seldom speak of the duty of helping others. The author of the *Milinda Panha**** declares that an Arahat should aim at the destruction of his own pain and sorrow. Some of the Sangha thought that one could be very wise and holy through personal self-culture without fulfilling the equally important duty of teaching and helping others.

From early Vedic times there had been in India ascetic tempers who had cut themselves adrift from the responsibilities of life and wandered free. The Brahminical codes recognized the right of these to sever themselves from the duties of life and the observance of rites. Many such beliefs and ascetic practices have been tacked on to the rationalistic Buddhist principles and ideals. Stress is laid on monasticism instead of the good life. Buddhism has been transformed into a system in which the celibate life is given paramount importance and the household life passes for something low (*hira*). There is no consistency in this teaching, for, according to the *Majjhima Nikaya*,† a man may attain Nirvana without being a bhikkhu.

The numerous accounts of conversions in the Pitakas, show clearly that the converts of the Buddha became Arahats, that is attained to Nirvana during their life on earth. The Buddhist tradition considers that the Sangha, or community of bhikkhus, at first consisted exclusively of Arahats, and large bodies of men attained to this state at the same time. Yasa attained Nirvana as a layman, but thereupon became a bhikkhu. It may be pointed out further that, in the *Maha-vagga*†† narrative, Yasa's father, the merchant prince, similarly attained salvation, but remained a layman. The *Maha-vagga* describes the conversion of King Bimbisara in practically the same terms. The case of the Buddha's father, Suddhodana, is similar. The idea that salvation was the monopoly of the Sangha was evidently a later notion, cultivated for priestly reasons, natural enough to a clerical order, but foreign to the mind of the great Teacher. The Buddha did not call men to the homeless life in order that they might live totally aloof from human society, but in order that they might serve the world by living a life of self-forgetful activity.

---

* *Way of Truth,* a short, very popular Pali canonical book of teaching.

** *Songs of the Elders,* a section of the Pali scripture.

*** *Questions of Milinda,* a Pali text written several centuries after the Buddha lived, which teaches Buddhist views through dialogues between the king Milinda and the monk Nagasena.

† *Division of Medium-length (Discourses),* an important section of Buddhist scripture.

†† From a section of the Pali scripture called *Vinaya* (rules of conduct).

The ascetic virtues cannot flourish side by side with the social and domestic. If you choose to be a recluse, you cannot be a lover of life. A hermit can know nothing of love or friendship nor can the social worker devote his strength to the advancement of knowledge. True asceticism is not indifference to the suffering of the world, but the building up of a silent centre even in the furious activity of life. We must be spiritual enough to possess ourselves in the noise of the blatant world, and not merely in the peace and silence of the cell of the monastery. By its abstract and negative tendencies the Theravāda became the incarnation of dead thought and the imprisonment of spirit. It gives us neither a warm faith for which to live nor a real ideal for which to work.

All this was the result of Brahminical accretions on the simple teaching of the Buddha and represents in reality a fall from that great Teacher's aim. These aberrations were surely infections from the superstitious environment. Detachment from the outer world always leads to a regression towards, or a revival of, juvenile or infantile states. As Amiel points out, the pleasure of the lonely, contemplative life ending in the blank trances "is deadly, inferior, in all respects, to the joys of action, to the sweetness of love, to the beauty of enthusiasm, or to the sacred savour of accomplished duty."

The Buddhism taught by some members of our Sangha is downright pessimism. They lay stress on the presence of suffering in the world to the exclusion of all else. Life, in their eyes, is a bleak and dismal procession to the grave. This emphasis on sorrow is a disastrous way of teaching the Buddha's Way of Life. The Sangha, by parodying sorrow and suffering, is tying, what are virtually mill-stones, round the necks of the people, and it becomes a great strain on the State, whose duty it is to make the people stand erect as men, and behave as men. Buddhism does, indeed, dwell much on suffering, but it does so in order to explain the way of deliverance from suffering. It goes further than Christianity in this respect, for it teaches that man, unaided, can effect his own deliverance. There is no pessimism here.

A section of the Sangha teaches the faithful to rest their hopes on charity (*dāna*) and gifts to them. It preaches that a man is born either rich or poor according to what he gives; those who have plenty of wealth are fortunate because they had given freely to charity in their past births. This sordid doctrine, that virtue deserves a material reward, is not Buddhism. It is the kind of preaching that makes people amass wealth and oppress the poor with unpricked conscience; their wealth, they are convinced, is a sign of their generosity in previous lives, the other fellow's poverty, of moral turpitude. The Sangha has invented the doctrine of transference of merit, and preaches that the right means of helping the dead is to make gifts to themselves. It encourages the erection of useless structures as places and objects of worship, all with an eye to one's own comfort and temporal gain. Today, the masses of the Buddhists are addicted to the ceremonies and observances prescribed by those who live on food provided by the faithful and whom the Buddha once described as "tricksters, droners out of holy words for pay, diviners, exorcists, ever hungering to add gain to gain."

The Ceylon Sangha, as a whole, have degenerated and no longer are they leading the selfless lives the Master exhorted them to do. The main reasons for the deterioration are the selfish motives and considerations of the bhikkhus themselves, their self-interest, greed and ignorance, and their failure to adhere to the principles of the teaching of the Master. The Siam *Nikaya,* the principal sect of the Sangha of Ceylon, is not only caste-ridden but also class conscious. They grant the *Upasampada* or higher Ordination to one particular caste only, and the Malwatta Chapter, which controls the largest number of bhikkhus, has always been dominated by Kandyan monks, although the largest number and the most learned bhikkhus of this sect are of the Low-country. *Nayakaships,* or High Priesthoods, are sold for considerations, and in some of these Chapters the bhikkhus are simple folk without any learning and not a few of them of a very low standard of morality. During the times of the Sinhalese kings they, as Protectors of the Faith, purged the Order of the undesirables who had crept into the ranks of the Sangha. The *Mahavaṃsa** mentions several instances when this was done; but now, without royal patronage and the guidance and supervision of a universally accepted leader, the Sangha is daily deteriorating and one shudders to think of the fate of the Order in the coming generations.

WHAT THE FUTURE DEMANDS

In the face of this sad picture, it is not strange that we should ask ourselves: "Has Buddhism failed?" But our times paint another picture. In it we see millions of men and women who are showing in their daily lives unselfishness, generosity, self-sacrifice, tolerance and compassion. These people are reflecting the Buddha's spirit. Yet, many of them have no temple affiliations, since theirs is fundamentally a religion of deeds, not of creeds; expressed in life, not in words. As we view this picture we say with renewed faith: "Buddhism has not failed; the Order to which the Buddha entrusted His doctrine may have failed, but Buddhism has not lost its hold on human life today."

Nevertheless if this vital force for good is to be conserved, Buddhism must have a new birth. Let us picture, for a moment, this reborn Buddhism. It would be a Social Religion. Its terms of admission would be the acceptance of the brotherhood of all mankind. It would welcome to its fellowship all those who are striving to live useful and worthy lives. For admission within its fold, it would pronounce dogma, ritual and creed all non-essential. A life, not a creed, would be the test. As its first concern it would encourage a Buddhist way of life lived seven days a week, fifty-two weeks a year, not only on *Poya* days** and on special occasions; the

---

* *The Great History,* a chronicle of early Buddhism (containing legendary material) and its expansion to Ceylon, written perhaps in the 5th century A.D.

** Buddhist sacred days related to the phases of the moon.

*Dhamma** is a way of life, meant to be followed every day, to influence every activity of ours. It would be a religion of all the people, the rich and the poor, the high and the low—a true kingdom of righteousness.

The sponsors of this revitalised religion, the Sangha, would pursue not a will-o'-the-wisp Nirvana secluded in the cells of their monasteries, but a Nirvana attained here and now by a life of self-forgetful activity. Theirs will not be a selfish existence, pursuing their own salvation, whilst living on the charity of others, but an existence full of service and self-sacrifice. To bring about this transformation the Sangha must be re-organised and the bhikkhus trained not only in Buddhist theory but also in some form of Social Service in order that they may acquire a personal knowledge of practical problems. Thus they would live in closer touch with humanity, would better understand and sympathize with human difficulties, and would exert their influence as much in living as in preaching.

The Sangha must be reformed and its lost prestige restored. The need for such an effort in a country with a predominantly Buddhist population will not be questioned by anyone. It is not an attempt to bring the breath of life to a relic of the past. There is an unbroken tradition which is woven into the pattern of the country's history. But today it is realised only too well that the Ceylon Sangha is not playing its proper part in the spiritual, social and cultural life of the people. It has lost its grip and is not only not pulling its weight, but is daily deteriorating materially and spiritually. The material side can automatically be corrected if only it devotes proper attention to the spiritual side.

There is in Ceylon today much talk of Buddhism being our "greatest assest"; of treating it as the "only remedy for all the political 'isms"; of using it "to put Ceylon on the map"; of taking it "to the West"; and of offering it as "a new way of life to the world." Have those who use these slogans ever thought what kind of Buddhism they mean to offer to a distracted world? If by "Buddhism" they mean the kind of Buddhism which is practised in everyday Ceylon and dosed out to the people from the temples, loud-speakers and the Broadcasting Service, we think there is very little likelihood of that Buddhism taking root in the West, or anywhere else, in these days of better education and increased knowledge.

Asoka** took Buddhism not only to the West but to the whole of the then known world; but it was principally in Ceylon that it took root. Other missions that he despatched failed. What was the reason for this set-back? Either those missionaries who took the Message failed to interpret it as an acceptable one to the particular people to whom it was delivered, or they failed to adapt themselves to the environment of those countries.

A modern instance of this failure is available in the case of a recent missionary enterprise, sponsored by the Maha Bodhi Society, to introduce Buddhism in England. It was not successful. One of the main reasons for its failure was the establishment of a Buddhist *Vihara* or place of worship

---

* The Buddha's teaching and practice.
** Third-century B.C. Indian ruler who fostered the growth of Buddhism.

in London. Buddhism is an intellectual doctrine, and its primary appeal is to people of intellect and of deep culture. These are the very people to whom the idea of a *Vihara,* or cathedral with statues and statue-worship, is irrelevant and indeed repellent.

The modern revolt against conventional religion is a sign of the quickening of conscience. Great social changes are generally brought about by a few individuals who throw aside their prejudices and get at the reality of things. Every moral reformer is an immoral force in the eyes of the conservative. Anyone who insists on doing differently from established custom is immoral, though his immorality acquires ethical value in the next generation and becomes a part of the tradition in another. The Buddha was the greatest moral reformer ever. He not only rebelled against the reactionary forces of His time, but when He said: "Do not go merely by hearsay or tradition, but what has been handed down from olden time, by cherished opinions and speculations, nor believe merely because I am your Master. But, when you yourselves have seen that a thing is evil and leads to harm and suffering, then you should reject it. And when you see that thing is good and blameless, and leads to blessing and welfare, then you should adopt such a thing"—He exhorted His followers to be rebels all the time.

All progress is due to the rebels, and it is to those few who are in advance of the highest life-conception of the time that all progress is due. No progress is possible if religion and ethics are held as sacrosanct; by showing that all things are subject to the law of change (*anicca*), and asking man to adapt himself to changing conditions, the Buddha brought the highest freedom to man.

The Buddha preached to a feudal society. Although that social structure was to last two thousand three hundred years more, the Buddha foresaw that it would yield place to other forms of society. Two hundred years ago feudal society gave way to capitalist society, and this system too is now giving way to yet another form of society. We are living through a civilization that is changing, following the law of change. We are today in the midst of two worlds, one dying and another struggling to be born; humanity is on the march towards the building of a lasting peace.

TRANSITION SECTION
The Shift to
Nontrancendent Ultimates

...[T]he evolutionary future of religion is extinction. The belief
in supernatural beings and in supernatural forces which affect
nature without obeying nature's laws will erode and become only
an interesting historical memory. This is not to say that this
event is likely to occur in the next decade; the process very likely
will take several hundred years, and there probably will always
remain individuals, or even occasional small cult groups, who
respond to hallucinations, trance, and obsession with a
supernaturalist interpretation. But as a cultural property, belief
in supernatural powers is doomed to die out, all over the world,
as a result of the increasing adequacy and diffusion of scientific
knowledge and of the realization by secular faiths that supernatural
belief is not necessary to the effective use of ritual. The question
of whether such a denouement will be good or bad for humanity
is irrelevant to the prediction; the process is inevitable. (Anthony
F. C. Wallace, "Rituals: Sacred And Profane," Zygon, Vol. I,
March 1966, p. 76.)

AT THE BEGINNING of this book we stated that we would consider not only traditionally recognized ways of being religious but also concerns, attitudes, and practices that many people regard as "secular" but that serve to transform life for some people. Were we to have edited a book like this some three hundred years ago, we probably would not have needed to include a section like this. No doubt nontraditional means of ultimate transformation were present then too. But they did not have the visibility or cultural power they have today. The reasons for this development are complex, and we cannot go into them here. But we can point to some of the themes in terms of which traditional ways have been rejected and new approaches to the meaning and character of human life have been justified. This is the function of this section.

Starting with the 18th century and continuing through our time, a growing number of moral philosophers and social scientists have called on mankind to "grow up." Among the "childish things" human beings are asked to put away are the "illusions" of a Transcendent Being on whom (which) man depends for his existence, of a moral and good universe based on an eternal principle of order, or of appeals to ecstatic experience through which to overcome the terror of the unknown. If man can let go of these "crutches," they say, he can develop capacities for the enjoyment of life that only a few sensitive people now perceive to be possible. To construct this new world, they call on us to perfect and extend some of the basic aspects of human life (or modes of human awareness) through the use of various applied sciences, creative education, and astute political and economic management. Even if we object that the realization of this vision will not come in our lifetime, these prophets insist that we live in a world in which appeals to transcendent agents, orders, and states of consciousness are no longer credible. Although man may reject transcendent absolutes, however, he still needs guidance, support, and inspiration. For these needs man has the same human capacities as before (at least for 700,000 years), and can further develop techniques for bettering the world that former generations did not know. These capacities and techniques, then, are mankind's ultimate means of transformation.

1. The "Immoralist,"
F. Nietzsche

Our first spokesman for this section is the brilliant, controversial, and enigmatic German scholar, Friedrich Nietzsche (1844–1900). In this excerpt from one of his last works, we encounter an early version of an idea found in many later existentialists, that man's being or existence precedes his essence. This carries with it the implication that there is no moral order in the universe which prescribes man's purpose. Values are the inventions of men. ("...there are altogether no moral facts.") We must ponder slowly and carefully what is meant by such an assertion. It clearly did not lead Nietzsche to stand for nothing at all, to have no values. Rather, it allowed him to go beyond traditional values. Nietzsche was concerned to attack traditional European (Judeo-Christian) morality, which he regarded as a "slave" morality, and which he predicted would lead to the downfall of Western civilization. Nietzsche, influenced by Arthur Schopenhauer (1788–1860), approved whatever conforms to nature, but he believed that conforming to nature meant striving for creature power, and the morality he prescribed was meant not for the "common herd" but for the few, superior "free spirits" of his time. To go "beyond good and evil," then, meant to go beyond the slave-morality to a master-morality. It meant to assume one's true role, that of creator and destroyer of ultimate values and purposes. What would be the consequence of this attitude for the religious types you have read so for?

...[W]e immoralists are trying with all our strength to take the concept of guilt and the concept of punishment out of the world again, and to cleanse psychology, history, nature, and social institutions and sanctions of them[;] there is in our eyes no more radical opposition than that of the theologians, who continue with the concept of a "moral world-order" to infect the innocence of becoming by means of "punishment" and "guilt." Christianity is a metaphysics of the hangman.

What alone can be *our* doctrine? That no one *gives* man his qualities—neither God, nor society, nor his parents and ancestors, nor he himself. (The nonsense of the last idea was taught as "intelligible freedom" by Kant—perhaps by Plato already.) No one is responsible for man's being there at all, for his being such-and-such, or for his being in these circumstances or in this environment. The fatality of his essence is not to be disentangled from the fatality of all that has been and will be. Man is not the effect of some special purpose, of a will, and end; nor is he the object of an attempt to attain an "ideal of humanity" or an "ideal of happiness" or an "ideal of morality." It is absurd to wish to devolve one's essence on some end or other. We have invented the concept of "end": in reality there is no end.

One is necessary, one is a piece of fatefulness, one belongs to the whole, one is in the whole; there is nothing which could judge, measure, compare, or sentence our being, for that would mean judging, measuring, comparing, or sentencing the whole. But there is nothing besides the whole. That nobody is held responsible any longer, that the mode of being may not be traced back to a *causa prima,* that the world does not form a unity either as a sensorium or as "spirit"—that alone is the great liberation; with this alone is the innocence of becoming restored. The concept of "God" was until now the greatest objection to existence. We deny God, we deny the responsibility in God: only thereby do we redeem the world.

THE "IMPROVERS" OF MANKIND

My demand upon the philosopher is known, that he take his stand *beyond good and evil* and leave the illusion of moral judgment *beneath* himself. This demand follows from an insight which I was the first to formulate: that *there are altogether no moral facts.* Moral judgments agree with religious ones in believing in realities which are no realities. Morality is merely an interpretation of certain phenomena—more precisely, a misinterpretation. Moral judgments, like religious ones, belong to a stage of ignorance at which the very concept of the real and the distinction between what is real and imaginary, are still lacking; thus "truth," at this stage, designates all sorts of things which we today call "imaginings." Moral judgments are therefore never to be taken literally: so understood, they always contain mere absurdity. Semeiotically, however, they remain invaluable: they reveal, at least for those who know, the most valuable realities of cultures and inwardnesses which did not know enough to "understand" themselves. Morality is mere sign language, mere symptomatology: one must know what it is all about to be able to profit from it.

2. On Faith as Illusion, W. T. Stace

The author of this excerpt, the distinguished philosopher and teacher Walter T. Stace (1886–1967), was for many years concerned with showing how "the modern mind" has evolved and

From "Man Against Darkness" by Walter T. Stace, found in *The Atlantic Monthly,* September 1948, pp. 54–58, 57–58. Copyright © 1948, by The Atlantic Monthly Company, Boston, Mass. Reprinted by permission of Mrs. W. T. Stace.

*how the characteristics of the modern mind can be traced back
to the 17th-century scientific revolution. In the following article,
Stace argues that it is not the particular discoveries of any of
the sciences that make it difficult for "modern man" to retain
traditional religious views, but "the general picture of the
world" that scientists have: namely, a world without final causes
or purposes, and a world without objective moral principles.
What follows? That is, how are we moderns to live in such a
world? How will we prevent the downfall of civilization? What
suggestions does Stace make? What "illusions" does he refer to?
(Note: Stace wrote this essay in 1948. In 1952 he wrote a
book which treated this same topic in greater depth, and indicated
how his own stance had changed. By this time Stace had gone
beyond the heroic stoicism, the "keep a stiff upper lip"
philosophy of this 1948 essay, and had arrived at a view which
he identified as mysticism, or "the way of the saints." By this
time he believed in "the unifying vision in which all is one."
For Stace's later position, then, see his* Religion and the Modern
Mind *[Philadelphia: J. B. Lippincott, 1952, available in
paperback].)*

...It was Galileo and Newton—notwithstanding that Newton himself
was a deeply religious man—who destroyed the old comfortable picture of
a friendly universe governed by spiritual values. And this was effected, not
by Newton's discovery of the law of gravitation nor by any of Galileo's
brilliant investigations, but by the general picture of the world which these
men and others of their time made the basis of the science, not only of
their own day, but of all succeeding generations down to the present. That
is why the century immediately following Newton, the eighteenth century,
was notoriously an age of religious skepticism. Skepticism did not have to
wait for the discoveries of Darwin and the geologists in the nineteenth
century. It flooded the world immediately after the age of the rise of
science. Neither the Copernican hypothesis nor any of Newton's or Galileo's
particular discoveries were the real causes. Religious faith might well have
accommodated itself to the new astronomy. The real turning point between
the medieval age of faith and the modern age of unfaith came when the
scientists of the seventeenth century turned their backs upon what used to
be called "final causes." The final cause of a thing or event meant the
purpose which it was supposed to serve in the universe, its cosmic purpose.
What lay back of this was the presupposition that there is a cosmic order or
plan and that everything which exists could in the last analysis be explained in terms of its place in this cosmic plan, that is, in terms of its
purpose.

Plato and Aristotle believed this, and so did the whole medieval Christian world. For instance, if it were true that the sun and the moon were
created and exist for the purpose of giving light to man, then this fact
would explain why the sun and the moon exist. We might not be able to

discover the purpose of everything, but everything must have a purpose. Belief in final causes thus amounted to a belief that the world is governed by purposes, presumably the purposes of some overruling mind. This belief was not the invention of Christianity. It was basic to the whole of Western civilization, whether in the ancient pagan world or in Christendom, from the time of Socrates to the rise of science in the seventeenth century.

The founders of modern science—for instance, Galileo, Kepler, and Newton—were mostly pious men who did not doubt God's purposes. Nevertheless they took the revolutionary step of consciously and deliberately expelling the idea of purpose as controlling nature from their new science of nature. They did this on the ground that inquiry into purposes is useless for what science aims at: namely, the prediction and control of events. To predict an eclipse, what you have to know is not its purpose but its causes. Hence science from the seventeenth century onwards became exclusively an inquiry into causes. The conception of purpose in the world was ignored and frowned on. This, though silent and almost unnoticed, was the greatest revolution in human history, far outweighing in importance any of the political revolutions whose thunder has reverberated through the world.

For it came about in this way that for the past three hundred years there has been growing up in men's minds, dominated as they are by science, a new imaginative picture of the world. The world, according to this new picture, is purposeless, senseless, meaningless. Nature is nothing but matter in motion. The motions of matter are governed, not by any purpose, but by blind forces and laws. Nature in this view, says Whitehead—to whose writings I am indebted in this part of my essay—is "merely the hurrying of material, endlessly, meaninglessly." You can draw a sharp line across the history of Europe dividing it into two epochs of very unequal length. The line passes through the lifetime of Galileo. European man before Galileo—whether ancient pagan or more recent Christian—thought of the world as controlled by plan and purpose. After Galileo European man thinks of it as utterly purposeless. This is the great revolution of which I spoke.

It is this which has killed religion. Religion could survive the discoveries that the sun, not the earth, is the center; that men are descended from simian ancestors; that the earth is hundreds of millions of years old. These discoveries may render out of date some of the details of older theological dogmas, may force their restatement in new intellectual frameworks. But they do not touch the essence of the religious vision itself, which is the faith that there is plan and purpose in the world, that the world is a moral order, that in the end all things are for the best. This faith may express itself through many different intellectual dogmas, those of Christianity, of Hinduism, of Islam. All and any of these intellectual dogmas may be destroyed without destroying the essential religious spirit. But that spirit cannot survive destruction of belief in a plan and purpose of the world, for that is the very heart of it. Religion can get on with any sort of astronomy, geology, biology, physics. But it cannot get on with a purposeless and meaningless universe. If the scheme of things is purposeless and meaning-

"You know what I think? I think eternity is a drag."

Cartoon by Kenneth Mahood, found in *Saturday Review,*
March 13, 1971. Copyright 1971 by Saturday Review,
Inc. Reprinted by permission of the publisher and Ken-
neth Mahood.

less, then the life of man is purposeless and meaningless too. Everything is
futile, all effort is in the end worthless. A man may, of course, still pursue
disconnected ends, money, fame, art, science, and may gain pleasure from
them. But his life is hollow at the center. Hence the dissatisfied, disillusioned,
restless, spirit of modern man....

Along with the ruin of the religious vision there went the ruin of moral
principles and indeed of all values. If there is a cosmic purpose, if there
is in the nature of things a drive towards goodness, then our moral systems
will derive their validity from this. But if our moral rules do not proceed
from something outside us in the nature of the universe—whether we say
it is God or simply the universe itself—then they must be our own inventions. Thus it came to be believed that moral rules must be merely an
expression of our own likes and dislikes. But likes and dislikes are notoriously variable. What pleases one man, people, or culture displeases another.
Therefore morals are wholly relative. This obvious conclusion from the
idea of a purposeless world made its appearance in Europe immediately
after the rise of science, for instance in the philosophy of Hobbes. Hobbes
saw at once that if there is no purpose in the world there are no values
either. "Good and evil," he writes, "are names that signify our appetites
and aversions; which in different tempers, customs, and doctrines of men
are different.... Every man calleth that which pleaseth him, good; and
that which displeaseth him, evil." ...

No civilization can live without ideals, or to put it in another way, without a firm faith in moral ideas. Our ideals and moral ideas have in the past been rooted in religion. But the religious basis of our ideals has been undermined, and the superstructure of ideals is plainly tottering. None of the commonly suggested remedies on examination seems likely to succeed. It would therefore look as if the early death of our civilization were inevitable.

Of course we know that it is perfectly possible for individual men, very highly educated men, philosophers, scientists, intellectuals in general, to live moral lives without any religious convictions. But the question is whether a whole civilization, a whole family of peoples, composed almost entirely of relatively uneducated men and women, can do this. It follows, of course, that if we could make the vast majority of men as highly educated as the very few are now, we might save the situation. And we are already moving slowly in that direction through the techniques of mass education. But the critical question seems to concern the time-lag. Perhaps in a hundred years most of the population will, at the present rate, be sufficiently highly educated and civilized to combine high ideals with an absence of religion. But long before we reach any such stage, the collapse of our civilization may have come about. How are we to live through the intervening period?

I am sure that the first thing we have to do is to face the truth, however bleak it may be, and then next we have to learn to live with it. Let me say a word about each of these two points. What I am urging as regards the first is complete honesty. Those who wish to resurrect Christian dogmas are not, of course, consciously dishonest. But they have that kind of unconscious dishonesty which consists in lulling oneself with opiates and dreams. Those who talk of a new religion are merely hoping for a new opiate. Both alike refuse to face the truth that there is, in the universe outside man, no spirituality, no regard for values, no friend in the sky, no help or comfort for man of any sort. To be perfectly honest in the admission of this fact, not to seek shelter in new or old illusions, not to indulge in wishful dreams about this matter, this is the first thing we shall have to do.

I do not urge this course out of any special regard for the sanctity of truth in the abstract. It is not self-evident to me that truth is the supreme value to which all else must be sacrificed. Might not the discoverer of a truth which would be fatal to mankind be justified in suppressing it, even in teaching men a falsehood? Is truth more valuable than goodness and beauty and happiness? To think so is to invent yet another absolute, another religious delusion in which Truth with a capital T is substituted for God. The reason why we must now boldly and honestly face the truth that the universe is non-spiritual and indifferent to goodness, beauty, happiness, or truth is not that it would be wicked to suppress it, but simply that it is too late to do so, so that in the end we cannot do anything else but face it. Yet we stand on the brink, dreading the icy plunge. We need courage. We need honesty.

Now about the other point, the necessity of learning to live with the truth. This means learning to live virtuously and happily, or at least contentedly, without illusions. And this is going to be extremely difficult because what we have now begun dimly to perceive is that human life in the past, or at least human happiness, has almost wholly depended upon illusions. It has been said that man lives by truth, and that the truth will make us free. Nearly the opposite seems to me to be the case. Mankind has managed to live only by means of lies, and the truth may very well destroy us. If one were a Bergsonian one might believe that nature deliberately puts illusions into our souls in order to induce us to go on living.

The illusions by which men have lived seem to be of two kinds. First, there is what one may perhaps call the Great Illusion—I mean the religious illusion that the universe is moral and good, that it follows a wise and noble plan, that it is gradually generating some supreme value, that goodness is bound to triumph in it. Secondly, there is a whole host of minor illusions on which human happiness nourishes itself. How much of human happiness notoriously comes from the illusions of the lover about his beloved? Then again we work and strive because of the illusions connected with fame, glory, power, or money. Banners of all kinds, flags, emblems, insignia, ceremonials, and rituals are invariably symbols of some illusion or other. The British Empire, the connection between mother country and dominions, used to be partly kept going by illusions surrounding the notion of kingship. Or think of the vast amount of human happiness which is derived from the illusion of supposing that if some nonsense syllable, such as "sir" or "count" or "lord" is pronounced in conjunction with our names, we belong to a superior order of people.

There is plenty of evidence that human happiness is almost wholly based upon illusions of one kind or another. But the scientific spirit, or the spirit of truth, is the enemy of illusions and therefore the enemy of human happiness. That is why it is going to be so difficult to live with the truth. There is no reason why we should have to give up the host of minor illusions which render life supportable. There is no reason why the lover should be scientific about the loved one. Even the illusions of fame and glory may persist. But without the Great Illusion, the illusion of a good, kindly, and purposeful universe, we shall *have* to learn to live. And to ask this is really no more than to ask that we become genuinely civilized beings and not merely sham civilized beings.

I can best explain the difference by a reminiscence. I remember a fellow student in my college days, an ardent Christian, who told me that if he did not believe in a future life, in heaven and hell, he would rape, murder, steal, and be a drunkard. That is what I call being a sham civilized being. On the other hand, not only could a Huxley, a John Stuart Mill, a David Hume, live great and fine lives without any religion, but a great many others of us, quite obscure persons, can at least live decent lives without it. To be genuinely civilized means to be able to walk straightly and to live honorably without the props and crutches of one or another of the childish dreams which have so far supported men. That such a life is likely to be ecstatically happy I will not claim. But that it can be lived in quiet content, accepting resignedly what cannot be helped, not expecting the impossible, and being thankful for small mercies, this I would maintain. That it will be difficult for men in general to learn this lesson I do not deny. But that it will be impossible I would not admit since so many have learned it already.

Man has not yet grown up. He is not adult. Like a child he cries for the moon and lives in a world of fantasies. And the race as a whole has perhaps reached the great crisis of its life. Can it grow up as a race in the same sense as individual men grow up? Can man put away childish things and adolescent dreams? Can he grasp the real world as it actually is, stark and bleak, without its romantic or religious halo, and still retain his ideals, striving for great ends and noble achievements? If he can, all may yet be well. If he cannot, he will probably sink back into the savagery and brutality from which he came, taking a humble place once more among the lower animals. —Bullshit!

3. A Humanist Manifesto

One way of illustrating some of the changes in Western thinking about religion during the last few decades is to note the rise of a movement variously known as scientific/naturalistic/evolutionary Humanism. (The three adjectives distinguish this kind of humanism from Renaissance humanism, which was mainly devoted to the study of Greek and Latin literature and culture.) The next three readings show some of the concerns of Humanists. The "Humanist Manifesto," first published in 1933, was signed by several clergymen, educators, and progressive intellectuals. Since it so systematically lists the beliefs of its signers, it can be conveniently used to inventory your own beliefs, thereby indicating how close or how distant you are from many Humanists. In any case, it sounds out many themes that will be evident in the materials of the next four sections of this book—new attitudes about the universe, man's nature and destiny, supernatural forces or the absence thereof, the breakdown of the sacred/profane dichotomy, the importance of human individual personality, the emphasis upon this earthly life and human well-being, and the reliance upon man's own intellectual powers. In each of the fifteen "affirmations," what traditional ideas are being rejected?

From *The Philosophy of Humanism* by Corliss Lamont, 5th ed., rev. and enlarged; (New York: Frederick Ungar Publishing Company, 1949, 1957, 1965, 1969, fourth printing), pp. 285–89. First published in *The New Humanist*, Vol. VI, No. 3, 1933.

Are there any of these affirmations that seem to you to be inadequately based or dangerous in their implications? Which ones, if any?

The time has come for widespread recognition of the radical changes in religious beliefs through the modern world. The time is past for mere revision of traditional attitudes. Science and economic change have disrupted the old beliefs. Religions the world over are under the necessity of coming to terms with new conditions created by a vastly increased knowledge and experience. In every field of human activity, the vital movement is now in the direction of a candid and explicit humanism. In order that religious humanism may be better understood we, the undersigned, desire to make certain affirmations which we believe the facts of our contemporary life demonstrate.

There is great danger of a final, and we believe fatal, identification of the word *religion* with doctrines and methods which have lost their significance and which are powerless to solve the problem of human living in the Twentieth Century. Religions have always been means for realizing the highest values of life. Their end has been accomplished through the interpretation of the total environing situation (theology or world view), the sense of values resulting therefrom (goal or ideal), and the technique (cult), established for realizing the satisfactory life. A change in any of these factors results in alteration of the outward forms of religion. This fact explains the changefulness of religions through the centuries. But through all changes religion itself remains constant in its quest for abiding values, an inseparable feature of human life.

Today man's larger understanding of the universe, his scientific achievements, and his deeper appreciation of brotherhood, have created a situation which requires a new statement of the means and purposes of religion. Such a vital, fearless, and frank religion capable of furnishing adequate social goals and personal satisfactions may appear to many people as a complete break with the past. While this age does owe a vast debt to the traditional religions, it is none the less obvious that any religion that can hope to be a synthesizing and dynamic force for today must be shaped for the needs of this age. To establish such a religion is a major necessity of the present. It is a responsibility which rests upon this generation. We therefore affirm the following:

First: Religious humanists regard the universe as self-existing and not created.

Second: Humanism believes that man is a part of nature and that he has emerged as the result of a continuous process.

Third: Holding an organic view of life, humanists find that the traditional dualism of mind and body must be rejected.

Fourth: Humanism recognizes that man's religious culture and civilization, as clearly depicted by anthropology and history, are the product of a gradual development due to his interaction with his natural environment and with his social heritage. The individual born into a particular culture is largely molded by that culture.

Fifth: Humanism asserts that the nature of the universe depicted by modern science makes unacceptable any supernatural or cosmic guarantees of human values. Obviously humanism does not deny the possibility of realities as yet undiscovered, but it does insist that the way to determine the existence and value of any and all realities is by means of intelligent inquiry and by the assessment of their relations to human needs. Religion must formulate its hopes and plans in the light of the scientific spirit and method.

Sixth: We are convinced that the time has passed for theism, deism, modernism, and the several varieties of "new thought."

Seventh: Religion consists of those actions, purposes, and experiences which are humanly significant. Nothing human is alien to the religious. It includes labor, art, science, philosophy, love, friendship, recreation—all that is in its degree expressive of intelligently satisfying human living. The distinction between the sacred and the secular can no longer be maintained.

Eighth: Religious Humanism considers the complete realization of human personality to be the end of man's life and seeks its development and fulfillment in the here and now. This is the explanation of the humanist's social passion.

Ninth: In the place of the old attitudes involved in worship and prayer the humanist finds his religious emotions expressed in a heightened sense of personal life and in a co-operative effort to promote social well-being.

Tenth: It follows that there will be no uniquely religious emotions and attitudes of the kind hitherto associated with belief in the supernatural.

Eleventh: Man will learn to face the crises of life in terms of his knowledge of their naturalness and probability. Reasonable and manly attitudes will be fostered by education and supported by custom. We assume that humanism will take the path of social and mental hygiene and discourage sentimental and unreal hopes and wishful thinking.

Twelfth: Believing that religion must work increasingly for joy in living, religious humanists aim to foster the creative in man and to encourage achievements that add to the satisfactions of life.

Thirteenth: Religious humanism maintains that all associations and institutions exist for the fulfillment of human life. The intelligent evaluation, transformation, control, and direction of such associations and institutions with a view to the enhancement of human life is the purpose and program of humanism. Certainly religious institutions, their ritualistic forms, ecclesiastical methods, and communal activities must be reconstituted as rapidly as experience allows, in order to function effectively in the modern world.

Fourteenth: The humanists are firmly convinced that existing acquisitive and profit-motivated society has shown itself to be inadequate and that a radical change in methods, controls, and motives must be instituted. A socialized and co-operative economic order must be established to the end that the equitable distribution of the means of life be possible. The goal of humanism is a free and universal society in which people voluntarily and intelligently co-operate for the common good. Humanists demand a shared life in a shared world.

Fifteenth and last: We assert that humanism will: (a) affirm life rather than deny it; (b) seek to elicit the possibilities of life, not flee from it; and (c) endeavor to establish the conditions of a satisfactory life for all, not merely for a few. By this positive *morale* and intention humanism will be guided, and from this perspective and alignment the techniques and efforts of humanism will flow.

So stand the theses of religious humanism. Though we consider the religious forms and ideas of our fathers no longer adequate, the quest for the good life is still the central task for mankind. Man is at last becoming aware that he alone is responsible for the realization of the world of his dreams, that he has within himself the power for its achievement. He must set intelligence and will to the task.

(Signed) J. A. C. Fagginger Auer, E. Burdette Backus, Harry Elmer Barnes, L. M. Birkhead, Raymond B. Bragg, Edwin Arthur Burtt, Ernest Caldecott, A. J. Carlson, John Dewey, Albert C. Dieffenbach, John H. Dietrich, Bernard Fantus, William Floyd, F. H. Hankins, A. Eustace Haydon, Llewellyn Jones, Robert Morss Lovett, Harold P. Marley, R. Lester Mondale, Charles Francis Potter, John Herman Randall, Jr., Curtis W. Reese, Oliver L. Reiser, Roy Wood Sellars, Clinton Lee Scott, Maynard Shipley, W. Frank Swift, V. T. Thayer, Eldred C. Vanderlaan, Joseph Walker, Jacob J. Weinstein, Frank S. C. Wicks, David Rhys Williams, Edwin H. Wilson.*

4. Evolution and Transhumanism, *J. Huxley*

Sometimes one gains insight into the future by inquiring into the pattern of the past. It is on this foundation that the famous biologist, philosopher, and humanist (Sir) Julian S. Huxley (b. 1887) constructs his vision of the future. He is convinced that

---

From Julian Huxley, "Transhumanism," in *New Bottles for New Wine: Essays by Julian Huxley* (London: Chatto & Windus Ltd., 1959), pp. 13–17. Reprinted by permission of A. D. Peters & Company.

* Note: *The Manifesto is a product of many minds. It was designed to represent a developing point of view, not a new creed. The individuals whose signatures appear, would, had they been writing individual statements, have stated the propositions in differing terms. The importance of the document is that more than thirty men have come to general agreement on matters of final concern and that these men are undoubtedly representative of a large number who are forging a new philosophy out of the materials of the modern world. It is obvious that many others might have been asked to sign the Manifesto had not the lack of time and the shortage of clerical assistance limited our ability to communicate with them.*

there have been two critical points in the evolution of life, and that we are presently on the threshold of a third phase of evolution. The first occurred when inorganic matter evolved into organic matter (the biological phase); the second, when biological life evolved into psychosocial life (human life); and the third, which is taking place now, occurs as we pass from the psychosocial to the consciously purposive phase of evolution. He believes that we will not pass safely into this third phase unless we bring into being a comprehensive system of ideas which draw from man's various areas of knowledge. To do this is man's "cosmic office," and the thought of doing it excites him greatly: "A vast New World of uncharted possibilities awaits its Columbus." We are using this essay to suggest something characteristic of the "modern" world generally, something that is seen in different ways in the four following chapters: namely, man's exuberant sense that the future is open and in his hands to control if he will but develop his potentialities. Now begins the new age when we will construct "true human destiny." Why does Huxley call this "Transhumanism"? Do you find his optimism securely based? What implications does Huxley's thesis have for man's physical, social, and "spiritual" life? Do you agree that if man is able to do what Huxley proposes, we will in fact be fulfilling our "real destiny"?

TRANSHUMANISM

As a result of a thousand million years of evolution, the universe is becoming conscious of itself, able to understand something of its past history and its possible future. This cosmic self-awareness is being realized in one tiny fragment of the universe—in a few of us human beings. Perhaps it has been realized elsewhere too, through the evolution of conscious living creatures on the planets of other stars. But on this our planet, it has never happened before.

Evolution on this planet is a history of the realization of ever new possibilities by the stuff of which earth (and the rest of the universe) is made—life; strength, speed and awareness; the flight of birds and the social polities of bees and ants; the emergence of mind, long before man was ever dreamt of, with the production of colour, beauty, communication, maternal care, and the beginnings of intelligence and insight. And finally, during the last few ticks of the cosmic clock, something wholly new and revolutionary, human beings with their capacities for conceptual thought and language, for self-conscious awareness and purpose, for accumulating and pooling conscious experience. For do not let us forget that the human species is as radically different from any of the microscopic single-celled animals that lived a thousand million years ago as they were from a fragment of stone or metal.

The new understanding of the universe has come about through the new knowledge amassed in the last hundred years—by psychologists, biologists, and other scientists, by archaeologists, anthropologists, and historians. It has defined man's responsibility and destiny—to be an agent for the rest of the world in the job of realizing its inherent potentialities as fully as possible.

It is as if man had been suddenly appointed managing director of the biggest business of all, the business of evolution—appointed without being asked if he wanted it, and without proper warning and preparation. What is more, he can't refuse the job. Whether he wants to or not, whether he is conscious of what he is doing or not, he *is* in point of fact determining the future direction of evolution on this earth. That is his inescapable destiny, and the sooner he realizes it and starts believing in it, the better for all concerned.

What the job really boils down to is this—the fullest realization of man's possibilities, whether by the individual, by the community, or by the species in its processional adventure along the corridors of time. Every man-jack of us begins as a mere speck of potentiality, a spherical and miscroscopic egg-cell. During the nine months before birth, this automatically unfolds into a truly miraculous range of organization: after birth, in addition to continuing automatic growth and development, the individual begins to realize his mental possibilities—by building up a personality, by developing special talents, by acquiring knowledge and skills of various kinds, by playing his part in keeping society going. This post-natal process is not an automatic or a predetermined one. It may proceed in very different ways according to circumstances and according to the individual's own efforts. The degree to which capacities are realized can be more or less complete. The end-result can be satisfactory or very much the reverse: in particular, the personality may grievously fail in attaining any real wholeness. One thing is certain, that the well-developed, well-integrated personality is the highest product of evolution, the fullest realization we know of in the universe.

The first thing that the human species has to do to prepare itself for the cosmic office to which it finds itself appointed is to explore human nature, to find out what are the possibilities open to it (including, of course, its limitations, whether inherent or imposed by the facts of external nature). We have pretty well finished the geographical exploration of the earth; we have pushed the scientific exploration of nature, both lifeless and living, to a point at which its main outlines have become clear; but the exploration of human nature and its possibilities has scarcely begun. A vast New World of uncharted possibilities awaits its Columbus.

The great men of the past have given us glimpses of what is possible in the way of personality, of intellectual understanding, of spiritual achievement, of artistic creation. But these are scarcely more than Pisgah glimpses. We need to explore and map the whole realm of human possibility, as the realm of physical geography has been explored and mapped. How to create new possibilities for ordinary living? What can be done to bring out the latent capacities of the ordinary man and woman for understanding and enjoyment; to teach people the techniques of achieving spiritual experience (after all, one can acquire the technique of dancing or tennis, so why not of mystical ecstasy or spiritual peace?); to develop native talent and intelligence in the growing child, instead of frustrating or distroying them? Already we know that painting and thinking, music and mathematics, acting and science can come to mean something very real to quite ordinary average boys and girls—provided only that the right methods are adopted for bringing out the children's possibilities. We are beginning to realize that even the most fortunate people are living far below capacity, and that most human beings develop not more than a small fraction of their potential mental and spiritual efficiency. The human race, in fact, is surrounded by a large area of unrealized possibilities, a challenge to the spirit of exploration.

The scientific and technical explorations have given the Common Man all over the world a notion of physical possibilities. Thanks to science, the under-privileged are coming to believe that no one need be underfed or chronically diseased, or deprived of the benefits of its technical and practical applications.

The world's unrest is largely due to this new belief. People are determined not to put up with a subnormal standard of physical health and material living now that science has revealed the possibility of raising it. The unrest will produce some unpleasant consequences before it is dissipated; but it is in essence a beneficent unrest, a dynamic force which will not be stilled until it has laid the physiological foundations of human destiny.

Once we have explored the possibilities open to consciousness and personality, and the knowledge of them has become common property, a new source of unrest will have emerged. People will realize and believe that if proper measures are taken, no one need be starved of true satisfaction, or condemned to sub-standard fulfilment. This process too will begin by being unpleasant, and end by being beneficent. It will begin by destroying the ideas and the institutions that stand in the way of our realizing our possibilities (or even deny that the possibilities are there to be realized), and will go on by at least making a start with the actual construction of true human destiny.

Up till now human life has generally been, as Hobbes described it, "nasty, brutish and short"; the great majority of human beings (if they have not already died young) have been afflicted with misery in one form or another—poverty, disease, ill-health, over-work, cruelty, or oppression. They have attempted to lighten their misery by means of their hopes and their ideals. The trouble has been that the hopes have generally been unjustified, the ideals have generally failed to correspond with reality.

The zestful but scientific exploration of possibilities and of the techniques for realizing them will make our hopes rational, and will set our ideals within the framework of reality, by showing how much of them are indeed realizable.

Already, we can justifiably hold the belief that these lands of possibility exist, and that the present limitations and miserable frustrations of our existence could be in large measure surmounted. We are already justified in the conviction that human life as we know it in history is a wretched makeshift, rooted in ignorance; and that it could be transcended by a state of existence based on the illumination of knowledge and comprehension, just as our modern control of physical nature based on science transcends the tentative fumblings of our ancestors, that were rooted in superstition and professional secrecy.

To do this, we must study the possibilities of creating a more favourable social environment, as we have already done in large measure with our physical environment. We shall start from new premisses. For instance, that beauty (something to enjoy and something to be proud of) is indispensable, and therefore that ugly or depressing towns are immoral; that quality of people, not mere quantity, is what we must aim at, and therefore that a concerted policy is required to prevent the present flood of population-increase from wrecking all our hopes for a better world; that true understanding and enjoyment are ends in themselves, as well as tools for or relaxations from a job, and that therefore we must explore and make fully available the techniques of education and self-education; that the most ultimate satisfaction comes from a depth and wholeness of the inner life, and therefore that we must explore and make fully available the techniques of spiritual development; above all, that there are two complementary parts of our cosmic duty—one to ourselves, to be fulfilled in the realization and enjoyment of our capacities, the other to others, to be fulfilled in service to the community and in promoting the welfare of the generations to come and the advancement of our species as a whole.

The human species can, if it wishes, transcend itself—not just sporadically, an individual here in one way, an individual there in another way, but in its entirety, as humanity. We need a name for this new belief. Perhaps *transhumanism* will serve: man remaining man, but transcending himself, by realizing new possibilities of and for his human nature.

"I believe in transhumanism": once there are enough people who can truly say that, the human species will be on the threshold of a new kind of existence, as different from ours as ours is from that of Pekin man. It will at last be consciously fulfilling its real destiny.

5. Ethics without Religion, K. Nielsen

One of the pervasive questions that is being asked as traditional views weaken is the question, "What will happen to morality?" For as we have seen in all of the preceding four units of this book, but especially in the units on cosmic law and myth/ritual, these traditional religious ways did provide guidelines for one's conception of his obligations. What will happen to one's sense of duty when he lacks all sense of the divine? Is there a problem here? Kai Nielsen, Professor of Philosophy at New York University, believes there is none. Earlier in this same article, but prior to our excerpt from it, Nielsen sets himself against the view, once propounded by Blaise Pascal (1623–1662) that "no purely human purposes are ultimately worth striving for." By contrast, Nielsen's concern is to show that "we do not need God or any religious conception to support our moral convictions." His first sentence (as excerpted) sounds out his main thesis, and is illustrative of the mind-set of many of our contemporaries. Do you find Nielsen's appeal to "happiness" deficient in any respects? (You might list his "relatively permanent sources of human happiness" and see what is important to you that he has omitted.) How does the "secularist" deal with the problem of suffering? Note his appeal to and belief in the claims of existentialists.

. . . I do not see why purposes of purely human devising are not ultimately worth striving for. There is much that we humans prize and would continue to prize even in a Godless world. Many things would remain to give our lives meaning and point even after "the death of God."*

Take a simple example. All of us *want* to be happy. But in certain bitter or sceptical moods we question what happiness is or we despairingly ask ourselves whether anyone can really be happy. Is this, however, a sober, sane view of the situation? I do not think that it is. Indeed we cannot adequately define "happiness" in the way that we can "bachelor," but neither can we in that way define "chair," "wind," "pain," and the vast majority of words in everyday discourse. For words like "bachelor," "triangle," or "father" we can specify a consistent set of properties that all

---

From "Ethics without Religion" by Kai Nielsen, found in *The Ohio University Review,* Vol. VI (1964), pp. 50–53, 55–56. Reprinted by permission of *The Ohio University Review,* Ohio University, Athens, Ohio.

* This is a term with various and disputed uses. Normally, it expresses the conviction of some contemporary Protestant theologians that contemporary Christians must learn how to live their faith without relying on special help from Someone who acts outside the framework of everyday life.

the things and only the things denoted by these words have, but we cannot do this for "happiness," "chair," "pain," and the like. In fact, we cannot do it for the great majority of our words. Yet there is no great loss here. Modern philosophical analysis has taught us that such an essentially Platonic conception of definition is unrealistic and unnecessary.[1] I may not be able to define "chair" in the way that I can define "bachelor," but I understand the meaning of "chair" perfectly well. In normal circumstances, at least, I know what to sit on when someone tells me to take a chair. I may not be able to define "pain," but I know what it is like to be in pain, and sometimes I can know when others are in pain. Similarly, though I cannot define "happiness" in the same way that I can define "bachelor," I know what it is like to be happy, and I sometimes can judge with considerable reliability whether others are happy or sad. "Happiness" is a slippery word, but it is not so slippery that we are justified in saying that nobody knows what happiness is.

A man could be said to have lived a happy life if he had found lasting sources of satisfaction in his life and if he had been able to find certain goals worthwhile and to achieve at least some of them. He could indeed have suffered some pain and anxiety, but his life must, for the most part, have been free from pain, estrangement, and despair, and must, on balance, have been a life which he has liked and found worthwhile. But surely we have no good grounds for saying that no one achieves such a balance or that no one is ever happy even for a time. We all have some idea of what would make us happy and of what would make us unhappy; many people, at least, can remain happy even after "the death of God." At any rate, we need not strike Pascalian attitudes, for even in a purely secular world there are permanent sources of human happiness for anyone to avail himself of.

What are they? What are these relatively permanent sources of human happiness that we all want or need? What is it which, if we have it, will give us the basis for a life that could properly be said to be happy? We all desire to be free from pain and want. Even masochists do not seek pain for its own sake; they endure pain because this is the only psychologically acceptable way of achieving something else (usually sexual satisfaction) that is so gratifying to them that they will put up with the pain to achieve it. We all want a life in which sometimes we can enjoy ourselves and in which we can attain our fair share of some of the simple pleasures that we all desire. They are not everything in life, but they are important, and our lives would be impoverished without them.

We also need security and emotional peace. We need and want a life in which we will not be constantly threatened with physical or emotional harassment. Again this is not the only thing worth seeking, but it is an essential ingredient in any adequate picture of the good life.

Human love and companionship are also central to a significant or happy life. We prize them, and a life which is without them is most surely an impoverished life, a life that no man, if he would take the matter to heart, would desire. But I would most emphatically assert that human love and companionship are quite possible in a Godless world, and the fact that life will some day inexorably come to an end and cut off love and companionship altogether enhances rather than diminishes their present value.

Furthermore, we all need some sort of creative employment or meaningful work to give our lives point, to save them from boredom, drudgery, and futility. A man who can find no way to use the talents he has or a man who can find no work which is meaningful to him will indeed be a miserable man. But again there is work—whether it be as a surgeon, a farmer, or a fisherman—that has a rationale even in a world without God. And poetry, music, and art retain their beauty and enrich our lives even in the complete absence of God or the gods.

We want and need art, music, and the dance. We find pleasure in travel and conversation and in a rich variety of experiences. The sources of human enjoyment are obviously too numerous to detail. But all of them are achievable in a Godless universe. If some can be ours, we can attain a reasonable measure of happiness. Only a Steppenwolfish personality* beguiled by impossible expectations and warped by irrational guilts and fears can fail to find happiness in the realization of such ends. But to be free of impossible expectations people must clearly recognize that there is no "one big thing" or, for that matter, "small thing" which would make them permanently happy; almost anything permanently and exclusively pursued will lead to that nausea that Sartre has so forcefully brought to our attention. But we can, if we are not too sick and if our situation is not too precarious, find lasting sources of human happiness in a purely secular world.

It is not only happiness for ourselves that can give us something of value, but there is the need to do what we can to diminish the awful sum of human misery in the world. I have never understood those who say that they find contemporary life meaningless because they find nothing worthy of devoting their energies to. Throughout the world there is an immense amount of human suffering, suffering that can, through a variety of human efforts, be partially alleviated. Why can we not find a meaningful life in devoting ourselves, as did Doctor Rieux in Albert Camus's *The Plague,* to relieving somewhat the sum total of human suffering? Why cannot this give our lives point, and for that matter an overall rationale? It is childish to think that by human effort we will someday totally rid the world of suffering and hate, of deprivation and sadness. This is a permanent part of the human condition. But specific bits of human suffering can be alleviated. The plague is always potentially with us, but we can destroy the Nazis and we can fight for racial and social equality throughout the world. And as isolated people, as individuals in a mass society, we find people turning to us in dire need, in suffering and in emotional deprivation, and we can as individuals respond to those people and alleviate or at least acknowledge

---

* Refers to the hero of the novel *Steppenwolf* by the German author Hermann Hesse.

that suffering and deprivation. A man who says, "If God is dead, nothing matters," is a spoilt child who has never looked at his fellow men with compassion.

Yet, it might be objected, if we abandon a Judaeo-Christian *Weltanschauung*,* there can, in a secular world, be no "one big thing" to give our lives an overall rationale. We will not be able to see written in the stars the final significance of human effort. There will be no architectonic purpose to give our lives such a rationale. Like Tolstoy's Pierre in *War and Peace,* we desire *somehow* to gather the sorry scheme of things entire into one intelligible explanation so that we can finally crack the riddle of human destiny. We long to understand why it is that men suffer and die. If it is a factual answer that is wanted when such a question is asked, it is plain enough. Ask any physician. But clearly this is not what people who seek such answers are after. They want some *justification* for suffering; they want some way of showing that suffering is after all for a good purpose. It can, of course, be argued that suffering sometimes is a good thing, for it occasionally gives us insight and at times even brings about in the man who suffers a capacity to love and to be kind. But there is plainly an excessive amount of human suffering—the suffering of children in childrens' hospitals, the suffering of people devoured by cancer, and the sufferings of millions of Jews under the Nazis—for which there simply is no justification. Neither the religious man nor the secularist can explain, that is justify, such suffering and find some overall "scheme of life" in which it has some place, but only the religious man needs to do so. The secularist understands that suffering is not something to be justified but simply to be struggled against with courage and dignity. And in this fight, even the man who has been deprived of that which could give him some measure of happiness can still find or make for himself a meaningful human existence. . . .

I cannot prove that happiness is good, but Christian and non-Christian alike take it in practice to be a very fundamental good. I can, in sum, only appeal to your sense of psychological realism to get you to admit intellectually what in practice you *do* acknowledge, namely, that happiness is good and that pointless suffering is bad. If you *will* acknowledge this, I can show, as I have, that man can attain happiness even in a world without God.

Suppose some Dostoyevskian "underground man" does not care a fig about happiness. Suppose he does not even care about the sufferings of others. How then can you show him to be wrong? But suppose a man doesn't care about God or about doing what He commands either. How can you show that such an indifference to God is wrong? If we ask such abstract questions, we can see a crucial feature about the nature of morality. Sometimes a moral agent may reach a point at which he can give no further justification for his claims but must simply, by his own deliberate decision, resolve to take a certain position. Here the claims of the existen-

---

* World-view.

tialists have a genuine relevance. We come to recognize that nothing can in the last analysis take the place of a decision or resolution. In the end we must simply decide. This recognition may arouse our anxieties and stimulate rationalization, but the necessity of making a decision is inherent in the logic of the situation.

NOTES

1. This is convincingly argued in Michael Scriven's essay "Definitions, Explanations, and Theories," in *Minnesota Studies in the Philosophy of Science,* III, ed. Herbert Feigl, Michael Scriven, and Grover Maxwell (Minneapolis, 1958), pp. 99–195.

6. The Lost Dimension in Religion, P. Tillich

The author of the following excerpt, Paul Tillich (1886–1965), is widely regarded as one of the most distinguished Western philosophers of religion in the twentieth century. He here calls our attention to the loss of the "dimension of depth," which he feels is the key to our understanding not only of the predicament of Western man in these times, but of man generally. What does he mean by the metaphor "dimension of depth"? How does he define "religion"? How does his own definition differ from the more usual, "narrow" definition? Does his phrase "ultimate concern" help you to locate the focus of your own life and personality? What does he mean by "the horizontal dimension" in life? What does he suggest as a way of recovering depth? Among whom does he find the most profound asking of "the religious question"? In what way, if any, is Tillich's understanding of religion different from those found in the other selections in the Transition Section?

Every observer of our Western civilization is aware of the fact that something has happened to religion. It especially strikes the observer of the American scene. Everywhere he finds symptoms of what one has called

From "The Lost Dimension in Religion" by Paul Tillich. Reprinted with permission from *The Saturday Evening Post* © 1958, The Curtis Publishing Company. Pp. 29, 76.

religious revival, or more modestly, the revival of interest in religion. He finds them in the churches with their rapidly increasing membership. He finds them in the mushroomlike growth of sects. He finds them on college campuses and in the theological faculties of universities. Most conspicuously, he finds them in the tremendous success of men like Billy Graham and Norman Vincent Peale, who attract masses of people Sunday after Sunday, meeting after meeting. The facts cannot be denied, but how should they be interpreted? It is my intention to show that these facts must be seen as expressions of the predicament of Western man in the second half of the twentieth century. But I would even go a step further. I believe that the predicament of man in our period gives us also an important insight into the predicament of man generally—at all times and in all parts of the earth.

There are many analyses of man and society in our time. Most of them show important traits in the picture, but few of them succeed in giving a general key to our present situation. Although it is not easy to find such a key, I shall attempt it and, in so doing, will make an assertion which may be somewhat mystifying at first hearing. The decisive element in the predicament of Western man in our period is his loss of the dimension of depth. Of course, "dimension of depth" is a metaphor. It is taken from the spatial realm and applied to man's spiritual life. What does it mean?

It means that man has lost an answer to the question: What is the meaning of life? Where do we come from, where do we go to? What shall we do, what should we become in the short stretch between birth and death? Such questions are not answered or even asked if the "dimension of depth" is lost. And this is precisely what has happened to man in our period of history. He has lost the courage to ask such questions with an infinite seriousness—as former generations did—and he has lost the courage to receive answers to these question, wherever they may come from.

I suggest that we call the dimension of depth the religious dimension in man's nature. Being religious means asking passionately the question of the meaning of our existence and being willing to receive answers, even if the answers hurt. Such an idea of religion makes religion universally human, but it certainly differs from what is usually called religion. It does not describe religion as the belief in the existence of gods or one God, and as a set of activities and institutions for the sake of relating oneself to these beings in thought, devotion and obedience. No one can deny that the religions which have appeared in history are religions in this sense. Nevertheless, religion in its innermost nature is more than religion in this narrower sense. It is the state of being concerned about one's own being and being universally.

There are many people who are ultimately concerned in this way who feel far removed, however, from religion in the narrower sense, and therefore from every historical religion. It often happens that such people take the question of the meaning of their life infinitely seriously and reject any historical religion just for this reason. They feel that the concrete religions

fail to express their profound concern adequately. They ar'
rejecting the religions. It is this experience which forces
the meaning of religion as living in the dimension of dep'
expressions of one's ultimate concern in the symbols and institc
concrete religion. If we now turn to the concrete analysis of the religic
situation of our time, it is obvious that our key must be the basic meaning
of religion and not any particular religion, not even Christianity. What
does this key disclose about the predicament of man in our period?

If we define religion as the state of being grasped by an infinite concern
we must say: Man in our time has lost such infinite concern. And the
resurgence of religion is nothing but a desperate and mostly futile attempt to
regain what has been lost.

How did the dimension of depth become lost? Like any important
event, it has many causes, but certainly not the one which one hears often
mentioned from ministers' pulpits and evangelists' platforms, namely that
a widespread impiety of modern man is responsible. Modern man is neither
more pious nor more impious than man in any other period. The loss of
the dimension of depth is caused by the relation of man to his world
and to himself in our period, the period in which nature is being subjected
scientifically and technically to the control of man. In this period, life in
the dimension of depth is replaced by life in the horizontal dimension. The
driving forces of the industrial society of which we are a part go ahead
horizontally and not vertically. In popular terms this is expressed in phrases
like "better and better," "bigger and bigger," "more and more." One
should not disparage the feeling which lies behind such speech. Man is
right in feeling that he is able to know and transform the world he encounters without a foreseeable limit. He can go ahead in all directions
without a definite boundary.

A most expressive symbol of this attitude of going ahead in the horizontal
dimension is the breaking through of the space which is controlled by the
gravitational power of the earth into the world-space. It is interesting that
one calls this world-space simply "space" and speaks, for instance, of space
travel, as if every trip were not travel into space. Perhaps one feels that the
true nature of space has been discovered only through our entering into
indefinite world-space. In any case, the predominance of the horizontal
dimension of depth has been immensely increased by the opening up of
the space beyond the space of the earth.

If we now ask what does man do and seek if he goes ahead in the
horizontal dimension, the answer is difficult. Sometimes one is inclined to
say that the mere movement ahead without an end, the intoxication with
speeding forward without limits, is what satisfies him. But this answer is
by no means sufficient. For on his way into space and time man changes
the world he encounters. And the changes made by him change himself. He
transforms everything he encounters into a tool; and in doing so he himself
becomes a tool. But if he asks, a tool for what, there is no answer.

One does not need to look far beyond everyone's daily experience in
order to find examples to describe this predicament. Indeed our daily life

in office and home, in cars and airplanes, at parties and conferences, while reading magazines and watching television, while looking at advertisements and hearing radio, are in themselves continuous examples of a life which has lost the dimension of depth. It runs ahead, every moment is filled with something which must be done or seen or said or planned. But no one can experience depth without stopping and becoming aware of himself. Only if he has moments in which he does not care about what comes next can he experience the meaning of this moment here and now and ask himself about the meaning of his life. As long as the preliminary, transitory concerns are not silenced, no matter how interesting and valuable and important they may be, the voice of the ultimate concern cannot be heard. This is the deepest root of the loss of the dimension of depth in our period —the loss of religion in its basic and universal meaning. . . .

. . . We have become aware of the degree to which everyone in our social structure is managed, even if one knows it and even if one belongs himself to the managing group. The influence of the gang mentality on adolescents, of the corporation's demands on the executives, of the conditioning of everyone by public communication, by propaganda and advertising under the guidance of motivation research, et cetera, have all been described in many books and articles.

Under these pressures, man can hardly escape the fate of becoming a thing among the things he produces, a bundle of conditioned reflexes without a free, deciding and responsible self. The immense mechanism, set up by man to produce objects for his use, transforms man himself into an object used by the same mechanism of production and consumption.

But man has not ceased to be man. He resists this fate anxiously, desperately, courageously. He asks the question, for what? And he realizes that there is no answer. He becomes aware of the emptiness which is covered by the continuous movement ahead and the production of means for ends which become means again without an ultimate end. Without knowing what has happened to him, he feels that he has lost the meaning of life, the dimension of depth.

Out of this awareness the religious question arises and religious answers are received or rejected. Therefore, in order to describe the contemporary attitude toward religion, we must first point to the places where the awareness of the predicament of Western man in our period is most sharply expressed. These places are the great art, literature and, partly at least, the philosophy of our time. It is both the subject matter and the style of these creations which show the passionate and often tragic struggle about the meaning of life in a period in which man has lost the dimension of depth. This art, literature, philosophy is not religious in the narrower sense of the word; but it asks the religious question more radically and more profoundly than most directly religious expressions of our time. . . .

V

Attaining an Integrated Self Through Creative Interaction

"Religion is a relationship to the highest or strongest value,
be it positive or negative. The relationship is voluntary as well as
involuntary, that is, you can accept, consciously, the value
by which you are possessed unconsciously. That psychological
fact which is the greatest power in your system is the god,
since it is always the overwhelming psychic factor which is called
god. As soon as a god ceases to be an overwhelming factor, he
becomes a mere name. His essence is dead and his power is gone.
Why have the antique gods lost their prestige and their effect
upon human souls? It was because the Olympic gods had served
their time and a new mystery began: God became man."
(C. G. Jung, Psychology and Religion [New Haven: Yale
University Press, 1938], p. 98.)

THE MATERIALS IN THE SECTION entitled "Transition" present a challenge to contemporary man to find ultimate joy and fulfillment without the help of a Transcendent Being. How is man to do this? The answer is that he will do it just the way he has always done it, but without the assumptions and models that have dominated human self-expression for the past nine or ten thousand years. This means that he will have to take some basic human enterprises that have formerly been associated with traditional religious beliefs and activities, and then develop their techniques and achieve the same measurable goals without reference to traditional religious forms. One such enterprise seen by a considerable number of people to function as "a means of ultimate transformation" (religion) is psychotherapy and related efforts of psychological integration. In pre-modern societies, medicine was closely tied to religious belief and practice. The word "psyche" itself comes from a Greek word meaning "soul" or "spirit"; thus, in its root meaning psycho-therapy could be translated "care of souls." However, at present the term "psychology" usually refers to the study of the development and conditioning of personality (as a result of its socio-biological environment); and psychotherapy is regarded as a branch of medicine which attempts to be completely disassociated (at least overtly) from theological or metaphysical assumptions. What was once seen as an activity in service of a transcendent goal is now a "means for salvation" intended to develop a fully-functioning personality.

In this chapter we include exponents of various psychological therapies, both one-to-one relationships (as in psychoanalysis) and group situations, attempting to avoid an identification with any single therapeutic method, for example, Freudian psychoanalysis, Jungian analysis, or Gestalt therapy. Many of the statements, however, are expressive of the more humanistic trends of recent psychology and psychiatry. By including them in this volume of readings we suggest that the claims made, and their interpretation of the human situation, should be studied in the context of their ultimate commitment to these techniques and perspectives. You may, as a result, reject these as *adequate* means of ultimate transformation—as do the critics at the end of the chapter. However, we believe that the psychotherapeutic effort, as a matter of fact, functions religiously for some people in terms of their own warrants and judgments. It is a process whereby the evils of alienation (from self and others), insincerity (facade), and depersonalization can be overcome, and such values as love (trust, understanding), integrity, and relatedness are affirmed and can be realized. Such a transformation is not only an ideal or a speculation (fantasy); rather it is seen to result from various personal and group techniques which have been successful in dispelling demonic "hang-ups" and nurturing a "new" person. Thus, as part of a new "humanist" attempt to deal at a fundamental level (ultimately) with basic human problems, the following selections are regarded as depicting another way of being religious.

ADVOCACY

1. Education in Approval,
A. S. Neill

*The author of this excerpt is the headmaster and founder of
a well-known experimental school in England known as
"Summerhill." He is a psychologist, and he believes it to be
the main purpose of psychology, and of the school, to cure the world
of unhappiness. In the education of children, his "radical approach"
(note the subtitle of the book from which this excerpt comes)
is to allow persons, in this case youth, to be free, to trust them
to be themselves. He sees this as a departure from past methods,
including those of the traditional church. Like the authors
of the previous items, Neill witnesses to the conviction that our
daily interpersonal relationships with other people determine our
identities. Evil arises from distorted personal relationships, while
virtue or goodness arises from sound relationships. Why, according
to Neill, do some children have difficulties? What understanding
does Neill have of innate human nature? What reason does
he give that many parents find it hard to love and approve of
their children? In what ways is Neill's proposal for a "new religion"
different from traditional religion as he describes it? Would you
like to have been sent to Summerhill as a child? Why, or why not?*

...In psychology, no man knows very much. The inner forces of human life are still largely hidden from us.

Since Freud's genius made it alive, psychology has gone far; but it is still a new science, mapping out the coast of an unknown continent. Fifty years hence, psychologists will very likely smile at our ignorance of today.

Since I left education and took up child psychology, I have had all sorts of children to deal with—incendiaries, thieves, liars, bed-wetters, and bad-tempered children. Years of intensive work in child training has convinced me that I know comparatively little of the forces that motivate life. I am convinced, however, that parents who have had to deal with only their own children know much less than I do.

It is because I believe that a difficult child is nearly always made difficult by wrong treatment at home that I dare address parents.

What is the province of psychology? I suggest the word *curing*. But what kind of curing? I do not want to be cured of my habit of choosing the colors orange and black; nor do I want to be cured of smoking; nor of my liking for a bottle of beer. No teacher has the right to cure a child

From *Summerhill: A Radical Approach to Child Rearing* by A. S. Neill, (New York: Hart Publishing Co., Inc., 1960), pp. xxiii–xxiv, 4, 117–19, 241–42. Used by permission of the publisher.

of making noises on a drum. The only curing that should be practiced is the curing of unhappiness.

The difficult child is the child who is unhappy. He is at war with himself; and in consequence, he is at war with the world.

The difficult adult is in the same boat. No happy man ever disturbed a meeting, or preached a war, or lynched a Negro. No happy woman ever nagged her husband or her children. No happy man ever committed a murder or a theft. No happy employer ever frightened his employees.

All crimes, all hatreds, all wars can be reduced to unhappiness. This book is an attempt to show how unhappiness arises, how it ruins human lives, and how children can be reared so that much of this unhappiness will never arise.

More than that, this book is the story of a place—Summerhill—where children's unhappiness is cured and, more important, where children are reared in happiness. . . .

Summerhill began as an experimental school. It is no longer such; it is now a demonstration school, for it demonstrates that freedom works.

When my first wife and I began the school, we had one main idea: *to make the school fit the child*—instead of making the child fit the school.

I had taught in ordinary schools for many years. I knew the other way well. I knew it was all wrong. It was wrong because it was based on an adult conception of what a child should be and of how a child should learn. The other way dated from the days when psychology was still an unknown science.

Well, we set out to make a school in which we should allow children freedom to be themselves. In order to do this, we had to renounce all discipline, all direction, all suggestion, all moral training, all religious instruction. We have been called brave, but it did not require courage. All it required was what we had—a complete belief in the child as a good, not an evil, being. For almost forty years, this belief in the goodness of the child has never wavered; it rather has become a final faith.

My view is that a child is innately wise and realistic. If left to himself without adult suggestion of any kind, he will develop as far as he is capable of developing. Logically, Summerhill is a place in which people who have the innate ability and wish to be scholars will be scholars; while those who are only fit to sweep the streets will sweep the streets. . . .

LOVE AND APPROVAL

The happiness and well-being of children depend on the degree of love and approval we give them. We must be on the child's side. Being on the side of the child is giving love to the child—not possessive love not sentimental love—just behaving to the child in such a way that the child feels you love him and approve of him.

It can be done. I know scores of parents who are on the side of their children, demanding nothing in return, and therefore getting a lot. They realize that children are not little adults.

When a son of ten writes home, "Dear Mommy, please send me fifty cents. Hope you are well. Love to Daddy," the parents smile, knowing that

that is what a child of ten writes if he is sincere and not afraid to express himself. The wrong type of parent sighs at such a letter, and thinks: *The selfish little beast, always asking for something.*

The right parents of my school never ask how their children are getting along; they see for themselves. The wrong type keep asking me impatient questions: *Can he read yet? When is he ever going to be tidy? Does she ever go to lessons?*

It is all a matter of faith in children. Some have it; most haven't it. And if you do not have this faith, the children feel it. They feel that your love cannot be very deep, or you would trust them more. When you approve of children you can talk to them about anything and everything, for approval makes many inhibitions fly away.

But the question arises, Is it possible to approve of children if you do not approve of yourself? If you are not aware of yourself, you cannot approve of yourself. In other words, the more conscious you are of yourself and your motives, the more likely you are to be an approver of yourself.

I express the earnest hope, then, that more knowledge of oneself and of child nature will help parents to keep their children free from neurosis. I repeat that parents are spoiling their children's lives by forcing on them outdated beliefs, outdated manners, outdated morals. They are sacrificing the child to the past. This is especially true of those parents who impose authoritative religion on their children just as it was once imposed on them.

I know well that the most difficult thing in the world is to renounce things we consider important, but it is only through renunciation that we find life, find progress, find happiness. Parents must renounce. They must renounce hate that is disguised as authority and criticism. They must renounce the intolerance that is the outcome of fear. They must renounce old morals and mob verdicts.

Or more simply, the parent must become an individual. He must know where he really stands. It is not easy. For a man is not just himself. He is a combination of everyone he has met, and he retains many of their values. Parents impose the authority of their own parents because every man has in him his own father, every woman her own mother. It is the imposing of this rigid authority that breeds hate, and with it, problem children. It is the opposite of giving the child approval.

Many a girl has said to me, "I can't do a thing to please Mommy. She can do everything better than I can, and she flies into a temper if I make a mistake in sewing or knitting."

Children do not need teaching as much as they need love and understanding. They need approval and freedom to be naturally good. It is the genuinely strong and loving parent who has the most power to give children freedom to be good.

The world is suffering from too much condemnation, which is really a fancier way of saying that the world is suffering from too much hate. It is the parents' hate that makes a child a problem, just as it is society's hate that makes the criminal a problem. Salvation lies in love, but what makes it difficult is that no one can *compel* love.

The parent of the problem child must sit down and ask himself or herself these questions: *Have I shown real approval of my child? Have I shown trust in him? Have I shown understanding?* I am not theorizing. I know that a problem child can come to my school and become a happy, normal child. I know that the chief ingredients in the curing process are the showing of approval, of trust, of understanding. . . .

RELIGION

A recent woman visitor said to me, "Why don't you teach your pupils about the life of Jesus, so that they will be inspired to follow in his steps?" I answered that one learns to live, not by *hearing* of other lives, but by *living;* for words are infinitely less important than acts. Many have called Summerhill a religious place because it gives out love to children.

That may be true; only I dislike the adjective as long as religion means what it generally means today—antagonism to natural life. Religion as I remember it, practiced by men and women in drab clothes, singing mournful hymns of tenth-rate music, asking forgiveness for their sins—this is nothing I wish to be identified with.

I personally have nothing against the man who believes in a God—no matter what God. What I object to is the man who claims that *his* God is the authority for his imposing restrictions on human growth and happiness. The battle is not between believers in theology and nonbelievers in theology; it is between believers in human freedom and believers in the suppression of human freedom.

Some day we will have a new religion. You may gape and exclaim, "What? A *new* religion?" The Christian will be up in arms and protest: "Is not Christianity eternal?" The Jew will be up in arms and protest: "Is not Judaism eternal?"

No, religions are no more eternal than nations are eternal. A religion—*any* religion—has a birth, a youth, an old age, and a death. Hundreds of religions have come and gone. Of all the millions of Egyptians who believed in Amon Ra through the better part of 4,000 years, not a single adherent of that religion can be found today. The idea of God changes as culture changes: in a pastoral land, God was the Gentle Shepherd; in warlike times, He was the God of Battles; when trade flourished, He was the God of Justice, weighing out equity and mercy. Today, when man is so mechanically creative, God is Wells' "Great Absentee," for a creative God is not wanted in an age that can make its own atom bombs.

Some day a new generation will not accept the obsolete religion and myths of today. When the new religion comes, it will refute the idea of man's being born in sin. A new religion will praise God by making men happy.

The new religion will refuse the antithesis of body and spirit. It will recognize that the flesh is not sinful. It will know that a Sunday morning spent in swimming is more holy than a Sunday morning spent in singing hymns—as if God needs hymns to keep Him contented. A new religion will find God on the meadows and not in the skies. Just imagine all that would be accomplished if only ten percent of all the hours spent in prayer and churchgoing were devoted to good deeds and acts of charity and helpfulness.

2. Education and Ecstasy, *G. B. Leonard*

This selection describes an encounter session at Esalen Institute, one of the best-known personality development centers, located at Big Sur, California. One of the session leaders, and author of this writing, is a widely read journalist on educational problems and an educational consultant. Education, for Leonard, is a process of change; and this excerpt, better than any definition, portrays what "creative interaction" can mean for producing fundamental changes in evaluating other human beings.

The particular problem being dealt with in this session is racial tension; and the means for change is a series of exercises in interpersonal encounter which emphasize feelings—for example, anger, hate, depression, weakness, compassion, need for another person. Why is a discussion of "an intellectual or political nature" of so little use for the resolution of fundamental conflicts?

In what sense, if any, did the members of this encounter group achieve something "transcendental"? What kinds of transformation took place in the weekend Leonard described? Would you agree with his claim in the last paragraph: "The Esalen experience shows that a new education is possible"? Why? Can educational pursuits be religious?

Education's new domain is not bound in by the conceptual, the factual, the symbolic. It includes every aspect of human existence that is relevant to the new age. To move into it, we don't have to wait for the twenty-first century. Experimenters all around the U.S. and in some other nations as well already have established beachheads in the new domain. Some of these experimenters work within the academies, some without. Powerful and respected institutions have begun to show strong interest in helping education break out of the old subject-matter entrapment. . . .

The one place you would go to find most of the new domain drawn together in some sort of coherent whole is an unlikely institute that psychologist Abraham Maslow has called "probably the most important educational institute in the world." To get there, you would drive south from Monterey, California, forty-five miles along the edge of the Pacific on one of the more spectacular roads in this hemisphere. Of this Coast Road, that at some places soars over a thousand feet above the sea, poet Robinson Jeffers wrote: "Beautiful beyond belief/ The heights glimmer in the sliding cloud, the great bronze gorge-cut sides of the mountain tower up invincibly/ Not the least hurt by this ribbon of road carved on their sea-foot."

From *Education and Ecstasy* by George B. Leonard. Copyright © 1968 by George B. Leonard. Reprinted by permission of the publisher, Delacorte Press, and of The Stering Lord Agency, Inc. Pp. 193–95, 197–210.

The road would lead you to a cluster of cabins, a small dome, a rustic lodge, some meeting rooms, a swimming pool and hot mineral baths—all thrusting seaward on a point of land above the Pacific. This site was the home, up into the nineteenth century, of a tribe of Indians who called themselves the "Esalen." They fished in the ocean and the cold stream that cascades down an adjoining redwood canyon, hunted small in the canyon, foraged for acorns and roots in fertile soil and worshiped the medicial powers of the hot springs that gush from the hills all around. It is from this Indian tribe, not an acronym, that Esalen Institute takes its name. . . .

Like Synanon, Esalen resists description at less than book length. Any single episode, out of context, may make it *harder* to understand. Two visitors may report quite accurately on their particular experiences and discover little in common. Since so much of Esalen is truly experimental, nothing can be guaranteed to "work." Yet, most people who participate come away with the conviction that they have somehow been changed. And many of the Esalen experiments resonate with a characteristic sense of hope and an assumption that even the most intractable human problems contain within them the seeds of their own solution.

One such experiment took place on a July weekend in 1967, at a time when race riots were troubling many of the nation's cities. The experiment had been announced in the Esalen brochure under the rather unfortunate title "Racial Confrontation as Transcendental Experience." The brochure went on in the same vein:

> Racial segregation exists among people with divided selves. A person who is alien to some part of himself is invariably separated from anyone who represents that alién part. The historic effort to integrate black man and white has involved us all in a vast working out of our divided human nature. Racial confrontation can be an axmple for all kinds of human encounter. When it goes deep enough—past superficial niceties and role-playing—it can be a vehicle for transcendental experience. Price Cobbs, a Negro psychiatrist from San Francisco, and George Leonard, a white journalist and author born and raised in Georgia, will conduct a marathon group encounter between races. The group will try to get past the roles and attitudes that divide its participants, so that they may encounter at a level beyond race.

Price Cobbs and I had okayed that brave overstatement some months before the event was to occur. On the Friday night the confrontation began both of us were feeling qualms. Here they were, thirty-five people of mixed race who had driven for miles over tricky roads to "work out their divided human natures." Could we help them past "superficial niceties and role-playing"? Could we deliver "transcendence" in a weekend?

The question gained urgency from the fast-worsening situation in the cities. It was the weekend of the Newark Black Power conference, and Price had been asked to go as a speaker. Only with considerable guilt had he begged off in favor of the improbable experiment at Big Sur.

We had planned the experiment out of a growing need, almost a desperation, for *some*thing that could show a way, even if a small one, through the racial impasse that had almost brought the civil-rights movement to a halt. The traditional ways weren't working. The Black Power militants screamed their hurt, anger and hatred. By revealing themselves and voicing the truth, they begged for encounter. The white leaders responded with conventional language, revealing nothing of their own feelings. How could there be understanding without self-revelation? Didn't the whites feel outrage, fear, repressed prejudice? The measured, judicious response seemed to us a lie. Nor was there real encounter in the biracial committees set up in some cities. Blacks and whites sat around tables, mouthed slogans, established "positions" and made "decisions" of an intellectual and political nature. They generally left the meetings unchanged. Little education took place. What would happen when we ventured into the dangerous territory where nothing is hidden?

We sat in a circle in a rustic meeting room, warmed against the cool sea air by candlelight and an open fire. Price and I outlined tentative plans for the weekend, after which each person around the circle introduced himself and offered reasons for attending—awkward, neatly wrapped statements that would be utterly shattered before the weekend was through. We started the confrontation with a technique borrowed from Dr. William Schutz. In this "Microlab," participants would have a chance to practice several ways of revaling and communicating feelings in the shortest possible time.

We asked people to take their chairs and form four separate circles of about eight each. I invited them to go along with a series of simple exercises in human relations. I suggested they start with the assumption that, within the hour, they would be relating on levels generally unknown in the community at large. Throughout the exercises, they would follow the familiar encounter rules: (1) Be completely honest and open. Forget about conventional politeness and reverve. Express anything you wish, no matter how shocking it may seem. (2) Relate on the level of feelings. Don't theorize or rationalize. (3) Stay in the here and now. Don't escape into past events or future plans. Only one prohibition: No physical violence, please.

In the first exercise, the groups would try this on their own for about ten minutes. Soon the room was alive with the kind of chatter you hear at cocktail parties. Price and I moved from circle to circle, listening in. After about seven minutes, we stopped them and offered our reactions. We had heard a lot of polite laughter. Expressions of negative feelings had been accompanied by humor that might soften the impact and take the heat off the speaker. Not that we had anything against humor, but it could so easily serve to avoid the kind of confrontation we were hoping for this weekend. Charm, too, could be a cop-out; several people were practicing it quite skillfully. The group by the door had somehow slid into the past tense, talking about former experiences and attitudes toward race, dodging the dangers and rewards of the present. As for the group nearest the fire, it was hopelessly tangled in the abstract. Members were vying with one another to spin theories that would "explain" just why they were there and how they felt. The realm of ideas is powerful, fascinating and always to be valued. But at this moment it wouldn't help us attain our goal. We asked the groups to try once more.

Now there was a change in tone. The room became quieter, more somber. We sensed premonitions of the tensions that might erupt. Tentatively, hesitantly, people began revealing themselves. But they softened each "insult" with a self-deprecatory grimace; they smiled gently at what might bring tears. And the group near the fire was back at its intellectualizing again.

After about ten minutes, we stopped the groups. Several people protested that they were just getting started. Price and I considered this an encouraging sign. We went on to the next exercise. The groups would stand in circles. Each person, in turn, would go around confronting each other person in the circle. He would look him in the eyes, touch him in some honest way (a handshake, an embrace, a finger in the chest, whatever), and tell him what he felt about him at that moment. This one-to-one situation encouraged a more direct and honest dialogue. Theorizing became more difficult. And the participants were introduced to the use of physical touch as a medium of communication.

Price and I sensed a new intentness in the room, but again we stopped the exercise before its completion. More vehement sounds of protest. We asked the groups if they would sit and try communicating for ten minutes without the use of words. They could touch, move, hum, dance—anything but talk. And they could practice a skill generally forgotten or forbidden by our culture: they could look directly and openly at another person for an extended period without having to justify it. This kind of engaged silence has a particular potency. Several people later told us it was only here they really began to feel something happening.

Ten minutes passed. We were reluctant to intervene. Most people in the circles had joined hands; though some, true to their feelings, had refused. Fifteen minutes. Complete dialogues transpired without words. People learned. Finally, Price broke the silence.

In the last exercise, the circles stood again and were asked to move slowly closer together. Inevitably, most people ended up tightly linked, arms around each other's shoulders. An artificial, manipulated integration? Perhaps. Nevertheless, people experienced a kind of closeness with strangers of various races they might previously have considered only in the abstract.

We asked the groups to sit again and try what they had tried at the beginning. Use words, sounds, touch, movement, silence—anything that would express true, here-and-now feelings. The difference was startling. It was by no means a deep confrontation, but it was a beginning. Entirely departed was the cocktail-party chatter. A few barriers had been crossed and a few eyes were moist with the wonder or relief that often accompanies such crossings. Price and I let the groups go without further interference. Gradually, the participants drifted out, most of them down the steep seaside path that leads to the hot mineral baths. The bathhouse juts out on a cliff high above a rocky beach. It is open to starlight, moonlight, the sound of surf, the chill ocean air. Up to my neck in the steaming water with members of the group, I felt comforted and mellow. Here were people of good will who were willing to be close. How could they harbor calamitous hostilities?

The next morning I began to find out. Contrary to usual practice, we held the whole group together rather than breaking it into two. This was mainly Price's idea. He wanted to keep the two of us in the same encounter. The example of our relationship, he felt, might prove useful, especially if the group ran into a complete impasse.

The first confrontations started, however, not between black and white, but among the blacks. The morning was shattered by their bitter accusations. "Racist," "Uncle Tom," and "fink" were among the milder words that went slashing back and forth across the room. "When they come with machine guns and barbed wire," one Negro said, "all I want to know is, baby, are you for me or against me?" By lunchtime, the atmosphere was electric. But there had been more accusation than true encounter. No one had really changed very much. There had been little education.

After lunch, the marathon began. We would stay in uninterrupted session through the night. Dinner would be brought to us. We would keep at it until the conventional defenses against feeling were broken down, even if it took until noon the next day. It didn't take nearly that long.

We had planned to begin the marathon with a period of sensory awakening, led by Bernard Gunther, an innovator in the field. Gunther would take us through exercises designed to make us aware of a bit of the rich sensory universe this culture commonly denies us. Because of the multiracial nature of the group, he planned to have us keep our eyes closed during the entire session. Prejudice, he felt, is visual. When we touched an unseen stranger, we would have to deal with him in a way that would bypass racial stereotypes. But a hitch developed. Many people were anxious to get on with the encounter. Only about half the group went out on the sunlit terrace to do the exercises. I accompanied them. Price stayed with the ones inside.

It was a bizarre experience for me. As I went through Gunther's exercises, I could hear the voices but not the words from the meeting room. Eyes closed, we groped our way around the terrace and found a partner. Touching hands, we "got acquainted," had a "quarrel," "made up," tried to express love or liking, and so on. At the same time, the counterpoint from inside rose: excitement, anger, pleading and finally a burst of loud sobbing and wailing. I knew the encounter was finally under way. (Who could deeply and truly experience the reality of racial prejudice without crying?) Sweat ran down my chest and sides. I wanted to continue the Gunther experiment and at the same time be inside. At last the outside group ended with a long, unrestrained shout. Those inside found this counterpoint equally bizarre.

We crowded back into the meeting room to find that everything had changed. The dialogue was on an unfamiliar level. The faces looked unashamedly tragic and yet strangely radiant. We seemed to come from a different world. We were an intrusion, yet grudgingly accepted as the encounter rushed on.

What had caused the breakthrough, I later learned, was this: A young

Japanese-American named Larry had driven up from Los Angeles with his friend, a personable light-skinned Negro named Cliff. Both of them were college students in business administration. They were making it in the white world and had tried to numb themselves to racial hurt. They were cool and cynical. They wore their masks well. But all the vehement racial talk, and especially the attacks among the blacks, had turned something upside down in them. Larry had begun talking. He had not realized how deeply he had felt racial prejudice or how much it had ruled his life. But now he knew he was a yellow man, a "Jap," and was ready to admit it. He declared himself to be a soul brother. With this declaration, all of his reserve collapsed and he "burst" into tears. The dikes were down then, and several of the Negroes poured out their hurt. "How many of you people can realize," a mother asked, "what it's like to send your children off to school and know they'll probably be called 'nigger' or spat on? And there's nothing, *nothing* you can do about it?"

When the outside group came in, Larry's friend, Cliff, was locked in a bitter encounter with a beautiful young white schoolteacher named Pam. She had told him she wanted his friendship, and he had responded scathingly, denouncing her "pitiful, condescending" overtures. Now her eyes were filled with tears.

"*Please.* What can I do? I'm trying. Please help me."

Cliff rocked his chair back and forth, looking across the room at her with contempt.

"No, baby, I'm not going to help you. I'm not going to take you off the hook. I want you to feel just what I feel. I want you to feel what I've felt for twenty one years. Go on. Cry."

"Please," she begged. Tears streamed down her checks.

Cliff kept rocking back and forth, his eyes fixed on hers. No one came to her aid. Somehow it seemed right that this interval in time should be fully realized by everyone in the room. The silence intensified, became in itself a powerful medium of communication. We began to *know* each other. At last, the silence seemed to unfold and we were talking again, the exchanges crackling around the room faster than the rational mind could follow.

Though any number of "subjects" came up in the hours that followed, the main theme through dinner and for some time thereafter was the Negroes' hurt and anger and despair, their absolute distrust of all whites. (Several times Price said that he did trust me. This had the effect of taking me off the hook, something always wished for in the hot and heavy of an encounter, but regretted afterwards.) At one point I suggested that whites, too, have their problems, their tragedies. But this was not accepted. A Negro mother said, "I just can't buy that. Whatever's wrong with you, you can do something about. But I can't do *anything* about the color of my skin—or my children's. Compared to us, you've got it made."

After darkness fell, we split the group in two for the night. Price took his half to a meeting room in another building. Without him, I felt forlorn in the vortex of all the anger and hate. But it was something we had to get through. There was no way *around* it if we wanted to accomplish our goal. By ten o'clock every white in my group was in utter despair. "I had no *idea* it was this bad," a middle-aged white woman said. "I work with Negroes. That's my *job*. And I didn't realize. My best friend of fifteen years is a Negro, and I had no idea she felt these kind of things, and now I know she does and has just been keeping them from me to spare me. I don't want to go back home. I'm afraid to see my friend. I don't see how the race problem can *ever* be solved." I told her I was glad it was all coming out in the open. The race problem could certainly never be solved so long as we *didn't* know and feel and experience the truth.

About this time, an episode began that was to occupy us, off and on, for most of the night. We had let a newcomer join the group at dinnertime. Chuck was in his early twenties, almost jet black, with a wary face and a body as taut as a steel spring. He began telling the group how he had successfully "transcended" the entire matter of race. He was utterly lacking in bad feelings against whites. He disliked the system, but not the man. He thought that racial incidents were extremely rare, especially in his own life. He never felt anger or hostility.

No one believed him. "It makes me nervous just to hear your voice," I told him. "That singsong way you have of talking, like there's no relation between what you're saying and what you feel. It puts me on edge. I feel like yelling at you." Someone suggested that I do so, and I did. Others followed me, cursing, yelling and cajoling as they expressed their feelings toward him and his professed attitude. But nothing moved Chuck. His face became a mask of stone. He had nothing but love for all mankind, the stone said. The group united in trying to get through to him. Black and white worked together. Cliff and Pam, the afternoon's bitterness forgotten, operated like a team. There was an unspoken accord among the eighteen people in the group that somehow, no matter how long it took, we would get through to Chuck. It was grinding, exhausting work, as if we were trying to penetrate a huge granite boulder with a hand drill.

At about 2:30 A.M. there came a moment of relief. A tall engineer with a thin moustache, excoriated earlier as the last of the old-time white liberals, began boasting about how many social contacts he had with Negroes. Then, with a slight smile of self-revelation, he said: "Actually, I collect Negroes." Perhaps it was not that the remark struck us as funny, but that we all needed so desperately to laugh. In any case, we exploded. "Do you have a good connection?" someone managed to gasp. "Oh, yes, the very best." "What's your source?" another blurted. The engineer named a ghetto near San Francisco. Between whoops of laughter, a good-looking Negro house-wife said, "I collect Negroes, too. My source is my uterus." That was all it took. For a good ten minutes we had our laugh of relief. Gradually, we subsided into silence. Wearily we looked over toward Chuck. There still was work to be done. If Chuck had asked us to take the pressure off him, we would have. Or he could have simply left. The principle of the free learner applies strongly to encounter groups; leaving would constitute an honest and appropriate response. But we sensed that Chuck was as fascinated by the confrontation as we were. Just as he was gradually learning, so were we.

Another hour passed. At last, Chuck's voice was beginning to sound more natural. He was talking about his sexual prowess. "I could take any woman here," he said, his eyes flashing around the room.

"How would you take Pam?" I asked him.

"I'll tell you."

"Tell *her*."

He turned toward the teacher. "All right. First I'd rap you, then I'd take you."

"Rap?"

"Talk. You know, establish rapport. I'd rap you, then I'd take you."

Pam looked at him with scorn. "You'd never take me. I wouldn't let you *touch* me. *Ever*."

"I'd take you, all right, baby." A fury lay just beneath his words.

Voices broke out around the group as various women denied or affirmed his sexual attraction. The Negro housewife leaned over toward him.

"You could never take me, and I'm going to tell you why." Something in her voice reduced us all to silence. "Because you're just a dirty little black nigger."

Chuck almost leaped from his chair. Clenching his fists on the armrests, he loosed his hidden fury in a savage and frightening tirade. Finally, he caught himself, looked around the room with dazed eyes and covered his face with his hands. He sat that way as members of the group comforted him. Then he looked up and smiled. His face was different.

A little later, after a surprisingly tender interchange, he said, "I want to thank all of you. I've learned more in the last two hours than in the last two years."

Near dawn, some of us went down through a dense fog to the baths. Others slept for an hour or two. All of us seemed illumined in the peculiar clarity of sleeplessness when we gathered in the meeting room after breakfast. Almost immediately, the group took an unexpected turn. The whites began revealing themselves, baring the most tragic and painful moments of their lives. *And the Negroes wept for the whites.* Without question of race, they *felt*, they *knew*. One after another, the revelations poured forth. The group took life of its own. There were no leaders now. We were all swept along.

An attractive white woman in her thirties had told us brightly the first night that she had come to tape some interviews. Now she was telling us the real reason. She had a half-Negro son. She hated the child's father, who had left her, and she feared that she would become prejudiced against the boy. The years were passing; she despaired of ever getting another husband. The son hurt her chances of remarriage. She resented Negro men and yet found herself dating them.

"I'll tell you why I'm dating spades," she said, near breakdown. "Because I've given up on white men." She collapsed in racking sobs. Though her words might previously have been construed as prejudiced, it was a black man who took her in his arms and comforted her.

Almost everyone in the room was crying. We were unashamed of our tears. We were not Negroes or whites or Orientals. We were human beings joined in a very precious, fragile awareness of our common plight, of the waste and loss in every life, and of hope for something better. For many of us, that morning was transcendental, a space in life when ordinary objects seem to shimmer, when all faces are beautiful and time can be taken at the crest like a great onrushing wave. That was the way it was for me.

Noon came and passed, but we wouldn't leave. At one-thirty, the dining-room crew came and told us we would have to go. We rose and moved, without a word, to the center of the room in a mass, moist-eyed embrace.

Since then, Price and I had planned further racial confrontations in San Francisco, sponsored by Esalen and the Episcopal Diocese of California. Other organizations have taken up the idea, and like meetings are spreading through the city. We can't predict what will eventually happen. Perhaps some education will take place.

But the racial confrontation described was only one of more than 650 Esalen meetings, each one unique and unpredictable. Esalen remains truly experimental; if an approach doesn't work, it is dropped, not made into a rigid doctrine. It is a place where new things that don't fit into the old structure can and do happen. One key reason may be that it is self-supporting, tied to no major corporation or foundation grant, and that it operates outside the restrictive latticework of university academic departments. Though thirty-two of its forty-three officers and advisors hold doctorates, the leadership is nonacademic—whether the leader happens to have a "Dr." by his name or not.

The Esalen experience shows that a new education is possible. It is not important that educators, parents and teachers follow the Esalen example or that they aim toward a Kennedy School. It *is* important that they know they can change more in their schools than the window dressing. They have a real choice—now.

3. Eupsychia—The Good Society, A. Maslow

Abraham H. Maslow was, until his recent death, chairman of the Department of Psychology at Brandeis University and one of the leaders in the development of a movement called "humanistic" or "third force" psychology. He conceived of human

From "Eupsychia—The Good Society" by Abraham H. Maslow, Ph.D. found in *Journal of Humanistic Psychology,* Vol. I, No. 2 (fall 1961), pp. 1–6, 8. Copyright © 1961 by Brandeis University. Used by permission.

life as a process of growth that was essentially independent both of supernatural and of natural determinism. He characterized this process as being one of "self-actualization." Note the essentially positive view of man's nature implied by this term. This excerpt is based on an interview by Trevor Thomas of the Pacifica Foundation, over radio station KPFA–FM, August 1960. Dr. Maslow is being interviewed about various Utopian ideas, particularly his own vision of "Eupsychia," the psychologically healthy society. What belief about man and his needs does he state early in the interview? What characteristics does he list of psychologically healthy people? What is the basis for his judgment that a healthy society (eupsychia) is possible? What does he regard as the chief obstacle to psychological health? Does Maslow think of himself as a cultural relativist? Does he appeal to a transcendent (Divine) force to help man attain psychological health? What technique does Maslow suggest we rely upon for assisting the healing process? Compare and contrast Maslow with the previous readings of this chapter regarding (1) the definition of the human situation, (2) the problems to be solved, and (3) the means of transforming human sorrow into joy, beauty, and goodness.

MR. THOMAS: "Dr. Maslow, during the next few minutes we are going to be talking about good societies and about your ideas on the psychological foundations of good societies. I remarked as we were coming into the studio that these were rather peculiar times to be discussing Utopias. Utopian societies have traditionally been descriptions of economic achievement—a place where the material needs of food, clothing, shelter, were completely filled. Why, then, in America where we have apparently solved these material problems, do we still feel compelled to reach out, to define better societies? Why are we dissatisfied? Why do we go on imagining Utopias?"

DR. MASLOW: "I think we're simply witnessing a human phenomenon that has appeared down through the ages. What man does not have, he struggles for. When the need is fulfilled, he moves to a different and higher need. The picture of the ideal society reflects the level of poverty or wealth of the current culture and, incidentally, of the individual's own concept of how rich *he* is, and how rich he wants to become. The fact that America is very rich—that all the things for which most cultures have struggled throughout history have been achieved here—is tending to push our thoughts to higher needs and therefore to higher levels of frustration."

MR. THOMAS: "Would you say something about the difference between 'higher' and 'lower' needs?"

DR. MASLOW: "Well, I think most psychologists now agree that our needs are arranged in a kind of hierarchy, with food and shelter the lowest on the scale. When our bellies are full and we are sheltered, we turn towards the problems of safety and security in the world. We want a good police force and good doctors. Then, we think of education, and we want good schools. This reminds me of that old cartoon where the wife says to the husband 'You are always wanting what you haven't got,' and he answers, 'Well, what else can you want?'

"Now, I think of love as a higher need, and beyond love there are the sitll higher needs for respect from others, for self respect, and so on. You can see that the higher the need, the less it is directly related to the basic material and physical needs. For these reasons I think it is entirely valid to be imagining better societies in America at this point in our history; but, I think we are now ready to conceive of a 'Eupsychia'—a psychologically healthy culture—rather than just another materially-based Utopia." . . .

"My own research was simply to pick out the healthiest people I could find, and then to study them directly. It was a small sampling, for there certainly aren't very many truly healthy individuals in this society. I just tried to find out what they were like. How did they feel? What kind of humor, interpersonal relations, families, demeanors did they have? What were their relationships to society? These were the kind of questions I asked, and I found to my satisfaction that it was possible to make some important preliminary generalizations from their answers—generalizations which on the whole have stood up remarkably well in the light of my own additional findings since then, and of those of many other psychologists which have accumulated during the fifteen years since this survey was first carried out."

MR. THOMAS: "And what were some of these generalizations?"

DR. MASLOW: "Well, for instance, just to pick out the most important ones, it was very clear in my pilot study that either the most important or one of the most important characteristics of psychological health was simply the ability to perceive clearly—that is, to see the truth, to penetrate falsehood, phoniness, hypocrisy, and so on. This was very clear and has been supported a dozen times over by other people, by the results of psychotherapy, which is after all, an effort to make a good man, too. This is pretty clear now; I think it is safe to say that psychologically healthy people are just more perceptive, they can see the truth more clearly, they are less fooled by masks, conventions, and expectations. They can penetrate through to the truth more easily, more clearly."

MR. THOMAS: "I guess this leads to the next obvious question, then: What is the factor in psychologically healthy people that permits them to be more capable of this perception?"

DR. MASLOW: "We don't have the time to talk about it at length, but for our purposes here we can call it a unique lack of fear. It is *fear* that puts blinders on our eyes and that puts shackles on us. You could also call it anxiety, inhibition, or lack of confidence. Whatever the term, it is the main psychological block to a Eupsychia—a society of psychologically healthy people.

"I might then go on and describe the second most important characteristic of healthy people—and the second basic foundation of Eupsychia

—as spontaneity, or the capacity to function fully, to live with a certain naturalness, simplicity, lack of artificiality or guile."

MR. THOMAS: "Dr. Maslow, this word 'spontaneity' is quite common in much current popular literature. I would see the word as being tied in with the concept of creativity. Would you see it this way?"

DR. MASLOW: "Very definitely."

MR. THOMAS: "Would you sort of nip the two concepts together for us?"

DR. MASLOW: "Being creative is being spontaneous—and it takes courage. Certainly one aspect of the creative person is that he must be strong, or let us say, unafraid. The creative person sticks his neck out when he has an idea. He may be defying the whole culture, even the whole of history. He is saying that what everyone accepts as the whole truth just isn't good enough. He is evidencing a certain defiance and perhaps a certain loneliness. To maintain this spontaneity—and thus, creativeness, he must overcome the fear of being in this very vulnerable position. Since we are all creative to some extent, perhaps those of our culture who evidence creativeness are simply those people with the ability to overcome a fear of spontaneity."

MR. THOMAS: "The fear is always present then, but the successful person is able to overcome it and 'be spontaneous' and thus 'creative'?"

DR. MASLOW: "Yes. When he overcomes his fear he can then permit what is inside of him to emerge even if other people laugh at him, even if he looks ridiculous, even if his emerging idea is a mistake, as so many creations are, and he has to throw it away and be laughed at even more for this. He must be strong to withstand this.

"Now in our Eupsychia, where everyone by definition would be psychologically healthy, everyone would be able to handle spontaneous ideas, and because there would be fewer personal hostilities there would be very little fear—and thus great spontaneity and creativity. People would trust themselves; they would look forward to new ideas, to novelty, to change. There would be no need to hang on to the past—people would happily adapt to changing conditions. . . .

It is certainly true that mankind, throughout history, has looked for guiding values, for principles of right and wrong. But he has tended to look outside of himself, outside of mankind, to a God, to some sort of sacred book perhaps, or to a ruling class. What I am doing is to explore the theory that you can find the values by which mankind must live, and for which man has always sought, by digging into the best people in depth. I believe, in other words, that I can find ultimate values which are right for mankind by observing the best of mankind. If under the best conditions and in the best specimens I simply stand aside and describe in a scientific way what these human values are, I find values that are the old values of truth, goodness, and beauty and some additional ones as well, for instance, gaiety, justice and joy. I do not say we should look for goodness because we *ought* to, or because there is some principle outside of ourselves that tells us to. I am saying that if you examine human beings fairly, you will find that they themselves have innate knowledge of and yearning for, goodness and beauty. Now there is an important reason why we don't see more of these good instincts; we are afraid of them, we tend to block their expression—the fear that I was mentioning earlier—even though we have a deep yearning for their expression. Our task is to create an environment where more and more of these innate instincts can find expression. This is what would characterize Eupsychia." . . .

MR. THOMAS: . . .How, in our present cultures, can we work toward the healthy society?"

DR. MASLOW: "The primary technical tool we now have for doing this, and I suppose the best way for doing it, is by psychoanalysis or by some other form of depth analysis with the help of a skilled person. However, since this is not a very practical suggestion for most of us, certainly not for most of mankind, we must turn our attention more and more to mass techniques of helping the person to discover this precious human nature deep within himself—this nature that he is afraid of expressing. Education, for example, certainly should help the person discover his own human nature, as should self-therapy. Self-therapy is applicable to all of us, although it is an extremely difficult job; we have only a few guide lines, a few models. One good guide, one which I frequently recommend to my students, is a paperback by Joanna Field called *A Life of One's Own*. It is a model for self-search and a description of a technique for doing it. Another good help is a book by the same author but under her own name, Marion Milner. *On Not Being Able to Paint.*

"In general, the consequences of psychotherapy are moves toward better values. The person in successful therapy generally comes out a better citizen, a better husband, a better wife—certainly a better person. He is more perceptive and more spontaneous—this practically always happens. These results are achieved through self-knowledge—the main path to discovering within ourselves the best values for all mankind. The more clearly we know these values, the more easily, spontaneously, effortlessly we can grope toward them.

4. On the Religious Character of "Integrity Groups," *O. H. Mowrer*

In this brief statement, the clinical psychologist O. H. Mowrer analyzes and describes specific forms of several themes discussed more generally in J. Seeley's article (reading 5). He first describes how recent the shift has been in this country from an ethic

From O. H. Mowrer, "The Problem of Good and Evil Empirically Considered, with Reference to Psychological and Social Adjustment," *Zygon: Journal of Religion and Science*, IV, No. 4 (December, 1969), 308–13. Used by permission of the author and The University of Chicago Press.

linked to the notions of "devil," "heaven," "hell," and "God"
to one defined entirely in an objective, naturalistic, and humanistic
frame of reference. Then he describes three contemporary
institutional expressions of the effort made to develop and nurture
personal character. Mowrer regards these (and other) "integrity
groups" as profoundly religious. Why? Do you regard overcoming
the problem of estrangement through the means of practicing
honesty, responsibility, and involvement within a structured
group of fellow human beings as "a religious reformation"
more important than the Protestant Reformation of the 16th
century, as Mowrer suggests? What is the significance of the shift
in calling the small groups "integrity groups" rather than
"integrity therapy"? How does Mowrer define religion? If people
assume that God is "dead," why do they seem to continue their
need for "religious" groups at all?

Today I can recall, clearly and with some discernment, the span of
more than half a century of life in our society; and I remember that when
I was eleven or twelve years old, there was a book in our family library
(housed in the small, glass-enclosed "bookcase" in our "parlor") which
fascinated me far more than any of the other rarely consulted volumes
there. As I remember it, this book had very little text and was made up
largely of pictures (actually engravings) of the devil carrying out his varied
and far-reaching responsibilities on earth and in hell. Although he was a
terrible-looking fellow, he did not seem, to my youthful eyes at least, altogether unlikeable or unhappy. And this much was certain: he took his
work very seriously and gave every indication of enjoying it. Stated most
generally, the devil's primary duty on earth was to *tempt* living mortals
and to superintend the punishment in hell of those who yielded to his
blandishments and failed to repent soon enough. On Sundays, the ministers
of the Protestant church which my family and I regularly attended pictured
hell to us even more vividly than did the book (in color and with sound
effects) and assured us that the fires burned brightly and that the place was
doing a thriving business. But our ministers, for some reason, did not seem
to want to appear to know too much about the general overseer of this
institution—perhaps this is why I found our old book, appropriately bound
in red, so uniquely instructive and interesting. Our ministers also, of course,
discoursed on heaven—and were much freer to talk about God, whose
supreme objective was to help human beings *be good* in this life so they
could share eternity with him.

It now appears, in retrospect, that by roughly 1920, the devil was failing to command full credence, rather generally—which was, from one point
of view, a grave misfortune; for if he was allowed to disappear from the
minds of men, it was predictable that the fires of hell would cool and the
place itself would eventually disappear. I have, of course, no way of
knowing just how rapidly this indeed happened—I have often thought how
instructive it would be if we had available today the results of a Gallup
poll taken, let us say, at five-year intervals, during the half-century between

1920 and 1970, on the decline of "belief" in this general area. But it seems fairly certain that the devil went first, and then hell likewise gradually faded into oblivion.

Hell's obsolescence was officially recognized in theological circles when E. Stanley Jones announced that "hell is portable," that is, that it is a human condition and not a place. And if our assumption be correct that man himself is *both* good and evil, we could have predicted that if this personal and spatial way of representing evil and its fruits disappeared, Heaven and God would also be endangered. Sometime in the 1950s, I recall hearing a sermon entitled "What's Happened to Heaven?" Suddenly I said to myself: "As a matter of fact, you don't hear much about heaven anymore, do you?" The dissolution of hell had, it seems, created an unnatural imbalance. With this "institution" gone, everyone now presumably went to heaven; and if this were the case, the whole "other world" arrangement seemed rather pointless. Furthermore, about the same time, the existentialists descended upon us with the revelation that, as a matter of fact, no one was "going" anywhere! Tillich's terms "human finitude" and "our creatureliness" became household expressions, all of which left God without a permanent address and, as someone observed, "largely unemployed." Small wonder that it was only a few years until the "rumor" that God was dead had developed into a vigorous, if somewhat paradoxical, "theological movement," which was launched by Vahanian's book[1] and has been "reviewed" by Adolfs.[2] And today it is generally conceded that our society is basically secular[3] and that the "three-storied universe" of traditional Christianity is "mythical."[4]

The sequential process whereby this scheme of supernatural entities and sanctions disappeared from the modern scene thus seems to have been: first to go was the devil, then hell, then heaven, and finally—at least in any naïvely anthropomorphic sense—God. Many of us recall that if, as children, we asked *why* this or that act was bad, we were likely to be told either that God did not *want* us to perform it or that the devil would *get* us if we did. It is, therefore, perhaps not surprising that the disappearance of the "all-seeing, sleepless daimonic eye" and its accoutrements has also badly shaken our faith in and respect for many human institutions which have claimed support and authentication from divine sources. For more than a decade now, we have been in an acute moral crisis, uncertain and confused as to where we can look for moral clarity and reliable guidance to the good life. In the earlier sections of this paper, some suggestions have been put forward as to how we can reapproach the problem of good and evil, in an entirely objective, naturalistic, humanistic frame of reference. In the next and concluding section we shall take a look at certain enterprises which are specifically interested in putting such a conceptual approach into practice.

THE PROBABLE SHAPE
OF THINGS TO COME
IN CHARACTER DEVELOPMENT AND NURTURANGE

It is not without significance, surely, that the institution or movement which is today most effective in producing personal *change* in adult human beings is one which (*a*) has no truck with any form of supernaturalism and (*b*) does not even use the traditional terminology of secular ethical theory. I refer to Synanon Foundation, whose "houses" are located mainly in major cities on the West Coast and whose specialty is the rehabilitation of hard-core drug addicts. Here there is, officially, no prayer or worship in the conventional sense, and even the terms "good" and "bad" are generally eschewed. Instead, behavior is likely to be characterized as *smart or stupid,* in the self-actualizing, self-defeating, selfishly hedonic sense previously discussed. That the power and effectiveness of this approach lies not in the personal charisma of Synanon's founder, Charles Dederich, but in clearly articulated principles and processes[5] is indicated by the fact that a very similar organization, known as Daytop Village, Inc., has come into existence in New York City and is now spreading up and down the Atlantic seaboard.[6] And both organizations owe much of their inspiration and know-how to Alcoholics Anonymous, which specializes in another admittedly "impossible" task, namely, the rehabilitation of alcoholics.

Being neither an addict nor an alcoholic, I have had only tangential (but very cordial) contact with Synanon, Daytop, and AA; but I have been persuaded for a full quarter of a century now that functional personality disorders or so-called neuroses are intrinsically associated with basically moral problems and their persistent mismanagement. This conviction eventuated first in what was called "integrity therapy";[7] but the name, and the process for which it stood, was attractive only to persons who were actively "hurting," and when they became reasonably comfortable, they, sensibly enough, disappeared. Who needs "therapy" if he is no longer "sick"? But we are now seeing the problem increasingly in educational rather than medical terms and have therefore dropped the term "therapy" and speak only of *"integrity groups."* As a result of this and related changes, people are now coming into our groups and *staying,* not because they are "still hurting," but because their pain has turned to a form of joy, which they feel they can continue to experience in no other way. In our groups, *personal change* and a form of *special training* go hand in hand. As a person becomes increasingly comfortable as a result of such change, he also begins to take deep satisfaction in new competences and skills which can then be exercised *in behalf of others.*

This is not the place to speak at length about integrity groups.[8] But this much is pertinent: we believe that these groups, as a facet of what is coming to be known, generally, as the small-groups movement, represent the emergence of a new *primary social institution.* In an era when the traditional primary social groups—home, church, school, and community— are badly shaken and confused, it is increasingly difficult for many persons to find identity, intimacy, emotional support, and cosmic meaning. It seems that the small-groups movement, of which integrity groups are one facet, represents an increasingly successful effort, on the part of more and more people, to avoid anonymity, alienation, and despair. And the part of this movement with which I am most closely associated has frankly moral or ethical objectives: to help oneself and others to become more *honest, responsible,* and *emotionally involved.* And *help* in the attainment or at least approximation of these objectives is found in the hope of heaven and the fear of hell, not as places but as human conditions in this life.

Within the past six months, there has been an unprecedented upsurge of interest in small groups, which has been reflected, among other ways, by the fact that several large-circulation magazines have run very thoughtful and competently written articles on this phenomenon. A long list of such articles could be cited, but one of the most recent and best will suffice: namely, a piece by Sam Blum entitled, "Group Therapy: A Special Report."[9] Personally, I think there is a good possibility that these groups represent the emerging form of the church of the twenty-first century. They will very likely differ from conventional Catholic and Protestant churches in that they will not be specifically christocentric, nor will they be explicitly theistic (compare Confucianism and Buddhism). But they will, I think, be *profoundly religious.* This may seem like a contradiction in terms to some, who will ask: "But how can anyone be religious without also believing in God?" The answer is very simple. The term "religion," in its literal derivation, has no necessary relation to "theology." The former term comes from the Latin root *ligare,* which means connection; and *re-ligare,* from which our term "religion" comes, means reconnection. And this, more than perhaps anything else, is what the small-groups movement is concerned with: the reconnection, reintegration, reconciliation of lost, lonely, isolated, alienated, estranged persons back into a loving, concerned, and orderly fellowship or group of some sort.

Dietrich Bonhoeffer was apparently envisioning something of this sort when toward the end of his life,[10] he spoke about "man coming of age" and of a "religionless Christianity." But his choice of terms was, I think, unfortunate. We would prefer to speak of a "nontheistic religion," of the sort which one already sees explicitly embodied in many forms of contemporary small groups. Yet in one sense there is a striking continuity and kinship here between the contemporary small-groups movement and Christianity. The early or apostolic church was basically a small-groups movement and was based, not in churches as we know them today, but typically in individual homes, where a "congregation" would consist of perhaps only ten or a dozen persons; and when the group got larger than this, it would divide and provide the nucleus of two new groups. Thus the early church was also known as a house church; and when, as in Rome, it was not safe to meet in private homes, these little bands found refuge and a degree of safety in the catacombs. Here honesty (confession, exomologesis), responsibility (restitution, penance), and involvement (loving kindness) were all practiced, with the same salubrious effects we see them capable of producing today. But there is, of course, the very significant difference that the small groups ("congregations," "house churches") with which we are here particularly concerned are naturalistic and humanistic, rather than metaphysical and deistic, in their basic orientation.

And why do human beings continue to need "religious" groups, regardless of their cosmology or world view? Because, as previously noted in this paper, we all need help in pursuing the good and avoiding evil. Socially isolated, estranged man is weak and highly prone to evil, self-defeating behavior. Bonhoeffer, in his book *Life Together,* puts it this way: "In confession the break-through to community takes place. Sin demands to have a man by himself. It withdraws him from the community. The more isolated a person is, the more destructive will be the power of sin over him, and the more deeply he becomes involved in it, the more disastrous is his isolation. Sin wants to remain unknown. It shuns the light. In the darkness of the unexpressed it poisons the whole being of a person."[11]

The most reliable means yet discovered for obtaining help in overcoming estrangement and building resistance to temptation ("ego strength") comes from commitment to and earnest participation in a properly conceived and contractually structured group of fellow human beings, that is, of one's *peers.* The best safeguard of legal rights and justice ever evolved is probably the principle, in English law, of the "right to trial before a jury of one's peers"; and it is no accident that the kind of small groups discussed in this paper are now being commonly referred to as "peer self-help groups."[12]

Today there is manifestly widespread uncertainty, conflict, and pain in the area of morality and "values." This is perhaps the price we have to pay as we move through a religious "reformation" which, in historical retrospect, may prove to be far more important, sounder, and unifying than that of the sixteenth century.

NOTES

1. G. Vahanian, *The Death of God* (New York: George Braziller, Inc., 1961).
2. R. Adolfs, *The Grave of God: Has the Church a Future?* (New York: Harper & Row, 1966).
3. See Harvey Cox, *The Secular Society* (New York: Macmillan Co., 1965).
4. See the writings of Rudolf Bultmann, *Kerygma and Myth: A Theological Debate,* ed. H. Bartsch, trans. R. H. Fuller (London: SPCK Press, 1953), 1:1–44; see also W. Hordern, *New Directions in Theology Today* (Philadelphia: Westminster Press, 1966), chap. 2.
5. See, for example, L. Yablonsky, *The Tunnel Back: Synanon* (New York: Macmillan Co., 1965).
6. See J. A. Shelly and A. Bassin, "Daytop Lodge: A New Treatment Approach for Drug Addicts," *Corrective Psychiatry* 11 (1965):186–95; see also A. Bassin, "Daytop Village," *Psychology Today* (December 1968), pp. 48 ff.
7. See, for example, J. W. Drakeford, *Integrity Therapy: A Christian Evaluation to a New Approch to Mental Health* (Nashville, Tenn.: Broadman Press, 1967).

8. See, for example, O. H. Mowrer, "Integrity Groups Today," mimeographed (Urbana: Department of Psychology, University of Illinois, 1969).
9. *Redbook* (March 1970), p. 134.
10. *Prisoner for God: Letters and Papers from Prison* (New York: Macmillan Co., 1953).
11. New York: Harper & Bros., 1954, p. 112.
12. See N. Hurvitz, "The Characteristics of Peer Self-Help Psychotherapy Groups and Their Implications for the Theory and Practice of Psychotherapy," *Psychotherapy: Theory, Research, and Practice* 7 (1970): 41–49.

INTERPRETATION

5. On the Religious Function of the Mental Health Movement, *J. Seeley*

In the first selection of the interpretation section John Seeley, who teaches sociology and psychiatry at the University of Toronto, provides a general description of the present American scene in which "the mental health movement" is seen to be taking over many functions in the "cure of souls" formerly performed by the Christian Church in the Western world—especially the function of defining ideals and values. What reasons does he give for the rise of this movement? What similarities does he see between the growth of this movement and the growth of the early church? In what ways does it differ from the church? There are two attitudes of mental hygienists regarding whether they are mediators of their own ultimate values. With which position do you agree? Why? If a contemporary social movement takes over the functions of religious institutions of the past, is there any reason we should not interpret that movement as "religious"? Even if it would be argued that the functions of the mental health movement and of the church are essentially different, would this movement qualify as a religious movement defined as "a means of ultimate transformation"?

From *The Americanization of the Unconscious* by John Seeley (New York: Science House, Inc., 1967), pp. 52–61. First published as "Social Values, The Mental Health Movement and Mental Health," *Annals of the American Academy of Political and Social Sciences,* 286 (March 1953). Used by permission of Science House, Inc.

SOCIAL VALUES
AND THE MENTAL HEALTH MOVEMENT

...[T]here has grown up in the Western world an increasingly powerful movement concerned with problems of "mental health." The growth of that movement is of extraordinary interest to the social scientist whether or not he is directly interested in mental health, and since it affects the layman deeply and is likely to affect him more, it should also be of extraordinary concern to him. Let us therefore examine the origin, the nature, and the effects of this movement.

When the going and settled order of the Middle Ages was disturbed and broken up, perhaps chiefly through the introduction of money, there was radical change in an old social structure, the feudal order, inevitably involving changes in the economics, the politics, the ethics, and the theologies of all the Western world. Unavoidably, man's relation to things, man's relation to man, and man's relation to what he projected as the ideal had to alter.

How men did things to and with things altered; these alterations constituted the "revolutions in technology." *What* men knew about things altered, enlarged, and expanded, giving birth to natural science viewed as a body of knowledge. And *how* men knew about things changed; natural science as a method came to dominate over revelation and tradition, and the testimony of scientists came to have greater weight than the opinion of priests or ancestors.

In the relation of man to man, somewhat the same sequence followed. Men, related to one another primarily by force, authority, tradition, and love, were reorganized in relations that depended more nearly on force, advantage, calculation, cupidity, interest, distrust, and fear. The market became the dominant institution, virtually replacing all such mystical bodies as family, church, and, later, guild. Similarly, what men knew about themselves and one another changed, giving birth to the social sciences viewed as a body of knowledge. And the ground upon which they accepted or rejected knowledge about themselves or one another changed to some degree also as the social sciences provided new methods of securing reliable knowledge about man. This revolution is by no means complete, and the traditional sources of knowledge still compete openly and forcefully in both popular and scholarly literature for the right to have their testimony accepted and its source accredited.

In the realm of value, or the ideal, the revolution is hardly well begun. Save for the obvious passing of the dominance of the one institution, the church, which formerly exerted almost undisputed sway in defining both what is and what ought to be the order of goods, nothing is clear. That no church any longer organizes the lives of men in so many respects or at so deep a level as the church once did, it would be difficult to doubt. But what has passed clearly—and, the author believes, finally—from the church has devolved exclusively upon no other body, nor has it even become dominantly concentrated in any. Who today has the right—for whom—to an authoritative pronouncement of what is the good life, of what is the order of the virtues, of whether there is a supernatural order, and if so, what it is and whether it matters? Has scientist, priest, artist, philosopher, psychiatrist, or Man of Distinction this right?

Into this power vacuum the mental health movement has been drawn—together with a variety of competitors from neo-orthodoxies to new inventions, such as the omnicompetent State. With one foot in humanism and the other in science, it seeks to perform, and to a degree does perform, many if not most of the functions of the relinquishing institution—plus, perhaps, some others. A revolution in social values is what gives birth to the movement, and it is a revolutionary doctrine that the movement is moved by and expresses.

The power vacuum created by the bankruptcy of other institutions, however, furnished only the condition in which a new institution could "move in," and does not fully explain it. There are three other roots of the mental health movement in the "great revolution."

First, such a time of radical and widespread change is likely to be (or to be *felt* as) a time of acute stress and deep distress. It will in and of itself (and it has done so) cause people to turn sustained attention and effort not only to the life without, but also to the nature and vicissitudes of the life within. And the latter is precisely the area of specialization and concern of the mental health movement.

Second, such a time will tend to call out (and it has) a spate of new social inventions—ways of dealing with human problems; and these, if they appear at a sufficiently rapid rate, will in turn call out mediators of the new ideas. And this is precisely where the mental health movement operates —between the scientific pen and the lay eye.

Third, whether or not there has been a net increase in misery of a psychological nature, the existence of a movement directed to its remedy or alleviation will tend to focus concern upon the problem; that is, in effect, to expand the market which it is equipped to supply.

This will tend to be more readily possible in a situation in which there is a diminution of suffering from natural disaster, famine, or the want of material objects. Lightning rods, ever-normal granaries, and the mass production of goods *permit* us to pay some increased attention to the inner life. The mental health movement *encourages* us to do so; the nature of present-day life virtually *forces* it upon us; and the disappearance of the formerly accepted and accredited ways of so doing inclines us to the trial and adoption of new methods. So we move from the "cure of souls" in either of its senses to "psychotherapy" and "mental hygiene"; from preoccupation with salvation to preoccupation with adjustment or peace of mind; from the attack upon evil to the war against anxiety; and from obedience in a service which was perfect freedom to a search for autonomy in a freedom without which no service can have dignity.

That the situation described presents some remarkable parallels with the situation confronting the early Christian Church should occasion no surprise. That the general shape and form of the resultant movement should in many vital particulars resemble those of any other church ought also to occasion no great astonishment.

Like the early church, the mental health movement unites and addresses itself to "all sorts and conditions of men," so only they be "for" mental health as they were formerly for virtue and (more mildly) against sin. Like the church, it consists of a body of laymen and specialists, with the latter having as their special charge the psychological welfare of the former, to be worked out, however, by both together. Like the church, there is a "fellowship of all believers" that transcends great variety of belief, but differentiates from the unbelievers—those who are against "all that" or simply not for it.

As in the church, a vast variety of activities are carried on whose principal unifying element is that they are all thought to lead in some degree to the furthering of the common end, though they are not all of equal importance; the monastic work of research, somewhat abstracted from the trials, tribulations, and rewards of this life, is frequently thought more important than the life of teaching and rescuing "in the world" with double risk of reward and seduction.

But much more important than these incidental analogies is the fact that the movement occupies or seeks to occupy the heartland of the old ·territory. The protagonists and practitioners of mental health are increasingly called upon to pronounce on what used to be called moral questions, in the small and in the large, in general and in particular.

The pronouncements cover matters of both substance and method. Breast feeding of infants, for instance, is currently "good," not under divine dispensation or because it is "natural," but because the mental hygienists say—probably quite rightly—it will help to produce a "good" child from the viewpoint of mental hygiene. The production of "good" children in another sense—what used to be called well-behaved children—by bad means such as fear or conditioning or seduction is held to be bad because it militates against integration, which is close to the mental hygienist's *summum bonum*.

Divorce is good or bad, not in and of itself, but insofar as it increases or decreases the mental health of the parties thereto; or, in a rare, wider view, all the parties concerned, including nonparticipants.

To say these things is by no means to attack or make fun of the mental health movement—quite the contrary. What is being said, in effect, is that of necessity it has the form and flavor of a church: organization, a message or mission, a set of central values, committed servants—lay and professional—activities, orthodoxies and heresies, celebrations and observances, excommunications at need, and the felt power in moral matters to bind and loose.

This is also not to say that there are no distinctions to be drawn between this movement and the movements it wholly or partly replaces. There are profound and important differences. How else and why else should it be on the wax as they wane?

First, the values embodied in the movement are this-worldly and secular, as opposed to other-worldly and supernatural. Second, it is man-centered—

sometimes perhaps too narrowly (taking account only of this patient, and taking the social context for granted), but often with a wide view and a full sweep. Third, it is to an unusual degree nondogmatic (unless the dictum that there is to be no dogma is itself held to be a dogma) despite what has been said above about orthodoxies and heresies. In close touch with the changing deliverances of science, it has itself to partake to a large degree of the tentative attitude, and in this respect it resembles more the mystic wing of the churches which for analogical reasons had to keep themselves largely unfettered and open to "the free sweep of the spirit." Fourth, its role is to facilitate an ongoing process, to remove obstacles to action and enjoyment, to free and liberate rather than enmesh and enchain.

The mental health movement has thus arisen out of a collapse of ancient social values, it has caught up, shaped, and embodied new ones, and has made of "mental health," however vaguely apprehended or defined, an important if not dominant social value, and seen to its incorporation to a degree in the beliefs and practices of other institutions.

THE MENTAL HEALTH MOVEMENT
AND SOCIAL VALUES

In the process of its own growth, the movement has, as already intimated, had reciprocal effects on the general social value scheme. To a very large degree, as the mediator of the inquiring spirit of the social sciences, it has acted with the other "acids of modernity" as a solvent of hitherto stable beliefs. Where are yesteryear's open champions of obedience, of the innate superiority of men over women, of the quiet, well-mannered child (at any price), of belief in "original sin" or the fundamental baseness of man (or virtue, for that matter), in the unitary character of intelligence, in corporal punishment, in proprietary rights in children and women? They are still with us, as the wheelbarrow is compresent with the airplane; but in much the same places.

The mental health movement has not unaided made these beliefs and a thousand others unfashionable, not to say disreputable, but it has helped. But it has done far more than render discreditable beliefs discredited. It has created or helped create something that is new in history, or as new in history as anything ever is. It has focused attention on the inner life—or perhaps more exactly, the inner life in relation to the outer. And while every church has sought to do that, the difference is that this movement is in somewhat more intimate contact with scientific methods of discovering what the inner life is.

This is a difference indeed—a difference that makes a difference. For good or ill, the movement is a mediator or interpreter of the scientific message, rather than an opponent of it, giving ground gracelessly and step by step.

The movement has not only focused attention on the inner life and its quality, but it bids fair to make that the touchstone of all other goods. This also is not new. But again, what is new is the gradual development of methods of increased sureness and reliability for the discovery of what that inner life is really like. "Know thyself," said the Greeks; but they hardly suspected the structure, not to say the content, of that which man least knows and most needs to know—his "unconscious."

This concentration upon, and heightened consciousness of, the nature of mental life is now so widespread as to ensure an appreciative audience for "New Yorker" cartoons about psychiatrists, Hollywood films about alcoholism or amnesia, mothers'-aid books about the emergent little super-egos and their resurgent little ids.

On the whole, the mental health movement has been content with its role of facilitation of ongoing process, and has had very little to say about final ends, or ultimate values. There are, of course, striking exceptions, as when a leader in the field says that Santa Claus (and his equivalents) must go, and as a consequence finds leagued against him a powerful combination of the sophisticated who have much to lose and the unsophisticated who have nothing to lose but their strains. But the two persistent positions taken by the majority in the field have interesting consequences.

The first of the two positions states or takes for granted that mental hygienists are not concerned with ultimate values as such: they function at the *means* level, and their aid should be equally welcome under almost any scheme of ultimate values. The church, industry, the Nazi party, the socialist society, all have mental health problems, and the mental hygienist can help all equally. Some have reservations, but the position is essentially that within a wide range of moral schemes, or in all of them, mental hygienists can aid and operate.

This is not quite moral indifference, though to many it will seem so. It is the precise analog of the position of at least one church: that it is above and beyond politics, and that—provided certain of its criteria are met—it can live in any form of polity and reach a concordat with any bargain-keeping government.

The alternate position consists largely in the attitude that ultimate values are matters for continuing discovery, and that therefore the business of the mental hygienist is to facilitate and further the endless common search. In this view, no values are ultimate; all are tentative and temporary, *except the values implicit in and necessary to the method of discovery itself.* This view puts a high premium on curiosity, honesty, intelligence, care, and boldness; and also, by implication, on due humility and proper responsibility in the human enterprise.

It may be felt that there is a great and unbridgeable gulf between these views; I feel that there is; and that this represents the latent first great schism within the movement. But in at least one important respect, the effect of each view upon social values has been, unwittingly, much the same.

That joint effect has been to shake confidence in any existent scheme of ultimate values, to lead people quite generally to conclude that such questions are unanswerable and that the answers are matters of indifference. No mental hygienist known to me actually holds such views; many people known to me draw such inferences from what mental hygienists say.

Selection between the two positions is as difficult as it is important, for the second is quite capable of making the search for ultimate values central to the human enterprise, which is where, in my judgment, it properly belongs. But the first position has behind it the authoritative weight of the medical and priestly tradition that the profession is there to serve all comers, regardless of the use to which they intend to put regained health or grace. The alternative is very uncomfortable ethically and politically. Ethically it raises the problem of forgiveness: to whom, under what circumstances, may the means of health or grace be refused? Politically it means the return of the power to bind or loose to a body of professionals, with all the risks of corruption of one side and spoliation of the other that such power situations always have implied.

No matter which course is chosen, the effects on social values are already profound, and are likely to be increasingly so as money and power and prestige accrue to the movement, as they may well do at steadily increasing rates.

6. Man's Search for Himself, R. May

From the previous excerpts the reader might gain the impression that the concerns of "humanistic psychology" are relatively recent. In one sense this is true. In its present form this movement is dependent on such events as the development of psychoanalysis. But in this excerpt by Rollo May, who is a practicing psychotherapist in New York, we are reminded that this "new" concern is directed toward an ancient problem—the relation between freedom and authority, between legitimate independence and guilt, and between confidence and anxiety. What interpretation does he give to the ancient Christian myth of Adam and Eve, and the ancient Greek myth of Prometheus? (In what ways does he differ from traditional interpretations of the former story with which you are familiar?) What possible positive meaning does May suggest for the mythical portrayal of the gods' fight against man's creativity? What is his attitude toward "the authoritarian side" of all religious traditions? Does May imply that those who simply obey and conform to society and church are

Reprinted from *Man's Search for Himself* by Rollo May, Ph.D. By permission of W. W. Norton & Company, Inc., and George Allen & Unwin Ltd. Copyright 1953 by W. W. Norton & Company, Inc. Pp. 180–94.

less than human? Do you feel you are "human" in his terms?
What are the characteristics of full, human life, for this author?

ADAM AND PROMETHEUS

Man is the ethical animal: but his achievement of ethical awareness is not easy. He does not grow into ethical judgment as simply as the flower grows toward the sun. Indeed, like freedom and the other aspects of man's consciousness of self, ethical awareness is gained only at the price of inner conflict and anxiety.

This conflict is portrayed in that fascinating myth of the first man, the Biblical story of Adam. This ancient Babylonian tale, rewritten and carried over into the Old Testament about 850 B.C., pictures how ethical insight and self-awareness are born at the same time. Like the story of Prometheus and other myths, this tale of Adam speaks a classic truth to generation after generation of people not because it refers to a particular historical event, but because it portrays some deep inward experience shared by all men.

Adam and Eve, so the story goes, live in the Garden of Eden where God "had made all sorts of trees grow that were pleasant to the sight and good for food." In this delightful land they know neither toil nor want. Even more significantly, they have no anxiety and no guilt: they "do not know they are naked." They have no struggle with the earth in wresting their living, nor psychological conflict within themselves, nor spiritual conflict with God.

But Adam had been commanded by God not to eat of the trees of the knowledge of good and evil and the tree of life in the Garden, "lest he become like God in knowing good and evil." When Adam and Eve did eat of the fruit of the first tree, "their eyes were opened"; and the first evidence of their knowing good and evil was in their experiencing anxiety and guilt. They were "aware of their nakedness," and when at noon God walked through the garden for his daily airing, as the author says in his childlike and charming style, Adam and Eve hid from his sight among the trees.

In his anger at their disobedience, God meted out punishments. The woman was condemned to have sexual cravings for her husband and to experience pain in childbirth, and to man God gave the punishment of work.

> By the sweat of your brow shall you earn your living,
> Until you return to the ground. . . .
> For dust you are,
> And to dust you must return.

This remarkable story is actually describing in the primitive way of the early Mesopotamian people what happens in every human being's development some time between the ages of one and three, namely the emergence of self-awareness. Before that time the individual has lived in the Garden of Eden, a symbol of the period of existence in the womb and early infancy when he is entirely taken care of by parents, and his life is warm and comfortable. The Garden stands for that state reserved for infants, animals and angels, in which ethical conflict and responsibility do not exist; it is the period of innocence in which one "knows neither shame nor guilt." Such pictures of paradise without productive activity appear in many different forms in literature, and they are typically a harking back in romantic longing to the early state preceding self-awareness, or to that more extreme state with which the period of innocence has much in common psychologically, namely the existence in the womb.

With the loss of "innocence" and the rudimentary beginnings of ethical sensitivity, the myth goes on to indicate, the person falls heir to the particular burdens of self-consciousness, anxiety and guilt feeling. He likewise has an awareness—though it may not appear till later—that he is "of dust." That is to say, he realizes that he will some time die; he becomes conscious of his own finiteness.

On the positive side, this eating of the tree of knowledge and the learning of right and wrong represent the birth of the psychological and spiritual person. Indeed, Hegel spoke of this myth of the "fall" of man as a "fall upward." The early Hebrew writers who put the myth into the book of Genesis might well have made it the occasion for celestial song and rejoicing, for this is the day—rather than at the creation of Adam—when man the human being was born. But what is amazing is that all this is pictured as happening *against* God's will and commandments. God is portrayed as being angry that "man has become like one of us, in knowing good from evil; and now, suppose he were to reach out his hand and take the fruit of the tree of life also, and eating it, live forever!"

Are we to believe that this God did not wish man to have knowledge and ethical sensitivity—this God who, we are told just the chapter before in the book of Genesis, created man in his own image, which, if it means anything at all, means likeness to God in the respects of freedom, creativity and ethical choice? Are we to suppose that God wished to keep man in the state of innocence and psychological and ethical blindness?

These implications are so out of keeping with the astute psychological insight of the myth, that we must find some other explanations. To be sure, the myth, coming as it does out of that dim period of three thousand to a thousand years before Christ, represents the primitive viewpoint. It is understandable that primitive storytellers would be unable to distinguish between constructive self-consciousness and rebellion, considering the fact that many people even today find it very hard to make that distinction. Furthermore, the God in the myth is Yahweh, the earliest and most primitive Hebrew tribal deity, who is notorious as the jealous and vindictive God. It was against the cruel and unethical ways of Yahweh that the later Hebrew prophets protested.

We can get light on this strange contradiction in the Adam myth if we look at the parallel Greek myths of Zeus and the other gods on Mount

Olympus which arose in the same archaic epoch. The Greek myth closest to the story of Adam is that of Prometheus, who stole fire from the gods and gave it to human beings for their warmth and productivity. The enraged Zeus, noting one night from a glow on earth that the mortals had fire, seized Prometheus, bore him off to the Caucasus, and chained him to a mountain peak. The torture devised by Zeus' skillful imagination was to have a vulture feast by day on Prometheus' liver, and then, when the liver had grown back during the night, the vulture would tear at it again the next day, thus ensuring perpetual torment for the hapless Prometheus.

So far as punishment goes, Zeus had an edge over Yahweh in cruelty. For the Greek god, smoldering in anger that man should now have fire, crammed all the diseases, sorrows and vices into a box in the form of mothlike creatures, and had Mercury take the box to the earthly paradise (very much like the Garden of Eden) in which Pandora and Epimetheus lived in untroubled happiness. When the curious woman opened it, out flew the creatures, and mankind was visited with these neverending afflictions. These demonic elements in the god's dealings with man certainly do not present a pretty picture.

As the Adam story is the myth of self-consciousness, Prometheus is the symbol of creativity—the bringing of new ways of life to mankind. Indeed, the name Prometheus means "forethought"—and as we have pointed out, the capacity to see into the future, to plan, is simply one aspect of self-consciousness. Prometheus' torture represents the inner conflict which comes with creativity—it symbolizes the anxiety and guilt to which—as creative figures like Michelangelo, Thomas Mann, Dostoevski and countless others have told us—the man who dares to bring mankind new forms of life is subject. But again, as in the Adam myth, Zeus is jealous of man's upward strivings and vindictive in punishment. So we are left with the same problem—what does it mean that the gods fight against man's creativity?

To be sure, there is rebellion against the gods in the actions of both Adam and Prometheus. This is the angle from which the myths as they stand make sense. For the Greeks and Hebrews knew that when a man tries to leap over his human limitations, when he commits the sin of overreaching himself (as David did in taking Uriah's wife), or commits *hubris** (as did the proud Agamemnon when he conquered Troy), or arrogates to himself universal power (as in modern fascist ideology) or holds that his limited knowledge is the final truth (as does the dogmatic person, whether he be religious or scientific), then he becomes dangerous. Socrates was right: the beginning of wisdom is the admission of one's ignorance, and man can creatively use his powers, and to some extent transcend his limitations, only as he humbly and honestly admits these limitations to begin with. The myths are sound in their warning against false pride.

But the rebellion these myths portray is clearly good and constructive at the same time; and hence they cannot be dismissed merely as pictures of

---

* Greek word for arrogance, insolence.

man's struggle against his finiteness and pride. They portray the psychological truth that the child's "opening his eyes," and gaining self-awareness, always involves potential conflict with those in power, be they gods or parents. But why is this potential rebellion—without which the child would never acquire potentialities for freedom, responsibility, and ethical choice, and the most precious characteristics of man would lie dormant—why is this rebellion to be condemned?

We submit that in these myths there speaks the age-old conflict between entrenched authority, as represented by the jealous gods, and the upsurging of new life and creativity. The emergence of new vitality always to some extent breaks the existing customs and beliefs, and is thus threatening and anxiety-provoking to those in power as well as to the growing person himself. And those who represent the "new" may find themselves in deadly conflict with the entrenched powers—as Orestes and Oedipus found out. The anxiety in Adam and the torture experienced by Prometheus also tell us psychologically that within the creative person himself there is fear of moving ahead. In these myths there speaks not only the courageous side of man, but the servile side which would prefer comfort to freedom, security to one's own growth. The fact that in the myth of Adam and Eve the punishments meted out are *sexual desire* and *work* further proves our point. For is it not the longing to be perpetually taken care of which would lead us to conceive of work—the opportunity to till the soil and produce food, to create by the power of one's own hand—as a *punishment?* Would it not be the anxious side of one's self which would conceive of sexual desire as in itself a burden—and to castrate one's self, as Origen actually did, to avoid conflict by cutting out desire? To be sure, anxiety and guilt which accompany having to produce one's own sustenance, and the problems involved in sexual desire as well as other aspects of self-awareness, are painful. At times they certainly do bring in their train great conflict and suffering. But who would argue that, except in extreme cases such as psychosis, anxiety and guilt feelings are too great a price to pay for the venture of self-knowledge, of creativity—in short too great a price to pay for the power to be a human being rather than an innocent infant?

These myths show the authoritarian side in all religious traditions—Greek, Hebrew or Christian as it may be—which wars against new ethical insights. It is the voice of Yahweh, the jealous and vindictive God; it is the voice of the king who, jealous of his position and power, would abandon his son to the wolves, as did Oedipus' father; it is the tribal chief or priest who tends to crush the young, the new, the growing; it is the dogmatic beliefs and rigid customs which resist new creativity.

To be sure, every society must have both sides—the influences which bring new ideas and ethical insights into birth, and the institutions which conserve the values of the past. No society would survive long without both new vitality and old forms, change and stability, the prophetic religion which attacks existing institutions and the priestly religion which protects the institutions.

But our particular problem in the present day, as we have seen, is an overwhelming tendency toward comformity. The radar-directed person, who is desperately trying to live by what the group expects of him, will obviously think of morality as "adjustment" to the standards of his group. In such times ethics tend more and more to be identified with *obedience*. One is "good" to the extent that one obeys the dictates of society and church. An uncritical view of the Adam myth, of course, makes a very good rationalization for such tendencies—one can point out that if Adam had not disobeyed, he would never have been forced out of paradise. This is much more appealing to people in our upset times than one might think, for the state symbolized by paradise where there is no care or want or anxiety or conflict or need for personal responsibility is devoutly to be wished in an age of anxiety.

Thus a premium is implicitly placed on *not* developing consciousness of one's self. It is as though the more unquestioning obedience the better, and as though the less personal responsibility the better.

But what really is ethical about obedience? If one's goal were simple obedience, one could train a dog to fulfill the requirements very well. In fact, the dog would then be more "ethical" than his human masters, for a dog won't carry with him the ever-present possibility of a neurotic outbreak, in the form of some "accident" of disobedience, as a protest from his repressed and denied freedom. And on the sociological level, what is ethical about conforming to accepted norms? The person fulfilling that ideal would in 1900 have been repressed sexually like almost everyone else in that period; in 1925 he would have been mildly rebellious according to the then accepted mode; in 1945 he would have guided his actions by the average of what's done as presented in the Kinsey report. Whether you dignify the standards by calling them "cultural" or moral rules or absolute religious doctrines, what is ethical about such conformity? Obviously such behavior leaves out the essence of human ethics—one's sensitive awareness of the unique relationship with the other person, and the working out, in some degree of freedom and personal responsibility, of the creative relationship.

One of the most remarkable pictures of the conflict between ethical sensitivity and existing institutions and of the anxiety which ethical freedom brings, is in Dostoevski's story of the Grand Inquisitor. Christ came back to earth one day, quietly and unobtrusively healing people in the streets but recognized by all. It happened to be during the Spanish Inquisition, and the old Cardinal, the Grand Inquisitor, met Christ on the street and had him taken to prison.

In the dead of night the Inquisitor comes to explain to the silent Christ why he never should have returned to earth. For fifteen centuries the church has been struggling to correct Christ's original mistake in giving man freedom, and they will not allow Him to undo their work. Christ's mistake, says the Inquisitor, was that "in place of the rigid ancient law," he placed on man the burden of having "with free heart to decide for himself what is good and what is evil," and "this fearful burden of free choice" is too much for men. Christ respected man too much, argues the

Inquisitor, and forgot that actually people want to be treated as children and be led by "authority" and "miracle." He should have merely given them bread, as the devil suggested in the temptation, but "thou wouldst not deprive man of freedom and didst reject the offer, thinking, what is that freedom worth if obedience is bought with bread?...But in the end they will lay their freedom at our feet, and say to us, 'Make us your slaves, but feed us.' ... Didst thou forget that man prefers peace and even death, to freedom of choice in the knowledge of good and evil?"

There are few heroic, strong persons who could follow Christ's way of freedom, continues the old Inquisitor, but what most men seek is to be united "all in one unanimous and harmonious ant heap.... I tell Thee that man is tormented by no greater anxiety than to find some one quickly to whom he can had over that gift of freedom with which the ill-fated creature is born." The church accepts the gift: "We shall allow or forbid them to live with their wives and mistresses, to have or not to have children—according to whether they have been obedient or disobedient—and they will submit to us gladly and cheerfully...for it will save them from the great anxiety and terrible agony they endure at present in making a free decision for themselves." The old Inquisitor, asking somewhat sadly the rhetorical question, "Why hast Thou come back to hinder our work?" states as he takes his leave that tomorrow Christ will be burned.

Dostoevski does not mean, of course, that the Inquisitor speaks for all religion, either Catholic or Protestant. He means, rather, to portray the life-thwarting side of religion which seeks the "unanimous...ant heap," the element in religion which enslaves the person and would tempt him to surrender, like Esau for a mess of pottage, his most precious possessions—his freedom and responsibility.

The person in our day, therefore, who seeks values around which he can integrate his living, needs to face the fact that there is no easy and simple way out. He cannot merely "return to religion" any more than he can healthily return to his parents when the freedom and responsibility of choice becomes too great a burden. For there is a double relation between ethics and religion, the same double relation we find between parents and offspring. On one hand, the ethical prophets throughout history are born and nourished in the religious tradition—one has only to call to mind Amos, Isaiah, Jesus, St. Francis, Lao-tzu, Socrates, Spinoza and countless others. But on the other hand, a bitter warfare exists between ethically sensitive people and religious institutions. Ethical insights are born in attacks upon conformity to existing mores. In the Sermon on the Mount, Jesus precedes each new ethical insight he offers with the refrain, "It was said unto you of old, but I say unto you...." This is the constant refrain of the man of ethical sensitivity: new wine "cannot be put into old bottles, else the bottles burst and the wine is spilt." Thus it is always: the ethically creative persons, like Socrates, Kierkegaard and Spinoza, are engaged in finding new ethical "spirit" as opposed to the formalized "law" of the traditional system.

There is always tension and sometimes even outright warfare between these ethical leaders and existing religious and social institutions, with the ethical leader often attacking the church and the church as frequently branding the other an enemy. Spinoza, the "God-intoxicated philosopher," was excommunicated; one of Kierkegaard's books is entitled *Attack on Christendom;* Jesus and Socrates were executed as "threats" to moral and social stability. It is amazing to note how often the saints of one period have been, in historical fact, the so-called atheists of the previous period.

In our own day the examples of those who attack existing religious institutions as opposed to ethical growth include Nietzsche, in his protest that Christian morality is motivated by resentment, and Freud, in his criticism of religion as ensconcing people in infantile dependency. Regardless of their theoretical beliefs, they represent the ethical concern for man's well-being and fulfillment. Though in some quarters their teachings are regarded as inimical to religion (as some of them are), I believe that in future generations the main insights of both Freud and Nietzsche will be absorbed into the ethical-religious tradition, and religion will become the richer and more effective for their contributions.

John Stuart Mill points out, for example, that his father James Mill considered religion the "enemy of morality." The elder Mill had been educated in a Presbyterian theological seminary in Scotland, but had later withdrawn from the church because he refused to believe that God could have created hell with the knowledge, as implied in predestination, that people were going there without their own choice. He held that religion "radically vitiated the standard of morals, making it consist of doing the will of a being, on whom it lavishes indeed all the phrases of adulation, but whom in sober truth it depicts as eminently hateful." Mill adds a point with respect to this type of "unbeliever" in the middle nineteenth century: "The best among them...are more genuinely religious, in the best sense of the word religion, than those who exclusively arrogate to themselves the title."[1]

Nicolai Berdyaev, the Russian Orthodox theologian and philosopher, protests against the same sadistic doctrines as the elder Mill referred to, and also against the fact that "Christians have expressed their piety in bows, fawnings and prostrations—gestures that are symbolic of servility and humiliation." As has every ethical prophet in history, Berdyaev remarks that he would "fight against God in the name of God," and adds that it is "impossible to revolt, except with reference to and in the name of some ultimate value by which I judge that which I resolve to oppose; that is to say in the name of God..."[2]

There is a common motif in these struggles between new insight and entrenched authorities as they appear in the conflict of Adam and Yahweh, Prometheus and Zeus, Oedipus and his father, Orestes and the matriarchal powers, or in the prophets in man's actual ethical history. Is it not the same psychological motif, on a different level, as we discovered in the conflict between child and parent? *Or, more accurately, is it not the conflict between every human being's need to struggle toward enlarged self-awareness, maturity, freedom and responsibility, and his tendency to remain a child and cling to the protection of parents or parental substitutes?*

RELIGION—SOURCE
OF STRENGTH OR WEAKNESS?

In any discussion of religion and personality integration the question is not whether religion itself makes for health or neurosis, but *what kind* of religion and how is it used? Freud was in error when he held that religion is per se a compulsion neurosis. Some religion is and some is not. Any area in life may be used as a compulsive neurosis: philosophy may be a flight from reality into a harmonious "system" as a protection from the anxiety and disharmonies of day-to-day life *or* it may be a courageous endeavor to understand reality better. Science may be used as a rigid, dogmatic faith by which one escapes emotional insecurity and doubt, *or* it may be an open-minded search for new truth. Indeed, since faith in science has been more acceptable in intelligent circles in our society and therefore is less apt to be questioned, it may well be that in our day this faith more frequently plays the role of a compulsive escape from uncertainties than does religion. Freud, however, was correct technically—as he so often was—in that he asked the right question with respect to religion: does it increase dependency and keep the individual infantile?

Nor are those on the other side correct who say glibly and with comfort to the masses that religion makes for mental health. Some religion certainly does and some decidedly does not. All of these blanket statements would relieve us of the much more difficult question of penetrating to the inner meaning of the religious attitudes, and assessing them not as theoretical beliefs but as functioning aspects of the person's organic relation to his life.

The questions we propose are: Does a given individual's religion serve to break his will, keep him at an infantile level of development, and enable him to avoid the anxiety of freedom and personal responsibility? Or does it serve him as a basis of meaning which affirms his dignity and worth, which gives him a basis for courageous acceptance of his limitations and normal anxiety, but which aids him to develop his powers, his responsibility and his capacity to love his fellow men?

NOTES

1. John Stuart Mill, *Autobiography.*
2. Nicolai Berdyaev, *Spirit and Reality,* New York, Charles Scribner's Sons, 1935.

7. Psychoanalyst— Physician of the Soul, E. Fromm

Like Seeley and May, Erich Fromm sees psychotherapy as continuing an essential element in the history of religious effort, but wants to purify this effort from an authoritarian stance. Dr. Fromm (b. 1900) is a practicing psychoanalyst and well-known author of several books on the nature of the human situation and psychoanalysis as a healing art. In the book from which this excerpt is taken, Fromm distinguishes between "humanistic religion" and "authoritarian religion," the latter being one in which man is seen to be controlled by a higher power outside himself. He also points out that there is a difference between a kind of psychotherapy that aims primarily at social adjustment and one that is concerned with the "cure of the soul." In the latter, the physician moves beyond the removal of a pathological symptom—for example, a headache or inordinate anxiety—to "a therapy of difficulties in living rooted in the neurotic character." Just prior to the beginning of our selection he has stated that a therapeutic solution at the level of social adjustment— for example, winning friends and influencing people—may be merely an expression of the problem seem at a deeper level— for example, lack of self-acceptance. Thus, what is regarded by one therapist as a cure is held to be a form of sickness by another. Nevertheless, Fromm is quite clear that he refers to a depth therapy, a "cure of the soul," when he explains how psychotherapy functions religiously. What criteria does he give for mental health? Do you agree that therapeutic goals are the same as "religious" goals? Would you agree with Fromm's description of religious elements as distinguished from ethical concerns? Fromm's next chapter following this except is entitled "Is Psychoanalysis a Threat to Religion?"; how would you expect Fromm to answer this question? How do you answer this question?

We see that it is not easy to determine what we consider to be the sickness and what we consider to be the cure. The solution depends on what one considers to be the aim of psychoanalysis. We find that according to one conception *adjustment* is the aim of analytic cure. By adjustment is meant a person's ability to act like the majority of people in his culture. In this view those existing patterns of behavior which society and the culture approve provide the criteria for mental health. These criteria are not critically examined from the standpoint of universal human norms but rather express a social relativism which takes this "rightness" for granted and considers behavior deviant from them to be wrong, hence unhealthy. Therapy aiming at nothing but social adjustment can only reduce the excessive suffering of the neurotic to the average level of suffering inherent in conformity to these patterns.

In the second view the aim of therapy is not primarily adjustment but optimal development of a person's potentialities and the realization of his individuality. Here the psychoanalyst is not an "adjustment counselor" but, to use Plato's expression, the "physician of the soul." This view is based on the premise that there are immutable laws inherent in human nature and human functioning which operate in any given culture. These laws cannot be violated without serious damage to the personality. If someone violates his moral and intellectual integrity he weakens or even paralyzes his total personality. He is unhappy and suffers. If his way of living is approved by his culture the suffering may not be conscious or it may be felt as being related to things entirely separate from his real problem. But in spite of what he thinks, the problem of mental health cannot be separated from the basic human problem, that of achieving the aims of human life: independence, integrity, and the ability to love.

In making this distinction between adjustment and the cure of the soul I have described *principles* of therapy but I do not intend to imply that one can make such a clear-cut distinction in practice. There are many kinds of psychoanalytic procedure in which both principles are blended; sometimes the emphasis is on one, sometimes on the other. But it is important to recognize the distinction between these principles because only then can we recognize their respective weight in any given analysis. Nor do I wish to give the impression that one must chose between social adjustment and concern with one's soul, and that choosing the path of human integrity necessarily leads one into the desert of social failure.

The "adjusted" person in the sense in which I have used the term here is one who has made himself into a commodity, with nothing stable or definite except his need to please and his readiness to change roles. As long as he succeeds in his efforts he enjoys a certain amount of security, but his betrayal of the higher self, of human values, leaves an inner emptiness and insecurity which will become manifest when anything goes wrong in his battle for success. And even if nothing should go wrong he often pays for his human failure with ulcers, heart trouble, or any of the other psychically determined kinds of illness. The person who has attained inner strength and integrity often may not be as successful as his unscrupulous neighbor but he will have security, judgment, and objectivity which will make him much less vulnerable to changing fortunes and opinions of others and will in many areas enhance his ability for constructive work.

It is obvious that "adjustment therapy" can have no religious function, provided that by religious we refer to the attitude common to the original teachings of humanistic religions. I wish now to show that psychoanalysis as a cure of the soul has very definitely a religious function in this sense, although it will usually lead to a more critical attitude toward theistic dogma.

In trying to give a picture of the human attitude underlying the thinking of Lao-tse, Buddha, the Prophets, Socrates, Jesus, Spinoza, and the philosophers of the Enlightenment, one is struck by the fact that in spite of significant differences there is a core of ideas and norms common to all of these teachings. Without attempting to arrive at a complete and precise formulation, the following is an approximate description of this common core: man must strive to recognize the truth and can be fully human only to the extent to which he succeeds in this task. He must be independent and free, an end in himself and not the means for any other persons's purposes. He must relate himself to his fellow men lovingly. If he has no love, he is an empty shell even if his were all power, wealth, and intelligence. Man must know the difference between good and evil, he must learn to listen to the voice of his conscience and to be able to follow it.

The following remarks attempt to show that the aim of the psychoanalytic cure of the soul is to help the patient attain the attitude which I just described as religious.

In our discussion of Freud I have indicated that to recognize the *truth* is a basic aim of the psychoanalytic process. Psychoanalysis has given the concept of truth a new dimension. In pre-analytic thinking a person could be considered to speak the truth if he believed in what he was saying. Psychoanalysis has shown that subjective conviction is by no means a sufficient criterion of sincerity. A person can believe that he acts out of a sense of justice and yet be motivated by cruelty. He can believe that he is motivated by love and yet be driven by a craving for masochistic dependence. A person can believe that duty is his guide though his main motivation is vanity. In fact most rationalizations are held to be true by the person who uses them. He not only wants others to believe his rationalizations but believes them himself, and the more he wants to protect himself from recognizing his true motivation the more ardently he must believe in them. Furthermore, in the psychoanalytic process a person learns to recognize which of his ideas have an emotional matrix and which are only conventional clichés without root in his character structure and therefore without substance and weight. The psychoanalytic process is in itself a search for truth. The object of this search is the truth about phenomena not outside of man but in man himself. It is based on the principle that mental health and happiness cannot be achieved unless we scrutinize our thinking and feeling to detect whether we rationalize and whether our beliefs are rooted in our feeling.

I have tried to show in this chapter that the psychoanalytic cure of the soul aims at helping the patient to achieve an attitude which can be called religious in the humanistic though not in the authoritarian sense of the word. It seeks to enable him to gain the faculty to see the truth, to love, to become free and responsible, and to be sensitive to the voice of his conscience. But am I not, the reader may ask, describing here an attitude which is more rightly called ethical than religious? Am I not leaving out the very element which distinguishes the religious from the ethical realm? I believe that the difference between the religious and the ethical is to a large extent only an epistemological one, though not entirely so. Indeed, it seems that there is a factor common to certain kinds of religious experience which goes beyond the purely ethical.[1] But it is exceedingly difficult if not impossible to formulate this factor of religious experience. Only those who experience it will understand the formulation, and they do not need any formulation. This difficulty is greater but not different in kind from that of expressing any feeling experience in word symbols, and I want to make at least an attempt to indicate what I mean by this specifically religious experience and what its relation is to the psychoanalytic process.

One aspect of religious experience is the wondering, the marveling, the becoming aware of life and of one's own existence, and of the puzzling problem of one's relatedness to the world. Existence, one's own existence and that of one's fellow men, is not taken for granted but is felt as a problem, is not an answer but a question. Socrates' statement that wonder is the beginning of all wisdom is true not only for wisdom but for the religious experience. One who has never been bewildered, who has never looked upon life and his own existence as phenomena which require answers and yet, paradoxically, for which the only answers are new questions, can hardly understand what religious experience is.

Another quality of religious experience is what Paul Tillich has called the "ultimate concern." It is not passionate concern with the fulfillment of our desires but the concern connected with the attitude of wonder I have been discussing: an ultimate concern with the meaning of life, with the self-realization of man, with the fulfillment of the task which life sets us. This ultimate concern gives all desires and aims, inasmuch as they do not contribute to the welfare of the soul and the realization of the self, a secondary importance; in fact they are made unimportant by comparison with the object of this ultimate concern. It necessarily excludes division between the holy and the secular because the secular is subordinated to and molded by it.

Beyond the attitude of wonder and of concern there is a third element in religious experience, the one which is most clearly exhibited and described by the mystics. It is an attitude of oneness not only in oneself, not only with one's fellow men, but with all life and, beyond that, with the universe. Some may think that this attitude is one in which the uniqueness and individuality of the self are denied and the experience of self weakened. That this is not so constitutes the paradoxical nature of this attitude. It comprises both the sharp and even painful awareness of one's self as a separate and unique entity and the longing to break through the confines of this individual organization and to be one with the All. The religious attitude in this sense is simultaneously the fullest experience of individuality and of its opposite; it is not so much a blending of the two as a polarity from whose tension religious experience springs. It is an attitude of pride and integrity and at the same time of a humility which stems from experiencing oneself as but a thread in the texture of the universe.

Has the psychoanalytic process any bearing on this kind of religious experience?

That it presupposes an attitude of ultimate concern I have already indicated. It is no less true that it tends to awaken the patient's sense of wondering and questioning. Once this sense is awakened the patient will find answers which are his own. If it is not awakened, no answer the psychoanalyst can give, not even the best and truest one, will be of any use. This wondering is the most significant therapeutic factor in analysis. The patient has taken his reactions, his desires and anxieties for granted, has interpreted his troubles as the result of the actions of others, of bad luck, constitution, or what not. If the psychoanalysis is effective it is not because the patient accepts new theories about the reasons of his unhappiness but because he acquires a capacity for being genuinely bewildered; he marvels at the discovery of a part of himself whose existence he had never suspected.

It is this process of breaking through the confines of one's organized self—the ego—and of getting in touch with the excluded and disassociated part of oneself, the unconscious, which is closely related to the religious experience of breaking down individuation and feeling one with the All. The concept of the unconscious however, as I use it here, is neither quite that of Freud nor that of Jung.

In Freud's thinking the unconscious is essentially that in us which is bad, the repressed, that which is incompatible with the demands of our culture and of our higher self. In Jung's system the unconscious becomes a source of revelation, a symbol for that which in religious language is God himself. In his view the fact that we are subject to the dictates of our unconscious is in itself a religious phenomenon. I believe that both these concepts of the unconscious are one-sided distortions of the truth. Our unconscious—that is, that part of our self which is excluded from the organized ego which we identify with our self—contains both the lowest and the highest, the worst and the best. We must approach the unconscious not as if it were a God whom we must worship or a dragon we must slay but in humility, with a profound sense of humor, in which we see that other part of ourselves as it is, neither with horror nor with awe. We discover in ourselves desires, fears, ideas, insights which have been excluded from our conscious organization and we have seen in others but not in ourselves. It is true, by necessity we can realize only a limited part of all the potentialities within us. We have to exclude many others, since we could not live our short and limited life without such exclusion. But outside the confines of the particular organization of ego are all human potentialities, in fact, the whole of humanity. When we get in touch with this disassociated part we retain the individuation of our ego structure but we experience this unique and individualized ego as only one of the infinite versions of life, just as a drop from the ocean is different from and yet the same as all other drops which are also only particularized modes of the same ocean.

In getting in touch with this disassociated world of the unconscious one replaces the principle of repression by that of permeation and integration. Repression is an act of force, of cutting off, of "law and order." It destroys the connection between our ego and the unorganized life from which it springs and makes our self into something finished, no longer growing but dead. In dissolving repression we permit ourselves to sense the living process and to have faith in life rather than in order.

I cannot leave the discussion of the religious function of psychoanalysis —incomplete as it is—without mentioning briefly one more factor of great significance. I am referring to something which has frequently been one of the greatest objections to Freud's method, the fact that so much time and effort is devoted to a single person. I believe that there is perhaps no greater evidence of Freud's genius than his counsel to take the time even if it should require many years to help one person to achieve freedom and happiness. This idea is rooted in the spirit of the Enlightenment which, crowning the whole humanistic trend of Western civilization, emphasized the dignity and uniqueness of the individual beyond everything else. But closely as it is in accord with these principles, such an idea is in contrast to much in the intellectual climate of our time. We tend to think in terms of mass production and of gadgets. As far as production of commodities is concerned this has proven exceedingly fruitful. But if the idea of mass production and gadget worship is transferred to the problem of man and into the field of psychiatry it destroys the very basis which makes producing more and better things worth while.

NOTES

1. The kind of religious esperience which I have in mind in these remarks is the one characteristic of Indian religious experience, Christian and Jewish mysticism, and Spinoza's pantheism. I should like to note that, quite in contrast to a popular sentiment that mysticism is an irrational type of religious experience, it represents—like Hindu and Buddhistic thought and Spinozism—the highest development of rationality in religious thinking. As Albert Schweitzer has put it: "Rational thinking which is free from assumptions ends in mysticism." *Philosophy of Civilization* (Macmillan Company, 1949), p. 79.

CRITIQUE

Imagine a traditional theologian sitting back and listening to the testimonials presented thus far in Chapter V: John Seeley announcing that the mental health movement is taking over the functions of the church; George Leonard claiming that Esalen Institute can bring the races together where churches have failed; A. S. Neill ridding the world of nothing less than unhappiness itself; Abraham Maslow studying the healthy people so that he can draw up plans for Eupsychia; and Rollo May announcing that what Christians have called sin is nothing but the effect of creative individuals marking off new ethical boundaries. They seem uniformly convinced that a proper understanding of man's psychology allied to a proper educational technique will suffice to dispel mankind's childish fears (the Devil), immature loyalties (God), and adult disorders (hatred, emotional poverty, and irrational behavior). It is enough to outrage some theologians, who would exclaim: How naive! How shallow! How utopian! These critics, as exemplified in the two selections following, assert that the psychological approach to man's problems fails to take into account the full extent of the final purpose of human life if it is to be meaningful (reading 8), or the extent of the transformation required if men are to be made whole (reading 9).

8. On Man as God's Creation—
Not Man's,
A. C. Outler

*In the first selection Albert Outler, a prominent Methodist
ecumenist and Professor of Theology at SMU Perkins School
of Theology, indicates that for all the positive value of
psychotherapy, the rational and empirical assumptions of most
psychotherapists do not allow them to deal with the most
profound of human experiences—death. Although the Christian
can affirm the positive joys of life quite as much as the humanist,
he says, the Christian sees his existence in a context that extends
beyond the limits of existence; and even within the realm
of this life the psychotherapist promises more than he can deliver.*

From Albert C. Outler, *Psychotherapy and the Christian Message* (New York: Harper and Row, 1954), pp. 170–78, 185–86.

*For instance, granted that some dependency-linked loyalties are
masochistic, does it follow that all are? Could it be that the
problem in these cases lies not in this form of loyalty as such
but rather a mistaken dependence on something less than
ultimate? In any case, he insists, one cannot escape the question
of the widest relevant framework within which human life
has its meaning. Why, from Outler's standpoint, does the
humanist's handling of "death" make life literally unintelligible?
Why does the realization of human potential become possible
only when man relies on God's love and grace? Outler's statement
that God does thwart man's freedom when it leads to a presumed
individual sovereignty (autarchy) seems to be in agreement
with Rollo May's interpretation of the myths of Adam and
Prometheus regarding the danger of man's attempt to leap over
his own limitations. But do you think that Outler would ever
regard rebellion against God as Creator-Spirit to be constructive
and liberating of self-hood—as May suggests in his analysis of
these myths? Why?*

As he looks at the ethical aspects of psychotherapy, the Christian thinker
might very well be impressed by the insistence that growth toward the
best can only follow knowledge of the worst. From this we can understand
why all therapies based primarily upon support, reassurance and advice
are superficial and harmful. We can see why accurate *diagnosis* does not
suffice, especially if it is offered in an arbitrary or pontifical manner. It is
only as a person, conscious of his disorder, comes to see, for himself, the
shape of that disorder, and the psychodynamic patterns at work in his
life, that he can come to true knowledge of his actual situation, enabled to
form a fair estimate of it. To know oneself as one really is—this is the
precondition to all cure, and growth and maturation. The Christian further
recognizes in this emphasis on self-knowledge a close similarity of the
Christian demand that men come to God in genuine contrition—that is,
without the illusions of merit or even the pride of spectacular demerit.

The Christian, then, may very well acknowledge and gratefully receive
the practical services of psychotherapy in keeping people away from their
psychic disabilities and toward their actual, productive possibilities. But he
must then stand ready to face the challenge of the rival faith which, as
we have seen, is so often the context for psychotherapeutic thought. He must
consider the charge that Christianity produces, in actual results, an inferior
pattern of personality organization and that the Christian world view is
psychologically invalid. He must weigh the claim that a humanistic religion
and ethic is able to take up into it itself and conserve the real values of
the Christian wisdom while it rightly discards the psychological disvalues
which are so apparent.

If the Christian wisdom were as harmful as Fromm and Flugel and
Brierley allege, we should all have seriously to consider the choice of aban-

doning it. In the name of our commitment to the essential biblical faith, we should have to reject any wisdom about life which inevitably and systematically distorts the evident design of human existence. If "the religion of humanity" were, in actual results, as vital and valid as its devotees affirm, we should all have seriously to consider the choice of adopting it. For at least one of the basic justifications of any religious faith is that it affords the widest, deepest, truest wisdom concerning both the ends and means of human life.

Such a choice, however, cannot be made simply by direct appeal to the authority of science or dogma. The humanist faith greatly exceeds any warrant of scientific authority, and the Christian dogmas are expressly founded upon prior choices of faith. Thus, the matter lies quite beyond the range of coercive demonstration. We come then to the persuasive force of sincere witness to one's faith, which makes no other demands than that it be considered with utmost seriousness and that a decision be made in full knowledge that it is the meaning of life and death that hangs in the balance and not mere rival opinions.

The secularist, humanist faith maintains that all the crucial questions of the meaning and value of life lie *inside* the *parenthesis of being* which is the locus of birth and growth and death. The Christian faith focuses the question of life's meaning *on the parenthesis itself.* Whatever life means and whatever final quality it may have must, therefore, be derived from the relation between man and the reality on which he does, in fact, depend—the finite on the infinite. Fromm contends that men may acknowledge the fact of their dependence without any corresponding need for insight into the nature and disposition of the reality involved.[1] Further, he claims that "clinical examination of masochistic character traits" supports his view that "to worship the forces on which one depends" is "masochistic and self-destructive." He must know that this is an illicit appeal to fragmentary evidence unless he can show that all such worship is invariably masochistic and that the humanist attitude toward the given is invariably nonneurotic. Indeed, one might more reasonably contend that men do—and must—worship that upon which they *believe* they depend. This is, in fact, what worship is: Man's acknowledgment and celebration of his fundamental reliance on what he takes to be reliable, his trust in what he takes to be trustworthy, his devotion to what he takes to be the shaping forces of his destiny. Thus, in humanism, man may refuse to worship God *or* nature. Thus he proclaims his faith that God does not exist and that nature is not man's final arbiter. But he still will worship that on which he *does* rely—humanity and himself! Christians, similarly, worship that on which, as they believe, they and all existence depend—the Living God, who bounds life with the parentheses of finite limitations but who is Himself boundless in His power and love.

In the Christian view, the basic fault of the humanist account of the human possibility is that all the meanings and values which may be achieved in human life stand surrounded by a bracket of inexorable, inscrutable *givenness*. "The development of the self is never completed; even under the best conditions only part of man's potentialities is realized. Man always dies before he is fully born."[2] Is this not, finally, a verdict of ultimate meaningless on life: that it should produce beings capable of self-realization in a process which finally negates the total enterprise? Nature, conceived as the ultimate context or process of existence, is itself without meaning or purpose beyond the infinite occurrence of life items in a dynamic system which defies further explanation—or inquiry. A human life, which by dint of good use of rational and moral powers (themselves "given," without further explanation) has enjoyed a brief episode of insight and productivity, must then, *of necessity* (also unexplained) dissolve back into the nonbeing from which the whole occurrence-sequence is continually renewed.

The Christian is bound to claim that this is simply and literally unintelligible. It makes no sense of the process of existence and the role in it of the rational structures and objective values which men can discern and verify. It disregards the problems of origin and cause, purpose and end—all of which require an answer if one is to talk of structure and value. It makes no sense of the existential issues men decide in their living or dying—for it points to events but not to an end or ground in which the meaning of these events is gathered up, or focused.

Nature is not intelligible in and of itself. It cannot be interpreted as a final and comprehensive frame of reference. Man's existence as an item-in-nature is no more intelligible in itself than is nature. If nature's final meaning is *occurrence,* then human life can find no higher meaning for itself than as an instance of this endless occurrence. One lives, one dies—the tense thereafter is past! But what then of reason in its service to man in improving the quality (and duration!) of his existence? It would seem, in fact, to be delusive, since reason works with an eye toward its vision of the ultimate and the whole.

The Christian message holds that life has meaning and value in and beyond the *occurrence* of this life or that. Life is more than coming to be and passing away. The parenthesis of finite being is surrounded by the mystery and fullness of infinite being. The meaning and value of life come from the intent and purpose in the production of life. If it just happened—then this is the sum of its meaning and value. But if human life is the crown of God's creation and if "the end for which God created the world" is His love of being, then it is a part of a grand design that contingent being should come to be and should actualize its possibilities in space-time and history—and beyond. Man is in nature—an item in the natural process—but it is his unique power and task to transcend nature in the exercise of his reason, his freedom and his love. To him God discloses something of the knowledge of creation as a divine project—and with this knowledge the freedom to participate in creation as a human project.

Man is God's creature, who bears the image and stamp of God's will and purpose in his inmost self. His existence and his destiny are valued by God's love and concern, which means that the accidental and the arbitrary events of life are never final or fully meaningful in themselves. Man is finite and is, therefore, not *self*-sufficient or *self*-explanatory or *self*-fulfilled! No finite creature can be. But it is God's design for him—and, therefore, the human possibility—that he should grow up into sufficiency and fulfillment in God's providence and through his own trustful responding to God's grace. The same love that gives us being and sustains us in existence moves in us toward our true and full maturity. The primordial purpose of God remains unaltered and still empowers and directs both history and the cosmic drama. And a part of that purpose was a human community on this earth, living in the maturity of love, exercising the powers of finite freedom and rationality, with reliant faith to buoy them up, humility to aid in self-acceptance and community, faith to bind them to God and to their fellows, grace to purify and ennoble their self-assertions. In the beginning, God projected a human community of righteousness, faith and glory. And this, in the end, is what will come to pass—that is what, indeed, has already begun. This is the human possibility.

We have spoken, however, of the shadow of estrangement which falls over God's project and blocks its fulfillment. The human possibility has become impossible—for man on his own. God will not interdict man's freedom; it is His gift to man and He will not force him into faith or virtue. But man in un-faith uses his freedom to create unfreedom, his reason to construct the idol systems by which he thinks to save himself. And man sees God as a threat to his freedom, because God *does* thwart man's successful use of freedom when it is devoted to the cause of autarchy. Faith in God, then, is never easy for men. Instead, it comes normally in times of genuine and profound disturbance in the self. Faith and crisis go hand in hand.

For the human possibility to become possible requires a genuine alteration of human concern from the self and its powers to God and His providence, from self-reliance to reliance upon God's love and grace, from fear to faith, from self-confidence to confidence born of a new pattern of involvement in God's creative and redemptive work. This is the Gospel's demand for conversion, for depth regeneration, for a reorientation of motive and inner dependence. All these bring a man to a new level of self-acceptance in God's love, in which he responds, with glad acknowledgment, to God's control of his life, in the sure confidence that such a control is *not* self-mutilating nor a loss of true dignity, but, literally, justification![3]

The Christian message proclaims the possibility of men entering into the way of abundant life that leads to fulfillment and blessedness. Beyond the pivot of life, turned by man's basic faith in God's rightful rule of existence, opens up a process of growth and maturation which is replete with crisis, ordeal and the full opportunity for the use and exercise of all human gifts. But it is a process which is everywhere sustained by the consciousness of God's grace and suffused with the quiet joys of spiritual communion. Historic Christianity, at its best, stands for and works toward the highest and fullest development of human selves, for the fulfillment of God's design in human life and history. The Christian evangel, when rightly proclaimed, emphasizes that men should, in actual relations with God and their fellows, experience genuine spontaneity of love and trust; they must come to know the meaning of justice, mercy and community (Micah 6:8). The Christian ethic is an ethic of responsibility which puts concern for persons foremost because of the abundant revelation of God's concern for all and each of His children. It aims at the transformation of culture through the mind and will and heart of Christ.[4] Christianity, at least in basic intent, is a true and integral humanism, as deeply and urgently committed to human self-fulfillment as any secular humanism can be. But it steadily maintains that the human possibility and its attainment is a project which God and man share together: God as Creator-Spirit; man the wayward creature of God's love and care.

Christianity is a religion of high hopes, of great expectations! It is confident of God's loving intent for men and of God's ultimate victory over all that would obstruct and defeat man's fulfillment. The Christian wisdom points to a power at work in life and history, beyond our full knowledge, possession or manipulation, which moves in us and draws us into its mysterious workings. It calls this power God's grace—God's intent and concern made operable in the complex web of personal life and the human community. It goes before us in all our crises, preparing our hearts for faith; it sustains us in all our doings, transforming nature into its sacramental medium; and it enables us with power and hope for life's journey through death to destiny.... The acid test of every human hope is set by the fact of death. Man dies, as every other living thing also dies, but unlike the others, man foreknows he dies. The shadow of his forthcoming and unevadable end falls over his life, confronts him with the threat of nonbeing, prompts him to decisions which reach to the very heart of his existence. Man must do something about death—the deaths of loved ones and friends and his own death. But what is there to do? One possibility is to develop ideas, with rituals and funerary practices to match, which, in effect, deny that death is real or final. This general concept of "survival" can range from the doctrines reflected in the tombs of Egypt to the Greek belief in the external existence of the soul down to the modern mortician who disposes of death with flowers, cosmetics and soft music. Another possibility is to conclude that death is indeed real and final—and face it, with calm and reasoned fortitude. This idea of "extinction" calls for courage—the courage to be and the courage not to be. This is, by and large, the attitude taken by the faithful humanist. When a man dies, "he is as completely insensible to all such things [sorrow or gladness] as any piece of earth or non-living matter. He is just exactly as non-existent as a potential human being that is unborn and unconceived."[5] Facing such a fact, rationally and calmly, men can "give of our best to the continuing affirmation of life on behalf of the greater glory of man."[6] This general view, with its show of reason and scientific authority, has been taken up by a majority of psychotherapists, without much attention to the questions about life, personal values it leaves unanswered.[7]

The Christian hope of man's attainment of his full possibility is based upon convictions which differ quite radically from either of these two notions of "survival" or "extinction." The hope of survival, as such, is of no great significance for man's moral and spiritual fulfillment. As for extinction, it means that what man becomes and has and gives and enjoys come to a final, irretrievable end at death. The "hope of heaven" based on the idea of the survival or the persistence of life beyond bodily death normally expresses itself in visions of the compensation in another world of denials and frustrations men have suffered in this. The hope of "social immortality" based on the thought of the continuation of one's influence on posterity often expresses itself in a cult of memorials of one kind or another—not unlike the Renaissance cult of fame and honor. The Christian hope, on the contrary, is based exclusively upon Christian faith in the reality and power of God's love to accomplish what God has set out to do. There are good arguments for the intelligibility and cogency of this hope—better than the humanists have ever supposed or inspected[8]—but the certitude and confidence with which it is held rests on an inner awareness of how God's grace can draw a man up onto new levels of responsiveness and responsibility, to new experiences of joy and fellowship, to new visions of God's purposes to "finish His creation." *co-creatures, Gods will is done by us.*

NOTES

1. Cf. *Escape from Freedom*, pp. 155–56.
2. Fromm, *Man for Himself*, p. 91.
3. Cf. my essay, "For Us Men and Our Salvation," *Religion in Life* (Spring, 1951), pp. 163–79, for a summary treatment on the mode and meaning of Christian salvation. For an ampler exploration, see H. R. Mackintosh, *The Christian Experience of Forgiveness*, or Leonard Hodgson, *The Doctrine of the Atonement* (Nisbet, 1951).
4. Cf. Richard Niebuhr, *Christ and Culture* (Harper, 1951), especially chap. 6.
5. C. Lamont, *The Illusion of Immortality* (Philosophical Library, 1950), p. 278.
6. *Ibid.*, p. 288.
7. Cf. Fromm, *Man for Himself*, pp. 42–44.
8. Cf. A. E. Taylor, *The Christian Hope of Immortality* (Centenary Press, 1938); John Baillie, *And the Life Everlasting* (Scribner's, 1933); R. J. Campbell, *The Life of the World to Come* (Longmans, 1948) as quite various analyses of the common Christian hope of man's destiny.

9. Nice People or New Men,
C. S. Lewis

What would it mean to be a perfect man? Is it enough just to be nice—even very nice indeed? In this excerpt, C. S. Lewis, a British essayist and popular defender of the Christian faith, points out that Christianity is concerned not merely to improve people but to transform them. As a spokesman for traditional Christian faith, Lewis clearly distinguishes between human capacities for improving created life and the completely different divine offer of new life. The psychologists, he suggests, have failed to take the measure of man's ideal possibility. In the light of this distinction, how does Lewis understand the next step in "evolution"? According to him, how might one seek this transformation? Would you agree that "eternal life" is something radically different from the development of meaning, responsibility, and a capacity to love which Rollo May spoke about? Compare Lewis' perspective on evolution with that found in J. Huxley (Transition Section, reading 4).

NICE PEOPLE OR NEW MEN

He meant what He said. Those who put themselves in His hands will become perfect, as He is perfect—perfect in love, wisdom, joy, beauty, and immortality. The change will not be completed in this life, for death is an important part of the treatment. How far the change will have gone before death in any particular Christian is uncertain. . . .

"Niceness"—wholesome, integrated personality—is an excellent thing. We must try by every medical, educational, economic, and political means in our power, to produce a world where as many people as possible grow up "nice"; just as we must try to produce a world where all have plenty to eat. But we must not suppose that even if we succeeded in making everyone nice we should have saved their souls. A world of nice people, content in their own niceness, looking no further, turned away from God, would be just as desperately in need of salvation as a miserable world—and might even be more difficult to save.

For mere improvement is not redemption, though redemption always improves people even here and now and will, in the end, improve them to a degree we cannot yet imagine. God became man to turn creatures into sons: not simply to produce better men of the old kind but to produce a new kind of man. It is not like teaching a horse to jump better and better but like turning a horse into a winged creature. Of course, once it has got its wings, it will soar over fences which could never have been jumped and thus beat the natural horse at its own game. But there may be a period, while the wings are just beginning to grow, when it cannot do so: and at that stage the lumps on the shoulders—no one could tell by looking at them that they are going to be wings—may even give it an awkward appearance.

But perhaps we have already spent too long on this question. If what you want is an argument against Christianity (and I well remember how eagerly I looked for such arguments when I began to be afraid it was true) you can easily find some stupid and unsatisfactory Christian and say, "So there's your boasted new man! Give me the old kind." But if once you have begun to see that Christianity is on other grounds probable, you will know in your heart that this is only evading the issue. What can you ever really know of other people's souls—of their temptations, their opportunities, their struggles? One soul in the whole creation you do know: and it is the only one whose fate is placed in your hands. If there is a God, you are, in a sense, alone with Him. You cannot put Him off with speculations about your next door neighbours or memories of what you have read in books. What will all that chatter and hearsay count (will you even be able to remember it?) when the anæsthetic fog which we call "nature" or "the real world" fades away and the Presence in which you have always stood becomes palpable, immediate, and unavoidable?

THE NEW MEN

In the last chapter I compared Christ's work of making New Men to the process of turning a horse into a winged creature. I used that extreme example in order to emphasise the point that it is not mere improvement but Transformation. The nearest parallel to it in the world of nature is be found in the remarkable transformations we can make in insects by applying certain rays to them. Some people think this is how Evolution worked. The alterations in creatures on which it all depends may have been produced by rays coming from outer space. (Of course once the alterations are there, what they call "Natural Selection" gets to work on them: i.e., the useful alterations survive and the other ones get weeded out.)

Perhaps a modern man can understand the Christian idea best if he takes it in connection with Evolution. Everyone now knows about Evolution (though, of course, some educated people disbelieve it): everyone has been told that man has evolved from lower types of life. Consequently, people often wonder "What is the next step? When is the thing beyond man going to appear?" Imaginative writers try sometimes to picture this next step—the "Superman" as they call him; but they usually only succeed in picturing someone a good deal nastier than man as we know him and then try to make up for that by sticking on extra legs or arms. But supposing the next step was to be something even more different from the earlier steps than they ever dreamed of? And is it not very likely it would be?...

Now, if you care to talk in these terms, the Christian view is precisely that the Next Step has already appeared. And it is really new. It is not a change from brainy men to brainier men: it is a change that goes off in a totally different direction—a change from being creatures of God to being sons of God....

On this view the thing has happened: the new step has been taken and is being taken. Already the new men are dotted here and there all over the earth. Some, as I have admitted, are still hardly recognisable: but others can be recognised. Every now and then one meets them. Their very voices and faces are different from ours; stronger, quieter, happier, more radiant. They begin where most of us leave off. They are, I say, recognisable; but you must know what to look for. They will not be very like the idea of "religious people" which you have formed from your general reading. They do not draw attention to themselves. You tend to think that you are being kind to them when they are really being kind to you. They love you more than other men do, but they need you less. (We must get over wanting to be needed: in some goodish people, specially women, that is the hardest of all temptations to resist.) They will usually seem to have a lot of time: you will wonder where it comes from. When you recognised one of them, you will recognise the next one much more easily. And I strongly suspect (but how should I know?) that they recognise one another immediately and infallibly, across every barrier of colour, sex, class, age, and even of creeds. In that way, to become holy is rather like joining a secret society. To put it at the very lowest, it must be great *fun*.

But you must not imagine that the new men are, in the ordinary sense, all alike. A good deal of what I have been saying in this last book might make you suppose that that was bound to be so. To become new men means losing what we now call "ourselves." Out of ourselves, into Christ, we must go. His will is to become ours and we are to think His thoughts, to "have the mind of Christ" as the Bible says. . . .

It is something like that with Christ and us. The more we get what we now call "ourselves" out of the way and let Him take us over, the more truly ourselves we become. There is so much of Him that millions and millions of "little Christs," all different, will still be too few to express Him fully. He made them all. He invented—as an author invents characters in a novel—all the different men that you and I were intended to be. In that sense our real selves are all waiting for us in Him. . . .

At the beginning I said there were Personalities in God. I will go further now. There are no real personalities anywhere else. Until you have given up your self to Him you will not have a real self. Sameness is to be found most among the most "natural" men, not among those who surrender to Christ. How monotonously alike all the great tyrants and conquerors have been: how gloriously different are the saints.

But there must be a real giving up of the self. You must throw it away "blindly" so to speak. Christ will indeed give you a real personality: but you must not go to Him for the sake of that. As long as your own personality is what you are bothering about you are not going to Him at all. The very first step is to try to forget about the self altogether. Your real, new self (which is Christ's and also yours, and yours just because it is His) will not come as long as you are looking for it. It will come when you are looking for Him. Does that sound strange? The same principle holds, you know, for more everyday matters. Even in social life, you will never make a good impression on other people until you stop thinking about what sort of impression you are making. Even in literature and art, no man who bothers about originality will ever be original: whereas if you simply try to tell the truth (without caring twopence how often it has been told before) you will, nine times out of ten, become original without ever having noticed it. The principle runs through all life from top to bottom. Give up your self, and you will find your real self. Lose your life and you will save it. Submit to death, death of your ambitions and favourite wishes every day and death of your whole body in the end: submit with every fibre of your being, and you will find eternal life. Keep back nothing. Nothing that you have not given away will ever be really yours. Nothing in you that has not died will ever be raised from the dead. Look for yourself, and you will find in the long run only hatred, loneliness, despair, rage, ruin, and decay. But look for Christ and you will find Him, and with Him everything else thrown in.

VI

Achievement of Human Rights Through Political and Economic Action

[The social idealist]...has a deep prophetic sense of the urgency of solving problems which threaten the integrity of our social life. He is in the forefront of the fight for racial equality, for peaceful settlement of disputes, for freedom for the oppressed, for alleviation of the distress of the unfortunate, for protection of the widow and the fatherless in their affliction.... He is often the conscience of the community, yet his uneasy conscience is not born of theological discontent, but rather of acute sympathy and penetrating insight into the causes of moral indifference. When he encounters the churchman who regards him as unduly disturbed because he lacks a steadying religious faith, he flares up with resentment against what he regards as hypocrisy. (E. E. Aubrey, Secularism a Myth *[New York: Harper & Brothers, 1954], p. 163.)*

THERE ARE PEOPLE WHO BELIEVE that all of the transformations sought after and promised in the previous five chapters are seriously inadequate. Few of them are inclined to view themselves as "religious," and yet they too seek a transformation that is, for them, ultimate. They are reluctant to employ the language used by the proponents of "rebirth through personal encounter with the Holy" (Chapter I), but if asked to do so they might say this much: that they seek not so much salvation from sin as deliverance from the evil acts of sinners who have too much power and employ it unjustly. They are suspicious of the truths of the myths (Chapter II), and have no desire to celebrate such myths in sacrament and ritual. They perhaps like some of what they hear from the advocates of "living harmoniously through conformity with the Cosmic Law" about doing one's duty in daily life (Chapter III), but they hesitate to announce that they have discovered moral laws of cosmic or transcendent significance, or that they know God's will for all mankind. They might welcome the day when the problems of the masses of the peoples of the world are so few that they can afford the luxury of withdrawing from the marketplace and crossroads into the peace and contentment of nirvana or satori or union with God (Chapter IV); but they are convinced that such a day has not yet arrived.

Even the goal of "attaining an integrated self through creative interaction" (Chapter V) is seen by them as a luxury which must not be indulged (or overindulged) in until more basic problems of survival have been solved— for how, they might ask, can personal growth be pursued by men whose stomachs are empty or whose bodies are enslaved or whose countries are embroiled in wars. There is no commonly used term or name for such persons. They are the revolutionaries and reformers, the political activists and organizers, the economic planners and socialists of the world. If they could reach more earthly goals, such as peace, freedom, equality, justice, and economic well-being, then in their terms—they would have achieved the ideal and highest state of being for humanity. We consider them in this book because their activism functions for them in a "religious" way. When political structures and social justice are matters of life-and-death, "the condition of being morally related to other human beings can be a means of ultimate transformation within a variety of historical religions expressions, as well as outside religious communities."[1]

---

[1] Frederick J. Streng, *Understanding Religious Man* (Belmont, California: Dickenson Publishing Company, Inc., 1969), p. 112.

ADVOCACY

1. Bread and Freedom,
A. Camus

> *Albert Camus (1913–1960), the existentialist philosopher and*
> *novelist, was well known for his resistence to political absolutism*
> *and his insistence on individual integrity. In this excerpt from*
> *a speech given at the Labor Exchange of Saint-Etienne on May*
> *10, 1953, he asserts that freedom—freedom expressed in common*
> *everyday political and economic life—should be an ultimate*
> *concern of mankind. "For even if society were suddenly*
> *transformed and became decent and comfortable for all, it would*
> *still be a barbarous state unless freedom triumphed." In this*
> *framework of values he concludes that the Russian Revolution*
> *(1917) was "the world's greatest hope [that] hardened into*
> *the world's most efficient dictatorship." What does he perceive to*
> *be the chief threat to freedom in his time? What is the difference*
> *between "bourgeois freedom," "freedom," and "total liberation"?*
> *Who does Camus assert to be the real protectors of freedom?*
> *Why did the revolutionary socialistic movement fail to bring*
> *about freedom? Who (what) is the true victim of injustice and*
> *enslavement whether these are found in Communist or bourgeois*
> *societies? Does Camus appeal to any sources outside of man*
> *for achieving total Liberation? Considering the title "Bread and*
> *Freedom," does Camus feel that bread has something to do with*
> *freedom? Is freedom ever won once and for all?*

If we add up the examples of breach of faith and extortion that have just been pointed out to us, we can foresee a time when, in a Europe of concentration camps, the only people at liberty will be prison guards who will then have to lock up one another. When only one remains, he will be called the "supreme guard," and that will be the ideal society in which problems of opposition, the headache of all twentieth-century governments, will be settled once and for all. . . .

The simplest, and hence most tempting, thing is to blame governments or some obscure powers for such naughty behavior. Besides, it is indeed true that they are guilty and that their guilt is so solidly established that we have lost sight of its beginnings. But they are not the only ones responsible. After all, if freedom had always had to rely on governments to encourage her growth, she would probably be still in her infancy or else definitively buried with the inscription "another angel in heaven." The society of money and exploitation has never been charged, so far as I know, with assuring the triumph of freedom and justice. Police states have never been suspected of opening schools of law in the cellars where they interrogate their subjects. So, when they oppress and exploit, they are merely doing their job, and whoever blindly entrusts them with the care of freedom has no right to be surprised when she is immediately dishonored. If freedom is humiliated or in chains today, it is not because her enemies had recourse to treachery. It is simply because she has lost her natural protector. Yes, freedom is widowed, but it must be added because it is true: she is widowed of all of us.

Freedom is the concern of the oppressed, and her natural protectors have always come from among the oppressed. In feudal Europe the communes maintained the ferments of freedom; those who assured her fleeting triumph in 1789 were the inhabitants of towns and cities; and since the nineteenth century the workers' movements have assumed responsibility for the double honor of freedom and justice, without ever dreaming of saying that they were irreconcilable. Laborers, both manual and intellectual, are the ones who gave a body to freedom and helped her progress in the world until she has become the very basis of our thought, the air we cannot do without, that we breathe without even noticing it until the time comes when, deprived of it, we feel that we are dying. And if freedom is regressing today throughout such a large part of the world, this is probably because the devices for enslavement have never been so cynically chosen or so effective, but also because her real defenders, through fatigue, through despair, or through a false idea of strategy and efficiency, have turned away from her. Yes, the great event of the twentieth century was the forsaking of the values of freedom by the revolutionary movement, the progressive retreat of socialism based on freedom before the attacks of a Caesarian and military socialism. Since that moment a certain hope has disappeared from the world and a solitude has begun for each and every free man.

When, after Marx, the rumor began to spread and gain strength that freedom was a bourgeois hoax, a single word was misplaced in that definition, and we are still paying for that mistake through the convulsions of our time. For it should have been said merely that bourgeois freedom was a hoax—and not all freedom. It should have been said simply that bourgeois freedom was not freedom or, in the best of cases, was not yet freedom. But that there were liberties to be won and never to be relinquished again. It is quite true that there is no possible freedom for the man tied to his lathe all day long who, when evening comes, crowds into a single room with his family. But this fact condemns a class, a society and the slavery it assumes, not freedom itself, without which the poorest among us cannot get along. For even if society were suddenly transformed and became decent and comfortable for all, it would still be a barbarous state unless freedom triumphed. And because bourgeois society talks about freedom without practicing it, must the world of workers also give up practicing it and boast merely of not talking about it? Yet the confusion took place and in the revolutionary movement freedom was gradually condemned because bourgeois society used it as a hoax. From a justifiable and healthy distrust of the way that bourgeois society prostituted freedom, people came to distrust freedom itself. At best, it was postponed to the end of time, with the request that meanwhile it be not talked about. The contention was that we needed justice first and that we would come to freedom later on, as if slaves could ever hope to achieve justice. And forceful intellectuals announced to the worker that bread alone interested him rather than freedom, as if the worker didn't know that his bread depends in part on his freedom. And, to be sure, in the face of the prolonged injustice of bourgeois society, the temptation to go to such extremes was great. After all, there is probably not one of us here who, either in deed or in thought, did not succumb. But history has progressed, and what we have seen must now make us think things over. The revolution brought about by workers succeeded in 1917 and marked the dawn of real freedom and the greatest hope the world has known. But that revolution, surrounded from the outside, threatened within and without, provided itself with a police force. Inheriting a definition and a doctrine that pictured freedom as suspect, the revolution little by little became stronger, and the world's greatest hope hardened into the world's most efficient dictatorship. The false freedom of bourgeois society has not suffered meanwhile. What was killed in the Moscow trials and elsewhere, and in the revolutionary camps, what is assassinated when in Hungary a railway worker is shot for some professional mistake, is not bourgeois freedom but rather the freedom of 1917. Bourgeois freedom can meanwhile have recourse to all possible hoaxes. The trials and perversions of revolutionary society furnish it at one and the same time with a good conscience and with arguments against its enemies.

In conclusion, the characteristic of the world we live in is just that cynical dialectic which sets up injustice against enslavement while strengthening one by the other. When we admit to the palace of culture Franco, the friend of Goebbels and of Himmler—Franco, the real victor of the Second World War—to those who protest that the rights of man inscribed in the charter of UNESCO are turned to ridicule every day in Franco's prisons we reply without smiling that Poland figures in UNESCO too and that, as far as public freedom is concerned, one is no better than the other. An idiotic argument, of course! If you were so unfortunate as to marry off your elder daughter to a sergeant in a battalion of ex-convicts, this is no reason why you should marry off her younger sister to the most elegant detective on the society squad; one black sheep in the family is enough. And yet the idiotic argument works, as is proved to us every day. When anyone brings up the slave in the colonies and calls for justice, he is reminded of prisoners in Russian concentration camps, and vice versa. And if you protest against the assassination in Prague of an opposition historian like Kalandra, two or three American Negroes are thrown in your face. In such a disgusting attempt at outbidding, one thing only does not change—the victim, who is always the same. A single value is constantly outraged or prostituted—freedom—and then we notice that everywhere, together with freedom, justice is also profaned.

How then can this infernal circle be broken? Obviously, it can be done only by reviving at once, in ourselves and in others, the value of freedom —and by never again agreeing to its being sacrificed, even temporarily, or separated from our demand for justice. The current motto for all of us can only be this: without giving up anything on the plane of justice, yield nothing on the plane of freedom. In particular, the few democratic liberties we still enjoy are not unimportant illusions that we can allow to be taken from us without a protest. They represent exactly what remains to us of the great revolutionary conquests of the last two centuries. Hence they are not, as so many clever demagogues tell us, the negation of true freedom. There is no ideal freedom that will someday be given us all at once, as a pension comes at the end of one's life. There are liberties to be won painfully, one by one, and those we still have are stages—most certainly inadequate, but stages nevertheless—on the way to total liberation. If we agree to suppress them, we do not progress nonetheless. On the contrary, we retreat, we go backward, and someday we shall have to retrace our steps along that road, but that new effort will once more be made in the sweat and blood of men.

2. Agenda for a Generation, Students for a Democratic Society

According to this 1962 statement from Students for a Democratic Society (SDS), American life is more and more characterized by anxiety masked by physical comfort, and this muffled unease is seen to arise from the very structure of society. It alienates people from power, from relevant knowledge, and from reality, and it simultaneously produces lethargy and fear, conformity and disengagement. In their opposition to this situation, there is a sense of urgency and emergency. Note that the basic problem of human life is here defined in terms that were also found in the preceeding chapter: "fragmented man," "deeply felt anxieties," and fear. There is also an affirmation of human capacities that unfortunately so far are "unrealized potential for self-cultivation, self-direction, self-understanding, and creativity." The chief difference is in the understanding of the social-political dimension of life, which in this chapter is the essential dimension

From "The Port Huron Statement" of Students for a Democratic Society (SDS) convention at Port Huron, Michigan, in 1962. Found in *The Revolutionary Imperative: Essays Toward a New Humanity,* ed. Alan D. Austin (Nashville, Tennessee: Board of Education of the Methodist Church, National Methodist Student Movement, 1966), pp. 154–60.

*in which the transformation must take place. Consider their
claim that "the search for truly democratic alternatives to
the present...is a worthy and fulfilling human enterprise."
What questions do they raise which they feel are being neglected?
When they admit they have "no sure formulas, no closed theories,"
note how unlike the advocates of "living harmoniously through
conformity with the Cosmic Law" (Chapter III) they are
in this respect. But does this mean they thereby renounce an
interest in value questions? Compare the claim made by
the advocates in Chapter III, that eternal or natural social
and ethical relationships exist and can be rediscovered, with
this SDS statement that human values have to be created.
What vision of a just society do they suggest? In their criticism
of the campus scene, do they have an alternative life style
in mind that befits a "citizen"?*

We are people of this generation, bred in at least modest comfort, housed in universities, looking uncomfortably to the world we inherit.

Our work is guided by the sense that we may be the last generation in the experiment with living. But we are a minority—the vast majority of our people regard the temporary equilibriums of our society and the world as eternally functional parts. In this is perhaps the outstanding paradox: we ourselves are imbued with urgency, yet the message of our society is that there is no viable alternative to the present. Beneath the reassuring tones of the politicians, beneath the common opinion that America will "muddle through," beneath the stagnation of those who have closed their minds to the future, is the pervading feeling that there simply are no alternatives, that our times have witnessed the exhaustion not only of Utopias, but of any new departures as well. Feeling the press of complexity upon the emptiness of life, people are fearful of the thought that at any moment things might thrust out of control. They fear change itself, since change might smash whatever invisible framework seems to hold back chaos for them now. For most Americans, all crusades are suspect, threatening. The fact that each individual sees apathy in his fellows perpetuates the common reluctance to organize for changes. The dominant institutions are complex enough to blunt the minds of their potential critics, and entrenched enough to swiftly dissipate or entirely repel the energies of protest and reform, thus limiting human expectancies. Then, too, we are a materially improved society, and by our own improvements we seem to have weakened the case for change.

Some would have us believe that Americans feel contentment amidst prosperity—but might it not better be called a glaze above deeply felt anxieties about their role in the new world? And if these anxieties produce a developed indifference to human affairs, do they not as well produce a yearning to believe there *is* an alternative to the present, that something *can* be done to change circumstances in the school, the workplaces, the bureaucracies, the government? It is to this latter yearning, at once the spark and engine of change, that we direct our present appeal. The search for truly democratic alternatives to the present, and a commitment to social experimentation with them, is a worthy and fulfilling human enterprise, one which moves us and, we hope, others today. . . .

Making values explicit—an initial task in establishing alternatives—is an activity that has been devalued and corrupted. The conventional moral terms of the age, the politician moralities ("free world," "peoples democracies") reflect realities poorly, if at all, and seem to function more as ruling myths than as descriptive principles. But neither has our experience in the universities brought us moral enlightenment. Our professors and administrators sacrifice controversy to public relations; their curriculums change more slowly than the living events of the world; their skills and silence are purchased by investors in the arms race; passion is called unscholastic. The questions we might want raised—what is really important? can we live in a different and better way? if we wanted to change society, how would we do it?—are not thought to be questions of a "fruitful, empirical nature," and thus are brushed aside.

Unlike youth in other countries we are used to moral leadership being exercised and moral dimensions being clarified by our elders. But today, for us, not even the liberal and socialist preachments of the past seem adequate to the forms of the present. Consider the old slogans: Capitalism Cannot Reform Itself, United Front Against Fascism, General Strike, All Out on May Day. Or, more recently, No Cooperation with Commies and Fellow Travelers, Ideologies Are Exhausted, Bipartisanship, No Utopias. These are incomplete, and there are few new prophets. It has been said that our liberal and socialist predecessors were plagued by vision without program, while our own generation is plagued by program without vision. All around us there is astute grasp of method, technique—the committee, the *ad hoc* group, the lobbyist, the hard and soft sell, the make, the projected image—but, if pressed critically, such expertise is incompetent to explain its implicit ideals. It is highly fashionable to identify oneself by old categories, or by naming a respected political figure, or by explaining "how we would vote" on various issues.

In suggesting social goals and values, therefore, we are aware of entering a sphere of some disrepute. Perhaps matured by the past, we have no sure formulas, no closed theories—but that does not mean values are beyond discussion and tentative determination. A first task of any social movement is to convince people that the search for orienting theories and the creation of human values is complex but worthwhile. We are aware that to avoid platitudes we must analyze the concrete conditions of social order. But to direct such an analysis we must use the guideposts of basic principles. Our own social values involve conceptions of human beings, human relationships, and social systems.

We regard *men* as infinitely precious and possessed of unfulfilled capacities for reason, freedom, and love. In affirming these principles we are aware of countering perhaps the dominant conceptions of man in the twentieth century: that he is a thing to be manipulated, and that he is inherently incapable of directing his own affairs. We oppose the depersonalization that reduces human beings to the status of things. If anything, the brutalities of the twentieth century teach that means and ends are intimately related, that vague appeals to "posterity" cannot justify the multilations of the present. We oppose, too, the doctrine of human incompetence because it rests essentially on the modern fact that men have been "competently" manipulated into incompetence. We see little reason why men cannot meet with increasing skill the complexities and responsibilities of their situation, if society is organized not for minority participation but for majority participation in decision-making.

Men have unrealized potential for self-cultivation, self-direction, self-understanding, and creativity. It is this potential that we regard as crucial and to which we appeal—not to the human potentiality for violence, unreason, and submission to authority. The goal of man and society should be human independence: a concern not with image or popularity but with finding a meaning in life that is personally authentic; a quality of mind not compulsively driven by a sense of powerlessness, nor one which unthinkingly adopts status values, nor one which represses all threats to its habits, but one which has full, spontaneous access to present and past experiences, one which easily unites the fragmented parts of personal history, one which openly faces problems which are troubling and unresolved—one with an intuitive awareness of possibilities, an active sense of curiosity, an ability and willingness to learn.

This kind of independence does not mean egoistic individualism; the object is not to have one's way so much as it is to have a way that is one's own. Nor do we deify man—we merely have faith in his potential.

Human relationships should involve fraternity and honesty. Human interdependence is contemporary fact; human brotherhood must be willed, however, as a condition of future survival and as the most appropriate form of social relations. Personal links between man and man are needed, especially to go beyond the partial and fragmentary bonds of function that bind men only as worker to worker, employer to employee, teacher to student, American to Russian.

Loneliness, estrangement, isolation describe the vast distance between man and man today. These dominant tendencies cannot be overcome by better personnel management, nor by improved gadgets, but only when a love of man overcomes the idolatrous worship of things by man.

As the individualism we affirm is not egoism, the selflessness we affirm is not self-elimination. On the contrary, we believe in generosity of a kind that imprints one's unique individual qualities in the relation to other men, and to all human activity. Further, to dislike isolation is not to favor the abolition of privacy; the latter differs from isolation in that it occurs or is abolished according to individual will.

•   •   •

In the last few years, thousands of American students demonstrated that they at least felt the urgency of the times. They moved actively and directly against racial injustices, the threat of war, violations of individual rights of conscience and, less frequently, against economic manipulation. They succeeded in restoring a small measure of controversy to the campuses after the stillness of the McCarthy period. They succeeded, too, in gaining some concessions from the people and institutions they opposed, especially in the fight against racial bigotry.

The significance of these scattered movements lies not in their success or failure in gaining objectives—at least not yet. Nor does the significance lie in the intellectual "competence" or "maturity" of the students involved —as some pedantic elders allege. The significance is in the fact that the students are breaking the crust of apathy and overcoming the inner alienation—facts that remain the defining characteristics of American college life.

If student movements for change are rarities still on the campus scene, what is commonplace there? The real campus, the familiar campus, is a place of private people, engaged in their notorious "inner emigration." It is a place of commitment to business-as-usual, getting ahead, playing it cool. It is a place of mass affirmation of the Twist, but mass reluctance toward the controversial public stance. Rules are accepted as "inevitable," bureaucracy as "just circumstances," irrelevance as "scholarship," selflessness as "martyrdom," politics as "just another way to make people, and an unprofitable one, too."

Almost no students value activity as a citizen. Passive in public, they are hardly more idealistic in arranging their private lives; Gallup concludes they will settle for "low success, and won't risk high failure." There is not much willingness to take risks (not even in business), no setting of dangerous goals, no real conception of personal identity except one manufactured in the image of others, no real urge for personal fulfillment except to be almost as successful as the very successful people. Attention is being paid to social status (the quality of shirt collars, meeting people, getting wives or husbands, making solid contacts for later on) ; much, too, is paid to academic status (grades, honors, the med school rat-race). But neglected generally is real intellectual status, the personal cultivation of the mind.

Look beyond the campus, to America itself. That student life is more intellectual, and perhaps more comfortable, does not obscure the fact that the fundamental qualities of life on the campus reflect the habits of society at large. The fraternity president is seen at the junior manager levels; the sorority queen has gone to Grosse Pointe; the serious poet burns for a place, any place, to work; the once-serious and never-serious poets work at the advertising agencies. The desperation of people threatened by forces about which they know little and of which they can say less, the cheerful emptiness of people giving up all hope of changing things, the faceless ones polled by Gallup who listed "international affairs" fourteenth on their list of problems but who also expected thermonuclear war in the next few years—in these and other forms, Americans are in withdrawal from public life, from any collective effort at directing their own affairs.

Some regard these national doldrums as a sign of healthy approval of the established order, but is it approval by consent or by manipulated acquiescence? Others declare that the people are withdrawn because compelling issues are fast disappearing; perhaps there are fewer breadlines in America, but is Jim Crow gone, is there enough work and is work more fulfilling, is world war a diminishing threat, and what of the revolutionary new peoples? Still others think the national quietude is a necessary consequence of the need for elites to resolve complex and specialized problems of modern industrial society. But, then, why should business elites help decide foreign policy, and who controls the elites anyway, and are they solving mankind's problems? Others finally shrug knowingly and announce that full democracy never worked anywhere in the past—but why lump qualitatively different civilizations together, and how can a social order work well if its best thinkers are skeptics, and is man really doomed forever to the domination of today?

There are no convincing apologies for the contemporary malaise.... The apathy is, first, subjective—the felt powerlessness of ordinary people, the resignation before the enormity of events. But subjective apathy is encouraged by the objective American situation—the actual separation of people from power, from relevant knowledge, from pinnacles of decision-making. Just as the university influences the student way of life, so do major social institutions create the circumstances in which the isolated citizen will try hopelessly to understand his world and himself.

The very isolation of the individual—from power and community and ability to aspire—means the rise of a democracy without publics. With the great mass of people structurally remote and psychologically hesitant with respect to democratic institutions, those institutions themselves attenuate and become, in a fashion of the vicious circle, progressively less accessible to those few who aspire to serious participation in social affairs. The vital democratic connection between community and leadership, between the mass and the several elites, has been so wrenched and perverted that disastrous policies go unchallenged time and again....

The first effort, then, should be to state a vision: What is the perimeter of human possibility in this epoch?...The second effort, if we are to be politically responsible, is to evaluate the prospects for obtaining at least a substantial part of that vision in our epoch: What are the social forces that exist, or that must exist, if we are to be successful? And what role have we ourselves to play as a social force?

3. The Human Being
and Social Alienation,
J. Cone

Black Power: What image is triggered in your mind when
you hear those two words? Molotov cocktails and urban riots?
For James Cone, the Black Power movement has religious
significance. Cone is a young, black Christian theologian, Associate
Professor of Theology at Union Theological Seminary in
New York City. Earlier in the book from which this excerpt
comes, he claims that "Black Power is the most important
development in American life in this century," and that it is
"Christ's central message to twentieth-century America."
If you have difficulties in understanding and/or appreciating
this claim, you might ask yourself these questions: How does
one live in a world that denies one's existence as a human being?
How does one deal with a world that one finds absurd?
Black Power is the black person's way of affirming his or her being.
Note the emphasis on the importance of social and political
(including legal) structures that define man's being. Would you
agree that rebellion against a society that threatens your humanity
is the only valid action to take? Would you agree, from your
own experience, that life in America for the black man has
generally resulted in "existential absurdity"? In what sense, if any,
might Cone's position be termed "religious"?

If there is no struggle, there is no progress. Those who profess to favor
freedom, and yet depreciate agitation, are men who want crops without
plowing up the ground. They want rain without thunder and lightning.
...This struggle may be a moral one; or it may be a physical one;
or it may be both moral and physical; but there must be a struggle.

Frederick Douglass

WHAT IS BLACK POWER?

There has been and still is much debate among the critics of Black
Power regarding the precise meaning of the words. The term "Black Power"
was first used in the civil rights movement in the spring of 1966 by Stokely
Carmichael to designate the only appropriate response to white racism.[1]
Since that time many critics have observed that there is no common agreement regarding its definition. In one sense this fact is not surprising, since
every new phenomenon passes through stages of development, and the
advocates of Black Power need time to define its many implications. But
in another sense, this criticism is surprising, since every literate person knows

that imprecision, the inability of a word to describe accurately the object of reality to which it points, is characteristic of all languages. The complexity of this problem is evident in the development of modern analytical philosophy. We are still in the process of defining such terms as "democracy," "good," "evil," and many others. In fact the ability to probe for deeper meanings of words as they relate to various manifestations of reality is what makes the intellectual pursuit interesting and worthwhile.

But if communication is not to reach an impasse, there must be agreement on the general shape of the object to which a term points. Meaningful dialogue is possible because of man's ability to use words as symbols for the real. Without this, communication ceases to exist. For example, theologians and political scientists may disagree on what they would consider "fine points" regarding the precise meaning of Christianity and democracy, but there is an underlying agreement regarding their referents.

The same is true of the words "Black Power." To what "object" does it point? What does it mean when used by its advocates? It means *complete emancipation of black people from white oppression by whatever means black people deem neccessary.* The methods may include selective buying, boycotting, marching, or even rebellion. Black Power means black freedom, black self-determination, wherein black people no longer view themselves as without human dignity but as men, human beings with the ability to carve out their own destiny. In short, as Stokely Carmichael would say, Black Power means T.C.B., Take Care of Business—black folk taking care of black folks' business, not on the terms of the oppressor, but on those of the oppressed.

Black Power is analogous to Albert Camus's understanding of the rebel. The rebel says No and Yes. He says No to conditions considered intolerable, and Yes to that "something within him which 'is worthwhile'...and which must be taken into consideration."[2] To say No means that the oppressor has overstepped his bounds, and that "there is a limit beyond which [he] shall not go."[3] It means that oppression can be endured no longer in the style that the oppressor takes for granted. To say No is to reject categorically "the humiliating orders of the master" and by so doing to affirm that something which is placed above everything else, including life itself. To say No means that death is preferable to life, if the latter is devoid of freedom. *"Better to die on one's feet than to live on one's knees."*[4] This is what Black Power means.

It is in this light that the slogan "Freedom Now"[5] ought to be interpreted. Like Camus's phrase, "All or Nothing," Freedom Now means that the slave is willing to risk death because "he considers these rights more important than himself. Therefore he is acting in the name of certain values which...he considers are common to himself and to all men."[6] That is what Henry Garnet had in mind when he said "rather *die freemen, than live to be slaves.*"[7] This is what Black Power means.

A further clarification of the meaning of Black Power may be found in Paul Tillich's analysis of "the courage to be," which is "the ethical act in which man affirms his being in spite of those elements of his existence which conflict with his essential self-affirmation."[8] Black Power, then, is a humanizing force because it is the black man's attempt to affirm his being, his attempt to be recognized as "Thou," in spite of the "other,"[9] the white power which dehumanizes him. The structure of white society attempts to make "black being" into "nonbeing" or "nothingness." In existential philosophy, nonbeing is usually identified as that which threatens being; it is that ever-present possibility of the inability to affirm one's existence. The courage to be, then, is the courage to affirm one's being by striking out at the dehumanizing forces which threaten being. And, as Tillich goes on to say, "He who is not capable of a powerful self-affirmation in spite of the anxiety of nonbeing is forced into a weak, reduced self-affirmation."[10]

The rebellion in the cities, far from being an expression of the inhumanity of blacks, is an affirmation of their being despite the ever-present possibility of death. For the black man to accept the white society's appeal to wait or to be orderly is to affirm "something which is less than essential. . . being."[11] The black man prefers to die rather than surrender to some other value. The cry for death is, as Rollo May has noted, the "most mature form of distinctly human behavior."[12] In fact, many existentialists point out that physical life itself "is not fully satisfying and meaningful until one can consciously choose another value which be holds more dear than life itself."[13] To be human is to find something worth dying for. When the black man rebels at the risk of death, he forces white society to look at him, to recognize him, to take his being into account, to admit that he *is*. And in a structure that regulates behavior, recognition by the other is indispensable to one's being. As Franz Fanon says: "Man is human only to the extent to which he tries to impose his existence on another in order to be recognized by him."[14] And "he who is reluctant to recognize me opposes me. In a savage struggle I am willing to accept convulsions of death, invincible dissolutions, but also the possibility of the impossible."[15]

Black Power, in short, is an *attitude,* an inward affirmation of the essential worth of blackness. It means that the black man will not be poisoned by the stereotypes that others have of him, but will affirm from the depth of his soul: "Get used to me, I am not getting used to anyone."[16] And "if the white man challenges my humanity, I will impose my whole weight as a man on his life and show him that I am not that 'sho good eatin'' that he persists in imagining."[17] This is Black Power, the power of the black man to say Yes to his own "black being," and to make the other accept him or be prepared for a struggle.

> I find myself suddenly in the world and I recognize that I have one right alone: That of demanding human behavior from the other. One duty alone: That of not renouncing my freedom through my choices.[18]

BLACK POWER
AND EXISTENTIAL ABSURDITY

Before one can really understand the mood of Black Power, it is necessary to describe a prior mood of the black man in a white society. When he first awakens to his place in America and feels sharply the absolute contradiction between *what is* and *what ought to be* or recognizes the inconsistency between his view of himself as a man and America's description of him as a thing, his immediate reaction is a feeling of absurdity. The absurd

> is basically that which man recognizes as the disparity between what he hopes for and what seems in fact to be. He yearns for some measure of happiness in an orderly, a rational and a reasonably predictable world; when he finds misery in a disorderly, an irrational and unpredictable world, he is oppressed by the absurdity of the disparity between the universe as he wishes it to be and as he sees it.[19]

This is what the black man feels in a white world.

There is no place in America where the black man can go for escape. In every section of the country there is still the feeling expressed by Langston Hughes:

> I swear to the Lord
> I still can't see
> Why Democracy means
> Everybody but me.

I can remember reading, as a child, the Declaration of Independence with a sense of identity with all men and with a sense of pride: "We hold these truths to be self-evident: that all men are created equal; that they are endowed by their creator with certain unalienable rights; that among them is life, liberty and the pursuit of happiness." But I also read in the Dred Scott decision, not with pride or identity, but with a feeling of inexplicable absurdity, that blacks are not human.

> But it is too clear for dispute, that the enslaved African race were not intended to be included, and formed no part of the people who framed and adopted this declaration; for if the language, as understood in that day, would embrace them, the conduct of the distinguished men who framed the Declaration of Independence would have been utterly and flagrantly inconsistent with the principles they asserted; and instead of the sympathy of mankind...they would have deserved and received universal rebuke and reprobation.

Thus the black man *"had no rights which the white man was bound to respect."*[20]

But many whites would reply: "The Negro is no longer bought and sold as chattel. We changed his status after the Civil War. Now he is free." Whatever may have been the motives of Abraham Lincoln and other white Americans for launching the war, it certainly was not on behalf of black people. Lincoln was clear on this:

> My paramount object in this struggle is to save the Union, and is not either to save or to destroy slavery. If I could save the Union without freeing any slave, I would do it; and if I could save it by freeing some and leaving others alone, I would also do that.[21]

If that quotation still leaves his motives unclear, here is another one which should remove all doubts regarding his thoughts about black people.

> I will say then that I am not, nor ever have been in favor of bringing about in any way the social and political equality of the black and white races—that I am not nor ever have been in favor of making voters or jurors of Negroes, nor of qualifying them to hold office, nor to intermarry with white people; and I will say in addition to this that there is a physical difference between the white and black races which I believe will forbid the two races living together on terms of social and political equality. And inasmuch as they cannot so live, while they do remain together, there must be the position of superior and inferior, and I as much as any other man am in favor of having the superior position assigned to the white race.[22]

And certainly the history of the black-white relations in this country from the Civil War to the present unmistakably shows that as a people, America has never intended for blacks to be free. To this day, in the eyes of most white Americans, the black man remains subhuman.

Yet Americans continue to talk about brotherhood and equality. They say that this is "the land of the free and the home of the brave." They sing: "My country 'tis of thee, sweet land of liberty." But they do not mean blacks. This is the black man's paradox, the absurdity of living in a world with "no rights which the white man [is] bound to respect."

It seems that white historians and political scientists have attempted, perhaps subconsciously, to camouflage the inhumanity of whites toward blacks.[23] But the evidence is clear for those who care to examine it. All aspects of this society have participated in the act of enslaving blacks, extinguishing Indians, and annihilating all who question white society's right to decide who is human.

I should point out here that most existentialists do not say that "man is absurd" or "the world is absurd." Rather, the absurdity arises as man confronts the world and looks for meaning. The same is true in regard to my analysis of the black man in a white society. It is not that the black man is absurd or that the white society as such is absurd. Absurdity arises as the black man seeks to understand his place in the white world. The black man does not view himself as absurd; he views himself as human. But as he meets the white world and its values, he is confronted with an almighty No and is defined as a thing. This produces the absurdity.

The crucial question, then, for the black man is, "How should I respond to a world which defines me as a nonperson?" That he is a person is beyond question, not debatable. But when he attempts to relate as a person, the world demands that he respond as a thing. In this existential absurdity, what should he do? Should he respond as he knows himself to be, or as the world defines him?

The response to this feeling of absurdity is determined by a man's ontological perspective. If one believes that this world is the extent of reality, he will either despair or rebel. According to Camus's *The Myth of Sisyphus,* suicide is the ultimate act of despair. Rebellion is epitomized in the person of Dr. Bernard Rieux in *The Plague.* Despite the overwhelming odds, Rieux fights against things as they are.

If, perchance, a man believes in God, and views this world as merely a pilgrimage to another world, he is likely to regard suffering as a necessity for entrance to the next world. Unfortunately Christianity has more often than not responded to evil in this manner.[24]

From this standpoint the response of Black Power is like Camus's view of the rebel. One who embraces Black Power does not despair and take suicide as an out, nor does he appeal to another world in order to relieve the pains of this one.[25] Rather, *he fights back with the whole of his being.* Black Power believes that blacks are not really human beings in white eyes, that they never have been and never will be, until blacks recognize the unsavory behavior of whites for what it is. Once this recognition takes place, they can make whites see them as humans. The man of Black Power will not rest until the oppressor recognizes him for what he is—man. He further knows that in this campaign for human dignity, freedom is not a gift but a right worth dying for.

NOTES

1. Richard Wright used the term as early as 1954 in reference to Africa.
2. Camus, *The Rebel,* trans. Anthony Bower (New York: Random House, 1956), p. 13.
3. *Ibid.*
4. *Ibid.,* p. 15. Emphasis added.
5. Most Black Power advocates have dropped the slogan because of its misuse by white liberals.
6. Camus, *The Rebel,* p. 16.
7. Quoted in Floyd B. Barbour (ed.), *The Black Power Revolt* (Boston: Porter Sargent, 1968), p. 39.
8. Tillich, *The Courage to Be* (New Haven: Yale University Press, 1952), p. 3.
9. The word "other," which designates the neighbor, occurs frequently in Franz Fanon, *Black Skins, White Masks,* trans. C. L. Markmann (New York: Grove Press, 1967).
10. Tillich, *The Courage to Be,* p. 66.
11. *Ibid.*
12. Rollo May, *Psychology and the Human Dilemma* (Princeton: Van Nostrand, 1967), p. 73.
13. *Ibid.*
14. Fanon, *Black Skins,* p. 216.
15. *Ibid.,* p. 218.
16. *Ibid.,* p. 131.
17. *Ibid.*
18. *Ibid.,* p. 229.
19. W. R. Mueller and J. Jacobsen, "Samuel Beckett's Long Last Saturday: To Wait or Not to Wait" in Nathan Scott, Jr., *Man in Modern Theatre* (Richmond, Va.: John Knox Press, 1965), p. 77.
20. Quoted in L. H. Fishel, Jr., and Benjamin Quarles, *The Negro American* (Glenview, Ill.: Scott, Foresman and Co., 1967), pp. 204–205. Emphasis added.

21. "Reply to Horace Greeley," 1862, in *The American Tradition in Literature,* Vol. I; revised, S. Bradley, R. C. Beatty, and E. H. Long, eds. (New York: W. W. Norton, 1962), p. 1567.
22. Quoted in Charles Silberman, *Crisis in Black and White* (New York: Random House, 1964), pp. 92–93.
23. See John H. Franklin and Isidore Starr (eds.), *The Negro in Twentieth Century America* (New York: Random House, 1967), pp. 45–46. Here is an analysis by six American historians of how most scholars give a "white" twist to history.
24. A fuller discussion of Christianity and Black Power is found in the next chapter.
25. It should be pointed out here that another alternative for black people is to submit to the white view of blacks....

4. The Revolutionary as the Moral Ideal, *Liu Shao-Ch'i*

> *The author of this except, Liu Shao-Ch'i, was a close associate of Mao Tse-tung, and as a theoretician had authority second only to Mao. Although he suffered a purge from his position of party leadership in recent years, his thinking on the meaning of Communism remains important. This excerpt is taken from a series of lectures for indoctrination of party members given in 1939 at the Institute of Marxism-Leninism in Yenan; and the requirements and the benefits of Communist life are set forth forcefully. As you read, you might like to try this experiment: When you come to such names as Marx, Engels, Lenin, and Stalin, substitute the name Jesus Christ or Moses; when you come to the term Marxism-Leninism, substitute the term Christianity or Judaism; and when you come to the term Communist Party, substitute the term Christian Church or Jewish Community. The self-cultivation being enjoined here then will reflect more clearly the possibly "religious" nature of this document. What transformation do Communists seek? Is not the ideal world they envision similar, in psychological terms, to the "Kingdom of God"? Is the loyalty encouraged not similar to the "thou shalt*

From Liu Shao-Ch'i, *How to Be a Good Communist*, trans. William T. de Bary, in *Sources of Chinese Tradition,* ed. William T. de Bary et al. (New York: Columbia University Press, 1960), pp. 911–18. Originally published in China by Foreign Languages Press in 1951.

*have no other gods before me" theme of the Jews? Do they
require any less sacrifice of their party members than the
Christian Church required of its disciples in the past? Do they
promise any less happiness than that promised by Christianity?
Are there any crosses for them to bear? Does the "ultimate
emancipation of mankind" of which they speak give them any less
missionary zeal than Christians had during the 19th century?
In sum: Note how self-cultivation is related to public social and
political acts, and what moral or spiritual benefits one could
hope to attain through it.*

Comrades! In order to become the most faithful and best pupils of
Marx, Engels, Lenin, and Stalin, we need to carry on cultivation in all
aspects in the course of the long and great revolutionary struggle of the
proletariat and the masses of the people. We need to carry on cultivation
in the theories of Marxism-Leninism and in applying such theories in
practice; cultivation in revolutionary strategy and tactics; cultivation in
studying and dealing with various problems according to the standpoint and
methods of Marxism-Leninism; cultivation in ideology and moral character; cultivation in Party unity, inner-Party struggle, and discipline; cultivation in hard work and in the style of work; cultivation in being skillful in
dealing with different kinds of people and in associating with the masses
of the people; and cultivation in various kinds of scientific knowledge, etc.
We are all Communist Party members and so we have a general cultivation
in common. But there exists a wide discrepancy today between our Party
members. Wide discrepancy exists among us in the level of political consciousness, in work, in position, in cultural level, in experience of struggle,
and in social origin. Therefore, in addition to cultivation in general we also
need special cultivation for different groups and for individual comrades.

Accordingly, there should be different kinds of methods and forms of
cultivation. For example, many of our comrades keep a diary in order to
have a daily check on their work and thoughts or they write down on small
posters their personal defects and what they hope to achieve and paste
them up where they work or live, together with the photographs of persons
they look up to, and ask comrades for criticism and supervision. In ancient
China, there were many methods of cultivation. There was Tseng Tze[1] who
said: "I reflect on myself three times a day." The *Book of Odes* has it that
one should cultivate oneself "as a lapidary cuts and files, carves and
polishes." Another method was "to examine oneself by self-reflection" and
to "write down some mottoes on the right hand side of one's desk" or "on
one's girdle" as daily reminders of rules of personal conduct. The Chinese
scholars of the Confucian school had a number of methods for the cultivation of their body and mind. Every religion has various methods and forms
of cultivation of its own. The "investigation of things, the extension of
knowledge, sincerity of thought, the rectification of the heart, the cultivation
of the person, the regulation of the family, the ordering well of the state
and the making tranquil of the whole kingdom" as set forth in *The Great
Learning*[2] also means the same. All this shows that in achieving one's

progress one must make serious and energetic efforts to carry on self-cultivation and study. However, many of these methods and forms cannot be adopted by us because most of them are idealistic, formalistic, abstract, and divorced from social practice. These scholars and religious believers exaggerate the function of subjective initiative, thinking that so long as they keep their general "good intentions" and are devoted to silent prayer they will be able to change the existing state of affairs, change society, and change themselves under conditions separated from social and revolutionary practice. This is, of course, absurd. We cannot cultivate ourselves in this way. We are materialists and our cultivation cannot be separated from practice.

What is important to us is that we must not under any circumstances isolate ourselves from the revolutionary struggles of different kinds of people and in different forms at a given moment and that we must, moreover, sum up historical revolutionary experience and learn humbly from this and put it into practice. That is to say, we must undertake self-cultivation and steel ourselves in the course of our own practice, basing ourselves on the experiences of past revolutionary practice, on the present concrete situation and on new experiences. Our self-cultivation and steeling are for no other purpose than that of revolutionary practice. That is to say, we must modestly try to understand the standpoint, the method and the spirit of Marxism-Leninism, and understand how Marx, Engels, Lenin and Stalin dealt with people. And having understood these, we should immediately apply them to our own practice, i.e., in our own lives, words, deeds, and work. Moreover, we should stick to them and unreservedly correct and purge everything in our ideology that runs counter to them, thereby strengthening our own proletarian and Communist ideology and qualities. That is to say, we must modestly listen to the opinions and criticisms of our comrades and of the masses, carefully study the practical problems in our lives and in our work and carefully sum up our experiences and the lessons we have learned so as to find an orientation for our own work. In addition, on the basis of all these, we must judge whether we have a correct understanding of Marxism-Leninism and whether we have correctly applied the method of Marxism-Leninism, found out our own shortcomings and mistakes and corrected them. At the same time, we must find out in what respects specific conclusions of Marxism-Leninism need to be supplemented, enriched and developed on the basis of well-digested new experiences. That is to say, we must combine the universal truth of Marxism-Leninism with the concrete practice of the revolution.

These should be the methods of self-cultivation of us Communist Party members. That is to say, we must use the methods of Marxism-Leninism to cultivate ourselves. This kind of cultivation is entirely different from other kinds of cultivation which are idealistic and are divorced from social practice.

In this connection, we cannot but oppose certain idle talk and mechanicalism on the question of cultivation and steeling.

First of all, we must oppose and resolutely eliminate one of the biggest evils bequeathed to us by the education and learning in the old society—

the separation of theory from practice. In the course of education and study in the old society many people thought that it was unnecessary or even impossible to act upon what they had learned. Despite the fact that they read over and over again books by ancient sages they did things the sages would have been loath to do. Despite the fact that in everything they wrote or said they preached righteousness and morality they acted like out-and-out robbers and harlots in everything they did. Some "highranking officials" issued orders for the reading of the *Four Books* and the *Five Classics*,[3] yet in their everyday administrative work they ruthlessly extorted exorbitant requisitions, ran amuck with corruption and killing, and did everything against righteousness and morality. Some people read the *Three People's Principles* over and over again and could recite the *Will of Dr. Sun Yat-sen,* yet they oppressed the people, opposed the nations who treated us on an equal footing, and went so far as to compromise with or surrender to the national enemy. Once a scholar of the old school told me himself that the only maxim of Confucius that he could observe was: "To him food can never be too dainty; minced meat can never be too fine," adding that all the rest of the teachings of Confucius he could not observe and had never proposed to observe. Then why did they still want to carry on educational work and study the teachings of the sages? Apart from utilizing them for window-dressing purposes, their objects were: 1) to make use of these teachings to oppress the exploited and to make use of righteousness and morality for the purpose of hoodwinking and suppressing the culturally backward people; 2) to attempt thereby to secure better government jobs, make money and achieve fame, and reflect credit on their parents. Apart from these objects, their actions were not restricted by the sages' teachings. This was the attitude and return of the "men of letters" and "scholars" of the old society to the sages they "worshiped." Of course we Communist Party members cannot adopt such an attitude in studying Marxism-Leninism and the excellent and useful teachings bequeathed to us by our ancient sages. We must live up to what we say. We are honest and pure and we cannot deceive ourselves, the people, or our forefathers. This is an outstanding characteristic as well as a great merit of us Communist Party members. [pp. 15–18]*

What is the most fundamental and common duty of us Communist Party members? As everybody knows, it is to establish Communism, to transform the present world into a Communist world. Is a Communist world good or not? We all know that it is very good. In such a world there will be no exploiters, oppressors, landlords, capitalists, imperialists, or fascists. There will be no oppressed and exploited people, no darkness, ignorance, backwardness, etc. In such a society all human beings will become unselfish and intelligent Communists with a high level of culture and technique. The spirit of mutual assistance and mutual love will prevail among mankind. There will be no such irrational things as mutual decep-

---

* The page numbers and subsequent page numbers in brackets are in the original and do not apply to this book.

tion, mutual antagonism, mutual slaughter and war, etc. Such a society will, of course, be the best, the most beautiful, and the most advanced society in the history of mankind. Who will say that such a society is not good? Here the question arises: Can Communist society be brought about? Our answer is "yes." About this the whole theory of Marxism-Leninism offers a scientific explanation that leaves no room for doubt. It further explains that as the ultimate result of the class struggle of mankind, such a society will inevitably be brought about. The victory of Socialism in the U.S.S.R. has also given us factual proof. Our duty is, therefore, to bring about at an early date this Communist society, the realization of which is inevitable in the history of mankind.

This is one aspect. This is our ideal.

But we should understand the other aspect, that is, in spite of the fact that Communism can and must be realized it is still confronted by powerful enemies that must be thoroughly and finally defeated in every respect before Communism can be realized. Thus, the cause of Communism is a long, bitter, arduous but victorious process of struggle. Without such a struggle there can be no Communism. [p. 24]

Comrades! If you only possess great and lofty ideals but not the spirit of "searching for the truth from concrete facts" and do not carry on genuinely practical work, you are not a good Communist Party member. You can only be a dreamer, a prattler, or a pedant. If on the contrary, you only do practical work but do not possess the great and lofty ideals of Communism, you are not a good Communist, but a common careerist. A good Communist Party member is one who combines the great and lofty ideals of Communism with practical work and the spirit of searching for the truth from concrete facts.

The Communist ideal is beautiful while the existing capitalist world is ugly. It is precisely because of its ugliness that the overwhelming majority of the people want to change it and cannot but change it. In changing the world we cannot divorce ourselves from reality, or disregard reality; nor can we escape from reality or surrender to the ugly reality. We must adapt ourselves to reality, understand reality, seek to live and develop in reality, struggle against the ugly reality and transform reality in order to realize our ideals. [pp. 29–30]

At all times and on all questions, a Communist Party member should take into account the interests of the Party as a whole, and place the Party's interests above his personal problems and interests. It is the highest principle of our Party members that the Party's interests are supreme. [p. 31]

If a Party member has only the interests and aims of the Party and Communism in his ideology, if he has no personal aims and considerations independent of the Party's interests, and if he is really unbiased and unselfish, then he will be capable of the following:

1. He will be capable of possessing very good Communist ethics. Because he has a firm outlook he "can both love and hate people." He can show loyalty to and ardent love for all his comrades, revolutionaries, and working

people, help them unconditionally, treat them with equality, and never harm any one of them for the sake of his own interests. He can deal with them in a "faithful and forgiving" spirit and "put himself in the position of others." He can consider others' problems from their points of view and be considerate to them. "He will never do to others anything he would not like others to do to him." He can deal with the most vicious enemies of mankind in a most resolute manner and conduct a persistent struggle against the enemy for the purpose of defending the interests of the Party, the class, and the emancipation of mankind. As the Chinese saying goes: "He will worry long before the rest of the world begins to worry and he will rejoice only after the rest of the world has rejoiced." Both in the Party and among the people he will be the first to suffer hardship and the last to enjoy himself. He never minds whether his conditions are better or worse than others, but he does mind as to whether he has done more revolutionary work than others, or whether he has fought harder. In times of adversity, he will stand out courageously and unflinchingly, and in the face of difficulties he will demonstrate the greatest sense of responsibility. Therefore, he is capable of possessing the greatest firmness and moral courage to resist corruption by riches or honors, to resist tendencies to vacillate in spite of poverty and lowly status, and to refuse to yield in spite of threats or force.

2. He will also be capable of possessing the greatest courage. Since he is free from any selfishness whatever and has never done "anything against his conscience," he can expose his mistakes and shortcomings and boldly correct them in the same way as the sun and the moon emerge bright and full following a brief eclipse. He is "courageous because his is a just cause." He is never afraid of truth. He courageously upholds truth, expounds truth to others, and fights for truth. Even if it is temporarily to his disadvantage to do so, even if he will be subjected to various attacks for the sake of upholding truth, even if the opposition and rebuff of the great majority of the pepole forces him into temporary isolation (glorious isolation) and even if on this account his life may be endangered he will still be able to stem the tide and uphold truth and will never resign himself to drifting with the tide. So far as he himself is concerned, he has nothing to fear.

3. He will be best capable of acquiring the theory and method of Marxism-Leninism, viewing problems and perceiving the real nature of the situation keenly and aptly. Because he has a firm and clear-cut class standpoint, he is free from personal worries and personal desires which may blur or distort his observation of things and understanding of truth. He has an objective attitude. He tests all theories, truths, and falsehoods in the course of revolutionary practice and is no respecter of persons.

4. He will also be capable of being the most sincere, most candid, and happiest of men. Since he has no selfish desires and since he has nothing to conceal from the Party, "there is nothing which he is afraid of telling others" as the Chinese saying goes. Apart from the interests of the Party and of the revolution, he has no personal losses or gains or other things to worry about. He can "look after himself when he is on his own." He takes care not to do wrong things when he works independently and without

supervision and when there is ample opportunity for him to do all kinds of wrong things. His work will be found in no way incompatible with the Party's interests no matter how many years later it is reviewed. He does not fear criticism from others and he can courageously and sincerely criticize others. That is why he can be sincere, candid and happy.

5. He will be capable of possessing the highest self-respect and self-esteem. For the interests of the Party and of the revolution, he can also be the most lenient, most tolerant, and most ready to compromise, and he will even endure, if necessary, various forms of humiliation and injustice without feeling hurt of bearing grudges. As he has no personal aims or designs, he has no need to flatter others and does not want others to flatter him, either. He has no personal favors to ask of others, so he has no need to humble himself in order to ask help from others. For the interests of the Party and the revolution he can also take care of himself, protect his life and health, raise his theoretical level and enhance his ability. But if for the sake of certain important aims of the Party and of the revolution he is required to endure insults, shoulder heavy burdens and do work which he is reluctant to do, he will take up the most difficult and important work without the slightest hesitation and will not pass the buck.

A Communist Party member should possess all the greatest and noblest virtues of mankind. He should also possess the strict and clear-cut standpoint of the Party and of the proletariat (that is, Party spirit and class character). Our ethics are great precisely because they are the ethics of Communism and of the proletariat. Such ethics are not built upon the backward basis of safeguarding the interests of individuals or a small number of exploiters. They are built, on the contrary, upon the progressive basis of the interests of the proletariat, of the ultimate emancipation of mankind as a whole, of saving the world from destruction and of building a happy and beautiful Communist world. [pp. 32–34]

NOTES

1. A disciple of Confucius.
2. *The Great Learning* is said to be "a Book handed down by the Confucian school, which forms the gate by which beginners enter into virtue."
3. The *Four Books* and *Five Classics* are nine ancient Chinese classics of philosophy, history, poetry, etc., of the Confucian Canon.

5. Toward Revolutionary Humanism,
   D. Dellinger

> *"You and I are murderers against our wills" (Dave Dellinger,*
> *1943). One of the important characteristics of a devotee of*
> *"achievement of human rights through political and economic action"*
> *is not only a vision of a just society, but a commitment to*
> *implement the vision, which implies a strong sense of moral*
> *responsibility and the quality of responsiveness to human needs.*
> *Not many persons have demonstrated this with their lives as*
> *dramatically as David T. Dellinger. While attending Union*
> *Theological Seminary he became a pacifist and was one of the first*
> *men to refuse induction through the draft during World War II*
> *(for which he served a two-year sentence at Lewisberg*
> *Penitentiary). He has been active in civil rights, socialist and*
> *pacifist groups for over thirty years, attempting to form a coalition*
> *against what he views as U.S. militarism, capitalism, imperialism,*
> *and racism. Recently he was one of the "Chicago Seven"*
> *defendents (originally eight, with Bobby Seale) in the trial arising*
> *from their alleged activities outside the Democratic Party*
> *Convention at Chicago in 1968. This particular essay was written*
> *in 1969, and shows his concern to find a moral equivalent and*
> *a politically effective substitute for revolution, war, and violence.*
> *It betrays the ignorance of those who claim that the New Left has*
> *no internal critics, for Dellinger is sensitive to the ineffectiveness,*
> *in terms of a truly liberated and humanistic society, of mere*
> *militancy, or of "by any means necessary" tactics. How does*
> *Dellinger attempt to steer a middle course between what he sees*
> *as an ineffective liberalism and "infantile leftism"? Do you think*
> *his practical concern with tactics makes him any less convinced*
> *that what he is struggling for is of ultimate importance?*

To the best of my memory it was Countée Cullen, a sensitive black poet who later committed suicide, who wrote in the thirties that the reason black people laughed so much was because when they opened their mouths they had to laugh so that they wouldn't cry.

For different reasons, those of us who advocate nonviolent revolution find it hard these days to know whether to exult or to weep. On the positive side, conflict and confrontation are growing more intense every day, in the ghetto, on the campus, in the streets and public places of the country. There is a growing consciousness on the part of nonwhites, young people, welfare recipients, women, draftees, and others that the present society denies them their heritage of dignity, economic well-being, and egalitarian control over their own lives. Moreover, a growing number of these people-in-revolt now perceive that the cause of their privation is not personal inadequacy, bad rulers, or the temporary malfunctioning of a desirable system. Rather it is the nature and purpose of capitalism to create a class society, both nationally and internationally, with vast inequalities in wealth, power, and privilege. If Randolph Bourne discovered, during World War I, that war is the health of the state, the youth of our country know in their bones today that inequality is the health of capitalism. And in their bones they reject this inequality, even when (especially when) they find themselves being channeled into privileged positions, either as apprentices to the ruling class or as trainees (both white and black) for the role of "house niggers."

Along with this growing rejection of a society of class divisions and delegated democracy is a rejection of the channels for social change within this society. It's not so much a question of "lacking patience," as is sometimes charged, but rather of realizing that the traditional methods do not lead in the right direction. The most that can be accomplished through electoral politics, lobbying, governmental commissions, polite negotiations with the authorities, or nonviolent demonstrations within the framework of law and order, is to shake loose a few benefits around the edges. These benefits may have immediate practical value for the recipients, but they are a small part of what is their legitimate birthright and leave them in the position of second- or third-class citizens. At best a few beneficiaries are raised to a slightly more privileged position within the established pecking order. This is what happened to skilled workers under the reforms of the thirties, which legitimized labor unions and divided the working class, making business unionism a co-optive substitute for the liberating goal of worker-control.

The movement has not yet discovered how to challenge the existing power centers effectively, but the built-in assumptions of the present society are gradually losing their legitimacy in the eyes of its victims, including many who would normally be expected to become its future rulers. At least there is heightened consciousness of what the real issues are, and the first experimental steps toward raising the level of the debate, both in the rhetoric of the demands and in the methods of raising them. The movement has discovered that in the absence of forceful confrontation (brought about by the seizure of buildings, strikes, the destruction of draft files and induction notices, or other direct disruptions of established procedures) the "rational discourse" so lauded by university authorities, editorial writers and other addicts of the status quo is slow, superficial and for the most part irrelevant.

All of this represents tremendous growth in a few short years, a growth for which the country owes a debt of gratitude to the Cuban revolutionaries, the incredibly heroic Vientamese, and the black insurgency within our own country. Currently the Black Panthers and the Black Conference for Economic Development, together with the student revolutionaries of

S.D.S., are continuing to transform the context within which the movement as a whole frames its questions and examines its tactics.

But history has taught that being anti-capitalist, courageous, and militant are not sufficient guarantees for contributing to the birth of a liberated and humanistic society. If the U.S. persistence in its agression in Vietnam is an historical fact which is contributing to the deepening anti-capitalist consciousness, the Soviet invasions of Hungary and Czechoslovakia and the continued post-Stalin repression of individuals and groups advocating alternative forms and tactics for the building of communism make clear that non-capitalist societies can be brutal and dehumanizing as well.

Even without the warnings of history, one can look around and see a distressing recrudescence of Old Leftist tendencies and attitudes in the once New Left. The discovery that the forces of oppression are deep, deceitful and brutal, and cannot be dislodged by polite debate, has led some people to conclude that *all* debate is futile, except perhaps within the secret confines of a theoretically democratic and assuredly centralist vanguard party. In practice such self-elected vanguards rarely level with other revolutionary groups or with that vast reservoir of potential revolutionaries who must be won over (not just manipulated) if the revolution is to succeed. Some movement people have inferred from the reformist nature of the nonviolent movement of the late fifties and early sixties that smashing windows, beating up police, and roughing up our antagonists are necessarily part of becoming a serious revolutionary.

But these are bad ways to educate people and win them to the real freedom and universal solidarity of our cause. If, as the saying goes, we are what we eat, a potentially revolutionary movement becomes what it does. Today people are still being won to the movement because they are revolted by what the system does to Vietnamese, G.I.'s, nonwhites, students, and the poor; and, conversely, because they are attracted to the fraternal, humanistic, and liberating goals and style of the insurgents. But if the rhetoric and practice of some of the present adovates of "by any means necessary" becomes the dominant reality, the new recruits will include more and more persons who enjoy street-fighting for its own sake or get a neurotic kick out of beating up other people. If the movement succumbs to the notion that there is one vanguard party which has *the* correct ideology, tactic, and style and that all deviation is counterrevolutionary, it will attract and encourage those who are doctrinaire and repressive. Instead of becoming a family of revolutionaries who are united in some concepts and activities but have family differences about other matters, we will become a group of feuding sects, incapable of learning from our allies or of mounting a genuine united front. Already S.D.S. was treated to the spectacle of a caucus of about 200 members who refused to join in the applause, at the National Council meeting in Austin, when it was announced that the Oakland Seven had been acquitted of the conspiracy charges brought against them for their activities in Stop the Draft Week. Already some of the articles in movement publications which purport to describe the positions of rival groups are as grossly inaccurate as the statements of the government which led to the well-known credibility gap.

On the one hand, it is unfortunate that some of the criticisms of the type that are appearing in *Liberation* are also being made by people who do not share either the movement's revolutionary goals or its awareness of the need for increased militance. It is absurd that both the privileged elite and the timid moderates have become spokesmen these days for "nonviolence." University presidents and government officials condemn the seizure of buildings as "violent," but have no words of condemnation for the real violence of R.O.T.C., police and court repression, or university complicity in war and counter-insurgency. The authorities who frame the Black Panthers on imaginary plots to bomb department stores are themselves engaged in blowing up every store, home, church, and village in liberated Vietnam. In the general debasement that the word "nonviolence" has suffered, it may be necessary for those of us who are anxious to preserve the humanistic sensitivity and content of the revolution to find another word to sum up what we are advocating.

On the other hand, there is substantial evidence that the police and the government send infiltrators into the movement not only to spy but to advocate harebrained schemes of violence which will discredit the movement and obscure what the revolution is genuinely about. There have been repeated instances when the guy who shouted "Kill the pigs," or "Charge the barricades," turned out to be a cop himself. The authorities would love to make the struggle a conflict of violence rather than of rival institutions and ways of life.

Clearly the movement must feel its way through the present period, continuing to deepen its anti-capitalist and anti-militarist consciousness, experimenting with militant ways of disrupting the smooth functioning of the system. It must refuse to retreat either into liberalism or into the pseudo-revolutionary "infantile leftism" which plays at revolution while leaving the movement bereft of allies and credibility, because of the gap between its goals and its methods. In the long run the dynamics of the movement will be determined not by the words we use but by the tactics we develop. To be truly liberating the tactics must combine the newly developed anti-capitalist consciousness and the socialist humanism we are seeking to nourish and make real.

6. Female Liberation and Revolution, R. Dunbar

In spite of the fact that most oppressed peoples have been fighting for their freedom for all human history, the 1960s has nevertheless been the decade when Americans have witnessed in more visible ways the emergence of dozens of liberation movements— black liberation, brown liberation, red (Indian) liberation, "third world" liberation, gay liberation, teenage minority liberation, drug liberation, and women's liberation, to name a few. Different as these movements are from each other, they share a conviction that the conventions of our society as expressed in law, custom, and major institutions deny, distort, or destroy the full humanity of some "minority" group. Consequently, political action, conceived rather broadly, appears to them to be an inescapable requirement of their personal integrity. To affirm their essential humanity, they must transform society.

This excerpt illustrates the last of the revolutionary movements listed above—women's liberation. This movement has spawned a wide array of organizations: NOW (National Organization for Women), with its Bill of Rights; Valerie Solanis's SCUM (Society for Cutting Up Men); New York Radical Women, with their claim that "Until Everywoman is free, no woman will be free"; No More Miss America, with its protest against the well-known annual pageant and the observation that since its inception in 1921 there has never been a black finalist, nor a Puerto Rican, Alaskan, Hawaiian, or Mexican-American winner; WAR (Women of the American Revolution), with its condemnation of the concept of illegitimacy; The Redstockings Manifesto, with its attempt to develop female class consciousness; WITCH, aiming hexes at oppressive financial corporations in America, disrupting bridal fairs, and holding un-wedding ceremonies (WITCH stands for, among other things, Women Inspired to Commit Herstory); and many others could be cited.

The author of this except, Roxanne Dunbar (b. 1939) has been active in both the black and the women's liberation movement. Her basic themes are that women's liberation is best understood if seen as a part of the worldwide struggle for human liberation, and that women must fight on many fronts

From "Female Liberation as the Basis for Social Revolution" by Roxanne Dunbar, found in *Sisterhood is Powerful: An Anthology of Writings from the Women's Liberation Movement*, ed. Robin Morgan (New York: Random House, Vintage Books, 1970), pp. 483–92. Used by permission of the Southern Female Rights Union.

at once. Do you feel that her history of the oppression of women
overstates the case? Do you think there is something more
ultimate for her than the tactics of and the values expressed in
the struggle for women's liberation? If not, may we properly
call that struggle her religion?

In order to understand the power relations óf white and black in
American society, of white imperialist America and the Third World, and
of male and female in all human societies, we must comprehend the caste
system which structures power, and within which caste roles we are conditioned to remain.

Often, in trying to describe the way a white person oppresses or exploits
a black person, or a man oppresses or exploits a woman, we say that the
oppressor treats the other person as a "thing" or as an "object." Men treat
women as "sex objects," we say; slavery reduced black human beings to
"mere property," no different from horses or cattle. This interpretation of
caste oppression overlooks the crucial importance of the fact that it is
human beings, not objects, which the person in the higher caste has the
power to dominate and exploit. Imagine a society becoming as dependent
upon cattle as Southern plantation society was upon black people, or as
men are upon women. The value of slaves as property lay precisely in their
being persons, rather than just another piece of property. The value of a
woman for a man is much greater than the value of a machine or animal
to satisfy his sexual urges and fantasies, to do his house work, breed and
tend his offspring. Under slavery, the slave did what no animal could do—
planting and harvest, as well as every other kind of backbreaking labor for
which no machines existed. But the slave served a much larger purpose
in terms of power. It is convenient and "fun" for a man to have satisfactions from "his woman," but his relation to her as a *person*, his position of
being of a higher caste, is the central aspect of his power and dominance
over her and his need for her.

(A further example of the importance to the higher castes of dominating human beings, not mere objects, is the way men view their sexual
exploitation of women. It is not just the satisfaction of a man's private,
individual, sexual urge which he fantasizes he will get from a woman he
sees. In addition, and more central to his view of women, he visualizes
himself taking her, dominating her through the sexual act; he sees her as
the *human* evidence of his own power and prowess. Prostitution, however
exploitative for the woman, can never serve this same purpose, just as wage
labor, however exploitative to the wage slave, could not have served the
same purpose in Southern society that black slaves served.)

Black people fell under two patterns of dominance and subservience
which emerged under slavery, and which are analogous to patterns of male-
female relations in industrial societies. One pattern is the paternalistic one
(house servants, livery men, entertainers, etc.). The second pattern is the
exploitative pattern of the fieldhands. Among females today, housewives
and women on welfare are subject to the paternalistic pattern. The exploita-

tive pattern rules the lives of more than a third of the population of females (those who work for wages, including paid domestic work) in the United States. But it is important to remember that females form a caste within the labor force; that their exploitation is not simply double or multiple, but is *qualitatively* different from the exploitation of workers of the upper caste (white male).

Though the paternalistic pattern may seem less oppressive or exploitative for females, it is actually only more insidious. The housewife remains tied by emotional bonds to a man and children, cut off from the more public world of work; she is able to experience the outside world only through the man or her children. If she were working in public industry, however exploitative, she could potentially do something about her situation through collective effort with other workers.

However, even for women who hold jobs outside the home, their caste conditioning and demands usually prevail, preventing them from knowing even that they have the *right* to work, much less to ask for something more. Also, the jobs women are allowed to have are most often "service" and domestic ones, demanding constant contact with men and children. Females and blacks, even under the alienating capitalist system, are subject to the paternalistic pattern of caste domination every minute of their lives. White men, however exploited as laborers, rarely experience this paternalism, which infantilizes and debilitates its victims.

A caste system provides rewards that are not entirely economic in the narrow sense. Caste is a way of making human relations "work," a way of freezing relationships, so that conflicts are minimal. A caste system is a *social system,* which is economically based. It is not a set of attitudes or just some mistaken ideas which must be understood and dispensed with because they are not really in the interest of the higher caste. No mere change in ideas will alter the caste system under which we live. The caste system does not exist just in the mind. Caste is deeply rooted in human history, dates to the division of labor by sex, and is the very basis of the present social system in the United States.

The present female liberation movement, like the movements for black liberation and national liberation, has begun to identify strongly with Marxist class analysis. And like other movements, we have taken the basic tools of Marxist analysis (dialectical and historical materialism) and expanded the understanding of the process of change. Our analysis of women as an exploited caste is not new. Marx and Engels as well as other nineteenth-century socialist and communist theorists analyzed the position of the female sex in just such a way. Engels identified the family as the basic unit of capitalist society, and of female oppression. "The modern individual family is founded on the open or concealed domestic slavery of the wife, and modern society is a mass composed of these individual families as its molecules." And "within the family, he (the man) is the bourgeois and the wife represents the proletariat." (Frederick Engels, *Origin of The Family, Private Property, and the State*).

Marx and Engels thought that the large-scale entrance of women into the work force (women and children were the first factory workers) would destroy the family unit, and that women would fight as workers, with men, for the overthrow of capitalism. That did not happen, nor were women freed in the socialist revolutions that succeeded. In the West (Europe and the United States) where proletarian revolutions have not succeeded, the family ideology has gained a whole new lease on life, and the lower caste position of women has continued to be enforced. Even now when 40 percent of the adult female population is in the work force, woman is still defined completely within the family, and the man is seen as "protector" and "breadwinner."

In reality, the family has fallen apart. Nearly half of all marriages end in divorce, and the family unit is a decadent, energy-absorbing, destructive, wasteful institution for everyone except the ruling class, the class for which the institution was created. The powers that be, through government action and their propaganda force, the news media, are desperately trying to hold the family together. Sensitivity, encounter, key clubs, group sex, income tax benefits, and many other devices are being used to promote the family as a desirable institution. Daniel Moynihan and other government sociologists have correctly surmised that the absence of the patriarchal family among blacks has been instrumental in the development of "anti-social" (revolutionary) black consciousness. Actually, in the absence of the patriarchal family, which this society has systematically denied black people, a sense of community life and collective effort has developed. Among whites, individualism and competitiveness prevail in social relations, chiefly because of the propagation of the ideology of the patriarchal family. The new sense of collective action among women is fast destroying the decadent family ideology along with its ugly individualism and competitiveness and complacency. Our demand for collective public child care is throwing into question the private family (or individual) ownership of children.

Yet, under this competitive system, without the family unit and without the tie with a male, the female falls from whatever middle-class status she has gained from the family situation. She quickly falls into the work force or has to go on welfare. Such was the case for black slaves when a master voluntarily freed them, and when slavery was ended as an institution. In both cases, the "helplessness" is used as the rationale for continued domination. Lower caste status almost always means lower class status as well. For women who are supported by and gain the status of their husbands, working class status is always a potential threat, if they do not perform their wifely duties properly. However, many of these supported women have chosen to enter the work force in the vast pool of female clerical workers, in order to gain the economic independence that is necessary to maintain self-respect and sanity. On these jobs, women are still subjected to patterns of masculine dominance. But often on the less personal ground of workplace, a woman can begin throwing off the bonds of servitude.

How will the family unit be destroyed? After all, women must take care of the children, and there will continue to be children. Our demand for full-time child care in the public schools will be met to some degree all over, and perhaps fully in places. The alleviation of the duty of full-time child care in private situations will free many women to make decisions they could not before. But more than that, the demand alone will throw the whole ideology of the family into question, so that women can begin establishing a community of work with each other and we can fight collectively. Women will feel freer to leave their husbands and become economically independent, either through a job or welfare.

Where will this leave white men and "their" families? The patriarchal family is economically and historically tied to private property and, under Western capitalism, with the development of the national state. The masculine ideology most strongly asserts home and country as primary values, with wealth and power an individual's greatest goal. The same upper class of men who created private property and founded nation-states also created the family. It is an expensive institution, and only the upper classes have been able to maintain it properly. However, American "democracy" has spread the ideology to the working class. The greatest pride of a working man is that he can support "his" wife and children and maintain a home (even though this is an impossibility for many and means misery for most). The very definition of a bum or derelict is that he does not maintain a wife, children, and home. Consequently, he is an outcast. It is absurd to consider the possibility of women sharing with men the "privilege" of owning a family. Even though 5.2 million families are headed by females in this country, they gain no prestige from doing so. In fact, the family without a male head or support is considered an inferior family. A woman supporting her family actually degrades the family in terms of social status.

At this point in history, white working-class men will fight for nothing except those values associated with the masculine ideology, the ideology of the ruling class—family, home, property, country, male supremacy, and white supremacy. This force, the organized or organizable working class, has been vital in other social revolutions. However, because of the caste system which reigns here, the American democracy of white males, and the power of the nation in the world with which white workers identify, white male workers are not now a revolutionary group in America. Among the most oppressed part of the white working-class males—Irish, Italian, French Canadian (in the U.S.), Polish immigrants—the patriarchal Catholic church buttresses the masculine ideology with its emphasis on family. Even among lower caste (color) groups, Puerto Ricans and Mexican-Americans the church reinforces masculine domination.

However, the women who "belong" to these men are going to revolt along with the women who belong to middle-class men, and women on welfare and women not yet in the cycle of marriage and family. Black women will probably continue to fight as blacks alongside black men with a reversal of the trend toward taking second place to the black man in order for him to gain his "due" masculine status according to the prevailing masculine ideology. When the white working-class man is confronted with the revolt of women against the family and the society, he will no longer have the escape valve of supremacy over those beneath him in the caste system.

Feminism is opposed to the masculine ideology. I do not suggest that all women are feminists, though many are; certainly some men are, though very few. Some women embrace the masculine ideology, particularly women with a college education. But most women have been programmed from early childhood for a role, maternity, which develops a certain consciousness of care for others, self-reliance, flexibility, non-competitiveness, cooperation, and materialism. In addition, women have inherited and continue to suffer exploitation which forces us to use our wits to survive, to know our enemy, to play dumb when necessary. So we have developed the consciousness of the oppressed, not the oppressor, even though some women have the right to oppress others, and all have the right to oppress children. If these "maternal" traits, conditioned into women, are desirable traits, they are desirable for everyone, not just women. By destroying the present society, and building a society on feminist principles, men will be forced to live in the human community on terms very different from the present. For that to happen, feminism must be asserted, by women, as the basis of revolutionary social change. Women and other oppressed people must lead and structure the revolutionary movement and the new society to assure the dominance of feminist principles. Our present female liberation movement is preparing us for that task, as is the black liberation movement preparing black people for their revolutionary leadership role.

The female liberation movement is developing in the context of international social revolution, but it is also heir to a 120-year struggle by women for legal rights. The nineteenth-century feminist movement as well as its child, the women's suffrage movement, were comparatively modest in their demands. They fought from a basis of no rights, no power at all. In the first movement, women began fighting for the right of females to speak publicly for abolition of slavery. The cause of female rights and the abolition of slavery were inexorably linked. The early feminists did not see the family as a decadent institution. They wanted to find a way to force men to share responsibility in the institution they created by supporting their families. They saw alcohol as an enemy of family solidarity.

With the end of slavery, only black males received citizenship. Black women and white women remained unenfranchised. Women then began the long struggle for the vote. They felt they could make the large-scale and basic changes in society which they saw as necessary by their influence in politics. They believed that woman's political involvement would bring her out of privacy. Many of them questioned the very foundations of civilization, but their strategy and tactics for gaining the desired upheaval of their society revolved around political influence within the System.

In the process of their struggle, the feminists and suffragists opened the door for our present female liberation movement. They won not only the right to vote, but other legal rights as well, including the custodial rights to their children. More than that, women began to fight their oppression and lift up their heads. At the same time, working women were fighting their wage slavery. Women began to emerge from privacy and to know that they did in fact have rights for which they must fight. They gained confidence in the struggle, and asserted a new independence, which we all inherited.

We also inherited an understanding of the weakness of single issue tactics, and of "organizing" women around issues rather than teaching a complete analysis of female oppression. We learned that there is no key to liberation. We must fight on many fronts at once. Thanks to gains made by our feminist predecessors, though, we have the confidence to assert feminism as a positive force, rather than asking for equality in the man's world. We can demand that men change. We can consider leading a social revolution, not just working in supportive positions, and hope for the justness, benevolence, and change of heart of men. We can assert the necessity of industrializing all housework, and for right now to have school cafeterias open to adults as well as children. We can demand the extension of public education facilities and funds to include infant and child care. We can demand the development of maternal skills and consciousness in men. We can insist on the necessity for revolution to be based on the needs and consciousness of the most oppressed of women. We can revoke any privileges we have which divide us from other women.

We are developing necessary skills—self-defense and physical strength, the ability to work collectively and politically, rather than privately and personally, and the ability to teach our ideas to many other women in such a way that they then can become teachers as well. From these new relations and skills will be built the values of the new society. Right now they are our tools of struggle. Though we may work in isolated and difficult and dangerous situations, we can know our larger strategy and goals, and know that we are a part of a worldwide struggle for human liberation.

INTERPRETATION

7. The Civil State, J. J. Rousseau

> *Jean Jacques Rousseau (1712–1778) was a French philosopher, essayist, novelist, and letter-writer. In* The Social Contract *(1762) he describes a theory of government based on the consent of the governed, to be ruled by the general will. Despite its obscurity and the self-contradictions found in many sections, this writing has become a classic statement on the formation of society.*

From the book *The Social Contract and Discourses* by Jean Jacques Rousseau. Trans. and with an intro. by G. D. H. Cole. Everyman's Library Edition. Published by E. P. Dutton & Co., Inc. and used with their permission and of J. M. Dent & Sons Ltd.

Rousseau is well-known for his celebration of man in his "natural state" and he is sometimes quoted as an advocate of a return to "primitivism." However, he did not urge a return to a state of "animal nature"; he attempted to give legitimacy to political man as he exists in a civil state. He tried to resolve a basic issue in political philosophy: the relation between individual liberty and social order. His solution was to affirm that a truly human society is possible where people recognize and unite two things: social order as the indispensible basis for any claim of personal rights, and personal dignity as the inalienable birthright of human beings. Rousseau recognized the social order as a sacred right, the basis of all other rights, but he insisted that this right did not come from nature, but from conventions (the social contract). This notion can be contrasted with the notion, found in Chapter III, of society as an expression of an eternal cosmic order. In any case, for Rousseau the act of association in creating a society is a moral act. The following brief excerpt includes Rousseau's description of the transformation ("a very remarkable change in man") that takes place when man forms a civil state. Some of the changes he suggests are:

Man in the state of nature (animal man)	Man in the civil state (political man)
a. Conduct by instinct	Conduct by justice
b. Actions: amoral	Actions: moral
c. Physical impulses & right of appetite	Duty
d. Consult inclinations	Consults his reason
e. Advantages: —natural liberty—bound by individual strength —unlimited right to everything he gets (possession) —slavery (impulse of appetite)	(Greater) Advantages: —civil liberty—bound by general will —proprietorship of all he possesses (property) —moral liberty (obedience) to laws we prescribe to ourselves

The passage from the state of nature to the civil state produces a very remarkable change in man, by substituting justice for instinct in his conduct, and giving his actions the morality they had formerly lacked. Then only, when the voice of duty takes the place of physical impulses and right of appetite, does man, who so far had considered only himself, find that he is forced to act on different principles, and to consult his reason before listening to his inclinations. Although, in this state, he deprives himself of some advantages which he got from nature, he gains in return others so great, his faculties are so stimulated and developed, his ideas so extended, his feelings so ennobled, and his whole soul so uplifted, that, did not the abuses of this new condition often degrade him below that which he left, he would be bound to bless continually the happy moment which took him from it for ever, and, instead of a stupid and unimaginative animal, made him an intelligent being and a man.

Let us draw up the whole account in terms easily commensurable. What man loses by the social contract is his natural liberty and an unlimited right to everything he tries to get and succeeds in getting; what he gains is civil liberty and the proprietorship of all he possesses. If we are to avoid mistake in weighing one against the other, we must clearly distinguish natural liberty, which is bounded only by the strength of the individual, from civil liberty, which is limited by the general will; and possession, which is merely the effect of force or the right of the first occupier, from property, which can be founded only on a positive title.

We might, over and above all this, add, to what man acquires in the civil state, moral liberty, which alone makes him truly master of himself; for the mere impulse of appetite is slavery, while obedience to a law which we prescribe to ourselves is liberty.

8. The Revolted,
C. Oglesby

Why do people become civil rights activists, protestors, reformers, and revolutionaries? Is it because they do not appreciate law and order? Are they rebelling against parental and other authority figures, playing out neuroses produced in childhood? Do they not know their place? Is it because they are naive about the swiftness with which change can take place in the sphere of history? Do they lack gratitude for the progress that has already come about? Do they suffer from an excess of impatience? Do they place too much emphasis upon freedom, equality, justice, and economic well-being? Are they too "this-worldly"? What answers would you give? The explanation provided in the following excerpt is by Carl Oglesby, a former president of Students for a Democratic Society (SDS) and a leading figure in "the movement." In a chapter from a book he co-authored with Richard Shaull, Oglesby describes the kinds of personal, social, and physical forces that bring about the evolution of "the rebel." What three assumptions about the rebel does he make? What other realizations are crucial before

Reprinted with permission of The Macmillan Company from *Containment and Change* by Carl Oglesby and Richard Shaull. Copyright © by Carl Oglesby and Richard Shaull 1967. pp. 140–56.

the non-rebel becomes the rebel? Would you say that insofar
as revolt is the rebel's ultimate concern and the revolution
his means of (what he considers to be) ultimate transformation,
he is to that degree and in that way "religious"?

Why do men rebel? Let us try to find out what could possibly be so wrong with so many of the world's men and women that they should fight so hard to stay outside the Eden we think we are offering them.

I make three assumptions. First, everyone who is now a rebel *became* a rebel; he was once upon a time a child who spoke no politics. The rebel is someone who has changed.

Second, men do not imperil their own and others' lives for unimpressive reasons. They are sharp accountants on the subject of staying alive. When they do something dangerous, they have been convinced that not to do it was more dangerous. There are always a few who can evidently be persuaded by some combination of statistics and principles to put their lives on the line. Lenin, for example, did not materially *need* the Russian Revolution. His commitment was principled and it originated from a basic detachment. But I am not trying to describe the Lenins. I am after those nameless ones but for whom the Lenins would have remained only philosophers, those who (as Brecht put it) grasp revolution first in the hand and only later in the mind.

Third, I assume that the rebel is much like myself, someone whom I can understand. He is politically extraordinary. That does not mean that he is psychologically so. My assumption is that what would not move me to the act of rebellion would not move another man.

It is safe to say first that revolutionary potential exists only in societies where material human misery is the denominating term in most social relationships. No one thinks that bankers are going to make disturbances in the streets. Less obviously, this also implies that privation can be political only if it is not universal. The peasant who compares his poverty to someone else's richness is able to conceive that his poverty is special, a social identity. To say that hunger does not become a rebellious sensation until it coexists with food is to say that rebellion has less to do with scarcity than with maldistribution. This states a central theme: revolutionary anger is not produced by privation, but by understood injustice.

But the self-recognized victim is not at once his own avenger. He is first of all a man who simply wants to reject his humiliation. He will therefore recreate his world via social pantomimes which transfigure or otherwise discharge that humiliation. "They whipped Him up the hill," sang the black slave, "and He never said a mumbling word." That divine reticence is clearly supposed to set an example. But it also does much more. In such a song, the slave plays the role of himself and thus avoids himself, puts his realities at the distance of a pretense which differs from the realities only to the extent that it *is* a pretense. The slave creates for the master's inspection an exact replica of himself, of that slave which he is; and even as the master looks, the slave escapes behind the image. It is not that he pretends to be other than a slave. Such an act would be quickly punished. He instead pretends to be what he knows himself to be, acts out the role of the suffering and humiliated, in order to place a psychic foil between himself and the eyes of others. The American Negro's older Steppinfetchit disguise, or the acutely ritualized violence of ghetto gangs: these are intentional lies which intentionally tell the truth. The victim-liar's inner reality, his demand for freedom, precludes telling the truth. His outer reality, his victimhood, precludes telling a lie. Therefore he *pretends* the truth, pretends to hold the truth in his hand and to pass judgment on it. And by choosing to enact what he *is* he disguises from himself the fact that he had no choice.

A crucial moment comes when something ruptures this thin membrane of pretense. What can do that? A glimpse of weakness in his master sometimes; sometimes the accidental discovery of some unsuspected strength in himself. More often it will be the master's heightened violence that confronts the slave with the incorrigible authenticity of his slave act. A black man sings blues about his powerlessness, his loneliness; he has taken refuge behind that perfect image of himself. The white master, for no reason, in mid-song, takes the guitar away, breaks it, awaits the slave's reaction. The slave is at that moment forced into his self-image space, is psychologically fused with this truth-telling pretense of his: He *is* powerless; he *is* lonely. He cannot now enact himself; he must *be* that man of whom he had tried to sing. This encounter strips life of its formality and returns it to pure, primitive substance. For the victim, there is no longer even the fragile, rare escape of the simultaneous re-enactment of reality. He lives wholly now in his victim space, without manners, not even allowed to mimic the horror of victimhood in the same gesture that expresses it. He is nothing now but the locus of injustice.

Grown less random, injustice becomes more coherent. Confronted at every instant by that coherence, the victim may find that it is no longer so easy to avoid the truth that his suffering is *caused,* that it is not just an accident that there are so many differences between his life and the life of the round, white-suited man in the big hillside house. He begins to feel singled out. He rediscovers the idea of the system of power.

And at that same moment he discovers that he also may accuse. When the victim sees that what had seemed universal is local, that what had seemed God-given is man-made, that what had seemed quality is mere condition—his permanent immobility permanently disappears. Being for the first time in possession of the stark idea that his life could be different were it not for others, he is for the first time someone who might move. His vision of change will at this point be narrow and mundane, his politics naive: Maybe be only wants a different landlord, a different mayor, a different sheriff. The important element is not the scope or complexity of his vision but the sheer existence of the idea that change can happen.

Then who is to be the agent of this change? Surely not the victim himself. He has already seen enough proof of his impotence, and knows better than anyone else that he is an unimportant person. What compels him to hope nevertheless is the vague notion that his tormentor is answerable to a higher and fairer authority. This sheriff's outrageous conduct, that is, belongs strictly to this particular sheriff, not to sheriffness. Further, this sheriff represents only a local derangement within a system which the victim barely perceives and certainly does not yet accuse, a hardship which High Authority did not intend to inflict, does not need, and will not allow. (Once Robin Hood meets King Richard, the Sheriff of Nottingham is done for.)

We meet in this the politics of the appeal to higher power, which has led to some poignant moments in history. It is the same thing as prayer. Its prayerfulness remains basic even as it is elaborated into the seemingly more politically aggressive mass petition to the king, a main assumption of which is that the king is not bad, only uninformed. This way of thinking brought the peasants and priests to their massacre at Kremlin Square in 1905. It prompted the so-called Manifesto of the Eighteen which leading Vietnamese intellectuals published in 1960. It rationalized the 1963 March on Washington for Jobs and Freedom. The Freedom Rides, the nonviolent sit-ins, and the various Deep South marches were rooted in the same belief: that there was indeed a higher power which was responsive and decent.[1]

Sometimes mass-based secular prayer has resulted in change. But more often it has only shown the victim-petitioners that the problem is graver and change harder to get than they had imagined. The bad sheriffs turn out to be everwhere; indeed, there seems to be no other kind. It turns out that the king is on their side, that the state's administrative and coercive-punitive machinery exists precisely to serve the landlords. It turns out that the powerful know perfectly well who their victims are and why there should be victims, and that they have no intention of changing anything. This recognition is momentous, no doubt the spiritual low point of the emergent revolutionary's education. He finds that the enemy is not a few men but a whole system whose agents saturate the society, occupying and fiercely protecting its control centers. He is diverted by a most realistic despair.

But this despair contains within itself the omen of that final shattering reconstitution of the spirit which will prepare the malcontent, the fighter, the wino, the criminal for the shift to insurgency, rebellion, revolution. He had entertained certain hopes about the powerful: They can tell justice from injustice, they support the first, they are open to change. He is now instructed that these hopes are whimsical. At the heart of his despair lies the new certainty that there will be no change which he does not produce by himself.

The man who believes that change can only come from his own initiative will be disinclined to believe that change can be less than total. Before he could see matters otherwise, he would have to accept on some terms, however revised, the power which he now opposes. The compromises which will actually be made will be arranged by his quietly "realistic" leaders and will be presented to him as a total victory. He himself is immoderate and unconciliatory. But the more important, more elusive feature of this immoderation is that he may be powerless to change it. He could only compromise with rebelled-against authority if he were in possession of specific "solutions" to those "problems" that finally drove him to revolt. Otherwise there is nothing to discuss. But the leap into revolution has left these "solutions" behind because it has collapsed and wholly redefined the "problems" to which they referred. The rebel is an incorrigible absolutist who has replaced all "problems" with the one grand claim that the entire system is an error, all "solutions" with the single irreducible demand that change shall be total, all diagnoses of disease with one final certificate of death. To him, total change means only that those who now have all power shall no longer have any, and that those who now have none—the people, victimized—shall have all. Then what can it mean to speak of compromise? Compromise is whatever absolves and reprieves an enemy who has already been sentenced. It explicitly restores the legitimacy of the very authority which the rebel defines himself by repudiating. This repudiation being total, it leaves exactly no motive—again, not even the *motive*—for creating that fund of specific proposals, that *conversation,* without which a compromise is not even *technically* possible.

"What do you want?" asks the worried, perhaps intimidated master. "What can I give you?" he inquires, hoping to have found in this rebel a responsible, realistic person, a man of the world like himself. But the rebel does not fail to see the real meaning of this word *give*. Therefore he answers, "I cannot be purchased." The answer is meant mainly to break off the conference. But at one level, it is completely substantive comment, not at all just a bolt of pride. It informs the master that he no longer exists, not even in part.

At another level, however, this answer is nothing but an evasion. The master seems to have solicited the rebel's views on the revolutionized, good society. The rebel would be embarrassed to confess the truth: that he has no such views. Industry? Agriculture? Foreign trade? It is not such matters that drive and preoccupy him. The victorious future is at the moment any society in which certain individuals no longer have power, no longer exist. The rebel fights for something that will not be like *this*. He cannot answer the question about the future because that is not his question. It is not the future that is victimizing him. It is the present. It is not an anticipated Utopia which moves him to risk his life. It is pain. "Turn it over!" he cries, because he can no longer bear it as it is. The revolutionary is not *by type* a Lenin, a Mao, a Castro, least of all a Brezhnev. He is neither an economist nor a politician nor a social philosopher. He may become these; ultimately he must. But his motivating vision of change is at root a vision of something absent—not of something that *will* be there, but of something that will be there *no longer*. His good future world is elementally described by its empty spaces: a missing landlord, a missing mine owner, a missing sheriff. Who or what will replace landlord, owner, sheriff? Never mind, says the revolutionary, glancing over his shoulder. Something better. If he is thereupon warned that this undefined "something" may turn out to make things worse than ever, his response is a plain one: "Then we should have to continue the revolution."

The fundamental revolutionary motive is not to construct a Paradise but to destroy an Inferno. In time, Utopian ideas will appear. Because the world now has a revolutionary past, it may seem that they appear at the same moment as destructive anger, or even that they precede and activate or even cause it. This is always an illusion produced by the predictive social analytic which revolutionist intellectuals claim to have borrowed from history. We may be sure that the people have not said: Here is a plan for a better life—socialism, Montes called it. He has proved to us that it is good. In its behalf, we shall throw everything to the wind and risk our necks. Rather, they have said: What we have here in the way of life cannot be put up with anymore. Therefore, we must defend ourselves.

It happens that at least the spirit of socialism will be implied by the inner dynamics of mass revolt: What was collectively won should be collectively owned. But it cannot be too much emphasized that the interest in developing other social forms, however acute it will become, follows, *does not precede,* the soul-basic explosion against injustice which is the one redemption of the damned. When Turcios takes his rebel band to a Guatemalan village for "armed propaganda," there is no need to talk of classless societies. Someone kneels in the center of the circle and begins to speak of his life, the few cents pay for a hard day's labor, the high prices, the arrogance of the *patrón,* the coffins of the children. It is this talk—very old talk, unfortunately always new—which finally sets the circle ringing with the defiant cry, "*Sí, es cierto!*" Yes, it is true. Something will have to be done.

Revolutionary consciousness exists for the first time when the victim elaborates his experience of injustice into an inclusive definition of the society in which he lives. *The rebel is someone for whom injustice and society are only different words for the same thing.* Nothing in the social world of the master is spared the contempt of this definition, which, as soon as it exists, absorbs everything in sight. No public door is marked overnight with a device that permits its survival. The loanshark's corner office and the Chase Manhattan Bank, Coney Island and Lincoln Center, look very much the same from 137th Street. They are all owned by someone else.

Everywhere he looks, the man-who-is-being-revolted sees something which is not his. The good land which the *campesino* works belongs to the *hacienda.* That belongs to the *patrón.* As often as not, the *patrón* belongs to the United Fruit Company. And that prime mover unmoved belongs to nothing. It can only be for a brief moment that the *campesino* gazes with unashamed wonder at these skyscrapers. For all the justice they promise him, they might as well be so many rocks. He is soon unimpressed and grows apathetic toward Western grandeur. *The rebel is someone who has no stakes.* He is an unnecessary number, a drifter into a life that will be memorable chiefly for its humiliations. No use talking to him about the need to sustain traditions and preserve institutions or to help society evolve in an orderly way toward something better bit by bit. He very well knows that it is not in his name that the virtue of this orderliness is being proved. *The rebel is an irresponsible man whose irresponsibility has been decreed by others.* It is no doing of his own that his fantasy is now filled with explosions and burning Spanish lace.

But this new consciousness, this radical alienation from past and present authority, does not lead straightway to political action. A commitment to violence has only just become possible at this point. We have a man who certainly will not intervene in a streetcorner incident in behalf of the "law and order" of which he considers himself the main victim. He will even betray a government troop movement or shelter an "outlaw." But he may also find a tactical rationale for joining a "moderate" march or applauding a "reasonable" speech or doing nothing at all. At odd moments, he will abide talk of reform. Maybe things left to themselves will get better. He will keep the conversation open and the switchblade closed.

What is wrong with this man who thinks things can change without being changed? Who knows everything and does nothing?

Nothing is wrong with him but the fact that he is a human being. All these excuses, these cautions and carefully rationalized delays, add up to one thing: *He wants to be free.* He therefore temporizes with freedom. His desire for an independent private life has been intensified everywhere by the conditions that prohibit it. He has understood his situation and the demands it makes. He knows he is being asked to become a historical object. But he seems to recognize in this demand an old familiar presence. He has been drafted before by this history, has he not? Is the new allurement of rebellion really so different at bottom from the old coercion of slavery! Are his privacy and freedom not pre-empted equally by both? Is the rebel anything more than the same unfree object in a different costume, playing a new role? When the slave kills the master, argues Sartre, two men die. He meant that the slave dies too and the free man materializes in his place. Very well, the image is nearly overwhelming. But where is the freedom of this ex-slave who, instead of cutting cane, is now sharpening knives? That he has removed himself from one discipline to another does not hide the fact that he remains under discipline. It will be said that he at least chose the new one. But that does not diminish the servitude. When the slave conceives rebellion and remains a slave, one may say that he has chosen his slavery. That makes him no less a slave, no more a free man. In fact, the free man was glimpsed only in the moment at which he said: *I can! I may!* At that moment, the whole world shook with his exhilaration. Everywhere, he saw commotion and uncertainty where there had been only stillness and routine before. He stops at the window of a firearms dealer. He does not go in. He proceeds to the window of an agency of escape. This is not irresolution; it is freedom, the liquidity of choice. When he changes *I may* into *I will,* when he has taken the rifle and changed *I will* into *I am,* this man who was for one moment a profuse blur of possibilities, a fleeting freedom, has disappeared into another pose, has transformed himself into another image: that of the rebel.

NOTES

1. What was new was the way these forms enlarged the concept of petition. Instead of merely writing down the tale of grievance, they reproduced the grievance itself in settings that forced everyone to behold it, tzar included, and to respond. The Vietnam war protest demonstrations are no different. The

speeches they occasion may sometimes seem especially pugnacious. But inasmuch as the antiwar movement has never been able to dream up a threat which it might really make good, this fiercer face-making has remained basically a kind of entertainment. The main idea has always been to persuade higher authority—Congress, the UN, Bobby Kennedy—to do something. Far from calling higher authority into question these wildly militant demonstrations actually dramatize and even exaggerate its power.

9. Revolutionary Immortality,
R. J. Lifton

We have already implied, by our inclusion of Liu Shao-Ch'i's article, that Communism may function religiously for its adherents. A most interesting interpretation of the Cultural Revolution in China is provided, next, by Robert Jay Lifton (b. 1926), who is a psychiatry professor at Yale University. He has long been interested in China and Japan, and in the problems suffered by individuals during historical crises. In 1968, in his book Revolutionary Immortality: Mao Tse-Tung and the Chinese Cultural Revolution *(Random House), he made the striking observation that our misunderstanding of China had less to do with our lack of information about China than with our lack of a conceptual scheme for interpreting what information is available. Being a psychiatrist, his own conceptual scheme is one that he calls "psychoformation," an attempt to find connections between individual and collective patterns. For example, Lifton sees the Cultural Revolution in China as a quest for revolutionary immortality, an attempt to transcend individual death by "living on" indefinitely within the continuing Chinese revolution. Such a conceptual scheme, it should be noted, goes beyond those who see the revolution in China as merely, and nothing else than, a* power *struggle. The real "power struggle" in China is, according to Lifton, a struggle for power over death. The following excerpt, from another book by Lifton, discusses this same theme. What biographical facts about Mao Tse-Tung does he recall in order to substantiate his thesis? Has your own education and socialization up to this point in your life prepared you to view the Chinese Communists as Lifton does? Does his thesis help you to understand how ultimacy saturates the involvement of many (Chinese) revolutionaries?*

From *Boundaries: Psychological Man in Revolution* by Robert Jay Lifton. First published in *Partisan Review.* Copyright © 1967, 1968, 1969 by Robert Jay Lifton. Reprinted by permission of Random House, Inc. and Robert Jay Lifton c/o IFA. pp. 69–78, 80–82.

I should like to suggest that much of what has been taking place in China recently can be understood as a quest for revolutionary immortality. By revolutionary immortality I mean a shared sense of participating in permanent revolutionary ferment, and of transcending individual death by 'living on' indefinitely within this continuing revolution. Some such vision has been present in all revolutions and was directly expressed in Trotsky's ideological principle of "permanent revolution" (even if other things were also meant by this term); but it has taken on unprecedented intensity in present-day Chinese Communist experience.

Central to this point of view is the concept of symbolic immortality I have described in earlier chapters—man's need for a *sense* of immortality as a form of connectedness with prior and future people and events. While this may at first seem a rather abstract approach to the passions and actions of old revolutionaries and young followers, I believe that only by recognizing such life-and-death components of the revolutionary psyche can we begin to comprehend precisely these passions and actions.

Applying these modes of symbolic immortality to the revolutionary, we may say that he becomes part of a vast 'family' reaching back to what he perceives to be historical beginnings of his revolution and extending infinitely into the future. This socially created 'family' tends to replace the biological one as a mode of immortality; moreover, it can itself take on an increasingly biological quality, as, over the generations, revolutionary identifications become blended with national, cultural, and racial ones. The revolutionary denies theology as such, but embraces a secular Utopia through images closely related to the spiritual conquest of death and even to an afterlife. His revolutionary 'works' are all important, and only to the extent that he can perceive them as enduring can he achieve a measure of acceptance of his own eventual death. The natural world to which he allies himself is one that must be transformed by revolution while continuing to contain all that revolution creates. And his experiential transcendence can approach that of religious mystics, as a glance at some of the younger participants in China's Cultural Revolution confirms.

What all this suggests, then, is that the essence of the "power struggle" taking place in China, as of all such "power struggles," is power over death. It also suggests that revolution itself is centrally concerned with the boundaries of individual and group existence.

It is impossible to know Mao's exact physical or mental state. But let us assume, on the basis of evidence we have, that the seventy-six-year-old (born December 26th, 1893) man has generally been vigorous, that he has experienced rather severe illness in recent years, and that he has always been a man of strong revolutionary passions. We can go a bit further, however, especially on the basis of a valuable interview with him conducted by Edgar Snow, perhaps the American who over the years has been closest to Mao, in January 1965.

During that interview, Mao made several references to his "getting ready to see God" (using the theological idiom somewhat wryly, as Snow noted). He also spoke of his amazing sequence of survivals in the face of the repeated deaths of so many close family members and equally close revolutionary comrades—the two categories of people more or less merging in his imagery—including several very narrow escapes in which men standing right next to him were killed.

In these ways and others Mao is surely the survivor *par excellence.* He is the hero of a truly epic story of revolutionary survival, that of the Long March of 1934–1935, in which it is believed that more than eighty percent of the original group perished along a six-thousand-mile trek, in order that the remainder, and the Revolution itself, might stay alive. To transcend his guilt over remaining alive while others die, the survivor must be able to render significant the death immersions he has experienced—and in Mao's case, done much to bring about. This kind of survivor formulation...faces both ways: justification of the past, and contribution to the future. Thus for a man in Mao's position, of his age and special commitments, the affirmation of a sense of immortality becomes crucial. The overwhelming threat is not so much death itself as the suggestion that his 'revolutionary works' will not endure.

We sense the passion behind his apparent calm as he goes on, during that same interview, to describe what he calls the "two possibilities" for the future: the first, "the continued development of the revolution toward Communism"; and the second, "that youth could negate the Revolution and give a poor performance: make peace with imperialism, bring the remnants of the Chiang Kai-shek clique back to the Mainland and take a stand beside the small percentage of counter-revolutionaries still in the country." The first is an image of continuous life; the second of death and extinction, of impaired immortality.

Mao's ultimate dread, the image of extinction which stalks him, is the death of the revolution. And when he speaks of the possible "poor performance" of the young, his overriding concern is that the immortal revolutionary legacy will be squandered, that in such unknowing hands, the sacred thing itself—the Revolution—could be abused, neglected, permitted to die. Such "historical death" can, for the revolutionary, represent an "end of the world," an ultimate deformation and "de-symbolization."

During the Cultural Revolution (and of course before that), Maoists have repeatedly called forth certain specific images to suggest the danger of the death of the revolution. These images include "American imperialism," "feudalism," "the capitalist road," "bourgeois remnants," and "modern revisionism." Without trying to describe each of these in detail, one may say that the image of modern revisionism is the one that has been recently expressed with greatest intensity and perhaps greatest fear. For modern revisionism represents both an external danger, as embodied by the visible friend-turned-enemy, the Soviet Union, and an internal one of an insidious personal nature. It is a form of degeneracy, of inner death, experienced by those who once knew the true path to revolutionary immortality but, through a combination of moral weakness or shadowy conspiracy, strayed from it. Much more than the other negative images, modern revisionism also looms closer to an immediate possibility.

But why now? Why the crisis in boundaries—in revolutionary immortality—at this time? There is much evidence that the Cultural Revolution represents the culmination of a series of conflicts surrounding totalistic visions and national campaigns, of an increasing inability to fulfill the visions or achieve the transformations of the physical and spiritual environment claimed by the campaigns. And these conflicts went on all through the late 1950s and early 1960s, and found dramatic expression in what was surely the most remarkable campaign of all prior to the Cultural Revolution, that of the Great Leap Forward of 1958.

The "Great Leap," in brief, was a heroic attempt to achieve rapid industrialization and collectivization by making extensive use of the bare hands and the pure minds of the Chinese people. It was really an attempt to break through ordinary boundaries of revolutionary accomplishment, and to outdo revolutionary rivals in the rapid march toward a state of communism. Such visions of transformation had become very basic to Chinese Communist (and more specifically Maoist) practice—and in many cases had been so brilliantly realized—that they could not be abandoned without a sense that the fundamental momentum of the revolution, its life force, was ebbing. But whether one attributed the Great Leap's failure (and, despite some accomplishments, it was essentially a failure) to insufficient revolutionary zeal, as Mao clearly did, or to an excess of the same, as did Liu Shao-chi and other so-called pragmatists, all came to feel anxious about the life of the revolution.

Moreover, the regime's subsequent economic backtracking and cultural liberalization (during the year 1961 to 1962), which was apparently implemented by the pragmatists, despite Mao's resistance, also contributed to these conflicts. That is, measures deemed necessary for national recovery encouraged precisely the kinds of personal freedom and self-interest readily viewed later on, within Chinese Communist ideology, as "decadent" forms of "individualism" and "economism"—as forms of "degeneracy" and "decay"—as death-tainted threats to the immortal revolutionary vision.

The Chinese have also had to cope with a more concrete form of death anxiety, as stimulated by America's aggressive policy in Vietnam, and by the fear of war with America. It is very difficult to evaluate how great a part the fear of war with America has played in the Cultural Revolution. Generally speaking, the Cultural Revolution seems to stem from within Chinese Communist revolutionary practice, but its shape could well have been influenced by this fear. What one can say is that the Cultural Revolution itself appears to be more a quest for a collective sense of revolutionary power than an actual mobilization of military power to combat an outside enemy.

The activist response to symbolic death, or to what might be called unmastered death anxiety, is a quest for rebirth. One could in fact view the entire Cultural Revolution as a demand for the renewal of Communist life. It is, in other words, a call for reassertion of revolutionary immortality. Now, in Maoist China, this has meant nothing less than an all-consuming experience of death and rebirth, an induced catastrophe, together with a prescription for reconstituting the world being destroyed.

The agents of this attempted rebirth are of great importance: I refer to those called upon to extend revolutionary boundaries, the Red Guards. The tenderness of their years—they included not only youths in their early twenties or late teens, but children of thirteen and fourteen—has been striking to everyone, and then much too quickly attributed to political necessity alone. The assumption here is that, having alienated most of the more mature population by his extreme policies, Mao had no choice but to call upon the young. But I believe one must look beyond such explanations (whatever their partial truth) to the wider symbolism of the Red Guard movement.

The Red Guards first began to appear during the early summer of 1966. Without going into detail about their emergence, one can say that they were called forth by the Maoists and continuously manipulated from above, but that there were also elements of spontaneity, as there inevitably are in such movements, especially in youth movements. Only after an official public confirmation and blessing from Mao Tse-tung, during a gigantic dawn rally on August 18th of that year, did the Red Guard really take on national, and even international, significance. Within a few days after that, tens of thousands of youngsters, with identifying red armbands, were roaming throughout Peking, and before long, throughout the entire country.

From the beginning, the battle cry of the Red Guard was the triumph of youth over age, of the new over the old. Hence the Red Guard's announced early goal of totally destroying the "four olds": old ideas, old culture, old customs, and old habits. The human targets selected by the young militants for mental and physical abuse were referred to as "old fogies of the landlord and bourgeois class," as "the revisionist clique of old men," and a bit later, as "old men in authority" and "old gentlemen who follow the capitalist road." The Red Guards themselves were heralded as "young people who had declared war on the old world." But in their attack upon old age and decay, they were, psychologically speaking, declaring war upon death itself.

Great stress was also placed on their 'purity', and at the beginning only those who had certain kinds of class and family backgrounds were permitted to become Red Guards. Their targets, in contrast, were associated with ultimate impurity, as designated members of the "five black" categories: landlords, rich peasants, counter-revolutionaries, "bad elements," and rightists. One observer of the official Chinese film taken of that August 18th rally—noting the extraordinary dawn scene of a million people gathered in the great square, singing "The East is Red," Mao Tse-tung, powerful in his presence though walking slowly and stiffly, then moving out among the masses on the arm of a teen-age girl—spoke of the formation of a "new community." I would suggest that this new community, in a symbolic sense, is a community of immortals, of men, women and children entering into a new relationship with the eternal revolutionary process. An event of this kind is meant to convey a blending of the immortal cultural and racial substance of the Chinese as a people with the equally immortal Communist revolution.

On other occasions as well, the Red Guard created an image of young people touched by grace, bestowing their anointed state on everyone around them. But they have also had a different face. Theirs has been the task of inducing the catastrophe, of, in their own words, "breaking and smashing," of initiating widespread agitation and disruption while spreading the message that this was what the country required. They became a strange young band of wandering zealots in search of evil and impurity, in their own terms "anti-bureaucratic" and "anti-authority."

The objects of Red Guard activism varied enormously. There was the invasion of homes of people in the "five black" categories, with confiscation of belongings. There were various forms of physical and verbal abuse, including the ritual of parading certain people through the streets in dunce caps; attacks upon temples and churches; destruction of art objects; destruction of certain forms of clothing, and of foreign made objects of various kinds, including dolls and playing cards; and the replacement of certain forms of burial ceremonies with simple cremation. And then there were the somewhat ludicrous dimensions of such things as the demand that traffic signals be reversed, that the red have the properly positive connotation of "go," or that military drill be changed from "eyes right" to "eyes left" and so on, even to the point of renaming Peking "East Is Red." But the Red Guard embodied a consistent principle, and that was the principle of renewal—an image of perpetual youth, really perpetual life, that was both revolutionary and Chinese. . . .

If we examine more closely Mao's thought, the usual commentary about it has stressed (perhaps rightly) its preoccupation with principles of "struggle" and "contradictions" and of "rectification" and reform. But what I think has not been adequately recognized is a special quality of tone and content that, more than any other, shaped the psychic contours of the Cultural Revolution. I refer here to a kind of *existential absolute, an insistence upon all-or-none confrontation with death.* Mao always further insists that the confrontation be rendered meaningful, that it be associated with a mode of transcendence. One must risk all, not only because one has little to lose but because even in death one has much to gain.

This quality of thought is amply illustrated by many selections contained in the little red bible of the Cultural Revolution, *Quotations from Chairman Mao Tse-tung.* One important chapter takes its title from Mao's 1944 essay, "Serve the People," and includes two comments about death and dying taken from the earlier essay. The first presents a simple definition of a "worthy death": "Wherever there is struggle there is sacrifice, and death is a common occurrence. But we have the interests of the people and the sufferings of the great majority at heart, and when we die for the people it is a worthy death." The cautionary sentence that follows—"Nevertheless, we should do our best to avoid unnecessary sacrifices"—does not alter the message. The second and more probing passage makes use of a classical image: "All men must die, but death can vary in its significance. The ancient Chinese writer Szuma Chien said, 'Though death befalls all men alike, it may be heavier than Mount Tai or lighter than a feather.' To die for the people is heavier than Mount Tai, but to work for the fascists and die for the exploiters and oppressors is lighter than a feather." Here "weight" is equated with lasting significance: a death becomes "heavier than Mount Tai" because it contributes to the immortal revolutionary process of the Chinese people. Mao encourages everyone to cultivate such a death and thereby, during life, enhance his individual *sense* of immortality.

One could also point to Mao's famous "paper tiger" image which has been applied to imperialism, to all reactionaries, to America and, as everybody knows, to nuclear weapons. What Mao keeps telling his people, in a great variety of ways, is that, above all, one need not fear death at the hands of the enemy. He speaks in a tone of transcendence, and conveys to the revolutionary a message which seems to say: Death does not really exist for you; there is nothing to fear. Mao put forth this message very vividly as early as 1919 during the cultural revolution of that year, the epochal May Fourth Movement: "What is the greatest force? The greatest force is that of the union of the popular masses. What should we fear? We should not fear heaven. We should not fear ghosts. We should not fear the dead. We should not fear the bureaucrats. We should not fear the militarists. We should not fear the capitalists."

A leader who can instill these transcendent principles in his followers can turn the most extreme threat of disintegration into an ordered certainty of mission, convert the most incapacitating death anxiety into a death-conquering calm of near invincibility. He can, in fact, become the omnipotent guide sought by all totalist movements—precisely the meaning of the characterization of Mao during the Cultural Revolution as the "Great Leader, Great Teacher, Great Supreme Commander and Great Helmsman." The Thought of Mao becomes not so much a precise theory of society as, in the traditional Chinese sense, a Way, a call to a particular mode of being on behalf of a transcendent purpose.

10. A Passion for Justice, R. Clark

"Crime reflects more than the character of the pitiful few who commit it. It reflects the character of the entire society. How do people...come to be that way?" These are the thoughts of Ramsey Clark (b. 1928), former Attorney General of the

United States. The title of the epilogue to his book Crime in
America *reflects his ultimate concern: "A Passion for Justice."
His practical tactic for bringing about more justice in America
has been to find ways to deal* meaningfully *with crime.
For him this means to treat the causes of crime, rather than
merely the symptoms. "What they [criminals] are and what they
experienced came largely from society—from its influences
on them and on their forebears." Such basic convictions give
Clark a sensitivity to the problems of criminals themselves,
as well as their victims. But basic to his solution is the conviction
that institutions can serve humanity if they are capable of
enough change, and this is mainly a question of the* will *of the
citizens of America. Education must be "a first priority,"
and all of our institutions—churches, government, business,
industry, trade, labor, and schools—must make an "all-fronts
effort" to meet the challenges of change. Do you find Clark overly
optimistic about what we can accomplish if we will just put
our minds to it? Can one expect a nation state to have justice
as its "passion"? Can a nation long exist without such a passion?*

The days and years ahead will be turbulent. Nothing else is possible.
We cannot cringe at the prospect, rather we must welcome it—for it is to
be. Turbulence is life force, the manifestation of change. It offers happiness
and fulfillment if we have the courage to master it. Shaw called Beethoven
"the most turbulent spirit that ever found expression in pure sound." He
was, and without his turbulence he would not be remembered two hundred
years after his birth. The power of the Ninth Symphony is the turbulent
joy of humanity.

We can fear change. Or we can withdraw into the apathy of affluence
and indifference. Neither reaction is alien to the human spirit. Both turn
us to narrow self-interest and incapacitate our will to find solutions and
meet needs. Together they pose the greatest threat to our future. As turbulence increases, fear will turn to force—brute force—as its technique for
preventing change it does not want, and apathy will not object. But force
cannot stop the irresistible movement of change. The result, if fear prevails,
can only be violence.

Change will accelerate with increasing population and proliferating
technology. We will experience more change in the way people live their
lives in the remaining three decades of the twentieth century than in all
history to date. The trauma of change with its uncertainties and newness,
the anonymity of mass populations and the dehumanization of technology
will cause dislocations in people's habits and well-being, with accompanying
frustrations and anxieties far beyond anything we have ever known.

As we approach absolute interdependence, the welfare of each nation
will depend on the welfare of all. Stability and the good life will not be
known by any if they are not shared by all. Park Avenue can no longer
be placid while Harlem seethes nor Beverly Hills dignified while Berkeley

is tumultuous. Crowded in urban dwellings, moved by mass transit systems and supersonic aircraft, instantly informed of major events and made aware of all living styles by electronics and other communications, every person will depend for his essential needs on the uninterrupted performance of millions of others. Food, water, clothing and shelter were simple wants. Now we must have not only the means to obtain those, but systems of production, distribution and delivery to supply them—and much more. Our fragile cities, barely functioning, must effectively provide transportation, education, power, labor, telephone service, mass communications, garbage collection, sewage disposal, health services, police and fire protection, parks, recreation opportunity, and environments free of pollution, noise, anxiety and violence.

Interdependence makes the consequences of violent revolution unbearably inhumane. These are not the simple days of Concord. Castro cannot harvest Cuba's sugar cane without help. What revolutionary leadership could seize and operate the essential services of an American megalopolis? What happens to man when no water flows from the faucet, the supermarket shelves are empty, buses trains and planes stop, gasoline is gone, electricity fails and with it, television, radio, telephones, elevators, stoves and heating systems; when truck drivers, teachers, firemen and police do not show up for work? Romanticists notwithstanding, violent revolution is no longer tolerable. We must reform without disruption.

Change will create new conditions of proverty unlike—and more severe than—the gentle poverty of simple wants. Antisocial conduct will find new forms reflecting the greater strains on the individual arising from poverties of health, opportunity, power, decent living conditions, humaneness, dignity, peace and love. The new poverty will feed crime among the young, the anxious, the unstable and the powerless. The impact of that crime will be felt by all. There is no place to escape. New Prophets of Doom will cry with Ezekiel, "The land is full of bloody crimes and the city is full of violence."

The different meanings of racism in technologically advanced societies and a world divided into continents of emerging blacks and browns and yellows will requite an early resolution of injustices and inequalities. Integration will be essential in America to avoid violent conflict and to show the world, which will have billions more blacks, browns and yellows in three decades, that the races can live together with dignity, respect and love.

If the challenge of change seems staggering, our capacity to meet it is overwhelming. There was never a people that so clearly had the means to solve their problems as Americans today. Movers, builders, doers—we have proven the ability of man to dramatically change his destiny. Now we must show that he can control that destiny. A nation that doubled its productive capacity in four years during World War II can supply the needs of its people and the techniques and assistance by which other nations can supply theirs. It is only a question of will. How much do we care? How much foresight, initiative and energy will we devote to the quality of life and the human condition in the exciting years ahead?

If institutions are to serve people meaningfully, provide for their needs and afford them a chance to participate in decisions vitally affecting their future, they will have to learn to change with conditions. The science of institutional change must become a major endeavor. Old institutions will have to adapt constantly to be relevant to developing situations, and new institutions with new techniques must be devised to meet new problems. Ways must be found to release the energies of our people. Today we fail to find constructive outlets for half of our energies. A million people now on welfare in New York City alone could add greatly to the wealth of the nation, provide needed goods and services and fulfill themselves if we work to find the way.

That we permit conditions of ill health to prevail among millions is perhaps the most devastating contemporary commentary on our character. We could end this in a few short years. Malnutrition, brain damage, retardation, mental illness, high death rates, infant mortality, addiction, alcoholism —these are principal causes of crime. But crime is a small part of the pain they inflict on society. Health is a key measure of the human condition. There is little chance for quality in life with poor health. Doctors, nurses, medicines, vaccines, clinics, hospitals, research, counseling and physical fitness facilities, clean air and water, some quiet and reasonably orderly environments are essential to reduce violence. We can supply them abundantly if we care. We can build 20 million housing units in five years if we want to and tear down the ugliness of the slums where crime is cultivated.

With vision, courage and compassion, America can unleash forces that will bring us through the turbulence ahead. We can devote our greatest talents to our most important business—education. We can give everyone the opportunity to absorb all the education he can. Education in its largest sense—understanding and individual fulfillment—is a major end of civilization. Through it we can salvage thousands of lost lives and avoid future losses. Education must be more than something we suffer through because it is the thing to do. It must be a first priority, a growing, reaching, searching quest for each of us through which we seek to know the truth, to understand, to prepare to make our contribution.

An all-fronts efforts [sic] to meet the challenges of change will be required of our institutions. Churches, government, business, industry, trade, labor, schools, health services, charities—all must disenthrall themselves, think anew and act anew. Law must be in the vanguard as an effective instrument for social change. It will have to create new rights adequate to the needs of the individual in mass society. The old laws, such as *caveat emptor* and negligence as the basis for liability, are not sufficient. New rights constantly refined to assure human dignity will require effective means of enforcement. The law must devise effective techniques for fulfilling its word, and where the law is unable to do so, it must help regiment the power within society necessary to that fulfillment. We cannot continue to deny essential rights and expect our system of government to survive.

In the main, regulation and control of technology must be through law. Man will have to make moral judgments by democratic processes, encase them in the rule of law and enforce them equally throughout his society.

The delicate balances of interpersonal relationships in crowded urban life must be sensitively defined and carefully enforced by law. Law must soon be brought to the solution of all international disputes. Our capacity for violence is too great to tolerate its further use in international problem solving.

Science must also be brought to bear on human attitudes. Old instincts must be altered. Our reflex to violence can be conditioned out of the American character. We should work to make violence socially unacceptable and personally unthinkable. Today we glorify the power of violence while ignoring the pity of it. Violence is ugly and in its criminal forms is the ultimate human degradation. We must see it as such.

We must also contain our acquisitive instinct. Selfishness must be relegated to the past, when scarcity created preciousness and made man covetous. We can produce more than enough for all. We must understand that if we fail to do so and to distribute our product equitably, all will suffer. There will be no social stability if major segments of society are excluded from the mainstream and millions go on living in poverty. There is no longer room enough for us to ignore one another. Service to others now best serves oneself. Social injustice will be shared by all in the form of anxiety, frustration and crime.

A conscious, constant and effective effort will be necessary to maintain freedom. The pressures of population and technology on the chance of the individual to be himself will overwhelm us if society does not strive to create liberty. There is no contest between liberty and safety. We have the means of enlarging both. Unless we do, we will lose both, because neither freedom nor security can long endure without the other.

Divisions arise over injustice. Underlying such divisions as those between the powerful and the powerless, young and old, rich and poor, educated and ignorant and black and white are different perceptions of and experiences with the quality of justice in America. St. John told us, "And if a house be divided against itself then that house cannot stand." He was right. Injustice in its many forms is the basic cause of disorder. It takes rather substantial injustice to arouse man from lethargy. From one side of America's house divided we hear the demand for order: There must be order! It is the voice of those who resist change. From the other side of our house comes the plea for justice: Give us justice! This is the voice of those who seek change. But the long history of mankind says you will have neither order nor justice unless you have both.

We are divided with repressive inference when we must join with constructive purpose. The fear and anger of the too comfortable and the unconcerned is catered to at the cost of greater alienation of the miserable and the involved. Behind the phrase "law and order" many conceal their opposition to civil rights enforcement and to dissent—to the supreme law of the land. Blinded by prejudice, they will not see that through decades of civil wrongs we have bred crime, caused it, and will continue to do so until wrongs are righted. People cry for order, but blush at the mention of justice. One of the blessings of technologically advanced mass society is that it makes injustice intolerable. We must not be ashamed to speak of humaneness, to be gentle, to seek rehabilitation—these are essential to the spirit of man. Without them he will be hard, cruel and violent.

Will the immensity of our problems—population, world peace, nuclear arms, rising racial strife, student unrest, the decaying hearts of our great cities, crime, pollution, the sheer numbers in our environment—so strain our understanding that we confuse essential liberties with the cause of our grief? Will we come to fear the strength of diversity, the virtue of difference? Will we see some nonexistent contest between liberty and security, between the rights of the individual and the safety of society? Will we seek a little more safety by giving a little less liberty? Can fear, affluence or lethargy overpower our will to enlarge both liberty and security? Can complexity and anxiety cause us to doubt that fulfillment is the flower of freedom, borne of no other tree, that freedom is the child of courage? Shall we fail to remember that nothing can so weaken security as the loss of liberty?

Tolerance, patience, humaneness and a gentle untiring hand will be essential to avoid division. Too, we must create ways for the exchange of views among all of our people. Agencies of criminal justice must be fair and effective if they are to hold us together in the tubulence of the years ahead until we have removed the underlying causes of crime in America. Our laws must provide moral leadership and cannot therefore be themselves immoral. Our purpose as a people must have a clear and generous meaning of equality for all. We must strive to fulfill the obligations of a great nation, to achieve needed reforms, to offer fulfillment, human dignity and reverence for life.

Guided by reason, America will soar on wings of humane concern. Passion is the vital spring to human action. Fertilized by ideas, passion alone has the power to activate millions. America's passion must be justice.

CRITIQUE

11. Religion and Morality,
J. E. Smith

John E. Smith, Professor of Philosophy at Yale University, here defends one of the traditional positions taken by the Christian churches on the relation between religion and morality. In common with the writers in this chapter, he holds that morality is autonomous—that is, that to be ethical the good

From John E. Smith, "Religion and Morality," *Journal of Religion*, Vol. 29, 1949, pp. 85–94. Used by permission of The University of Chicago Press.

act must be done because it is good and not for reasons of supernatural reward or punishment. But in contrast to these advocates, he argues that a sound ethic is dependent finally on religious conviction. Note that Smith means by "religion" an activity that specifically involves reference to some supernatural agency. What two questions does Smith ask of those philosophers who affirm the value of morality without religious foundation? What are the three reasons that the author gives for claiming that morality without religion is ultimately impossible? Do you find Smith persuasive? Thinking back to the advocates encounted in this chapter, how do you think they would respond to Smith's critique?

The relation of religion to morality is a theme well known to every student of the history of religion. Not only has it been the subject of much discussion within the various religious traditions themselves, but it has been at the center of the philosophical discussion of ethics in Western culture since the age of the Enlightenment. When in ancient times the Old Testament prophets first apprehended the ideal of justice and preached the necessity of righteousness before God, they were at the same time criticizing both directly and indirectly certain popular religious beliefs about God on the basis of their newly acquired standard. From such criticism it was inevitable that there should arise the question concerning the relation between the standard regulating the conduct of life, on the one hand, and traditional belief about God's nature, on the other. . . .

Since our problem has, like the problem of evil, been raised not merely by the critics of religion but within the very confines of the Judeo-Christian tradition itself, it seems best to try to develop a certain contrast within that tradition for the purpose of making clear from the beginning the distinguishing marks both of the specifically religious concern and of morality. Such clarification is absolutely essential, since, contrary to both popular belief and the opinions of some philosophers, religion and morality are not synonymous terms signifying some vague concern for "values" or ideals as distinct from "facts." Not only are the religious concern and the concern for the correct regulation of conduct not identical, but it is precisely the fact that they are distinct, although related in some essential way, that generates the problem with which this analysis will deal.

Since the development of a complete philosophy of religion is not possible here, it is necessary to proceed simply by indicating the essential features of both religion and morality. There is no better way of accomplishing this than by setting forth a familiar contrast within Western Cristianity between what we may call the "pietistic"[1] and the "activistic" poles within the religious community.* The former pole, as will be shown, while

---

* Smith's conviction that this is the best way to state the problem arises not simply from the need for economy of argument (to which he refers) but also from the way he defines "religion."

not unmindful of the moral problem, tends to stress the exclusively religious aspect of experience, while the latter tends to put the greatest emphasis on morality and the ideal relations between man and man, often to the exclusion of what is more definitely the concern of religion. The pietistic pole raises the question of man's ultimate destiny and looks to God as the supreme object of trust and devotion, at the same time recognizing the gulf between man and God (sin) and the consequent need for reconciliation (salvation). The activistic pole, on the other hand, is impatient with this concern for ultimate questions and foundations, and being tremendously impressed by the concrete historical situation with its multitudinous evils, it wants to be engaged in some concrete task in this world. Its watchword may be summed up in the questions: What are we to do? What is our duty? Here the concern is for action that will have, in this world, a noticeable effect upon the existing state of affairs. Here the concern is for economic and social justice, for the care of the weak and the poor, and for the establishment of that society on earth which shall be, if not actually the Kingdom of God, the closest approximation to that ideal that is possible for man. Both these tendencies are present in the Judeo-Christian tradition, and they represent not so much two mutually exclusive concerns (for there are pietistic elements in the activistic pole and vice versa) as a difference of emphasis upon either one of two strains that were always present in both Old and New Testament religion. From these two poles develops the problem of the relation of religion and morality. . . .

. . . We must ask the extent to which morality is dependent for its content on the norms and concepts derived from historical religion, and also from what source comes the inspiration to shun pleasure, wealth, and worldly success in order to live that type of life which is in accord with the most exalted moral principles. In biblical religion the answer to these questions is clear; the ideals (content) which are to govern human existence in society are derived from the nature of the divine, and it is the love of God (form) that furnishes the power to live the good life in a world which often thwarts our most determined attempts to embody Christian perfection. In biblical religion man is required to be just and merciful because God is both just and merciful in all relations with his people. Man is required to manifest love in his earthly life because, according to the essence of Christian faith, God is of the nature of love. And in all cases the love of God dwelling within the person of the individual believer is what provides the motive and inspiration for all our human efforts. The relation between religion and morality here stressed is well stated in a blunt and poignant remark in the First Epistle of John: "If a man say, I love God, and hateth his brother, he is a liar."[2] In this passage morality, the principle of order among men, is determined by the object of religion, the nature of God; and the writer regards it as an express contradiction if a man professes love of God and yet fails to manifest this love toward his fellow men. The nature of God provides the norm for conduct (the context of the passage quoted makes this more clear than does the passage itself), and the love of God provides the motive and passion necessary to perform.

Yet those who do not share this view of the relation between the religious and the moral fail to do so generally because they believe that religion at the basis of morality inevitably means that authoritarian sanctions are employed and that human conduct in such a situation is ultimately determined not by a pure love of God but by a craven fear of either divine or ecclesiastical retribution, or both. Historically, this charge cannot be denied; certainly, history offers many illustrations of the perversion of a religious morality in which the pure motive of love has been obscured and replaced by an external (i.e., nonpersonal) authority. We should not, however, too hastily reject the religious foundations of morality simply because of the possibility of perversion. Love of God, as the foundation for the good life, meant both for Old Testament prophetism and for classical Christianity a basic orientation of the person as a whole toward the divine perfection and from such an orientation (the same as the Platonic turning toward [*converto*] the light or good) the good life was believed to follow as a consistent expression of the personality whose life is turned toward and centered in God. Hence love of God as the basis of morality involves us in no subjugation to an external authority necessitating conduct through fear, but it is rather the underlying attitude and motive of the person who seeks to live the good life and whose life as a member of society then becomes a consistent expression of an individual will and personality rooted in God.

A true morality, as was said above, should be autonomous, i.e. it should be free from any external authority that coerces the personality or that subjects the good life to some further end by reducing it to the status of a means. The protest against religious morality is justified when the religious basis is perverted into an authority. An autonomous morality, however, is not necessarily one that is divorced from religious foundations, and the question remains as to what constitutes the religious basis of morality. Prophetic Judaism and classical Christianity are at one in maintaining that morality without religion is ultimately impossible. Only the main points in this regard can be stated here, but the following relations between the two are defensible:

1. No criticism of the existing state of affairs in any society is possible without the assumption (whether implicit or explicit) of the unconditional validity of standards by reference to which such criticism is made. All critical assertions about human activity of the nature of evaluations (excluding rigorously *descriptive* assertions) either contain or imply a proposition like "such and such *ought* to be done," and the term "ought" or some logical equivalent never fails to occur. This holds whether, for example, we are criticized for not loving our neighbors, for not seeking clarity in philosophical thought, or for not employing the method of intelligence in conducting all our affairs. Furthermore, standards intended to tell us what ought to be done (some idea of what is a good life) cannot and, in fact, do not remain neutral with respect to the question which is the properly religious one: the question of and concern for man's final destiny as a creature in his world. Just as surely as moral criticism implies moral standards, so moral standards themselves imply some view concerning the final

destiny of man. An analysis of every critical discussion of human conduct containing assertions that are evaluations will reveal that a proposition like "The truth about man's final destiny is such and such" is implied. This fact has been overlooked to an extent that is a scandal for moral philosophy. There is no better way of showing this than by pointing to the ethical writing of Dewey. He calls himself a naturalist, and he is certainly an opponent of the view of religious morality outlined here; yet it is clear to anyone who takes the trouble to raise questions about his thought, that some such proposition as "The final destiny of man is to control his own destiny through technology or the method of intelligence" is assumed throughout. This assumption is an assumption about the basically religious question, and that it functions as an ultimate premise in Dewey's thought is clear from the fact that not only is there nowhere any proof of it, but it is not ever brought up for discussion.[3]

Ultimately, no view of the good life, no serious doctrine of what man ought to do, is ever possible apart from some view of his final destiny; and such a view introduces the religious element. This is the most important consideration in showing that morality is necessarily related to religion.

2. One of the prevalent dangers confronting all morality is that it may degenerate and become ideology or a cloak for the hypocrisy of self-righteousness. A morality that has no foundation in a reality transcending itself is inevitably subject to corruption precisely because it recognizes no judge beyond its own commands. A morality, however, truly based on a love of God that is religious in character and one that recognizes the power of God as judge is protected, in principle, from such corruption and consequent transformation into ideology. A morality so grounded in religion recognizes that it is subject to the same ultimate principle of criticism (divine judgment) by which it judges existing persons and societies, and a morality rooted in that which transcends all times because it belongs exclusively to no one time possesses within itself its own principle of criticism. Such criticism is brought to bear subjectively by self-conscious judgment on the part of the holders of that morality, and objectively through the medium of historical events at the same time. No morality not based on religion possesses a principle of self-criticism, precisely because it possesses no transcendent reference to which it is itself subject and which judges it. This is not to say that, in fact, religiously grounded morality has not been corrupted in the past. Such an assertion could be made only in ignorance of the facts; but, nevertheless, it remains true that, in addition to determining the content of morality, religion is the final judge of morality. It stands as an ever present guardian, warning morality of its possible pretensions and enabling it to be free from transformation into ideology.

3. Finally, religion supplies the inspiration for the moral life and provides, at the same time, something even more important: the meaning and purpose of moral striving. The man who has morality and nothing more, as Royce once put it, is like a man who serves an ideal master who is forever in a far country. The servant not only toils on without ever seeing the master, but he may well come to doubt whether there is any master at all.

The man, however, whose morality is founded on religion knows the master intimately and believes fully in the ultimately purposeful character of his striving. Furthermore, his vision of the ideal society, the kingdom of God, gives form and substance to his attempts both to regulate his personal life on the basis of certain standards and to labor for the remaking of present society into a likeness of the ideal. Without the vision, the hope, and, finally, the faith of religion, such labor is forever incomplete.

In the above ways[4] religion is a genuine foundation for morality without at the same time being an authoritarian force behind it compelling the good life through fear. Since it is the threat of authority that the opponents of religious morality usually deplore (and rightly so), a religious foundation that eliminates this threat and that at the same time provides the basis without which all morality must be destroyed is able to overcome the objection. Morality is both unsure and incomplete without a living connection with religious faith. The sure recognition of this truth can be hastened if it is made clear, first, that a true religious morality should be free from authoritarianism and, second, that, for the reasons cited above, morality implies religion and when it is not founded on religion it is continually threatened with destruction.

NOTES

1. This term may have for some a derogatory connotation. Nothing of the kind is meant here. What the term refers to is made clear enough in the body of the discussion. The term "mystical" might be better here, but it has a great variety of connotations.
2. I John 4:20.
3. Why this is the case is beyond the scope of this discussion, but the answer is probably to be sought in an examination of the basic assumptions of modern culture.
4. All the possible relations between religion and morality have not been discussed here. The question of sin and morality, for example, needs extended treatment, for this raises the question of man's ability to live the good life without grace.

12. The Spiritual Source
of Morality,
S. Radhakrishnan

*The next critique is closely related in content to the preceding one.
The author, S. Radhakrishnan (b. 1888), is the same man
who explained the Hindu concept of dharma in Chapter III.
In this excerpt he distinguishes between being rational
(or logical) and being reasonable. Admitting that the truths
of religion cannot be substantiated by reason (logic) alone,
we are nevertheless being* unreasonable *if we do not hold to them,
since life cannot be lived without religion. Now, Radhakrishnan
suspects that many people attempt to fill the void of loneliness,
caused by their conviction that the universe is hostile to human
purposes, by becoming involved in family attachments or civic
duties. "The prophets of disillusion call upon us to seek truth,
create beauty and achieve goodness." What charges does he level,
then, at those who put all their hopes in planning and
organizing society? What deficiency does he point to in socialism?
Why does he find humanism empty and insufficient as an answer
to life's problems? Can it (humanism) supply the "great mood"
needed for the "great gift" of life? Does he find* implicit
*in humanism, however blind to it humanists themselves may be,
a spiritual view of the universe? In what way?*

We cannot live if we do not recover our faith in life and the universe.
It is true that we should oppose a passionless disillusion to the lies which
cripple our minds. Rationality is essential, but so is religion if disintegration
is to be averted. It may be that religion does not rest on purely speculative
grounds. But it is not enough to be logical. We have also to be reasonable.
Loyalty to life requires us to know the creative mystery and serve it to the
best of our power. If we feel ourselves to be unwanted in the universe, we
may try to cover up our inner crisis by family attachments or civic duties,
but the essential loneliness of the soul is worse than solitary confinement.
The felt solitude of the human soul, its strange isolation in an incomprehensible world, breaks the vital rhythm that sustains the world. The
prophets of disillusion call upon us to seek truth, create beauty and achieve
goodness. We cannot strive for these ideals if we are convinced that we are
unimportant accidents in a universe which is indifferent, if not hostile, to
them. If the nature of the world is malign, our duty is to defy. . . .

However ingeniously we might plan and organize our society and adjust
human relationships, so long as the world is what it is, the best of us cannot

From S. Radhakrishnan, *An Idealist View of Life* (London: George Allen &
Unwin Ltd., 1932; rev. 2d ed. 1937; paperback ed. 1961, 1964), pp. 42–43, 53–55.
Reprinted with permission of the publisher.

escape sorrow and suffering. Socialism cannot remove human selfishness. Even if we by some stroke of good fortune escape from the usual annoyances of life, we cannot free ourselves from death. Our bodily organism has in it seeds of dissolution. Mortality seems to be native to our world. Can humanism make death trivial and service significant? It is easy to ask us to draw on our capacity for endurance and heroism and go down into the valley, strong, alone and conquering, but when we are uncertain of the meaning of the world such advice is stupid. In the second book of the *Republic,* Plato tells us of an absolutely just man who yet passes for an unjust one, and suffers the most severe penalties with no hope of relief in this life and no expectation of reward in the next. When Socrates is asked whether such a one tortured on the rack and crucified can yet be happy, he answered in the affirmative, simply because he was not a mere humanist, but believed in the spirit in man and the significance of the world. Humanism has no consolation for those who bear in pain the burden of defeated hopes and suffer sorrow and contempt. Kant's chief argument for theism is that since the good man is often defeated on earth, we require a superhuman power to adjust virtue and happiness. When the foundations of life are shaken, when the ultimate issues face us demanding an answer, humanism does not suffice. Life is a great gift, and we have to bring to it a great mood; only humanism does not induce it.

When the humanist admits the ultimateness of the values, he is implicitly accepting the spiritual view of the universe. For him the ethical self is a power above the ordinary self in which all men may share, in spite of the diversity of personal temperament and to which our attitude must be one of subjection. The question is inevitable whether the ethical ideal is a mere dream or has the backing of the universe. Is man ploughing his lonely furrow in the dark or is there a transcending purpose that is co-operating with him in his quest for ideals, securing him against the ultimate defeat of his plans? Are the values mere empirical accidents, creations at best of the human mind, or do they reveal to us an order of being which is more than merely human, a spiritual reality which is the source of the significance of what happens in the temporal process? Does human life point beyond the contingent to another world, absolute and eternal though in contact with the human, and exerting a transforming influence on it? Professor Alexander is of opinion that the world of values arises as a secondary emergent product out of a simpler ultimate existent. For him values are "incidents in the empirical growth of things, within what is really the primary reality of space-time."[1] Alexander denies priority to value, but finds it difficult to account for the development of space-time without the postulation of a *nisus.** The *nisus* is not space-time. If it were, it could not serve the purpose for which it is assumed; if, on the other hand, it is something that makes space-time move on to higher forms, it is something different from space-time and prior to it. The principle of

---

* "Nisus" is S. Alexander's term (from the Latin "nisus," to strive) for an urge in nature toward ever higher levels and qualities of existence.

explanation seems to be space-time and the *nisus,* the void and God, to use Old Testament terminology. Kant's ethical theory shows that we glimpse the spiritual reality superior to the human by means of the ethical consciousness. Though Kant distinguishes religion from ethics as an independent activity of the human spirit, somewhat subordinate to the ethical, his system as a whole sets right the balance. While virtue is good in its own right, it is not the whole good, which is virtue combined with happiness. Perfect virtue and perfect happiness are two sides of the unconditioned good which the practical reason sets before itself. Our moral consciousness is offended if there is a divorce between the two. Perfect happiness, however, is dependent on natural causes which do not seem to have any direct relation with virtue. A proper adjustment of happiness to virtue is possible only if we assume a divine being who is able to bring the cosmic into conformity with the moral and regulate the combination of happiness and virtue. Our moral consciousness *postulates* God, who is adequate to the realization of the *summum bonum.* Kant is convinced that this world is not all, and that the disproportion between the claims of virtue and the rewards of life will be set right. If we do not accept the postulate of God, we shall be faced by a dualism between the moral law which claims our allegiance and a universe which is apparently indifferent if not hostile to the demands of morality. If the authority of the moral law is to be justified, if the ultimateness of man as a moral being is to be vindicated, then the world process which has resulted in the formation of human personalities has significance and the structure of things is spiritual. Humanism thus leads to a view of itself as rooted in a reality deeper and more comprehensive, in which it finds its completion. Humanism is concerned with value; religion relates value to reality, human life to the ultimate background against which it is set. However crude and misconceived the savage's religion may be, it gives him the security that the real is friendly to his values, and is not indifferent to his welfare. From the totemic principle of the savage to the absolute spirit of the philosopher, there is right through a confident belief that man is a fragment of the larger scheme of things which contains the secret of his life and his surroundings and exerts a mysterious power over his destiny.

NOTES

1. *Space Time and Deity,* vol. ii (1920), p. 314.

VII

The New Life
Through Technocracy

*About a million years ago, an unprepossessing primate discovered
that his forelimbs could be used for other purposes besides
locomotion. Objects like sticks and stones could be grasped—and,
once grasped, were useful for killing game, digging up roots,
defending or attacking, and a hundred other jobs. On the third
planet of the Sun, tools had appeared; and the place would
never be the same again.*

    The first users of tools were not *men—a fact appreciated
only in the last year or two—but prehuman anthropoids;
and by their discovery they doomed themselves. . . .*

    *Now the cycle is about to begin again; but neither history
nor prehistory ever exactly repeats itself, and this time there
will be a fascinating twist in the plot. The tools the ape-men
invented caused them to evolve into their successor, Homo sapiens.
The tool we have invented is our successor. Biological evolution
has given way to a far more rapid process—technological
evolution. To put it bluntly and brutally, the machine is going
to take over. (Arthur C. Clarke,* Profiles of the Future: An Inquiry
into the Limits of the Possible [*Harper & Row, 1963; Bantam
Books, 1964*], pp. 212–13.)

BESIDES MAN'S CAPACITIES to integrate his psychic being through interpersonal relations and to establish economic-political structures to provide responsible social relations, mankind has a capacity to change his physical environment. This capacity is related to man's perception of himself as a temporal-physical being. At first glance it may seem unimportant to note man's sensitivity to his physical experience because it appears to be self-evident that he is part of a physical world. However, man's awareness of his physical being has special importance in contemporary discussions of values and meaning. There are at least two reasons for this: (1) a growing technology seems to take the place of several traditional religious practices; and (2) the common assumption that "the physical world" is just something "out there"—external to man—fails to recognize that man's experience of his physical world is, in part, an interpretation. In this chapter we want to focus on the role that man's world view has in his self-definition, with special consideration of the claims, and assumptions behind the claims, of contemporary Western technology. The self-image of modern man as "technological man" plus the power and control he seems to be gaining through scientific analysis of himself and his environment (technocracy) provides one of the most dramatic reinterpretations of man's selfhood and of his role in deciding his own future. As you read the excerpts in this chapter, compare both the possibilities and hazards in a scientific, technologically oriented world view with those world views found earlier in human history, for example, the world as God's creation, the world as an ambiguous fabrication.

ADVOCACY

1. How to Make the World Work, R. B. Fuller

*How does a modern, rational man confront today's world?
In this selection, the renowned inventor, mathematician, and
visionary, winner of the Nobel Peace Prize and University
Professor at Southern Illinois University, R. Buckminster Fuller,
proposes a straightforward answer. He defines his aims,
his resources, and his limitations; then he puts them all together
rationally. The outcome of this procedure is a plan "to make
the world work." Do you find this an attractive picture?
What is the role of political leadership in this scheme? Who is
in charge? What does Fuller mean when he tells us to think
"transcendentally"?*

To start with, here is an educational bombshell: Take from all of today's industrial nations all their industrial machinery and all their energy-distributing networks, and leave them all their ideologies, all their political leaders, and all their political organizations and I can tell you that within six months two billion people will die of starvation, having gone through great pain and deprivation along the way.

However, if we leave the industrial machinery and their energy-distribution networks and leave them also all the people who have routine jobs operating the industrial machinery and distributing its products, and we take away from all the industrial countries all their ideologies and all the politicians and political machine workers, people would keep right on eating. Possibly getting on a little better than before.

The fact is that now—for the first time in the history of man for the last ten years, all the political theories and all the concepts of political functions—in any other than secondary roles as housekeeping organizations —are completely obsolete. All of them were developed on the you-or-me basis. This whole realization that mankind can and may be comprehensively successful is startling.

In pursuance of this theme and under auspices to be announced later we are going to undertake at Southern Illinois University, in the next five years, a very extraordinary computerized program to be known as "How to Make the World Work."

Here on Southern Illinois' campus we are going to set up a great computer program. We are going to introduce the many variables now known to be operative in economics. We will store all the basic data in the machine's memory bank; where and how much of each class of the physical resources; where are the people, what are the trendings— all kinds of trendings of world man?

Next we are going to set up a computer feeding game, called "How Do We Make the World Work?" We will start playing relatively soon. We will bring people from all over the world to play it. There will be competitive teams from all around earth to test their theories on how to make the world work. If a team resorts to political pressures to accelerate their advantages and is not able to wait for the going gestation rates to validate their theory they are apt to be in trouble. When you get into politics you are very liable to get into war. War is the ultimate tool of politics. If war develops the side inducing it loses the game.

Essence of the world's working will be to make every man able to become a world citizen and able to enjoy the whole earth, going wherever he wants at any time, able to take care of all the needs of all his forward days without any interference with any other man and never at the cost of another man's equal freedom and advantage. I think that the communication problem—of "How to Make the World Work"—will become extremely popular the world around.

The game will be played by competing individuals and teams. The comprehensive logistical information upon which it is based is your Southern Illinois University-supported Inventory of World Resources Human Trends and Needs. It is also based upon the data and grand world strategies already evolved in the Design Science Decade being conducted, under our leadership here at Southern Illinois University, by world-around university students who, forsaking the political expedient of attempting to reform man, are committed to reforming the environment in such a manner as to "up" the performance per each unit of invested world resources until so much more is accomplished with so much less that an even higher standard of living will be effected for 100% of humanity than is now realized by the 40% of humanity who may now be classified as economically and physically successful.

"The game" will be hooked up with the now swiftly increasing major universities information network. This network's information bank will soon be augmented by the world-around satellite-scanned live inventorying of vital data. Spy satellites are now inadvertently telephotoing the whereabouts and number of beef cattle around the surface of the entire earth. The exact condition of all the world's crops is now simultaneously and totally scanned and inventoried. The interrelationship of the comprehensively scanned weather and the growing food supply of the entire earth are becoming manifest.

In playing "the game" the computer will remember all the plays made by previous players and will be able to remind each successive player of the ill fate of any poor move he might contemplate making. But the ever-changing inventory might make possible today that which would not work yesterday. Therefore the successful strategems of the live game will vary from day to day. The game will not become stereotyped.

If a player resorts to political means for the realization of his strategy, he may be forced ultimately to use the war-waging equipment with which all national political systems maintain their sovereign power. If a player fires a gun—that is, if he resorts to warfare, large or small—he loses and must fall out of the game.

The general-systems-theory controls of the game will be predicated upon employing within a closed system the world's continually updated total resource information in closely specified network complexes designed to facilitate attainment, at the earliest possible date, by every human being of complete enjoyment of the total planet earth, through the individual's optional traveling, tarrying, or dwelling here and there. This world-around freedom of living, work, study, and enjoyment must be accomplished without any one individual interfering with another and without any individual being physically or economically advantaged at the cost of another.

Whichever player or team first attains total success for humanity wins the first round of the gaming. There are alternate ways of attaining success. The one who attains it in the shortest time wins the second round. Those who better the record at a later date win rounds 3, 4, and so on.

All the foregoing objectives must be accomplished not only for those who now live but for all coming generations of humanity. How to make humanity a continuing success at the earliest possible moment will be the objective. The game will also be dynamic. The players will be forced to improve the program—failure to improve also results in retrogression of conditions. Conditions cannot be pegged to accomplishment. They must also grow either worse or better. This puts time at a premium in playing the game.

Major world individuals and teams will be asked to play the game. The game cannot help but become major world news. As it will be played from a high balcony overlooking a football field-sized Dymaxion Airocean World Map* with electrically illumined data transformations, the game will be visibly developed and may be live-televised the world over by a multi-Telstar relay system.

The world's increasing confidence in electronic instrumentation in general—due to the demonstrated reliability of its gyrocompasses, and its "blind" instrument landings of airplanes at night in thick fog, and confidence in opinion-proof computers in particular, will make the "world game" playing of fundamental and spontaneous interest to all of humanity.

Ultimately its most successful winning techniques will become well known around the world and as the game's solutions gain world favor they will be spontaneously resorted to as political emergencies accelerate.

---

* A designation coined by Fuller for a map, devised by him, which eliminates all visual distortion.

Nothing in the game can solve the problem of two men falling in love with the same girl, or falling in love with the same shade under one specific tree. Some are going to have to take the shade of another equally inviting tree. Some may end up bachelors. Some may punch each other's noses. For every problem solved a plurality of new problems arise to take their place. But the problems need not be those of physical and economic survival. They can be perplexing and absorbing in entirely metaphysical directions such as those which confront the philosophers, the artists, poets, and scientists.

The game must, however, find ways in which to provide many beautiful shade trees for each—that is to say a physical and economic abundance adequate for all. There will, of course, have to be matchings of times and desires, requiring many initial wait-listings. As time goes on, however, and world-around information becomes available, the peaks and valleys of men's total time can be ever-improvedly smoothed out. Comprehensive coordination of bookings, resource, and accommodation information will soon bring about a 24-hour, world-around viewpoint of society which will operate and think transcendentally to local "seasons" and weathers of rooted botanical life. Humanity will become emancipated from its mental fixation on the seven-day-week frame of reference. I myself now have many winters and summers per year as I cross the equator from northern to southern hemisphere and back several times annually. I have now circled the earth so many times that I think of it and literally sense it in my sight as a sphere. I often jump in eight- and nine-hour time-zone air strides. As a consequence my metabolic coordination has become independent of local time fixations.

It is my intention to initiate on several occasions in a number of places anticipatory discussion of the necessary and desirable parameters to establish for playing the world game. I intend to nominate as participants both in these preliminary discussions and in formal play only those who are outstandingly capable of discussing these parameters. The participants must also be those well known for their lack of bias as well as for their forward-looking competence and practical experience.

2. The Immortalist,
A. Harrington

In the Hebrew Bible, both Joshua and King David say,
when they are about to die, that they are going "the way of all
the earth" (Joshua 23:14; I Kings 2:2). Death was then
regarded as inevitable and universal; most human beings have
regarded themselves as mortal. (Even for those who believe in
rebirth, it comes only after death.) More than any other
facet of our lives, then, death confronts us with a decisive limit.
If man is seriously to bring his destiny within rational, technical
control (as the advocates of this chapter assert) he must, somehow,
overcome death. In this article from Playboy, *Alan Harrington*
pulls out many emotional stops to present his thesis that man's
basic problem is physical death. Is the desire to overcome death
the ultimate concern of as many people as the author claims?
Do you agree that the single cause of meaninglessness,
alienation, isolation, aggressiveness, paranoia, and the inability
to believe, commit, or care is the fact that we grow old and die?
In what ways have human beings dealt with the fact of death
up to this point in history? Do you agree that these ways are,
as the author puts it, "psychotic, shameful and ludicrous"?
What are some of the current ways of dealing with death?
What is the solution according to the "immortalist"?
"Our new faith must accept as gospel that salvation belongs to
medical engineering and nothing else..." What do you think will
be the role, if any, of religious worship and devotion in this new age?

Death is an imposition on the human race, and no longer acceptable.
Man has all but lost his ability to accommodate himself to personal extinction; he must now proceed physically to overcome it. In short, to kill
death: to put an end to his own mortality as a certain consequence of being
born. Our survival without the God we once knew comes down now to a
race against time. The suspicion or conviction that God is dead has lately
struck home not merely to a few hundred thousand freethinkers but to
masses of the unprepared. Ancient orthodoxies may linger, but the content
of worship has begun to collapse. This is what makes our situation urgent:
Around the world, people are becoming increasingly less inclined to pray to
a force that kills them.

The most imaginative philosophical and religious answers to the "problem" of death have become irrelevant to the fact that we die. Humanity's
powers of self-deception seem to be running out. Modern theological word

From *The Immortalist* by Alan Harrington. Originally appeared in *Playboy*
Magazine, May 1969, pp. 116–18, 220–34. Copyright © 1969 by Alan Harrington,
Reprinted by permission of Random House, Inc. and International Famous Agency.

games may be pleasing to seminarians. Let jazz be permitted in the old spiritual gathering places. Such developments must be understood as gallant but altogether pathetic holding operations. Emotionally, growing millions of us are in crisis. "Men are so necessarily mad," wrote Pascal, "that not to be mad would amount to another form of madness." Three hundred years later, with the mass communication of anxiety, and new weaponry and drugs in our possession, we need only open the morning paper or sit down to television, or look into our own lives, to observe signs of a growing spiritual insurrection. . . .

Civilized humanity is signaling. It seems to be both an SOS and a warning. In many languages and forms, the coded sign repeats: "Change this scene or *we* will!" The message has by no means gone unnoticed. Governments, the professions, universities, the clergy and social agencies of every description have paid close attention to the semaphore. (When they don't, their sanctums are frequently invaded by large crowds carrying signs and shouting obscenities.)

What does this violent mood portend? A revolution of some kind would seem already to be under way. Young people carry most of the signs. "The new majority," they seem to be taking over everything. They appear determined to seize the day, and possibly the world. But there is something desperate as well as knowing in the way they are going about it, for theirs has really been a revolt against *meaninglessness*—which, at the present time, they are attempting to cover up by mass action, but which they covertly fear will outlast that action. And this mood is not confined to the young. Mature, wearying, old—so many of us are conducting our affairs in a peculiarly nervous fashion, as though time were short.

Quite evidently, the people of our time are reporting an emotional displacement; a condition not new but, some say, "aggravated by the complexities of modern life." The diagnosis, roughly speaking: angst, alienation. The treatment? Any public-library catalog offers an assortment of prescriptions. Also a host of new preachers and messiahs. Their life plans usually involve one or a combination of these choices: spiritual uplift; psychiatric consultation; group action; drunkenness; embracing the outdoors; making love as often as possible to the very edge of consciousness and forgetting about anything else; burying oneself in work, games or large families; trying to follow the complicated religio-philosophical excuses for what Reinhold Niebuhr* described as man's "natural contingency"; and, in more recent years, the skillful employment of narcotics, blowing your mind and seeking rebirth in the psychedelic voyage.

Unfortunately, these panaceas have a single fault in common: They are all varieties of *self-hypnosis*. Without exception, they aim to cover up our condition, rather than change it. Tiptoeing around like the old man with a young bride, they dare not come to grips—because the bride is death.

The "problem," expressed in whatever form—feelings of isolation, aggressive behavior toward one another, massive paranoia and the common

---

* See introduction to reading 9, Chapter VIII.

inability to believe, commit or care—derives from a single cause, which must be identified, simply and without sham, as the fact that we grow old and die. The fear of aging and death, and in the long run *nothing else,* is at the heart of our distress. All else is peripheral and finally unimportant. Hence, no therapeutic treatment, however inspirational, can do more than apply a coating of salve to our concern. The problem is neither social nor philosophical, not religious nor even psychiatric. Rather, it is based solidly on an intolerable recognition only now emerging to general consciousness: not merely the knowledge but the gut realization that the void is waiting for everybody and that each of us is going to vanish into it. . . .

We do our best to put the vision off somewhere, make it remote. Or close it off with black jokes. Any new religion is eagerly grasped for a little while. We must *kick* the vision by whatever means. The members of our species have never been reconciled to the brutal circumstance that we must die. Through the centuries, we have invented an incredible number of explanations to account for our individual forms decomposing in agony and returning to the earth. Hope of setting things right with the gods has driven us to lunacies of self-denial, cruelties, persecutions, elaborate ceremonies with incense and smoke, dancing around totem poles, the thumbscrewing of heretics; from Mexico to India, the casting of shrieking innocents into pits, and all kinds of psychotic, shameful and ludicrous practices such as would make whatever gods might be watching hide their eyes.

In the East, we have been more subtle, attempting to placate destiny by an elaborate pretense of not wanting to survive, or preferring nirvana to the eternal return. But elsewhere, listen to the wails, songs, shouts, hymns and chants. The voices of Islam, Judaism, Christianity and atheism join as one. Massed units in Red Square as well as Vatican City combine their energies in a single mighty appeal: *Save us.* For the beauty and the cruelty in the world; the kindness and the murder; our art trying to illuminate this wilderness; speculations of philosophers; the descent into drugs and drunkenness; today's wildly emotional crowds rushing around the world's streets—all are organized around death and designed to protect each of us from annihilation here or elsewhere.

Dostoievsky penetrates our situation with one quick thrust. In *The Possessed,* Kirillov, the engineer, about to become his own god by committing suicide, says: "Man simply invented God in order not to kill himself. That is the sum of universal history down to this moment." . . .

Having lost faith, a great many men and women have returned to old superstitions now cloaked in new disguises. God may have retreated, but the *gods* today are by no means dead. Though disposed to destroy them, we simultaneously bow down to the weirdest assortment of deities ever known, such as History, Success and Statistics. We worship purveyors of Luck, Fashion and Publicity. We follow shifting gospels based on journalistic graffiti passing for honest news. We humbly receive the word from makeshift divinities seated at the heads of couches, sexual statisticians, psychological testers, poll takers, various merchants of paranoia, the manipulators of public relations, television personalities—the multiple gods of our quickening century.

This is to say that increasing numbers of civilized men and women are progressing, or retrogressing, to a pagan state of mind. The most sophisticated as well as humble people—and atheists most of all—live in fear of these gods and are guided by the need either to live up to their examples or to compete for their approval. What emerges, astonishingly, is that the old gods in new forms live on in our heads, not metaphorically but, for all practical purposes, *alive,* and that they exert a dominating influence over the great bulk of modern affairs. One development is new here. For want of any other way, the publicizing of one's excellence (fitness for survival beyond death)—publicity great and small—has become the path to immortality. The lust for do-it-yourself immortality has produced an emotional transformation in which the ideal of right conduct (formerly the passport to heaven) is being replaced everywhere by the ideal of printing one's image on all things.

Among the middle-class masses, God, supposedly dead, has reappeared in the form of a gigantic Computer of Excellence. The faith of the anxious, climbing mortal is that degrees of excellence, or at least public visibility, are somehow calibrated in the stars. If we are persistent enough, our presence can be Xeroxed all over heaven. Our scores are being tabulated and processed by a master calculator. Imaginary keepers of immortality pass our data into this system. By some nameless procedure, each of us will be tested out. Our reward, a passing grade, will be that of life beyond death; our punishment for failure, annihilation. This accounts for the intensified publicity hunting and status seeking we see around us today. The only way to make sense out of the immortality hunters in the crowd (to a varying degree, nearly everyone) is to understand that they are trying to post scores on an imaginary record.

Yet, seeking to remedy his condition, civilized man also wildly contradicts himself. Expending his energies at one and the same time to placate, impress, destroy and replace his gods, he also exhibits a craving to *share consciousness* with all other beings, including the divine. The attempt at spiritual fusion with others can take many forms—destructive, saintly (that is to say, charitable) and quiescent. Consider some recent effects.

Writing in the context of Nazism, Jacques Maritain* heard "the voices of a base multitude whose baseness itself appears as an apocalyptic sign." These voices cry out: " 'We have had enough of lying optimism and illusory morality, enough of freedom and personal dignity and justice and peace and faithfulness and goodness which make us mad with distress. Let us give ground to the infinite promises of evil, and of swarming death, and of blessed enslavement, and of triumphant despair.' "

In contrast—growing out of San Francisco and New York and spreading across the country—we have had the hippie subculture, originally based on the ideal of natural saintliness or, at any rate, of free-form living. This has been made possible by a union bringing together the wisdom of the East and Western pharmacology, with LSD and other substances providing the means for prolonged and repeated escapes from time (which marks the

---

* A contemporary, French, Roman Catholic, neo-Thomist philosopher.

minutes leading to extinction). The movement should be understood—and generally is not—as an attempt to achieve *immortality now*: freedom from time, money, history and death. It also attempts to realize a general sharing of consciousness; in other words, collective immortality.

"The basic unit of the culture," one young man calling himself Billy Digger says, "would be the commune, instead of a house with one man and one woman in it. The commune would not be owned by one person or one group but would be open to all people at all times, to do whatever they wish to do in it." (In a different way, searching for communal immortality through violence, California's Hell's Angels and the Red Guards of China have been into the same thing: knocking down the uncles of the world and putting dunce caps on them.)

If such movements appear to deny old-fashioned responsibility and traditional modes of achievement, it is not surprising. The ideal of achievement has to do with a *reach* for immortality, which, if you feel already in that state, even in simulation, is obviously no longer necessary.

Yet, these starts at saintly living (including, glibly, saintliness through violence), whether genuine or make-believe, fail to hide the phenomenon of flight. Saintliness in our time will not be able to generate corrective measures against our one long-range problem, which is death. Lacking a dynamic principle beyond that of shattering present life forms, it can only turn into another short-term holding operation. Saintliness can further charity, farming and simple craftsmanship. It can create motorcycles for the road to nowhere. It can promote measures to restore dignity at least temporarily, such as mass sweeping of refuse-strewn neighborhoods. It can sponsor brotherhood Happenings in the park; create sweet afternoons with flowers, balloons and kites; and encourage people to draw closer to one another. But finally, the uses of saintliness are defensive. Resisting technological inroads on the soul, they represent an attempt to deal with a neurotic industrial society by dropping out of it. Possibly the goal of all these efforts is that of agrarian return, or return to the small machine shop.

But with all the love and kindness in the world, no agrarian retreat or machine-shop rendezvous can prevail for long against the thought of death, except by encouraging the participants to ignore it—and as the body grows older, this cannot be done. The enlarged families of the "now" people will grow older. The measures they have undertaken are not wrong but right before their time. They must be reserved for the day when we gain utopia *beyond* time. They are eternally right but temporally inadequate. For the near future, dropout brotherhood will not be good enough, because the struggle against real death—as opposed to the simulated death and rebirth experienced under LSD and the other psychedelics—requires training and must be fought out industrially and in the laboratory....

Today, we are in a race against time—racing, as Maritain suggests, our own apocalypse. Man's inexorable though hardly remorseless drive to divinity is taking new, noninstitutionalized forms. This comes down to the simplest of propositions: The species must solve the problem of death very soon, blow itself up or blow its mind.

Medical help is on the way. But so, too, are firepower and despair. All have computer technology behind them. Any one of the three might win. Will medical advances to arrest the aging of human tissues prevail over weaponry and mass psychosis? That has become the question of our time, and conceivably of all time.

The immortalist position is that the usefulness of philosophy has come to an end, because all philosophy teaches accommodation to death and grants it static finality as "the human condition." Art, too, insofar as it celebrates or merely bemoans our helplessness, has gone as far as it can. The beautiful device of tragedy ending in helplessness has become outmoded in our absurd time, no longer desirable and not to be glamorized. The art that embellishes death with visual beauty and celebrates it in music belongs to other centuries. . . .

It comes as no surprise that traditional forms of art are being shattered, with the editing and fixing of life no longer allowed. Our participation is demanded in these works; we cannot be spectators. The *discothèque* takes its place as an electric art form. We loosen our anxieties with the help of enormous guitars in a temple of fragmentation. Kinetic and luminous forms that reach out and bring us into the action, declaimed poetry now so often set to music, multiple screens, Happenings that frequently involve orgy and obscenity—all have one purpose: to smash the separateness of everyone present; to expose feeling and break through thinking, to make us live, in the prase Alan Watts* has quoted from Ananda K. Coomaraswamy,** "a perpetual uncalculated life in the present." And all this, too, amounts to one more attempt to hide from the end—this time by substituting Dionysian togetherness for romance, and a bombardment of the senses, lightworks of the soul, a sort of electronic Buddhism in place of sequential perception. In this environment, the lost self finds a comforting and protective nonexistence—if the self does not really exist, it cannot be killed. The use of kinetic environment as an art form thus *removes death*, creating the illusion of an eternal *now*—an illusion in that it seems to guarantee eternal youth, which, of course, is what this generation is really after.

The immortalist thesis is that the time has come for man to get rid of the intimidating gods in his own head. It is time for him to grow up out of his cosmic inferiority complex (no more "dust thou art, and unto dust shalt thou return"), bring his disguised desire into the open and go after what he wants, the only state of being he will settle for, which is divinity.

The moment has come also to stop yielding to hysteria, or to its opposite extreme, sinking into indifference and fashionable despair. Action, not passion, is called for to lift humanity out of this mortal predicament.

We have circled the moon, harnessed nuclear energy, and now have the biochemical means to control birth; why must death itself, called in *I Corinthians* "the last enemy," be considered sacred and beyond con-

---

* See introduction to reading 6, Chapter VIII.
** A well-known writer 1887–1947 on Indian art, religious images, and philosophy.

quest? A new act of faith we might have had a few decades ago, and did not, when Dr. R. H. Goddard* was bravely projecting his rockets into the atmosphere and a band of futurists was insisting that not just in comic strips but in reality we could lift ourselves beyond any space that could be seen from the earth. This new faith we must have is that with the technology at our disposal in the near future, death can be conquered. This faith must also weld salvation to medical engineering. We must drive away the gods of doubt and self-punishment.

Our new faith must accept as gospel that salvation belongs to medical engineering and nothing else; that man's fate depends first on the proper management of his technical proficiency; that we can only engineer our freedom from death, not pray for it; that our only messiahs will be wearing white coats, not in asylums but in chemical and biological laboratories.

3. Chart of the Future,
A. Clarke

> *Arthur C. Clarke is a Fellow of the Royal Astronomical Society and author of many books on space travel and science. He has achieved some notoriety from his accurate predictions of the future developments of science—for example, in 1945 he predicted the use of communication satellites for world television, and in 1947 he predicted that a rocket would land on the moon in 1959. This chart comes from a book in which Clarke predicts what technological advances will come about in the one hundred and fifty years after 1960. Check the chart for projections of what may happen in your lifetime at the present rate of acquiring technological proficiency. If a nation like the U.S. would "turn on" to technology as the highest religious expression "in orienting man to the universe" (See reading 5, following) and double the rate of technological achievement, would you want to experience life as projected here for the year 2100? As you read Clarke's list of predictions, do you think they add up to an unusual transformation for man? Are the changes of the sort that could be regarded as ultimate transformations?*

Chart "The Past, Now, The Future" from *Profiles of the Future* by Arthur C. Clarke. Copyright © 1962 by Arthur C. Clarke. By permission of Harper & Row, Publishers, Inc. Pp. 232–33.

* An American physicist (d. 1945) who pioneered in rocket research. The Goddard Space Flight Center near Washington D.C. is named after him.

THE PAST

Date	Transportation	Communication Information	Materials Manufacturing	Biology Chemistry	Physics
1800			Steam engine	Inorganic chemistry	Atomic theory
	Locomotive	Camera Babbage calculator		Urea synthesized	
	Steamship	Telegraph	Machine tools		Spectroscope
1850					Conservation of energy
			Electricity	Organic chemistry	
		Telephone Phonograph Office machines			Electromagnetism Evolution
	Automobile		Diesel engine		
1900	Airplane		Gasoline engine	Dyes	X-rays Electron
		Vacuum tube	Mass production Nitrogen fixation	Genetics Vitamines Plastics	Radioactivity
1910					Isotopes
		Radio			Quantum theory
1920				Chromosomes Genes	
					Relativity Atomic structure
1930				Language of bees Hormones	
		TV			Indeterminacy Wave mechanics Neutron
1940	Jet Rocket Helicopter	Radar			
		Tape recorders Electronic computers Cybernetics	Magnesium from sea Atomic energy	Synthetics Antibiotics Silicones	Uranium fission Accelerators Radio astronomy
1950	Satellite GEM	Transistor Maser Laser	Automation Fusion bomb	Tranquilizers	I.G.Y. Parity overthrown

Date	Transportation	Communication Information	Materials Manufacturing	Biology Chemistry	Physics
1960	Spaceship	Communication satellite		Protein structure	Nucleon structure

THE FUTURE

Date	Transportation	Communication Information	Materials Manufacturing	Biology Chemistry	Physics
1970	Space lab Lunar landing Nuclear rocket	Translating machines	Efficient electric storage	Cetacean languages	
1980	Planetary landings	Personal radio		Exobiology	Gravity waves
1990		Artificial intelligence	Fusion power "Wireless" energy	Cyborgs	
2000	Colonizing planets	Global library	Sea mining	Time, perception enhancement	Sub-nuclear structure
2010	Earth probes	Telesensory devices	Weather control		
2020	Interstellar probes	Logical languages Robots		Control of heredity	Nuclear catalysts
2030		Contact with extraterrestrials	Space mining	Bioengineering	
2040			Transmutation	Intelligent animals	
2050	Gravity control "Space drive"	Memory playback		Suspended animation	
2060		Mechanical educator Coding of artifacts	Planetary engineering	Artificial life	Space, time distortion

Date	Trans-portation	Communi-cation Information	Materials Manu-facturing	Biology Chemistry	Physics
2070					
	Near-light speeds		Climate control		
2080		Machine inteligence exceeds man's			
	Interstellar flight				
2090					
	Matter transmit-ter		Replicator		
	Meeting with extra-terres-trials	World brain	Astronom-ical engineer-ing	Immor-tality*	
2100					

4. On Programming Society, B. F. Skinner

Burrhus F. Skinner (b. 1904) is an American behavioral psychologist and an author of many books (including a novel about a scientific utopia, Walden Two *and, more recently, a comprehensive statement entitled* Beyond Freedom and Dignity*); he has been a professor at Harvard University since 1948. He has long advocated more scientific control of human life by using the principles of behavioral psychology—namely, a system of rewards and punishments as environmental stimuli for preferred behavior. In this essay Skinner (who is also mentioned in Ferkiss' excerpt) not only expresses his confidence that man can "lift himself by his own bootstraps," but attempts to give a defense of psychological conditioning against five common objections. He recognizes that objections to betterment through scientific designs are based on a reluctance to let go*

From Burrhus F. Skinner, *Cumulative Record* (New York: Appleton-Century-Crofts, 1961), pp. 4–18. Reprinted by permission of the publisher.
*See reading 2.

of a traditional view of man. How does the "scientific conception
of man" differ from "the traditional democratic conception"?
Why does he conclude that "some kind of control of human
behavior is inevitable"? How does Skinner answer the criticism
that a scientific conception of man precludes the possibility
of unplanned genius and that it leads to excessive uniformity in
its products? Why are veneration of heroes and moral judgments
regarded to be without value in Skinner's social program for
human improvement? What benefits result from developing
a science of man, and what harm can be predicted if the science
of man is not allowed to play an important role in building
a new political community? Can you see any reason(s) to resist
the kind of control Skinner advocates?

History records many foolish and unworkable schemes for human betterment, but almost all the great changes in our culture which we now regard
as worthwhile can be traced to perfectionistic philosophies. Governmental,
religious, educational, economic, and social reforms follow a common
pattern. Someone believes that a change in a cultural practice—for example,
in the rules of evidence in a court of law, in the characterization of man's
relation to God, in the way children are taught to read and write, in
permitted rates of interest, or in minimal housing standards—will improve
the condition of men: by promoting justice, permitting men to seek salvation more effectively, increasing the literacy of a people, checking an in-
flationary trend, or improving public health and family relations, respectively. The underlying hypothesis is always the same: that a different
physical or cultural environment will make a different and better man.

The scientific study of behavior not only justifies the general pattern of
such proposals; it promises new and better hypotheses. The earliest cultural
practices must have originated in sheer accidents. Those which strengthened
the group survived with the group in a sort of natural selection. As soon as
men began to propose and carry out changes in practice for the sake of
possible consequences, the evolutionary process must have accelerated. The
simple practice of making changes must have had survival value. A further
acceleration is now to be expected. As laws of behavior are more precisely
stated, the changes in the environment required to bring about a given
effect may be more clearly specified. Conditions which have been neglected
because their effects were slight or unlooked for may be shown to be
relevant. New conditions may actually be created, as in the discovery and
synthesis of drugs which affect behavior.

This is no time, then, to abandon notions of progress, improvement or,
indeed, human perfectibility.* The simple fact is that man is able, and
now as never before, to lift himself by his own bootstraps. In achieving con-

---

* Cf. the apparent similarity in the notion of perfectibility and the difference of
the means for attaining it with claims made in Chapter V, reading 3 and Chapter
VI, reading 4.

trol of the world of which he is a part, he may learn at last to control himself.

Timeworn objections to the planned improvement of cultural practices are already losing much of their force. Marcus Aurelius* was probably right in advising his readers to be content with a haphazard amelioration of mankind. "Never hope to realize Plato's republic," he sighed, "...for who can change the opinions of men? And without a change of sentiments what can you make but reluctant slaves and hypocrites?" He was thinking, no doubt, of contemporary patterns of control based upon punishment or the threat of punishment which, as he correctly observed, breed only reluctant slaves of those who submit and hypocrites of those who discover modes of evasion. But we need not share his pessimism, for the opinions of men can be changed. The techniques of indoctrination which were being devised by the early Christian Church at the very time Marcus Aurelius was writing are relevant, as are some of the techniques of psychotherapy and of advertising and public relations. Other methods suggested by recent scientific analyses leave little doubt of the matter.

The study of human behavior also answers the cynical complaint that there is a plain "cussedness" in man which will always thwart efforts to improve him. We are often told that men do not want to be changed, even for the better. Try to help them, and they will outwit you and remain happily wretched. Dostoevsky claimed to see some plan in it. "Out of sheer ingratitude," he complained, or possibly boasted, "man will play you a dirty trick, just to prove that men are still men and not the keys of a piano.... And even if you could prove that a man is only a piano key, he would still do something out of sheer perversity—he would create destruction and chaos—just to gain his point.... And if all this could in turn be analyzed and prevented by predicting that it would occur, then man would deliberately go mad to prove his point." This is a conceivable neurotic reaction to inept control. A few men may have shown it, and many have enjoyed Dostoevsky's statement because they tend to show it. But that such perversity is a fundamental reaction of the human organism to controlling conditions is sheer nonsense.

So is the objection that we have no way of knowing what changes to make even though we have the necessary techniques. That is one of the great hoaxes of the century—a sort of booby trap left behind in the retreat before the advancing front of science. Scientists themselves have unsuspectingly agreed that there are two kinds of useful propositions about nature—facts and value judgments—and that science must confine itself to "what is," leaving "what ought to be" to others. But with what special sort of wisdom is the non-scientist endowed? Science is only effective knowing, no matter who engages in it. Verbal behavior proves upon analysis to be composed of many different types of utterances, from poetry and exhortation to logic and factual description, but these are not all equally useful in talking about cultural practices. We may classify useful propositions

---

* A second century A.D. Roman emperor and Stoic philosopher.

according to the degrees of confidence with which they may be asserted. Sentences about nature range from highly probable "facts" to sheer guesses. In general, future events are less likely to be correctly described than past. When a scientist talks about a projected experiment, for example, he must often resort to statements having only a moderate likelihood of being correct; he calls them hypotheses.

"I think I'll stick it out here, but thanks, anyway."

Cartoon by Joseph Ferris. Found in the April 17, 1971
Saturday Review. Copyright 1971 Saturday Review, Inc.

Designing a new cultural pattern is in many ways like designing an experiment. In drawing up a new constitution, outlining a new educational program, modifying a religious doctrine, or setting up a new fiscal policy, many statements must be quite tentative. We cannot be sure that the practices we specify will have the consequences we predict, or that the consequences will reward our efforts. This is in the nature of such proposals. They are not value judgments—they are guesses. To confuse and delay the improvement of cultural practices by quibbling about the word *improve* is itself not a useful practice. Let us agree, to start with, that health is better than illness, wisdom better than ignorance, love better than hate, and productive energy better than neurotic sloth.

Another familiar objection is the "political problem." Though we know what changes to make and how to make them, we still need to control certain relevant conditions, but these have long since fallen into the hands of selfish men who are not going to relinquish them for such purposes. Possibly we shall be permitted to develop areas which at the moment seem unimportant, but at the first signs of success the strong men will move in. This, it is said, has happened to Christianity, democracy, and communism. There will always be men who are fundamentally selfish and evil, and in the long run innocent goodness cannot have its way....

An optimistic historian could defend a different conclusion. The principle that if there are not enough men of good will in the world the first step is to create more seems to be gaining recognition. The Marshall Plan (as originally conceived), Point Four, the offer of atomic materials to power starved countries—these may or may not be wholly new in the history of international relations, but they suggest an increasing awareness of the power of governmental good will. They are proposals to make certain changes in the environments of men for the sake of consequences which should be rewarding for all concerned. They do not exemplify a distinterested generosity, but an interest which is the interest of everyone. We have not yet seen Plato's philosopher-king, and may not want to, but the gap between real and utopian government is closing.

But we are not yet in the clear, for a new and unexpected obstacle has arisen. With a world of their own making almost within reach, men of good will have been seized with distaste for their achievement. They have uneasily rejected opportunities to apply the techniques and findings of science in the service of men, and as the import of effective cultural design has come to be understood, many of them have voiced an outright refusal to have any part in it. Science has been challenged before when it has encroached upon institutions already engaged in the control of human behavior; but what are we to make of benevolent men, with no special interests of their own to defend, who nevertheless turn against the very means of reaching long-dreamed-of goals?

What is being rejected, of course, is the scientific conception of man and his place in nature. So long as the findings and methods of science are applied to human affairs only in a sort of remedial patchwork, we may continue to hold any view of human nature we like. But as the use of science increases, we are forced to accept the theoretical structure with which science represents its facts. The difficulty is that this structure is clearly at odds with the traditional democratic conception of man. Every discovery of an event which has a part in shaping a man's behavior seems to leave so much the less to be credited to the man himself; and as such explanations become more and more comprehensive, the contribution which may be claimed by the individual himself appears to approach zero. Man's vaunted creative powers, his original accomplishments in art, science, and morals, his capacity to choose and our right to hold him responsible for the consequences of his choice—none of these is conspicuous in this new self-portrait. Man, we once believed, was free to express himself in art, music, and literature, to inquire into nature, to seek salvation in his own way. He could initiate action and make spontaneous and capricious changes of course. Under the most extreme duress some sort of choice remained to him. He could resist any effort to control him, though it might cost him his life. But science insists that action is initiated by forces impinging upon the individual, and that caprice is only another name for behavior for which we have not yet found a cause.

In attempting to reconcile these views it is important to note that the traditional democratic conception was not designed as a description in the scientific sense but as a philosophy to be used in setting up and maintaining a governmental process. It arose under historical circumstances and served political purposes apart from which it cannot be properly understood. In rallying men against tyranny it was necessary that the individual be strengthened, that he be taught that he had rights and could govern himself. To give the common man a new conception of his worth, his dignity, and his power to save himself, both here and hereafter, was often the only resource of the revolutionist. When democratic principles were put into practice, the same doctrines were used as a working formula. This is exemplified by the notion of personal responsibility in Anglo-American law. All governments make certain forms of punishment contingent upon certain kinds of acts. In democratic countries these contingencies are expressed by the notion of responsible choice. But the notion may have no meaning under governmental practices formulated in other ways and would certainly have no place in systems which did not use punishment.

The democratic philosophy of human nature is determined by certain political exigencies and techniques, not by the goals of democracy. But exigencies and techniques change; and a conception which is not supported for its accuracy as a likeness—is not, indeed, rooted in fact at all—may be expected to change too. No matter how effective we judge current democratic practices to be, how highly we value them or how long we expect them to survive, they are almost certainly not the *final* form of government. The philosophy of human nature which has been useful in implementing them is also almost certainly not the last word. The ultimate achievement of democracy may be long deferred unless we emphasize the real aims rather than the verbal devices of democratic thinking. A philosophy which has been appropriate to one set of political exigencies will defeat its purpose if, under other circumstances, it prevents us from applying to human affairs the science of man which probably nothing but democracy itself could have produced.

Perhaps the most crucial part of our democratic philosophy to be reconsidered is our attitude toward freedom—or its reciprocal, the control of human behavior. We do not oppose all forms of control because it is "human nature" to do so. The reaction is not characteristic of all men under all conditions of life. It is an attitude which has been carefully engineered, in large part by what we call the "literature" of democracy. With respect to some methods of control (for example, the threat of force), very little engineering is needed, for the techniques or their immediate consequences are objectionable. Society has suppressed these methods by branding them "wrong," "illegal," or "sinful." But to encourage these attitudes toward objectionable forms of control, it has been necessary to disguise the real nature of certain indispensable techniques, the commonest examples of which are education, moral discourse, and persuasion. The actual procedures appear harmless enough. They consist of supplying information, presenting opportunities for action, pointing out logical relationships, appealing to reason or "enlightened understanding," and so on. Through a masterful piece of misrepresentation, the illusion is fostered that these procedures do not involve the control of behavior; at most, they are simply ways of "getting someone to change his mind." But analysis not only reveals the presence of well-defined behavioral processes, it demonstrates a kind of control no less inexorable, though in some ways more acceptable, than the bully's threat of force.

Let us suppose that someone in whom we are interested is acting unwisely—he is careless in the way he deals with his friends, he drives too fast, or he holds his golf club the wrong way. We could probably help him by issuing a series of commands: don't nag, don't drive over sixty, don't hold your club that way. Much less objectionable would be "an appeal to reason." We could show him how people are affected by his treatment of them, how accident rates rise sharply at higher speed, how a particular grip on the club alters the way the ball is struck and corrects a slice. In doing so we resort to verbal mediating devices which emphasize and support certain "contingencies of reinforcement"—that is, certain relations between behavior and its consequences—which strengthen the behavior we wish to set up. The same consequences would possibly set up the behavior without our help, and they eventually take control no matter which form of help we give. The appeal to reason has certain advantages over the authoritative command. A threat of punishment, no matter how subtle, generates emotional reactions and tendencies to escape or revolt. Perhaps the controllee merely "feels resentment" at being made to act in a given way, but even that is to be avoided. When we "appeal to reason," he "feels freer to do as he pleases." The fact is that we have exerted *less* control than in using a threat; since other conditions may contribute to the result, the effect may be delayed or, possibly in a given instance, lacking. But if we have worked a change in his behavior at all, it is because we have altered relevant environmental conditions, and the processes we have set in motion are just as real and just as inexorable, if not as comprehensive, as in the most authoritative coercion. . . .

The methods of education, moral discourse, and persuasion are acceptable not because they recognize the freedom of the individual or his right to dissent, but because they make only *partial* contributions to the control of his behavior. The freedom they recognize is freedom from a more coercive form of control. The dissent which they tolerate is the possible effect of other determiners of action. Since these sanctioned methods are frequently ineffective, we have been able to convince ourselves that they do not represent control at all. When they show too much strength to permit disguise, we give them other names and suppress them as energetically as we suppress the use of force. Education grown too powerful is rejected as propaganda or "brain-washing," while really effective persuasion is decried as "undue influence," "demagoguery," "seduction," and so on.

If we are not to rely solely upon accident for the innovations which give rise to cultural evolution, we must accept the fact that some kind of control of human behavior is inevitable. We cannot use good sense in human affairs unless someone engages in the design and construction of environmental conditions which affect the behavior of men. Environmental changes have always been the condition for the improvement of cultural patterns, and we can hardly use the more effective methods of science without making changes on a grander scale. We are all controlled by the world in which we live, and part of that world has been and will be constructed by men. The question is this: Are we to be controlled by accident, by tyrants, or by ourselves in effective cultural design? . . .

Science has turned up dangerous processes and materials before. To use the facts and techniques of a science of man to the fullest extent without making some monstrous mistake will be difficult and obviously perilous. It is no time for self-deception, emotional indulgence, or the assumption of attitudes which are no longer useful. Man is facing a difficult test. He must keep his head now, or he must start again—a long way back.

Those who reject the scientific conception of man must, to be logical, oppose the methods of science as well. The position is often supported by predicting a series of dire consequences which are to follow if science is not checked. A recent book by Joseph Wood Krutch, *The Measure of Man,* is in this vein. Mr. Krutch sees in the growing science of man the threat of an unexampled tyranny over men's minds. If science is permitted to have its way, he insists, "we may never be able really to think again." A controlled culture will, for example, lack some virtue inherent in disorder. We have emerged from chaos through a series of happy accidents, but in an engineered culture it will be "impossible for the unplanned to erupt again." But there is no virtue in the accidental character of an accident, and the diversity which arises from disorder can not only be duplicated by design but vastly extended. The experimental method is superior to simple observation just because it multiplies "accidents" in a systematic coverage of the possibilities. Technology offers many familiar examples. We no longer wait for immunity to disease to develop from a series of accidental exposures, nor do we wait for natural mutations in sheep and cotton to produce better fibers; but we continue to make use of such accidents when they occur, and we certainly do not prevent them. Many of the things we value have emerged from the clash of ignorant armies on darkling plains, but it is not therefore wise to encourage ignorance and darkness. . . .

Another predicted consequence of a science of man is an excessive uniformity. We are told that effective control—whether governmental, religious, educational, economic, or social—will produce a race of men who differ from each other only through relatively refractory genetic differences. That would probably be bad design, but we must admit that we are not now pursuing another course from choice. In a modern school, for example, there is usually a syllabus which specifies what every student is to learn by the end of each year. This would be flagrant regimentation if anyone expected every student to comply. But some will be poor in particular subjects, others will not study, others will not remember what they have been taught, and diversity is assured. Suppose, however, that we someday possess such effective educational techniques that every student will in fact be put in possession of all the behavior specified in a syllabus. At the end of the year, all students will correctly answer all questions on the final examination and "must all have prizes." Should we reject such a system on the grounds that in making all students excellent it has made them all alike? Advocates of the theory of a special faculty might contend that an important advantage of the present system is that the good student learns *in spite of* a system which is so defective that it is currently producing bad students as well. But if really effective techniques are available, we cannot avoid the problem of design simply by preferring the status quo. At what point should education be deliberately inefficient?...

Apart from their possibly objectionable consequences, scientific methods seem to make no provision for certain admirable qualities and faculties which seem to have flourished in less explicitly planned cultures; hence they are called "degrading" or "lacking in dignity." (Mr. Krutch has called the author's *Walden Two* an "ignoble Utopia.") The conditioned reflex is the current whipping boy. Because conditioned reflex may be demonstrated in animals, they are spoken of as though they were exclusively subhuman. It is implied, as we have seen, that no behavioral processes are involved in education and moral discourse or, at least, that the processes are exclusively human. But men do show conditioned reflexes (for example, when they are frightened by all instances of the control of human behavior because some instances engender fear), and animals do show processes similar to the human behavior involved in instruction and moral discourse. When Mr. Krutch asserts that " 'Conditioning' is achieved by methods which bypass or, as it were, short-circuit those very reasoning faculties which education proposes to cultivate and exercise," he is making a technical statement which needs a definition of terms and a great deal of supporting evidence.

If such methods are called "ignoble" simply because they leave no room for certain admirable attributes, then perhaps the practice of admiration needs to be examined. We might say that the child whose education has been skillfully planned has been deprived of the right to intellectual heroism. Nothing has been left to be admired in the way he acquires an education. Similarly, we can conceive of moral training which is so adequate to the demands of the culture that men will be good practically automatically, but to that extent they will be deprived of the right to moral heroism, since we seldom admire automatic goodness. Yet if we consider the end of morals rather than certain virtuous means, is not "automatic goodness" a desirable state of affairs? Is it not, for example, the avowed goal of religious education? T. H. Huxley* answered the question unambiguously: "If some great power would agree to make me always think what is true and do what is right, on condition of being a sort of clock and wound up every morning before I got out of bed, I should close instantly with the offer." Yet Mr. Krutch quotes this as the scarcely credible point of view of a "proto-modern" and seems himself to share T. S. Eliot's contempt for ". . . systems so perfect/That no one will need to be good."

"Having to be good" is an excellent example of an expendable honorific. It is inseparable from a particular form of ethical and moral control. We distinguish between the things we *have* to do to avoid punishment and those we *want* to do for rewarding consequences. In a culture which did not resort to punishment we should never "have" to do anything except with respect to the punishing contingencies which arise directly in the physical environment. And we are moving toward such a culture, because the neurotic, not to say psychotic, by-products of control through punishment have long since led compassionate men to seek alternative techniques. Recent research has explained some of the objectionable results of punishment and has revealed resources of at least equal power in "positive reinforcement." It is reasonable to look forward to a time when man will seldom "have" to do anything, although he may show interest, energy, imagination, and productivity far beyond the level seen under the present system (except for rare eruptions of the unplanned).

What we have to do we do with *effort*. We call it "work." There is no other way to distinguish between exhausing labor and the possibly equally energetic but rewarding activity of play. It is presumably good cultural design to replace the former with the latter. But an adjustment in attitudes is needed. We are much more practiced in admiring the heroic labor of a Hercules than the activity of one who works without having to. In a truly effective educational system the student might not "have to work" at all, but that possibility is likely to be received by the contemporary teacher with an emotion little short of rage. . . .

To those who are stimulated by the glamorous heroism of the battlefield, a peaceful world may not be a better world. Others may reject a world without sorrow, longing, or a sense of guilt because the relevance of deeply moving works of art would be lost. To many who have devoted their lives to the struggle to be wise and good, a world without confusion and evil might be an empty thing. A nostalgic concern for the decline of moral heroism has been a dominating theme in the work of Aldous Huxley. In *Brave New World* he could see in the application of science to human affairs only a travesty on the notion of the Good (just as George Orwell, in *1984*, could foresee nothing but horror). In a recent issue of *Esquire*,

---

* English biologist (1825–1895) and grandfather of Julian Huxley, who is the author of reading 4 in the Transition Section.

Huxley has expressed the point this way: "We have had religious revolutions, we have had political, industrial, economic and nationalistic revolutions. All of them, as our descendants will discover, were but ripples in an ocean of conservatism—trivial by comparison with the psychological revolution toward which we are so rapidly moving. *That* will really be a revolution. When it is over, the human race will give no further trouble." (Footnote for the reader of the future: This was not meant as a happy ending. Up to 1956 men had been admired, if at all, either for causing trouble or alleviating it. Therefore—)

It will be a long time before the world can dispense with heroes and hence with the cultural practice of admiring heroism, but we move in that direction whenever we act to prevent war, famine, pestilence, and disaster. It will be a long time before man will never need to submit to punishing environments or engage in exhausting labor, but we move in that direction whenever we make food, shelter, clothing, and labor-saving devices more readily available. We may mourn the passing of heroes but not the conditions which make for heroism. We can spare the self-made saint or sage as we spare the laundress on the river's bank struggling against fearful odds to achieve cleanliness. . . .

Far from being a threat to the tradition of Western democracy, the growth of a science of man is a consistent and probably inevitable part of it. In turning to the external conditions which shape and maintain the behavior of men, while questioning the reality of inner qualities and faculties to which human achievements were once attributed, we turn from the ill-defined and remote to the observable and manipulable. Though it is a painful step, it has far-reaching consequences, for it not only sets higher standards of human welfare but shows us how to meet them. A change in a theory of human nature cannot change the facts. The achievements of man in science, art, literature, music, and morals will survive any interpretation we place upon them. The uniqueness of the individual is unchallenged in the scientific view. Man, in short, will remain man. (There will be much to admire for those who are so inclined. Possibly the noblest achievement to which man can aspire, even according to present standards, is to accept himself for what he is, as that is revealed to him by the methods which he devised and tested on a part of the world in which he had only a small personal stake.)

If Western democracy does not lose sight of the aims of humanitarian action, it will welcome the almost fabulous support of its own science of man and will strengthen itself and play an important role in building a better world for everyone. But if it cannot put its "democratic philosophy" into proper historical perspective—if, under the control of attitudes and emotions which it generated for other purposes, it now rejects the help of science—then it must be prepared for defeat. For if we continue to insist that science has nothing to offer but a new and more horrible form of tyranny, we may produce just such a result by allowing the strength of science to fall into the hands of despots. And if, with luck, it were to fall instead to men of good will in other political communities, it would be perhaps a more ignominious defeat; for we should then, through a mis-carriage of democratic principles, be forced to leave to others the next step in man's long struggle to control nature and himself.

INTERPRETATION

5. On the Meaning of the Technological Revolution, *V. C. Ferkiss*

Can man's cultural creations and scientific discoveries produce a new kind of creature, a "superman"? This excerpt suggests that a basic capacity in human existence, man's technological capacity, can be cultivated as a means of ultimate transformation. As in the six ways of being religious we have already investigated, man has a process or technique of becoming a new being; but in this chapter the "means" are science and technology. Through advancing his knowledge of such areas as psychological conditioning, genetics, and electronics, man is gaining control of his own development. The author of this excerpt is Professor of Government at Georgetown University, and has taught political science at the University of the West Indies. In the preface to the book from which this material comes, Ferkiss notes that technology has made human society into a seamless web, so that to study politics today "is to study all aspects of human life." Here we have, then, a political scientist reflecting in an interdisciplinary way about the present human condition; and he concludes that "technological man" is both myth and reality. This excerpt includes only his discussion of "technological man" as a reality—though not a completed reality; for he announces: "Man as we have known him is on the verge of becoming something else." What characterizes the "existential revolution" in which modern man lives? What "radically new moral position" results from chemical and psychological discoveries about controlling human beings? According to the technology prophets, what will be the future relation between man and machines? What are some of the projected life-techniques for man when

Reprinted with permission of the publishers from *Technological Man: The Myth and Reality* by Victor C. Ferkiss (George Braziller, Inc., New York 1969, and William Heinemann Ltd., London). Copyright © 1969 by Victor Ferkiss. Pp. 17–22, 101–11.

*he extends his environment into space and the ocean?
Do you agree that the distinction between "natural" and
"artificial" life forms should be eliminated? Since we emphasize
"transformation" in this volume, pay special attention to
the last paragraph of Ferkiss' article.*

Existential Revolution
and Social Inertia

Humanity today is on the threshold of self-transfiguration, of attaining new powers over itself and its environment that can alter its nature as fundamentally as walking upright or the use of tools. No aspect of man's existence can escape being revolutionized by this fundamental fact—all his self-consciousness that we call culture, his patterns of interaction that we call society, his very biological structure itself. At the same time there are certain patterns of human institutional and personal behavior that are almost as resistant to change as those of the lower animals and the social insects. Man is fundamentally oriented to scarcity, conflict, insecurity, fear, irrationality, self-centeredness and a host of social and cultural institutions that reflect these or seek to transcend the problems they are traditionally considered to pose. The juxtaposition of these two factors is not just an overwhelming intellectual paradox, nor is it simply a moral scandal. It poses both a danger and a hope of cosmic proportions.

In what sense is it meaningful to say that an existential revolution is taking place, that technological man is more reality than myth? To speak of reality in this context is to assume that the term itself has meaning, that there is some sense in which our perceptions of the world correspond to something "out there." Debating this question is a favorite and not completely useless occupation of philosophers, but for most of us we can act only as if our words and ideas had some objective meaning. It is less simple to assume that there are different levels of reality, yet our "common sense" seems to tell us that the invention of agriculture, the advent of Christianity, the liberation of atomic power were somehow events of profound significance, and not merely in terms of the numbers of persons directly affected. So, too, the transition from feudalism to capitalism is regarded as more important than the decline of the Hapsburgs and the rise of Prussia, the French Revolution as more significant than the freeing of Greece from the Ottomans. We know that beneath the surface of day-to-day events there is a beneath-the-surface, a larger context in which ordinary social and individual behavior takes place.

Since Darwin, we are all dimly aware that man was not always man, that there was a long process of ascent from something else, and that this was somehow marked by specific changes such as upright posture and the opposed thumb that were physical, and others—the development of speech, the use of tools and the discovery of fire—that were in a sense technological and social. But we have assumed that at a certain point in the distant past man became man and evolution stopped. Everything since then is of a lower order of significance in that human nature is fixed, and man's economic and political and cultural life, while admitting of change and perhaps great improvement, is fundamentally unchanging. Man is here and his relation to the world of nature, his place in it, is a given. All of his achievements, however great, are variations on a theme, incremental and in the last analysis not very important. He has always eaten vegetation and animals; used tools; constructed dwellings; lived in families, usually in the company of a realtively large group of other men; been ruled by a combination of persuasion, coercion and inertia; traded with others, whether in goods or services; amused himself, and sought to find meaning in life and to express it in cultural forms. With a fixed biological heritage, a limited choice among social forms and a limited control over his environment, he has gone on his way from birth to death. Death and Taxes—basic biological and social facts—are inevitable.

But from a more meaningful perspective on evolution, the above is simply not true. Man is still capable of fundamental change, since evolution has not come to an end. Biologically speaking, it is true that every newborn infant is a brother to the cave-man's child. In that sense there has been no change; "test-tube" babies will still be of the species *Homo sapiens,* and if Cro-Magnons or Neanderthals still existed presumably it would be possible for the "test-tube" men to interbreed with them. But this is not the whole story. Babies are born into society, and depend on it for their survival. Culture is part of the human inheritance even if it is not built into the genetic code. As a distinguished biologist puts it, in man there is "a fundamentally new sort of heredity, the inheritance of learning."[1] Changes in human cluture can be changes so fundamental as to be of significance even on the evolutionary scale. Man can become a new kind of creature. This is the message of men such as Teilhard de Chardin, Julian Huxley and Sir Charles Sherrington: evolution is still taking place and man is aware of it and can consciously direct its course.

But what could take place in the realm of culture so fundamental as to alter the basic nature of the human animal? What discovery could rank with those forces that turned animal into man? No one thing, certainly. But a complex of events has altered the nature of man, the complex of discoveries and powers that we glibly speak of as modern technology. Technology is altering life to its existential roots before our very eyes.[2] How? Simply by giving man almost infinite power to change his world and to change himself. In the words of Emmanuel Mesthene, director of the Harvard Program in Science and Technology, "We have now, or know how to acquire, the technical capability to do very nearly anything we want. Can we transplant human hearts, control personality, order the weather that suits us, travel to Mars or Venus? Of course we can, if not now or in five or ten years, then certainly in 25 or in 50 or 100."[3] The space race and atomic energy are not the most telling evidence for man's new existential position. More fundamental yet is what is going on in medicine and biology. "We cannot duplicate God's work," is a typical comment of the emerging new man, "but we can come very close."[4]

How close can man come? What is left to do to challenge his Creator? He must be able to create life out of nonliving substances and to guide its development. Recent work on viruses and DNA brings him fairly close to that. He must be able to postpone death indefinitely. This he cannot yet do, but the existence of cryogenics (freezing bodies in the hope of reviving them after certain diseases have been conquered) is an index of how close some believe man has come. Actually, organ transplants may make the question meaningless. If the brain can be transplanted, especially if its contents can somehow be transferred to another, fresher brain, then death of the original body will have little meaning. Man is destined to be forever frustrated in not being able to create the world *de novo*; it is already there. But he is now close to being able to render the planet absolutely uninhabitable and perhaps to so skew its orbit as to cause it to be physically destroyed.

To the extent that man can do all the things that he can do and knows it, we are entitled to speak of the end of the modern world and the advent of an existential revolution. For these new powers are not merely extensions of the old. The whole is greater than the sum of its parts, and absolute power over himself and his environment puts man in a radically new moral position. Throughout his history he has lived with certain concepts of freedom and identity. Freedom was doing what you wanted to do. You were restricted by other men or an intractable physical environment. But the degree to which other men could control you or restrict your freedom was limited by the fact that the environment limited their powers also. You lived in a society, an economy, a physical environment that was difficult to alter. If worst came to worst you could run away. You could hide. Or you could remain true to yourself to the stake. Identity, by the same token, was a limited problem. You were the result of a combination of circumstances—your childhood, your surroundings, your own desires. These might be determined by fate, but not by anyone else, certainly not by yourself.

In the era of absolute technology, freedom and identity must take on new meanings or become meaningless. Other men can change your society, your economy and your physical environment. Eventually, they will be able to force you to live in a world with neither trees nor oceans if they choose. Running and hiding become increasingly difficult. They can make you love them so that you need not go to the stake. They can alter your identity by controlling how you are brought up and what your experiences are; they can even program your children genetically in advance of birth. But perhaps more disturbing is the fact that you can do all these things yourself: you can change your appearance or even your sex, your moods and your memories, you can even decide what you want your children to look like. But if you can be whatever you want to be, how will you distinguish the "real" you from the chosen? Who is it that is doing the choosing?

Not all of these changes affecting the nature of freedom and identity are yet practicable, but all are implicit in the new powers being developed by modern technology. Not whether they can exist but how long it will be before these futures come into existence seems to be the only question. The fact that postmodern man knows that they are coming must already begin to alter his self-image and his actions. No, there is no doubt but that the era of the new man will soon be upon us. For the existential revolution is a reality. At the deepest level of human existence man as we have known him is on the verge of becoming something else. . . .

THE EXISTENTIAL REVOLUTION

Mankind, it is alleged by the prophets of the new man, is on the threshold of a new age. He has, so they tell us, within or almost within his grasp new powers over himself and his environment that will radically transform the whole character and meaning of human existence. But before we can affirm or deny the reality or extent of this existential revolution we need to be more specific about the changes technology is making possible that threaten the persistence of civilization as we have known it or that herald the coming of the new technological man.

Trying to understand what is happening to man today is difficult for several reasons. Many of the new scientific and technological breakthroughs, like the development of the atomic bomb or the circumnavigation of the earth by astronauts, are or appear to be isolated events. It is not at once apparent what effect they are having on man's social life and self-image; most of us go about our daily business as if they had never occurred. We may once have thought of building a fallout shelter or we may have stayed at home to watch the first manned rocket launchings on television, but soon we are once again caught up in the daily routine of bills, promotions, vacations and lawns to mow. Other triumphs of science, like the successful transplantation of the human heart, strike us as novel and possibly important to a few humans with medical problems, but they seem like more of the same thing: further steps in a long upward spiral of medical progress, added conveniences like faster cars and color TV. Isn't it wonderful, we say, and then belie our words by going on about our business.

Still other additions to man's power over nature, such as the synthesis of DNA, involve such esoteric scientific problems that to most of us (though not necessarily to our more alert offspring) they are largely meaningless. Not understanding the scientific issues involved, we soon lose interest (though we may feel guilty about this if we are middle class and college trained, for today not being interested in science is not unlike admitting to being bored by classical music). Having no philosophical or scientific context within which to place these discoveries, we soon forget about them.

Finally there are a great number of possibilities that never enter our consciousness at all simply because through lack of background knowledge and interest we never hear about them or, if we do, we unconsciously dismiss them as mere speculation or even fantasy. Gene banks and artificial brains, extrasensory perception and the ability to derive atomic energy from ordinary rocks may crop up in the headlines of our newspapers, but they become a kind of background noise to the stock-market reports and the war news, filtered out like the television program our children are watching in the next room. If we do notice these items, we may simply suppress them, as many of us do with information relating to the dangers of nuclear war or a world population that will more than double in the next generation. The power of the ordinary to reclaim our attention is enormous, and is in part a necessary condition of our sanity. It also may represent a healthy acceptance of fate. An early modern saint is famous for his reply to a question about what he would do if he knew that God was going to bring his life to an end within the hour. His reply was that he would go on playing billiards. But his faith in the state of his soul and the beneficence of the Almighty may not be an appropriate response for those whose civilization is threatened by developments all of which might not be beneficent (in part because the present civilization is not as morally healthy as it might be), developments that it still has some power to affect.

There exists today a sizable literature about the foreseeable future (the period from today until the era of our great-grandchildren) in which the leading experts in various fields set forth their views as to what technological developments are likely to occur. Ability to predict technological change is far from absolute, but usually the unanticipated event occurs in addition to the anticipated rather than as a substitute for it, so most of what is predicted probably will occur. Many predictions necessarily rest on assumptions about how much effort will go into certain lines of research as well as about what appears to be intrinsically possible, but increasingly the prophets take this complication into account. Some predictions are to a certain extent mutually incompatible, in practice even if not in theory. Thus improvements in communications technology might lead to a slackening of efforts to improve transportation or vice versa, or an increased ability to convert ordinary substances such as sand and rock into scarce minerals might make interplanetary mining uneconomic; but this does not negate the possibility of any of the alternatives or the need to take cognizance of them.

While not all futurists agree on details—and today every competent scientist, businessman, military leader or government official is continually involved in predicting the future through sheer necessity to plan ahead in his own activity—there is considerable consensus on basic trends in technological development.[5] (In part, of course, this may be due to common orientations or to the fact that there is developing a futurist Establishment that dominates most studies and conferences.) Most disagreements are about probabilities rather than possibilities and about timing. When one realizes the magnitude and probable impact of the events forecast, one is struck by the wide measure of agreement rather than by the minor disagreements. If only a small fraction of the developments predicted take place, the existential revolution will present humanity with psychological shocks and practical problems on a scale unknown to recorded history.

The Extension of Environment

Because of its remoteness from ordinary human life, progress in the conquest of space presents perhaps the fewest immediately disturbing elements for contemporary civilization to assimilate. We are already getting used to the intercontinental missile and its cousin, the satellite that can observe or destroy any part of the earth's surface unless prevented from doing so. Mechanical contact with or electronic observation of the surface of the moon and Venus is already a reality. What does the future hold? Some predictions are so certain that a consensus exists as to the actual date of their probable occurrence—a permanent lunar base by 1975, permanent manned stations on some planets by 1990—given certain assumptions about budgetary commitments on the part of the governments concerned.

There is nothing very startling about these predictions. Less expected by most of us, however, is the probable discovery of an antigravity drive on a principle other than rocket propulsion, which one panel of experts expects soon after the year 2020.[6] Such an event would open the door to travel beyond the solar system, in addition to being a contribution toward nullifying the force of gravity (rather than merely overcoming it) here on earth. Some predictions such as competition for the raw materials of other planets and extraterrestrial farming by about the same time would have important economic and psychological effects if fulfilled.[7] But even if they came to pass they would simply mean that man's conquest of the solar system was essentially Europe's conquest of the earth in the colonial era writ large: colonies, bases, plantations, economic exploitation.

More significant are those technological developments associated with the conquest of space that have direct implications for the nature of man himself. Journeys into outer space—especially beyond the solar system— would take vast amounts of time with any immediate foreseeable techniques. Scientists therefore predict placing voyagers in a state of coma from which they would automatically recover at a set time. An even more significant alternative would be multigeneration missions in which those who arrived at their destination would be the descendants of the original crew. Should this occur, man would really have left earth behind, scattering his seed far into the universe. Those born and reared in space would be in a sense a different kind of man. They might never be able to communicate with the planet that sent them forth. But the impact of their going on the consciousness of those who remained behind would still be immense.

The difficulties of operating in and adjusting to the physical conditions of outer space and strange planets have led to speculation that the astronauts of the future would be Cyborgs, men who would have many artificial organs and thus would be better able to cope with harsh and novel surroundings. An alternative or supplementary means of exploration (at least within shorter distances where something like real-time communication was possible) would be a kind of machine-man symbiosis, in which there would be direct electromagnetic connection between the human nervous system and equipment that was receiving transmissions from sensors elsewhere in space. Those humans involved would control the exploring machines and receive impressions (muted, if necessary) as if they were actually physically experiencing the exploration themselves. Space would thus become part of the human environment, since even those not in the direct symbiotic relationship would be part of a culture that knew the sights and sounds of the expanses of space firsthand.[8]

Not only in space but also on earth itself is the environment about to be radically extended. The oceans will in a generation or two become part of the human habitat.[9] They will not merely be crossed by travelers, fishermen or the world's navies, or explored by a few aquanauts for scientific, military or recreational purposes; they will become as domesticated as the land surface of the planet. Men will farm the waters, breed and herd fish, and mine the bottom of the high seas. The conquest of the 70 per cent of the earth's surface that is under water will mean changes in man, society and nature. Permanent undersea colonies will be established; individuals and even whole families may eventually spend most of their lives under water. Cetaceans, many of whom exhibit a high level of natural intelligence, will be bred and trained as helpers; already the U.S. Navy is using dolphins in undersea recovery work.[10] Man himself will learn to breathe water through medical alteration of his lungs or other means; the U.S. Navy's leading expert's target for the creation of "gillmen" is 1972.[11] Extensive research in breathing water impregnated with compressed gas is currently underway at Duke University under the direction of Dr. Johannes Klystra. Whether or not any particular developments now foreseen actually will take place, man's over-all relation to the oceans is about to change inexorably and irrevocably. Just as we soon will no longer see the moon primarily as an aid to romance but rather as a revolving mining camp or military base, our children standing on the shores of the Pacific will see not a vastness of untamed water stretching far beyond the horizon to Cathay, but a pond full of derricks, mines, ranches and perhaps even suburbs.

What of man's economic life? Some predict that the race between technological progress and population growth will be won by the former. How likely this is we must judge in due course. Certainly there seems to be increasing consensus among scientists that new weapons will soon be available for the war on hunger and scarcity. Most startling and important, it is even hoped that the alchemist's ancient dream of transmuting base metals into precious ones will be fully realized at last. Man already can create new sources of energy and new elements through his mastery of the atom. But this ability is so far restricted by the need to use naturally unstable radioactive minerals as a point of departure. If man can unlock the energy in ordinary iron or hydrogen and use it to turn the common elements of the land and seas into mechanical or electrical energy or into other elements, scarcity would lose most of its meaning. Some predict that the world's need for fresh water soon could be remedied by economically feasible desalination using radioactive materials; if ordinary minerals could be substituted this would remove all obstacles to unlimited water supplies. It is already technically possible to create synthetic protein from petroleum; once we are able to do this on a large scale no one need ever go hungry or suffer the physical or mental defects caused by lack of protein; for petroleum itself can probably be made available without limit through chemical alchemy.

In time man should be able to use any part of the earth's surface or interior for any purpose he wishes, through recycling he could use it over and over again.

Today natural forces still get in the way of man's productive activities, especially in agriculture. This, too, will soon be a thing of the past. Completely accurate prediction of the weather over the globe is almost unanimously expected in a relatively short time; many foresee control of the most significant aspects of the weather within a generation.[12]

The single factor that most distinguishes the coming civilization, whatever one chooses to call it, is the substitution of "communication" processes for traditional "work" as man's primary activity. That automation in one form or another will be the basis of the new civilization is generally held by futurists. Teaching machines will become the norm, and in time information will be directly transmitted to the human brain electronically. Use of the computer will lead to what, in effect, will be a universal language for some purposes, based on the computer's needs. By 1990, many confidently predict, computers will be available with the equivalent of IQ's of 150 in terms of their ability to respond to directions, understand their environment and initiate activity. Routine labor will be taken over by robot household servants (though many see as an alternative the breeding of intelligent animals, particularly primates, for low-grade routine labor on the land as well as in the sea). The climax of this process will come when machine-man symbiosis begins to play its role on earth; a median date predicted for its large-scale practicability is 2010.[13]

The progress of technology will increase vastly the means available to men to control other men. New biological and pharmacological weapons will be available that will coerce without destroying men or property, largely through their direct effect on the will. Electronics will increase greatly the means of centralized surveillance available to ruling groups (a national data bank is already a subject of controversy in Washington, and it could be instituted tomorrow, Congress permitting).[14]

The Impact of Biology

But neither the extensions of man's effective environment into the depths of space or the oceans, nor the vision of automated affluence, nor even the greater social controls that are predicted for the near future most radically affect man's existential situation. He has always sought knowledge, ease and power over his fellows. The coming of the new man is foreshadowed most by the contemporary revolution in the biological sciences.[15] We have noted already the extent to which man's biological integrity could be affected by various kinds of symbiosis with the machine, whether through increased use of artificial organs or by being literally plugged into a computer. But increasing understanding of the processes underlying biological activity will also make it possible to subject organic processes to human control. Drugs may become widespread not only as means of social control but as accepted means of self-realization. General and permanent immunization against most diseases is considered increasingly feasible. Physical and chemical treatment for psychological and psychotic states may soon relegate the Freudian analyst to the role of witch doctor that many scientists feel is only appropriate. New contraceptive techniques are constantly being developed to bring fecundity under control, and increasingly the aspiration of researchers is something (a capsule implanted in the body that permanently inhibits formation of appropriate cells unless neutralized, for instance) that would make breeding, rather than prevention, require a special medical act. New medical discoveries lead researchers to expect the lengthening of the human life span fifty years, which in their view would only be a return to the normal. It is already virtually certain that even the brain can be rejuvenated by injections of DNA, thus making it possible to maintain memory and problem-solving ability unimpaired into old age.[16]

However, it is not the curing of disease but the control of genetic processes and the shape of man that most excites speculation. Man's physical shape will be alterable by new and radical forms of medical cosmetology; the nose job and the paraffin-inflated breasts of today will be succeeded by a variety of techniques to alter color of hair, skin or eyes or to change contours or even sex, with only the basic skeletal structure constituting any limitation. Mental states will be alterable as well: intelligence and character affected by chemical means, dreams stimulated or even preprogramed. Biochemical processes may make possible the growing of new organs to replace old ones; the year 2007 is predicted by some as the date for this breakthrough.

But at best the human mind and body, once formed, present a difficult problem for the biologist. Far better to "adjust" them beforehand. The breaking of the genetic code will in the reasonably near future make it possible to predetermine not only sex but other characteristics. Genetic defects could be countered by excision or addition of genes in embryo; if suitable artificial wombs being worked on at present are perfected, "foetal therapy" is well on the way. New knowledge of the mechanisms of heredity, storage of genetic materials and artificial insemination will make it possible for women to order the kind of child they wish as they would order a new car. For parents with higher self-esteem, techniques are being developed that will make it possible to produce exact duplicates of the father or mother by substituting the cell nuclei of the desired parent for that in the fertilized human egg. This has already been done with frogs.[17] Alternatively, society could breed sub-types of men as it now does dogs for various roles and functions. Biologist Bentley Glass predicts artificial production of children "will probably be realized by the end of the 20th century."[18]

What do all these discoveries in biology and the increasing symbiosis of man and machine, even if only on the social and intellectual rather than on the physical plane, add up to? Physicist Herman Kahn, in these respects more conservative than other futurists, perhaps because he is not a biologist, lists two "far-out" predictions that, he holds, nevertheless deserve serious consideration. One is the almost complete genetic control of man, wherein he still remains, however, *Homo sapiens*; the other is the end of *Homo sapiens* and the creation of a new species by man's own actions.[19] If in time, as some predict, man is able to create new species of plants and animals directly in the laboratory rather than through the more time-consuming process of selective breeding, just as he already can create live viruses from inanimate matter, why not a new species built up from human genetic materials? But whatever the specifics, man is about to enter upon a new plane of existence. "The logical climax of evolution can be said to have occurred when, as is now imminent, a sentient species deliberately and directly assumes control of its own evolution," is the way a leading medical researcher describes man's new status in the cosmos.[20]

NOTES

1. George Gaylord Simpson, *The Meaning of Evolution,* p. 286.
2. Robert Heilbroner in Foreword to Ben B. Seligman, *Most Notorious Victory,* p. ix.
3. Quoted in Walter Sullivan, "Our Future Is Incomputable," New York *Times,* March 26, 1967.
4. Unidentified medical research worker, quoted in "The New Medicine and Its Weapons," *Newsweek,* April 24, 1967, p. 68.
5. In assessing the future I have leaned most heavily on Herman Kahn and Anthony J. Weiner, *The Year* 2000; T. J. Gordon and Olaf Helmer, *Report on a Long-Range Forecasting Study;* Daniel Bell and his associates who prepared the special issue of *Daedalus,* "Toward the Year 2000: Work in Progress" (Summer, 1967); Walter Gilman, *Science: U.S.A.;* Nigel Calder (ed.), *The World in 1984;* Arthur C. Clarke, *Profiles of the Future; Wall Street Journal, Here Comes Tomorrow;* Sir George Thompson, *The Foreseeable Future; Foreign Policy Association, Toward the Year 2018;* and and Sergei Gouschev and Michael Vassilev, *Russian Science in the 21st Century.* Not all of these prophets are in agreement, of course. See also Stuart Chase, *The Most Probable World,* and Harrison Brown, James Bonner and John Weir, *The Next Hundred Years.*
6. Gordon and Helmer, *Report of a Long-Range Forecasting Study,* p. 25. Clarke's estimate is between 2050 and 2060 (*Profiles of the Future,* p. 235).
7. Gordon and Helmer, *Report,* p. 25.
8. For early and somewhat timid looks at the impact of space travel on humanity see Lincoln P. Bloomfield (ed.), *Outer Space: Prospects for Man and Society;* Lillian Levy (ed.), *Space: Its Impact upon Man and Society;* Harold Leland Goodwin, *Space: Frontier Unlimited;* and Howard J. Taubenfeld (ed.), *Space and Society.* But see also Arthur C. Clarke, *The Promise of Space.*
9. On the oceans see Harris B. Stewart, Jr., *The Global Sea;* Marine Technology Society, *Exploiting the Ocean;* John Bardach, *Harvest of the Sea;* Elisabeth Mann Borghese, "The Republic of the Deep Seas"; and Athelstan Spilhaus, "Oceanography: A Wet and Wondrous Journey."
10. "Dolphins Operate Sea Lost and Found," New York *Times,* March 23, 1967.
11. "Breathing Water Seen in 5 Years," Washington *Post,* November 12, 1967.
12. See D. S. Halacy, Jr., *The Weather Changers;* Thomas F. Malone, "Weather Modification"; and W. R. Derrick Sewall, "Humanity and the Weather."
13. Gordon and Helmer, *Report,* p. 21.
14. Alan Westin, "The Snooping Machine."

15. On man's future biological self-control see John D. Roslansky (ed.), *Genetics and the Future of Man;* Jean Rostand, *Peut-on Modifier l'Homme?;* Max Gunther, "Second Genesis"; Kurt Hirschorn, "On Re-Doing Man"; Dwight J. Ingle, "The Biological Future of Man"; Hermann J. Muller, "The Prospects of Genetic Change"; and Albert Rosenfeld, "Will Man Direct His Own Evolution?"

16. "Brain Renewal Object of Science," Washington *Post,* May 3, 1968.

17. "Genes Are Held Able to Cure Disease," New York *Times,* October 22, 1967.

18. "There Is Peril, Too, In Growing Technology," New York *Times,* March 24, 1968.

19. Kahn and Weiner, *The Year* 2000, p. 56.

20. John Heller, quoted in Max Gunther, "Second Genesis," p. 117.

CRITIQUE

The revolutionary impact of technology on the modern world cannot be denied. But is this impact to be a source of hope or of fear? And are the problems and possibilities created by it to be dealt with primarily by the technologists themselves, or must we look elsewhere for help? These issues are open to dispute as we see in the following excerpts.

6. The Present Evolutionary Crisis,
Sri Aurobindo

> *Sri* Aurobindo Ghose (1872–1950) is one of the most notable mystic-philosophers of India during the last century. During the last four decades of his life, he was a practicing devotee of the Divine Mother (the transcendent and creative power in all existence), a Yogi, and the founder of a religious community. In his view, mankind cannot survive the modern age unless it undergoes a profound spiritual transformation. He argues in effect that those who place their faith in technology have mistaken the problem for the answer. It is precisely the disproportion between our present "system of civilization" and our spiritual immaturity that poses the critical threat. The creations of life and of mind need the power of Spirit to bring them*

From *The Future Evolution of Man* by Sri Aurobindo Ghose (Pondicherry, India: Sri Aurobindo Ashram Press, 1963), pp. 51–56, 67–71. Used by permission of the publisher.

* Sri is a title translated by such terms as "Sir" or "The Honorable," and is pronounced "shree."

to that unity, mutuality and harmony which is the proper and
now evolving possibility of human life. In his philosophy he
attempts to reconcile the notions of spirit and of matter,
to view all existence as a continuum of matter, life, mind, and
spirit (soul). And in this excerpt he attempts to show how our
present state of civilization marks a critical stage in the evolving
forms of this continuum. In what way has man's developed
"system of civilization" brought him to an evolutionary crisis?
Why is the order provided by rational thought and political
systems inadequate to the needs of our time? How about
organized religion? How is spirit related to life and to mind,
and why is its appearance man's only hope at this stage
of evolution? What would his attitude likely be toward
Skinner's thought?

At present mankind is undergoing an evolutionary crisis in which is concealed a choice of its destiny; for a stage has been reached in which the human mind has achieved in certain directions an enormous development while in others it stands arrested and bewildered and can no longer find its way. A structure of the external life has been raised up by man's ever-active mind and life-will, a structure of an unmanageable hugeness and complexity, for the service of his mental, vital, physical claims and urges, a complex political, social, administrative, economic, cultural machinery, an organized collective means for his intellectual, sensational, aesthetic and material satisfaction. Man has created a system of civilization which has become too big for his limited mental capacity and understanding and his still more limited spiritual and moral capacity to utilize and manage, a too dangerous servant of his blundering ego[1] and its appetites. For no greater seeing mind, no intuitive soul of knowledge has yet come to his surface of consciousness which could make this basic fullness of life a condition for the free growth of something that exceeded it. This new fullness of the means of life might be, by its power for a release from the incessant unsatisfied stress of his economic and physical needs, an opportunity for the full pursuit of other and greater aims surpassing the material existence, for the discovery of a higher truth and good and beauty, for the discovery of a greater and diviner spirit which would intervene and use life for a higher perfection of the being: but it is being used instead for the multiplication of new wants and an aggressive expansion of the collective ego. At the same time Science has put at his disposal many potencies of the universal Force and has made the life of humanity materially one; but what uses this universal Force is a little human individual or communal ego[2] with nothing universal in its light of knowledge or its movements, no inner sense or power which would create in this physical drawing together of the human world a true life unity, a mental unity or a spiritual oneness. All that is there is a chaos of clashing mental ideas, urges of individual and collective physical want and need, vital claims and desires, impulses of an ignorant life-push, hungers and calls for life satisfaction of individuals, classes, nations, a rich fungus of political and social and economic nostrums and notions, a hustling medley of slogans and panaceas for which men are ready to oppress and be oppressed, to kill and be killed, to impose them somehow or other by the immense and too formidable means placed at his disposal, in the belief that this is his way out to something ideal. The evolution of human mind and life* must necessarily lead towards an increasing universality; but on a basis of ego and segmenting and dividing mind this opening to the universal can only create a vast pollulation of unaccorded ideas and impulses, a surge of enormous powers and desires, a chaotic mass of unassimilated and intermixed mental, vital and physical material of a larger existence which, because it is not taken up by a creative harmonizing light of the spirit, must welter in a universalized confusion and discord out of which it is impossible to build a greater harmonic life.

LD.**II, 28

Without an inner change man can no longer cope with the gigantic development of the outer life.

A life of unity, mutuality and harmony born of a deeper and wider truth of our being is the only truth of life that can successfully replace the imperfect mental constructions of the past which were a combination of association and regulated conflict, an accommodation of egos and interests grouped or dovetailed into each other to form a society, a consolidation by common general life-motives, a unification by need and the pressure of struggle with outside forces. It is such a change and such a reshaping of life for which humanity is blindly beginning to seek, now more and more with a sense that its very existence depends upon finding the way. The evolution of mind working upon life has developed an organization of the activity of mind and use of matter which can no longer be supported by human capacity without an inner change. An accommodation of the ego-centric human individuality, separative even in association, to a system of living which demands unity, perfect mutuality, harmony, is imperative. But because the burden which is being laid on mankind is too great for the present littleness of the human personality and its petty mind and small life-instincts, because it cannot operate the needed change, because it is using this new apparatus and organization to serve the old infraspiritual and infrarational life-self of humanity, the destiny of the race seems to be heading dangerously, as if impatiently and in spite of itself, under the drive of the vital ego seized by colossal forces which are on the same scale as the huge mechanical organization of life and scientific knowledge which it has evolved, a scale too large for its reason and will to handle, into a prolonged confusion and perilous crisis and darkness of violent shifting incertitude. Even if this turns out to be a passing phase or appearance and a tolerable structural accommodation is found which will enable man-

---

* See diagram later in this selection.
** *The Life Divine* (Calcutta: Arya Publishing House, 1947), 2 vols.

kind to proceed less catastrophically on its uncertain journey, this can only be a respite. For the problem is fundamental and in putting it evolutionary Nature in man is confronting herself with a critical choice which must one day be solved in the true sense if the race is to arrive or even to survive.

LD.II, 28

The exaltation of the collectivity, of the State, only substitutes the collective ego for the individual ego.

A rational and scientific formula of the vitalistic and materialistic human being and his life, a search for a perfected economic society and the democratic cultus of the average man are all that the modern mind presents us in this crisis as a light for its solution. Whatever the truth supporting these ideas, this is clearly not enough to meet the need of a humanity which is missioned to evolve beyond itself or, at any rate, if it is to live, must evolve far beyond anything that it at present is. A life-instinct in the race and in the average man himself has felt the inadequacy and has been driving towards a reversal of values or a discovery of new values and a transfer of life to a new foundation. This has taken the form of an attempt to find a simple and ready-made basis of unity, mutuality, harmony for the common life, to enforce it by a suppression of the competitive clash of egos and so to arrive at a life of identity for the community in place of a life of difference. But to realize these desirable ends the means adopted have been the forcible and successful materialization of a few restricted ideas or slogans enthroned to the exclusion of all other thought, the suppression of the mind of the individual, a mechanized compression of the elements of life, a mechanized unity and drive of the life-force, a coercion of man by the State, the substitution of the communal for the individual ego. The communal ego is idealized as the soul of the nation, the race, the community; but this is a colossal and may turn out to be a fatal error. A forced and imposed unanimity of mind, life, action raised to their highest tension under the drive of something which is thought to be greater, the collective soul, the collective life, is the formula found. But this obscure collective being is not the soul or self of the community; it is a life-force that rises from the subconscient and, if denied the light of guidance by the reason, can be driven only by dark massive forces which are powerful but dangerous for the race because they are alien to the conscious evolution of which man is the trustee and bearer. It is not in this direction that evolutionary Nature has pointed mankind; this is a reversion towards something that she had left behind her.

LD.II, 28

If humanity is to survive, a radical transformation of human nature is indispensable.

But it has not been found in experience, whatever might have once been hoped, that education and intellectual training by itself can change man; it only provides the human individual and collective ego[3] with better information and a more efficient machinery for its self-affirmation, but leaves it the same unchanged human ego. Nor can human mind and life be cut into perfection—even into what is thought to be perfection, a constructed substitute—by any kind of social machinery; matter can be so cut, thought can be so cut, but in our human existence matter and thought are only instruments for the soul and the life-force. Machinery cannot form the soul and life-force into standardized shapes; it can at best coerce them, make soul and mind inert and stationary and regulate the life's outward action; but if this is to be effectively done, coercion and compression of the mind and life are indispensable and that again spells either unprogressive stability or decadence.

There is the possibility that in the swing back from a mechanistic idea of life and society the human mind may seek refuge in a return to the religious idea and a society governed or sanctioned by religion. But organized religion, though it can provide a means of inner uplift for the individual and preserve in it or behind it a way for his opening to spiritual experience, has not changed human life and society; it could not do so because, in governing society, it had to compromise with the lower parts of life and could not insist on the inner change of the whole being; it could insist only on a credal adherence, a formal acceptance of its ethical standards and a conformity to institution, ceremony and ritual. Religion so conceived can give a religio-ethical colour or surface tinge—sometimes, if it maintains a strong kernel of inner experience, it can generalize to some extent an incomplete spiritual tendency; but it does not transform the race, it cannot create a new principle of the human existence. A total spiritual direction given to the whole life and the whole nature can alone lift humanity beyond itself. Another possible conception akin to the religious solution is the guidance of society by men of spiritual attainment, the brotherhood or unity of all in the faith or in the discipline, the spiritualization of life and society by the taking up of the old machinery of life into such a unification or inventing a new machinery. This too has been attempted before without success; it was the original founding idea of more than one religion: but the human ego and vital nature were too strong for a religious idea working on the mind and by the mind to overcome its resistance. It is only the full emergence of the soul,[4] the full descent of the native light and power of the Spirit and the consequent replacement or transformation and uplifting of our insufficient mental and vital nature by a spiritual and supramental supernature that can effect this evolutionary miracle.

At first sight this insistence on a radical change of nature might seem to put off all the hope of humanity to a distant evolutionary future; for the transcendence of our normal human nature, a transcendence of our mental, vital and physical being, has the appearance of an endeavour too high and difficult and at present, for man as he is, impossible. Even if it were so, it would still remain the sole possibility for the transmutation of life; for to hope for a true change of human life without a change of human nature is an irrational and unspiritual proposition; it is to ask for something unnatural and unreal, an impossible miracle. But what is demanded by this change is not something altogether distant, alien to our existence and radically impossible; for what has to be developed is there in our being and not something outside it: what evolutionary Nature presses for, is an awakening to the knowledge of self, the discovery of self, the manifestation of the self and spirit within us and the release of its self-knowledge, its self-power, its native self-instrumentation. It is, besides, a step for which the whole of evolution has been a preparation and which is brought closer at each crisis of human destiny when the mental and vital evolution of the being touches a point where intellect and vital force reach some acme of tension and there is a need either for them to collapse, to sink back into a torpor of defeat or a repose of unprogressive quiescence or to rend their way through the veil against which they are straining. What is necessary is that there should be a turn in humanity felt by some or many towards the vision of this change, a feeling of its imperative need, the sense of its possibility, the will to make it possible in themselves and to find the way. That trend is not absent and it must increase with the tension of the crisis in human world-destiny; the need of an escape or a solution, the feeling that there is no other solution than the spiritual cannot but grow and become more imperative under the urgency of critical circumstance. To that call in the being there must always be some answer in the Divine Reality and in Nature.

LD.II, 28

THE DEVELOPMENT
OF THE SPIRITUAL MAN

> *Spirituality is something else than intellectuality; its appearance is the sign that a Power greater than mind is striving to emerge in its turn.*

Is is quite true that to a surface view life seems only an operation of Matter, mind an activity of life, and it might seem to follow that what we call the soul or spirit is only a power of mentality, soul a fine form of mind, spirituality a high activity of the embodied mental being. But this is a superficial view of things due to the thought's concentrating on the appearance and process and not looking at what lies behind the process. One might as well on the same lines have concluded that electricity is only a product or operation of water and cloud matter, because it is in such a field that lightning emerges; but a deeper inquiry has shown that both cloud and water have, on the contrary, the energy of electricity as their foundation, their constituent power or energy-substance: that which seems to be a result is—in its reality, though not in its form—the origin; the effect is in the essence pre-existent to the apparent cause, the principle of the emergent activity precedent to its present field of action. So it is throughout evolutionary Nature;* Matter could not have become animate if the principle of life had not been there constituting Matter and emerging as a phenomenon of life-in-matter; life-in-matter could not have begun to

---

* Note the common recognition of the present phase of evolution as a consciously purposive one in Sri Aurobindo's thought and that of J. Huxley (Transition Section,

feel, perceive, think, reason, if the principle of mind had not been there behind life and substance, constituting it as its field of operation and emergent in the phenomenon of a thinking life and body: so too spirituality emerging in mind is the sign of a power which itself has founded and constituted life, mind and body and is now emerging as a spiritual being in a living and thinking body. How far this emergence will go, whether it will become dominant and transform its instrument, is a subsequent question; but what is necessary first to posit is the existence of spirit as something else than mind and greater than mind, spirituality as something other than mentality and the spiritual being therefore as something distinct from the mental being: spirit is a final evolutionary emergence because it is the original involutionary element and factor. Evolution is an inverse action of the involution[5]: what is an ultimate and last derivation in the involution is the first to appear in the evolution; what was original and primal in the involution is in the evolution the last and supreme emergence.

LD.II, 24

> *Spirituality is a progressive awakening to the inner reality of our being, to a spirit, self, soul which is other than our mind, life and body. It is an inner aspiration to know, to enter into contact and union with the greater Reality beyond, which also pervades the universe and dwells in us, and, as a result of that aspiration, that contact and that union, a turning, a conversion, a birth into a new being.*

reading 4); but observe the contrasting views of the nature and source of evolution in each position as depicted in the following diagram:

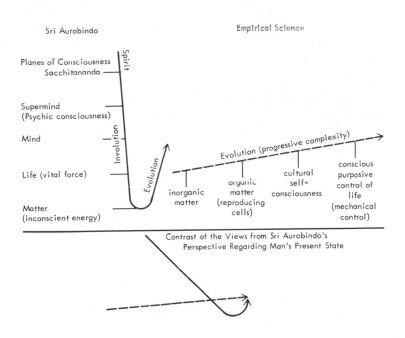

Contrast of the Views from Sri Aurobindo's
Perspective Regarding Man's Present State

In the animal mind is not quite distinct from its own life-matrix and lifematter; its movements are so involved in the life movements that it cannot detach itself from them, cannot stand separate and observe them; but in man mind has become separate, he can become aware of his mental operations as distinct from his life operations, his thought and will can disengage themselves from his sensations and impulses, desires and emotional reactions, can become detached from them, observe and control them, sanction or cancel their functioning: he does not as yet know the secrets of his being well enough to be aware of himself decisively and with certitude as a mental being in a life and body, but he has that impression and can take inwardly that position. So too at first soul in man does not appear as something quite distinct from mind and from mentalised life; its movements are involved in the mind movements, its operations seem to be mental and emotional activities; the mental human being is not aware of a soul in him standing back from the mind and life and body, detaching itself, seeing and controlling and moulding their action and formation: but, as the inner evolution proceeds, this is precisely what can, must and does happen—it is the long-delayed but inevitable next step in our evolutionary destiny. There can be a decisive emergence in which the being separates itself from thought and sees itself in an inner silence as the spirit in mind, or separates itself from the life movements, desires, sensations, kinetic impulses and is aware of itself as the spirit supporting life, or separates itself from the body sense and knows itself as a spirit ensouling Matter: this is the discovery of ourselves as the Purusha,[6] a mental being or a life-soul or a subtle self supporting the body. This is taken by many as a sufficient discovery of the true self and in a certain sense they are right; for it is the self or spirit that so represents itself in regard to the activities of Nature, and this revelation of its presence is enough to disengage the spiritual element: but self-discovery can go farther, it can even put aside all relation to form or action of Nature. For it is seen that these selves are representations of a divine Entity to which mind, life and body are only forms and instruments: we are then the Soul looking at Nature, knowing all her dynamisms in us, not by mental perception and observation, but by an intrinsic consciousness and its direct sense of things and its intimate exact vision, able therefore by its emergence to put a close control on our nature and change it. When there is a complete silence in the being, either a stillness of the whole being or a stillness behind unaffected by surface movements, then we can become aware of a Self, a spiritual substance of our being, an existence exceeding even the soul individuality, spreading itself into universality, surpassing all dependence on any natural form or action, extending itself upward into a transcendence of which the limits are not visible. It is these liberations of the spiritual part in us which are the decisive steps of the spiritual evolution in Nature.

When there is the decisive emergence, one sign of it is the status or action in us of an inherent, intrinsic, self-existent consciousness which knows itself by the mere fact of being, knows all that is in itself in the same way, by identity with it, begins even to see all that to our mind seems external in the same manner, by a movement of identity or by an intrinsic direct consciousness which envelops, penetrates, enters into its object, discovers itself in the object, is aware in it of something that is not mind or life or body. There is, then, evidently a spiritual consciousness which is other than the mental, and it testifies to the existence of a spiritual being in us which is other than our surface mental personality. But at first this consciousness may confine itself to a status of being separate from the action of our ignorant surface nature, observing it, limiting itself to knowledge, to a seeing of things with a spiritual sense and vision of existence. For action it may still depend upon the mental, vital, bodily instruments, or it may allow them to act according to their own nature and itself remain satisfied with self-experience and self-knowledge, with an inner liberation, an eventual freedom: but it may also and usually does exercise a certain authority, governance, influence on thought, life movement, physical action, a purifying uplifting control compelling them to move in a higher and purer truth of themselves, to obey or be an instrumentation of an influx of some diviner Power or a luminous direction which is not mental but spiritual and can be recognized as having a certain divine character—the inspiration of a greater Self or the command of the Ruler of all being, the Ishwara.[7] Or the nature may obey the psychic[8] entity's intimations, move in an inner light, follow an inner guidance. This is already a considerable evolution and amounts to a beginning at least of a psychic and spiritual transformation. But it is possible to go farther; for the spiritual being, once inwardly liberated, can develop in mind the higher states of being that are its own natural atmosphere and bring down a supramental energy and action which are proper to the Truth-consciousness; the ordinary mental instrumentation, life-instrumentation, physical instrumentation even, could then be entirely transformed and become parts no longer of an ignorance however much illumined, but of a supramental creation which would be the true action of a spiritual truth-consciousness and knowledge.

It must therefore be emphasized that spirituality is not a high intellectuality, not idealism, not an ethical turn of mind or moral purity and austerity, not religiosity or an ardent and exalted emotional fervour, not even a compound of all these excellent things; a mental belief, creed or faith, an emotional aspiration, a regulation of conduct according to a religious or ethical formula are not spiritual achievement and experience. These things are of considerable value to mind and life; they are of value to the spiritual evolution itself as preparatory movements disciplining, purifying or giving a suitable form to the nature; but they still belong to the mental evolution—the beginning of a spiritual realization, experience, change is not yet there. Spirituality is in its essence an awakening to the inner reality of our being, to a spirit, self, soul which is other than our mind, life and body, an inner aspiration to know, to feel, to be that, to enter into contact with the greater Reality beyond and pervading the universe which inhabits also our own being, to be in communion with It and union with It, and a turning, a conversion, a transformation of our whole being as a result of the aspiration, the contact, the union, a growth or waking into a new becoming or new being, a new self, a new nature.

LD.II, 24

NOTES*

1. Whether for the individual or the collectivity, Sri Aurobindo stresses the fundamental difference which exists between the true *Self*, immutable and free, one with the supreme *Self*, and the *ego*, a transient separative individual consciousness identified with the mind, vital and physical, open and more or less subject to the forces of all kinds belonging to these planes.

   In the evolution, the ego has a role of protection; it is necessary as long as the individual is not conscious of the true Self. But it becomes unnecessary when the psychic being, which is a delegate of the true Self, openly asserts itself, and in order that the psychic being may take possession of the nature, the ego has to abdicate and disappear.

2. *Ibid.*
3. *Ibid.*
4. Man is made up of a temporary surface personality and a deeper eternal soul with an individual Self (Jivatman) presiding from above. The personality has three principal parts: *body, life* and *mind.*

   The individual soul is called the *psychic being* by Sri Aurobindo. It stands, so to speak, behind mind, life and body, which are its instruments in the manifestation, and supports them at first in a veiled manner, then, as it grows, more and more openly.

   The psychic being is immortal while the body, the vital [power] and the mind are dissolved at death, or a little later. It passes from life to life, gathering the essence of its life experiences and makes that its basis of growth in the evolution of the individual through the ages.

   The true central being, the individual Self or Spirit (*Jivatman*), presides over the individual evolution, but it remains above the cosmic manifestation: it is not born nor does it evolve. It puts forward, as a representative of itself, the psychic being, which stands behind the manifestation in mind, life and body, and ensures the continuity of the individual evolution.

   The psychic being should not be confused with the vital being which governs the activities of life and is the seat of desires, passions and emotions. The true individual Self should also be distinguished from its distorted reflection, the *ego*. The ego, the little self, which regards itself as separate from others and from the world, is a physical, vital and mental formation; it belongs to the transitory personality and dissolves with it.

5. The present cosmic manifestation is the result of a double movement: *involution* and *evolution*. Involution is a process of self-limitation, of densification, by which the universal Consciousness-Force veils itself by stages until it assumes the appearance of a dense cosmic Inconscience. In this way a series of universal principles, worlds, or planes of consciousness have been created, each characterized by certain powers of consciousness.

---

* [These notes are supplied by P. B. Saint-Hilaire, editor of *The Future Evolution of Man.*]

The three superior planes of this universe are called *the planes of Sachchidananda*. They form universal and fundamental states of the spiritual Reality in which the unity of the Divine Existence, the power of the Divine Consciousness, the bliss of the Divine Delight of existence are put in front. They are far above the reach of normal human consciousness and experience.

Then comes an intermediate plane, called *the Supramental plane, or the plane of Supermind*. It can be characterized as a self-effectuating Truth-Consciousness.

The series of descending planes ends with
—*the mental plane* or plane of Mind,
—*the vital plane* or plane of Life,
—*the physical or material plane,* or plane of Matter.

In the physical plane the involution reaches its last stage in a total inconscience which becomes the starting point of a gradual evolution. This Inconscience is a stark and utter negation of the Spirit—an indeterminable original chaos, as it were.

In each plane all the powers of consciousness belonging to the planes above it are involved, so that all the powers of the original and universal Consciousness-Force are really involved or hidden even in the Inconscient.

These universal planes are worlds in themselves: they have their own forces, forms and beings. We are partly immersed in them and influenced by them (see Note 6 below [not included]), although it is only in the material plane that we have developed sense organs which bring the forces, forms and beings of the world of matter within our normal perception.

Evolution is an opposite process, by which the Consciousness-Force emerges again gradually from the apparent cosmic Inconscience and manifests its hidden powers.

Out of the Inconscient, *Matter* has been organized by the urge of the involved Consciousness-Force and under the pressure of the subtler forces of the physical plane. It has gradually developed into the physical cosmos as we know it. Matter, again by the working of the secret Consciousness-Force and that of the forces of the vital plane above, has produced *Life* and living physical beings: plants and animals. In the animal, once more by a double action, the forces of the mental plane have successfully fashioned an instrument permitting them to come in contact with Matter and organize it: *Mind* is born in the physical world and, with it Man, the self-conscious thinking animal. The next step of the ascent of the embodied consciousness will be taken under the pressure of the forces from the supramental plane: *Supermind* will emerge in the earthly manifestation. Sri Aurobindo's principal works are a comprehensive study of this new power of consciousness, the conditions of its emergence on earth and the resultant transformation of mankind.

"Mind, Life and Matter are the realized powers of the evolution and well-known to us; Supermind and the triune aspects of Sachchidananda are the secret principles which are not yet put in front and have still to be realized in the forms of the manifestation and we know them only by hints and a partial and fragmentary action still not disengaged from the lower movements and therefore not easily recognizable." (Sri Aurobindo, *The Life Divine,* II, 15).

It must be noted that, as Sri Aurobindo uses the terms, evolution is not exactly the reverse of involution. Evolution is not a withdrawing, a subtilization, plane after plane, leading to a reabsorption into the One Unmanifest. It takes place in Matter itself: it is a gradual emergence of higher powers of consciousness, leading to an ever greater manifestation of the divine Consciousness-Force *in the material universe*. This is the secret significance of the terrestrial evolution.

6. The Spirit is the Atman, Brahman, the essential Divine. When the One manifests the Many, that are always inherent in it, it assumes two aspects: *Purusha* and *Prakriti,* the Conscious Being or Soul, and Nature.

   The *Purusha* is the true being, or at least represents the true being, on whatever plane he manifests. But in ordinary man, he is covered by the ego and by the ignorant play of the Prakriti, and remains veiled as a 'witness' which upholds and observes the play of the Ignorance. When he emerges, he is perceived at first as a calm, immovable consciousness, detached from the play of Nature. Thereafter he gradually asserts himself as the sovereign Master of Prakriti. Even when he is covered up, he is always present. The emergence of Purusha is the beginning of liberation.

   What is commonly meant by *Prakriti* is Nature; it appears to be a play of unconscious and mechanical forces. But behind it is the ever present living Consciousness and Force of the Divine: the divine Shakti. Truly speaking Nature is only the outer or executive aspects of the Shakti or Conscious Force that forms and moves the worlds.

   It can be said also that *Nature* is only the lower Prakriti, the Prakriti of mind, life and matter. There exists also a Higher Prakriti (Paraprakriti), the *Supernature* or divine Nature of the Sachchidananda, which has the power of manifesting the Supermind and remains always conscious of the Divine and free from Ignorance and its consequences.

7. *Ishwara,* the Divine as Lord and Master of the universe, and *Shakti,* the conscious creative Power, form of a fundamental duality somewhat different from the *Purusha-Prakriti* duality (Note 8, above [Note 6]). Purusha and Prakriti are separate powers, while Ishwara and Shakti are contained in each other. Ishwara is Purusha who contains Prakriti and rules by the power of the Shakti within him. Shakti is Prakriti ensouled by Purusha and acts by the will of the Ishwara, whose presence in her movements she carries always with her.

   The Shakti of the Ishwara (*Ishwari-Shakti*) is the divine *Consciousness-Force* or *World-Mother*, who contains all and carries all within herself, and to manifest it in Time and Space is her role. She thus appears as the mediatrix between the eternal One and the manifested Many.

   These two dualities, as also the third fundamental duality *Brahman-Maya*, correspond to different spiritual experiences or realizations in Yoga (see *The Synthesis of Yoga,* Part II, Chapter IV, and *The Life Divine,* Vol. II, Chapter II).

8. See footnote 4.

7. Modern Technology as an Expression of Rebellion, E. Brunner

Emil Brunner, a neo-orthodox Swiss Protestant theologian (whom we have read before in Chapter I), renders a more severe verdict on technology than does Sri Aurobindo. Although he points to roughly the same set of problems as Aurobindo, Brunner's view of their religious significance is different.
Our problems, he insists, arise not merely from the disproportion between man's technology and his spiritual development, but from an impulse that is positively evil. Man is attempting to replace God. According to Brunner, man has turned technics (his God-given capacity to make things) into technology (a presumed science of self-redemption). For faithful man, he argues, technics would have been an unqualified boon. But because of his perverted use of it, man, like the Zauberlehrling (sorcerer's apprentice), is caught by the destructive energies of his own creations. And from this dilemma, there can be no escape through further reliance on his technical skills.
Do you perceive the role of the technological revolution since the 18th century as changing man's self image toward a destructive egotism? Do you recognize the dangers of technology in dehumanizing man? What does Brunner mean by the "world-voracity" of modern man? Are you impressed by the fact that Brunner wrote this over twenty years ago, before many people were aware of the crisis of which he speaks? What solution to the problem does Brunner suggest?

. . . Amongst all the problems of civilisation with which we are dealing in these lectures, the problem of "technics" is the youngest. All the others have worried Western mankind and Christianity for centuries; not so technics. In earlier times people had hardly become conscious of it, much less did they think of it as a problem. To-day, however, it is in the front line, because—to a degree previously unheard of—technics—or shall I say technology?—determines the life of man, endangers the human character of civilisation, and even threatens the very existence of mankind. Whilst half a century ago the startling progress of technology was the basis of an optimistic philosophy of life and progress, since the two world wars, and particularly since the first atomic bomb was dropped on Hiroshima, the conception of technics has become more and more connected with gloomy, even desperate, perspectives for the future. . . . Whether civilisation and mankind will survive has become *the* problem of the hour, so that we cannot but start with it.

This fact—that technology has recently become the most urgent of all problems—contrasts strangely with the other fact that technics is as old as humanity. Human history begins with the invention of the first stone tool, that is, with technics. It is in the shape of *homo faber** that man first shows himself as a being transcending nature. From this beginning technics, that is, the creation and use of artificial tools serving the life of man, has increasingly distinguished man's life from that of the animal, and imprinted upon it a specifically human character. The history of technics from its beginning to, say, the time of James Watt, is characterised by an almost unbroken, more or less equable and, therefore, quite unobtrusive progress. Step by step man makes headway in solving the task which he recognises as his own, to subdue nature by his technical inventions.

We distinguish the first epochs of human history by their technical character, speaking of the stone age, the bronze age and the iron age, where an almost unnoticeable transition from one to the other makes the distinction difficult. The same is true of what we call historical man, as we find him first in the Delta of the Nile, in Mesopotamia, in the great valleys of China and of India, where the history of civilisation has its origin. Everywhere the development of technics is the hardly perceptible and therefore often forgotten basis of political, social and cultural change. Nowhere does this technical evolution assume a revolutionary aspect, never does it appear as a break with the past. All epochs and all nations in history are equally technical and therefore none is so in an outstanding sense. That is true also of Western history as it first appears as a characteristic unity in the Roman Empire; it is true of the Middle Ages and up to the beginning of the 18th century; but at that moment it is as if this underground current suddenly broke through the surface. The curve of development which hitherto had been a continuously and almost imperceptibly rising straight line, abruptly takes the form of a parabola becoming steeper and steeper. Technology begins to become a great revolutionary power and within the last few decades it has taken the lead in the life of the Western nations, and even of the whole world. It has become the dominating factor of modern civilisation. The changes which technology has wrought in the last two centuries are beyond all comparison with those in previous ages. That is why our epoch is called the age of technics, and why the problem of technology, unknown to previous epochs, has suddenly become the most urgent problem of all.

Why is this so? We *might* answer this question first by pointing to the tempo of technical inventions and the changes created by them. The mad speed of technical progress makes mankind breathless; with one invention pressing fast on another, man cannot get any rest. The growth of technics is out of proportion to the progress made in other departments of life, and puts to shame all attempts of society to adapt itself to the technical change

---

* Man as maker (of tools).

in order to make it useful and beneficent. It is like what happens when a youth suddenly begins to grow at a great pace. His spiritual development cannot keep pace with his bodily growth and therefore there are disturbances. There is a disproportion between bodily and spiritual growth, the one taking place at the cost of the other. This comparison, with its emphasis on the time-aspect of technical evolution, is certainly legitimate. It is true that technical evolution and change acquired such a speed that the balance of power within society was disturbed and that the social changes, which would have been necessary to adapt life to them, could not be made adequately. We might say that the mushroom growth of giant cities, with their apparent poverty of structure and their production of a mass-society and mass-psychology, was a kind of surprise-effect produced by lack of time for adaptation. In a similar way, one can attribute the preponderance of technical interest in our generation to this speedy development of technics.

But such an analysis remains wholly on the surface. More than that: it falsifies the picture of real history by making the cause the effect and the effect the cause. This idea of social adaptation lagging behind technical progress rather hides than reveals the truth. It is not technics which has created the modern man, but it is the modern man who has created technics. The technical man existed before technics. Take as an example the most famous novel hero of the age immediately preceding the technical revolution, Robinson Crusoe. Compare Robinson Crusoe with his colleague in suffering, Ulysses. How differently they face their identical lot of being cast by shipwreck on a solitary island! There is not much difference, technically, between Robinson Crusoe and Odysseus. Perhaps the most important difference is that Defoe's hero, in distinction from Homer's, has and uses gunpowder. But the main difference is this, and this is exactly what Defoe wants to show: how Crusoe masters technically his hopeless condition. This is the inspiring idea which has made the book a favorite of youth: the idea of the man who helps himself out of the difficulties, the man who—ingenious in quite another sense than Ulysses—is capable of subduing hostile nature step by step.

Behind the technical evolution of the last two hundred years there is a much deeper spiritual process, with which the first part of these lectures has dealt. This process begins with the Renaissance, leading on to the Enlightenment, and beyond it to the radically positivist secularised man of to-day. Modern technics is the product of the man who wants to redeem himself by rising above nature, who wants to gather life into his hand, who wants to owe his existence to nobody but himself, who wants to create a world after his own image, an artificial world which is entirely his creation. Behind the terrifying, crazy tempo of technical evolution, there is all the insatiability of secularised man who, not believing in God or eternal life, wants to snatch as much of this world within his lifetime as he can. Modern technics is, to put it crudely, the expression of the world-voracity of modern man, and the tempo of its development is the expression of his inward unrest, the disquiet of the man who is destined for God's eternity, but has himself rejected this destiny. The hypertrophy of technical interest, resulting in a hyper-dynamism of technical evolution, is the necessary consequence of man's abandonment to the world of things, which follows his emancipation from God.

Let us return for a moment to those quiet periods which nobody would call technical, though even then technics had reached a high measure of development and was incessantly progressive. What do we mean by "technics"? In the first place, domination over nature, emancipation from its hazards by intensifying and multiplying the functions of bodily organs. The hammer and the crane are the fortified fist and the prolonged arm, the car is the improved foot, and so on. The whole of technics is a continuation of what nature has given to man as his particular character: upright walk. That is why technics is, as such, a task given to man by the Creator, that Creator who gave man the upright spine and thereby the freedom of the use of his hands and the eye directed to infinitude. God wants man to use his intelligence in order to rise above nature and *"subdue the earth."* This phrase is found on the first page of the Bible. It immediately follows that other phrase in which the specific nature and destiny of man is expressed: *"and God created man in His own image."* It is not by chance that the second precedes the first. The task of subduing the earth follows from the first. The task of subduing the earth follows from the nature and the destiny given to man by the Creator. It is most likely that the author of this first chapter of Genesis was thinking of the upright walk of man, but this physical presupposition of his superiority is the expression of a deeper reason for superiority. Man is called to transcend nature, because he is called to be godlike. Technics is only one of the forms of nature-transcendence, but it is that which presupposes the others, higher civilisation and spiritual life.

So long as man does not use artificial means, he remains dependent on what nature gives, here and now. That is, he necessarily remains on a low, more or less animal, level of development. He is completely at the mercy of natural hazard and tied to the moment; he cannot look into the future, he cannot shape his life, he must live it as nature gives it. By the invention of artificial tools, man emancipates himself to a certain degree from the dictates of nature. The technics of housebuilding and agriculture make him independent of what nature gives at each particular time and place. With a roof over his head and four walls around him, he can defy the weather and live where he chooses. By agriculture he dictates to the earth what to produce for him and to produce it in such a measure that he can store up enough for the future. He makes water or wind drive his mill. He captures the wind in his sail and forces it to carry him over the seas. The spinning-wheel and the loom make him independent of the scarce animal-skins for clothing. One by one he cuts the thousand ties by which his body and its needs are linked to the fortuitous formation and production of the ground. The development of crafts of all sorts leads to differentiation of human society and to the specialised training and development of spiritual capacities; it leads to exchange, to the communal life of the city, to communication between town and town, between country and country. The crafts are at the same time a preparation for higher arts and, in the form of artistic trade, they play their part in aesthetic ennoblement.

Technical skill can be learned and, therefore, transmitted from generation to generation. That is why in this sphere of life there is an unambiguous and more or less continuous progress. Each generation learns from the one before and adds new inventions. In this process of technical education the mind is trained for methodical work. The multiplicity of crafts makes for a rich differentiation of the spirit. It cannot be denied that cities, with their differentiated crafts, are pre-eminently the seats and nurseries of higher culture and education. All these organic types of technics—if I may so call them—are easily forgotten in our age of highly abstract mechanical and therefore inhuman technics. But they belong to the true picture and show the close relation between technics and truly human civilisation.

Even in this picture of pre-modern technics, however, there are traits of a more sinister quality. Closely related to the tool, and often expressed by the same word, is the weapon. The development of crafts almost everywhere gives rise to the development of war technics. There are exceptions to this rule, one of the most interesting being that of the older China, where an almost unique development of crafts did not lead to a parallel development of war technics, because war and fighting were stigmatised, culturally and morally. Not even the invention of gunpowder, which in Europe had such pernicious consequences, could be come dangerous among this peaceful people. The moral discredit of war was so deep that gunpowder was never allowed to be used for war purposes, and its dangerous energy was puffed out in harmless fire-works. But apart from this most honourable exception, the development of technics generally resulted in increasingly dangerous weapons and wars. The Roman technics of road-building was developed primarily for military purposes. The technics of shipbuilding created the navy, and so on. Still, all this remained within limits which prevented technics from being the dominating potential of war.

Another danger to society resulting from technical development is the formation of social classes. Technical, like military, superiority creates differences of property, social privilege and power. These differences, however, so far as they were conditioned by technics, did not become very dangerous in the premodern ages, because it was not so difficult to acquire technical skill and technical means. From all this, we can conclude that on the whole the positive, beneficial aspects of technical progress by far outweighed the negative or evil ones. In the "golden age of the crafts" nobody would have thought of technics as a serious danger or even a problem of civilisation.

All this is suddenly changed with the introduction of machine technics. It had a sort of prelude in the invention of gunpowder and its application to warfare. The consequences of this invention were far-reaching and could give a premonition of what further similar leaps in the development might mean. It is strange and somehow shameful that Christian Europe did not succeed in doing—perhaps did not even attempt to do— what had been achieved by the Chinese. At any rate, with gunpowder, technics begin to acquire a negative trait in European history. But incomparably more revolutionary was the invention of the steam engine and the locomotive, and later on the discovery and technical use of electricity and of petrol, the invention of light metals and the development of chemistry. Now begins the technical age. As we said before, we should not look upon these inventions as the real causes of the technical revolution; they had to come, because men wanted them. They had to develop at such an unparalleled rate, because men did not want to limit their development in any way. Still, once technics had become what it is now, its effects upon the social and spiritual life of mankind are tremendous.

It has often been said, and it is obviously true, that all the technical changes which took place in the life of men from the stone age to James Watt are not nearly as great as those since James Watt. The life of a farmer or craftsman before the invention of the steam engine was not so different from that of Jeremiah's time as from that under modern agriculture and industry. Machine industry in the broadest sense of the word, including transport and communication, has changed not only the life of Europe and America, but that of the whole surface of the world, in a tempo and in a measure completely unparalleled before.

This technical revolution has its positive as well as its negative side. By it man has indeed subdued the earth in a measure inconceivable before. By the radio he has eliminated distance completely, so far as mental communication is concerned; by the aeroplane he has eliminated it almost completely, so far as bodily communication is concerned. The techniques of production are capable of nourishing, clothing, housing every inhabitant of this earth in more than sufficient degree and with almost complete certainty. Hunger and want are no more inevitable. That they are still amongst us is entirely conditioned by political, social, international power-relations, preventing the reasonable use of technical possibilities. Medical and hygienic techniques would be sufficient to create everywhere conditions of life which would guarantee to a high degree a healthy life and development of the child and double the average age of man. The invention of cinema and radio, perfecting that of the printing-press, allows an almost unlimited spreading of cultural assets. In a measure then, present day technics places at the disposal of man the means which would safeguard a high standard of life and give access to cultural advantages to everyone capable of understanding and valuing them. Technical mankind has a superabundance of all things needed, and a superabundance of means to transport them wherever they are needed. If there were no war, if there were only just and reasonable laws, if all men were well-intentioned, technics would provide, so it seems, almost a paradise. The technicians can claim that it is not their fault if, at this hour more than ever before, mankind presents features of the utmost misery and the most unworthy conditions. All this is meant by the phrase "technical progress," which up to recent years was used without hesitation. It seems as if technics—and particularly modern technics—was an indisputable gain for mankind.

Why is it, then, that nobody at this hour uses that word "progress" without hesitation, if at all? Let us be clear that there is no such thing as "technics in itself." The production of a cannon is a technical affair, but at the same time it is the expression of a certain political and military will. The production of dangerous narcotics is a matter of chemical industry, but it serves purposes which are medically and morally unsound and pernicious. Technics, therefore, is never purely technical. It always stands in the closest connection with the totality of social and cultural life and of man himself. "Technics" is an abstraction which does not exist. There are only men working technically for certain purposes. When modern man conceived the idea of redeeming himself and making himself master of his life by technics, he did not know or divine that such technics would have results of a very different order. What, then, are those effects of the technical revolution which an increasing majority of modern men abhor?

Modern technics does not mean merely a fantastic extension of man's power over nature; it also means millions of men working underground, uncounted millions of men massed together in soulless giant cities; a proletariat without connection with nature, without a native heath or neighbourhood; it means asphalt-culture, uniformity and standardisation. It means men whom the machine has relieved from thinking and willing, who in their turn have to "serve the machine" at a prescribed tempo and in a stereotyped manner. It means unbearable noise and rush, unemployment and insecurity of life, the concentration of productive power, wealth and prestige in a few hands or their monopolisation by state bureaucracy. It means the destruction of noble crafts with their standards of quality and their patriarchal working conditions; it means the transformation of the farmer into a specialised technician of agriculture, the rise of an office proletariat with infinitely monotonous work. It means also the speedy standardisation of all national cultures and the extinction of their historical originality. It means universal cliché-culture, the same films and musical hits from New York to Tokyo, from Cape Town to Stockholm, the same illustrated magazines all over the world, the same menus, the same dance-tunes. It means the increasing domination of quantity over quality, not only in production itself but also in the formation of social, political and international power.

Above all, there are two phenomena in very recent times which, like devilish monsters, rise from that progressively technified mankind: the modern totalitarian state and modern technical war industry. It cannot be said that the totalitarian state is the necessary product of technics, but its relation to technics is obvious. Without modern technics the totalitarian state is impossible. And the tendency towards totalitarianism lies within technical evolution: mechanisation, centralisation, mass-men. Modern war industry, however, is the direct product of modern technics. Let us remember it is not the technicians that are guilty, but man who has abandoned technics to itself, incapable of bridling its development, putting technics without hesitation, and, as if driven by necessity, at the service of his political power-aims. This war machinery displayed its terrifying force in the first world war. The second world war manifested its increased destructive force; but since then there has come that last step or leap: the use of atomic energy, which means a sudden increase in the capacity of annihilation without analogy in the previous history of technics. Now the development of technical warfare has reached the point where nothing is impossible to it. Mankind for the first time faces possible universal suicide.

This is the other, the dark side of the picture. It shows how dangerous it is to speak of technics *in abstracto*. One could have known from the history of technics that every technical advance does not change merely man's relation to nature, but also man's relation to man. Every invention is an increase in power, and every increase in power within society is a danger to its balance and order. This fact could remain unnoticed so long as technical progress could be assimilated socially and ethically. It is the tragic fact of modern history that the technical revolution took place at a time when mankind was in a process of social dissolution and ethical confusion. It was the era of progressive secularisation and mass-atheism, when all ethical standards were relativised and men became metaphysically and ethically homeless. Cause and effect mutually interpenetrate each other. We have already seen that modern technics could not have developed without a certain spirit of rationalism and secularisation. It is, however, equally true that secularised humanity was not socially and ethically equal to the technical revolution. Only a society which was incapable of subordinating the profit motive to higher motives, a society which was ethically, and even aesthetically callous and enfeebled, could allow the growth of those soulless, ugly, giant cities, with their speculative building and their proletarian quarters. Only such a society could watch without protest the dissolution of all natural community, and accept as inevitable the development of modern war technics.

In this connection we have to point out grave fault on the part of the Christian Church. The Church ought to have been on the watch-tower. She ought to have seen what was going on behind those beautiful slogans of freedom and progress. The Church might have been expected to protect men from enslavement and from becoming automatons. The Church ought to have seen that in such conditions, which upset all the order of creation, the preaching of the Gospel became almost illusory. Is it not shameful for the Christian society that Confucian China was capable of suppressing the military use of gunpowder, while the Christian Church could not prevent, and did not even try to prevent, the development of a war machinery incomparably more dreadful?

European industrial history is not altogether devoid of indications of what might have happened if modern industry had developed within a truly Christian society. I am thinking of a certain phase in the industrial development of Great Britain and Switzerland. Within a few decades of the invention of the steam engine these countries experienced a physical and social devastation within the working population which was definitely alarming. But then moral and religious forces reacted and were called to the defence. By social legislation, by the trade-union and co-operative movements, and by something like an awakening of social consciousness through prophetic personalities, much of the damage was repaired in a comparatively short time. What had been called technical necessity proved quite unnecessary. The techniques of fabrication, so often regarded as being beyond ethical control, was effectively put under such control. Many things remained bad enough, but yet the effect of this ethical-social reaction against the technical materialistic *laissez-faire* gives us a faint idea of what could have been avoided if society had awakened in time to the ethical dangers of so-called progress.

Nobody can say how far the disease of uncontrolled, unassimilated technics has progressed already, whether the disease has reached the point where it becomes incurable or not. It is our duty, however, to open our eyes to the imminent threat to life and to do whatever we can to make technics serve human ends.

The nature of technics is to place at man's disposal the means for certain purposes. Of course, the production and use of technical means is in itself a purpose, but it is never a *Selbstzweck,* an ultimate purpose. It is essential to the health of a society that this order of ends and means should be known and recognised, so that technics as the sum of means is subordinated to man's life. Where the means become more important than the end, where technics becomes autonomous, a social disease develops, which is analogous to cancer: autonomous growths, not useful but injurious to the organism, which develop independently of the organic centre and finally destroy the organism. When, for instance, a country rejoices over the growth of a city of millions of inhabitants, this is as stupid as if someone were to rejoice over the growth of a cancer. Giant cities are merely symptoms, but they are obvious symptoms of autonomous technical growth which finally leads to destruction.

The positive meaning of a human civilisation depends on this subordination of means to ends. The reversal of this order, therefore, results in civilisation becoming inhuman and finally perverted. For this reversal of the order of ends and means, which produces a demonic autonomy of technics, secularisation is more to blame than technics. It is because the world and its goods become to men more important than God, eternal life and love, that men throw themselves into the production of material goods with that passion of which the human soul, destined for infinitude, is capable. Technics was merely the means by which this insatiable desire for material goods could be, or seemed to be, stilled, because technics is capable of unlimited development. Once brought into action, this process of unlimited increase and expansion could no longer be controlled. The machine invented by man began to control man's will; whether he liked it or not he had to obey the logic of technical development. It was exactly as in Goethe's symbolic ballad, *Der Zauberlehrling,* about the spying apprentice who had found out his wizard master's magic word which summoned obedient spirits to his service. For a while he revelled in the service of the water-carrying spirits; but before long he became afraid, because the spirits could no longer be controlled, so that by their very service the poor apprentice was in peril of being drowned—*Die ich rief, die Geister,*

*wered ich nun nicht los**—a catastrophe from which the master's intervention saved him. This is very like our situation. Man has learned to
control the immeasurable powers of nature. Modern man dominates nature
to a degree unthinkable in previous ages. But whilst man controls nature
by technics he no longer controls his own technics, but is more and more
more dominated by it and threatened with catastrophe.

Last century saw the climax of technical enthusiasm and of belief in
progress by technics. It was then that people hoped technics would relieve
man of all impediments and troubles connected with his body. "Our saviour
is the machine," ran a sentence in a German newspaper. This enthusiasm
for technics can still take hold of peoples whose technical development has
lagged behind that of Western Europe. It can develop the more where the
ground is prepared by secularist thinking which recognises only earthly and
material goods. In Western Europe, however, this enthusiasm has been
followed by disillusionment, deep despondency and fear. The first part of
the story of the *Zauberlehrling* is finished. The second part is in full
process and, since the invention of the atomic bomb, is approaching its
climax.

Such disillusionment and despair might bring about a real turn of
the pendulum in the right direction, but only if man is capable of understanding something of the deeper causes of this fatal, automatic development of technics, if he comes to see the false order of means and ends—
that is, secularisation, loss of faith in God and in eternal values—as the
root of the whole matter. All other proposals to make technics subservient
again to human ends, and all attempts to heal the damage to social and
personal life produced by the technical revolution, are mere palliatives. I
do not mean that they are worthless, they may even be necessary, as the
treatment of symptoms—such as fighting the fever—is often necessary
until more radical therapy can begin. But unless there is a basic conversion,
technics will develop as before, and the tempo of its development will not
decrease but increase, because nowadays men not only make inventions but
have found the technique of making inventions. For this reason, all cor-
rections coming from outside always come too late. The crazy tempo of
technical revolution can only be reduced to a degree which is socially and
personally supportable, if the whole scale of values of European nations can
be changed. As long as material values indisputably take the first place, no
change for the better is to be expected.

The perversion of the order of means and ends was caused by the
decay of the consciousness of personality. And this in its turn was the
consequence of the decay of Christian faith. In our time many have come
to see, and are ready to admit, that moral values ought to be put in the
first place. This insight is good, but not sufficient. Mere ethics has never
displayed real dynamic. You cannot cure a demon-ridden technical world
with moral postulates. In contrast to mere ethics and morality, Christian
faith has the dynamic of passion, of surrender and sacrifice; it is capable

---

* The spirits whom I called upon, I now cannot get rid of.

of turning men to the eternal end, of unmasking demonic sin and thereby banning it, which no enlightened education is capable of doing.

Technics in itself is no problem for the Christian man. As long as technics is subordinate to human will, and human will is obedient to the divine will, technics is neutral, and as a means of goodwill is itself good. From the Christian point of view, there is no reason to condemn the machine and to return to the spinning-wheel. Even the use of atomic energy is not in itself harmful or bad. But we can hardly avoid the question whether technical evolution has not already passed the limits within which it is controllable by feeble, mortal men. This question cannot be theoretically decided. It is a question of the real dynamic. For us the only important question is whether mankind is ready, or may become ready, to perform that inward right-about-turn which alone will correct the fatal perversion of the order of means and ends.

VIII

Enjoyment of the Full Life Through Sensuous Experiences

For two thousand years or more man has been subjected to a systematic effort to transform him into an ascetic animal. He remains a pleasure-seeking animal. Parental discipline, religious denunciation of bodily pleasure, and philosophic exaltation of the life of reason have all left man overtly docile, but secretly in his unconscious unconvinced, and therefore neurotic. Man remains unconvinced because in infancy he tasted the fruit of the tree of life, and knows that it is good, and never forgets it. (Norman O. Brown, Life Against Death: The Psychoanalytical Meaning of History *[New York: Random House, Vintage Books, 1959], p. 31.)*

IN THE PRECEDING THREE CHAPTERS we have explored the possibilities for ultimate transformation which might lie in interpersonal relations (Chapter V), political and economic structures (Chapter VI), and technology (Chapter VII). Different as these three types are from each other, all presuppose the existence of some society within which the believer must act if he is to realize the transformation in question. In this last chapter we return to a theme sounded in Chapters I and IV—the possibility of transformation arising from experiences that are essentially personal. Like believers in Chapters I and IV, the advocates for this religious type find justification, direction, and power for their lives from experiences that are private in that only they can fully appreciate their meaning. Unlike more traditional believers, however, these find the power that transforms neither in some Holy One (Chapter I) nor in the discipline by which one attains special states of awareness (Chapter IV), but in man's natural sensuousness. Through the development of this capacity they seek to overcome the threats posed by the experience of emotional sterility, lifelessness, alienation, and atrophy of feeling. In perfect, *physical* communion with the world, they seek the fullness of life.

ADVOCACY

1. The Religion of Man,
R. Tagore

*Rabindranath Tagore (1861–1941), a prolific author and poet,
received the Nobel Prize in Literature in 1913. Raised in
Bengal, India, he studied law in England and traveled widely
in many parts of the world. Although he was consciously aloof
from the religion of his day, he was led by a recurring,
vivid sense of the world's beauty to a set of personal convictions
which he refers to as a "religion of man." What is important
for the presence of his account in this chapter is not so much
its content (much of which reflects themes of traditional Indian
thought) as its foundation in sensuous, personal experience.
Note the imagery in which he expresses his thought. He speaks
of the "wonder of the gathering clouds hanging heavy with
the unshed rain," the sense of "serene exaltation." He speaks
of experiencing "a current of feeling," an experience like a
"sudden spring breeze" in which he overcomes "the invisible
screen of the commonplace," of moments in which his mind
"touched the creative realm of expression" in which he received
"gladness [as] the one criterion of truth." It is this freedom
from convention combined with an openness to the wonder of
one's experienced world that leads us to agree with him
when he speaks of his religion as "a poet's religion." In what
realm does man live besides that of geography and history?
How does he define beauty? What is the artist's test for truth?
Would you agree that it is more profound than that of the scientist?
(Considering again the relation between Chapters I and VIII,
it is interesting to note that the Vaishnava sect that influenced
Tagore is the religious group from which the hymn excerpted from
"In Praise of Krishna"—found in Chapter I—comes.)*

Man has made the entire geography of the earth his own, ignoring the
boundaries of climate; for, unlike the lion and the reindeer, he has the
power to create his special skin and temperature, including his unscrupulous power of borrowing the skins of the indigenous inhabitants and mis-
appropriating their fats.

His kingdom is also continually extending in time through a great sur-

---

plus in his power of memory, to which is linked his immense facility of borrowing the treasure of the past from all quarters of the world. He dwells in a universe of history, in an environment of continuous remembrance. The animal occupies time only through the multiplication of its own race, but man through the memorials of his mind, raised along the pilgrimage of progress. The stupendousness of his knowledge and wisdom is due to their roots spreading into and drawing sap from the far-reaching area of history.

Man has his other dwelling-place in the realm of inner realization, in the element of an immaterial value. This is a world where from the subterranean soil of his mind his consciousness often, like a seed, unexpectedly sends up sprouts into the heart of a luminous freedom, and the individual is made to realize his truth in the universal Man. I hope it may prove of interest if I give an account of my own personal experience of a sudden spiritual outburst from within me which is like the underground current of a perennial stream unexpectedly welling up on the surface.

I was born in a family which, at that time, was earnestly developing a monotheistic religion based upon the philosophy of the Upanishad.* Somehow my mind at first remained coldly aloof, absolutely uninfluenced by any religion whatever. It was through an idiosyncrasy of my temperament that I refused to accept any religious teaching merely because people in my surroundings believed it to be true. I could not persuade myself to imagine that I had a religion because everybody whom I might trust believed in its value.

Thus my mind was brought up in an atmosphere of freedom—freedom from the dominance of any creed that had its sanction in the definite authority of some scripture, or in the teaching of some organized body of worshippers. And, therefore, the man who questions me has every right to distrust my vision and reject my testimony. In such a case, the authority of some particular book venerated by a large number of men may have greater weight than the assertion of an individual, and therefore I never claim any right to preach.

When I look back upon those days, it seems to me that unconsciously I followed the path of my Vedic** ancestors, and was inspired by the tropical sky with its suggestion of an uttermost Beyond. The wonder of the gathering clouds hanging heavy with the unshed rain, of the sudden sweep of storms arousing vehement gestures along the line of coconut trees, the fierce loneliness of the blazing summer noon, the silent sunrise behind the dewy veil of autumn morning, kept my mind with the intimacy of a pervasive companionship.

Then came my initiation ceremony of Brahminhood when the *gayatri* verse of meditation*** was given to me, whose meaning, according to the explanation I had, runs as follows:

---

* A group of texts embodying the mystical teaching of ancient Hindu philosophy.
** The Vedas are the earliest sacred expression of the Aryan Indians.
*** One of the most sacred verses from the Rig-veda.

Let me contemplate the adorable splendour of Him who created the earth, the air and the starry spheres, and sends the power of comprehension within our minds.

This produced a sense of serene exaltation in me, the daily meditation upon the infinite being which unites in one stream of creation my mind and the outer world. Though to-day I find no difficulty in realizing this being as an infinite personality in whom the subject and object are perfectly reconciled, at that time the idea to me was vague. Therefore the current of feeling that it aroused in my mind was indefinite, like the circulation of air—an atmosphere which needed a definite world to complete itself and satisfy me. For it is evident that my religion is a poet's religion, and neither that of an orthodox man of piety nor that of a theologian. Its touch comes to me through the same unseen and trackless channel as does the inspiration of my songs. My religious life has followed the same mysterious line of growth as has my poetical life. Somehow they are wedded to each other and, though their betrothal had a long period of ceremony, it was kept secret to me.

When I was eighteen, a sudden spring breeze of religious experience for the first time came to my life and passed away leaving in my memory a direct message of spiritual reality. One day while I stood watching at early dawn the sun sending out its rays from behind the trees, I suddenly felt as if some ancient mist had in a moment lifted from my sight, and the morning light on the face of the world revealed an inner radiance of joy. The invisible screen of the commonplace was removed from all things and all men, and their ultimate significance was intensified in my mind; and this is the definition of beauty. That which was memorable in this experience was its human message, the sudden expansion of my consciousness in the super-personal world of man. The poem I wrote on the first day of my surprise was named "The Awakening of the Waterfall." The waterfall, whose spirit lay dormant in its ice-bound isolation, was touched by the sun and, bursting in a cataract of freedom, it found its finality in an unending sacrifice, in a continual union with the sea. After four days the vision passed away, and the lid hung down upon my inner sight. In the dark, the world once again put on its disguise of the obscurity of an ordinary fact.

When I grew older and was employed in a responsible work in some villages I took my place in a neighbourhood where the current of time ran slow and joys and sorrows had their simple and elemental shades and lights. The day which had its special significance for me came with all its drifting trivialities of the commonplace life. The ordinary work of my morning had come to its close, and before going to take my bath I stood for a moment at my window, overlooking a market-place on the bank of a dry river bed, welcoming the first flood of rain along its channel. Suddenly I became conscious of a stirring of soul within me. My world of experience in a moment seemed to become lighted, and facts that were detached and dim found a great unity of meaning. The feeling which I had was like that which a man, groping through a fog without knowing his destination, might feel when he suddenly discovers that he stands before his own house.

I still remember the day in my childhood when I was made to struggle across my lessons in a first primer, strewn with isolated words smothered under the burden of spelling. The morning hour appeared to me like a once-illumined page, grown dusty and faded, discoloured into irrelevant marks, smudges and gaps, wearisome in its moth-eaten meaninglessness. Suddenly I came to a rhymed sentence of combined words, which may be translated thus—"It rains, the leaves tremble." At once I came to a world wherein I recovered my full meaning. My mind touched the creative realm of expression, and at that moment I was no longer a mere student with his mind muffled by spelling lessons, enclosed by classroom. The rhythmic picture of the tremulous leaves beaten by the rain opened before my mind the world which does not merely carry information, but a harmony with my being. The unmeaning fragments lost their individual isolation and my mind revelled in the unity of a vision. In a similar manner, on that morning in the village the facts of my life suddenly appeared to me in a luminous unity of truth. All things that had seemed like vagrant waves were revealed to my mind in relation to a boundless sea. I felt sure that some Being who comprehended me and my world was seeking his best expression in all my experiences, uniting them into an ever-widening individuality which is a spiritual work of art.

To this Being I was responsible; for the creation in me is his as well as mine. It may be that it was the same creative Mind that is shaping the universe to its eternal idea; but in me as a person it had one of its special centres of a personal relationship growing into a deepening consciousness. I had my sorrows that left their memory in a long burning track across my days, but I felt at that moment that in them I lent myself to a travail of creation that ever exceeded my own personal bounds like stars which in their individual fire-bursts are lighting the history of the universe. It gave me a great joy to feel in my life detachment at the idea of a mystery of a meeting of the two in a creative comradeship. I felt that I had found my religion at last, the religion of Man, in which the infinite became defined in humanity and came close to me so as to need my love and co-operation.

This idea of mine found at a later date its expression in some of my poems addressed to what I called *Jivan devata,* the Lord of my life. Fully aware of my awkwardness in dealing with a foreign language, with some hesitation I give a translation, being sure that any evidence revealed through the self-recording instrument of poetry is more authentic than answers extorted through conscious questionings.

> Thou who art the innermost Spirit of my being,
> art thou pleased,
> > Lord of my Life?
> For I gave to thee my cup
> filled with all the pain and delight

that the crushed grapes of my heart had surrendered,
I wove with the rhythm of colours and songs the cover
   for thy bed,
and with the molten gold of my desires
I fashioned playthings for thy passing hours.

I know not why thou chosest me for thy partner,
   Lord of my life!
Didst thou store my days and nights,
my deeds and dreams for the alchemy of thy art,
and string in the chain of thy music my songs of autumn
   and spring,
and gather the flowers from my mature moments for thy
   crown?

I see thine eyes gazing at the dark of my heart,
   Lord of my Life,
I wonder if my failures and wrongs are forgiven.
For many were my days without service
and nights of forgetfulness;
futile were the flowers that faded in the shade not offered
   to thee.
Often the tired strings of my lute
slackened at the strain of thy tunes.
And often at the ruin of wasted hours
my desolate evenings were filled with tears.

But have my days come to their end at last,
   Lord of my life,
while my arms round thee grow limp,
my kisses losing their truth?
Then break up the meeting of this languid day.
Renew the old in me in fresh forms of delight;
and let the wedding come once again
in a new ceremony of life.

You will understand from this how unconsciously I had been travelling toward the realization which I stumbled upon in an idle moment on a day in July, when morning clouds thickened on the eastern horizon and a caressing shadow lay on the tremulous bamboo branches, while an excited group of village boys was noisily dragging from the bank an old fishing-boat; and I cannot tell how at that moment an unexpected train of thoughts ran across my mind like a strange caravan carrying the wealth of an unknown kingdom.

From my infancy I had a keen sensitiveness which kept my mind tingling with consciousness of the world around me, natural and human. We had a small garden attached to our house; it was a fairyland to me, where miracles of beauty were of everyday occurrence....

I had been blessed with that sense of wonder which gives a child his right of entry into the treasure house of mystery in the depth of existence. My studies in the school I neglected, because they rudely dismembered me from the context of my world and I felt miserable, like a caged rabbit in a biological institute. This, perhaps, will explain the meaning of my religion. This world was living to me, intimately close to my life, permeated by a subtle touch of kinship which enhanced the value of my own being.

It is true that this world also has its impersonal aspect of truth which is pursued by the man of impersonal science. . . .

The details of reality must be studied in their differences by Science, but it can never know the character of the grand unity of relationship pervading it, which can only be realized immediately by the human spirit. And therefore it is the primal imagination of man—the imagination which is fresh and immediate in its experiences—that exclaims in a poet's verse:

> Wisdom and spirit of the universe!
> Thou soul, that art the eternity of thought,
> And giv'st to forms and images a breath
> And everlasting motion.

And in another poet's words it speaks of

> That light whose smile kindles the universe,
> That Beauty in which all things work and move.

The theologian may follow the scientist and shake his head and say that all that I have written is pantheism. But let us not indulge in an idolatry of name and dethrone living truth in its favour. When I say that I am a man, it is implied by that word that there is such a thing as a general idea of Man which persistently manifests itself in every particular human being, who is different from all other individuals. If we lazily label such a belief as "pananthropy" and divert our thoughts from its mysteriousness by such a title it does not help us much. Let me assert my faith by saying that this world, consisting of what we call animate and inanimate things, has found its culmination in man, its best expression. Man, as a creation, represents the Creator, and this is why of all creatures it has been possible for him to comprehend this world in his knowledge and in his feeling and in his imagination, to realize in his individual spirit a union with a Spirit that is everywhere.

There is an illustration that I have made use of in which I supposed that a stranger from some other planet has paid a visit to our earth and happens to hear the sound of a human voice on the gramophone. All that is obvious to him and most seemingly active, is the revolving disc. He is unable to discover the personal truth that lies behind, and so might accept the impersonal scientific fact of the disc as final—the fact that could be touched and measured. He would wonder how it could be possible for a machine to speak to the soul. Then, if in pursuing the mystery, he should suddenly come to the heart of the music through a meeting with the composer, he would at once understand the meaning of that music as a personal communication.

That which merely gives us information can be explained in terms of measurement, but that which gives us joy cannot be explained by the facts of a mere grouping of atoms and molecules. Somewhere in the arrangement of this world there seems to be a great concern about giving us delight, which shows that, in the universe, over and above the meaning of matter and forces, there is a message conveyed through the magic touch of personality. This touch cannot be analysed, it can only be felt. We cannot prove it any more than the man from the other planet could prove to the satisfaction of his fellows the personality which remained invisible, but which, through the machinery, spoke direct to the heart....

Fortunately for me a collection of old lyrical poems composed by the poets of the Vaishnava sect came to my hand when I was young. I became aware of some underlying idea deep in the obvious meaning of these love poems. I felt the joy of an explorer who suddenly discovers the key to the language lying hidden in the hieroglyphs which are beautiful in themselves. I was sure that these poets were speaking about the supreme Lover, whose touch we experience in all our relations of love—the love of nature's beauty, of the animal, the child, the comrade, the beloved, the love that illuminates our consciousness of reality. They sang of a love that ever flows through numerous obstacles between men and Man the Divine, the eternal relation which has the relationship of mutual dependence for a fulfilment that needs perfect union of individuals and the Universal.

The Vaishnava poet sings of the Lover who has his flute which, with its different stops, gives out the varied notes of beauty and love that are in Nature and Man. These notes bring to us our message of invitation. They eternally urge us to come out from the seclusion of our self-centred life into the realm of love and truth. Are we deaf by nature, or is it that we have been deafened by the claims of the world, of self-seeking, by the clamorous noise of the market-place? We miss the voice of the Lover, and we fight, we rob, we exploit the weak, we chuckle at our cleverness, when we can appropriate for our use what is due to others; we make our lives a desert by turning away from our world that stream of love which pours down from the blue sky and wells up from the bosom of the earth....

Mere information about facts, mere discovery of power, belongs to the outside and not to the inner soul of things. Gladness is the one criterion of truth, and we know when we have touched Truth by the music it gives, by the joy of greeting it sends forth to the truth in us. That is the true foundation of all religions. It is not as ether waves that we receive light; the morning does not wait for some scientist for its introduction to us. In the same way we touch the infinite reality immediately within us only when we perceive the pure truth of love or goodness, not through the explanations of theologians, not through the erudite discussion of ethical doctrines.

I have already made the confession that my religion is a poet's religion. All that I feel about it is from vision and not from knowledge. Frankly, I acknowledge that I cannot satisfactorily answer any questions about evil, or about what happens after death. Nevertheless, I am sure that there have come moments in my own experience when my soul has touched the infinite and has become intensely conscious of it through the illumination of joy. It has been said in our Upanishad that our mind and our words come away baffled from the Supreme Truth, but he who knows truth through the immediate joy of his own soul is saved from all doubts and fears.

In the night we stumble over things and become acutely conscious of their individual separateness. But the day reveals the greater unity which embraces them. The man whose inner vision is bathed in an illumination of his consciousness at once realizes the spiritual unity reigning supreme over all differences. His mind no longer awkwardly stumbles over individual facts of separateness in the human world, accepting them as final. He realizes that peace is in the inner harmony which dwells in truth and not in any outer adjustments. He knows that beauty carries an eternal assurance of our spiritual relationship to reality, which waits for its perfection in the response of our love.

2. Letting Go, R. Kaiser

You may find it somewhat abrupt to move from the high-minded, religious aesthetic of Tagore to the gut sensualism of "Letting Go." These works are certainly directed to different audiences; but the difference is more one of cultural sophistication than it is of basic approach. For Kaiser—as for Tagore—the way to truth lies through education of the senses. The author is a reporter, and his subject is the new emphasis many persons, such as many of those at Esalen Institute (Big Sur, California; already mentioned in Chapter V, reading 2), are placing on spontaneous sensuality and feeling. Corresponding to this is a devaluation of convention, rational control, intellectual analysis, and technological development. Body massage and (an interpretation of) Tantric Yoga are described as means to achieve a re-eroticization of human life. What justifications are given for "letting go"?

"FEELINGS AREN'T NICE." To most of the people in the U.S., the message has been drummed in: Cover up your feelings, don't give yourself away, hold back, stay cool, because your feelings will get you into trouble.

But now there is another message coming through—let go—and it comes from unexpected people in unexpected places. It is often spoken without words.

Nuns dance: In San Francisco, Sister Mary Gertrude Ann's young body is draped in a flowing habit, and her feet are bare as she whirls and spins up to the altar in the middle of Mass.

Ph.D.s strip: At the Esalen Institute in the Big Sur, California, four men with advanced degrees in psychology, three psychiatric social workers and an aerospace scientist climb nude into a hot tub together, abandon all talk—and float, touch, rub, fiddle in a sea of feeling.

Executives cry: At TRW Systems, a rocket corporation near Los Angeles, upper management convenes for weekly "sensitivity sessions," where they are encouraged into honesty jags, to shout and scream about their private hurts, to unbottle hidden resentments and fears.

Rock groups urge: "Let go. Let the world know you're alive. Let go." Their tone is joyful, exhilarating. Letting go is fun, the opposite of holding back, which is narrow and mean.

For several years, people from some sectors of society—especially the so-called intellectuals—have devalued commitments to the life of the mind and placed a new importance on feeling. In their work, calculation, control and conformity to the rules assure "success." They get places, even as far as the moon, by following certain norms, being rational and careful. But somehow that isn't enough. The sensualists need a little freedom as well, and many are turning toward what is spontaneous, personal, natural and real.

There may be some cyclic force built into men that causes them, like snakes, to shuck off the skins of reason and revert to primal states for a season or so. In the 1800s, the citizens of various European states rejected minuets and rhyming couplets for passionate waltzes and songs of nature and political revolution. An elite forsook proprieties for novelties of expression and behavior. Now, in 1969, it is obvious that many in America are adopting a new romanticism. Their thrust is anti-intellectual, anti-ideological and toward the eroticization of practically everything. Their influence may be pushing America into a new Elizabethan age or at least into the life styles of Shelley, Keats and Wordsworth.

Paul Hilsdale, a Jesuit priest from California, is a dramatic and significant example of the new romantic. At 40, Father Hilsdale had received the rigorous training of his rigorous order. In his novitiate, he had practiced all the virtues and learned to keep his "lower" self under submission by various ascetic means—prayer, fasting and self-administered lashings twice a week with a small cord whip. His subsequent studies had made him a modern Erasmus, God's spare-but-well-oiled thinking machine. And then, after 20 years of preparation for missionary work in the jungles of Asia—or possibly Los Angeles—he was seduced to the wilds of Big Sur, where he became a resident fellow at the Esalen Institute.

In order to regain his natural being, Hilsdale was told that he had to lose all the hard-won control, rediscover his emotions and learn to express them in a variety of ways: through phantasy, psychodrama and hypnosis. He was told that his eloquence with words was a barrier to self-knowledge. He was then led into nonverbal encounters, in which he tried to communicate with others with his eyes alone, or by touch, kisses, hugs and slaps. He bathed with others in the hot mineral pools. He started laughing a lot, eating well and painting bright water colors. And he met several beautiful girls. "At last," he says, "I was in touch with myself and the world. I had refound the forgotten joys of feeling. I had learned to let go. And it was good."

Hilsdale is now living comfortably in his own home in the Hollywood Hills. He is trying to turn on the underground church in Los Angeles with OM chants and marathon encounter weekends, and is leading scores of persons into his little subsection of the letting-go movement. . . .

The strongest put-down at Esalen is "You're up in your head"—a place where most people live most of their waking lives and definitely not as good as living in the total self, here and now. Thinking about the future is contemptuously called mind fucking—obviously no substitute for the real thing. If people are strictly up in their heads, they are turned off. In touch with their entire being, they are turned on. The constant query, "Where are you?!" is a call to come out of your head, where all is idea, abstracted from time and place, into the here and now, in touch with reality, where life is lived.

At Esalen, on a craggy cliff on the California coast, you don't talk about it, you do it—whatever might help reawaken the life you are capable of living, in yourself, with others. "We had it as kids, that joy in living," says burly, bearded Bill Schutz, a staff member at Esalen. "But something happened." In his book called *Joy*, Schutz gives a tiny intimation of what it was that turned us off:

"The golden era of physical pleasure is the first 15 months of life," says Schutz, and he recalls his own son Ethan "being thrown up in the air, sliding off the refrigerator into his father's arms, being tickled and hugged, having his cheeks chewed, his behind munched, his face caressed, rubbing his cheek against another's cheek. . . . Ethan *is* joy."

The seekers at Esalen will try anything that might help restore that early innocence. There's pragmatic eclecticism about the place, a borrowing from psychotherapy, group dynamics, dance, drama, Eastern mystical philosophy, Western existential philosophy—whatever turns them on enough so they can let go.

The casual visitor may, in fact, have the opposite reaction. He may be initially frozen with fear at the very thought that anyone is going to chew *his* cheeks or munch *his* behind. His anxieties are not allayed by the bold looks he receives from the bra-less girl with the see-through top who presides over the registration desk, nor by the subsequent calls to instant intimacy by the workshop leaders. Grown men and women engaging in childlike games of blindman's buff! Locking together in a "Gunther Hero Sandwich" (man-woman-man-woman-man-woman, arms around each other, chest to shoulder blades)! Exploring one another under a large white sheet! Lying down on your stomach to be slapped gently all over by all the other members of the group! Will the visitor have to make an ass of himself, too? Or be able to verbalize his honest feelings about it? Tossed in the midst of all this, he may have a rather hard time letting go. After all, his training in the uptight culture has taught him *not* to. What's so good about letting go?

The people at Esalen answer that with another question: What's so good about being alive? Some of them point to a prime kind of letting go— genuine orgasmic release—as the ultimate analog of all life. They are concerned with a wider extension of orgasmic life, but they do not put down good, old-fashioned sexual transport. In fact, one of the hottest trends in the movement is a proliferation of "bioenergetics workships" designed to promote just that kind of release. I attended one of them at Kairos (Greek for "unfolding"), a center for "intensive group experience" somewhat like Esalen, at Rancho Santa Fe, California, where Stanley Keleman did some fascinating work with a group of 14 men and women. . . .

Keleman is a disciple of Wilhelm Reich, studied psychology in Vienna and Zurich and worked for eight years in New York with Dr. Alexander Lowen, the psychologist-author of a book called *Love and Orgasm*. Keleman, who does not have a Ph.D., is a big man with a shaggy mane and bushy eyebrows. He is also something of a miracle worker. "I guess I'm engaged in something you might call the re-eroticization process." Keleman told me, describing his work as a counselor in Berkeley, "I help people restore feeling they've forgotten or had beaten out of them." How? By helping them remove blocks that impede a normal flow of emotions. There is something in people he identifies as a life force or life energy (he doesn't care what the psychologists call it) and he gets it flowing again by leading them into a kind of simulated madness. They kick and scream and moan. They let go. "Letting go," says Keleman, "is one of the keys—to all kinds of pleasurable activity. Fucking. Writing. Laughing." . . .

Keleman is one of the new frontiersmen of sex in America, who hope to find in the erotic an answer to "the alienation of the age" and a new sense of wholeness for men and women. He is on the Esalen circuit, a loose confederation of no fewer than 35 experimental communities of seekers exploring ways to "help us come out of ourselves."

Horny young men may believe they have exactly the opposite problem. They may think they are already too turned on, if anything. But the letting-go therapists call that an illusion. They tell you that you may imagine turning on by climbing into a hot mineral pool with a dozen other men and women, all of you stark-naked, after talking with them all day and wondering which of the women you'd like to lie with, because it's hard to imagine being encouraged to "go with your feelings" without having a little guilt-free affair. But being in a warm pool with those people may shatter that fantasy. Nothing, apparently, could be more erotic than rubbing against those warm bodies in a darkened pool; but you find there is genuine affection—without erection. There, in the baths, you learn the false separation of mind and sex, that there is more to you than head and penis.

In the Esalen massage, that lesson is rubbed in: You are a pleasure body—all of you, head to toe. My lesson came at nine o'clock on a quiet Friday morning. I was in one of the pools, alone, soaking, getting warm and soft, as instructed. Shortly, Linda appeared, smiling winsomely, and said, "Are you ready?" Linda was small but beautiful, about 22 or 23, with straight, long blonde hair falling halfway down her back. My type altogether, in the altogether, and we were alone. My libido was high, but, it seemed, well, *distributed* throughout my being. "Sure, I'm ready," I said. She said, "Follow me."

I padded after her toward the room set aside for massage. She climbed into a brief black leotard while I dried off, then told me to lie on my back. She told me I shouldn't talk but, instead, try to get in touch with my body, to focus my awareness wherever her fingers led.

She moistened her hands with an aromatic pine oil and began to rub the crown of my head. I focused my attention there and began to relax. She worked on the muscles behind my ears, gently but firmly, and then on my forehead, my eyes, my nose, the muscles in my jaw, my lips, my neck. When she got to my arms, I felt a slight stirring in my loins. I refocused my attention on the sensation in my shoulders and upper arms and calmed down below. I stopped trying to hold my breath and went with the feelings Linda was creating on the surface of me. She moved lithely back and forth around the table, sometimes swinging my arms and legs in huge arcs, never removing her hands from me, giving my body a kind of continuity I had never felt before. At times, her touch was heavy; at other times, like the fluttering of hummingbird wings. There are limits, even at Esalen: She did not touch my genitals. But then, that was not the point. I was *supposed* to know I had feelings there. The massage was aimed at eroticizing the rest of me. Linda proceeded down my legs, to my ankles and feet (at that moment, I wished I'd never worn shoes): she ended that stage of the action by holding, holding, holding the tips of my toes between her palms.

Then she had me flip over on my stomach and started again, with more of the pine oil. The same process. A slight shock when her fingers lingered on my *yoni*, that spot midway between my anus and the base of my penis, which I later learned was one of the *cakras*, the six primary centers of physical energy, according to the canons of Kundalini yoga (which is very big today in the movement). Linda finished as before, the tips of my toes warmed between her clasped palms and held, tenderly. Then she stopped. I could hear the sound of the surf on the rocks below and feel a slight breeze off the morning waters of the Pacific and the sound of my own breathing and the heavier breathing of Linda, who had been moving over me for an hour and a half. I opened one eye and saw that she was now sitting on the adjoining table, tucked in a kind of lotus position, contemplating my body. The Esalen massage is supposed to be more than a massage; it is a kind of contemplation. I had an idea that Linda was finishing her meditation and I went to sleep while she did. . . .

3. Turning On,
R. Gustaitis

In this excerpt Rasa Gustaitis, a journalist-reporter, reflects on her exposure to "the turned-on view of life" at Esalen Institute (California). Although her statement is somewhat less erotic in its imagery, its basic outlook is much like that of Kaiser's. The good life is conceived of as immediate, intense, childlike, and honest. What does "turning-on" mean? What ways are there of turning-on? How is it related to "going through changes" or "getting hung up"? Gustaitis shares the view of Michael Murphy, the president of the Esalen Institute, that there is emerging a new Western spiritual growth process (sadhana) that can transform a person who is anxious, isolated from life, and self-destructive into a healthy human being. The process is to restimulate the senses, which in turn makes it possible to get "into direct contact with the nature of your being." From this perspective, can the intellect aid in knowing the truth about oneself? Note the three aspects of the Western sadhana mentioned. Do you see some similarities between the solution to the spiritual hunger in America suggested here with that expressed in Chapter V? Do you think the spiritual hunger Gustaitis refers to is centrally related to the disillusionment of many Americans with their social-political system, as Hans Morgenthau asserts?

...At Big Sur I was inundated by a flood of entirely new experiences. I flipped—freaked out—forgot about the deadline for the book and found out what it was I had been missing by discovering the turned-on point of view. Before coming to Esalen, I thought "turning on" referred only to turn-ons such as marijuana, LSD, or encountering sessions. But out there I saw that it was developing into a whole *Weltanschauung* that was spreading through the middle class of the West Coast and, from there, reaching toward the rest of the country.

In essence, the turn-on message is: clean your perception and you will see that your childhood dream is true. The only obstacle is your own blindness. We have bolloxed ourselves in so that we miss the obvious. Aren't all great discoveries obvious later? Well, turn on—take what is yours. The way is clear and simple. Dig! Life is art. Thou art God. God enjoys being God.

To be turned-on is to be with it, into it, right there; to be fully present at whatever one is in at a particular moment and ready to accept the next moment, whatever it might bring. It is not a matter of performing well but of fully being; not a question of developing a mature attitude toward adult responsibilities but of experiencing anger, love, grief and joy, perceiving subtle inner and outer events and relationships and responding to them clearly and directly.

Nobody is turned on all the time all the way, except perhaps some master gurus and saints. But to the extent that an uptight person turns on, his anxiety becomes excitement. Energy that went toward holding him together radiates outward. Mind, body and senses are freed to reach toward the limits of the possible.

The turned-on person recognizes that continuous change is the nature of the universe. Everything is part of a constantly flowing pattern of particles. Nothing stands still or is ever repeated. All systems are temporary. There is nothing to cling to. We, as part of it all, change and shift, move and evolve, level beyond level.

So, he says, groove with it. The only way of life that makes sense builds on acceptance of change. We have forgotten this and have built, with our intellects, an illusion of fixed forms and dualities. These, not being natural, have cut us off from life's rhythm and the source of our existence. We have become deformed and are blocked in our growth; the intellect has turned tyrannical and cut us off from our senses, the major vehicles of experience. Perception is dulled and distorted by an endless word-chatter. Our emotions embarrass us and we take tranquilizers to quiet them. We become afraid of risk and fail to realize that to stop is to die.

Now someone who builds his life on acceptance of change cannot rely on the usual props—family, friends, status, property. Nor can he live by a scheme, system or philosophy, on plans for the future or memories of the past. His sense of security must come from within, through a transcendence of self and the capacity to go with changes. This is basic to the turned-on view of life. LSD, Zen, the Maharishi Mahesh Yogi, the Esalen experiences, all lead to this.

Turned-on people tend to think less of risk and security than of "going through changes," and "getting hung up" as alternatives. A man who moves is alive, so motion and change have intrinsic value. Any experience that takes one "far out" is valuable. ("Far out" and "out of sight" is high praise in the hip idiom.) But you cannot stay far out or that too becomes a hangup.

It is not enough—or even necessary—to move physically. The movement is within perception and experience. There are many ways to travel there. Drugs are one, meditation another; encounter groups, fasting, sensory awareness practice, music and dancing, sex and sensuality are still others. Anything that will "blow your mind," blast you out of your frame of reference and into direct contact with the nature of your being and the world around you is a trip. Looking at a flower may do it under the right conditions. So might a sexual orgy. The important thing is to break through mind-sets.

Out of this new attitude there may be emerging a Western *sadhana,* in the view of Michael Murphy, the founder and president of Esalen Institute. Murphy is super-turned-on. He is boyish, charming, enthusiastic, meditates daily, runs a million-dollar-a-year institution without being frantic, and has great hopes for the future of Western man. In the fifties be spent eighteen months meditating at the Sri Aurobindo Ashram* in Pondicherry, India, and returned with a new vision of man as a creature emerging through levels of consciousness. He founded Esalen (named after a local Indian tribe) as a forum for exploring that idea. Since then he has become one of the spokesmen for the new life style.

The West lacks a concept of *sadhana,* which is a Sankrit word that may be roughly translated as "the way." Almost every other culture has some growth discipline to guide man in his unconscious groping toward ecstasy, knowledge and meaning, he says. The West, without one, has been spiritually impoverished. But now he sees the emergence of a new *sadhana* that could become the greatest ever developed because of the enormous resources available to Western man.

Most sadhanas have been ascetic and stressed the development of inner states. One got one's life and affairs in order and proceeded to concentrate on the spirit. The new Western *sadhana,* as Murphy sees it emerging, involves three things: the inner state, sensory and kinesthetic development, and human relationships as something mysterious and ecstatic.

He suggests that in other cultures asceticism was a necessity because there was no other way to overcome the problem of hunger, poverty and physical suffering. But in the affluent society, the struggle for that kind of survival is largely over. In other cultures, barriers to the senses were needed because sensual involvement meant children and serious limits to a man's freedom. Now this too is no longer a problem. So, says Murphy, the Western *sadhana* can be rich and subtle, joyous and expansive.

Huston Smith, professor of philosophy at the Massachusetts Institute of Technology, advances a related view. There is now emerging, he says, a new world culture that draws from the strengths of the Chinese, Indian and Western cultures. The Chinese developed social stability, the Indians developed spiritual growth as ways to survive in the midst of a hostile and overwhelming nature. The West has won man's struggle for survival against nature and also developed a concept of individual liberty. Now all three are learning and adapting from the others and a new great world civilization may be coming.

All this is grand and speculative. But to many Americans, the turned-on attitude is extremely frightening. It threatens values that are held dear, even though many of them no longer make sense in the present context. Hard work, material prosperity, duty, marital stability and sexual constancy are all up for reexamination. The turned-on person will point out that perhaps man's ultimate evolution will bring him to a state where he will no longer work, only play. There is no work, after all, in the Western idea of heaven.

The turned-on life style grows directly out of the psychedelic experi-

---

* The school and spiritual retreat founded by Sri Aurobindo, author of reading 6, Chapter VII.

ence, which has led to new forms of art and music, a new interest in Eastern philosophy and religion, to the hippies and other evolving life-styles. But, particularly on the West Coast, many people outside of artistic and bohemian circles—psychologists, physicians, journalists, businessmen, teachers—also took LSD, began to smoke grass regularly, and found themselves veering in new directions. They became aware that our culture emphasizes action but does not train us adequately to watch, listen, and allow things to happen. The forward-thrusting individual, they found, has lost touch with his context. He feels isolated because he no longer senses how he is part of the whole flow of life.

Through LSD, these people became interested in meditation, in subtler sensory awareness, in expanding the power and energies of the mind, body and spirit. They gathered around yogis and gurus who had been working quietly for years in isolated corners and who until now many had viewed as quacks, if they had heard of them at all. And so the new life-style took shape and spread far beyond the psychedelic drug scene. Now people who would never think of trying LSD or even grass are turning on.

But though drugs were the direct catalyst for the new world view, it caught on because the time was ripe for it. In the 1960s, almost all prophets and wise men agreed, something was dreadfully wrong with the state of the nation.

A sense of wholeness, which healthy men and healthy societies have, was missing in urban America. Everything—man and his world—was fractured, compartmentalized and contradictory: the country had never been so rich, yet poverty was an ever more stubborn and divisive condition. Never had so much material comfort been available to so many, yet millions found life too hard to bear without daily tranquilizers or stimulants. Civil liberties were expanding, yet imaginative and intelligent people complained that their chance to contribute to society creatively was shrinking. The more life was compartmentalized, the more did people write, talk and study the subject of creativity. Corporations even had departments of creativity. And the more the preoccupation with creativity grew, the less did many people feel it as part of the daily flow of their lives.

The spiritual hunger was aggravated, in the mid-1960s, by a growing awareness that the entire social-political structure was somehow out of control.

Hans J. Morgenthau, the author of *Politics of Power,* wrote in the *New Republic* of October 28, 1967, "It is the distinctive and ominous mark of the present crisis that it has produced no remedy consonant with the ideals of America. It could not have produced one, for the inability to do so is an element of the crisis itself. The democratic state is in a blind alley, and so is American democracy."

The basic safeguard to the people's interest in democratic states has always been their power to overthrow the government, Morgenthau pointed out. This is no longer possible now when the government has a monopoly of most destructive weapons and can take over control of most effective transportation and communication facilities at an instant, he argued. The people's recourse now is voting.

But the vote has lost much of its meaning because most important government decisions are now enormously complex. "Thus the great national decisions of life and death are rendered by technological elites, and both the Congress and the people at large retain little more than the illusion of making the decisions which the theory of democracy supposes them to make."

The citizen feels powerless. He is also ambivalent toward his government, knowing that, should it make a serious error in its peacekeeping operations, it would cease to be his protector and become his destroyer.

In the United States, Morgenthau wrote, this general crisis of democracy was further aggravated by a widening racial conflict and the war in Vietnam.

Morgenthau's view of the future was gloomy. He saw a trend toward violence and repression rather than toward democratic solutions. By the time the gravity of the situation becomes clear to the powers that make decisions, he suggested, it may be too late for democratic solutions.

In recent years, many social reformers lost faith in the possibility of change through the political process and sought them through demonstrations, civil disobedience and the disruption of government machinery. But as the Vietnam war and racial guerrilla warfare in the cities continued to grow, even direct action of this sort began to seem futile.

And so people—especially young people—who, under other circumstances, might have become political leaders, now withdrew completely from the political process and began to look for areas where individual effort and dedication would yield creative satisfaction. They turned their energies to themselves and their immediate surroundings. Travelers on the turn-on circuit tend to be apolitical but interested in social experiments such as communes, tribal and extended families. They talk a lot about building world peace through the search for personal peace.

4. High Priest,
T. Leary

As indicated in the materials of Chapter I, personal awareness of the Holy has been a common form of, and justification for, religious life in various religious traditions. The use of drugs in the form of liquid, seeds, or pulp also has been evident during the last three millennia as a means for at least some people in a society to achieve a profoundly different awareness of life.

*What for most people in Western society is a social problem and
a crime is, for others a wonderful experience. Some even
speak of it as their religion. Such is the case with Timothy Leary,
who has a Ph.D. in psychology and was, until the summer of 1963,
a lecturer in clinical psychology at Harvard University.
Leary's contract was not renewed at Harvard after his own
research with colleague Richard Alpert became controversial.
Leary has set up the League for Spiritual Discovery (LSD),
which he describes as "a legally incorporated religion dedicated
to the ancient sacred sequence of turning on, tuning-in, and
dropping out," and whose aim is "to help recreate every man as
God and every woman as Goddess." The book from which the
following excerpt comes is intended by Leary as "the first
of a four-volume biblical account of the birth, structural growth,
exile, return, persecution, redemption, and flowering of the LSD
religious cult." The excerpt shows one of Leary's experiences
in 1960, with what he calls the "bemushroomed state," caused by
eating some of the Sacred Mushrooms of Mexico. Leary elsewhere
in the book informs his readers that the Aztecs, before the
Spanish arrived, called these mushrooms "God's flesh"
(Teonanacatl), and that they functioned for the Aztecs much
like the elements of the Eucharist function for Christians,
except that whereas the miracle of the latter occurs beyond vision,
the miracle of the former occurs by means of it.*

We know that today there are many *curanderos* who carry on the cult, each according to his lights, some of them consummate artists, performing the ancient liturgy in remote huts before minuscule congregations.

Gerhart had talked with the University botanists and had researched the field thoroughly. So while he supervised the cleaning he started to lecture on the mushrooms. Known and used by the Aztecs. Banned by the Catholic church. Said by leading botanists not even to exist! The trance-giving mushrooms. Pushed out of history's notice until the last decade when they had been discovered by Weitlinger and Schultes and the American mycologists, Valentina and Gordon Wasson. Pause to clear throat. By now they had been been eaten by a few scientists, a few poets, a few intellectuals looking for mystical experiences. They produced wondrous trances. Oh yeah? What does he mean by that?

There were two kinds, females and males. The lady mushrooms were the familiar umbrella shape, but black, ominous, bitter-looking. The male's anatomy was so phallic there was no need to ask why they were called males. Wondrous trances. The words meant nothing. We moved out to the pool.

They are hard to reach, these *curanderos.*

Do not think that it is a question of money.

Perhaps you will learn the names of a number of renowned *curanderos,* and your emissaries will even promise to deliver them to you, but then you wait and wait and they never come.

You will brush past them in the marketplace, they will know you, but you will not know them.

The judge in the town hall may be the very man you are seeking: And you may pass the time of day with him, yet never learn that he is your *curandero.*

The mushrooms were in two large bowls, male and female separate, on the table under the huge beach umbrella. Gerhart was still lecturing, now about the dosage. Six females and six males. The effect should begin after an hour. Then he stuffed a big, black, moldy-damp mushroom is his mouth and made a face and chewed and I watched his Adam's apple bounce as it went down. Gerhart was voyager number one.

I picked one up. It stank of forest damp and crumbling logs and New England basement. Are you sure they are not poisonous?

Gerhart shrugged. That's what I asked the old witch and she swore that they were okay and she popped a few in her mouth to demonstrate.

I looked around. Joan, following Gerhart's example, was munching somewhat unhappily. She was explorer number two.

Mandy, my girl friend, was miserably chewing. She was number three.

Dick Dettering was looking down so that the loose pouches under his eyes sagged. Well, Dicko? He gave a fierce scared look and began to nibble at his palm with squirrelly movement. He was number four.

I went next. They tasted worse than they looked. Bitter, stringy. Filthy. I took a slug of Carta Blanca and jammed the rest in my mouth and washed them down. Number five.

Poet Betty standing by the edge of the terrace was suddenly vomiting black strings in the bushes. Then she ate more. She was number six.

Gerhart was telling us that the males had no effect and served only a ceremonial function. Everyone was listening to his own stomach expecting to be poisoned. Quite a picture, six of us sitting around on the sunlit terrace in our bathing suits waiting, waiting: asking each other, how many did you take? Males or females? Do you feel anything?

Two people fasted. Ruth Dettering was eager to eat but she was pregnant and Dick scolded her with froggy harumphs until she agreed to wait. She had been a nurse and I was glad that she was going to be out of trance. I talked to her about how to call for an ambulance and stomach pumps.

And Whiskers fasted.

Whiskers was a friend of a friend and had arrived the night before. He was slight in build, sweet in demeanor—a sensitive logician just flunked out of Michigan, clipping his words, hesitant, pedantic, anxious about sending a cable to his mother. To his mother?

After all, would you have it any different? What priest of the Catholic Church will perform mass to satisfy an unbeliever's curiosity?

Religion in primitive society was an awesome reality, "terrible" in the original meaning of the word, pervading all life and culminating in ceremonies that were forbidden to the profane.

He claimed he suffered from nervous fits and so he passed up the visions. He was sitting next to Gerhart and was dressed in bathing trunks over flowered undershorts, and green garters and black socks and leather shoes and a silken robe. He had been appointed scientist and was taking elaborate notes of Gerhart's reactions.

Suddenly
        I begin
                to feel
Strange.
Going under dental gas. Good-bye.
Mildly nauseous. Detached. Moving away
                        away
                          away

Let me point out certain parallels between our Mexican rite and the mystery performed at Eleusis.

From the group in bathing suits.
On a terrace
        under the bright
                Mexican sky.
When I tell this the others scoff
Hah, hah. Him. Power of suggestion.
Skepticism? Of my mind? Of me? Of mind?
Of my?
Oh, now no. No matter.
Dettering says he feels it too.

O muses, O great genius, aid me now! O memory that wrote down what I saw, here shall your noble character be shown. (Inferno II)

At the heart of the mystery of Eleusis lay a secret. In the surviving texts there are numerous references to the secret, but in none is it revealed.

Oh my friend. Do you feel tingling in face?
Yes.
Dental gas?
Yes.
Slight dizziness?
Yes. Exactly.

Whiskers making notes. Rapid whiz pencil.
Lips obscene gash brown stained beard.
Flowered underpants peeping out
from bathing trunks, green socks, black shoes,
thin shoulders
Bending over note pad.

From the writings of the Greeks, from a fresco in Pompeii, we know that the initiate dank a potion.

Viennese analyst.
Comic. Laugh. Laugh. Laugh. Laugh. Can't stop.
Laugh. Laugh.
All look at me.
Astonishment

Then, in the depths of the night, he beheld a great vision, and the next day he was still so awestruck that he felt he would never be the same man as before.

More laugh laugh laugh laugh
Whiskers looks up, red tongue flicks from shrubbery.
Lick lips.
Stomach laugh. So funny that I. . . .
Laughing pointing. . . .
The rabbi! Psychoanalytic rabbinical rabbit!
Convulsed in laughahafter.

When, at the beginning of summer, thunder—electrical energy—comes rushing forth from the earth again, and the first thunderstorm refreshes nature, a prolonged state of tension is resolved. Joy and relief make themselves felt. (I Ching XVI)

What the initiate experienced was "new, astonishing, inaccessible to rational cognition."

     pomposity of scholars
      impudence of the mind
       smug naïveté of words
If Whiskers could only see!
Stagger in hahahouse. Roaring. Into bedroom.
Fahahalling on bed
Doubled in laughahafter.
Detterings follow, watch curiously, maybe scared.
Funnier.
Then
Dettering begins to lafhahahaf.
Yes, he laughs too.
You see, Dickohoho? The impudent mind?
Comedy? Yes.
Only Ruth standing there grinning quizzically.

The king is told not to be anxious, but to study how he may always be like the sun in his meridian height, cheering and enlightening all.

It also seems significant that the Greeks were wont to refer to mushrooms as "the food of the gods," *broma theon,* and that Porphyrius is quoted as having called them "nurslings of the gods," *Theotrophos.*

They were not for mortal man to eat, at least not every day. We might be dealing with what was in origin a religious tabu. . . .

The music assumes harmonious shapes, giving visual form to its harmonies, and what you are seeing takes on the modalities of music—the music of the spheres.

All your senses are similarly affected:

The cigarette with which you occasionally break the tension of the night smells as no cigarette before had ever smelled: The glass of water is infinitely better than champagne.

Starting back to terrace
My walk has changed
Rubber legs
Room is full of water
Under water
Floating
Floating in air-sea
Room
Terrace
People
All

Water
BUT NO WORDS CAN DESCRIBE . . .

Swim along veranda to bedroom
Shades drawn. Dark.
Betty feels isolated. All woman un-tilled earth.
I am sorry tender.
Her black hair
drawn back big pony tail.
Cherokee princess great beauty.
Humming bird words swoop from mouth.
How do you feel?

I sit trying answer. Can't talk.
Can only look jeweled patterns,
swirling tapestry work in closed eyes.
What is she asking me? Oh yes, how do I feel.
Far far gone.
She sits silently behind bead-work face. Do you have anything on your mind? Do you want to talk?
She wants close. Intimacy. But,
I drift off to cavern of sea light.

Gerhart and Joan come in.
Fall on another bed.

In Mandy's arms
Her body warm foam rubber
Marshmallow flesh
My body gone
Fallen into her
Two leafy water plants
Twined together, undulating warm bermuda sea
deep

The bemushroomed person is poised in space, a disembodied eye, invisible, incorporeal, seeing but not seen.

In truth, he is the five senses disembodied, all of them keyed to the height of sensitivity and awareness, all of them blending into one another most strangely, until the person, utterly passive, becomes a pure receptor, infinitely delicate, of sensations.

As your body lies there in its sleeping bag, your soul is free, loses all sense of time, alert as it never was before, living an eternity in a night, seeing infinity in a grain of sand.

Entangled so that no one
Not even plants themselves can tell
Which leaf
Which stem
Belongs to which.

Gone again, gone into
Palace by Nile
Temple near Hong Kong
Babylonian boudoir, Bedouin pleasure tent
Gem-flash jewel
Woven color silk gown movement
Mosaics flaming color Muzo emerald Burma rubies
Ceylon sapphire
Mosaics lighted from within glowing, moving, changing.
Hundred reptiles, Jewel encrusted. Hammered Moorish patterned
Snakeskin.
Snake mosaic, reptiles piled in
Giant, mile-square chest
Slide, slither, tumble down central
                                    drain
                                    One

                                    By
                                    One
                                    One
                                    By
                                    One
Such happy beauty
I lift up head to laugh
From around come answering chuckles.
Who? There are others here?
Eye open
Gerhart and Joan on next bed laughing
Next to me mermaid, laughing.
Put hand on hip where
Skin pokes through bikini lacings
Hand up soft back until fingers
Sink in quicksand of flesh through skin through ribs
Closed eyes
Moving belts like
Inlaid Moorish patterns

Plummeting back through time,
snake time,
fish time
Down through giant jungle palm time,
greeny lacy ferny leaf time.
Watching first life oozing,
writhing,
twisting up.
Watching first sea thing crawl to shore
Lie with her. Sand-rasp under cheek
Then float sea-thing, down
Deep green sea dark
I am first living
Thing I
Am

What you have seen and heard is cut as with a burin into your memory, never to be effaced.

Laughter in dark room IT IS INTERESTING TO CONTEMPLATE A TANGLED BANK CLOTHED WITH MANY PLANTS OF MANY KINDS Gerhart sitting up in dark shouting WITH BIRDS SINGING ON THE BUSHES WITH VARIOUS INSECTS FLITTING ABOUT Oh God don't let this end AND WITH WORMS CRAWLING THROUGH THE DAMP EARTH Gerhart goatee bobbing AND TO REFLECT THAT THESE ELABORATELY CONSTRUCTED FORMS SO DIFFERENT FROM EACH OTHER Gerhart gone in ecstasy AND DEPENDENT ON EACH OTHER IN SO COMPLEX A MANNER I know his ecstasy HAVE ALL BEEN PRODUCED BY LAWS ACTING AROUND US We are high. High Priests

At last you know what the ineffable is and what ecstasy means.

The mind harks back to the origin of that word. For the Greeks *ekstasis* meant the flight of the soul from the body. I can find no better word to describe the bemushroomed state.

THESE LAWS TAKEN IN ancient evolution trail THUS FROM THE WAR OF NATURE, FROM FAMINE AND DEATH down to fishy bottom Float with plankton THE MOST EXALTED OBJECT WHICH WE ARE CAPABLE OF CONCEIVING NAMELY down the littoral Tumbling past coral reef THE PRODUCTION OF THE HIGHER ANIMALS DIRECTLY FOLLOWS AND barnacled sea cliff Fathoms down through tangled jungle THERE IS GRANDEUR IN THIS VIEW OF LIFE Once we were all double-celled creatures Remember THAT WHILE THIS PLANET HAS GONE ON CYCLING ON ACCORDING TO THE FIXED LAWS OF GRAVITY Once we all drifted down soft red-walled caverns FROM SO SIMPLE A BEGINNING ENDLESS FORMS MOST

In common parlance, among the many who have not experienced ecstasy, ecstasy is fun, and I am frequently asked why I do not reach for mushrooms every night.

BEAUTIFUL AND MOST WONDERFUL Our neurons remember HAVE BEEN AND ARE BEING EVOLVED Do you remember

Then begins Blake's long red voyage EVERY TIME LESS THAN A PULSATION OF THE ARTERY down the blood stream IS EQUAL IN ITS PERIOD AND VALUE TO SIX THOUSAND YEARS floating, bouncing along labyrinthian tunnels FOR IN THIS MOMENT THE POET'S WORK IS DONE artery, arteriole AND ALL THE GREAT EVENTS OF TIME START FORTH through every capillary AND ARE CONCEIVED IN SUCH A PERIOD through pink honey-comb tissue world WITHIN A MOMENT: A PULSATION OF ARTERY along soft watermelon channels EVERY SPACE LARGER THAN A RED GLOBULE OF MAN'S BLOOD part clotted scarlet swamps coagulate IS VISIONARY, AND IS CREATED BY THE HAMMER OF LOS tumbling thru caverned heart hall, ventricular AND EVERY SPACE SMALLER THAN A GLOBULE sliding down the smooth aortic shute OF MAN'S BLOOD OPENS slow bumping into narrow tunneled plexus INTO ETERNITY, OF WHICH THE VEGETABLE EARTH feel

But ecstasy is not fun. Your very soul is seized and shaken until it tingles.

After all, who will choose to feel undiluted awe, or to float through that door yonder into the divine presence?

heart's muscle motor prodding us
Chuckles from across room
All fall soft laugh
Some scene
Four sprawl in darkened room
Opium den of purest dreams
    Oh you worldling looking in think
    you evil no you wrong evil in your
    mental coin your evil makes me
    compassion laugh
    here is no evil
    but

The unknowing abuse the word, but we must recapture its full and terrifying sense.

Diamond virtue
Pure blue pureness
Beyond desire
Only
Needle moment
Buddha unity

This uniting of the human past with the Divinity in solemn moments of religious inspiration established the bond between God and man. The ruler who revered the Divinity in revering

> his ancestors became thereby the Son of
> Heaven, in whom the heavenly and the earthly
> world met in mystical contact. (I Ching XVI)

INTERPRETATION

5. Do Drugs Have
Religious Import?
H. Smith

> Earlier in this chapter we considered one rather unconventional
> claim for the religious significance of drug-induced experiences.
> In this excerpt the question of defining these experiences as
> religious in a more traditional sense is specifically raised.
> The author, Professor of Philosophy at Massachusetts Institute
> of Technology, examines the possibilities of regarding some present
> use of psychedelic drugs in America as having religious import.
> He argues affirmatively from authority, from analogy with
> other religious experiences resulting from a physical crisis,
> and from a hypothetical description of the biological mechanism
> that may be at work in the sense of participation with one's
> environment evoked by the drug experience. Can you correctly
> distinguish between the description of a drug-induced experience
> and the mystic's description of his religious experience quoted by
> Smith? If the descriptions of drug-induced experience and
> a mystic's experience appear to be indistinguishable, is there any
> justification to say they are basically different? How does
> Smith account for the resistance that many traditional religious
> believers have shown to the claim that these experiences are
> the same? Does he go on to say that drug experiences which
> are descriptively like mystical experiences produce religious lives?
> What three components of man's nature does Smith think
> every adequate religion or faith must arouse and involve?
> Would you agree that drug-induced experiences can have
> religious significance? If yes, in what way? In view of Smith's
> understanding of the role of drugs in man's religious life, would
> you say that his is a type VIII religious structure? Some other type?
> A combination?

Until six months ago, if I picked up my phone in the Cambridge area
and dialed KISS-BIG a voice would answer, "If-if." These were coinci-

From "Do Drugs Have Religious Import?" by Huston Smith, found in *The Journal of Philosophy,* Vol. LXI, No. 18 (October 1, 1964), pp. 517–30. Used by permission of the publisher and the author.

dences: KISS-BIG simply happened to be the letter equivalents of an arbitrarily assigned telephone number, while I.F.I.F. represented the initials of an organization with the improbable name of the International Federation for Internal Freedom. But the coincidences were apposite to the point of being poetic. "Kiss big" caught the euphoric, manic, life-embracing attitude that characterized this most publicized of the organizations formed to explore the newly synthesized consciousness-changing substances, while the organization itself was surely one of the "iffy-est" phenomena to appear on our social and intellectual scene in some time. It produced the first firings in Harvard's history, an ultimatum to get out of Mexico in five days, and "the miracle of Marsh Chapel" in which during a two-and-one-half hour Good Friday service ten theological students and professors ingested psilocybin and were visited by what they generally reported to be the deepest religious experiences of their lives.

Despite the last of these phenomena and its numerous if less dramatic parallels, students of religion appear by and large to be dismissing the psychedelic drugs which have sprung to our attention in the sixties as having little religious relevance. The position taken in one of the most forward-looking volumes of theological essays to have appeared in recent years[1] accepts R. C. Zaehner's *Mysticism Sacred and Profane* as having "fully examined and refuted" the religious claims for mescaline which Aldous Huxley sketched in *The Doors of Perception*. This closing of the case strikes me as premature, for it looks as if the drugs have light to throw on the history of religion, the phenomenology of religion, the philosophy of religion, and the practice of the religious life itself. . . .

DRUGS AND RELIGION
VIEWED PHENOMENOLOGICALLY

Phenomenology attempts a careful description of human experience. The question the drugs pose for the phenomenology of religion, therefore, is whether the experiences they induce differ from religious experiences reached *au naturel,* and if so how.

Even the Bible notes that chemically induced psychic states bear *some* resemblance to religious ones. Peter had to appeal to a circumstantial criterion—the early hour of the day—to defend those who were caught up in the Pentecostal experience against the charge that they were merely drunk: "These men are not drunk, as you suppose, since it is only the third hour of the day" (Acts 2:15); and Paul initiates the comparison when he admonishes the Ephesians not to "get drunk with wine...but [to] be filled with the spirit" (Ephesians 5:18). Are such comparisons, paralleled in the accounts of virtually every religion, superficial? How far can they be pushed?

Not all the way, students of religion have thus far insisted. With respect to the new drugs, Professor R. C. Zaehner has drawn the line emphatically. "The importance of Huxley's *Doors of Perception*," he writes, "is that in it the author clearly makes the claim that what he experienced under the influence of mescalin is closely comparable to a genuine mystical experience. If he is right...the conclusions...are alarming."[2] Zaehner thinks that Huxley is not right, but Zaehner is mistaken.

There are, of course, innumerable drug experiences which haven't a religious feature; they can be sensual as readily as spiritual, trivial as readily as transforming, capricious as readily as sacramental. If there is one point about which every student of the drugs agrees, it is that there is no such thing as the drug experience per se—no experience which the drugs, as it were, merely secrete. Every experience is a mix of three ingredients: drug, set (the psychological makeup of the individual) and setting (the social and physical environment in which it is taken). But given the right set and setting, the drugs can induce religious experiences indistinguishable from ones that occur spontaneously. Nor need set and setting be exceptional. The way the statistics are currently running, it looks as if from one-fourth to one-third of the general population will have religious experiences if they take the drugs under naturalistic conditions, meaning by this conditions in which the researcher supports the subject but doesn't try to influence the direction his experience will take. Among subjects who have strong religious inclinations to begin with, the proportion of those having religious experiences jumps to three-fourths. If they take them in settings which are religious too, the ratio soars to nine out of ten.

How do we know that the experiences these people have really are religious? We can begin with the fact that they say they are. The "one-fourth to one-third of the general populous" [sic] figure is drawn from two sources. Ten months after they had had their experiences, 24 percent of the 194 subjects in a study by the California psychiatrist Oscar Janiger characterized them as having been religious.[3] Thirty-two percent of the 74 subjects in Ditman and Hayman's study reported that in looking back on their LSD experience it looked as if it had been "very much" or "quite a bit" a religious experience; 42 percent checked as true the statement that they "were left with a greater awareness of God, or a higher power, or ultimate reality."[4] The statement that three-fourths of subjects having religious "sets" will have religious experiences comes from the reports of sixty-nine religious professionals who took the drugs while the Harvard project was in progress.[5]

In the absence of (a) a single definition of a religious experience acceptable to psychologists of religion generally, and (b) foolproof ways of ascertaining whether actual experiences exemplify any definition, I am not sure there is a better way of telling whether the experiences of the 333 men and women involved in the above studies were religious than by noting whether they seemed so to them. But if more rigorous methods are preferred, they exist; they have been utilized and confirm the conviction of the man in the street that drug experiences can indeed be religious. In his doctoral study at Harvard University, Dr. Walter Pahnke worked out a typology of religious experience (in this instance of the mystical variety) based on the classic cases of mystical experiences as summarized in Walter Stace's *Mysticism and Philosophy*. He then administered psilocybin to ten theology students and professors in the setting of a Good Friday service. The drug was given "double-blind," meaning that neither Dr. Pahnke nor his subjects would know which ten were getting psilocybin and which ten placebos to constitute a control group. Subsequently the reports the subjects wrote of their experiences were laid successively before three college-graduate housewives who, without being informed about the nature of the study, were asked to rate each statement as to the degree (strong, moderate, slight, or none) to which it exemplified each of the nine traits of mystical experience as enumerated in the typology of mysticism worked out in advance. When the test of significance was applied to their statistics, it showed that "those subjects who received psilocybin experienced phenomena which were indistinguishable from, if not identical with...the categories defined by our typology of mysticism."[6]

With the thought that the reader might like to test his own powers of discernment on the question being considered, I insert here a simple test I gave to a group of Princeton students following a recent discussion sponsored by the Woodrow Wilson Society.

Below are accounts of two religious experiences. One occurred under the influence of drugs, one without their influence. Check the one you think *was* drug-induced.

I

Suddenly I burst into a vast, new, indescribably wonderful universe. Although I am writing this over a year later, the thrill of the surprise and amazement, the awesomeness of the revelation, the engulfment in an overwhelming feeling-wave of gratitude and blessed wonderment, are as fresh, and the memory of the experience is as vivid, as if it had happened five minutes ago. And yet to concoct anything by way of description that would even hint at the magnitude, the sense of ultimate reality... this seems such an impossible task. The knowledge which has infused and affected every aspect of my life came instantaneously and with such complete force of certainty that it was impossible, then or since, to doubt its validity.

II

All at once, without warning of any kind, I found myself wrapped in a flame-colored cloud. For an instant I thought of fire...the next, I knew that the fire was within myself. Directly afterward there came upon me a sense of exultation, of immense joyousness accompanied or immediately followed by an intellectual illumination impossible to describe. Among other things, I did not merely come to believe, but I saw that the universe is not composed of dead matter, but is, on the contrary, a living Presence; I became conscious in myself of eternal life.... I saw that all men are immortal: that the cosmic order is such that without any peradventure all things work together for the good of each and all; that the foundation principle of the world...is what we call love, and that the happiness of each and all is in the long run absolutely certain.

On the occasion referred to, twice the number of students (46) answered incorrectly as answered correctly (23). I bury the correct answer in a footnote to preserve the reader's opportunity to test himself.[7] . . .

DRUGS AND RELIGION
VIEWED PHILOSOPHICALLY

Why do people reject evidence? Because they find it threatening, we may suppose. Theologians are not the only professionals to utilize this mode of defense. In his *Personal Knowledge,* Michael Polanyi recounts the way the medical profession ignored such palpable facts as the painless amputation of human limbs, performed before their own eyes in hundreds of successive cases, concluding that the subjects were impostors who were either deluding their physician or colluding with him. One physician, Esdaile, carried out about 300 major operations painlessly under mesmeric trance in India, but neither in India nor in Great Britain could he get medical journals to print accounts of his work. Polanyi attributes this closed-mindedness to "lack of a conceptual framework in which their discoveries could be separated from specious and untenable admixtures."

The "untenable admixture" in the fact that psychotomimetic drugs can induce religious experience is their apparent implicate: that religious disclosures are no more veridical than psychotic ones. For religious skeptics, this conclusion is obviously not untenable at all; it fits in beautifully with their thesis that *all* religion is at heart an escape from reality. Psychotics avoid reality by retiring into dream worlds of make-believe; what better evidence that religious visionaries do the same than the fact that identical changes in brain chemistry produces both states of mind? Had not Marx already warned us that religion is the "opiate" of the people? Apparently he was more literally accurate than he supposed. Freud was likewise too mild. He "never doubted that religious phenomena are to be understood only on the model of the neurotic symptoms of the individual."[8] He should have said "psychotic symptoms."

So the religious skeptic is likely to reason. What about the religious believer? Convinced that religious experiences are not fundamentally delusory, can he admit that psychotomimetic drugs can occasion them? To do so he needs (to return to Polanyi's words) "a conceptual framework in which [the discoveries can] be separated from specious and untenable admixtures," the latter being in this case the conclusion that religious experiences are in general delusory.

One way to effect the separation would be to argue that despite phenomenological similarities between natural and drug-induced religious experiences, they are separated by a crucial *ontological* difference. Such an argument would follow the pattern of theologians who argue for the "real presence" of Christ's body and blood in the bread and wine of the Eucharist despite their admission that chemical analysis, confined as it is to the level of "accidents" rather than "essences," would not disclose this presence. But this distinction will not appeal to many today, for it turns on an essence-accident metaphysics which is not widely accepted. Instead of fighting a rearguard action by insisting that if drug and nondrug religious experiences can't be distinguished empirically there must be some trans-empirical factor which distinguishes them and renders the drug experience profane, I wish to explore the possibility of accepting drug-induced experiences as religious in every sense of the word without relinquishing confidence in the truth claims of religious experience generally.

To begin with the weakest of all arguments, the argument from authority: William James didn't discount *his* insights which occurred while his brain chemistry was altered. The paragraph in which he retrospectively evaluates his nitrous oxide experiences has become classic, but it is so pertinent to the present discussion that it merits quoting again.

> One conclusion was forced upon my mind at that time, and my impression of its truth has ever since remained unshaken. It is that our normal waking consciousness, rational consciousness as we call it, is but one special type of consciousness, whilst all about it, parted from it by the filmiest of screens, there lie potential forms of consciousness entirely different. We may go through life without suspecting their existence; but apply the requisite stimulus, and at a touch they are there in all their completeness, definite types of mentality which probably somewhere have their field of application and adaptation. No account of the universe in its totality can be final which leaves these other forms of consciousness quite disregarded. How to regard them is the question—for they are so discontinuous with ordinary consciousness. Yet they may determine attitudes though they cannot furnish formulas, and open a region though they fail to give a map. At any rate, they forbid a premature closing of our accounts with reality. Looking back on my own experiences, they all converge toward a kind of insight to which I cannot help ascribing some metaphysical significance.[9]

To this argument from authority, I add two that try to provide something by way of reasons. Drug experiences that assume a religious cast tend to have fearful and/or beatific features, and each of my hypotheses relates to one of these aspects of the experience.

Beginning with the ominous, "fear of the Lord," awe-ful features, Gordon Wasson, the New York banker-turned-mycologist, describes these as he encountered them in his psilocybin experience as follows: "Ecstasy! In common parlance...ecstasy is fun.... But ecstasy is not fun. Your very soul is seized and shaken until it tingles. After all, who will choose to feel undiluted awe...? The unknowing vulgar abuse the word; we must recapture its full and terrifying sense." Emotionally the drug experience can be like having forty-foot waves crash over you for several hours while you cling desperately to a life raft which may be swept from under you at any minute. It seemes quite possible that such an ordeal, like any experience of a close call, could awaken rather fundamental sentiments respecting life and death and destiny and trigger the "no atheists in foxholes" effect. Similarly, as the subject emerges from the trauma and realizes that he is not going to be insane as he had feared, there may come over him an intensified appreciation like that frequently reported by patients recovering from critical illness. "It happened on the day when my bed was pushed out of doors to the open gallery of the hospital," reads one such report.

> I cannot now recall whether the revelation came suddenly or gradually; I only remember finding myself in the very midst of those wonderful moments, beholding life for the first time in all its young intoxication of loveliness, in its unspeakable joy, beauty, and importance. I cannot say exactly what the mysterious change was. I saw no new thing, but I saw all the usual things in a miraculous new light—in what I believe is their true light. I saw for the first time how wildly beautiful and joyous, beyond any words of mine to describe, is the whole of life. Every human being moving across that porch, every sparrow that flew, every branch tossing in the wind, was caught in and was a part of the whole mad ecstasy of loveliness, of joy, of importance, of intoxication of life.[10]

If we do not discount religious intuitions because they are prompted by battlefields and *physical* crises; if we regard the latter as "calling us to our senses" more often than they seduce us into delusions, need comparable intuitions be discounted simply because the crises that trigger them are of an inner, *psychic* variety?

Turning from the hellish to the heavenly aspects of the drug experience, *some* of the latter may be explainable by the hypothesis just stated; that is, they may be occasioned by the relief that attends the sense of escape from high danger. But this hypothesis cannot possibly account for *all* the beatific episodes for the simple reason that the positive episodes often come first, or to persons who experience no negative episodes whatever. Dr. Sanford Unger of the National Institute of Mental Health reports that among his subjects "50 to 60 percent will not manifest any real disturbance worthy of discussion," yet "around 75" will have at least one episode in which exaltation, rapture, and joy are the key descriptions.[11] How are we to account for the drug's capacity to induce peak experiences, such as the following, which are *not* preceded by fear?

> A feeling of great peace and contentment seemed to flow through my entire body. All sound ceased and I seemed to be floating in a great, very very still void or hemisphere. It is impossible to describe the overpowering feeling of peace, contentment, and being a part of goodness itself that I felt. I could feel my body dissolving and actually becoming a part of the goodness and peace that was all around me. Words can't describe this. I feel an awe and wonder that such a feeling could have occurred to me.[12]

Consider the following line of argument. Like every other form of life, man's nature has become distinctive through specialization. Man has specialized in developing a cerebral cortex. The analytic powers of this instrument are a standing wonder, but it seems less able to provide man with the sense that he is meaningfully related to his environment, to life, the world and history in their wholeness. As Albert Camus describes the situation, "If I were...a cat among animals, this life would have a meaning, or rather this problem would not arise, for I should belong to this world. I would *be* this world to which I am now opposed by my whole consciousness."[13] Note that it is Camus' consciousness that opposes him to his world. The drugs do not knock this consciousness out, but while they leave it operative they also activate areas of the brain that normally lie below its threshold of awareness. One of the clearest objective signs that the drugs are taking effect is the dilation they produce in the pupils of the eyes, while one of the most predictable subjective signs is the intensification of visual perception. Both of these responses are controlled by portions of the brain that lie deep, further to the rear than the mechanisms that govern consciousness. Meanwhile we know that the human organism is interlaced with its world in innumerable ways it normally cannot sense—through gravitational fields, body respiration, and the like; the list could be multiplied until man's skin began to seem more like a thoroughfare than a boundary. Perhaps the deeper regions of the brain which evolved earlier and are more like those of the lower animals—"If I were...a cat...I should belong to this world"—can sense this relatedness better than can the cerebral cortex which now dominates our awareness. If so, when the drugs rearrange the neurohumors that chemically transmit impulses across synapses between neurons, man's consciousness and his submerged, intuitive, ecological awareness might for a spell become interlaced. This is, of course, no more than a hypothesis, but how else are we to account for the extraordinary incidence under the drugs of that kind of insight the keynote of which James described as

> invariably a reconciliation. It is as if the opposites of the world, whose contradictoriness and conflict make all our difficulties and troubles, were melted into one and the same genus, but *one of the species, the nobler and better one, is itself the genus, and so soaks up and absorbs its opposites into itself.*[14]

THE DRUGS AND RELIGION
VIEWED "RELIGIOUSLY"

Suppose that drugs can induce experiences that are indistinguishable from religious ones, and that we can respect their reports. Do they shed any light, not (we now ask) on life, but on the nature of the religious life?

One thing they may do is throw religious experience itself into perspective by clarifying its relation to the religious life as a whole. Drugs appear able to induce religious experiences; it is less evident that they can produce religious lives. It follows that religion is more than religious experiences. This is hardly news, but it may be a useful reminder, especially to those who incline toward "the religion of religious experience," which is to say toward lives bent on the acquisition of desired states of experience irrespective of their relation to life's other demands and components.

Despite the dangers of faculty psychology, it remains useful to regard man as having a mind, a will, and feelings. One of the lessons of religious history is that to be adequate a faith must rouse and involve all three components of man's nature. Religions of reason grow arid; religions of duty, leaden. Religions of experience have their comparable pitfalls, as evidenced by Taoism's struggle (not always successful) to keep from degenerating into quietism, and the vehemence with which Zen Buddhism has insisted that once students have attained *satori*, they must be driven out of it, back into the world. The case of Zen is especially pertinent here, for it pivots on an enlightenment experience—*satori* or *kensho*—which some (but not all) Zennists says resembles LSD.* Alike or different, the point is that Zen recognizes that unless the experience is joined to discipline, it will come to naught.

> Even the Buddha...had to sit.... Without *joriki,* the particular power developed through *zazen* [seated meditation], the vision of oneness attained in enlightenment...in time becomes clouded and eventually fades into a pleasant memory instead of remaining an omnipresent reality shaping our daily life.... To be able to live in accordance with what the Mind's eye has revealed through *satori* requires, like the purification of character and the development of personality, a ripening period of *zazen*.[15]

If the religion of religious experience is a snare and a delusion, it follows that no religion that fixes its faith primarily in substances that induce religious experiences can be expected to come to a good end. What promised to be a shortcut will prove to be a short circuit; what began as a religion will end as a religion surrogate. Whether chemical substances can be helpful *adjuncts* to faith is another question. The peyote-using Native American Church seems to indicate that they can be; anthropologists give this church a good report, noting among other things that members resist alcohol and alcoholism better than do nonmembers.[16] The conclusion to which evidence currently points would seem to be that chemicals *can* aid the religious life, but only where set within a context of faith (meaning by this the conviction that what they disclose is true) and discipline (meaning diligent exercise of the will in the attempt to work out the implications of the disclosures for the living of life in the every day, common sense world).

Nowhere today in Western civilization are these two conditions jointly fulfilled. Churches lack faith in the sense just mentioned, hipsters lack discipline. This might lead us to forget about the drugs, were it not for one fact: the distinctive religious emotion and the one drugs unquestionably can occasion—Otto's *mysterium tremendum, majestas, mysterium fascinans;* in a phrase, the phenomenon of religious awe—seems to be declining sharply. As Paul Tillich said in an address to the Hillel Society at Harvard several years ago:

> The question our century puts before us [is]: Is it possible to regain the lost dimension, the encounter with the Holy, the dimension which cuts through the world of subjectivity and objectivity and goes down to that which is not world but is the mystery of the Ground of Being?

Tillich may be right; this may be the religious question of our century. For if (as we have insisted) religion cannot be equated with religious experience, neither can it long survive its absence.

---

* See reading 10, Chapter IV.

NOTES

1. *Soundings: Essays Concerning Christian Understandings,* edited by A. R. Vidler. Cambridge: The University Press, 1962. The statement cited appears on page 72.
2. *Mysticism, Sacred and Profane.* New York: Oxford Galaxy Book, 1961, p. 12.
3. Quoted in McGlothlin, William H. "Long-lasting Effects of LSD on Certain Attitudes in Normals." Printed for private distribution by the RAND Corporation, p. 16.
4. *Ibid.,* pp. 45, 46.
5. Leary, Timothy. "The Religious Experience: Its Production and Interpretation." *The Psychedelic Review,* vol. I. no. 3 (1964), p. 325.
6. "Drugs and Mysticism: An Analysis of the Relationship Between Psychedelic Drugs and the Mystical Consciousness." A thesis presented to the Committee on Higher Degress in History and Philosophy of Religion, Harvard University, June 1963.
7. The first account is quoted anonymously in "The Issue of the Consciousness-Expanding Drugs." *Main Currents in Modern Thought* vol. XX, no. 1 (September–October 1963), pp. 10–11. The second experience was that of Dr. R. M. Bucke, the author of *Cosmic Consciousness,* as quoted in James, William. *The Varieties of Religious Experience.* New York: The Modern Library, 1902, pp. 390–391. The former experience occurred under the influence of drugs, the latter did not.
8. *Totem and Taboo.* New York: Modern Library, 1938.
9. *The Varieties of Religious Experience, op. cit.,* pp. 378–379.
10. Montague, Margaret Prescott. *Twenty Minutes of Reality.* Saint Paul, Minn.: Macalester Park Publishing Company, 1947, pp. 15, 17.
11. "The Current Scientific Status of Psychedelic Drug Research." A paper read at the Conference on Methods in Philosophy and the Sciences, New School for Social Research, May 3, 1964.
12. Quoted by Dr. Unger in the paper just mentioned.
13. *The Myth of Sisyphus.* New York: Vintage, 1955, p. 38.
14. James, William, *op. cit.,* p. 379.
15. Kapleau, Philip. *Zen Practice and Attainment.* A manuscript in process of publication.
16. Slotkin, James S., (*Peyote Religion* Glencoe, Ill.: Free Press, 1956).

6. Nature, Man, and Woman,
A. Watts

*"...there is really no other reason for creation than pure joy."
This claim, which appears in the following excerpt, is
characteristic of Watts' thought. A student of Eastern religions,
he has written much in an attempt to help Westerners
understand Eastern thought better and to meet their own needs
through such an understanding. In this excerpt, he presents
the philosophy of a "contemplative approach" to the male/female
sexual relationship. In the process he criticizes both the ascetic
and what he calls "the sensualist" because of their failure
to understand the unity of man and nature. Most readers will
probably do well to read this excerpt slowly, carefully, and
more than once, since at first glance Watts appears to be critical
of a certain kind of advocate for the pursuit of sensual experiences.
Indeed, he is; but he is critical of an ego-centered pursuit
(since it is self-defeating), not of the claim that sensual
experiences are in fact splendid and divine. For Watts, sexuality
properly experienced (we intentionally did not say "properly
used") can be a means by which all of life becomes an
intercourse with nature. There are, obviously, traces of mysticism
that pervade Watt's article. Have you experienced in your own
life the paradox with which Watts deals here: that the more one
pursues pleasure, the less pleasure one receives? Do you understand
Watts' point about spontaneity? Do you see in what sense
sexual activity can be a "religion" for some people? What
misunderstandings about Eastern techniques of sexual yoga does
Watts attempt to remove? Do you find his interpretation of
sexuality more profound that the various rationales for
"letting go" explored in Kaiser's article, earlier in this unit?
Do you suspect any deficiencies in Watts' "contemplative
approach"? Do you agree that "the height of sexual love...
is one of the most total experiences of relationship to the other
of which we are capable," and is worthy of being called
"mystical ecstasy" and "adoration in its full religious sense"?*

The failure to realize the mutuality and bodily unity of man and the
world underlies both the sensual and the ascetic attitudes. Trying to grasp
the pleasure of the senses and to make their enjoyment the goal of life
is already an attitude in which man feels divided from his experience, and
sees it as something to be exploited and pursued. But the pleasure so gained

is always fragmentary and frustrating, so that by way of reaction the ascetic gives up the pursuit, but not the sense of division which is the real root of the difficulty. He accentuates dividedness by pitting his will against the flesh, by siding with the abstract against the concrete, and so aggravates the very feeling from which the pursuit of pleasure arose. Ascetic spirituality is a symptom of the very disease which it intends to cure. Sensuality and conventional spirituality are not truly opposed; their conflict is a mock battle staged, unconsciously, by partisans to a single "conspiracy."[1]

Ascetic and sensualist alike confuse nature and "the body" with the abstract world of separate entities. Identifying themselves with the isolated individual, they feel inwardly incomplete. The sensualist tries to compensate for his insufficiency by extracting pleasure, or completeness, from the world which appears to stand apart from him as something lacking. The ascetic, with an attitude of "sour grapes," makes a virtue of the lack. Both have failed to distinguish between pleasure and the pursuit of pleasure, between appetite or desire and the exploitation of desire, and to see that pleasure grasped is no pleasure. For pleasure is a grace and is not obedient to the commands of the will. In other words, it is brought about by the relationship between man and his world. Like mystical insight itself, it must always come unsought, which is to say that relationship can be experienced fully only by mind and senses which are open and not attempting to be clutching muscles. There is obviously nothing degrading in sensuous pleasure which comes "of itself," without craving. But in fact there is no other kind of pleasure, and the error of the sensualist is not so much that he is doing something evil as that he is attempting the impossible. Naturally, it is possible to exercise the muscles in pursuing something that may, or may not, give pleasure; but pleasure cannot be given unless the senses are in a state of accepting rather than taking, and for this reason they must not be, as it were, paralyzed and rigidified by the anxiety to get something out of the object.

All this is peculiarly true of love and of the sexual communion between man and woman. This is why it has such a strongly spiritual and mystical character when spontaneous, and why it is so degrading and frustrating when forced. It is for this reason that sexual love is so problematic in cultures where the human being is strongly identified with the abstract separate entity. The experience neither lives up to expectations nor fulfills the relationship between man and woman. At the same time it is, fragmentarily, gratifying enough to be pursued ever more relentlessly for the release which it seems to promise. Sex is therefore the virtual religion of very many people, the end to which they accord more devotion than any other. To the conventionally religious mind this worship of sex is a dangerous and positively sinful substitute for the worship of God. But this is because sex, or any other pleasure, as ordinarily pursued is never a true fulfillment. For this very reason it is *not* God, but not at all because it is "merely physical." The rift between God and nature would vanish if we knew how to experience nature, because what keeps them apart is not a difference of substance but a split in the mind.

But, as we have seen, the problems of sexuality cannot be solved at their own level. The full splendor of sexual experience does not reveal itself without a new mode of attention to the world in general. On the other hand, the sexual relationship is a setting in which the full opening of attention may rather easily be realized because it is so immediately rewarding. It is the most common and dramatic instance of union between oneself and the other. But to serve as a means of initiation to the "one body" of the universe, it requires what we have called a contemplative approach. This is not love "without desire" in the sense of love without delight, but love which is not contrived or willfully provoked as an escape from the habitual empty feeling of an isolated ego.

It is not quite correct to say that such a relationship goes far beyond the "merely sexual," for it would be better to say that sexual contact irradiates every aspect of the encounter, spreading its warmth into work and conversation outside the bounds of actual "love-making." Sexuality is not a separate compartment of human life; it is a radiance pervading every human relationship, but assuming a particular intensity at certain points. Conversely, we might say that sexuality is a special mode or degree of the total intercourse of man and nature. Its delight is an intimation of the ordinarily repressed delight which inheres in life itself, in our fundamental but normally unrealized identity with the world.

A relationship of this kind cannot adequately be discussed, as in manuals of sexual hygiene, as a matter of techniques. It is true that in Taoism and Tantric Buddhism there are what appear to be techniques or "practices" of sexual relationship, but these are, like sacraments, the "outward and visible signs of an inward and spiritual grace." Their use is the consequence rather than the cause of a certain inner attitude, since they suggest themselves almost naturally to partners who take their love as it comes, contemplatively, and are in no hurry to grasp anything from it. Sexual yoga needs to be freed from a misunderstanding attached to all forms of yoga, of spiritual "practice" or "exercise," since these ill-chosen words suggest that yoga is a method for the progressive achievement of certain results—and this is exactly what it is not.[2] Yoga means "union," that is, the realization of man's inner identity with Brahman or Tao, and strictly speaking this is not an end to which there are methods or means since it cannot be made an object of desire. The attempt to achieve it invariably thrusts it away. Yoga "practices" are therefore sacramental expressions or "celebrations" of this union, in rather the same sense that Catholics celebrate the Mass as an expression of Christ's "full, perfect, and *sufficient* sacrifice." . . .

The importance of these ancient ideas to us lies not so much in their technicalities as in their psychological intent. They express an attitude to sexuality which, if absorbed by us today, could contribute more than anything else to the healing of the confusion and frustration of our marital and sexual relations. It remains, then, to separate the underlying sexual philosophy of Tantra and Taoism from symbolic and ritual elements which have no meaning for us, and to see whether it can be applied in terms of our own culture.

To clarify the basic intent of sexual yoga we must study its practice in context with the underlying principles of Buddhist and Taoist philosophy. For Buddhism the basic principle is to have one's consciousness undisturbed by *trishna,* or grasping desire, in such a way that the senses do not receive a distorted and fragmentary vision of the world. For Taoism the principle differs only in terminology: it is *wuwei,* or noninterference with the Tao or course of nature, which is the organic and spontaneous functioning of man-in-relation-to-his-environment. Both involve the contemplative or open-sensed attitude to experience, the Buddhist *dhyana* (in Japanese, *zen*) and the Taoist *kuan.* In their respective yogas, both practice "watching over the breath" because the rhythm of breathing determines the total disposition of the organism. Now, their attitude to breathing is one of the main keys to understanding their attitude to sexuality.

According to some accounts, perfect mastery of the breath is attained when its rhythm comes to a total stop—without loss of life. This is obviously a literalistic caricature, based on a crude version of the meaning of *nirvana*—"breathed out." Actually, "watching over the breath" consists in letting the breath come and go as it wants, without forcing it or clutching at it. In due course its rhythm automatically slows down, and it flows in and out so smoothly that all rasping and hissing ceases *as if* it had stopped. This is both a symbol of and a positive aid to letting one's whole life come and go without grasping, since the way a person breathes is indicative of the way he lives.

In the sexual sphere the stopping of the male orgasm is just as much of a literalism as the stopping of breath; the point in both instances is not to stop but not to grasp. As contemplation of the breathing process automatically slows it down, sexual contemplation naturally delays the orgasm. For there is no value in prolonged and motionless intercourse as such; the point is to allow the sexual process to become spontaneous, and this cannot happen without the prior disappearance of the ego—of the forcing of sexual pleasure. Thus the orgasm is spontaneous (*tzu-jan*) when it happens of itself and in its own time, and when the rest of the body moves *in response* to it. Active or forced sexual intercourse is the deliberate imitation of movements which should ordinarily come about of themselves. Given the open attitude of mind and senses, sexual love in this spirit is a revelation. Long before the male orgasm begins, the sexual impulse manifests itself as what can only be described, psychologically, as a melting warmth between the partners so that they seem veritably to flow into each other. To put it in another way, "physical lust" transforms itself into the most considerate and tender form of love imaginable. . . .

One of the first phases of contemplative love is the discovery of the depth and satisfaction of very simple contacts which are ordinarily called "preliminaries" to sexual activity. But in a relationship which has no goal other than itself, nothing is merely preliminary. One finds out what it can mean simply to look at the other person, to touch hands, or to listen to the voice. If these contacts are not regarded as leading to something else, but rather allowed to come to one's consciousness as if the source of activity lay in them and not in the will, they become sensations of immense subtlety and richness. Received thus, the external world acquires a liveliness which one ordinarily associates only with one's own bodily activity, and from this comes the sensation that one's body somehow includes the external world.

It was through the practice of *za-zen* or "sitting meditation" in this particular attitude that Japanese Zen Buddhists discovered the possibilities of such arts as the tea ceremony (*cha-no-yu*), wherein the most intense aesthetic delight is found in the simplest social association of drinking tea with a few friends. For the art developed into a contemplation of the unexpected beauty in the "primitive" and unpretentious utensils employed, and in the natural simplicity of the surroundings—the unchiselled mountain rocks in the garden, the texture of paper walls, and the grain of rough wooden beams. Obviously, the cultivation of this viewpoint can lead to an infinitely refined snobbery when it is done with an eye to oneself doing it—when, in other words, the point becomes not the objects of contemplation but the "exercise" of contemplating. For this reason, lovers who begin to relate themselves to each other in this way need not feel that they are practicing a skill in which there are certain standards of excellence which they *ought* to attain. It is simply absurd for them to sit down and *restrain* themselves just to looking at each other, while fighting off the intense desire to fall into each other's arms. The point is to discover the wonder of simple contacts, not the duty of it, for which reason it may be better at first to explore this type of relationship after intercourse than before.

The fact remains, however, that if they let themselves come gradually and gently into contact, they create a situation in which their senses can really work, so that when they have discovered what it can mean just to touch hands, the intimacy of a kiss or even of lips in near proximity regains the "electric" quality which it had at the first meeting. In other words, they find out what the kiss *really* involves, just as profound love reveals what other people really are: beings in relation, not in isolation.

If we say that from such contacts the movement toward sexual intercourse grows of itself, it may be supposed that this is no more than what ordinarily happens. Intimacy just leads to passion; it certainly does not have to be willed. But there is all the difference in the world between gobbling and actually tasting food when one is hungry. It is not merely that appetite needs restraint; it needs awareness—awareness of the total process of the organism-environment moving into action of itself. As the lead and response of good dancers appears to be almost simultaneous, as if they were a single entity, there comes a moment when more intimate sexual contact occurs with an extraordinary mutuality. The man does not lead and the woman follow; the man-and-woman relationship acts of itself. The feeling of this mutuality is entirely distinct from that of a man initiating sexual contact with a perfectly willing woman. His "advance" and her "response" seems to be the *same* movement.

At a particular but unpredetermined moment they may, for example, take off their clothes as if the hands of each belonged to the other. The gesture is neither awkward nor bold; it is the simultaneous expression of a unity beneath the masks of social roles and proprieties by the revelation and contact of the intimate and off-scene aspects of their bodies. Now, these aspects are ordinarily guarded because of their extreme sensitivity, or awareness of relationship. Only the eyes are as sensitive, and in ordinary social intercourse prolonged eye-contact is avoided because of its embarrassing intimacy—embarrassing because it creates a sense of relationship belying and overpassing the separative roles which we take so much trouble to maintain. For the sensitive organs of the body which we call most intimate and private are not, as might be supposed, the most central to the ego. On the contrary, they are those which most surpass the ego because their sensitivity brings the greatest contact with the outside world, the greatest intimacy with what is formally "other."

The psychic counterpart of this bodily and sensuous intimacy is a similar openness of attention to each other's thoughts—a form of communion which can be as sexually "charged" as physical contact. This is the feeling that one can express one's thoughts to the other just as they are, since there is not the slightest compulsion to assume a pretended character. This is perhaps the rarest and most difficult aspect of any human relationship, since in ordinary social converse the spontaneous arising of thought is more carefully hidden than anything else. Between unconscious and humorless people who do not know and accept their own limitations it is almost impossible, for the things which we criticize most readily in others are usually those of which we are least conscious in ourselves. Yet this is quite the most important part of a deep sexual relationship, and it is in some way understood even when thoughts are left unsaid.[3]

It is significant that we commonly say that those with whom we can express ourselves most spontaneously are those with whom we can most fully be ourselves. For this already implies that the full and real self is not the willing and deliberating function but the spontaneous. In the same way that our most sensitive organs are guarded because they transcend and break the bonds of the ego, the flow of thought and feeling—though called one's "inner self"—is the most spontaneous and role-free activity of all. The more inward and central the form of activity, the less it partakes of the mask of the ego. To unveil the flow of thought can therefore be an even greater sexual intimacy than physical nakedness.

In contemplative love we do not speak of the sexual "act," since this puts intercourse into its own special dissociated compartment, where it becomes what Albert Jay Nock called very properly and humorously the "culbatising exercise." Perhaps one of the subordinate reasons why sex is a matter for laughter is that there is something ridiculous in "doing" it with set purpose and deliberation—even when described with so picturesque a phrase as the Chinese "flowery combat." Without wanting to make rules for this freest of all human associations, it is certainly best to approach it inactively. For when the couple are so close to each other that the sexual parts are touching, it is only necessary to remain quietly and unhurriedly still, so that in time the woman can absorb the man's member into herself without being actively penetrated.[4]

It is at this juncture that simple waiting with open attention is most rewarding. If no attempt is made to induce the orgasm by bodily motion, the interpenetration of the sexual centers becomes a channel of the most vivid psychic interchange. While neither partner is working to make anything happen, both surrender themselves completely to whatever the process itself may feel like doing. The sense of identity with the other becomes peculiarly intense, though it is rather as if a new identity were formed between them with a life of its own. This life—one might say this Tao—lifts them out of themselves so that they feel carried together upon a stream of vitality which can only be called cosmic, because it is no longer what "you" and "I" are doing. Although the man does nothing either to excite or withhold the orgasm, it becomes possible to let this interchange continue for an hour or more, during which the female orgasm may occur several times with a very slight amount of active stimulation, depending upon the degree of her receptivity to the experience as a process taking charge of her.

In due course, both partners feel relieved of all anxiety as to whether orgasm will or will not happen, which makes it possible for them to give themselves up to whatever forms of sexual play may suggest themselves, however active or even violent. We say "suggest themselves" because this is a matter of immediate feeling rather than learned technique—a response to the marvellously overwhelming urge to turn themselves inside out for each other. Or it may happen that they prefer simply to remain still and let the process unfold itself at the level of pure feeling, which usually tends to be the deeper and more psychically satisfying way.

Feelings which at the height of intercourse are often taken for the extremity of lust—that question-begging word—are simply the *ananda,* the ecstasy of bliss, which accompanies the experience of relationship as distinct from isolated selfhood. "Abandon" expresses the mood better than "lust," because the two individuals give themselves up to the process or relationship between them, and this abandonment of wills can become so intense that it feels like the desire to give up life itself—to die into the other person. De Rougemont maintains—I think wrongly—that this "death wish" distinguishes mere passion or *eros* from divine love or *agape.* He feels that the former, being a purely creaturely love, seeks the nonbeing which was its origin, and that the latter is the love of the Creator which seeks life because its origin is pure Being. This entirely neglects the Christian mystery of Death and Resurrection, which is the Christian version of the more widely held truth that death and life are not opposed, but mutually arising aspects of a Whole—so that life emerges from plunging into death, and death from plunging into life. But the death wish in love is figurative, the giving up of life being a poetic image for the mystical, self-transcending quality of sexual transport. Death in the same figurative sense, as "dying to oneself," is commonly used in mystical literature for the process whereby the individual becomes divine. It is no more literal than the "death" of a grain of corn planted in the soil, or of a caterpillar sleeping in its chrysalis.

The mood of intense sexual delight is not, however, always quite so overwhelming as a desire to "die." The sense of "abandon" or of being carried out of oneself may equally find expression in gaiety, and this is peculiarly true when the experience brings a strong sense of fulfillment. Rare as such gaiety may be in cultures where there is a tie between sex and guilt, the release from self brings laughter in love-making as much as in mysticism, for we must remember that it was Dante who described the song of the angels in heaven as "the laughter of the universe." "Love," said Coventry Patmore, "raises the spirit above the sphere of reverence and worship into one of laughter and dalliance." This is above all true when the partners are not *working* at their love to be sure that they attain a "real experience." The grasping approach to sexuality destroys its gaiety before anything else, blocking up its deepest and most secret fountain. For there is really no other reason for creation than pure joy.

It is no matter for timing by the clock how long this play should continue. Let it be repeated again, its timeless quality is not attained by endurance or even duration, but by absence of purpose and hurry. The final release of orgasm, neither sought nor restrained, is simply allowed to "come," as even the popular expression suggests from our intuitive knowledge that it is not a deed but a gift and a grace. When this experience bursts in upon fully opened feelings it is no mere "sneeze in the loins" relieving physical tension: it is an explosion whose outermost sparks are the stars.

This may seem irreverent, or just claiming too much, to those who are unwilling to feel it completely, refusing to see anything mystical or divine in the moment of life's origin. Yet it is just in treating this moment as a bestial convulsion that we reveal our vast separation from life. It is just at this extreme point that we must find the physical and the spiritual to be one, for otherwise our mysticism is sentimental or sterile-pure and our sexuality just vulgar. Without—in its true sense—the lustiness of sex, religion is joyless and abstract; without the self-abandonment of religion, sex is a mechanical masturbation.

The height of sexual love, coming upon us of itself, is one of the most total experiences of relationship to the other of which we are capable, but prejudice and insensitivity have prevented us from seeing that in any other circumstances such delight would be called mystical ecstasy. For what lovers feel for each other in this moment is no other than adoration in its full religious sense, and its climax is almost literally the pouring of their lives into each other. Such adoration, which is due only to God, would indeed be idolatrous were it not that in that moment love takes away illusion and shows the beloved for what he or she in truth is—not the socially pretended person but the naturally divine.

Mystical vision, as has always been recognized, does not remain at the peak of ecstasy. As in love, its ecstasy leads into clarity and peace. The aftermath of love is an anti-climax only when the climax has been taken and not received. But when the whole experience was received the aftermath finds one in a marvellously changed and yet unchanged world, and here we are speaking of spirituality and sexuality in the same breath. For the mind and senses do not now have to open themselves; they find themselves naturally opened, and it appears that the divine world is no other than the everyday world. Just as they come and just as they are, the simplest sights and sounds are sufficient, and do not have to be brushed aside in the mind's eagerness to find something more significant. One is thereby initiated from the world of clock time to the world of real time, in which events come and go of themselves in unforced succession—timed by themselves and not by the mind. As the accomplished singer does not *sing* a song but lets it sing itself with his voice—since otherwise he will lose the rhythm and strain the tone—the course of life is here seen to happen of itself, in a continuum where the active and the passive, the inward and the outward are the same. Here we have at last found the true place of man in nature which underlies the imagery of the Chinese poem:

> Let us live
> Among the white clouds and scarlet woodlands,
> Singing together
> Songs of the Great Peace.[5]

NOTES

1. See the marvelous discussion in L. L. Whyte [*The Next Development in Man* (New York: Henry Holt, 1948)], ch. 3, where the author attempts a physiological and historical analysis of the origins of the conflict. A current instance of this mock battle is the alliance of organized crime with conservative church groups to maintain the legal suppression of certain types of vice.
2. See the excellent discussion of this point in Guénon [*Introduction to the Study of the Hindu Doctrines* (London: Luzac, 1945)], pp. 261–67.
3. Obviously, we are speaking here of a very special relationship which is seldom to be found in the ordinary marriage contracted between emotionally immature and socially rigid people, when the more mature partner should express his or her mind only with the utmost consideration for the other. Complete self-expression is really a form of self-indulgence in circumstances where it cannot be received. While it may sometimes be "good" for another person to be frank with them, husbands and wives should be the last people to take on programs of mutual improvement. It may be cynical, but it is good-naturedly and humanly so, to assume that one's spouse is going to remain just as he or she is, and that one is going to have to live with these limitations. If they are going to change at all, this is the only way to begin. For this is already an act of deep acceptance of the other person, which may become mutual by a kind of psychic osmosis.
4. Von Urban [*Sex Perfection and Marital Happiness* (New York: Dial Press, 1955)] does not recommend the cross-legged "Tantric" posture, which is naturally difficult for those not used to sitting this way. Instead, he suggests lying at right angles to each other, the woman on her back with one leg between the man's thighs and the other resting on his hip. In this way the contact is purely genital and the whole relationship between the two "pours through" this center. While this is an excellent way of beginning,

there is no need to make it a fixed rule, though there is an extraordinary intensity in letting the whole feeling-relationship pass through the sexual centers alone. The "absorption" of the male member depends, of course, upon the sufficient secretion of vaginal moisture.

5. *Teiwa shu, ii.* Tr. Ruth Sasaki, in *Zen Notes*, III, 10. New York, 1956.

7. The Aesthetic in Religious Experience, F. D. Martin

> *In this excerpt, David Martin, Professor of Philosophy at Bucknell University, argues to support the claim that true aesthetic experience has religious significance. His argument is complex, but it has two foundations, essentially: (1) the concept of "rapt attention" and (2) his distinction between the ontic and the ontological. Note the meaning he gives to these terms. The thrust of his argument is that in the rapt attention of true aesthetic experience we penetrate the merely ordinary facade of the ontic and apprehend that ontological mystery, Being, of which the ontic is a sign. To understand how he believes this to be so, consider carefully his contrast between "spectator enjoyment" and "participative enjoyment" of a work of art. The first is transient, impervious to form, shallow and noncommittal. The latter is enduring (in significance, though it may not occupy much time), sensitive to form, deep, and self-involving. In this nearly total self-surrender to significant, sensuous form, the participant overcomes for a moment the (basically misleading) separation between observer and observed and finds a communion with reality that gives him a sense of lasting enrichment. For this reason art can (and often does) serve as a bridge to religious experience and Martin can join Heidegger in calling the artist the "Shepherd of Being." Martin's closing paragraph should provide a good summary of his convictions about the connections between aesthetic and religious experience. How does this view of the world as sacramental differ from the understanding of sacrament which characterizes the myth and ritual pattern discussed in Chapter II? (In this connection footnote 18 is especially pertinent.)*

From "The Aesthetic in Religious Experience," *Religious Studies* by F. David Martin, (London: Cambridge University Press), Vol. 4, No. 1 (October, 1968), pp. 3, 17–24. Reprinted by permission of the publisher.

The aesthetic experience in its pure mode is rapt or intransitive attention to a presented thing, the 'given', whether that thing be a colour, a cup of coffee, wallpaper, a pretty girl, or a work of art. When the 'given' attracts and holds our attention because of its intrinsic value, not for its utility in serving some practical end, it becomes an aesthetic object. Thus the red in the evening sky is enjoyed for its own sake, for its qualities such as brilliancy and texture, not as a sign of good weather tomorrow. The recognition of this sign function, however, can become a contributing factor in the aesthetic experience, provided that this recognition adds to the interest in the qualities of the red. The aesthetic experience accents the present tense, the here and now. References to the past and future may be involved, of course, but they are subordinated to making the present experience more complete and satisfactory. We halt at the present—"indulging in...self-enjoyment derived from the immediacy of the show of things."[1] There is "the present tense with the whole emphasis upon the present" (Kierkegaard), and "the primordial empirical given" (C. I. Lewis) is perceived for its own rather than its instrumental value. Thus the aesthetic experience is an intense ontical* experience, and this very intensity suspends us from functions.

Aesthetic experiences obviously are among the great joys of the world. Satisfaction is the *sine qua non* of the aesthetic experience, for without it we are not likely to keep our attention rapt for long. Surely the aesthetic experience, perhaps more than any other kind of experience, renews our faith in the ontical world, as Dewey saw quite clearly in *Art as Experience*. Thus the aesthetic experience would seem, like functions, fit to further bury our ontological sensitivities. But this by no means is always the case.

In the first place, in the aesthetic experience we look at things for their intrinsic rather than their extrinsic values. A rapport between ourselves and the 'given' releases us from the drive of functions. Thus scientists like Einstein, who are much more than technologists,[2] relax at times and sit still long enough to view their science as an aesthetic object and a 'silence' sets in. Noise—that permeating monstrous prodigy of our age that bores in even at night without respite—is shut out. Then the Being dimension of that object, or what Einstein calls "the mysterious side," has a chance to be heard, the "ringing silence" that Heidegger speaks about in his lectures on *Das Wesen der Sprache*. This is the basic point of Whitehead's oft-repeated

---

* Earlier in this article, Martin distinguishes between "ontical" and "ontological." See the following (from p. 3):

Following the distinctions of Heidegger, especially as modified after *Being and Time* (1927), I shall call sense data and objects 'beings' or 'things',[a] and the world of beings or things shall be called 'ontical reality'. This reality can be subjected to the procedures and uses of science, including therefore the technological and practical disciplines as well as the theoretical sciences. 'Ontological reality', on the other hand, is composed of 'Being' which reveals itself, if at all, not as a being or beings but as a 'presence' in our experience. Being is that temporal and yet permanent reality,[b] a continual coming and an endless origin, that is the source or ground of objects, and yet Being is not an object. Nor is Being a sense datum or data, for Being is that

remark that "religion is what the individual does with his own solitariness." For those of us who have not learned the ways of Eastern meditation, increasingly difficult in the West, the aesthetic experience is probably the best way to calm our noisy souls and achieve aloneness. Then in solitude and serenity the silent force of Being may have resonance in our inward listening.[3] "The times of spiritual history," says Buber, "in which anthropological thought has so far found its depth of experience have been those very times in which a feeling of strict and inescapable solitude took possession of man."[4] Without privacy we cannot commune with Being.

In the second place, the aesthetic experience of works of art usually is very different from the aesthetic experience of non-artistic artifacts and natural objects. In the latter cases, there is usually spectator enjoyment without insight, especially for those of us who are not artists. In the case of the aesthetic experience of works of art, however, there is much more likely to be participative enjoyment with insight. Spectator enjoyment, however refreshing, is of passing moment, a holiday from ontological reality except as it may be a preface to privacy, conducive to the silence that rings. Moreover, the ringing sounds after, not during, that kind of aesthetic experience. The spectator is dominated by curiosity for the show of things. The 'given' is a playground, not to be taken seriously except as an object of pleasure. The aesthetic object including the work of art is treated as decoration. There may be form, the relationships of part to part and part to whole, but the form is not experienced as informing.

---

intangible matrix and power that makes possible the existence of any sense datum at all. Nor is Being the common denominator of all beings. Rather Being refers to the to-be of whatever is, whereas being refers to anything that is as revealed by sensation. Being is that which renders possible all 'is', that familiar copula implying existence. Being gives beings their 'is'. Being is the primordial power that conditions and makes beings possible. Being is the depth dimension of all beings that both surpasses and includes them. Thus Being is a further reality.

a This is a free following at this point, for 'sense data' and 'objects' for Heidegger are abstractions from beings or things. "We never really first perceive a throng of sensations, e.g., tones and noises, in the appearance of things. . . . We hear the door shut in the house and never hear acoustical sensations or even mere sounds. In order to hear a bare sound we have to listen-away from things, divert our ear from them, i.e. listen abstractly." "The Origin of The Work of Art," trans. Albert Hofstadter, *Philosophies of Art and Beauty,* ed. Albert Hofstadter and Richard Kuhns (New York, 1964), p. 656.

b There are analogies here, although no more than that, with the Whiteheadian-Hartshornean concept of God. Heidegger has remained neutral on the question of the relation or identification of Being and God, and I will do likewise throughout this discussion. But, whatever the answer to that question may be, God is not a being. As Tillich puts it: "Both the theological and the scientific critics of the belief that religion is an aspect of the human spirit define religion as man's relation to divine beings, whose existence the theological critics assert and the scientific critics deny. But it is just this idea of religion which makes any understanding of religion impossible. . . . A God about whose existence or non-existence you can argue is a thing beside others within the universe of existing things [beings]." *Theology of Culture* (New York, 1959), pp. 4 f.

The form of a work of art, nevertheless, does inform, provided that we are capable of full or participative enjoyment. Every work of art has a "subject matter"—any aspect of human experience that is fundamentally related to man as a purposive and normative agent. A subject matter may be anything that involves a value dimension—that which is worth depicting because it is the object of some basic human interest—on the condition that this value dimension is susceptible or 'subject' to interpretation by an artist.

> If the true artist seeks to express in his art an interpretation of some aspect of the real world of human experience, every genuine work of art, however slight and in whatever medium, must have *some* subject matter. It is not *merely* an aesthetically satisfying organisation of sensuous particulars. The entire history of the fine arts and literature, from the earliest times on record down to the present, offers overwhelming evidence that art in the various media has arisen from the artist's desire to express and communicate to his fellows some pervasive human emotion, some insight felt by him to have a wider relevancy, some interpretation of a reality other than the work of art itself in all its specificity.[5]

Whereas a subject matter is a value before artistic interpretation, the 'content' is the significantly interpreted subject matter as revealed by the form. Form is the means whereby values are threshed from the husks of irrelevancies. "If the world were clear," as Camus says, "art would not exist."[6] The artist purges from our sight the films of familiarity. Whereas decorative form merely pleases, artistic form also informs, and it must inform about neither the arbitrary nor the unimportant. Rather, it must draw from the chaotic state of life, which as Van Gogh describes it is like "a sketch that didn't come off," a distillation, an economy that produces a lucidity which enables us better to understand and cope with what matters most. Thus the informing must be about subject matter with value dimensions that go beyond the artist's idiosyncracies and perversities.

A partial or spectator enjoyment of aesthetic objects, including works of art, floats on their surface, for it never gets to any content. This kind of aesthetic experience makes no lasting impact, for nothing has been learned. We brush off such experiences rather like dust off a coat. A complete or participative aesthetic experience of a work of art, on the other hand, involves the awareness of content, an insight that is life-enhancing because it sees something of the depth of reality. Anyone who has fully experienced one of Cézanne's interpretations of Mont St Victoire, for example, cannot help seeing the massiveness of mountains with a "higher coefficient of meaning," as Berenson puts it. Our enjoyment is participative because we cannot stay aloof from that which is seriously important to us. In turn the participative aesthetic experience (or simply the participative experience) is trans-objective, personal, dramatic, full of feeling, and wonder deepening into gratitude. "Grey cold eyes," wrote Nietzsche, "do not know the value of things." Whereas the aesthetic object lies wholly before the spectator and he scans it objectively as an onlooker or observer, the participator is an impassioned intelligence opening and committing the whole of himself as a purposive, normative agent to the significance of the object. In Edward Bullough's well-used terms: psychical distance is maximised by the spectator, whereas psychical distance is minimised by the participator. The spectator remains clearly aware of himself as distinct from the aesthetic object, whereas the participator becomes so absorbed in receiving and retaining the aesthetic object that in this profound intimacy he tends to lose any sense of subject-object duality. The difference is similar to my *knowing* about the love of another, and my own love which I *understand* because I am that love.

For the participator the object completely commands the foreground of his attention, thus pushing self-consciousness deeply into the background. Whatever has no relevance to the individuality of the object ceases to exist for consciousness. As Eliade describes it, "thought is freed from the presence of the 'I,' for the cognitive act ("I know this object," or "This object is mine") is no longer produced; it is thought that *is* (becomes) the given object. The object is no longer known through associations—that is to say, included in a series of previous representations, localised by extrinsic relations (name, dimensions, use, class) and, so to speak, impoverished by the habitual process of abstraction characteristic of secular thought—it is grasped directly, in its existential nakedness, as a concrete and irreducible datum."[7] When, for example, we have a participative experience of or rather *with* a flower, we are not making a botanical observation or thinking of it as an object. For if we did, the flower would pale into a mere instance of the appropriate ontical categories. The vivid impact of the flower would dim out as the focus of our attention shifted beyond in the direction of generality. The 'concrete suchness' of the object penetrates and permeates the participator's consciousness to the point that consciousness almost becomes opaque to itself, until, as Sartre describes it, "there is nothing more than a gigantic object in a desert world." The subjective and the objective aspects of experience melt into a unitary phenomenon. However self-consciousness is never totally abolished even in the most intense participative experience, for, as Sartre's analysis shows,[8] consciousness requires some degree of self-consciouness. But the participator ceases to be his ordinary self, almost possessed by one awareness in his fascinated self-surrender to the unfolding unto its fullness of the aesthetic object.[9] Perhaps this is what D. H. Lawrence was getting at in his description of the way Cézanne saw and painted: "For the intuitive perception of the apple is so *tangibly* aware of the apple that it is aware of it *all round,* not only just of the front. The eye sees only fronts, and the mind, on the whole, is satisfied with fronts. But intuition needs all-roundedness, and instinct needs insideness. The true imagination is for ever curving round to the other side, to the back of presented appearance.[10] Thus the participator is able to commune with the great simplicities of nature. This is the point of Henry Bugbee's insistence that "the existence of things, the standing out of the distinct, can only make sense, as we stand forth ourselves, as we are made to stand forth. In *ecstasis* (literally a "being made to stand forth") the meaning of the existent becomes clear, and the infinite importance of existent things becomes clear. . . . How apt are those Chinese scrolls which show men in harmony with all nature, men and things emerging *together* and not as over against one another.[11] The space between the aesthetic object and the participator is eliminated. And then, as Schopenhauer saw, it is "all one whether we see the sun set from the prison or the palace." The spectator perceives and enjoys the aesthetic object, and then more or less forgets. The participator also perceives and enjoys; but since the content forces him below the surface, his perception and enjoyment are extraordinary, ecstatic, and he is unlikely to forget. Whereas the spectator experience is a kind of window-shopping, 'stand-offish' and ephemeral,[12] the communion of the participative experience has a fascination, fullness and finality that transports us to lasting enrichment. Whitehead writes:

> Great art is the arrangement of the environment so as to provide for the soul vivid, but transient, values. Human beings require something which absorbs them for a time, something out of the routine which they can stare at. But you cannot subdivide life, except in the abstract analysis of thought. Accordingly, the great art is more than a transient refreshment. It is something which adds to the permanent richness of the soul's self-attainment. It justifies itself both by its immediate enjoyment, and also by its discipline of the inmost being. Its discipline is not distinct from enjoyment, but by reason of it. It transforms the soul into the permanent realisation of values extending beyond its former self.[13]

In the participative experience values have an ontological aspect because they over-run the ontically given and the passing moment. We find an importance that transcends the ontically given and yet, for that very reason, deepens our participation with that given. Thus we become coparticipants with the ontically given embraced in the power of Being. Thus ontical reality is not undermined, as in our experience of the tragic, or voided, as in our experience of the dreadful. And especially in a participative experience of a work of art there is a celebration of the sensuous in the very use and structuring of the artistic media. But within the rhapsody of sensations there is insight. Being comes into awareness because something of the depth dimension, the enduring value, of the ontical subject matter is revealed by the informing form.[14] The work of art never interprets all of Being, of course; for since Being is inexhaustible and therefore *essentially* mysterious, Being stretches beyond every interpretation. "The artist," Schelling noted in *Systems of Transcendental Idealism,* "seems to have presented in his work, as if instinctively, apart from what he has put into it with obvious intent, an infinity which no finite understanding can unfold." Thus works of art, despite the creed that Nietzsche called "aesthetic Socratism," can never be completely intelligible. Being as revealed is always inseparately mixed with concealment. Nevertheless, the work of art corners and illuminates Being. And so we cling with rapt gaze on both the unveiled and the veiled.

The artist is, in that wonderful phrase of Heidegger's, "The Shepherd of Being." By means of a participative experience with some area of ontical reality, the artist discovers the depth dimension of that area. This requires what might be called a "receptive creativity," a nonresistant consciousness, a letting Being be, and through the artist's "constructive creativity" he preserves his discovery, his unveiling of Being, in his art. That does not mean, as Croce claims, that these two kinds of creativity are necessarily chronologically distinct. With most artists it seems that the two creativities are inextricably combined. In any case, the artist shelters and tends to Being as Being emerges in things. The artist lets the 'is' of some thing shine forth.

Art is a gift of Being. That is why art, despite its autonomy, has always served as the principal sacred bridge—although, admittedly, very narrowly framed in the Puritan tradition—to the religious experience, and continues to do so even in these apparently post-religious times.[15] And that is why the participative experience of art is more than just a way back to Being, as in the tragic, dreadful, and spectator experiences. The participative experience of art consummates these preparatory experiences, for it always includes the presence and articulation of Being. And the participative experience of anything that is not a work of art is also an experience of consummation, as in, for example, the love for the sensuous or a river or a person or something brought forth from our memories or even a function.[16]

The participative experience requires for those of us who are not artists a receptive creativity that differs only in degree from the receptive creativity of the artist. To the degree that we are less ontologically sensitive than the artist, to that degree our understanding of Being in the participative experience is less adequate. And the enlightenment of our ontological sensitivity is beholden above all to the gifts of the artist. These gifts generate the growth of our authentic humanity. For the artist shows us the way "to abide with Being," as Heidegger puts it in his essays on the poetry of Hölderlin, "to be at home in the homeland." The gifts of the artist focus to a fine point that aboriginal light of Being, present to us all but usually as concealed or confused, that illuminates beings. To the degree that our ontological sensitivity is enlightened, to that degree we are saved from ontical slavery.[17] To be is to participate, to be creatively absorbed with the presence of Being. And then we may be at one with sun and stone, as Nabokov writes somewhere. And then the corroding acids of technology can be contained and even functions may partake of the beauty of Being. Every object and event, no matter how mundane, is potentially sacramental.[18]

Both the participative experience and the religious experience spring from the same empirical grounds; both involve love for Being; both are attuned to the call of Being; both are reverential in attitude to things as well as persons; both give a man a sense of being reunited with "that with which he is most familiar"; both give enduring value and serenity to existence; and thus both are profoundly regenerative. The participative experience, then, always has a religious quality, for the participative experience penetrates into the religious dimension. How deeply into this dimension the experience delves depends upon how seriously the participation with Being is believed to be of supreme importance, and this in turn, in so far as it is not a groundless belief, depends upon the convictional power of the participative experience itself, the pressure of the presence of Being.[19] From the coercive character of the participative experience flows religious belief and the feelings of ultimate concern, reverence, and peace, and in turn the various theoretical, practical, and sociological forms of religious expression. The tragic, the dreadful, and the spectator experiences open us to Being by freeing us from ontical obsession. But it is only in the participative experience that Being begins to grace our destinies.

NOTES

1. Alfred North Whitehead, *Symbolism: Its Meaning and Effect* (New York, 1927), p. 44.
2. Such scientists usually find the one-dimensional scientism of Ayer and the positivists at best only partially descriptive of their work and at worst a travesty. Pierre Duhem, for example: "If he wishes to be nothing but a physicist, and if, as an intransigent positivist, he regards everything not determinable by the method proper to the positive sciences as unknowable, he will notice this tendency powerfully inciting his own research as it has guided those of all times, but he will not look for its origin, because the only method of discovery which he trusts will not be able to reveal it to him. If, on the other hand, he yields to the nature of the human mind, which is repugnant to the extreme demands of positivism, he will want to know the reason for, or explanation of, what carries him along; he will break through the wall at which the procedures of physics stop, helpless, and he will make an affirmation which these procedures do not justify; he will be metaphysical [ontological]. What is this metaphysical affirmation that the physicist will make, despite the nearly forced restraint imposed on the method he customarily uses? He will affirm that underneath the observable data, the only data accessible to his methods of study, are hidden realities whose essence cannot be grasped by these same methods...." *The Aim and Structures of Physical Theory*, trans. Philip P. Wiener (New York, 1962), pp. 296 f.
3. Michel Seuphor stresses the same point: "I believe that religious sentiment, in all religions, resides first of all in an immobilization before life, a prolonged attention, a questioning and expectant attitude that suspends all corporeal activity and that is a prelude to an activity of a quite different nature that we call inner life, spiritual life." *The Spiritual Mission of Life* (New York, 1960), p. 26.
4. *Between Man and Man,* trans. Ronald Gregor Smith (Boston, 1955), p. 126.
5. Theodore Meyer Greene, *The Arts and the Art of Criticism* (Princeton, 1940), p. 231.
6. *The Myth of Sisyphus,* trans. Justin O'Brien (New York, 1959), p. 73.
7. *Yoga: Immortality and Freedom,* trans. Willard R. Trask (New York, 1958), p. 82. Cf. Bernard Berenson's description of what he calls "the aesthetic moment": *Aesthetics and History* (Garden City, N.Y., 1954), p. 93.
8. *Being and Nothingness,* esp. pp. 177 ff. See also my "On the Supposed Incompatibility of Expressionism and Formalism," *The Journal of Aesthetics and Art Criticism*, XV, I (September 1956), p. 98.
9. Such unity is also a characteristic of the mystic experience; but the mystic

experience, unlike the participative experience, is an awareness of the ontological free from the ontical.

10. *Paintings of D. H. Lawrence,* ed. Mervyn Levy (New York, 1964), p. 39.

11. *The Inward Morning,* p. 110. The Zen Buddhists put it this way: "The unreal life is a life forever unconsummated. The man who stands apart from things, unable to give himself to them, receives payment in kind; because his relation to things is an external one, these things, in turn, withhold their full reality from him. When life is contemplated objectively, nowhere is there to be found anything that is free of limitations, nothing that fully satisfies the yearning of the human heart. It is only when man's experience of life is integral that it 'means everything' to him; only when the subject is not outside the object, where each lives in the other as well as in itself—only then is life complete from moment to moment." Daisetz T. Suzuki, *The Essential of Zen Buddhism,* ed. Bernard Phillips, (London, 1962), p. xiv.

12. The spectator sensibility taken to its ultimate extreme is a cult now called "Camp." See Susan Sonntag, "Notes on 'Camp'," *Partisan Review,* XXI, 4 (Fall 1964). For a denial that the complete aesthetic experience is participative, see Ortega y Gasset, "The Dehumanization of Art," *Symposium,* ed. J. Burnham and P. Wheelwright, I (April 1930), pp. 194–205.

13. *Science and the Modern World* (New York, 1948), p. 202.

14. Cf. Heidegger's description in "Vom Ursprung des Kunstwerkes," *Holzwege* of a painting by Van Gogh: "The painting is of a pair of peasant's shoes— and nothing else. Just a pair of shoes; yet around and through them emerges the world in which the peasant traces his furrows, watches patiently for the wheat to bloom, or trudges tiredly at evening back from the fields. The cycles of time—Spring, Summer, Autumn, Winter—enfold these simple boots, which as serviceable and dependable, find their place in a world. Being, as presence, emerges through the painting of the shoes; yet in such a way that it enfolds them in their concrete thingness—just a pair of shoes, and nothing else—as the simple, serviceable gear that they are." Translation by William Barrett in "Art and Being," *Art and Philosophy,* ed. Sidney Hook (New York, 1966), p. 172.

15. How each of the arts does this in its distinctive way is another story. With respect to music, see my "Unrealized Possibility in the Aesthetic Experience," *The Journal of Philosophy,* LII, 15 (July 1955). With respect to painting, see my "The Beautiful as Symbolic of the Holy," *The Christian Scholar,* XLI, 2 (June 1958).

16. If Mark Twain is correct (see p. 13), it would seem that functions could never be experienced participatively. Bugbee has convinced me otherwise. See especially the moving descriptions of how his absorption in the functions of the life of a ship at sea became participative experiences. *The Inward Morning,* pp. 174–89. See also Antoine de Saint Exupéry, *Wind, Sand and Stars,* trans. Lewis Galantiere (New York, 1939). Functions directly dependent upon the vagaries of nature, such as sea-faring, space-exploration, and farming, are more likely, I believe, to involve us participatively than such functions as business and machine technology. For how technical objects can become aesthetic objects, see Mikel Dufrenne, "The Aesthetic Object and The Technical Object," *Aesthetic Inquiry: Essays on Art Criticism and the Philosophy of Art,* ed. Monroe C. Beardsley and Herbert M. Schueller (Belmont, Cal., 1967).

17. Unless the duality of subject and object is transcended to some significant degree through participative experiences, this slavery is of two basic kinds,

as Berdyaev points out: "The 'objective' either entirely engulfs and enslaves human subjectivity or it arouses repulsion and disgust and so isolates human subjectivity and shuts it up in itself.... Engulfed entirely by his own ego the subject is a slave, just as a subject which is wholly ejected into an object is a slave. Both in the one case and in the other personality is disintegrated or else it has not yet taken shape." *Slavery and Freedom,* trans. R. M. French (Glasgow, 1943), p. 138.

18. "Either all occurrences are in some degree revelation of God [Being], or else there is no such revelation at all; for the conditions of the possibility of any revelation require that there should be nothing which is not revelation." William Temple, *Nature, Man and God* (London, 1935), p. 306. Everything in ontical reality is a "cipher," in Jaspers' terminology, whose secret text can be deciphered not by scientific codes or keys but only through the participative experience.

19. Without this convictional power, as Bugbee points out, religious belief or faith is groundless and thus a deception. "I have encountered no attempt to accord the idea of faith a 'sympathetic' interpretation, 'a defence,' more misleading than the kind suggested by Pascal's 'wager' or William James' 'forced option': that faith means tipping the scale in favor of a set of beliefs which can be neither established nor disproven conclusively, because we have everything to gain and nothing to lose (*a*) if they are true, by believing so, and (*b*) by believing they are true even if they are not." *The Inward Morning,* p. 67. It seems to me, however, that second-hand religious belief or faith based entirely on traditional authority, even when that tradition is based on participative experiences, is equally misleading.

CRITIQUE

8. Guilt in the Social Sciences,
O. H. Mowrer

Consider what we have covered thus far in this chapter.
A clinical psychologist (Leary) and a professor of philosophy (Smith) have suggested that drugs make possible transformations that are equivalent to religious experiences. A poet (Tagore) has encouraged us to rely primarily on the immediacy of feeling and sensuous experiences of the beauty of the universe, using beauty and gladness as primary vehicles of truth. A scholarly

interpreter of participative enjoyment of aesthetic experience (Martin) has claimed that since aesthetic experiences enable us to understand Being itself, we are through art enabled to be transformed into "authentic humanity." Two persons who have been involved in the celebration of spontaneity and sensuality at Esalen Institute (Kaiser and Gustaitis) suggest the emergence of a new world culture, a new Western sadhana for people who are turned-on and letting-go. Finally, an interpreter of Eastern thought (Watts) claims that a contemplative approach to sexuality would allow us to experience the pure joy that is the very reason for creation. What would a critique of all of this look like? Obviously there are many possible critiques.

The first critique included here is by a psychiatrist who casts a suspicious eye on all new social customs. (Interestingly, this is the same author who sees religious significance in "integrity groups." See his article, Chapter V, reading 4.) Beginning with a study of Sumner and Keller that was made some thirty years ago, Mowrer criticizes the emphasis on immediate feeling, spontaneity, and new experience as the highest good. Do you agree that we are "threatened by a form of chaos as a result of the fetish we have made of so-called creativity"? Here Mowrer argues that social convention, coercion, and fear are essential to human well-being; for, just as the biological organism needs regulation to survive, so does society. The principles of regulation are the "old-fashioned virtues," which have been recognized by surviving societies to be those which in the long run are the most rewarding. Contrast Mowrer's view of the function of fear in education with that typically described in Chapter VIII. Which do you find more persuasive? Do you think that the possibility of chaos (societal neurosis) warrants the social limitation of possibilities for sensuous experience? Would you say that, all things considered, conscience and discipline are enemies of joy? Does Mowrer feel that social convention and constraint can be positively related to the ideals of spontaneity and creativity? Would you say that (some, most) artists, Esalen enthusiasts, and drug-users can be fairly charged with being sexually licentious, or are they, instead, trying to counterbalance a sexually repressive society? How does Mowrer's understanding of the prevalence of neurosis differ from that typical of this chapter? Do you think that society should limit the possibilities of sensuous experience among the masses but reserve a special place for those who emphasize insight through the senses? (If so, who should determine the size of the sensuously free group?) Is Mowrer's position expressed in this excerpt consistent with that found in his description of "integrity groups" in Chapter V?

CROSS-CULTURAL INDUCTIONS
CONCERNING SOCIAL MORALITY

If one examines the monumental four-volume work, *The Science of Society,* by Yale Professors William Graham Sumner and Albert Galloway Keller, which was published in 1927, one discovers that the entire second volume is devoted to moral and religious concerns and controls. With enormous erudition, these authors, drawing from a great wealth of both historical and cross-cultural materials which they had assembled over a lifetime, came to the conclusion that, despite their not infrequent arbitrariness and error, religious and moral concerns are not only found in all human societies but are, in the long run, functional and adaptive. In the last chapter of the second volume of their work, Sumner and Keller summarize this argument as follows:

> An evolutionist [which is the authors' term for a person who takes both a long and a broad approach to the understanding of social institutions and cultural mores], viewing the universal existence of religion throughout the races of mankind, cannot but believe that it has possessed survival-value, for there must once have been races without it and it must on a time have risen as a variation that has withstood selection and has persisted. If one considers, further, that it is precisely the most advanced races that have suffered most and longest under the cult-burdens and other alleged disadvantages accruing from religion, he comes unavoidably to the conclusion that religion constitutes for society an adjustment with high survival-value. Along with the family, property, and government, religion has taken its place as one of the major institutional adjustments in the evolution of society. (p. 1475)*

And then, with equal clarity and eloquence, these writers continue their analysis thus:

> There is always reason behind the success of a persisting adjustment, whether in the organic or the social realm; in fact, our very idea of reason is derived from observation of the constitution and operation of things that "work." Adjustments do not survive selection and last only when they are wrong-headed and contrary to reason or despite the fact that they are whimsical, capricious, and unamenable to law. If one looks dispassionately into the charges against religion and admits all of them, either wholly or in some degree, and then surveys and acknowledges the costs in capital, effort, and pain that religious systems have imposed cold-bloodedly and offensively upon mankind, he is yet, in the end, constrained to believe that the article was worth the cost. Exceedingly expensive, it has also been incomparably effective. (p. 1475)
>
> Not to prolong a discussion of relatively minor matters, much less try to combat the detailed complaints about religion and the priesthood, let us consider what is, after all, the first and last service of religion to a society, namely, the discipline it exercises. Not without justice has it been written that fear is the beginning of knowledge. It is certainly the

---

* The four-digit page numbers refer to the study by Sumner and Keller.

beginning of that discipline through which alone wisdom arrives. Discipline was precisely what men needed in the childhood of the race and have continued to require ever since. Men must learn to control themselves. Though the regulative organization exercised considerable discipline, its agents were merely human; the chief had to sleep occasionally, could not be everywhere at once, and might be deceived and evaded. Not so the ghosts and spirits. The all-seeing daimonic eye was sleepless; no time or place was immune from its surveillance. Detection was sure. Further, the penalty inflicted was awesome. Granted that the chief might beat or maim or fine or kill, there were yet limits to what he could do. The spirits, on the other hand, could inflict strange agonies and frightful malformations and transformations. Their powers extended even beyond the grave and their resources for harm outran the liveliest imaginings. In short, they inspired, not a daylight-fear but a grisly, gruesome terror—ghost-fear. Consider the threat of the taboo, and its effectiveness. It is beneath this unearthly whip of scorpions that humanity has cringed for long ages and there is no doubt that its disciplinary value has superseded all other compulsions to which mankind has ever been subject. (pp. 1478–1479)

I apologize to the reader for quoting at such length from an analysis which was published more than thirty years ago. But these are strangely prophetic words, which have special relevance for our time. Under the impact of forces that we shall consider shortly, the Sumner-Keller argument concerning the basic social value of discipline, morality, and religion fell, by and large, upon a generation of deaf ears. In 1927, when *The Science of Society* made its appearance, the movement to "debunk" religion, morality, tradition, and history itself was in full swing; and a major economic depression and a second world-wide war were yet to leave their scars upon the human mind and soul. But now, as we end the first decade of the second half of this century, we cannot look back upon the work of Sumner and Keller without being impressed by its deep insight and perspicacity. . . .

Creativity, Conscience,
and Coercion

Three features of the Sumner-Keller analysis invite our special attention. Recall first of all, if you will, the point that religious and moral traditions are to a society what physical heredity is to an individual organism. Without heredity an organism has no identity, biologically speaking; without it we would not know what an organism *is*. And the same is true of social tradition: without it we lack personal identity and do not know *who we are*. Social tradition and values give form and definition, without which organization is impossible; and society is an organization, an established, agreed-upon way of doing things, particularly very vital things of a personal and interpersonal nature. "If all were variation," Sumner and Keller say, "life would be an unrelated chaos, just as, if all were tradition, it would take on the immobility of death."

In our time, the first danger is obviously more immediate and real than the second. Certainly there is no prospect of our stagnating as a race of stodgy, sodden conformists. But we are, it seems, threatened by a form of chaos as a result of the fetish we have made of so-called creativity. Recently I spent a very illuminating day in company with a group of highly placed and able professional educators in southern California; and although there were some persons in the group who were willing to stand up for such old-fashioned virtues as personal integrity and character in children, the greater emphasis was upon education for spontaneity, variation, creativity. To what extent is this latter position empirically based, and to what extent is it a projection of a personal philosophy, which is today very widespread, to the effect that moral restraint and self-discipline are indeed "the bunk" and that "self-expression" is the measure of all things?

It is perhaps not without significance that in southern California one also meets so many persons who are "in therapy." Can it be that there is a *connection* between this philosophy of personal freedom, spontaneity, and "creativity" and the personal disorganization and crisis that we ambiguously refer to as "neurosis"? The dominant emphasis in psychotherapy has been in the direction of pushing the individual toward the belief that his difficulty lies in overrestraint, too much character, too much self-discipline; but now it looks very much as if, in trying to move toward greater personal freedom and spontaneity, we are making matters worse rather than better. Sumner and Keller insisted—and the more recent writers cited are also again holding—that the capacity for *self*-discipline is personally and socially indispensable.

One cannot, I think, escape the feeling that many persons who are today the devotees of The New Freedom have become "spontaneous" and "creative" without first attaining the balance and wisdom and perspective that comes from restraint and self-control. Someone once said of Christopher Morley that he "got mellow before he got ripe." Something of the same unfortunate type of development seems to have occurred in many of the apostles of so-called spontaneity and creativity. Let us have change, yes, but seasoned, ripened change, and not change merely for the sake of change. If one has never given a traditional, established way of life an extended trial, how can one argue convincingly against it? Inexperience hardly qualifies one as an expert in other areas; and it is not immediately apparent that it should do so in the moral realm. If a person has devoted a considerable piece of his life to a given moral principle and found it invalid and void of sense, and if he can obtain consensual support from others, both historically and contemporaneously, *then* he is perhaps in a position to speak out in favor of a different and supposedly better way of dealing with the problem. But ignorance must not be mistaken for evidence. Someone has said, "He who finds pleasure in vice or pain in virtue is inexperienced in both." Vice is what works and seems rewarding and attractive immediately; and virtue, as Sumner and Keller say, is what works and rewards us in the *long run*. Before we follow the prophets of the new personal liberty and of psychological and moral emancipation, we need to be sure that they have long-term rather than mere short-term support for their views.

The second conception put forward by Sumner and Keller in the passages quoted to which I wish particularly to call attention is this. Social controls, they say, cannot be adequate if they are entirely external and objective. By one means or another, the norms of the culture and the penalties for violating them must be internalized; and this, these authors hold, is the essence of morality and of religion. *"Discipline,"* they say, "was precisely what men needed in the childhood of the race and have *continued to require ever since.* Men must learn to *control themselves."* This, obviously, is the function of character, of conscience, to replace external supervision and sanctions by *internal* ones. "The chief," these writers say metaphorically and yet quite literally, "had to sleep occasionally, could not be everywhere at once, and might be deceived and evaded." Therefore, some system of beliefs and emotional forces had to be devised that would work toward the enforcement of morality even though the chief did indeed sleep.

For a generation now, we have been pummeled by the perverse argument that conscience is an impostor and morality a superstition, and that in combination they produce those states which we call mental illness. In one sense, this is, of course, true: as Sumner and Keller point out, conscience can indeed "inflict strange agonies and frightful malformations and transformations" upon us. But it does so for socially necessary and functional reasons; and we are at last waking up to the fact that we cannot solve the problem of "neurosis" by the naive expedient of abolishing conscience and moral principle. We are now realizing that such a procedure is tantamount to dehumanization and reverses the long social evolution that we call history and progress. . . .

We have been the victims of a strange misconception in recent decades, namely, the view that conscience is bent upon taking the joy out of life and imposing quite unnecessary and crippling limitations upon us. Anyone who has seen Walt Disney's "Seal Island" will recall that here, during the breeding season, a few powerful bull seals, in the height of their physical vigor, maintain large harems of females, whereas the young males, fallen monarchs, and males that have never made the grade even during the prime of life live together at one end of the island in what the makers of the film refer to as "bachelor quarters." It is not hard to imagine a similar state of affairs among human, or at least protohuman, beings forty or fifty thousand years ago. And why have we moved, evolved toward monogamy? Because it was a way of circumscribing and inhibiting sexuality? Not at all! It was rather because allotment of one woman to one man not only assured optimal care and training of the young, but also provided maximal sexual satisfaction for the greatest number of individuals and thus greatest social stability. George Bernard Shaw, with his acute sense of paradox, displays shrewd insight in this connection when he refers, in one of his plays, to marriage "as the most licentious of institutions." And yet we have had a spate of self-styled "therapists" and would-be social reformers literally selling us the pernicious notion that society and conscience are sexually repressive and must be fought back if one is to escape the neurotic state that such repression supposedly produces.[1] This is not, of course, to deny that society *is* in certain respects "repressive" as far as sexuality is concerned. For example, in our particular culture, we ask the young to forgo marriage during the second decade of life, until after, as we say, they get their education.[2] But what must be remembered is that this restraint is imposed, not for the sake of restraint as such, but for much larger and more far-reaching reasons.

Finally, I would call attention to the quite unabashed and unapologetic way in which Sumner and Keller recognize the necessity of force, coercion, and punishment in the socialization process. *Fear,* they remind us, is the beginning, not of neurosis, but of *knowledge.* It is true, of course, that without discipline and "fear of the Lord" a child never develops those inner conflicts and crises that we call mental illness; but neither does he become a complete, wise human being.

In the Chicago papers there was recently an account of the hearings that were held concerning the right of the Chicago School Board to dismiss Marie G. Thomas from her position as a teacher because of a failure to maintain classroom order and discipline. Mrs. Thomas' defense was that teachers are so circumscribed and delimited in what they can today do to enforce order that the task has become quite impossible and hopeless. Mrs. Thomas is probably going to lose her job, and there may be special, undisclosed reasons why she should; but on the face of it, the situation is one that makes a great deal of sense as she presented it.[3] We seem to have become completely unrealistic in our assumptions concerning the socialization of children and are in [the] process of reaping the practical consequences of our folly.

NOTES

1. Cf. the fact that unmarried persons in our society are often termed "old maids" and "bachelors" and viewed with mingled scorn and pity. Note also that marriage is an occasion for ceremony *and celebration.*
2. Professor William Cole has recently phrased the problem thus: "Man is the only animal that achieves sexual maturity before he achieves social maturity."
3. For further details, see *Chicago Daily News, March* 23, 1960.

9. Sin and Sensuality,
R. Niebuhr

Is innocent pleasure truly "innocent"? Does the cultivation of
sensuality have any deeper implications for human self-awareness,
such that man is directing himself thereby to less than his highest
capacity? In this excerpt Reinhold Neibuhr (1892–1971),
formerly a professor at Union Theological Seminary, New York,
and one of the most influential American Protestant theologians
of this century, argues against the claim that cultivating
the senses can itself reveal man's highest good. His approach
is much like that of Brunner's (Chapter VII, reading 7).
Both insist that one of man's good, God-given capacities
("technics" or sensual responsiveness) has been corrupted by sin
(excessive self-love), and has consequently become an agent
of man's enslavement and destruction. In this excerpt he first
gives a background orientation of the orthodox Christian
view of sensuality: he refers to St. Paul (d. A.D. 67?), St. Augustine
(354–430), St. Thomas Aquinas (1225–1274), and Martin
Luther (1483–1546). His point is that sensuality is one form
of a more basic sin: love of self (vs. love of God). Seen in
this light, claims Niebuhr, an adequate "means of ultimate
transformation" must resolve the basic *problem—which resolution*
ultimately resides in God's grace. What are the various sinful
uses of sensuality according to the orthodox Christian tradition?
Can "letting-go" sexually be a vehicle of "self-deification"?
Does man feel ashamed of the sexual function because of religious
teachings, or does the shame antedate them? Why not repress
sex altogether? Do you think any of the advocates in
Chapter VIII are vulnerable to the charges made by Niebuhr?
What different assumptions about the nature of ultimate
reality lead Niebuhr to reject the positions of the advocates
in this chapter regarding the usefulness of senses for perceiving
reality?

The Pauline-Augustinian theological tradition interprets the relation of
sensuality to sin fairly consistently in the light of the first chapter of Paul's
epistle to the Romans. Here lust, particularly unnatural lust, is described as
a consequence of and punishment for the more basic sin of pride and self-
deification. Because men changed the glory of the incorruptible God into
the image of corruptible man, and because they "worshipped and served
the creature rather than the Creator," therefore "God gave them up unto

vile passions, for their women changed the natural use into that which is against nature...and even as they refused to have God in their knowledge God gave them up unto a reprobate mind, to do those things which are not fitting, being filled with all unrighteousness, fornication, wickedness, covetousness, maliciousness, etc." (Romans 1:26–30). In enumerating the various forms of sin, St. Paul makes no clear distinction between anti-social vices (selfishness) and lust, but in this instance his thought obviously is that the sins of lust (more particularly unnatural lust) are fruits of the more primal sin of rebellion against God.[1]

Augustine follows the Pauline interpretation literally and, quoting from the first chapter of Romans the words "and receiving in themselves that recompense of their error which was due" (v. 27), declares that "these things were not only sins in themselves but punishment for sins." He continues. "Here now let our opponents say: 'Sin ought not to have been punished in this way that the sinner through his punishment should commit more sins.' Perhaps he may say in answer: God does not compel men to do these things; He only leaves those alone who deserve to be forsaken."[2]

Sensuality as a secondary consequence of man's rebellion against God is explained in more explicit terms by Augustine in the following words: "When the first man transgressed the law of God, he began to have another law in his members which was repugnant to his mind; then he felt evil of disobedience when he experienced in the rebellion of his own flesh a most righteous retribution recoiling on himself.—For it certainly was not just and right that obedience should be rendered by his servant, that is, his body to him who had not obeyed his own Lord and Master."[3] Whatever Augustine may say about the passions of the flesh and however morbidly he may use sex as the primary symbol of such passions, his analyses always remain within terms of this general statement. He never regards sensuality as a natural fruit of the man's animal nature: "We should therefore wrong our Creator in imputing our vices to our flesh: the flesh is good but to leave the Creator and live according to this created good is mischief."[4]

The Thomistic version of the Pauline-Augustinian interpretation of sensuality as the consequence of and punishment for sin is fairly true to the original. St. Thomas writes: "God bestowed this favour upon man in his primitive state, that as long as his mind was subject to God, the lower powers of his soul would be subject to his rational mind, and his body to his soul. But inasmuch as through sin man's mind withdrew from subjection to God, the result was that neither were his lower powers wholly subject to his reason; and from this there followed so great a rebellion of carnal appetite against reason that neither was the body subject to the soul; whence arose death and other bodily defects."[5] Though St. Thomas defines original sin as concupiscence he still insists that concupiscence is a consequence of self-love: "Every sinful act proceeds from inordinate desire of a mutable good. Now the fact that some one desires a temporal good inordinately is due to the fact he loves himself inordinately."[6]

The Lutheran interpretation does not differ materially from the Thomistic one, except that Luther eliminates the implicit Aristotelian emphasis upon reason as the master of the body. For Luther, as for St. Thomas, sin is essentially lust (*concupiscentia* or *cupiditas*) but he does not mean by this the natural desires and impulses of physical life. Lust is the consequence of man's turning from God, which results in the corruption of his heart and will with evil desire.[7] This evil desire includes both self-love and sensuality. It is the preference of the self and that which pertains to the self (*se et quac sua*) instead of God. Thus while Luther, as St. Thomas, uses the word lust as the inclusive term for sin, he follows the general tradition in regarding lust, in the narrower sense of sinful pleasure, as a consequence of man's turning from God, of his disobedience and pride. Sensuality is, in effect, the inordinate love for all creaturely and mutable values which results from the primal love of self, rather than love of God. . . .

Inasfar as the explanation is precise it suffers from the contradiction that on the one hand the self is said to have lost control over the impulses of the body while on the other hand its undue gratification of these impulses is regarded as merely a further form of self-love. This inconsistency raises an interesting question.

The question is: does the drunkard or the glutton merely press self-love to the limit and lose all control over himself by his effort to gratify a particular physical desire so unreservedly that its gratification comes in conflict with other desires? Or is lack of moderation an effort to escape from the self? And does sexual license mean merely the subordination of another person to the ego's self-love, expressed in this case in an inordinate physical desire; or does undisciplined sex life represent an effort on the part of a disquieted and disorganized self to escape from itself? Is sensuality, in other words, a form of idolatry which makes the self god; or is it an alternative idolatry in which the self, conscious of the inadequacy of its self-worship, seeks escape by finding some other god?

The probable reason for the ambiguous and equivocal answers to this question in the whole course of Christian theology is that there is a little of both in sensuality. An analysis of various forms of sensuality may prove the point. Luxurious and extravagant living, the gratification of various sensual desires without limit, is on the one hand a form of self-love. Sometimes its purpose is to display power and to enhance prestige.[8] Sometimes it is not so much the servant of pride as the consequence of the freedom which power secures. Freed of the restraints, which poverty places upon all forms of expansive desires, the powerful individual indulges these desires without restraint. But sometimes luxurious living is not so much an advertisement of the ego's pride or even a simple and soft acquiescence with the various impulses of the physical life, as it is a frantic effort to escape from self. It betrays an uneasy conscience. The self is seeking to escape from itself and throws itself into any pursuit which will allow it to forget for a moment the inner tension of an uneasy conscience. The self, finding itself to be inadequate as the centre of its existence, seeks for another god amidst the various forces, processes and impulses of nature over which it obtensibly presides.

Drunkenness exhibits the same ambivalence of purpose. The drunkard sometimes seeks the abnormal stimulus of intoxicating drink in order to experience a sense of power and importance which normal life denies him. This type of intoxication represents a pathetic effort to make the self the centre of the world to a degree which normal reason with its consciousness of the ego's insignificance makes impossible. But drunkenness may have a quite different purpose. It may be desired not in order to enhance the ego but to escape from it.[9] It would not be inaccurate to define the first purpose of intoxication as the sinful ego-assertion which is rooted in anxiety and unduly compensates for the sense of inferiority and insecurity; while the second purpose of intoxication springs from the sense of guilt, or a state of perplexity in which a sense of guilt has been compounded with the previous sense of insecurity. The tension of this perplexity is too great to bear and results in an effort to escape consciousness completely. Thus drunkenness is merely a vivid form of the logic of sin which every heart reveals: Anxiety tempts the self to sin; the sin increases the insecurity which it was intended to alleviate until some escape from the whole tension of life is sought.

It has been previously noted that in all forms of Christian thought sexual passion is regarded as a particularly vivid form of, or at least occasion for, sensuality. The modern fashion is to deride this characteristic of Christian thought as morbid and as leading to an accentuation of sexual passion by its prurient repression. While it must be admitted that Christian thought on sex has frequently been unduly morbid and that dualistic forms of Christianity have regarded sex as evil of itself, there are nevertheless profound insights into the problem of sex in the Christian interpretation of sin, which modern thought has missed completely.

Both modern and traditional Christian thought would agree that sexual passion is a particularly powerful impulse which has expressed itself more vigorously throughout human history than the physical function of procreation requires. The usual modern explanation for this hypertrophy of the impulse is that it has been accentuated by repression.[10] This explanation fails to take account of the fact that the social disciplines, which civilized society has thrown about the satisfaction of the sex impulse, are made necessary by the very fact that the impulse has exceeded the necessities of the preservation of the species, from the very beginning; and that even in primitive man sex has never been merely "glandular and physiological." The sexual, as every other physical, impulse in man is subject to and compounded with the freedom of man's spirit. It is not something which man could conceivably leave imbedded in some natural harmony of animal impulses. Its force reaches up into the highest pinnacles of human spirituality; and the insecurity of man in the heights of his freedom reaches down to the sex impulse as an instrument of compensation and as an avenue of escape.

From the standpoint of "pure nature" the sex impulse is a natural basis of "alteregoism"; for it is the method by which nature insures that the individual shall look beyond himself to the preservation of the species. The fact that upon the purely instinctive basis both the self and the other are involved in sexual passion makes it possible for spirit to use the natural stuff of sex for both the assertion of the ego and the flight of the ego into another. The sexual act thus becomes, in human life, a drama in which the domination of one life over the desires of another and the self-abnegation of the same life in favour of another are in bewildering conflict, and also in baffling intermixture. Furthermore these corruptions are complexly interlaced and compounded with a creative discovery of the self through its giving of itself to another. Thus the climax of sexual union is also a climax of creativity and sinfulness. The element of sin in the experience is not due to the fact that sex is in any sense sinful as such. But once sin is presupposed, that is, once the original harmony of nature is disturbed by man's self-love, the instincts of sex are particularly effective tools for both the assertion of the self and the flight from the self. This is what gives man's sex life the quality of uneasiness. It is both a vehicle of the primal sin of self-deification and the expression of an uneasy conscience, seeking to escape from self by the deification of another. The deification of the other is almost a literal description of many romantic sentiments in which attributes of perfection are assigned to the partner of love, beyond the capacities of any human being to bear, and therefore the cause of inevitable disillusionment.[11] While the more active part of the male and the more passive part of the female in the relation of the sexes may seem to point to self-deification as the particular sin of the male and the idolatry of the other as the particular temptation of the woman in the sexual act, yet both elements of sin are undoubtedly involved in both sexes.

An analysis of sexual passion thus verifies the correctness of the seemingly contradictory Christian interpretation of the relation of sensuality to self-love. It contains both a further extension of the sin of self-love and an effort to escape from it, an effort which results in the futility of worshipping the "creature rather than the Creator." To complete the analysis it must be mentioned that sexuality is subject to the development of one further degree of sensuality. Sexual passion may, by the very power it develops in the spiritual confusion of human sin, serve exactly the same purpose as drunkenness. It may serve as an anodyne. The ego, having found the worship both of self and of the other abortive, may use the passion of sex, without reference to self and the other, as a form of escape from the tension of life. The most corrupt forms of sensuality, as for instance in commercialized vice, have exactly this characteristic, that personal considerations are excluded from the satisfaction of the sexual impulse. It is a flight not to a false god but to nothingness. The strength of the passion which makes this momentary escape possible is itself a consequence of sin primarily and of an uneasy conscience consequent upon sin secondarily. If this analysis be correct it verifies the Augustinian conception of sensuality as a further sin which is also a punishment for the more primary sin; and justifies his conclusion: "God does not compel men to do these things; He only leaves those alone who deserve to be forsaken."[12]

The proof that sex is a very crucial point in the spirituality of sinful man is that shame is so universally attached to the performance of the sexual function. The profundity of the account of the Fall in Genesis cannot be overestimated. For though the account describes sin as primarily disobedience to God through the temptation of pride and not as sensual passion, it understands that guilt becomes involved in sensual passion after the Fall, for man becomes suddenly conscious of his sexuality: "And the eyes of them both were opened, and they knew that they were naked; and they sewed fig leaves together, and made themselves aprons" (Gen. 3:7).

The idea of modern psychology, particularly Freudian psychology, that this sense of guilt is abnormal, unnecessary and entirely due to the repressions of civilization, is a consequence of a too superficial view of the complexities on the relationship of spirit to nature. The sense of shame in relation to sex antedates the conventions of civilized society, just as the inordinate expression of sexual passion is the cause and not the consequence of the social disciplines and restraints which society has set around this area of life. A sophisticated effort to destroy modesty and the sense of shame by the simple device of making the function of sex more public is therefore bound to aggravate rather than alleviate the difficulties of man's sex life.[13]

On the other hand it must be admitted that Christian puritanism and asceticism have usually been just as much in error in their effort to eliminate the sin attached to and expressed in sex by undue repressions. Such efforts have not only aggravated the sexual problem but have contributed to the self-righteous fury of those who sin covertly in matters of sex against those who sin overtly.[14]

The problem of sex, sensuality and sin is very complex and for that reason a constant source of confusion. Since sin is inevitably attached to sex, the dualist and ascetic is tempted to regard it as sinful *per se*. The anti-ascetic on the other hand, viewing the difficulties which arise from morbidity and undue prurience, imagines he can solve the problem by relaxing all restraints and by regarding minimal restraints only from the standpoint of social utility. The real situation is that man, granted his "fallen" nature, sins in his sex life but not because sex is essentially sinful. Or in other words, man, having lost the true centre of his life in God, falls into sensuality; and sex is the most obvious occasion for the expression of sensuality and the most vivid expression of it. Thus sex reveals sensuality to be first another and final form of self-love, secondly an effort to escape self-love by the deification of another and finally as an escape from the futilities of both forms of idolatry by a plunge into unconsciousness.

What sex reveals in regard to sensuality is not unique but typical in regard to the problem of sensuality in general. Whether in drunkenness, gluttony, sexual license, love of luxury, or any inordinate devotion to a mutable good, sensuality is always: (1) an extension of self-love to the point where it defeats its own ends; (2) an effort to escape the prison house of self by finding a god in a process or person outside the self; and (3) finally an effort to escape from the confusion which sin has created into some form of subconscious existence.

NOTES

1. In cataloguing the various vices and sins, St. Paul sometimes enumerates anti-social and sensual sins separately and sometimes lists them indiscriminately, without a clear distinction between them. *Cf.* 1 Cor. 5:10–11; 11 Cor. 12:20; Gal. 5:19–21; Eph. 5:3–5; Col. 3:5–8.
2. *Treatise on the Nature of Grace,* Chs. 24 and 25.
3. *On Marriage and Concupiscence,* Ch. 7.
4. *De civ. Dei,* Book XIV, Ch. v. Or again: "If any man say that flesh is the cause of the viciousness of the soul, he is ignorant of man's nature, for the corruptible body does not burden the soul.—For this corruption that is so burdensome to the soul is the punishment for the first sin and not the cause. The corruptible flesh made not the soul to sin, but the sinning soul made the flesh corruptible; from which corruption although there arise some incitements to sin, and some vicious desires, yet are not all sins of an evil life to be laid to the flesh, otherwise we shall make the devil, who has no flesh, sinless." *De civ. Dei,* Book XIV, Ch. 3.
5. *Summa theologiae,* Part II (Second Part), Question 164, Art. 1.
6. *Summa,* Part II (First Part), Question 77, Art. 4.
7. *Mala inclinatio cordis, inordinatio in volunte."* Werke, *Weimarausgabe,* Vol. III, 453.
8. *Cf.* Thorstein Veblen, *Theory of the Leisure Class.*
9. A modern psychoanalyst explains this twofold function of addiction to alcohol as follows: " 'Alcoholics' are almost invariably jolly, sociable, talkative fellows—who indeed seem obliged to make themselves well liked and are skillful in doing so. It takes very little penetration to discover, however, that this inordinate wish to be loved which compels them to be at so much pains to be charming...bespeaks a great underlying feeling of insecurity, a feeling which must constantly be denied, compensated for or anesthetized. ...Such feelings of insecurity and inferiority depend less upon actual reality comparisons than upon unconscious 'irrational' reasons, generally feelings of great frustration and rage and the fear and guilt which the rage induces.... A supplementary function of alcohol drinking is the further repression of such feelings and memories, which threaten to emerge and become again conscious." Karl A. Menninger, *Man Against Himself,* p. 169.
10. Thus a modern psychologist writes: "In the lower animals in a state of nature, and natively in man, the sex drive is a glandular and physiological one, satisfied by direct (though learned) mechanisms when it arises. In civilized man the direct satisfaction of the sexual urges is thwarted at their appearance in infancy and at their strengthening in the glandular changes of adolescence by social conventions and economic obstacles. This thwarting directs attention to the drive and attaches it to many substitute stimuli and substitute responses." L. F. Shaffer, *The Psychology of Adjustment,* p. 105.
11. *Cf.,* for a convincing analysis of this aspect of sexual attachment, Emil Brunner, *Man in Revolt,* Ch. 15.
12. The flight of the self into the other and the escape into oblivion are recurring themes in D. H. Lawrence's analysis of sex. Thus for instance he describes the experience of a man and woman in *Sons and Lovers:* "To know their own nothingness, to know the tremendous living flood which carried them always, gave them rest within themselves. If so great a magnificent power could overwhelm them, identify them altogether with itself, so that they knew that they were only grains in the tremendous heave that lifted every

grass blade its little height and living thing, then why fret about themselves? They could let themselves be carried by life and they felt a sort of peace each in the other" (p. 436). It will be noted that the motif of escape into subconscious nature is more dominant than the sense of loss in the other.

Sometimes Lawrence explicitly identifies the sex impulse with the longing for death.

13. The criticism of Augustine, directed against the Cynics, is strikingly applicable to these modern theories: "It was against the modesty of natural shame that the Cynic philosophers struggled so hard in the error of their astonishing shamelessness; they thought that the intercourse between husband and wife was indeed honourable and that therefore it should be done in public. Such barefaced obscenity deserved to receive a doggish name; and so they went by the title of 'Cynics'" (Kŭvikol—doglike) From *On Marriage and Concupiscence*, Book I, Ch. 25.

14. This is the point of criticism, for instance, in Ibsen's *The Wild Duck* and Hawthorne's *The Scarlet Letter*.

Index

A

Abraham, 63
absorption (*jhana*), 272, 273
absurdity, 431–34
abyss, 37, 298, 311, 314
act, priority of, 142
actions(s), 183, 187, 192, 198, 202, 225, 231,
    240, 256, 258, 266, 267, 275, 293, 297,
    308, 329, 330, 360, 365, 388, 392, 403
    (*See also* karma)
action(s), obsessive, 160 ff.
action, sacred, 162
action, sacrificial, 151
action, symbolic, 150
activistic Christians, 473–74
Adam, 115, 116, 120 f., 390–95, 406
aesthetic experience, 589–98
Africa(n), 1, 201, 228, 245
Africa, religions of, 99–105
agnostic, 73
Akhilananda, Swami, 305

Alenu, 118
Alexander, S., 479
alienation, 429–34, 489
Allah, 9, 62, 237, 293, 315–317
Alpert, Richard, 562
altar, 46, 66
America(n), 133 ff., 198–202, 228, 245, 246,
    248–52, 282, 305, 319, 324, 371, 375,
    376, 384, 390, 424–28, 467–72
amulet(s), 159
analysis, phenomenological, 150
ancestors, 183, 185, 191, 215, 220, 299, 385
angel(s), 26, 27, 29, 392
Anglican(s) (England, Church of), 4, 247,
    248
anguish, 62
al-Ansari, Abdullah, 62
anthropology, 155
anthropomorphism, 75 f.
anxiety, 157, 164, 283, 304, 376, 390, 391,
    393, 394, 396, 398, 403
Apollo, 10

613

Aquinas, St. Thomas, 200, 605, 606
Aristotle, 338
art, 12, 358, 415, 493, 502, 589–98
asceticism, 209, 262, 290, 328 (See also monasticism)
astrology, 171, 221, 222, 315
atheism, 490
atman, 16, 206, 303 (See also Self)
attention, 276, 278, 280, 285, 294, 386
Aubrey, E. E., 417
Augustine, Saint, 200, 237, 605, 606
aura, 37, 223
Aurelius, Marcus, 499
Auschwitz, 117
austerity, 191
authentic, 252
authoritarian, 400, 401
authority, 177 f.
authority, social-political, 111, 211, 241, 249, 364, 385, 394, 397, 399
automation, 516
Avalokiteśvara, 37, 282
avatar (divine incarnation), 43
awakening, 309–11, 313, 370
awareness, 275–79, 284, 285, 291, 301–303, 305, 310, 320, 364, 391, 395
awe, 32, 79, 141, 142, 146, 147, 403, 578
Aztecs, 562

B

Bach, Marcus, 50
Baptism (of the Holy Spirit), 29, 30, 50 ff.
baptism, sacrament of, 120, 122, 171
Baptist (Church), 8, 59
beatitude, 86
beauty, 35, 186, 187, 231, 377, 412, 545–52 (See also aesthetic)
behavior, scientific study of, 498, 504
being, 408, 409, 589–98
being, spiritual, 147, 150, 356, 520, 521
Being, Transcendent, 360
belief, 24, 43, 160, 174 ff., 180, 236, 298–301, 303, 327, 360, 363–65, 380, 382, 387, 388, 394, 398, 401
Bellah, R. N., 136
"bemushroomed state," 562, 567, 568
Benedict, Ruth, 19, 106
benevolence (charity), 187–89, 195, 196, 211
Berger, Peter, 87, 241
bias, religious, 3

Bible, 28, 48, 51, 56, 70, 150, 488, 534
biblical, 407, 414
birth (new or second), 23, 105, 168, 170 ff., 270, 313, 409, 412–14, 525
Black(s), 367, 370, 372, 373, 431 (See also Negroes)
Black Conference for Economic Development, 443
Black Muslim, 201
Black Panthers, 443, 445
Black Power, 368, 429–35
Black Theology, 429–34
bless, 26, 188, 236, 244, 331
bliss, supreme, 59, 86, 191, 193, 245, 265, 315–18
bodhisattva, 34
body awareness, 12, 552–56, 557–61
Bonhoeffer, Dietrich, 382, 383
Brahman, 171, 191, 264–68, 301, 308, 316, 582
Brahmin (Brāhmana), 189–91, 229, 231, 232, 244, 327, 328
bread, sacramental, 122, 125, 129, 149, 151 ff.
breath (breathing), 276, 277, 295
brotherhood, 426; see Chapter Six, passim
Brunner, Emil, 71, 531, 605
Buber, Martin, 200, 591
Buddha, 16, 35, 38, 173, 179, 220, 269–71, 274, 278, 282, 311, 315, 316, 325–31, 401
Buddhism (Buddhist), 4, 34, 207, 209, 219, 261, 263, 269, 274, 275, 280, 281, 285, 287, 316–18, 325, 327–31, 382

C

cakras, 556
Calvin, John, 237
Calvinists, 4
Campbell, Joseph, 168, 300
campus (student) movement, 423–28
Camus, Albert, 247, 248, 353, 420, 430, 433, 434, 576, 592
Carmichael, Stokely, 429, 430
caste, 225–29, 249, 265, 448–50 (See also varna and jāti)
Castro, Fidel, 458, 469
Catholic, Roman, see Roman Catholic
celebration, 117, 123, 145 f., 148, 387, 407
ceremonial, neurotic, 161 ff., 166

ceremony, civil-religious, 132 ff., 249
ceremony, initiation, 100, 170
ceremony, marriage, 113 ff., 165, 170
ceremony, sacred, 100, 106, 132 ff., 136, 146, 157, 160, 162, 164, 236, 328
Cézanne, 592
change, see transformation
change, technological, 513 ff.
Chardin, Teilhard de, 510
charity, 33 (*See also* benevolence)
Cherry, Conrad, 132
Chiang Kai-shek, 463
"Chicago Seven," 442
child(ren), 187, 188, 207, 227, 243, 260, 303, 362–65, 380, 394, 396, 397, 410 (*See also* filial piety)
Chinese, 171, 183, 185, 203–09, 440, 538
Chinese Cultural Revolution, 461–67
Christ, *see* Jesus
Christian, pietistic, 473–74
Christian(ity), 2–5, 32, 119 ff., 123 ff., 132, 156, 171, 177, 201, 234–37, 245, 247, 261, 308, 328, 339, 365, 380, 382, 384, 386, 405, 407–13, 430, 434, 490, 531
Chuang Tzu, 205, 288–90
Church, Christian, 128, 171, 499, 538
Church of Jesus Christ of the Latter-Day Saints, 47
circumcision, 102, 105
civilization, 141, 167, 520, 532 ff.
civil-rights movement, 368 (*See also* 423–35, 442–45 *passim*)
Civil War (the American), 137, 432, 433
Clarke, Arthur C., 494
Clark, Ramsey, 467–72
clergy, 489 (*See also* priest)
Clifford, W. K., 174
clitorectomy, 102, 105
commandment, 31, 33, 194
Communion (Holy), see Eucharist
communication, 369, 371, 430
Communist, 435–41
community, 97, 99, 100, 184, 225, 233, 242, 247, 248, 251, 262, 274, 297, 325, 327, 409, 410
compassion (pity), 36, 37, 39, 196, 220, 270, 282, 311, 326, 329, 366
compulsion (neurotic), 164
computer, 485, 486, 493
concentration (*samadhi*), 272, 276, 278–79, 300, 302, 307, 308

Cone, James H., 429–35
confession, 239, 382
conformity, 181, 425
confrontation, 369, 370, 372–74
Confucian, 8, 184, 185, 187, 193, 207, 209, 210, 234, 382, 436
Confucius, 208–209, 215, 438
conduct, virtuous, 193, 290, 294, 295, 316
conscience, 220, 235, 240, 242, 243, 331, 401, 402
consciousness, 41, 42, 44, 52, 220–21, 223, 264–66, 276, 281, 300–302, 308, 309, 311, 312, 322, 391, 395, 403, 409, 526
consecration, 150, 152
Constitution (of the United States), 133, 138
contemplation, 34, 147
control, 25, 499, 503, 506
conversion, 7, 100
Coomaraswamy, Ananda K., 172, 493
Copernicus, 338
Cragg, K., 237
"creative interaction," 11, 359, 366, 376, 377
creativity (human), 390, 393, 394, 405, 409, 426
creatureliness, sense of, 146
credulity, 176, 177
creeds, 49 (*See also* doctrine)
cross (Christian), 156, 159
Cullen, Counteé, 442
cult, 99, 148, 150
cultivation (of human qualities), 184, 227, 231–32, 435–41
cultus, 141, 142, 144
curanderos, 562 f.
Cyborg, 514

D

dance, 46, 110, 143, 558
darkness, 37, 48, 70, 310, 313
data, primary, 19
Darwin, 338, 509
dead, cult of the, 132, 135
death, 49, 119–22, 172, 223, 282, 287, 288, 312, 313, 315, 365, 396, 404–407, 410–12, 415, 430, 431, 461–67, 488 ff., 492, 494, 511, 586
De Rougemont, Denis, 586

Declaration of Independence (U. S.), 133, 136, 138, 432

deities, 8, 10, 14, 32 (*See also* God)

delight, 41, 52 (*See also* joy)

deliverance, 38 (*See also* salvation)

Dellinger, David T., 442–45

delusion, 265, 283, 300 (*See also* illusion)

democracy, 232, 233, 234, 250, 425, 430, 498, 502, 507

demon, 35 (*See also* devil)

Descartes, René, 68

desire, 185, 189, 192, 215, 220, 222, 254, 255, 257, 258, 270, 275, 281, 282, 284, 287, 295, 304, 326, 394, 401–403, (*See also* greed)

despair, 24, 44, 48 (*See also* anxiety)

devil, 49, 379, 380, 396, 405

devotion, 34, 39, 45, 60, 147, 283, 292, 295, 307, 308, 321, 407

Dewey, John, 476, 590

dhamma (Buddhist), 270, 274

dharma (Hindu), 7, 181, 182, 184, 224–33, 237 (*See also* law, sacred; conduct, virtuous)

dhyana, 583 (*See also* absorption, concentration, meditations)

"dimension of depth" (Tillich), 355–58

Dionysus, 141, 493

disciple(s), 30, 43

discipline, 208, 213, 261, 263, 291, 299–300, 307, 310–15, 363

dissociation, law of, 155, 157 ff., 166

displacement, see dissociation

distinctions (in society), 213–14, 220, 225, 228–29, 233, 254

distress, 24, 61 (*See also* anxiety)

divine (divinity), 9, 24, 33, 64, 99, 263, 292–97, 306, 317, 380, 412, 493

doctrine(s), 49, 177 (*See also* creeds, dogma)

dogma, 388, 394, 395, 398, 407

Dostoyevsky, 354, 490, 499

doubt(s), 177, 270, 296, 304, 309, 311, 312, 398

Douglass, Frederick, 429

dread, religious, 79, 80

dream(ing), 35, 134 f.

drug(s), 158, 381, 489, 557–79

drunkenness, 46, 63, 608

Dunbar, Roxanne, 446–52

Durkheim, E., 242

duty(ies), 188, 191, 239, 241, 327, 328, 379, 401

E

earth, 29, 185–86, 187–88, 194, 215, 238, 289, 294, 297–99, 391

ecstasy, 40, 49, 50, 54, 64, 366

Eden, Garden of, 114, 116

education, 185, 362, 366, 368, 374, 376, 378, 381, 405, 412, 499, 503, 522

ego, 264, 272, 297, 302, 304, 383, 403, 404, 409, 426

ego, collective, 520, 522, 528

Einstein, Albert, 590

election (spiritual), 33, 78 f.

"electronic Buddhism," 493

Eleusis, 564

Eliade, Mircea, 593

Eliot, T. S., 506

emotion, 77 ff., 186–87, 201, 213, 272, 281, 306, 310, 314, 320, 321, 382, 398, 401, 405

encounter (divine), 23, 24, 28, 31

encounter, interpersonal, 366, 370–72, 378

Engels, Frederick, 435–37, 448

enlightenment, 7, 220, 261, 270, 281–83, 287, 288, 314, 425 (*See also satori*)

Enlightenment Period, 533

environment, 220, 226–27, 482

environment, modification of, 498 f., 503, 513

eroticization, 552–56

Esalen Institute, 366, 367, 405, 553, 554, 557–61, 599

eternal, 121, 134, 184, 270, 298, 365, 379, 412

Ethical Culture, 234–37

ethic(s), 174, 187, 195, 207, 234, 236, 238–39, 241, 254, 255, 262, 307, 323, 379, 381, 382, 385, 390, 391, 394, 402, 405, 406, 410

Ethics and Religion (*See* religion and morality)

Eucharist, 97, 120, 150 ff., 562, 574

Eupsychia, 374–78, 405

evangelism, 54, 58, 159

Eve, 115, 116, 390–95

evidence (empirical), 174, 176, 177, 178

evil, 64, 176, 196, 197, 219, 220, 222, 232, 236, 238, 239, 254, 255, 259, 270, 326, 331, 362, 363, 380, 383, 391, 395, 396, 401, 403, 491

evolution, 227, 300, 346–50, 413, 509 ff., 522, 524, 525, 527

existence, profane, 146 ff.
existentialism, 429–34
Exodus, the, 75, 116
experience, 25, 26, 28, 40, 43, 47, 54, 56, 60, 101, 178, 264, 271, 272, 276, 281, 293, 296, 300, 301, 303, 306, 308, 310, 313–15, 367–72, 382, 391, 402, 403
experience, philosophical, assessment of, 91 ff.
experience(s), religious, 31, 51, 67, 95, 570–78
experience, sensuous, 12, 543 ff. (See Chapter Eight passim)
experiment(al), 366, 367, 374, 500
Ezekiel, 469

F

face, divine, 37
fact(s), judgment of, 499
faith, 27, 120, 126, 139, 235, 239, 246, 297, 301, 307, 308, 311, 328, 363, 364, 398, 406, 407, 409–11, 527
faith, Christian, 540
faith, Muslim, 62
Family, the, 449, 450
family, religion of the, 207, 208
Fanon, Franz, 431
Fate (destiny), 215–16, 239, 252, 303, 358, 408, 410, 413
fear, 26, 27, 28, 37, 41, 42, 46, 70, 270, 295, 297, 304, 376–78, 385, 387, 403, 405
fear of God (dread), 194, 293, 294, 296
feeling(s), 187, 231, 261, 276, 278–80, 284, 295, 302, 314, 326, 366, 368, 369, 372, 382, 402, 403 (See also Chapter Eight passim)
Fehl, N. E., 210
Feigl, H., 319, 320
fellowship, 69
female liberation (See women's liberation)
feminism (See women's liberation)
Ferkiss, V. C., 508
Ferré, Nels, 68
filial piety (hsiao), 187–88, 207
final cause(s), 338
finitude, sense of, 146
First Epistle of John, 474
fire, tongues of, 51
food, unclean, 29
forgiveness, 249, 365, 390
form(ing), 38, 98 ff.

Forsyth, Peter Taylor, 69
Francis, Saint, 69
Franco, 422
freedom, 52, 69, 401, 404, 408, 409, 417, 420–23, 425, 429–35, 503, 511, 527
freedom (total liberation), 420–23 (See also freedom, spiritual)
freedom, bourgeois, 420–23
freedom, political and economic, 135, 420–23
freedom, social, 198, 201, 363, 394
freedom, spiritual, 233, 238, 261, 263, 265–66, 281, 287, 296–98, 304, 307, 358, 362, 364, 365, 388, 390, 391, 396, 397
Freedom Rides, 457
Freud, Sigmund, 160, 243, 362, 397, 398, 401, 403, 404, 574
Fromm, Erich, 399, 406, 407
Fuller, R. Buckminster, 484
fusion, spiritual, 491
future, 222–23, 307, 314, 329, 381–83, 393
future, chart of the, 494–97
futurist(s), 513

G

Galileo, G., 338, 339
game, world, 485 ff.
Gandhi, M. K., 69, 198, 235
Ganges, 45, 64
Garnet, Henry, 430
"gayatri" (verse of Hindu meditation), 546
general-systems-theory, 486
genetic code, 510, 517
genius, Greek, 144
Gentiles, 29
Germany, 34
Gethsemane, 69
Gettysburg Address, 137
Ghose, Sri Aurobindo, 519, 531
ghosts, fear of, 79, 84 f.
gift, 27, 30
gift(s), sacrificial, 151, 152
gladness (as test of truth), 551
glory, 24, 29, 48, 57, 58
glossolalia, 52, 54
goal, 257, 258, 259, 261, 272, 296, 298, 300, 310, 314, 316, 318, 358, 360, 369, 395, 402, 407
god(s), 2, 7, 13, 16, 21, 23, 25–28, 30, 31, 33, 40, 42, 48, 50, 51, 54, 60, 62–65, 114, 117, 120, 171, 179, 180, 191, 194,

god(s) *(cont.)*
196–97, 201, 206, 207, 236, 237–41, 244,
247, 249, 260, 288, 291, 293–98, 301,
306–309, 317, 322, 336–37, 338–43, 359,
365, 377, 379, 380, 382, 391, 393, 394,
397, 403, 405, 406, 408–13, 414, 434,
490, 533, 562, 605–12
God, abstract idea of, 75
God, attributes of, 56, 58, 69, 70, 71, 72, 74,
78, 81–83, 119, 121
God, as creator, 534
God, death of, 351, 488
God, doctrine of, 72
God, as Father, 9
God, gift of, 121
God, glory of, 194
God, judgment of, 123
God, kingdom of, 118, 171
God, knowledge of, 68, 71 ff., 74 ff.
God, Lamb of, 129, 130
God, love of, 70
God, name of, 72 ff.
God, relations with and attitudes toward,
31, 32, 43, 69, 70, 74, 78, 79, 93, 97,
120, 149 ff., 151, 540
God, revelation of, 74 ff.
God, Shrine of, 31, 32
God, Son of, 129
God, will of, 184, 195, 238, 290, 292, 293,
392, 408, 414
God, word of, 29, 131, 195
God, worship of, 81
Goddard, Dr. R. H., 494
Goddess, 44, 46
Godless world, 351–55
godliness, form of, 49
gods, dancing, 111
gods, masked, cult of, 106, 109
good, 197, 209, 212, 239, 254–60, 303, 331,
362–64, 377, 379–81, 383, 386, 387, 391,
395, 396, 401
good and evil, 337
goodness, automatic, 506
gospel, 26
Gospel, Four Square, 54
gospel, preaching of, 538
government, 186, 208, 211, 229–30, 244, 425,
501
Govinda, Lama Anagarika, 34
grace, 21, 26, 27, 59, 237, 291, 306, 390, 406,
409, 410

Graham, Billy, 356
Great Leap Forward (China, 1958), 464
greed, 270 *(See also* desire)
Greek(s) (Greece), 212, 221, 226, 234, 236,
244, 254, 255, 271, 297, 389, 390, 392,
393
"group therapy," 382 *(See also* integrity
group)
growth, spiritual, 533
guilt, 29, 164, 166, 243, 244, 336, 506
gunpowder, invention of, 535
guru, 35, 38
Gustaitis, Rasa, 557–61, 599

H

happenings 493
happiness, infinite, 44
harmonious(ly), 181, 186
harmony, 39, 185, 195, 203, 213, 225, 227–
29, 230, 521
Harrington, Alan, 488
Hartshorne, M. H., 20
hatred, 201, 222, 366, 368, 373, 405
health, 352, 501
health, mental, 384–90, 398, 399, 405,
Chapter Five *passim*
heart, 28, 48
heart, gladness of, 37
heaven, 29, 32, 185–86, 187–89, 194, 206,
215, 216, 235, 289, 290, 293, 301, 379,
380, 411
Heidegger, Martin, 589, 590, 594–95
hell, 26, 28, 379, 380, 382, 397
help, 24
help, medical, 493
Herberg, Will, 246
heredity, 220, 225–27, 231
hermit, 34
heroism, value of, 507
Hesse, Hermann, 353 n.
High Priest, 30
Hindu, 183, 189, 193, 221, 224–31, 244,
263, 300, 305–307
Hinduism, 4, 43, 64, 172, 339
Hiroshima, 531
history, God's purposes in, 135
history and myth, 119 ff.
history, sacred, 150
history, saving, 150
Hobbes, Thomas, 340, 349

Hölderlin, 595
holiday, 133, 145
holiness, transcendent, 148
Holy, the, 23, 24, 27–29, 40, 147
holy, celebration of, 148
Holy, experience of the, 39, 62
holy, manifestation of the, 145
holy day, 133, 145
Holy Ghost, 2, 51, 52
holy men, 193, 327, 414
Holy One, 7, 9, 20, 21
Holy Power, experiences of, 43
Holy Presence, 263, 291, 310, 320
Holy Spirit, 29, 30, 53, 58, 120
Holy Spirit, baptism of, 56, 57
Holy Spirit, invocation of, 125
Holy Spirit, power of, 56, 57
homo faber, 532
honest, 304
honor, 43
hope, 24, 25, 120, 367, 374, 410, 411
Hsün Tzu (Hsün Ch'ing), 185–87, 209, 210–18, 254
Hu Tzu, 288–90
hubris (arrogance), 393
Hughes, Langston, 432
human rights, 11, chapter six *passim*
humanist(ic), 234–37, 343–46, 361, 365, 377, 380, 383, 386, 387, 390, 300 401, 404–407, 410, 479
Humanist Manifesto, 343–46
Hume, David, 342
humility, 25, 41, 42, 82, 307, 389, 403, 409
Humphreys, C., 291
Huxley, Aldous, 506, 571
Huxley, Julian S. (Sir), 346–50, 412, 510
Huxley, T. H., 342, 506
hymn, gospel, 59
hypnotism, 51, 55, 158
hypothesis, 500
hysteria, 51

I

I Ching, 570
ideals, exemplars of American, 135
ideology, 484
identity, human, 382, 511
idolatry, 75, 118
ignorance, 42, 171, 175, 178, 222, 267–69, 291, 300, 304, 329, 393 (*See also* illusion)

illumination (ultimate), 262, 265, 307 (*See also* enlightenment)
illusion, 177, 222, 232, 253, 300, 302, 303, 313, 406
image(s), paradigmatic, 120
imagery, religious, 64
imagery, sensuous, 64
imagination, mythic, 141
imagination, poetic, 144
immortality, 266, 267, 331, 411, 412, 491 ff., 497
immortality, symbolic, 461–67
immortality, revolutionary, 461–67
impermanence, 270, 272, 331
impulses, 270
inauthentic, 252
incarnation, 151 f., 172
India, 34, 43, 45, 64, 171, 184, 197–98, 219, 221, 224–33, 280, 299, 309, 327
individualistic, 25
individuality, mutuality and, 521
industrialism, 232
inequality, 214, 219–20, 232, 245
infinity, 408
injustice, 198, 202, 219, 220, 249 (*See also* justice)
iniquity, 62
initiation, necessity for, 101
initiation, rite of, 38
innovation, 366, 379, 380, 382, 385, 386
Inquisitor, Grand, 395
insight, 34, 272, 278, 288, 292, 300, 308, 316, 321, 325, 397, 403
instinct, sexual, 165 ff.
Institute of Marxism-Leninism, 435
instruction, secret, 101
insurrection, spiritual, 489
integrity, 361, 376, 377, 381, 400, 403, 404
"Integrity Group," 378, 379, 381, 382
intellect(ual), 265, 302, 310, 311, 331, 368, 400, 401, 404
intercourse, ritual, 103, 104
International Federation for Internal Freedom (I.F.I.F.), 571
interpretation, 67 ff.
interpretation, Freudian, 156
intimacy, 373–74, 382
intolerance, 364
intuition, 303, 321, 322, 324
involution, 525, 528 f.
Ishwara, 527, 530

Islam, 3, 32, 179, 237–39, 291, 490
isolation, 382, 383
isolation, feelings of, 489
isolation, self-centered, 77
Israel, 61, 115, 193
Israel, archetypical, 115
Israel, Covenant with, 75
Isracl, destiny of, 119
Israel, myth of, 119
Israel, people of, 30

J

James, Epistle of, 48
James, William, 575, 577
Japan, 31, 32, 171, 187, 280, 281, 283, 310,
    313, 371
jāti, 192
Jehovah's Witnesses, 139
jen (human-heartedness), 187, 203, 209
Jerusalem, 29, 114, 115
Jesus Christ, 2, 3, 10, 30, 58, 69, 120–22,
    198, 202, 236, 247–49, 365, 395–97, 400,
    410, 413–15
Jesus, bless you, 53, 54
Jesus, blood of, 53, 122, 123, 128, 130, 153
Jesus, body of, 122, 123, 128, 130, 131, 153
Jesus, death and resurrection of, 119–122,
    123, 125, 126
Jesus, to know, 50
Jesus, name of, 151
Jesus, presence of, 152
Jesus, sacrifice of, 151, 153
Jesus, self-offering of, 75
Jewish, 30, 116, 193, 200, 234–35, 365, 392,
    393 (*See also* Judaism)
Jim Crow laws, 478
John (the Baptist), 29
John (the disciple), 471
Joshua, 488
joy, 35, 52, 56, 58, 62, 66, 115, 282, 283, 290,
    298, 299, 304, 308, 315, 360, 363, 365,
    377, 381, 388, 404, 405, 409, 412, 554,
    565
Judaism, 4, 113, 139, 490 (*See also* Jewish)
Judea, 29
Jung, C. G., 3, 357, 403
justice, 61, 195, 201, 202, 211–12, 214–15,
    228, 377, 410, 454–61, 467–72, 486, 498
justice, freedom and, 422–23

K

Kachinas, 111
Ka'ba, 63
Kaibara, E., 187–89
Kairos, 555
Kaiser, Robert, 552–56, 599
Kalandra (opposition historian in Prague),
    422
Kali, 43, 44, 45, 46
Kama, 67
Kami, 7
kanrodai, 32
Kant, I., 336, 479
karma, 219–24 (*See also* action)
Kazantzakis, N., 263, 296
Keleman, Stanley, 555
Keller, Albert Galloway, 600–604
Kennedy, Robert, 132 ff.
kensho, 281, 578 (*See also satori*)
Kepler, Johannes, 339
Kierkegaard, Sören, 590
King, Jr., Martin Luther, 197–202
King (divine), 42
Kingdom of God, 40, 435, 474
kirtan (praise), 64
knowledge, 35, 104, 175, 178, 263, 320–25,
    330, 364, 385
knowledge (wisdom), eye of, 193, 310, 312
knowledge, religious, critique of, 89 ff.
knowledge, spiritual, 194, 264–67, 292–95,
    298–300, 303, 305, 306, 308, 316, 377,
    392, 397, 406, 410
koan, 281, 286, 310, 311
Koran, *see* Qur'an
Krishna, 9, 64
Krutch, Joseph Wood, 504, 505
kshatriya (rulers, protectors), 189, 190, 230
Kuan, 583
Kundalini Yoga, 556
Kunitokotachi-no-Mikoto, 32

L

Lamont, Corliss, 343 n.
Law, Cosmic, 10, 181, 183, 184, 203, 242,
    424 (*See also* natural law)
law, moral, 234–36, 260
law, natural, 13 (*See also* Cosmic Law)
law, social, 120, 189, 199, 200, 212, 225,
    230, 254

law, sacred (divine), 191, 193, 194, 198, 238, 241
law, transcendent, 191, 197, 292
law, unjust, 200, 254
Lawrence, D. H., 593
League for Spiritual Discovery, 562
Leary, Timothy, 561–70, 598
Lenin, 435–37, 458
Leonard, G. B., 366, 405
Lewis, C. I., 590
Lewis, C. S., 412
li (rites, propriety), 185–87, 193, 210–18, 237
liberation (liberated), 52, 266, 267, 269, 274, 300, 388 (*See also* freedom)
Liberation (magazine), 445
Lieh Tzu, 288–90
life, eternal, 147, 247
life, profane, 25, 39, 146, 147, 526
Lifton, Robert Jay, 461–67
light, 37–39, 44, 45, 48, 50, 52, 70
Lincoln, Abraham, 137, 202, 432
liturgy, 97, 123 ff., 249
living, standard of, 485
living-dead, 102, 104
Logos, 152
Lord, 26, 27, 29, 30, 39, 40, 49, 50, 52, 53, 55, 57, 58, 60–62, 65, 114, 128, 193, 265, 299
Lord, fear of, 61
Lord's Supper, 97, 125 (*See also* Eucharist)
lotus-flower, 35, 38
love, 26, 28, 35, 36, 37, 39, 42, 60, 131, 152, 202, 304, 306, 307, 361–65, 372, 376, 382, 398, 400, 401, 407, 408, 410–12, 414, 425, 492, 501
Lowen, Alexander (Dr.), 555
LSD, 491, 492, 558, 560, 578
Luther, Martin, 80, 82, 202, 237, 605, 606–607
Lutheran, 4, 249, 606, 607

M

McPherson, Aimee Semple, 54
machine(s), teaching, 516
machinery, industrial, 484
magic, 107, 156
Maharishi Mahesh Yogi, 558
Manifesto of the Eighteen, 457
Maitreya (Buddha), 34, 35, 37

majesty (of God), 35, 40, 41, 61
Majumdar, S. K., 299, 300, 305
mandala, 35
Mañjuśrī, 35
man (kind), 23, 24, 32, 177, 187, 189, 207, 216, 234, 238, 255, 269–70, 291, 297, 300, 304, 310, 314, 330, 331, 337, 358, 365, 366, 372, 375, 377, 378, 380, 382, 383, 391, 393, 397, 400, 403, 405, 407, 408, 426, 431, 504, 507, 517, 531 ff., 532, 537
mantra, 307
Manu, Law of, 183, 189–93, 226, 254
Mao Tse-tung, 435, 458, 461–67
marathon, encounter, 370
March on Washington (1963), 457
Maritain, Jacques, 491
marriage, 114, 115, 192, 225–26, 229
Martin, C. B., 89
Martin, F. David, 589–98, 599
martyr(s), 135
Marx, Karl, 3, 245, 421, 435, 436, 437, 448, 574
Marxism, 448
Marxism-Leninism, 435–41
Maslow, Abraham, 366, 374–78, 405
masochism, 87 ff.
Mass, Roman Catholic, 123–27, 134, 149, 151
master (spiritual), 271, 277, 279, 281, 287, 288, 291–92, 309, 310, 319, 320, 329
Matter, 524, 529
May Fourth Movement, 467
May, Rollo, 390, 399, 405, 406, 412, 431
Mbiti, John S., 100
Mead, Sidney E., 136
meaning, universal (ultimate), 358, 382, 402, 406–407
meaninglessness, revolt against, 489
means, 9–12, 13, 334, 409, 486
Mecca, 63
mediatrix, 31
medicine bundle, 110
meditation, 45, 261, 269, 271–88, 290, 299, 307, 308, 310, 315, 316, 326, 327
medium, 31
Memorial Day, 132–35
Messiah, coming of, 116
metaphysics, 320–22, 361, 383
Methodist, 47, 49, 59, 139
Micklem, Nathaniel, 69
mighty, 37, 39

Miki, 31, 32, 33

Mill, John Stuart, 342

mind, 51, 220, 222, 224, 233, 258, 261, 269, 271, 276, 279, 282, 285, 290, 295, 301–303, 305, 307, 308, 311, 321, 322, 324, 326, 379,, 386, 426, 491, 521, 524 ff. (*See also* consciousness)

mindfulness, 269–280, 316

Mohammed (Muhammed), 179, 180, 195

modern scientific views, 337–43

monasticism, 34, 39, 263, 326, 327, 330

monk, 34, 37, 287, 313, 325, 326

Montes, 459

moral(s), 435, 502

morality and religion (*See* religion and morality)

morality as invention, 336–37

morality, social, 183, 187, 203, 207, 210, 211, 239, 242, 243, 254–60, 291, 340, 363, 364, 380–83, 387, 395, 400, 408, 414, 417, 425, 488 (*See also* law, moral)

Morgenthau, Hans, 557, 560–61

Mormon, see Church of Jesus Chirst of the Latter-Day Saints

Morte, 26

Moses, 62, 75

Mother, Divine, 43–47, 519

motivation(s), 304, 364, 397, 401

Mowrer, O. Hobart, 378, 379, 598–604

Moynihan, Daniel, 449

Mueller, Max, 1

Murphy, Michael, 557–59

music, 186, 194

Muslim, 195, 237–40, 263, 290, 291 (*See also* Islam)

Muzzey, David S., 234

mysterious, 24, 32, 34

mysterium tremendum, 78 ff., 578

mystery, 67, 72 ff., 77 ff., 85, 146, 147, 151, 303, 359, 408, 410

mysticism, 10, 39, 40, 206, 261, 262, 272, 290, 291, 296, 301, 314–16, 319, 321–22, 324–26, 388, 402, 571, 573

myth, 10, 97 ff., 113, 119, 132–39, 141 ff., 156, 157, 184, 365, 380, 390–92, 394, 395, 406, 433

N

nation, as church, 137 ff.

National Organization for Women (NOW), 446

Native American Church, 578

natural, 183, 197, 203, 207, 210, 229, 237, 277, 282–84, 308, 313, 322, 327, 387, 408, 412

nature, 187, 188–89, 204, 205–206, 211–13, 215–16, 226–27, 230–33, 236, 241, 255, 257, 264, 266, 272, 281, 288, 300, 303, 304, 307, 362, 364, 375, 378, 400, 402, 407, 408, 413, 523, 526, 534

Nazism, 353, 354, 491

Negro(es), 200, 201, 245, 248, 249, 367, 371–74 (*See also* Blacks)

Neill, A. S., 362, 405

neurosis, 160 ff., 173

Neusner, Jacob, 113

New Left, 442, 444

New York Radical Women, 446

Newton, Sir Isaac, 338, 339

Niebuhr, Reinhold, 489, 605–12

Nielsen, Kai, 351–355

Nietzsche, Friedrich, 170, 245, 336–37, 397, 592, 594, 595

nirvāna, 7, 261, 315–18, 326, 327, 330, 583

No More Miss America, 446

Nock, Albert Jay, 585

numinous, 78

Nyanaponika Thera, 269, 300, 325

O

Oakland Seven, 444

obedience, 395, 396

obligation, moral, 188–89, 208, 225, 238, 239

Oedipus Complex, 169

Oglesby, Carl, 454–61

Old Left, 444

One, the Coming, 35, 37, 38

oneness, spiritual, 402, 403, 520

ontical experience, 590

openness, 25

oppression, racial, 202

oracle, divince, 33

order, cosmic, 203, 241

order, eternal, 185, 195

order, moral, 184, 333–37

order, natural, 99, 146, 183, 184, 190, 224

order, religious, 39

order, social, 213–14, 224, 244, 252–53

Orwell, George, 506

Other, the, 23, 24, 28

Otto, Rudolf, 77, 578

Otto, Walter F., 141
Outler, A. C., 405, 406

P

Pahnke, Walter, 572 f.
pagan, 72, 74
pain, 31, 32, 44 (*See also* suffering)
Paraclete, 53
paradigm, 117, 120, 137
paradise, 115, 392, 395
paradox, 7
parents, 188, 196, 227, 362–64, 394, 396, 397
parson, 42
Pascal, Blaise, 351, 352, 489
passion, 52
Passover, festival of, 113, 116 ff.
Patanjali, 302, 306–308
path, 30, 44, 70, 238, 314–18, 396
Patmore, Coventry, 587
Paul, the apostle, 29, 49, 119, 198, 202, 309, 571, 605, 606
peace, 27, 34, 186, 221–22, 225, 229, 304, 328, 331, 386, 396
Peale, Norman Vincent, 356
Pentecostal, 51, 54, 55
peoplehood, myth of, 118
perfect(ion), 7, 14, 208, 209, 231, 234, 265, 281, 286, 290, 303, 386, 412, 498
persecution(s), 42
personage(s), 48, 49, 50
personality, 77, 159, 360
persuasion, nature of, 503
Peter, Simon, 29
philosophy, 283, 284, 320, 322, 386, 397, 398, 493
phobia, 165
piety, Western, 60 (*See also* Christian, pietistic)
Plague, The, 353, 433
Plato, 336, 338, 352, 479, 499, 501
play, 506
pleasure, 187, 220, 231, 284, 304
Polanyi, Michael, 574
political acts as religious, see chapter six *passim*
"Port Huron Statement, The", 423 n.
postures, meditation, 273, 274, 277, 311
potential (human), 426
power(s), 25, 27, 39, 41, 42, 46, 48, 54, 55, 59, 67, 175, 244, 245, 258, 288, 298, 300,

power(s) *(cont.)*
304, 306, 309, 359, 367, 385, 393, 394, 398, 401, 404, 407, 410, 411, 511
praise, 26, 60
Prakriti, 530
prayer(s), 34, 35, 39, 42, 44, 50, 54, 68–71, 107, 111, 113, 114, 124, 126, 156, 165, 195, 201, 240, 261, 290, 381, 488
prayer-sticks, 108
prejudice, 368, 370, 373
"primitivism," 453
preach, 26, 28, 49, 54–55
Presbyterian, 397
presence, divine, 28, 141 ff., 143
priest(s), 31, 43, 99, 110, 164, 385–86, 394
principles, moral, 195, 258–60
procession(s), 143
profane, 145, 175
Prometheus, 390–91, 393, 394, 397, 406
propaganda, 503
Protestant, 57, 139, 379, 382, 396
proverb(s), 1
providence, God's 137, 409
Psalm, 60, 193, 194
psychedelic (drugs), 12, 570–79
psychic(ally), 359, 400, 406
psychoanalysis, 160, 168, 173, 308, 361, 378, 390, 399, 400, 403, 404
"psychoformation," 461
psychological, 307, 324, 359, 360, 375–77, 386, 387, 391, 392, 394, 397
psychology, 223, 300, 305, 307, 309, 321, 322, 359, 361, 363, 365, 374, 390, 405, 412, 497 ff.
psychology and religion, 3
psychosis, 493
psychotherapy, 360, 361, 375, 386, 390, 399, 405, 406, 410, 499
punishment, 196, 206, 211, 242, 243, 294, 295, 379, 391, 393, 394, 503, 506
punishment, capital, 247–49
pure, 265, 266, 292, 302
purification, 240, 272, 298, 399
purpose, ultimate, 539
Purusha, 526, 530

Q

Quakers, 4, 245, 247
Qur'an, 195–97, 237, 238, 293
Quotations from Chairman Mao Tse-tung, 466
al-Qushayri, 290, 292

R

races, equality of, 417, 419
Radhakrishnan, S., 221, 224, 225, 478–80
Rahu, 64
Ramakrishna, Sri, 43–47, 309
rapture, 40–42, 51, 86
reality, 24, 118, 152, 320, 525
reality, transcendent (Divine), 67, 183, 291, 292
Reality, Ultimate, 203, 264, 269, 288, 304, 306, 309, 324, 410
reason, 72, 76, 174, 237, 256–58, 300, 302, 312, 318, 368, 388, 405, 408, 409, 425
rebellion 454, 461, 531
rebirth, 168, 170 ff. (*See also* birth [second, new], reincarnation)
reconciliation, 119–22
redemption, 117, 135, 409, 412
Red Guards, 465, 466, 492
Reformation, Protestant, 379
Reformed-Evangelical Church, 51
reformer, religious, 39
regeneration, 172
Reich, Wilhelm, 555
reincarnation, 219, 244, 265, 315
reinforcement, positive, 506 (*See also* education)
rejoicing, 28 (*See also* joy)
religion, 1–22 *passim*, 32, 148, 157, 166, 333, 339, 523 (*See also* ceremony, rite, ritual, sacred, transformation, ultimate)
religion, civic, 135, 137–39, 246 (*See also* ceremony, civil-religious)
religion, evolution of, 4–5, 333
religion, morality and, 2, 8, 10, 174, 472–77
religion, study of, 1–22 *passim*
religiousness, type of, 24, 40, 197
remembrance, 291–96
renunciation, 364
repentance, 30, 240, 243
repression, police, 445
repression, psychological, 165
responsibility, 219, 379, 382, 394–96, 410–12, 502
responsibility, social, 134, 184–85, 224, 240, 389, 397
resurrection, 104, 172, 586 (*See also* Jesus, death and resurrection of)

retreat, religious, 109, 110, 112
revelation, 13, 19, 31, 32, 47, 72–74, 76, 77, 193, 210, 237, 239, 292, 297, 385, 401, 403, 410
revolution, 245, 454–61, 489, 509, 512
revolution, technological, 508 ff., 536, 538, 540
righteousness, 121, 185, 193, 194, 196, 202, 209, 236, 237, 330, 409
rites, 10, 14–16, 128, 157, 159, 185–86, 190, 246, 327 (*See also* ceremony, ritual, sacrifice)
rites, African, 101, 105
rites, initiation and puberty, 100 ff., 112, 172
rites, funeral, 186, 252, 410
ritual, 31, 44, 97 ff., 106 ff., 113, 141, 145 ff., 155 ff., 160, 162, 170, 185, 187, 210, 212, 239, 249, 292, 293, 329, 410, 523 (*See also* ceremony, rites)
Róheim, Géza, 168 ff.
Roman Catholic, 4, 39, 57, 123, 139, 149, 382, 396, 562
Rousseau, Jean Jacques, 452–54
Royce, Josiah, 476
ṛṣi (Hindu sage), 190–91, 231
rule(s) of conduct, 185, 191, 259, 260
Russian revolution, the, 420, 455

S

sacrament, 14, 122, 123, 126, 151, 191, 234, 239, 410, 572
Sacred, 3, 110, 145, 151, 155, 247, 291, 562
sacrifice, 14, 123, 132, 137, 143, 149, 151, 171, 186, 187, 190, 192
sadhana, 557–59
sadism, 87
sage, 208, 211–15, 271
salvation, 7, 27, 29, 128, 151, 159, 301, 327, 330, 360, 364, 386, 412, 498
samadhi, 300–302, 309, 310, 316 (*See also* concentration)
sanctification, 151
sanctuary, 34, 61
sanzen (personal Zen interview), 280–86, 311–13
Sartre, Jean-Paul, 353, 593
Satan, 27 (*See also* demon, devil)
satori, 310, 313, 314, 578
Savior, 38, 60, 239, 297, 298

sceptre, 35, 37

Schopenhauer, Arthur, 336, 594

Schutz, Bill, 554

science, 152, 157, 263, 302, 306, 320–24, 362, 377, 385–86, 388, 398, 407, 497–99, 502, 508, 512, 520

scriptures, 19, 48, 72, 225, 266, 291, 297, 377

Seale, Bobby, 442

secret, 101, 103, 105, 294, 296, 299, 414

secular, 380, 381, 410, 417, 533, 538–40

security, 169, 376

Seeley, J., 378, 384, 399, 404

segregation (of races), 198–202, 367

Self (real, ultimate), 26, 151, 204, 265–67, 282, 283, 291, 300–302, 304, 305, 312, 313, 358, 361, 414, 415, 488, 489, 509, 516, 526

self-actualizing, 375, 381

self-identity, 225, 390–94, 397, 402, 406, 407

Self, integrated, 359, 378, 409, 412

sensuality, 605–12

sexuality, 64 ff., 101 ff., 214, 373, 391, 394, 580–89

Shakti, 530

Shao-Ch'i, Liu, 435–41, 461, 464

shaman, 288–90

Shankara, 264, 315

Sharī'ah, 237–39

Shaull, Richard, 454

Shaw, George Bernard, 170, 468, 603

Sherrington, Sir Charles, 510

Shibayama, Z., 310, 315

shrine, 44

shuddering, 80

sign, 149–50, 491 (*See also* symbol)

silence, 296–98, 369, 371, 372, 425

sin(s), 27, 29, 53, 57, 60, 61, 63, 74, 120–22, 177, 191, 194, 196, 200, 209, 220, 237, 249, 265, 266, 279, 365, 383, 387, 405

skepticism, 338

Skinner, B. F., 497

"slave morality," 336

Smart, N., 314

Smith, John E., 145, 175, 472–77

Smith, Joseph, 19, 47

Smith, Huston, 559, 570–79, 598

social, 197, 198, 202, 207, 210, 212, 213, 225, 229–31, 233, 241–43, 249, 252, 254, 259, 260, 262, 263, 283, 301, 323, 325, 328–31, 358, 381, 384–90, 399, 400, 411, 414,

social (*cont.*) 417, 420

society, 169 ff., 176, 211–15, 225, 229, 230, 233, 239, 242–45, 247, 249–51, 271, 282, 300, 327, 331, 360, 364, 376, 379, 380, 394, 398, 399

society, withdrawal or separation from, 101, 103, 109, 110, 112, 158

Socrates, 339

Solanis, Valerie, 446

soul, 28, 40, 42, 190, 221, 233, 247, 297, 298, 321, 360, 399–401, 410, 412, 413, 523 ff., 528

Soviet Union, 444, 463

space, conquest of, 513–15

spirit, 33, 40, 148, 521, 523 ff.

Spirit, 29, 41, 51, 53, 54, 57, 171, 523 ff., 528

spontaneity, 377, 410, 426

Stace, Walter T., 337–43, 572

Stalin, 435–37

state, totalitarian, 537

Stop the Draft Week, 444

Straelen, Henry van, 31

stress, extreme, 158

strife, 39, 47

structure, 408

structure, mythic, definition of, 113 ff.

Students for a Democratic Society (SDS), 423–28, 444

stupor, 83–84

submission, religious, 12, 87

substance, 151, 152

Sudra (servants), 189–190, 192, 230

suffering (grief, pain), 37, 44, 220, 244, 245, 261, 265, 269, 272, 282, 298, 300–301, 315, 325–27, 331, 364, 381, 383, 386, 391, 394, 400

Sūfī, 263, 290–96, 316, 317

Summerhill, 362, 363, 365

Sumner, William Graham, 600–604

superconsciousness, 300–303, 305, 306, 309

supernatural, 160, 333, 345, 381, 386, 387

superstition, 3, 142, 146, 175, 490

supplication, 25, 35, 60

symbol(s), 10, 99, 149 ff., 162, 164, 245, 246, 262, 266, 366, 397, 402

symbol and reality, 149 ff.

symbolism, 139, 168, 169

synagogue, 118

Synanon Foundation, 367, 381

Szuma Chien, 467

T

Tagore, Rabindranath, 545–552, 598
Tantric Buddhism, 582
Tao, 203, 205, 213, 582
Taoism (Taoist), 171, 207, 209, 263, 288
Taylor, R., 254
tea ceremony (cha-no-yu), 584
teacher (teaching), 186, 190, 215, 269–72, 274, 282, 298, 305–309, 326, 327, 362, 371, 400, 401
technics, 531 ff. (See also technology)
technocracy, 12, 481 ff. (See also technology)
technology, 13, 385, 482, 494, 504, 508 ff., 510, 511, 531–33, 536
technology, evolution of, 513 ff., 533, 534, 541
temple, 29, 37, 43–46, 66, 142
Tenrikyo (The Religion of Divine Wisdom), 31–33
Teonanacatl, 562
Teresa of Jesus, Saint, 39–40
texts, revealed, 193, 265–67
theism, see God, theology
theocracy, 111
theology, 236, 320, 321, 360, 365, 380, 385, 397, 404
therapy, 361, 378, 381, 399, 403
Thompson, L. G., 203
throne, 26, 29, 35
Tibet, 34, 35
Tillich, Paul, 200, 355–58, 402, 430, 431, 578
time, escape from, 491
time(s), special, 117, 145
Tolstoy, Leo, 354
tongues, speaking in, 50–52, 55, 57
Torah, 117, 235 (See also law)
tradition, 28, 174, 191, 193, 208, 229, 238, 240, 330, 331, 385, 394, 498, 501
trance, 27, 32
transcendent, 184, 235, 320, 324, 334, 360, 366, 367, 374, 375
transformation, 6–12, 34, 115–17, 151, 153, 156, 301, 304, 325, 330, 360, 361, 384, 405, 410, 412, 413, 508, 527, 532
transgression, 196, 219
transhumanism, 346–50
transmigration, 192
tremor, 79

Trotsky, Leon, 462
trust (confidence), 307, 362, 364, 410
truth, 26, 34, 47, 50, 76, 176, 177, 179, 202, 247, 263, 266, 281, 283, 290, 296, 300–303, 308, 310, 311, 313, 319, 326, 368, 376, 377, 393, 398, 400, 415
Tseng, Tze, 436
"turning on," 557
"twice-born," 171
type(s), religious, 10, 12, 24, 40, 197 (See also religion)

U

ultimate, 3, 6–7, 10, 14, 265, 301, 303, 358, 377, 384, 389, 402, 403, 405–407, 410
"ultimate concern," 355–358
ultimates, nontranscendent, 333
unbeliever, 197
uncanny, 25, 80 ff.
understand(ing), 67, 208, 238, 241, 282, 295, 303, 305, 307, 317, 361, 364, 365, 367, 368, 398, 406
UNESCO, 422
Unger, Sanford, 576
union, 40, 41, 64
unity, 157, 520
universe, 31, 114, 297, 298, 313, 324, 402, 403
Upanishads, 171, 546
utopia(s), 375, 425, 492, 501

V

Vaishnava (sect), 551
Vaiśya (farmers, merchants), 189, 190, 192, 230
value(s), 214, 242–44, 246, 247, 286, 300, 301, 305, 306, 323, 324, 359, 377, 378, 383–90, 394, 396, 400, 405–408, 410, 425, 499
Van Gogh, 592
varna, 181, 190, 191, 224
Veda(s), 171, 190–93, 265–66, 546
Vedānta, 43, 264–67, 305
Vietnam War, 444–45
Vijayavardhana, D. C., 325
violence, physical, 368
virtue (virtuous), 187, 193, 203, 207–10, 224, 236, 237, 250, 260, 265, 266, 286, 325, 326, 328, 362, 409
Vishnu, 64

vision(s), 29, 30, 34, 41, 44, 45, 49, 50, 58, 135, 297, 563
Vivekananda, Swami, 308, 309
voodoo, 159

W

Wallace, Anthony F. C., 155, 333 n.
war, 219, 221, 222, 244, 269, 270, 362, 485, 486
Warnach, Victor, 149
Warner, Lloyd, 132
Washington, George, 137
Wasson, Gordon, 575
water, 29, 38, 40
Watt, James, 532, 536
Watts, Alan W., 493, 580–89, 599
"ways of being religious" (outline), 9
Weber, M., 244, 245
Wesley, John, 159
Weltanschauung, 354, 557
Whitehead, Alfred N., 339, 590, 591, 594
Whites, 367, 368, 370–74, 431
"wholly other," 83 ff., 263
wickedness, 60
will (divine), 33
will (human), 256–58, 307, 311, 313, 398
wine, sacramental, 149, 151 ff.
wisdom, 35, 37, 39, 48, 212, 213, 270, 271, 290–300, 302, 303, 305, 311, 313, 393, 402, 406, 407, 410, 412, 501
witness, 27, 54
WITCH, 446

Women of the American Revolution (WAR), 446
woman, 32, 42, 195, 196, 225, 226, 298, 371–73, 391, 393, 446–52
wonder (religious), 147, 402, 403, 414, 562
word, 27, 120, 151
works, good, 68, 71
world, 27, 35, 156, 193, 194, 233, 238, 313, 326, 370, 387, 412, 425, 482
"world brain," 497
worship, 2, 8, 43–46, 54, 60, 106, 118, 123, 146, 150, 242, 308, 328, 330, 367, 381, 403, 404, 407, 490 (*See also* prayer, rite, ritual)

Y

Yahweh, 74
yamabushi, 31
Yasutani Roshi, 280
yin-yang, 203–205
yoga (yogic concentration), 209, 262, 263, 273, 299–305, 316, 530, 582
yoni, 556
Yung-chia (Ch'an master), 286–88

Z

Zaehner, R. C., 571 f.
Zen, 148 n., 262, 263, 281–88, 310–14, 318, 558, 578
Zion, 114, 115
Zuni Indians, 19, 106 ff.

	Personal Experience of the Holy	Creation of Community Through Myth and Ritual	Daily Living That Expresses the Cosmic Law	Spiritual Fr⸱ Through Dis⸱ (Mysticis⸱
A) The Problem	• sin, pride, pretension • incapacity, imperfection, imperfect functioning	• the power of chaos; chaotic existence (physical, social, & personal); unreal existence; nonorder • willful alienation; or ignorant alienation; i.e., alienation from the real (sin) • sin, and/or ignorance • natural deterioration of secular activity	• social/cosmic disharmony (i.e., disharmony with the cosmic law, the transcendent ideal); disfunctionalism: i.e., imbalance with the "real" system (=Eastern) • immature man; disordered; out of step; disharmony in social/cosmic relationships • being unnaturally isolated; inauthenticity (=Roman Catholic) • moral imperfection (=Ethical Culture) • ignorant or willful rejection of one's social and cosmic relationships	• bondage, ignora⸱ separation from • bondage to self • ignorance (spir⸱ man's own maki⸱
B) The Answer	• the all-sufficiency of God (the Absolute Other) • the Divine Surprise, uncontrollable, nonprogrammed; the Inscrutable Mystery • "wakan"; "mana"; "maxpe" among American Indian and members of so-called pre-literate societies	• the power of the Divine Creation (of a specific order); a singular order transcendent creative activity; order through transcendent activity; Divine art • reconciliation—to the real; grace (the power of)	• a natural/cosmic/eternal/transcendent law to be followed • eternal harmony manifested (or implicit) in right social order	• transcendant (God, Self) • absolute freedor⸱ • absolute truth dent consciousn⸱
C) The Means as Appropriated Individually	• nonverbal feeling (a-intellectual, or anti-intellectual) • an individual, personal experience (inner); submission, obedience, dependency, trust, faith; a conversion • intense, dramatic, striking • historical, infrequent • unpredictable; cannot be encouraged • uncanny	• symbolic re-enactment through traditional creative activity; order through transcendent activity; Divine art • reconciliation—to the real; grace (the power of)	• proper self-identity cultivated through right social relationships (morality, ethics) • cultivating one's true nature in the eternal order by proper activity in relation to all life, and especially to other people • capacity and responsibility to cultivate (mature, grow, attain, realize) one's true nature • human existence is part of a natural order • the perfect is true humanity; perfection is maturity in being human	• personal discip⸱ sonal (inner) of immanent R⸱ • illumination th⸱ perconsciousnes⸱ • experience of p⸱ Kensho, Satori,
D) The Means as Expressed Socially	• illustrates confidence, demonstrates capacity • requires (produces) deviance from old ways and cultural habits • individualistic (minimally social, anti-institutional, iconoclastic) • witness required; or efficacy becomes apparent; witness to new being • exhuberance (exhuberant response)	• dependency upon sacred persons (priests), sacred times (holy days), sacred places (temples, churches, holy lands) • communal rituals (sacraments)	• culture should reflect knowledge of the eternal order • eternal order to be reflected in everyday actions • wisdom for harmonious living requires learning ancient truths	• rejection of soc⸱ tion; a detache⸱ • individualistic a⸱ ized training fr⸱ ter who is spir⸱ fected • may involve re⸱ clerical, intelle⸱ social expectati⸱ community